Letter of Welcome: "Built by ..."

Dear Students:

Welcome to First-Year Writing at the University of Alaba... you will learn and practice many skills that will prove ... suc-cess in college and after graduation. You'll read, think, an... ...uss. You'll create, challenge, and question. You'll research, revise, and publish. You'll establish close working relationships with your classmates and instruc-tors. You'll reflect on your work in this course with an eye to improving it. You'll develop a keen "rhetorical awareness"—a sense of how best to communicate a particular message to a particular audience. Your writing, in turn, will take many forms: formal essays, creative works, reflections, narratives, electronic communications, even workplace documents. Your writing will change (for the better!), and you will change, and you will grow as a writer. After all, the University of Alabama—like all institutions of higher learning—is *built by writers* just like you.

That brings us to this resource, *The Norton Field Guide to Writing*. It's one of my favorites, and I am excited to share it with you. Take some time—right now!—to get a feel for it. Here, you can learn about writing processes, strategies, and style. You can learn about grammar and punc-tuation. You can learn more about the First-Year Writing Program and its affiliated services, such as the Writing Center. And be sure to consult the *Analog* section, which features several student-authored essays from pre-vious First-Year Writing classes. Here, you'll see how past students have responded to many of the same writing prompts you'll receive. I hope their work challenges and motivates you. And I hope to include some of your work in future volumes of this resource. However you choose to use this guide, it will serve you well, and it will serve you for a very long time.

One piece of unsolicited advice, and I will sign off: Get to know your instructors. Walk up to them today, look them straight in the eyes, say hello, and shake their hands. Visit them during their office hours. Your instructors are there to support, guide, and challenge you as you undertake your new academic career. They want you to succeed. And so do I.

Happy writing!

Dr. Luke Niiler
Director, First-Year Writing Program

Program Contact Information

DIRECTOR OF THE FIRST-YEAR WRITING PROGRAM

Dr. Luke Niiler
208 Morgan Hall
205-348-8503
lpniiler@ua.edu

ASSOCIATE DIRECTOR OF THE FIRST-YEAR WRITING PROGRAM

Jessica Kidd
206 Morgan Hall
205-348-1763
kidd005@ua.edu

SENIOR OFFICE ASSOCIATE

Melinda Fields
207 Morgan Hall
(phone) 205-348-6488
(fax) 205-348-1388
mfields@ua.edu

WRITING CENTER DIRECTOR

Dr. Amy Dayton
323 Lloyd Hall
205-348-5049
adayton@ua.edu

ENGLISH DEPARTMENT

Joel Brouwer, Chair
111 Morgan Hall
205-348-0766
joel.brouwer@ua.edu

Main Office
103 Morgan Hall
(phone) 205-348-5065
(fax) 205-348-1388

Important Web Addresses

FIRST-YEAR WRITING PROGRAM

comp.ua.edu

- Descriptions of EN 101, 102, 103, 104
- Course policies
- Placement information

THE WRITING CENTER

writingcenter.ua.edu

- Information about services
- Make an appointment
- Writing resources

UA LIBRARIES AND LIBGUIDES

lib.ua.edu

- Access to library resources

guides.lib.ua.edu/en101

- Guide specifically for EN 1w01

guides.lib.ua.edu/en102

- Guide specifically for EN 102

guides.lib.ua.edu/en103

- Guide specifically for EN 103

guides.lib.ua.edu/en104

- Guide specifically for EN 104

OFFICE OF ACADEMIC INTEGRITY

academicintegrity.as.ua.edu

- Student Resources
- UA Policies

TURNITIN

https://guides.turnitin.com/01_Manuals_and_Guides/Student_Guides

- Student guide to submitting work
- Student guide to using the feedback studio

University of Alabama First-Year Writing at Alabama

First-Year Writing at the University of Alabama

Mission Statement

The University of Alabama's First-Year Writing Program (FWP) will develop deliberate and versatile student writers; provide FWP instructors with ongoing opportunities for professional growth; collaborate with UA faculty outside the FWP program to build writing instruction into their courses; and contribute to research on the teaching and assessment of composition.

Program Goals

Rhetorical Knowledge: Students will learn to analyze contexts and AUDIENCES and then to act on that analysis in comprehending and composing texts.

■ 57–60

Critical Thinking: Students will learn to ANALYZE, SYNTHESIZE, interpret and EVALUATE ideas, information, situations, and texts.

▶ 94–128
197–205
● 473–77

Processes: Students will learn to conceptualize, develop, and finalize writing projects through multiple drafts.

Knowledge of Conventions: Students will learn to work within the guidelines of specific GENRES, and in so doing, shape readers' and writers' perceptions of correctness and appropriateness. Conventions govern mechanics, usage, spelling, and citation practices, as well as content, style, organization, graphics, and document DESIGN.

■ 61–63

■ 68–70

*Source: The WPA Outcomes Statement for First-Year Composition (3.0), Approved July 17, 2014

First-Year Writing placement

AP (Advanced Placement) Scores

- A score of 3 on either AP English test (Language or Literature) earns a student EN 101 credit and places them nto EN 102.

- Scores of 3 on both AP English tests (Language and Literature) earns a student EN 101 and EN 102 credit, fulfilling their 6-hour core composition requirement, and placement into 200-level literature courses. (Note: Students who earn a 3 on one exam and a 4 on the other exam will not earn credit beyond EN 101 and 102.)

- A score of 4 or 5 on either AP English test (Language or Literature) earns a student EN 101 and EN 102 credit, fulfilling their 6-hour core composition requirement. A student with this score qualifies for optional placement into Honors sections of 200-level literature surveys (EN 215, 216, 219, and 220).

- A score of 4 or 5 on both AP English tests (Language and Literature) earns a student EN 101 and EN 102 credit, fulfilling their 6-hour core composition requirement, and 3 additional hours of elective humanities credit. This score also qualifies a student for optional placement into Honors sections of 200-level literature surveys (EN 215, 216, 219, and 220).

ACT and SAT Scores

- An ACT composite score of 28, an ACT English score of 30, an SAT composite score of 1250, or an SAT verbal score of 720 qualifies a student for optional placement into EN 103 (Honors Comp). Successful completion of EN 103 (C- or higher) with correct qualifying scores gives a student 3 hours of credit for EN 103 and 3 additional hours of placement credit, satisfying the 6-hour core composition requirement.

CLEP Scores

- The English Department does not accept CLEP test scores for placement credit.

IB (International Baccalaureate) Scores

- Please see https://catalog.ua.edu/undergraduate/about/academic-regulations/policies/credit-by-examination/ for current information.

Synopsis of EN 101

Description
English 101, the first in a two-course sequence, introduces students to college-level expository writing, critical reading, basic citation, and the rhetorical tools needed to participate successfully in the University of Alabama discourse community.

Prerequisites and Placement Procedures
None

Core Curriculum Credit*
3 hrs (FC)

Course Outcomes
See comp.ua.edu and your class syllabus for student learning outcomes for all FWP courses.

Synopsis of EN 102

Description
English 102, the second course in UA's first-year sequence, introduces students to the principles of academic **ARGUMENTATION**, advanced critical thinking, university-level research techniques, and source-based writing.

355–73

Prerequisites and Placement Procedures
Students must successfully pass EN 101 with a grade of C- or higher or receive a score of 3 or higher on either English AP exam (Language or

---

*All students are required to have 6 hours of freshman composition (FC) credit.

Literature), allowing them to obtain placement credit for EN 101 and enroll directly in EN 102.

Core Curriculum Credit*
3 hrs (FC)

Course Outcomes
See comp.ua.edu and your class syllabus for student learning outcomes for all FWP courses.

Synopsis of EN 103

Description
English 103, Advanced English Composition, is a one-semester course that introduces students to the challenges of expository writing and academic **ARGUMENTATION**. The course emphasizes critical reading, critical thinking, and writing as **SYNTHESIS**, along with university-level research techniques and source-based writing.

355–73
473–77

Prerequisites and Placement Procedures
Qualifying Scores:

- 28 ACT composite, or
- 1250 SAT composite, or
- 30 ACT English, or
- 720 SAT Verbal.

Core Curriculum Credit*
Students with necessary qualifying scores who successfully complete EN 103 with a grade of C- or higher receive 6 hours of composition credit (3 hours for EN 103 and 3 hours of placement credit).

Note: The 3 additional hours of placement credit received for successful completion of EN 103 generally do not appear on a student's transcript until a few weeks after the beginning of the following semester.

---

*All students are required to have 6 hours of freshman composition (FC) credit.

Course Outcomes

See comp.ua.edu and your class syllabus for student learning outcomes for all FWP courses.

Synopsis of EN 104

Description

English 104 is a one-semester composition course for students in the Blount Undergraduate Initiative Program. It has the same organizational and descriptive fundamentals as EN 103, differing only in the qualifying prerequisites and placement credit procedures.

Prerequisites and Placement Procedures

Students must be members of the Blount Undergraduate Initiative Program.

BUI students taking EN 104 who also meet the EN 103 prerequisite will receive 6 hours of composition credit for successfully completing EN 104 with a grade of C- or higher (3 hours for EN 104 and 3 hours of placement credit).

BUI students taking EN 104 who do not meet the EN 103 prerequisite must make a grade of A- or higher to receive 6 hours of composition credit. Otherwise, they must take an additional 3-hour composition course (EN 102).

Core Curriculum Credit*

3 hrs (FC) + 3 hrs placement credit (FC) with qualifying scores/grade

Course Outcomes

See comp.ua.edu and your class syllabus for student learning outcomes for all FWP courses.

---

*All students are required to have 6 hours of freshman composition (FC) credit.

Grade Appeals

- If you are assigned a grade of NC and you don't understand why, first speak to your instructor for an explanation of why you earned this grade.

- After that, if you feel there are extenuating circumstances, you may appeal to the Director of First-Year Writing. See the main office of the English Department for contact information.

- All appeals must be made within two weeks after final grades are submitted. No appeals will be considered before or after this time frame.

- To appeal your grade, e-mail Dr. Luke Niiler, Director of First-Year Writing (lpniiler@ua.edu), with your name, your CWID, your instructor's name, your section number, and a carefully written explanation of the extenuating circumstances that you believe warrant a grade change. You should be prepared to provide any necessary evidence such as doctor's notes, and so on. All appeals should be carefully proofread. Poorly written appeals will not be considered.

Student Opinions of Instruction

Toward the end of the semester, you will be asked to complete two surveys.

- The First-Year Writing Program Student Opinion Survey asks for you to provide feedback on a variety of things related to your EN 101, EN 102, EN 103, or EN 104 course, including what skills you learned and which activities were most helpful.

- The College of Arts and Sciences Faculty Teaching Evaluation Survey asks questions about the quality of your instruction and class experience.

Rhetorical situation for both surveys:
Your instructor will read survey results to find out what is working for students and what might be improved for future semesters. Program administrators will read the results to assess the effectiveness of the First-Year Writing Program.

Pointers for writing the most useful responses:

- Take the surveys. The FWP survey will be done during class time on your phone, tablet, or laptop, but if you are absent you can get the link from your instructor and complete the survey after class time. The FWP survey is available in the student tab of comp.ua.edu. The College of Arts and Sciences survey is available through MyBama.

- Write your best. Think through what you want to say; organize your thoughts; support your claims with details; pay attention to your ethos as an evaluator. (For example: Be specific in your responses. We can't tell what you liked if you say only, "Some of the readings were good but some sucked." As in all good writing, details matter. Whether you want to praise something or complain about something, include specific details so that your reader will understand your response.)

- We are not trolling for criticism with these surveys. If your class experience was good, tell us about that. You don't have to search for something negative to say.

- Your instructor and program administrators will not have access to your survey responses until after final grades have been posted.

The University of Alabama Writing Center

LOCATION

322 Lloyd Hall
(on the Quad, next to the Alabama Museum of Natural History)

FALL AND SPRING HOURS

- Monday through Thursday, 9:00 a.m. – 6:00 p.m.
- Friday, 9:00 a.m. – 3:00 p.m.
- Additional walk-in hours are available at Java City/Gorgas Library. Hours vary by semester and are posted at writingcenter.ua.edu.

SUMMER I AND II HOURS

- Monday through Friday, 9:00 a.m. – 3:00 p.m.

Located in 322 Lloyd Hall, the University of Alabama Writing Center provides professional writing assistance to all UA students. Appointments are recommended. Directions, information, and additional resources are available at writingcenter.ua.edu.

Our graduate and undergraduate writing consultants can help you with both general writing skills and more discipline-specific forms of writing, including research papers, lab reports, theses, **RÉSUMÉS**, cover letters, applications, and personal statements.

253–64 ▶

We will be pleased to help you

- review the requirements of your writing assignment,
- generate and focus your ideas,
- develop strong **ARGUMENTS**,
- integrate sources into your work,
- format your work, or
- work on punctuation, grammar, and spelling.

◆ 355–73

Before you visit us in person,

- make an appointment at writingcenter.ua.edu, or just walk in;
- have a copy of your paper and your assignment ready; and
- be prepared to work on your writing, as you will be asked to take an active role in your consultation by talking about your writing and, of course, by writing.

How Can I Create a Writing Center Account?

If you are an on-campus student:

1. Go to writingcenter.ua.edu.
2. Click on the "Make an Appointment" link.
3. On the next page, click on the "Register for an Account" link.
4. Fill in the required fields.
5. Click on the link at the bottom of the page that reads, "Register." This will return you to the login page.
6. Enter your username and password.
7. Available consulting slots will be shown as white boxes. Remember that, even if all appointments are filled, walk-in consultations are often available.

If you are a distance learner:

1. Go to writingcenter.ua.edu.
2. Click on the "Distance Learners" link for complete directions.
3. Contact us at (205) 348-5049 with any questions.

Using the University of Alabama Library System

Navigating UA Libraries

The University Libraries consist of five branches, all accessed via lib.ua.edu. In addition to the University Libraries, there are two independent libraries on campus for the law school and health sciences.

- Gorgas Library is the main library and houses the humanities collections. Much of what you will need for First-Year Writing research can be found in Gorgas or through the online resources.

- Hoole Special Collections Library, located in the Mary Harmon Bryant Building, and the A. S. Williams III Americana Collection, located in Gorgas Library, comprise the Division of Special Collections. Hoole Special Collections Library houses rare and unique research resources, including books, manuscripts, maps, photographs, and Alabama- and UA-specific materials. The A. S. Williams III Collection is a nineteenth-century Americana collection including materials related to the presidents of the United States, the Civil War, Southern history, Southern literature, and African American history. Both Hoole and the Williams Collection are noncirculating libraries. Materials cannot be checked out.

- Rodgers Library for Science and Engineering holds materials specific to the hard sciences, engineering, and nursing disciplines. Most of the material in Rodgers is available online and accessible 24/7 from any computer.

- McLure Education Library serves primarily the faculty, students, and staff of the College of Education and the Graduate School of Education.

In addition to the professional collections, McLure houses a collection of approximately twenty thousand trade books for preschool through young adult readers, as well as other materials relevant to education majors.

- Angelo Bruno Business Library serves the business information needs of the University of Alabama, and in particular, of the students and faculty of the Culverhouse College of Commerce and Business Administration (C&BA) and the Manderson Graduate School of Business.

Locating Resources

Locating Books, Magazines, and Journal Articles

To find sources for your paper, start with the libraries' search engine, Scout. Scout searches for books, magazines, and academic journals all at the same time, so you may not need to search in separate databases for them. You can access both primary and secondary source material using Scout. To search Scout, go to lib.ua.edu, and click the link to Scout. In Scout, you can type your keywords into the search box at the top of the page or you can click "advanced search" underneath the search box to immediately try more specific search parameters. Remember that Scout does not work well with natural language. For example, instead of typing "what are the consequences of using genetically modified organisms in breakfast cereals," try "'genetically modified organisms' AND 'breakfast cereal.'"

You can filter your results after you search by using the limiters in the left column. You have several options, including books, magazines, newspapers, trade journals, and academic journals. You can also limit by publication date.

Remember that not all items you find through Scout will be immediately available in full text. You may find a record for an item without the item (either a book or an article) attached. These are index records. When you find these, you will have to search for the item in a different way. This would be a great opportunity to use Ask a Librarian (see below).

Note that the big search box prominently displayed on lib.ua.edu searches Scout as well as information about the libraries. Going directly to Scout as described above often yields better results for your research.

Finding Print Books

Books are organized in the libraries using Library of Congress Classification (LCC), which is a subject-based system. So, when you go to the shelf to find a book, it will be located next to other books on the same subject. Be sure to write down the complete call number or use the catalog feature that will text you the call number before you go to look for a book.

Print books are located in all of the branch libraries and also at the Library Annex. Remember to check the location of the book, and go to the correct branch to find it. Also, remember that you cannot check out books or materials at Hoole or in the Williams Collection, but you can use them within the library.

LCC uses call numbers with an alphanumeric sequence that always begins with one or two letters. There are signs throughout the library building that tell you where to look to find certain call numbers based on this alphanumeric sequence. If you have trouble locating a book, remember to check with the information desk in each library. UA Libraries also provides access to more than one million electronic books.

Accessing Databases

Through the UA Libraries, you have access to nearly four hundred databases, but not all of the databases are searchable by Scout. You may want to access databases directly to find other sources. Go back to lib.ua.edu and click "Databases."

You can filter databases by subject, by type of source, or by publisher. You can also search for a specific database by name using the search box on the databases page. A description is included for each database, including the date range and subject of coverage.

Some databases are harder to use than others. If you have trouble with a database, use Ask a Librarian to get some help.

If you are off campus, remember that you will need to use your MyBama login information to access the databases.

Using Google Scholar

Google Scholar is a helpful tool through which you may search the UA Libraries resources using the familiar Google search algorithm. Find a link in the Research Tools at the top of the UA Libraries page. In addition to the comfort of searching in the Google environment, Google Scholar offers information about how sources are connected to other sources. If you are on campus, simply enter your keywords in the search box. If you are off campus, click "Access to Google Scholar for Off-Campus Users." You'll need to enter your MyBama ID and password.

Many of the UA Libraries resources are linked through Google Scholar. Look for the gray text to the right of your results. This gray text indicates articles that you can find in full-text form in the UA Libraries. Click on gray text to be taken to the article you want. Be careful when using Google Scholar—while it is nice to use such a familiar tool, Google Scholar doesn't always lead you to the best sources.

Using Ask a Librarian

Ask a Librarian is a great tool available on the UA Libraries website that functions as a frequently asked questions page. It also allows library users to contact librarians with specific questions (e.g., "How do I find sources related to crime rates in developing countries?").

Find a link to Ask a Librarian in the quicklinks section of the UA Libraries page, or go to ask.lib.ua.edu. Then, simply type your question in the search box. If your question is one that has already been asked and answered, the box may autofill with the question (e.g., "What are the hours for McClure Library?"). If your question is more specific and you cannot find an answer by searching, complete the form at the right on your search results page. A librarian will e-mail you back with an answer to your question as soon as possible. You can also:

- E-mail askalibrarian@ua.edu.

- Ask your question by text message: (205) 377-0920.

- Visit a reference desk at any of the UA Libraries.

- Request a research consultation through the libraries' website (lib.ua.edu).

More Helpful Information

For library resources and information related to your specific courses, please see the following Library Guides:

- EN 101: guides.lib.ua.edu/en101
- EN 102: guides.lib.ua.edu/en102
- EN 103: guides.lib.ua.edu/en103
- EN 104: guides.lib.ua.edu/en104

If you need help at any point during your writing or research process, remember that your instructor and a team of librarians are there for you. To speak with a librarian, visit any library location or simply use the Ask a Librarian feature on the UA Libraries website.

Last but certainly not least, visit the UA Libraries in person before you have the pressure of an assignment. If you need assistance, there is an information desk in each library, where staff are always available to answer questions.

Using Sources Ethically

Before You Begin that Paper

Adapted by the UA First-Year Writing Program with permission from UCLA Dean of Students Office

1. Be sure you understand your assignment. If you have any questions, do not hesitate to ask your instructor.

2. Be sure you understand the definition of plagiarism.

494–95 According to The Oxford Dictionary of Literary Terms (Oxford University Press, 2015. Oxfordreference.com 22 February 2018.), **PLAGIARISM** is "the theft of ideas (such as the plots of narrative or dramatic works) or of written passages or works, where these are passed off as one's own work without acknowledgement of their true origin."

Many college writing assignments—from small homework assignments to long research projects—will require you to incorporate the words and ideas of others. If your assignment directs you to consult outside sources, be sure to use and cite them correctly. If you are not sure how to do this, ask before submitting the work for credit.

If your assignment says not to use outside sources, be sure that you don't. College-level work involves personal growth, and often that involves wrangling with issues and ideas on your own before you turn to outside sources. Don't shortchange yourself. Do the assignment as assigned. If your instructor says "no outside sources," then be assured that he or she wants your ideas and not the ideas you gathered from a Google search or Wikipedia.

3. Be sure you understand the consequences of plagiarism.

When you plagiarize, you hand in work that is not your own (or not entirely your own). That means that you sabotage the quality of your own education and your own learning experience. When you plagiarize, you steal—from yourself and from others. The University assumes that the grades you earn in your courses represent your own work. When you plagiarize—even if you "get away with it"—you undermine the value of your own college degree.

When you plagiarize, chances are good that you will get caught. If that happens, you should be aware that there will be very real consequences, including possible suspension or expulsion from the University. Consider the impact on your financial aid, on your plans to attend graduate school, on your career, on your housing situation, on your family and friends!

4. Be sure you understand that there are alternatives to plagiarism.

- Your instructor will explain in class how you can avoid plagiarism. You can also ask your instructor for help in office hours or a conference.

- Consult your textbook for advice on **TAKING NOTES**, **QUOTING**, **PARA-PHRASING**, and **SUMMARIZING**, citing, and **ACKOWLEDGING SOURCES**.

478–80
480–83
483–86
486–87
491–95

- Ask your instructor if Turnitin is available for checking source usage in your draft.

- Visit the University of Alabama Writing Center (322 Lloyd Hall).

- Contact the Office of Academic Integrity Initiatives (ASAcademicintegrity@ua.edu).

5. Be sure you understand that UA instructors are required to refer possible cases of plagiarism to their divisional academic misconduct monitor.

This does not mean you are guilty of plagiarism; it means the situation needs further review. For English courses, the monitor is Dr. Tricia McElroy, Associate Dean of the College of Arts and Sciences.

Ethical Use of Wikipedia in Student Research

Wikipedia is a collaborative online encyclopedia. It may be a good place to get oriented or to find quick factual information about your research topic. It may also be a good source for identifying other outside sources (by using the links at the bottom of each article). But you need to be aware of a couple of cautions in using Wikipedia for college-level research:

- Wikipedia articles can be revised by anyone at any time, so the information may be subjective and is susceptible to change. (This means Wikipedia is not considered a good source for academic research, and some instructors ask you not to use it for this reason.)

510–38, 547–48

- If you use Wikipedia, it must be cited as a source and included on your **WORKS CITED** page. (You'll notice that Wikipedia itself tries to be an ethical source by providing their own citations and by flagging moments in the text that require citations.)

Many students get into trouble because of inappropriate and/or unacknowledged use of Wikipedia entries in research papers. If your instructor tells you not to use Wikipedia, then don't use it. But, if you do use Wikipedia, you must correctly cite and document the appropriate entries. Here's how to correctly integrate a source into your text:

483–87

1. Paraphrase correctly. **PARAPHRASING** means that you put the information provided in a source text into your own words entirely. All the language should be yours, including the sentence structure. Paraphrases must be cited and documented.

2. Quote correctly. In your papers, any time you use the exact words or phrases of a source text, you must place those words or phrases inside quotation marks and cite and **DOCUMENT** your source accordingly.

496–99

3. Cite and Document. Any use of Wikipedia should be accompanied by an internal citation within your paper that refers the reader to a correctly formatted entry in your Works Cited page.

How do You Know When to Paraphrase and When to Auote?

See Chapter 49 of this textbook, but a quick rule of thumb is "paraphrase for ideas, quote for language."

For more information on paraphrasing, quoting, and summarizing, or acknowledging and documenting sources, see chapters 49–51 of this textbook.

What can I Use Instead of Wikipedia?

- Articles found through the UA libraries' databases
- Material from websites ending in .gov or .edu
- Resources provided by or referred to you by your instructor

Example of Incorrect Use of Wikipedia

From Wikipedia article on plagiarism (accessed 22 February 2018):

> "Within academia, plagiarism by students, professors, or researchers is considered academic dishonesty or academic fraud, and offenders are subject to academic censure, up to and including expulsion."

Student writing based on the Wikipedia passage:

> Within higher education, plagiarism by researchers, students or professors is considered by some people to be academically dishonest or a fraud, and guilty people are subject to being censured, including being expelled.

What is Wrong with This Example?

- Incorrect paraphrasing, as well as overreliance on the sentence structure and language of the original passage
- Lack of quotation marks around quoted sections of the original text
- Lack of citation/documentation

How could You Use This Information Correctly in a Paper?

Revised student writing based on the Wikipedia passage:

> In an academic setting, people who plagiarize may be particularly harshly penalized, largely because inappropriately borrowing the ideas, words, and phrasing of others is considered to be "academic dishonesty or academic fraud" ("Plagiarism").

Works Cited

"Plagiarism." *Wikipedia.* Wikimedia, https://en.wikipedia.org/wiki/Plagiarism. Accessed 22 Feb. 2018.

Follow-up Assignment

Write a paragraph in which you define plagiarism and share your feelings on the subject. In your paragraph, please include both a paraphrase and a quotation from the Wikipedia passage below.

"Within academia, plagiarism by students, professors, or researchers is considered academic dishonesty or academic fraud, and offenders are subject to academic censure, up to and including expulsion. Some institutions use plagiarism detection software to uncover potential plagiarism and to deter students from plagiarizing. Some 'universities address the issue of academic integrity by providing students with thorough orientations, required writing courses, and clearly articulated honor codes. Indeed, there is a virtually uniform understanding among college students that plagiarism is wrong. Nevertheless, each year students are brought before their institutions' disciplinary boards on charges that they have misused sources in their schoolwork.'[11]"

Additional challenge: What does the [11] mean? How would you deal with it in a paper?

Office of Academic Integrity Initiatives

Questions About Writing with Sources?
For help determining correct

- use of web sources,
- summary and paraphrasing practices,
- use of quotations and quotation marks,
- citation practices, or
- documentation practices,

ask your instructor while writing your paper. Want a bit more help? Contact the Office of Academic Integrity Initiatives, College of Arts and Sciences (ASAcademicIntegrity@ua.edu).

First-Year Writing Program Policy on Academic Misconduct

All First-Year Writing Program courses adhere to the University of Alabama's Academic Misconduct Policy.

The Official Word on Academic Misconduct at UA

According to the University of Alabama 2017–2018 Undergraduate Catalog, "academic misconduct includes all acts of dishonesty in any academic or related matter and any knowing or intentional help, attempt to help, or conspiracy to help another student commit an act of academic dishonesty. Academic dishonesty includes, but is not limited to, the following acts, when performed in any type of academic or academically related matter, exercise, or activity:

- **Cheating:** using or attempting to use unauthorized materials, information, study aids, or computer-related information
- **Plagiarism:** representing the words, data, works, ideas, computer programs or output, or anything not generated in an authorized fashion, as one's own
- **Fabrication:** presenting as genuine any invented or falsified citation or material
- **Misrepresentation:** falsifying, altering, or misstating the contents of documents or other materials related to academic matters, including schedules, prerequisites, and transcripts."

To this list, the FWP adds the following:

- **Recycling:** presenting as new work, wholly or in part, any material previously submitted for another class—even if you wrote that material yourself.

Any of these actions may result in evidence being submitted to the academic dean of the College of Arts and Sciences for review and a possible hearing, the results of which may be appealed according to UA's Academic Misconduct Policy. Students should be aware that consequences "can range from a reprimand to a penalty as severe as suspension for a designated length of time or even indefinite suspension" and that verified second offenses are taken very seriously (see the UA Catalog: catalog. ua.edu/undergraduate/about/academic-regulations/student-expectations/ code-academic-conduct/).

Some Advice on How to Avoid Plagiarism

494–95

In addition to what your instructor and your textbooks say about **AVOIDING PLAGIARISM**, here are some guidelines to help you prevent it:

- Take extra precautions to safeguard your papers and computer files so that no one has an opportunity to copy your work without your knowledge (and if you become aware that this has happened, contact your instructor as soon as possible in order not to be held responsible).

298–300

- Write **DRAFTS** of your assigned papers without any source materials in front of you, workshop your drafts with your class, and then revise your drafts so that your final paper has substantially improved from the original draft.

- If your teacher allows, turn in your draft through Turnitin, check your originality report, and revise as needed.

486–87
483–87

- If you quote source material, copy it accurately, put quotation marks around it, and include a source citation. You should similarly cite materials you **SUMMARIZE** or **PARAPHRASE**.

Helping you improve your writing skills must involve trust. So, your instructor may require that you sign UA's Academic Honor Pledge, acknowledging that you have read and understand the above policy. The Capstone Creed further underscores UA's commitment to academic integrity.

Academic Honor Pledge

"I promise or affirm that I will not at any time be involved with cheating, plagiarism, fabrication, or misrepresentation while enrolled as a student at the University of Alabama. I have read the Academic Honor Code, which explains disciplinary procedures that will result from the aforementioned. I understand that violation of this code will result in penalties as severe as indefinite suspension from the University."

Capstone Creed

"As a member of The University of Alabama community, I will pursue knowledge, act with fairness, integrity and respect; promote equity and inclusion; foster individual and civic responsibility; and strive for excellence in all I do."

FOURTH EDITION

The Norton
Field Guide
to Writing

with readings and handbook

Richard Bullock

WRIGHT STATE UNIVERSITY

Maureen Daly Goggin

ARIZONA STATE UNIVERSITY

Francine Weinberg

University of Alabama

W. W. NORTON & COMPANY

New York • London

Editor: Marilyn Moller
Project Editors: Rebecca Homiski and Christine D'Antonio
Developmental Editor: John Elliott
Assistant Editor: Claire Wallace
Manuscript Editor: Jude Grant
Managing Editor, College: Marian Johnson
Managing Editor, College Digital Media: Kim Yi
Production Manager: Andy Ensor
Media Editor: Erica Wnek
Media Project Editor: Cooper Wilhelm

Media Editorial Assistant: Ava Bramson
Marketing Manager, Composition: Megan Zwilling
Design Director: Jillian Burr
Book Designer: Anna Palchik
Photo Editor: Nelson Colón
Photo Research: Dena Digilio Betz
Permissions Manager: Megan Jackson
Permissions Clearing: Bethany Salminen
Composition: Cenveo® Publisher Services
Manufacturing: LSC Communications, Crawfordsville

The Library of Congress has cataloged an earlier edition as follows:
Library of Congress Cataloging-in-Publication Data
Names: Bullock, Richard H. (Richard Harvey) author. | Goggin, Maureen Daly, author. | Weinberg, Francine, author.
Title: The Norton Field Guide to writing with readings and handbook / Richard Bullock ; Maureen Daly Goggin ; Francine Weinberg.
Description: Fourth Edition. | New York : W.W. Norton & Company, [2016] | Includes bibliographical references and index.
Identifiers: LCCN 2015044572 | ISBN 9780393264388 (pbk.)
Subjects: LCSH: English language—Rhetoric—Handbooks, manuals, etc. | English language—Grammar—Handbooks, manuals, etc. | Report writing—Handbooks, manuals, etc. | College readers.
Classification: LCC PE1408 .B883825 2016 | DDC 808/.042—dc23 LC record available at http://lccn.loc.gov/2015044572

This edition: **ISBN 978-0-393-67123-0**

W. W. Norton & Company, Inc., 500 Fifth Avenue, New York, NY 10110-0017
wwnorton.com

W. W. Norton & Company Ltd., Castle House, 75/76 Wells Street, London W1T 3QT
1 2 3 4 5 6 7 8 9 0

Preface

The Norton Field Guide to Writing began as an attempt to offer the kind of writing guides found in the best rhetorics in a format as user-friendly as the best handbooks, and on top of that, to be as brief as could be. We wanted to create a handy guide to help college students with all their written work. Just as there are field guides for bird watchers, for gardeners, and for accountants, this would be one for writers. In its first three editions, the book has obviously touched a chord with many writing instructors, and it's become the best-selling college rhetoric — a success that leaves us humbled and grateful. Student success is now on everyone's mind. As teachers, we want our students to succeed, and first-year writing courses offer one of the best opportunities to help them develop the skills and habits of mind they need to succeed, whatever their goals may be. To that end, we've added a new part on academic literacies, with chapters on reading and writing in academic contexts, summarizing and responding, and developing academic habits of mind.

The Norton Field Guide still aims to offer both the guidance new teachers and first-year writers need and the flexibility many experienced teachers want. From our own experiences as teachers and WPAs, we've seen how well explicit guides to writing work for students and novice teachers. But too often, writing textbooks provide far more information than students need or instructors can assign and as a result are bigger and more expensive than they should be. So we've tried to provide enough structure without too much detail—to give the information college writers need to know while resisting the temptation to tell them everything there is to know.

Most of all, we've tried to make the book easy to use, with menus, directories, a glossary/index, and color-coded links to help students find what they're looking for. The links are also the way we keep the book brief: chapters are short, but the links send students to pages elsewhere in the book *if* they need more detail.

What's in the Book

The Norton Field Guide covers 14 genres often assigned in college. Much of the book is in the form of guidelines, designed to help students consider the choices they have as writers. The book is organized into nine parts:

1. **ACADEMIC LITERACIES.** Chapters 1–4 focus on writing and reading in academic contexts, summarizing and responding, and developing academic habits of mind.

2. **RHETORICAL SITUATIONS.** Chapters 5–9 focus on purpose, audience, genre, stance, and media and design. In addition, almost every chapter includes tips to help students focus on their rhetorical situations.

3. **GENRES.** Chapters 10–23 cover 14 genres, 4 of them — literacy narrative, textual analysis, report, and argument — treated in greater detail. Chapter 24 helps students choose genres when they need to.

4. **PROCESSES.** Chapters 25–32 offer advice for generating ideas and text, drafting, revising and rewriting, editing, proofreading, compiling a portfolio, collaborating with others, and writing as inquiry.

5. **STRATEGIES.** Chapters 33–44 cover ways of developing and organizing text — writing effective beginnings and endings, titles and thesis statements, comparing, describing, taking essay exams, and so on.

6. **RESEARCH/DOCUMENTATION.** Chapters 45–53 offer advice on how to do academic research; work with sources; quote, paraphrase, and summarize source materials; and document sources using MLA and APA styles. Chapters 51 and 52 present the "official MLA style" introduced in 2016.

7. **MEDIA/DESIGN.** Chapters 54–58 give guidance on choosing the appropriate print, electronic, or spoken medium; designing text; using images and sound; giving spoken presentations; and writing online.

8. **ANALOG.**

9. **HANDBOOK.** At the end of the book is a handbook to help students edit what they write, organized around the intuitive categories of sentences, language, and punctuation to make it easy to use.

What's Online

Norton/write. Just a click away with no passcode required, find a library of model student papers; more than 1,000 online exercises and quizzes; research and plagiarism tutorials; documentation guidelines for MLA, APA, *Chicago*, and CSE styles; MLA citation drills — and more. All MLA materials reflect 2016 style. Access the site at wwnorton.com/write.

A companion website includes worksheets and templates, additional chapters, and more. Access the site at wwnorton.com/write/fieldguide.

What's Available for Instructors

A Guide to Teaching with *The Norton Field Guides.* Written by Richard Bullock and several other teachers, this is a comprehensive guide to teaching first-year writing, from developing a syllabus to facilitating group work, teaching multimodal writing to assessing student writing. Free of charge.

Coursepacks are available for free and in a variety of formats, including *Blackbaord*, *Desire2Learn*, *Moodle*, *Canvas*, and *Angel* — and work within your existing learning management system, so there's no new system to learn, and access is free and easy. The *Field Guide* Coursepack includes model student papers; reading comprehension quizzes; reading strategy exercises; quizzes and exercises on grammar and research; documentation guidelines; and author biographies. Coursepacks are ready to use, right from the start — but are also easy to customize, using the system you already know and understand. Access the Coursepack at wwnorton.com/instructors.

PowerPoints. Ready-made PowerPoints feature genre organization flowcharts and documentation maps from the book to help you show examples during class. Download the PowerPoints at wwnorton.com/instructors.

Worksheets available in Word and PDF can be edited, downloaded, and printed with guidance on editing paragraphs, responding to a draft, and more. Download the worksheets at wwnorton.com/instructors.

Highlights

It's easy to use. Menus, directories, and a glossary/index make it easy for students to find what they're looking for. Color-coded templates and documentation maps even make MLA and APA documentation easy.

It has just enough detail, with short chapters that include color-coded links sending students to more detail *if* they need more.

It's uniquely flexible for teachers. Short chapters can be assigned in any order — and color-coded links help draw from other chapters as need be.

A user-friendly handbook, with an intuitive organization around sentences, language, and punctuation to make it easy for students to find what they need. And we go easy on the grammatical terminology, with links to the glossary for students who need detailed definitions.

What's New

A new part on academic literacies: with chapters on writing and reading in academic contexts, summarizing and responding, and developing academic habits of mind. Chapter 1 lists the WPA outcomes, showing students what's expected of writers in colleges and universities across the nation. (Part 1)

A new chapter on summarizing and responding, two fundamental moves required of college writers across disciplines. The chapter also includes guidance in writing a summary-response essay, a common assignment in many composition classes today. (Chapter 3)

A new chapter on developing academic habits of mind: engagement, persistence, flexibility, creativity, and other such habits, including all the ones identified in the *Framework for Success in College Writing.* (Chapter 4)

New MLA guidelines: Chapters 51 and 52 have been updated to reflect the new "official MLA style" introduced in 2016. All the MLA-style essays in the book have been updated as well.

Chapters on literary analyses: with an album of 5 stories and poems. (Chapters 17, 64)

3 new chapters with help for students whose first language isn't English: idioms, prepositions, and Englishes. (L-3, L-5, L-10)

Ways of Teaching with *The Norton Field Guide to Writing*

The Norton Field Guide is designed to give you both support and flexibility. It has clear assignment sequences if you want them, or you can create your own. If, for example, you assign a position paper, there's a full chapter. If you want students to use sources, add the appropriate research chapters. If you want them to submit a topic proposal, add that chapter.

If you're a new teacher, the genre chapters offer explicit assignment sequences—and the color-coded links will remind you of detail you may want to bring in. The instructor's manual offers advice on creating a syllabus, responding to writing, and more.

If you focus on genres, there are complete chapters on all the genres college students are often assigned. Color-coded links will help you bring in details about research or other writing strategies as you wish.

If you organize your course thematically, a Thematic Guide will lead you to readings on 23 themes. Chapter 27 on generating ideas can help get students thinking about a theme. You can also assign them to do research on the theme, starting with Chapter 46 on finding sources, or perhaps with Chapter 25 on writing as inquiry. If they then write in a particular genre, there will be a chapter to guide them.

If you want students to do research, there are 9 chapters on the research process, including guidelines and sample papers for MLA and APA styles.

If you focus on modes, you'll find chapters on using narration, description, and so on as strategies for many writing purposes, and links that lead students through the process of writing an essay organized around a particular mode.

If you teach a stretch, ALP, IRW, or dual credit course, the academic literacies chapters offer explicit guidelines to help students write and read in academic contexts, summarize and respond to what they read, and develop academic habits of mind that will help them succeed in college.

If you teach online, the book is available as an ebook — and a companion Coursepack includes exercises, quizzes, video tutorials, and more.

Acknowledgments

As we've traveled around the country and met many of the students, teachers, and WPAs who are using *The Norton Field Guide*, we've been gratified to hear that so many find it helpful, to the point that some students tell us that they aren't going to sell it back to the bookstore when the term ends — the highest form of praise. As much as we like the positive response, though, we are especially grateful when we receive suggestions for ways the book might be improved. In this fourth edition, as we did in the third edition, we have tried to respond to the many good suggestions we've gotten from students, colleagues, reviewers, and editors. Thank you all, both for your kind words and for your good suggestions.

Some people need to be singled out for thanks, especially Marilyn Moller, the guiding editorial spirit of the *Field Guide* through all four editions. When we presented Marilyn with the idea for this book, she encouraged us and helped us conceptualize it — and then taught us how to write a textbook. The quality of the *Field Guide* is due in large part to her knowledge of the field of composition, her formidable editing and writing skills, her sometimes uncanny ability to see the future of the teaching of writing — and her equally formidable, if not uncanny, stamina.

Developmental editor John Elliott shepherded both the third and the fourth editions through their revisions and additions with a careful hand

and a clear eye for appropriate content and language. His painstaking editing shows throughout the book, and we're grateful for his ability to make us appear to be better writers than we are.

Many others have contributed, too. Thanks to project editors Christine D'Antonio, Rebecca Homiski, and Katie Callahan for their energy, patience, and great skill in coordinating the tightly scheduled production process for the book. Claire Wallace managed the reviewing process and brought her own astute eye to evaluating all the readings, and more. *The Norton Field Guide* is more than just a print book, and we thank Erica Wnek, Kim Yi, Mateus Teixeira, Patrick Cartelli, Ava Bramson, and Cooper Wilhelm for creating and producing the superb ebook and instructors' site. Anna Palchik designed the award-winning, user-friendly, and attractive interior, Carin Berger created the beautiful new cover design, and Debra Morton Hoyt, Michael Wood, and Tiani Kennedy further enhanced the design and coordinated it all, inside and out. Andy Ensor transformed a scribbled-over manuscript into a finished product with extraordinary speed and precision, while Jude Grant copyedited. Megan Jackson and Bethany Salminen cleared text permissions, coping efficiently with ongoing changes, and Nelson Colón cleared permission for the images found by Dena Digilio Betz. Steve Dunn, Lib Triplett, Megan Zwilling, Maureen Connolly, and Doug Day helped us all keep our eyes on the market. Thanks to all, and to Roby Harrington, Drake McFeely, and Julia Reidhead for supporting this project in the first place.

Rich has many, many people at Wright State University to thank for their support and assistance. Jane Blakelock has taught Rich most of what he knows about electronic text and writing on and for the web and has assembled an impressive list of useful links for the book's website. Adrienne Cassel, now at Sinclair Community College, and Catherine Crowley read and commented on many drafts. Peggy Lindsey (now at Georgia Southern University) shared her students' work and the idea of using charts to show how various genres might be organized. Brady Allen, Debbie Bertsch (now at Columbus State Community College), Vicki Burke, Melissa Carrion, Jimmy Chesire, Carol Cornett, Mary Doyle, Byron Crews, Deborah Crusan, Sally DeThomas, Stephanie Dickey, Scott Geisel, Karen Hayes, Chuck Holmes, Beth Klaisner, Nancy Mack, Marty Maner, Cynthia Marshall, Sarah McGinley, Kristie McKiernan, Michelle Metzner, Kristie Rowe, Bobby Rubin, Cathy Sayer, David Seitz, Caroline Simmons, Tracy Smith, Rick Strader, Mary Van Loveren, and A. J. Williams responded to drafts, submitted good models of student writing, contributed to the instructor's manual, tested the *Field Guide* in their classes, provided support, and shared with Rich some of their best teaching ideas. Henry Limouze and then Carol Loranger, chairs of the English Department, gave him room to work on this project with patience and good humor. Sandy Trimboli, Becky Traxler, and Lynn Morgan, the secretaries to the writing programs, kept him anchored. And he thanks especially the more than 300 graduate teaching assistants and 10,000 first-year students who class-tested various editions of the *Field Guide* and whose experiences helped — and continue to help — to shape it.

At Arizona State, Maureen wants to acknowledge the unwavering support of Neal A. Lester, Vice President of Humanities and Arts and former chair of the English Department, and the assistance of Jason Diller, her former graduate research assistant, and Judy Holiday, her former graduate mentee, for their reading suggestions. She thanks her colleagues, all exemplary teachers and mentors, for creating a supportive intellectual environment, especially Patricia Boyd, Peter Goggin, Mark Hannah, Kathleen Lamp, Elenore Long, Paul Matsuda, Keith Miller, Ersula Ore, Alice Robison, Shirley Rose, and Doris Warriner. Thanks also go to ASU instructors and first-year students who have used the *Field Guide* and have offered good suggestions. Finally, Maureen wants to pay tribute to her students, who are themselves among her best teachers.

Thanks to the teachers across the country who reviewed the third edition of the *Field Guide* and helped shape this fourth edition: Neal Abramson, Richland College; Marian Anders, Alamance Community College; Bonnie Asselin, Abraham Baldwin Agricultural College; Lillie Bailey, Virginia State University; Jacqueline Blackwell, Thomas Nelson Community College; Dean Blumberg, Horry–Georgetown Technical College; Ronald Brooks, Oklahoma State University; Belinda Bruner, Oklahoma State University; Laurie Buchanan, Clark State Community College; Judi Buenaflor, Northampton Community College; Jeaneen Canfield, Oklahoma State University; John Castellarin, Germanna Community College; Sheila Chase, Arkansas State University–Beebe; W. Scott Cheney, Collin College; Robert Ransom Cole, Auburn University at Montgomery; Candace Cooper, Collin College; Amy Decker, Germanna Community College; Regina Dickerson, University of Nevada, Las Vegas; Courtney Doi, Alamance Community College; Summer Doucet, Baton Rouge Community College; Barbara Dumont, Joliet Junior College; Julie Dunlop, Central New Mexico Community College;

Lexy Durand, Alamance Community College; Mary Sue Fox, Central New Mexico Community College; Deborah Goodwyn, Virginia State University; Bruce Gospin, Northampton Community College; Michael Hedges, Horry Georgetown Technical College; Kalissa Hendrickson, Arizona State University; Matthew Henry, Richland College; Missy James, Tallahassee Community College; David Jones, Arkansas State University–Beebe; Sheikh Umarr Kamarah, Virginia State University; Erin Kelley, Richland College; Cecilia Kennedy, Clark State Community College; Myleah Kerns, Thomas Nelson Community College; Guy Krueger, University of Mississippi; Sharon Gavin Levy, Northampton Community College; Jan Look, Joliet Junior College; Terri Mann, El Paso Community College; Margaret Marangione, Blue Ridge Community College; William McGee Jr., Joliet Junior College; Heath Mensher, Northampton Community College; Cathryn Meyer, Tallahassee Community College; Rosemary Mink, Mohawk Valley Community College; David Nackley, Mohawk Valley Community College; Michael Neil, Highland Park High School; Clarence Nero, Baton Rouge Community College; Tanya Nichols, Fresno State University; Nancy Noel, Germanna Community College; Stephen Nowka, Clark State Community College; Joseph Paretta, Northampton Community College; Eden Pearson, Des Moines Area Community College; Robert Pontious, Brunswick Community College; Donna Porche-Frilot, Baton Rouge Community College; Tony Procell, El Paso Community College; Bonnie Proudfoot, Hocking College; Sayanti Ganguly Puckett, Johnson County Community College; Anthony Rapino, Northampton Community College; Brenda Reid, Tallahassee Community College; Marilyn Senter, Johnson County Community College; Maureen Sherbondy, Alamance Community College; Vivian Walters, Arkansas State University–Beebe; Jay Branagan Webb, Richland College; Antoinette Whalen, Richland College; Tammy Wolf, Central New Mexico Community College.

The Norton Field Guide has also benefited from the good advice and conversations we've had with writing teachers across the country, including (among many others) Maureen Mathison, Susan Miller, Tom Huckin, Gae Lyn Henderson, and Sundy Watanabe at the University of Utah; Christa Albrecht-Crane, Doug Downs, and Brian Whaley at Utah Valley State College; Anne Dvorak and Anya Morrissey at Longview Community University; Jeff Andelora at Mesa Community College; Robin Calitri at Merced College; Lori Gallinger, Rose Hawkins, Jennifer Nelson, Georgia Standish, and John Ziebell at the Community College of Southern Nevada; Stuart Blythe at Indiana University–Purdue University Fort Wayne; Janice Kelly at Arizona State University; Jeanne McDonald at Waubonsee Community College; Web Newbold, Mary Clark-Upchurch, Megan Auffart, Matt Balk, Edward James Chambers, Sarah Chavez, Desiree Dighton, Ashley Ellison, Theresa Evans, Keith Heller, Ellie Isenhart, Angela Jackson-Brown, Naoko Kato, Yuanyuan Liao, Claire Lutkewitte, Yeno Matuki, Casey McArdle, Tibor Munkacsi, Dani Nier-Weber, Karen Neubauer, Craig O'Hara, Martha Payne, Sarah Sandman, and Kellie Weiss at Ball State University; Patrick Tompkins at Tyler Community College; George Kanieski and Pamela Hardman at Cuyahoga Community College; Daniela Regusa, Jeff Partridge, and Lydia Vine at Capital Community College; Elizabeth Woodworth, Auburn University–Montgomery; Stephanie Eason at Enterprise Community College; Kate Geiselman at Sinclair Community College; Ronda Dively at Southern Illinois University; Debra Knutson at Shawnee State University; Guy Shebat and Amy Flick at Youngstown State University; and Martha Tolleson, Toni McMillen, and Patricia Gerecci at Collin College.

We wouldn't have met most of these people without the help of the Norton travelers, the representatives who spend their days visiting faculty, showing and discussing the *Field Guide* and Norton's many other fine textbooks. Thanks especially to Hayley Bartholomew, Kathy Carlsen, Scott Cook, John Darger, Marilyn Rayner, Peter Wentz, Mary Helen Willett, Lauren Winkler, and all the other Norton travelers. And we'd especially like to thank Mike Wright, Lib Triplett, Ashley Cain, and Doug Day for promoting this book so enthusiastically and professionally.

It's customary to conclude by expressing gratitude to one's spouse and family, and for good reason. Writing and revising *The Norton Field Guide* over the past several years, we have enjoyed the loving and unconditional support of our spouses, Barb, Peter, and Larry, who provide the foundation for all we do. Thank you. We couldn't have done it without you.

How to Use This Book

There's no one way to do anything, and writing is no exception. Some people need to do a lot of planning on paper; others write entire drafts in their heads. Some writers compose quickly and loosely, going back later to revise; others work on one sentence until they're satisfied with it, then move on to the next. And writers' needs vary from task to task, too: sometimes you know what you're going to write about and why, but need to figure out how to do it; other times your first job is to come up with a topic. *The Norton Field Guide* is designed to allow you to chart your own course as a writer, offering guidelines that suit your writing needs. It is organized in nine parts:

1. **ACADEMIC LITERACIES**: The chapters in this part will help you know what's expected in the reading and writing you do for academic purposes, and in summarizing and responding to what you read. One chapter even provides tips for developing habits of mind that will help you succeed in college, whatever your goals.

2. **RHETORICAL SITUATIONS**: No matter what you're writing, it will always have some purpose, audience, genre, stance, and medium and design. This part will help you consider each of these elements, as well as the particular kinds of rhetorical situations created by academic assignments.

3. **GENRES**: Use these chapters for help with specific kinds of writing, from abstracts to lab reports to memoirs and more. You'll find more detailed guidance for four especially common assignments: literacy narratives, textual analyses, reports, and arguments. There's also help with choosing which genre to use when an assignment doesn't specify one.

4. **PROCESSES**: These chapters offer general advice for all writing situations—from generating ideas and text to drafting, revising and rewriting, compiling a portfolio—and more.

5. **STRATEGIES** : Use the advice in this part to develop and organize your writing—to write effective beginnings and endings, to guide readers through your text, and to use comparison, description, dialogue, and other strategies as appropriate.

6. **RESEARCH / DOCUMENTATION** : Use this section for advice on how to do research, work with sources, and compose and document research-based texts using MLA and APA styles.

7. **MEDIA / DESIGN** : This section offers guidance in designing your work and using visuals and sound, and in deciding whether and how to deliver what you write on paper, on screen, or in person.

8. **READINGS** : This section includes readings in 10 genres, and one chapter of texts that mix genres — 42 readings in all that provide good examples of the kinds of writing you yourself may be assigned to do.

9. **HANDBOOK** : Look here for help with sentence-level editing.

Ways into the Book

The Norton Field Guide gives you the writing advice you need, along with the flexibility to write in the way that works best for you. Here are some of the ways you can find what you need in the book.

Brief menus.   Inside the front cover you'll find a list of all the chapters; start here if you are looking for a chapter on a certain kind of writing or a general writing issue. Inside the back cover is a menu of all the topics covered in the **HANDBOOK**.

Complete contents.   Pages xiii–xxxiii contain a detailed table of contents. Look here if you need to find a reading or a specific section in a chapter.

Guides to writing.   If you know the kind of writing you need to do, you'll find guides to writing 14 common genres in Part 2. These guides are designed to help you through all the decisions you have to make— from coming up with a topic to editing and proofreading your final draft.

Color-coding.   The parts of this book are color-coded for easy reference: light blue for **ACADEMIC LITERACIES**, red for **RHETORICAL SITUATIONS**, green for **GENRES**, lavender for **PROCESSES**, orange for **STRATEGIES**, blue for **RESEARCH / DOCUMENTATION**, gold for **MEDIA / DESIGN**, apple green for the **READINGS**, and yellow for the **HANDBOOK**. You'll find a key to the colors on the front cover flap and also at the foot of each left-hand page. When you see a word highlighted in a color, that tells you where you can find additional detail on the topic.

Glossary / index. At the back of the book is a combined glossary and index, where you'll find full definitions of key terms and topics, along with a list of the pages where everything is covered in detail.

Directories to MLA and APA documentation. A brief directory inside the back cover will lead you to guidelines on citing sources and composing a list of references or works cited. The documentation models are color-coded so you can easily see the key details.

The website. You can also start at wwnorton.com/write/fieldguide. There you'll find model essays; worksheets; MLA and APA guidelines; more than 1,000 exercises focused on sentences, language, and punctuation; an online handbook; and more.

Ways of Getting Started

If you know your genre, simply turn to the appropriate genre chapter. There you'll find model readings, a description of the genre's Key Features, and a Guide to Writing that will help you come up with a topic, generate text, organize and write a draft, get response, revise, edit, and proofread. The genre chapters also point out places where you might need to do research, use certain writing strategies, design your text a certain way — and direct you to the exact pages in the book where you can find help doing so.

If you know your topic, you might start with some of the activities in Chapter 27, Generating Ideas and Text. From there, you might turn to Chapter 46, for help Finding Sources on the topic. When it comes time to narrow your topic and come up with a thesis statement, Chapter 34 can help. If you get stuck at any point, you might turn to Chapter 25, Writing as Inquiry; it provides tips that can get you beyond what you already know about your topic. If your assignment or your thesis defines your genre, turn to that chapter; if not, consult Chapter 25 for help determining the appropriate genre, and then turn to that genre chapter. The genre chapters point out places where you might need to do more research, use certain writing strategies, design your text a certain way — and direct you to the exact pages in the book where you can find help doing so.

Contents

Part 2   Rhetorical Situations   53

Part 4   Processes   279

Part 6   Doing Research   433

Part 8   Analog   637

Part 9   Handbook   HB-1

Sentences   HB-3

part 1

Academic Literacies

Whenever we enter a new community — start a new job, move to a new town, join a new club — there are certain things we need to learn. The same is true upon entering the academic world. We need to be able to **READ** and **WRITE** in certain ways. We're routinely called on to **SUMMARIZE** something we've heard or read, and to **RESPOND** in some way. And to succeed, we need to develop certain **HABITS OF MIND** — everyday things such as asking questions and being persistent. The following chapters provide guidelines to help you develop these fundamental academic literacies — and know what's expected of you in academic communities.

Academic Literacies

Writing in Academic Contexts   **1**

Write an essay arguing whether genes or environment do more to determine people's intelligence. Research and write a report on the environmental effects of electricity-generating windmills. Work with a team to write a proposal and create a multimedia presentation for a sales campaign. Whatever you're studying, you're surely going to be doing a lot of writing, in classes from various disciplines — the above assignments, for example, are from psychology, environmental science, and marketing. Academic writing can serve a number of different purposes — to **ARGUE** for what you think about a topic and why, to **REPORT** on what's known about an issue, to **PROPOSE A SOLUTION** for some problem, and so on. Whatever your topics or purposes, all academic writing follows certain conventions, ones you'll need to master in order to join the conversations going on across campus. This chapter describes what's expected of academic writing — and of academic writers.

▲ 156–82

129–55

235–42

What's Expected of Academic Writing

Evidence that you've considered the subject thoughtfully. Whether you're composing a report, an argument, or some other kind of writing, you need to demonstrate that you've thought seriously about the topic and done any necessary research. You can use various ways to show that you've considered the subject carefully, from citing authoritative sources to incorporating information you learned in class to pointing out connections among ideas.

academic literacies   rhetorical situations   genres   processes   strategies   research MLA / APA   media / design   readings   handbook

An indication of why your topic matters.   You need to help your readers understand why your topic is worth exploring and why your writing is worth reading. Even if you are writing in response to an assigned topic, you can better make your point and achieve your purpose by showing your readers why your topic is important and why they should care about it. For example, in "Throwing Like a Girl," James Fallows explains why his topic, the differences between the ways men and women throw a baseball, is worth writing about:

> The phrase "throwing like a girl" has become an embattled and offensive one. Feminists smart at its implication that to do something "like a girl" is to do it the wrong way. Recently, on the heels of the O. J. Simpson case, a book appeared in which the phrase was used to help explain why male athletes, especially football players, were involved in so many assaults against women. Having been trained (like most American boys) to dread the accusation of doing anything "like a girl," athletes were said to grow into the assumption that women were valueless, and natural prey.

By explaining that the topic matters because it reflects attitudes about gender that have potentially serious consequences, he gives readers reason to read on about the mechanics of "throwing like a girl."

A response to what others have said.   Whatever your topic, it's unlikely that you'll be the first one to write about it. And if, as this chapter assumes, all academic writing is part of a larger conversation, you are in a way adding your own voice to that conversation. One good way of doing that is to present your ideas as a response to what others have said about your topic — to begin by quoting, paraphrasing, or summarizing what others have said and then to agree, disagree, or both.

For example, in an essay arguing that organ sales will save lives, Joanna MacKay says, "Some agree with Pope John Paul II that the selling of organs is morally wrong and violates 'the dignity of the human person.'" But she then responds — and disagrees, arguing that "the morals we hold are not absolute truths" and that "peasants of third world countries" might not agree with the pope.

A clear, appropriately qualified thesis. When you write in an academic context, you're expected to state your main point explicitly, often in a **THESIS** statement. MIT student Joanna MacKay states her thesis clearly in her essay "Organ Sales Will Save Lives": "Governments should not ban the sale of human organs; they should regulate it." Often you'll need to **QUALIFY** your thesis statement to acknowledge that the subject is complicated and there may be more than one way of seeing it or exceptions to the generalization you're making about it. Here, for example, is a qualified thesis, from an essay evaluating the movie *Juno* by Ali Heinkamp, a student at Wright State University: "Although the situations *Juno's* characters find themselves in and their dialogue may be criticized as unrealistic, the film, written by Diablo Cody and directed by Jason Reitman, successfully portrays the emotions of a teen being shoved into maturity way too fast." Heinkamp makes a claim that *Juno* achieves its main goal, while acknowledging at the beginning of the sentence that the film may be flawed.

345–47
346–47

Good reasons supported by evidence. You need to provide good reasons for your thesis and evidence to support those reasons. For example, Joanna MacKay offers several reasons why sales of human kidneys should be legalized: there is a surplus of kidneys, the risk to the donor is not great, and legalization would allow the trade in kidneys to be regulated. Evidence to support your reasons sometimes comes from your own experience but more often from published research and scholarship, research you do yourself or firsthand accounts by others.

Compared with other kinds of writing, academic writing is generally expected to be more objective and less emotional. You may find *Romeo and Juliet* deeply moving or cry when you watch *Titanic* — but when you write about the play or the film for a class, you must do so using evidence from the text to support your thesis. You may find someone's ideas deeply offensive, but you should respond to them with reason rather than with emotional appeals or personal attacks.

Acknowledgment of multiple perspectives. Debates and arguments in popular media are often framed in "pro/con" terms, as if there were only two sides to any given issue. Once you begin seriously studying a topic, though, you're likely to find that there are several sides and that each of them deserves serious consideration. In your academic writing, you need to represent fairly the range of perspectives on your topic — to explore three, four, or more positions on it as you research and write. In her report, "Does Texting Affect Writing," Marywood University student Michaela Cullington, for example, examines texting from several points of view: teachers' impressions of the influence of texting on student writing, the results of several research studies, and her own survey research.

A confident, authoritative stance. If one goal of academic writing is to contribute to a larger conversation, your tone should convey confidence and establish your authority to write about your subject. Ways to achieve such a tone include using active verbs ("X claims" rather than "it seems"), avoiding such phrases as "in my opinion" and "I think," and writing in a straightforward, direct style. Your writing should send the message that you've done the research, analysis, and thinking and know what you're talking about. For example, here is the final paragraph of Michaela Cullington's essay on texting and writing:

> On the basis of my own research, expert research, and personal observations, I can confidently state that texting is not interfering with students' use of standard written English and has no effect on their writing abilities in general. It is interesting to look at the dynamics of the arguments over these issues. Teachers and parents who claim that they are seeing a decline in the writing abilities of their students and children mainly support the negative-impact argument. Other teachers and researchers suggest that texting provides a way for teens to practice writing in a casual setting and thus helps prepare them to write formally. Experts and students themselves, however, report that they see no effect, positive or negative. Anecdotal experiences should not overshadow the actual evidence.

Cullington's use of simple, declarative sentences ("Other teachers and researchers suggest ..."; "Anecdotal experiences should not overshadow ...") and her straightforward summary of the arguments surrounding texting, along with her strong, unequivocal ending ("texting is not interfering with students' use of standard written English"), lend her writing a confident tone. Her stance sends the message that she's done the research and knows what she's talking about.

Carefully documented sources.   Clearly acknowledging sources and documenting them carefully and correctly is a basic requirement of academic writing. When you use the words or ideas of others — including visuals, video, or audio — those sources must be documented in the text and in a works cited or references list at the end. (If you're writing something that will appear online, you may also refer readers to your sources by using hyperlinks in the text; ask your instructor if you need to include a list of references or works cited as well.)

Careful attention to correctness.   Whether you're writing something formal or informal, in an essay or an email, you should always write in complete sentences, use appropriate capitalization and punctuation, and check that your spelling is correct. In general, academic writing is no place for colloquial language, slang, or texting abbreviations. If you're quoting someone, you can reproduce that person's writing or speech exactly, but in your own writing you try hard to be correct — and always proofread carefully.

What's Expected of College Writers: The WPA Outcomes

Writing is not a multiple-choice test; it doesn't have right and wrong answers that are easily graded. Instead, your readers, whether they're teachers or anyone else, are likely to read your writing with various things in mind: does it make sense, does it meet the demands of the assignment, is the grammar correct, to name just a few of the things readers may look for. Different readers may notice different things, so sometimes it may seem to you that their response — and your grade — is unpredictable. It should be good to know, then, that writing teachers across the nation have come to some agreement on certain "outcomes," what college students should know and be able to do by the time you finish a first-year writing course. These outcomes have been defined by the National Council of Writing Program Administrators (WPA). Here's a brief summary of these outcomes and how *The Norton Field Guide* can help you meet them.

Knowledge of Rhetoric

- *Understand the rhetorical situation of texts that you read and write.* See Chapters 5–9 and the many prompts for Considering the Rhetorical Situation throughout the book.
- *Read and write texts in a number of different genres and understand how your purpose may influence your writing.* See Chapters 10–22 for guidelines on writing in thirteen genres, Chapter 23 on mixing genres, and Chapter 24 for help choosing genres when you need to.
- *Adjust your voice, tone, level of formality, design, and medium as is necessary and appropriate.* See Chapter 8 on stance and tone and Chapter 9 for help thinking about medium and design.
- *Choose the media that will best suit your audience, purpose, and the rest of your rhetorical situation.* See Chapters 9 and 54.

Critical Thinking, Reading, and Composing

- *Read and write to inquire, learn, think critically, and communicate.* See Chapters 1 and 2 on academic writing and reading, and Chapter 25 on writing as inquiry. Chapters 10–13 provide genre-specific prompts to help you think critically about a draft.
- *Read for content, argumentative strategies, and rhetorical effectiveness.* Chapter 7 provides guidance on reading texts with a critical eye, Chapter 11 teaches how to analyze a text, and Chapter 47 shows how to evaluate sources.
- *Find and evaluate popular and scholarly sources.* Chapter 46 teaches how to use databases and other methods to find sources, and Chapter 47 shows how to evaluate the sources you find.

- *Use sources in various ways to support your ideas.* Chapter 36 suggests strategies for supporting your ideas, and Chapter 49 shows how to incorporate ideas from sources into your writing to support your ideas.

Processes

- *Use writing processes to compose texts and explore ideas in various media.* Part 4 covers all stages of the processes writers use, from generating ideas and text to drafting to getting response and revising to editing and proofreading. Each of the thirteen genre chapters (10–22) includes a guide that leads you through the process of writing in that genre.
- *Collaborate with others on your own writing and on group tasks.* Chapter 26 offers guidelines for working with others, Chapter 30 provides general prompts for getting and giving response, and Chapters 10–13 provide genre-specific prompts for reading a draft with a critical eye.
- *Reflect on your own writing processes.* Chapters 10–13 provide genre-specific questions to help you take stock of your work, and Chapter 29 offers guidance in thinking about your own writing process. Chapter 32 provides prompts to help you reflect on a writing portfolio.

Knowledge of Conventions

- *Use correct grammar, punctuation, and spelling.* Chapter 31 provides tips to help you edit and proofread for your writing. Chapters 10–13 offer genre-specific advice for editing and proofreading.
- *Understand and use genre conventions and formats in your writing.* Chapter 7 provides an overview of genres and how to think about them. Part 3 covers thirteen genres, describing the key features and conventions of each one.
- *Understand intellectual property and document sources appropriately.* Chapter 50 offers guidance on the ethical use of sources, Chapter 51 provides an overview of documentation styles, and Chapters 52 and 53 provide templates for documenting in MLA and APA styles.

2 Reading in Academic Contexts

We read newspapers to know about the events of the day. We read textbooks to learn about history, chemistry, and other academic topics — and other academic sources to do research and develop arguments. We read tweets and blogs to follow (and participate in) conversations about issues that interest us. And as writers, we read our own writing to make sure it says what we mean it to say and proofread our final drafts to make sure they say it correctly. In other words, we read many kinds of texts for many different purposes. This chapter offers a number of strategies for various kinds of reading you do in academic contexts.

TAKING STOCK OF YOUR READING

One way to become a better reader is to understand your reading process; if you know what you do when you read, you're in a position to decide what you need to change or improve. Consider the answers to the following questions:

- What do you read for pleasure? for work? for school? Consider all the sorts of reading you do: books, magazines, and newspapers, websites, *Facebook*, texts, blogs, product instructions.

- When you're facing a reading assignment, what do you do? Do you do certain things to get comfortable? Do you play music or seek quiet? Do you plan your reading time or set reading goals for yourself? Do you flip through or skim the text before settling down to read it, or do you start at the beginning and work through it?

- When you begin to read something for an assignment, do you make sure you understand the purpose of the assignment — why you

academic literacies   rhetorical situations   genres   processes   strategies   research MLA / APA   media / design   readings   handbook

must read this text? Do you ever ask your instructor (or whoever else assigned the reading) what its purpose is?

- How do you motivate yourself to read material you don't have any interest in? How do you deal with boredom while reading?

- Does your mind wander? If you realize that you haven't been paying attention and don't know what you just read, what do you do?

- Do you ever highlight, underline, or annotate text as you read? Do you take notes? If so, what do you mark or write down? Why?

- When you read text you don't understand, what do you do?

- As you anticipate and read an assigned text, what attitudes or feelings do you typically have? If they differ from reading to reading, why do they?

- What do you do when you've finished reading an assigned text? Write out notes? Think about what you've just read? Move on to the next task? Something else?

- How well do your reading processes work for you, both in school and otherwise? What would you like to change? What can you do to change?

The rest of this chapter offers advice and strategies that you may find helpful as you work to improve your reading skills.

READING STRATEGICALLY

Academic reading is challenging because it makes several demands on you at once. Textbooks present new vocabulary and new concepts, and picking out the main ideas can be difficult. Scholarly articles present content and arguments you need to understand, but they often assume that readers already know key concepts and vocabulary and so don't generally provide background information. As you read more texts in an academic field and begin to participate in its conversations, the reading will become easier, but in the meantime you can develop strategies that will help you to read effectively.

Thinking about What You Want to Learn

To learn anything, we need to place new information into the context of what we already know. For example, to understand photosynthesis, we need to already know something about plants, energy, and air, among other things. To learn a new language, we draw on similarities and differences between it and any other languages we know. A method of bringing to conscious attention our current knowledge on a topic and of helping us articulate our purposes for reading is a list-making process called KWL+. To use it, create a table with three columns:

K: What I <u>K</u>now	W: What I <u>W</u>ant to Know	L: What I <u>L</u>earned

Before you begin reading a text, list in the "K" column what you already know about the topic. Brainstorm ideas, and list terms or phrases that come to mind. Then group them into categories. Also before reading, or after reading the first few paragraphs, list in the "W" column questions you have that you expect, want, or hope to be answered as you read. Number or reorder the questions by their importance to you.

Then, as you read the text or afterward, list in the "L" column what you learned from the text. Compare your "L" list with your "W" list to see what you still want or need to know (the "+") — and what you learned that you didn't expect.

Previewing the Text

It's usually a good idea to start by skimming a text — read the title and subtitle, any headings, the first and last paragraphs, the first sentences of all the other paragraphs. Study any illustrations and other visuals. Your goal is to get a sense of where the text is heading. At this point, don't stop to look up unfamiliar words; just mark them in some way to look up later.

Adjusting Your Reading Speed to Different Texts

Different texts require different kinds of effort. Some that are simple and straightforward can be skimmed fairly quickly. With academic texts, though, you usually need to read more slowly and carefully, matching the pace of your reading to the difficulty of the text. You'll likely need to skim the text for an overview of the basic ideas and then go back to read it closely. And then you may need to read it yet again. (But do try always to read quickly enough to focus on the meanings of sentences and paragraphs, not just individual words.) With visual texts, too, you'll often need to look at them several times, moving from gaining an overall impression to closely examining the structure, layout, and other visual features — and exploring how those features relate to any accompanying verbal text.

Looking for Organizational Cues

As you read, look for cues that signal the way the text's ideas are organized and how each part relates to the ones around it:

The introductory paragraph and thesis often offer a preview of the topics to be discussed and the order in which they will be addressed. Here, for example, is a typical thesis statement for a report: *Types of prisons in the United States include minimum and medium security, close security, maximum security, and supermax.* The report that follows should explain each type of prison in the order stated in the thesis.

Transitions help **GUIDE READERS** in following the direction of the writer's thinking from idea to idea. For example, "however" indicates an idea that contradicts or limits what has just been said, while "furthermore" indicates one that adds to or supports it.

349

Headings identify a text's major and minor sections, by means of both the headings' content and their design.

Thinking about Your Initial Response

Some readers find it helps to make brief notes about their first response to a text, noting their reaction and thinking a little about why they reacted as they did.

What are your initial reactions? Describe both your intellectual reaction and any emotional reaction, and identify places in the text that caused you to react as you did. An intellectual reaction might consist of an evaluation ("I disagree with this position because . . ."), a connection ("This idea reminds me of . . ."), or an elaboration ("Another example of this point is . . ."). An emotional reaction could include approval or disapproval ("YES! This is exactly right!" "NO! This is so wrong!"), an expression of feeling ("This passage makes me so sad"), or one of appreciation ("This is said so beautifully"). If you had no particular reaction, note that, too.

What accounts for your reactions? Are they rooted in personal experiences? aspects of your personality? positions you hold on an issue? As much as possible, you want to keep your opinions from interfering with your understanding of what you're reading, so it's important to try to identify those opinions up front.

Dealing with Difficult Texts

Let's face it: some texts are difficult. You may have no interest in the subject matter, or lack background knowledge or vocabulary necessary for understanding the text, or simply not have a clear sense of why you have to read the text at all. Whatever the reason, reading such texts can be a challenge. Here are some tips for dealing with them:

Look for something familiar.   Texts often seem difficult or boring because we don't know enough about the topic or about the larger conversation surrounding it to read them effectively. By skimming the headings, the abstract or introduction, and the conclusion, you may find something that relates to something you already know or are at least interested in — and being aware of that prior knowledge can help you see how this new material relates to it.

Look for "landmarks."   Reading a challenging academic text the first time through can be like driving to an unfamiliar destination on roads you've never traveled: you don't know where you're headed, you don't recognize anything along the way, and you're not sure how long getting there will take. As you drive the route again, though, you see landmarks along the way that help you know where you're going. The same goes for reading a difficult text: sometimes you need to get through it once just to get some idea of what it's about. On the second reading, now that you have "driven the route," look for the ways that the parts of the text relate to one another, to other texts or course information, or to other knowledge you have.

Monitor your understanding.   You may have had the experience of reading a text and suddenly realizing that you have no idea what you just read. Being able to monitor your reading — to sense when you aren't understanding the text and need to reread, focus your attention, look up unfamiliar terms, take some notes, or take a break — can make you a more efficient and better reader. Keep these questions in mind as you read: What is my purpose for reading this text? Am I understanding it? Does it make sense? Should I slow down, reread, annotate? skim ahead and then come back? pause to reflect?

Be persistent.   Research shows that many students respond to difficult texts by assuming they're "too dumb to get it" — and quit reading. Successful students, on the other hand, report that if they keep at a text, they will come to understand it. Some of them even see difficult texts as challenges: "I'm going to keep working on this until I make sense of it."

Remember that reading is an active process, and the more you work at it the more successful you will be.

Annotating

Many readers find it helps to annotate as they read: highlighting keywords, phrases, sentences; connecting ideas with lines or symbols; writing comments or questions in the margin or on sticky notes; circling new words so you can look up the definitions later; noting anything that seems noteworthy or questionable. Annotating forces you to read for more than just the surface meaning. Especially when you are going to be writing about or responding to a text, annotating creates a record of things you may want to refer to.

Annotate as if you're having a conversation with the author, someone you take seriously but whose words you do not accept without question. Put your part of the conversation in the margin, asking questions, talking back: "What's this mean?" "So what?" "Says who?" "Where's evidence?" "Yes!" "Whoa!" or even ☺ or ☹ or texting shorthand like LOL or INTRSTN. If you're reading a text online, you may be able to copy it and annotate it electronically. If so, make your annotations a different color from the text itself.

55–56 What you annotate depends upon your **PURPOSE**, or what you're most interested in. If you're analyzing a text that makes an explicit argu- 345–47 ment, you would probably underline the **THESIS STATEMENT**, and then 358–67 the **REASONS AND EVIDENCE** that support that statement. It might help to restate those ideas in your own words in the margins — in order to understand them, you need to put them in your own words! If you are trying to 28–29 **IDENTIFY PATTERNS**, you might highlight each pattern in a different color or mark it with a sticky note and write any questions or notes about it in that color. You might annotate a visual text by circling and identifying important parts of the image.

There are some texts that you cannot annotate, of course — library books, some materials you read on the web, and so on. Then you will need to use sticky notes or make notes elsewhere, and you might find it useful to keep a reading log for this purpose.

A Sample Annotated Text

Here is an excerpt from Justice: What's the Right Thing to Do?, *a book by Harvard professor Michael J. Sandel, annotated by a writer who was doing research for a report on the awarding of military medals:*

What Wounds Deserve the Purple Heart?

On some issues, questions of virtue and honor are too obvious to deny. Consider the recent debate over who should qualify for the Purple Heart. Since 1932, the U.S. military has awarded the medal to soldiers wounded or killed in battle by enemy action. In addition to the honor, the medal entitles recipients to special privileges in veterans' hospitals.

> *Purple Heart given for wounding or death in battle.*

Since the beginning of the current wars in Iraq and Afghanistan, growing numbers of veterans have been diagnosed with post-traumatic stress disorder and treated for the condition. Symptoms include recurring nightmares, severe depression, and suicide. At least three hundred thousand veterans reportedly suffer from traumatic stress or major depression. Advocates for these veterans have proposed that they, too, should qualify for the Purple Heart. Since psychological injuries can be at least as debilitating as physical ones, they argue, soldiers who suffer these wounds should receive the medal.

> *PTSD increasingly common among veterans.*

> *Argument: Vets with PTSD should be eligible for PH because psych. injuries are as serious as physical.*

After a Pentagon advisory group studied the question, the Pentagon announced, in 2009, that the Purple Heart would be reserved for soldiers with physical injuries. Veterans suffering from mental disorders and psychological trauma would not be eligible, even though they qualify for government-supported medical treatment and disability payments. The Pentagon offered two reasons for its decision: traumatic stress disorders are not intentionally caused by enemy action, and they are difficult to diagnose objectively.

> *2009: Military says no: PTSD injuries "not intentionally caused by enemy" and are hard to diagnose.*

Did the Pentagon make the right decision? Taken by themselves, its reasons are unconvincing. In the Iraq War, one of the most common injuries recognized with the Purple Heart has been a punctured eardrum, caused by explosions at close range. But unlike bullets and bombs, such explosions are not a deliberate enemy tactic intended to injure or kill; they are (like traumatic stress) a damaging side effect of battlefield action. And while traumatic disorders may be more difficult

> *PTSD is like punctured eardrums, which do get the PH.*

to diagnose than a broken limb, the injury they inflict can be more severe and long-lasting.

As the wider debate about the Purple Heart revealed, the real issue is about the meaning of the medal and the virtues it honors. What, then, are the relevant virtues? Unlike other military medals, <u>the Purple Heart honors sacrifice, not bravery</u>. It requires no heroic act, only an injury inflicted by the enemy. The question is what kind of injury should count.

PH "honors sacrifice, not bravery." Injury enough. So what kind of injury?

A veteran's group called the Military Order of the Purple Heart opposed awarding the medal for psychological injuries, claiming that doing so would "debase" the honor. A spokesman for the group stated that "shedding blood" should be an essential qualification. He didn't explain why bloodless injuries shouldn't count. But Tyler E. Boudreau, a former Marine captain who favors including psychological injuries, offers a compelling analysis of the dispute. He attributes the opposition to a deep-seated attitude in the military that views post-traumatic stress as a kind of weakness. "The same culture that demands tough-mindedness also encourages skepticism toward the suggestion that the violence of war can hurt the healthiest of minds . . . Sadly, <u>as long as our military culture bears at least a quiet contempt for the psychological wounds of war, it is unlikely those veterans will ever see a Purple Heart</u>."

Wow: one vet's group insists that for PH, soldier must <u>bleed</u>!

Good quote!

So the debate over the Purple Heart is more than a medical or clinical dispute about how to determine the veracity of injury. At the heart of the disagreement are rival conceptions of <u>moral character and military valor</u>. Those who insist that only bleeding wounds should count believe that post-traumatic stress reflects a weakness of character unworthy of honor. Those who believe that psychological wounds should qualify argue that veterans suffering long-term trauma and severe depression have sacrificed for their country as surely, and as honorably, as those who've lost a limb. The dispute over the Purple Heart illustrates the moral logic of Aristotle's theory of justice. We can't determine who deserves a military medal without asking what virtues the medal properly honors. And to answer that question, we have to assess competing conceptions of character and sacrifice.

Argument based on different ideas about what counts as a military virtue.

— Michael J. Sandel, *Justice: What's the Right Thing to Do?*

academic literacies ‖ rhetorical situations ‖ genres ‖ processes ‖ strategies ‖ research MLA / APA ‖ media / design ‖ readings ‖ handbook

Coding

You may also find it useful to record your thoughts as you read by using a coding system — for example, using "X" to indicate passages that contradict your assumptions, or "?" for ones that puzzle you. You can make up your own coding system, of course, but you could start with this one*:

- ✔ Confirms what you thought
- X Contradicts what you thought
- ? Puzzles you
- ?? Confuses you
- ! Surprises you
- ☆ Strikes you as important
- → Is new or interesting to you

You might also circle new words that you'll want to look up later and highlight or underline key phrases.

Summarizing

Writing a summary, boiling down a text to its main ideas, can help you understand it. To do so, you need to identify which ideas in the text are crucial to its meaning. Then you put those crucial ideas into your own words, creating a brief version that accurately sums up the text. Here, for example, is a summary of Sandel's analysis of the Purple Heart debate:

> In "What Wounds Deserve the Purple Heart?," Harvard professor Michael J. Sandel explores the debate over eligibility for the Purple Heart, the medal given to soldiers who die or are wounded in battle. Some argue that soldiers suffering from post-traumatic stress disorder

---

*Adapted from Harvey Daniels and Steven Zemelman, *Subjects Matter: Every Teacher's Guide to Content-Area Reading*.

should qualify for the medal because psychological injuries are as serious as physical ones. However, the military disagrees, since PTSD injuries are not "intentionally caused by enemy action" and are hard to diagnose. Sandel observes that the dispute centers on how "character" and "sacrifice" are defined. Those who insist that soldiers must have had physical wounds to be eligible for the Purple Heart see psychological wounds as reflecting "weakness of character," while others argue that veterans with PTSD and other psychological traumas have sacrificed honorably for their country.

Thinking about How the Text Works: What It Says, What It Does

Sometimes you'll need to think about how a text works, how its parts fit together. You may be assigned to analyze a text, or you may just need to make sense of a difficult text, to think about how the ideas all relate to one another. Whatever your purpose, a good way to think about a text

293–95

structure is by **OUTLINING** it, paragraph by paragraph. If you're interested in analyzing its ideas, look at what each paragraph *says*; if, on the other hand, you're concerned with how the ideas are presented, pay attention to what each paragraph *does*.

What it says. Write a sentence that identifies what each paragraph says. Once you've done that for the whole text, look for patterns in the topics the writer addresses. Pay attention to the order in which the topics are presented. Also look for gaps, ideas the writer has left unsaid. Such paragraph-by-paragraph outlining of the content can help you see how the writer has arranged ideas and how that arrangement builds an argument or develops a topic. Here, for example, is an outline of Michael Granof's proposal, "Course Requirement: Extortion"; the essay may be found on pages 235–37. The numbers in the left column refer to the essay's paragraphs.

1   College textbooks cost several times more than other books.

2   However, a proposed solution to the cost problem would only make things worse.

3   This proposal, to promote sales of used textbooks, would actually cause textbook costs to rise, because the sale of used books is a main reason new texts cost so much.

4   There is another way to lower costs.

5   Used textbooks are already being marketed and sold very efficiently.

6   Because of this, most new textbook sales take place in the first semester after they're published, forcing publishers to raise prices before used books take over the market.

7   In response, textbooks are revised every few years, whether or not the content is outdated, and the texts are "bundled" with other materials that can't be used again.

8–9   A better solution would be to consider textbooks to be like computer software and issue "site licenses" to universities. Once instructors choose textbooks, the university would pay publishers fees per student for their use.

10   Publishers would earn money for the use of the textbooks, and students' costs would be much lower.

11   Students could use an electronic text or buy a print copy for additional money. The print copies would cost less because the publisher would make most of its profits on the site license fees.

12   This arrangement would have no impact on teaching, unlike other proposals that focus on using electronic materials or using "no frills" textbooks and might negatively affect students' learning.

13   This proposal would reduce the cost of attending college and help students and their families.

What it does. Identify the function of each paragraph. Starting with the first paragraph, ask, What does this paragraph do? Does it introduce a topic? provide background for a topic to come? describe something? define something? entice me to read further? something else? What does the second paragraph do? the third? As you go through the text, you may identify groups of paragraphs that have a single purpose. Here is a functional outline of Granof's essay (again, the numbers on the left refer to the paragraphs):

1	Introduces the topic by defining a problem
2	Introduces a flawed solution
3	Explains the flawed solution and the problem with it
4	Introduces a better solution
5–7	Describes the current situation and the dynamics of the problem
8	Outlines the author's proposed solution
9–10	Explains the proposed solution
11–12	Describes the benefits and effects of the proposed solution
13	Concludes

Reading Visual Texts

Photos, drawings, graphs, diagrams, and charts are frequently used to help convey important information and often make powerful arguments themselves. So learning to read and interpret visual texts is just as necessary as it is for written texts.

Taking visuals seriously.　Remember that visuals are texts themselves, not just decoration. When they appear as part of a written text, they may introduce information not discussed elsewhere in the text. Or they might illustrate concepts hard to grasp from words alone. In either case, it's important to pay close attention to any visuals in a written text.

Looking at any title, caption, or other written text that's part of a visual will help you understand its main idea. It might also help to think about its purpose: Why did the writer include it? What information does it add or emphasize? What argument is it making? See, for example, how a psychology textbook uses visuals to help explain two ways that information can be represented:

academic literacies　rhetorical situations　genres　processes　strategies　research MLA / APA　media / design　readings　handbook

Analogical and Symbolic Representations

When we think about information, we use two basic types of internal representations: analogical and symbolic.

Analogical representations usually correspond to images. They have some characteristics of actual objects. Therefore, they are analogous to actual objects. For example, maps correspond to geographical layouts. Family trees depict branching relationships between relatives. A clock corresponds directly to the passage of time. **Figure 2.1a** is a drawing of a violin from a particular perspective. This drawing is an analogical representation.

Figure 2.1 Analogical Versus Symbolic Representations

(a)   (b)

(a) Analogical representations, such as this picture of a violin, have some characteristics of the objects they represent.
(b) Symbolic representations, such as the word *violin*, are abstract and do not have relationships to the physical qualities of objects.

By contrast, **symbolic representations** are abstract. These representations usually consist of words or ideas. They do not have relationships to physical qualities of objects in the world. The word *hamburger* is a symbolic representation that usually represents a cooked patty of beef served on a bun. The word *violin* stands for a musical instrument (**Figure 2.1b**).   — Sarah Grison, Todd Heatherton, and Michael Gazzaniga, *Psychology in Your Life*

The headings tell you the topic: analogical and symbolic representations. The paragraphs define the two types of representation, and the illustrations present a visual example of each type. The visuals make the information in the written text easier to understand by illustrating the differences between the two.

Title: Indicates the topic.

Legend: Explains the symbols used. Here, colors show the different categories.

Source: The origin of the data.

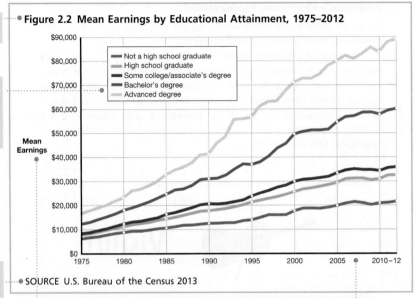

Figure 2.2 Mean Earnings by Educational Attainment, 1975–2012

Legend:
- Not a high school graduate
- High school graduate
- Some college/associate's degree
- Bachelor's degree
- Advanced degree

Mean Earnings (y-axis): $0, $10,000, $20,000, $30,000, $40,000, $50,000, $60,000, $70,000, $80,000, $90,000

X-axis: 1975, 1980, 1985, 1990, 1995, 2000, 2005, 2010–12

SOURCE U.S. Bureau of the Census 2013

Y-axis: Defines the independent variable (something that doesn't change depending on other factors).

X-axis: Defines the dependent variable (something that changes, depending on other factors).

Reading charts and graphs. To read the information in charts and graphs, you need to look for different things depending on what type of chart or graph you're considering. A line graph, for example, usually contains certain elements: title, legend, x-axis, y-axis, and source information. Figure 2.2 shows one such graph taken from a sociology textbook.

Other types of charts and graphs include some of these same elements. But the specific elements vary according to the different kinds of information being presented, and some charts and graphs can be challenging to read. For example, the chart in Figure 2.3, from the same textbook, includes elements of both bar and line graphs to depict two trends at once: the red line shows the percentage of women in the United States and the larger context within which a writer wrote and the argument the text makes.

Considering the Rhetorical Situation

As a reader, you need to think about the message that the writer wants to articulate, including the intended audience and the writer's attitude toward that audience and the topic, as well as about the genre, medium, and design of the text.

PURPOSE   What is the writer's purpose? To entertain? inform? persuade readers to think something or take some action? What is *your* purpose for reading this text? | 55–56

AUDIENCE   Who is the intended audience? Are you a member of that group? If not, should you expect that you'll need to look up unfamiliar terms or concepts or that you'll run into assumptions you don't necessarily share? How is the writer addressing the audience — as an expert addressing those less knowledgeable? an outsider addressing insiders? | 57–60

GENRE   What is the genre? Is it a report? an argument? an analysis? something else? Knowing the genre can help you to anticipate certain key features. | 61–63

STANCE   Who is the writer, and what is his or her stance? Critical? Curious? Opinionated? Objective? Passionate? Indifferent? Something else? Knowing the stance affects the way you understand a text, whether you're inclined to agree or disagree with it, to take it seriously, and so on. | 64–67

MEDIA / DESIGN   What is the medium, and how does it affect the way you read? If it's a print text, what do you know about the publisher? If it's on the web, who sponsors the site, and when was it last updated? Are there any headings, summaries, or other elements that highlight key parts of the text? | 68–70

Identifying Patterns

Look for notable patterns in the text — recurring words and their synonyms, as well as repeated phrases, metaphors and other images, and types of sentences. Some readers find it helps to highlight patterns in various colors. Does the author repeatedly rely on any particular writing strategies: **NARRATION**? **COMPARISON**? Something else?

419–27
380–87

Another kind of pattern it might be important to consider is the kind of evidence the text provides. Is it more opinion than facts? nothing but statistics? If many sources are cited, is the information presented in any patterns — as **QUOTATIONS**? **PARAPHRASES**? **SUMMARIES**? Are there repeated references to certain experts or sources?

478–90

In visual texts, look for patterns of color, shape, and line. What's in the foreground, and what's in the background? What's completely visible, partly visible, or hidden? In both verbal and visual texts, look for omissions and anomalies: What isn't there that you would expect to find? Is there anything that doesn't really fit in?

If you discover patterns, then you need to consider what, if anything, they mean in terms of what the writer is saying. What do they reveal about the writer's underlying premises and beliefs? What do they tell you about the writer's strategies for persuading readers to accept the truth of what he or she is saying?

See how color-coding an essay by *New York Times* columnist William Safire on the meaning of the Gettysburg Address reveals several patterns in the language Safire uses. In this excerpt from the essay, which was published just before the first anniversary of the September 11, 2001, terrorist attacks, Safire develops his analysis through several patterns. Religious references are colored yellow; references to a "national spirit," green; references to life, death, and rebirth, blue; and places where Safire directly addresses the reader, gray.

> But the selection of this poetic political sermon as the oratorical centerpiece of our observance need not be only an exercise. . . . now, as then, a national spirit rose from the ashes of destruction.
> Here is how to listen to Lincoln's all-too-familiar speech with new ears.

academic literacies   rhetorical situations   genres   processes   strategies   research MLA / APA   media / design   readings   handbook

> In those 266 words, you will hear the word *dedicate* five times. . . .
>   Those five pillars of dedication rested on a fundament of religious metaphor. From a president not known for his piety — indeed, often criticized for his supposed lack of faith — came a speech rooted in the theme of national resurrection. The speech is grounded in conception, birth, death, and rebirth.
>   Consider the barrage of images of birth in the opening sentence. . . .
>   Finally, the nation's spirit rises from this scene of death: "that this nation, under God, shall have a new birth of freedom." Conception, birth, death, rebirth. The nation, purified in this fiery trial of war, is resurrected. Through the sacrifice of its sons, the sundered nation would be reborn as one. . . .
>   Do not listen on Sept. 11 only to Lincoln's famous words and comforting cadences. Think about how Lincoln's message encompasses but goes beyond paying "fitting and proper" respect to the dead and the bereaved. His sermon at Gettysburg reminds "us the living" of our "unfinished work" and "the great task remaining before us" — to resolve that this generation's response to the deaths of thousands of our people leads to "a new birth of freedom."

The color coding helps us to see patterns in Safire's language, just as Safire reveals patterns in Lincoln's words. He offers an interpretation of Lincoln's address as a "poetic political sermon," and the words he uses throughout support that interpretation. At the end, he repeats the assertion that Lincoln's address is a sermon, inviting us to consider it differently. Safire's repeated commands ("Consider," "Do not listen," "Think about") offer additional insight into how he wishes to position himself in relation to his readers.

Analyzing the Argument

All texts make some kind of argument, claiming something and then offering reasons and evidence as support for any claim. As a critical reader, you need to look closely at the argument a text makes — to recognize all the claims it makes, consider the support it offers for those claims, and decide how you want to respond. What do you think, and why? Here are some questions to consider when analyzing an argument:

345–47
5
- *What claim is the text making?* What is the writer's main point? Is it stated as a **THESIS**, or only implied? Is it limited or **QUALIFIED** somehow? If not, should it have been?

358–59
359–67
- *How is the claim supported?* What **REASONS** does the writer provide for the claim, and what **EVIDENCE** is given for the reasons? What kind of evidence is it? Facts? Statistics? Examples? Expert opinions? Images? How convincing do you find the reasons and evidence? Is there enough evidence?

370
367
367–69
- *What appeals besides logical ones are used?* Does the writer appeal to readers' **EMOTIONS**? try to establish **COMMON GROUND**? demonstrate his or her **CREDIBILITY** as trustworthy and knowledgeable? How successful are these appeals?

368–69
- *Are any* **COUNTERARGUMENTS** *acknowledged?* If so, are they presented accurately and respectfully? Does the writer concede any value to them or try to refute them? How successfully does he or she deal with them?

- *What outside sources of information does the writer cite?* What kinds of sources are they, and how credible do they seem? Are they current and authoritative? How well do they support the argument?

370–72
- *Do you detect any* **FALLACIES**? Fallacies are arguments that involve faulty reasoning. Because they often seem plausible, they can be persuasive. It is important, therefore, that you question the legitimacy of such reasoning when you run across it.

Believing and Doubting

290–91
289–90
One way to develop a response to a text is to play the Believing and Doubting Game, sometimes called reading with and against the grain. Your goal is to **LIST** or **FREEWRITE** notes as you read, writing out as many reasons as you can think of for believing what the writer says (reading with the grain) and then as many as you can for doubting it (reading against the grain).

academic literacies | rhetorical situations | genres | processes | strategies | research MLA / APA | media / design | readings | handbook

First, try to look at the world through the writer's perspective. Try to understand his or her reasons for arguing as he or she does, even if you strongly disagree. Then reread the text, trying to doubt everything in it: try to find every flaw in the argument, every possible way it can be refuted — even if you totally agree with it. Developed by writing theorist Peter Elbow, the believing and doubting game helps you consider new ideas and question ideas you already have — and at the same time will see where you stand in relation to the ideas in the text you're reading.

Considering the Larger Context

All texts are part of ongoing conversations with other texts that have dealt with the topic of the text. An essay arguing for handgun trigger locks is part of an ongoing conversation on gun control, which is itself part of a conversation on individual rights and responsibilities. Academic texts document their sources in part to show their relationship to the ongoing scholarly conversation on a particular topic. In fact, any time you're reading to learn, you're probably reading for some larger context. Whatever your reading goals, being aware of that larger context can help you better understand what you're reading. Here are some specific aspects of the text to pay attention to:

Who else cares about this topic? Especially when you're reading in order to learn about a topic, the texts you read will often reveal which people or groups are part of the conversation — and might be sources of further reading. For example, an essay describing the formation of Mammoth Cave in Kentucky could be of interest to geologists, spelunkers, travel writers, or tourists. If you're reading such an essay while doing research on the cave, you should consider how the audience to whom the writer is writing determines the nature of the information provided — and its suitability as a source for your research.

What conversations is this text part of? Does the text refer to any concepts or ideas that give you some sense that it's part of a larger conversation? An argument on airport security measures, for example, is part of larger conversations about government response to terrorism, the limits of freedom in a democracy, and the possibilities of using technology to detect weapons and explosives, among others.

What terms does the writer use? Do any terms or specialized language reflect the writer's allegiance to a particular group or academic discipline? If you run across words like *false consciousness*, *ideology*, and *hegemony*, for example, you might guess that the text was written by a Marxist scholar.

What other writers or sources does the writer cite? Do the other writers have a particular academic specialty, belong to an identifiable intellectual school, share similar political leanings? If an article on politics cites Paul Krugman and Barbara Ehrenreich in support of its argument, you might assume that the writer holds liberal opinions; if it cites Ross Douthat and Amity Schlaes, the writer is likely a conservative.

IF YOU NEED MORE HELP

See Chapter 47, **EVALUATING SOURCES**, for questions to help you analyze a text's rhetorical situation. See also Chapter 27 on **GENERATING IDEAS AND TEXT**; you can adapt those methods as ways of looking at texts, especially clustering and cubing. And see also Chapter 29 on **ASSESSING YOUR OWN WRITING**, Chapter 30 on **GETTING RESPONSE AND REVISING**, and Chapter 31 on **EDITING AND PROOFREADING** if you need advice for reading your own writing.

Summarizing and Responding:
Where Reading Meets Writing

Summarizing a text helps us to see and understand its main points and to think about what it says. Responding to that text then prompts us to think about — *and say* — what we think. Together, summarizing and responding to texts is one way that we engage with the ideas of others. In a history course, you might summarize and respond to an essay arguing that Civil War photographers did not accurately capture the realities of the battle-field. In a philosophy course, you might summarize Plato's "Allegory of the Cave "and respond to its portrayal of knowledge as shadows on a wall.

And in much of the writing that you do, you'll need to cite the ideas of others, both as context for your own thinking and as evidence to support your arguments. In fact, unless you're Adam, there's probably no topic you'll write about that someone else hasn't already written about — and one way of introducing what you have to say is as a response to something others have said about your topic. A good way of doing that is by summarizing what they've said, using the summary as a launching pad for what you say. This chapter offers advice for summarizing and responding, writing tasks you'll have occasion to do in many of your college classes — and provides a short guide to writing a summary/response essay, a common assignment in composition classes.

SUMMARIZING

In many of your college courses, you'll likely be asked to summarize what someone else has said. Boiling down a text to its basic ideas helps you focus on the text, figure out what the writer has said, and understand (and remember) what you're reading. In fact, summarizing is an essential academic skill, a way to incorporate the ideas of others into your own writing. Following are some guidelines for summarizing effectively:

Read the text carefully. To write a good summary, you need to read the original text carefully to capture the writer's intended meaning as clearly and evenhandedly as you can. Start by SKIMMING the text to get a general sense of what it's saying. If some parts don't make sense, don't worry; at this point, you're reading just to get the gist. Then reread the text more slowly, ANNOTATING it paragraph by paragraph. If there's an explicit THESIS stating the main point, highlight it in some way. Then try to capture the main idea of each paragraph in a single sentence.

12–13 ✳

16–18 ✳
345–47 ◆

State the main points concisely and accurately. Summaries of a complete text are generally between 100 and 250 words in length, so you need to choose your words carefully and to focus only on the text's main ideas. Leave out supporting evidence, anecdotes, and counterarguments unless they're crucial to understanding the text. For instance, in summarizing "Throwing Like a Girl," James Fallows's essay explaining the mechanics of throwing baseballs (see p. 137), you would omit his discussion of Bill and Hillary Clinton throwing out the first ball at two Major League games.

Describe the text accurately and fairly — and using neutral language. Present the author's ideas evenhandedly and fairly; a summary isn't the place to share your opinion of what the text says. Use neutral verbs such as *states, asserts,* or *concludes,* not verbs that imply praise or criticism like *proves* or *complains.*

487–90 ●

Use SIGNAL PHRASES to distinguish what the author says from what you say. Introducing a statement with phrases such as "he says" or "the essay concludes" indicates explicitly that you're summarizing what the author said. When first introducing an author, you may need to say something about his or her credentials. For example:

> In "Always Living in Spanish," Spanish professor Marjorie Agosín describes her need to connect with her childhood by writing in Spanish.

James Fallows, a contributing editor at the *Atlantic,* explains the mechanics of throwing baseballs in "Throwing Like a Girl."

Later in the text, you may need to refer to the author again as you summarize specific parts of the text. These signal phrases are typically briefer: *In Agosín's view . . . , Fallows then argues . . .*

Use quotations sparingly, if at all. You may need to **QUOTE** keywords or memorable phrases, but most or all of a summary should be written in your own words, using your own sentence structures.

    DOCUMENT any text you summarize in a works-cited or references list. A summary of a lengthy work should include **IN-TEXT DOCUMENTATION** noting the pages summarized; they aren't needed with a brief text like the one summarized below (see p. 142).

480

496–99
MLA 503–9
APA 552–56

An Example Summary

In "The Reason College Costs More than You Think," Jon Marcus, a higher-education editor at the *Hechinger Report*, reports that a major reason why college educations are so expensive is the amount of time students stay in college. Although almost all first-year students and their families assume that earning a bachelor's degree will take four years, the reality is that more than half of all students take longer, with many taking six years or more. This delay happens for many reasons, including students changing majors, having to take developmental courses, taking fewer courses per term than they could have, and being unable to register for required courses. As a result, their expenses are much greater — financial aid seldom covers a fifth or sixth year, so students must borrow money to finish — and the additional time they spend in college is time they aren't working, leading to significant losses in wages.

This summary begins with a signal phrase stating the author's name and credentials and the title of the text being summarized. The summary includes only the main ideas, in the summary writer's own words.

RESPONDING

When you summarize a text, you show that you understand its main ideas; responding to a text pushes you to engage with those ideas — and gives you the opportunity to contribute your ideas to a larger conversation. You can respond in various ways, for instance, by taking a **POSITION** on the text's argument, by **ANALYZING THE TEXT** in some way, or by **REFLECTING** on what it says.

156–82
94–128
245–52

Deciding How to Respond

You may be assigned to write a specific kind of response — an argument or analysis, for instance — but more often than not, the nature of your response is left largely up to you. If so, you'll need to read closely and critically to understand what the text says; to get a sense of how — and how well — it does so; and to think about your own reaction to it. Only then can you decide how to respond. You can respond to what the text says (its ideas), to how it says it (the way it's written), or to where it leads your own thinking (your own personal reaction). Or you might write a response that mixes those ways of responding. You might, for example, combine a personal reaction with an examination of how the writing caused that reaction.

If you're responding to what a text says, you might agree or disagree with the author's argument, supporting your position with good reasons and evidence for your response. You might agree with parts of the argument and disagree with others. You might find that the author has ignored or downplayed some important aspect of the topic that needs to be discussed or at least acknowledged. Here are some questions to consider that can help you think about what a text says:

- What does the writer claim?
358–67
- What **REASONS** and **EVIDENCE** does he or she provide to support that claim?

- What parts of the text do you agree with? Is there anything you disagree with — and if so, why?

- Does the writer represent any views other than his or her own? If not, what other perspectives should be considered?

- Are there any aspects of the topic that the writer overlooks or ignores?

- If you're responding to a visual text, how do the design and any images contribute to your understanding of what the text "says"?

Here is a brief response to Jon Marcus's "The Reason College Costs More than You Think," one that responds to his argument:

> It's true that one reason college costs so much more is that students take longer than four years to finish their degrees, but Jon Marcus's argument in "The Reason College Costs More than You Think" is flawed in several ways. He ignores the fact that over the past years state governments have reduced their subsidies to state-supported colleges and universities, forcing higher tuition; and that federal scholarship aid has declined as well, forcing students to pay a greater share of the costs. He doesn't mention the increased number of administrators or the costs of fancy athletic facilities and dormitories. Ultimately, his argument places most of the blame for higher college costs on students, who, he asserts, make poor choices by changing majors and "taking fewer courses per term than they could." College is supposed to present opportunities to explore many possible career paths, so changing majors should be considered a form of growth and education. Furthermore, many of us are working full-time to pay the high costs of college, leaving us with little extra time to study for four or five courses at once and sometimes forcing us to take fewer classes per term because that's all we can afford. Marcus is partly right — but he gets much of the problem wrong.

If you're focusing on the way a text is written, you'll consider what elements the writer uses to convey his or her message — facts, stories, images, and so on. You'll likely pay attention to the writer's word choices and look for any patterns that lead you to understand the text in a particular way. To think about the way a text is written, you might find some of these questions helpful:

- What is the writer's message? Is there an explicit statement of that message?

- How well has the writer communicated the message?

- How does the writer support what he or she says: by citing facts or statistics? by quoting experts? by noting personal experiences? Are you persuaded?

- Are there any words, phrases, or sentences that you find notable, and that contribute to the text's overall effect?

116–22 - How does the text's design affect your response to it? If it's a **VISUAL TEXT** — a photo or ad, for example — how do the various parts of the text contribute to its message?

Here is a brief response to Marcus's essay that analyzes the various ways it makes its argument:

> In "The Reason College Costs More than You Think," *Time* magazine writer Jon Marcus argues that although several factors contribute to high college costs, the main one is how long it takes students to graduate. Marcus introduces this topic by briefly profiling a student who is in his fifth year of school and has run out of financial aid because he "changed majors and took courses he ended up not needing." This profile gives a human face to the topic, which Marcus then develops with statistics about college costs and the numbers of students who take more than four years to finish. Marcus's purpose is twofold: to inform readers that the assumption that most students finish college in four years is wrong, and to persuade them that poor choices like those this student made are the primary reason college takes so long and costs so much. He acknowledges that the extra costs are "hidden" and "not entirely the student's fault" and suggests that poor high school preparation and unavailable required courses play a role, as do limits on financial aid. However, his final paragraph quotes the student as saying of the extra years, "That's time you're wasting that you could be out making money." As the essay's final statement, this assertion that spending more time in school is time wasted and that the implicit goal of college is career preparation reinforces Marcus's argument that college *should* take only four years and that students who take longer are financially irresponsible.

academic literacies   rhetorical situations   genres   processes   strategies   research MLA / APA   media / design   readings   handbook

If you're reflecting on your own reaction to a text, you might focus on how your personal experiences or beliefs influenced the way you understood the text, or on how it reinforced or prompted you to reassess some of those beliefs. You could also focus on how it led you to see the topic in new ways — or note questions that it's led you to wonder about. Some questions that may help you reflect on your own reaction to a text include:

- How did the text affect you personally?
- Is there anything in the text that really got your attention? If so, what?
- Do any parts of the text provoke an emotional reaction — make you laugh or cry, make you uneasy? What prompted that response?
- Does the text bring to mind any memories or past experiences? Can you see anything related to you and your life in the text?
- Does the text remind you of any other texts?
- Does the text support (or challenge) any of your beliefs? How?
- Has reading this text given you any new ideas or insight?

Here is a brief response to Jon Marcus's essay that reflects on an important personal issue:

> Jon Marcus's "Why College Costs More than You Think" made me think hard about my own educational plans. Because I'm working to pay for as much of my education as I can, I'm taking a full load of courses so I can graduate in four years, but truth be told I'm starting to question the major I've chosen. That's one aspect of going to college that Marcus fails to discuss: how your major affects your future career choices and earnings — and whether or not some majors that don't lead immediately to a career, are another way of "wasting" your time. After taking several courses in English and philosophy, I find myself fascinated by the study of literature and ideas. If I decide to major in one or both of those subjects, am I being impractical? Or am I "following my heart," as Steve Jobs said in his Stanford commencement speech? Jobs did as he told those graduates to do, and it worked out well for him, so maybe majoring in something "practical" is less practical than it seems. If I graduate in four years and am "out making money" but doing something I don't enjoy, I might be worse off than if I take longer in college but find a path that is satisfying and enriching.

WRITING A SUMMARY/RESPONSE ESSAY

You may be assigned to write a full essay that summarizes and responds to something you've read. Following is one such essay. It was written by Jacob MacLeod, a student at Wright State University, and responds to a *New York Times* column by Nicholas Kristof, "Our Blind Spot about Guns" (see p. 161).

JACOB MacLEOD

Guns and Cars Are Different

In "Our Blind Spot about Guns," *The New York Times* columnist Nicholas Kristof compares guns to cars in order to argue for sensible gun regulation. Kristof suggests that gun regulations would dramatically decrease the number of deaths caused by gun use. To demonstrate this point, he shows that the regulations governments have instituted for cars have greatly decreased the number of deaths per million miles driven. Kristof then argues that guns should be regulated in the same way that cars are, that car regulation provides a model for gun regulation. I agree with Kristof that there should be more sensible gun regulation, but I have difficulty accepting that all of the regulations imposed on cars have made them safer, and I also believe that not all of the safety regulations he proposes for guns would necessarily have positive effects.

Kristof is right that background checks for those who want to buy guns should be expanded. According to Daniel Webster, director of the Johns Hopkins Center for Gun Policy and Research, state laws prohibiting firearm ownership by members of high-risk groups, such as perpetrators of domestic violence and the mentally ill, have been shown to reduce violence. Therefore, Webster argues, universal background checks would significantly reduce the availability of guns to high-risk groups, as well as reducing the number of guns diverted to the illegal market by making it easier to prosecute gun traffickers.

Kristof also argues that lowering the speed limit made cars safer. However, in 1987, forty states raised their top speed limit from 55 to 65 miles per hour. An analysis of this change by the University of California Transportation Center shows that after the increase, traffic fatality rates on interstate highways in those forty states decreased between 3.4 percent and 5.1 percent. After the higher limits went into effect, the study suggested, some drivers may have switched to safer interstates from other, more dangerous roads, and highway patrols may have focused less on enforcing interstate speed limits and more on activities yielding greater benefits in terms of safety (Lave and Elias 58–61). Although common sense might suggest that lowered speed limits would mean safer driving, research showed otherwise, and the same may be true for gun regulation.

Gun control advocates argue that more guns mean more deaths. However, an article by gun rights advocates Don B. Kates and Gary Mauser argues that murder rates in many developed nations have bear no relation to the rate of gun ownership (652). The authors cite data on firearms ownership in the United States and England that suggest that crime rates are lowest where the density of gun ownership is highest and highest where gun density is lowest (653) and that increased gun ownership has often coincided with significant reductions in violence. For example, in the United States in the 1990s, criminal violence decreased, even though gun ownership increased (656). However, the authors acknowledge that "the notion that more guns reduce crime is highly controversial" (659).

All in all, then, Kristof is correct to suggest that sensible gun regulation is a good idea in general, but the available data suggest that some of the particular measures he proposes should not be instituted. I agree that expanding background checks would be a good way to regulate guns and that failure to require them would lead to more guns in the hands of criminals. While background checks are a good form of regulation, however, lower speed limits and trigger locks are not. The problem with this solution is that although it is based on commonsense thinking, the empirical data show that it may not work.

Works Cited

Kates, Don B., and Gary Mauser. "Would Banning Firearms Reduce Murder and Suicide? A Review of International and Some Domestic Evidence." *Harvard Journal of Law and Public Policy*, vol. 30, no. 2, Jan. 2007, pp. 649-94, www.law.harvard.edu/students/orgs/jlpp/ Vol30_No2_KatesMauseronline.pdf. Accessed 4 Oct. 2014.

Kristof, Nicholas. "Our Blind Spot about Guns." *The New York Times,* 31 July 2014, www.nytimes.com/2014/07/31/opinion/nicholas-kristof-our-blind-spot-about-guns.html. Accessed 4 Oct. 2014.

Lave, Charles, and Patrick Elias. "Did the 65 mph Speed Limit Save Lives?" *Accident Analysis & Prevention*, vol. 26, no. 1, Feb. 1994, pp. 49-62, www.sciencedirect.com/science/article/pii/000145759490068X. Accessed 4 Oct. 2014.

Webster, Daniel. "Why Expanding Background Checks Would, in Fact, Reduce Gun Crime." Interview by Greg Sargent. *The Washington Post,* 3 Apr. 2013, www.washingtonpost.com/blogs/plum-line/wp/2013/04/03/why-expanding-background-checks-would-in-fact-reduce-gun-crime/. Accessed 5 Oct. 2014.

In his response, MacLeod both agrees and disagrees with Kristof's argument, using several sources to support his argument that some of Kristof's proposals may not work. MacLeod states his thesis at the end of the first paragraph, after his summary, and ends with a balanced assessment of Kristof's proposals. He cites several sources, both in the text with signal phrases and in-text documentation and at the end in a works-cited section.

Key Features of Summary / Response Essays

A clearly identified author and title.   Usually the author and title of the text being summarized are identified in a signal phrase in the first sentence. The author (or sometimes the title) may then be referred to in an abbreviated form if necessary in the rest of the essay: for example, "Kristof argues . . ." or "according to 'Our Blind Spot about Guns' . . ."

A concise summary of the text.   The summary presents the main and supporting ideas in the text, usually in the order in which they appear. MacLeod, for example, reduces Kristof's argument to four sentences that capture Kristof's main points while leaving out his many examples.

An explicit response.   Your essay should usually provide a concise statement (one sentence if possible) of your overall response to the text.

- *If you're responding to the argument,* you'll likely agree or disagree (or both), and so your response itself will constitute an argument, with an explicit thesis statement. For example, MacLeod first agrees with Kristof that "there should be more sensible gun regulation," but then introduces a two-part thesis: that not all automobile regulations have made cars safer, and that not all gun regulations would make guns safer.

- *If you're analyzing the text,* you'll likely need to explain what you think the author is saying and how the text goes about conveying that message. An analysis of Kristof's text, for example, might focus on his comparison of automobile regulations with gun regulations.

- *If you're responding with a reflection,* you might explore the ideas, emotions, or memories that the text evokes, the effects of its ideas on your own beliefs, or how your own personal experiences support or contradict the author's position. One response to Kristof's essay might begin by expressing surprise at the comparison of guns to cars and then explore the reasons you find that comparison surprising, leading to a new understanding of the ways regulations can work to save lives.

Support for your response.   Whatever your response, you need to offer reasons and evidence to support what you say.

- *If you're responding to what the text says,* you may offer facts, statistics, anecdotal evidence, and textual evidence, as MacLeod does. You'll also need to consider — and acknowledge — any possible counterarguments, positions other than yours.
- *If you're responding to the way the text is written,* you may identify certain patterns in the text that you think mean something, and you'll need to cite evidence from the text itself. For example, Kristof twice invokes a popular slogan among gun rights advocates, "Guns don't kill people. People kill people," changing "guns" to "cars" to advance his argument that regulating guns may make them safer, just as has happened with cars.
- *If you're reflecting on your own reaction to the text,* you may connect its ideas with your own experiences or beliefs or explore how the text reinforced, challenged, or altered your beliefs. A staunch gun-rights advocate, for example, might find in Kristof's essay a reasonable middle ground too often lacking in polarized debates like the one on gun control.

Ways of Organizing a Summary and Response Essay

You can organize a summary and response essay in various ways. You may want to use a simple, straightforward structure that starts out by

345–47

summarizing the text and then gives the **THESIS** of your response followed by details that develop the thesis.

[Summary, followed by response]

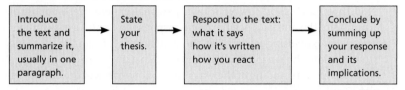

| Introduce the text and summarize it, usually in one paragraph. | State your thesis. | Respond to the text: what it says how it's written how you react | Conclude by summing up your response and its implications. |

Or you may want to start out with the thesis and then, depending on whether your response focuses on the text's argument or its rhetorical choices, provide a paired summary of each main point or each aspect of the writing and a response to it.

[Introduction and thesis, followed by point-by-point summary and response]

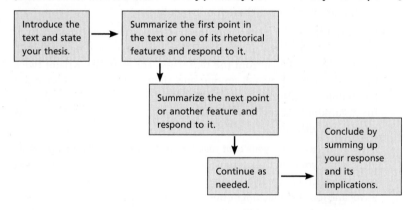

| Introduce the text and state your thesis. | Summarize the first point in the text or one of its rhetorical features and respond to it. |

| Summarize the next point or another feature and respond to it. |

| Continue as needed. | Conclude by summing up your response and its implications. |

IF YOU NEED MORE HELP

298–300
301–5
306–12
313–17
491–95

See Chapter 28 for guidelines on **DRAFTING** and Chapter 34 for help writing a thesis and coming up with a title. See Chapter 29 on **ASSESSING YOUR OWN WRITING**, Chapter 30 on **GETTING RESPONSE AND REVISING**, and Chapter 31 on **EDITING AND PROOFREADING**. See Chapter 50 on **ACKNOWLEDGING SOURCES AND AVOIDING PLAGIARISM**.

academic literacies   rhetorical situations   genres   processes   strategies   research MLA / APA   media / design   readings   handbook

Developing Academic Habits of Mind

A little advice from Serena Williams: "Stick to it and work hard." She wasn't just talking about tennis, and her words resonate for all of us, for everything we set out to do. And here's Michael Jordan, who tells us "Never quit!" and then goes on to issue a warning: "If you quit once, it becomes a habit." Serena Williams and Michael Jordan may be two of the greatest athletes ever, but neither of them was born a champion. They became great by working hard, hanging in there, never giving up.

They succeeded, in other words, by developing certain habits of mind that can serve us all well — and that are especially valuable when it comes to succeeding in school. This chapter is about developing *academic habits of mind*. Just as Serena Williams wasn't born with her powerful serve, none of us was born knowing how to write academic papers or ace exams. But we too can learn and can develop the habits we need to succeed. This chapter offers advice for developing habits of mind that writing teachers nationwide have identified as essential for college success.

Engage

We all know people who see school as a series of hoops to jump through, who seem uninvolved — and even bored. We also know people who are passionate about something — a video game, a hobby, a profession — and who invest themselves, their time, and their emotions wholeheartedly in those activities. Successful students make that investment in school.

In other words, they engage with what they're studying, what they're doing, and what they're learning.

Think about your purpose for being in college.   What are your goals? To get a degree? To qualify for a particular job or profession? To find intellectual stimulation? To explore life? Try to define why you are in school, both in larger terms ("to get a degree in accounting") and in terms of the specific courses you are taking ("Learning to write better will help me be a better student in general and communicate effectively at work").

Fight off boredom.   Every job, including the job of being a student, includes some tasks that are dull but need to be done. When you encounter such a task, ask yourself how it helps you reach a larger goal. Shooting a hundred free throws for practice may not seem interesting, but it can help you win games. When you're listening to a lecture or reading a textbook, take notes, highlight, and annotate; doing that forces you to pay attention and increases what you remember and learn. Trying to identify the main ideas as you listen to a lecture will help you stay focused. When you're studying, try alternating between different tasks: reading, writing, doing problem sets, drawing, and so on.

If you get distracted, figure out ways to deal with it.   It's hard to engage with what you're reading or studying when you're thinking about something else — paying a tuition bill, the last episode of *The Walking Dead*, whatever. Try taking a few moments to write out what's on your mind, in a journal or somewhere else. Sometimes that simple act frees your mind to think about your work, even if it doesn't solve anything.

Raise your hand.   When you think you know the answer to a teacher's question (or when you yourself have a question), raise your hand. Most teachers appreciate students who take chances and who participate in class. At the same time, be polite: don't monopolize discussion or interrupt others when they're speaking.

Get involved. Get to know other students; study with them; join a campus organization. People who see themselves as part of something larger, even just a study group with three or four others, engage more in what they're doing than those who try to go it alone.

Be Curious

When we're young, we're curious about everything, and we learn by asking questions (why? why *not*?) and by exploring our surroundings (digging holes, cutting up magazines, investigating attics and basements). As we get older, though, we focus on things that interest us — and may as a result start to ignore other things or even to forget how to explore. In college, you'll be asked to research, study, and write about many topics you know nothing about. Seize the opportunity. Be curious! And take a tip from Dr. Seuss: "The more that you read, the more things you will know. / The more that you learn, the more places you'll go."

Ask questions. It's tempting to stay within our comfort zones, thinking about things we know and like, listening to those whose views we tend to agree with — to say what we already think rather than to stop and think. Resist that temptation! Take every opportunity to ask questions, to learn more about things you're already interested in, and especially to learn about things you don't (yet) know anything about. As marine biologist Sylvia Earle says, "The best scientists and explorers have the attributes of kids! They ask questions and have a sense of wonder. They have curiosity. Who, what, where, why, when, and how! They never stop asking questions, and I never stop asking questions, just like a five year old."

Listen! Pay attention to what others say, including those who you don't necessarily agree with. The words and ideas of others can challenge the way we think, prompt us to rethink what we think — and spark our curiosity: Why does X think that? What do *I* think — *and why?* Why do my neighbors oppose the Common Core? What do educators think about it? Paying attention to all sides of an argument, doing research to find out what others have said about a topic, or searching social media to see the latest postings on a trending topic are all ways you can listen in on (and engage in) conversations on important issues of all kinds.

Be Open to New Ideas

No matter where you're in school, you're going to encounter ideas and concepts and even facts that challenge your own beliefs; you're also likely to meet people whose backgrounds and ways of looking at life are very different from your own. Be open-minded, open to new ideas and to what others think and say. Consider the perspectives and arguments of others. Learning involves accepting new ideas, acknowledging the value of different perspectives, and coming to understand our own beliefs in new ways. Listen to what others say, and think before you respond.

- *Treat the ideas of others with respect,* whether you agree with them or not, and encourage others to do the same. We don't open up if we don't feel safe.

- *Try to withhold judgment.* Be willing to listen to the thoughts of others and to consider ideas that may at first seem alien or weird (or wrong). Remember that your weird is likely someone else's normal — and the reverse.

- *Look for common ground between your perspectives and those of others* — places where you can agree, even in the midst of serious disagreement.

Be Flexible

Being flexible means being adaptable. In college, you'll likely face novel situations and need to find new ways to address problems, such as juggling school, work, and family; adjusting to roommates and making new friends; and figuring out how to do unfamiliar new assignments and how to take tests. You'll even have to do new kinds of writing: lab reports, reflections,

academic literacies | rhetorical situations | genres | processes | strategies | research MLA / APA | media / design | readings | handbook

literacy narratives, and many, many more; if your school writing up until this point has usually (or always) called for a five-paragraph theme, that's not going to be the case anymore.

Look for new ways to do things. As the saying goes, "If all you have is a hammer, everything looks like a nail." Look for other tools to add to your toolbox: try solving math problems with words or by drawing, or starting a writing project by sketching out the parts.

Try not to see things as right or wrong, good or bad. Be willing to consider alternative points of view and to withhold judgment. Often ideas or actions can only be judged in context; they may be true in some cases or in part, and you often need to understand the larger situation or take into account various perspectives. For example, you may believe that lying is wrong, but is it excusable if telling the truth will cause someone pain? You find a required reading assignment boring and useless, but why, then, did your instructor assign it?

Approach academic assignments rhetorically. Analyze each assignment's purpose, intended audience, and the rest of its **RHETORICAL SITUATION**. ■ 53–70 Think about what's required in terms of content and format — and also about what's appropriate in terms of language and style. And what's expected in the discipline: informal language, sentence fragments, and photographs without captions might be appropriate for a sociology blog, for example, whereas a research project for a history course might have different requirements for how it's organized, formatted, and documented.

Be Creative

If you think that creativity is something artists have (and are born with), think again. From the young man selling homemade granola at a local farm market to the woman who puts together an eye-catching outfit from thrift-store bins, many of us are at work expressing ourselves in distinctive ways. Psychologists tell us that acting creatively opens us up to becoming more creative — and it is safe to say that doing so will make your work more productive and very likely more fun.

289–97 ○

- *Play with ideas.* Freewrite. Make lists. Try looping, clustering, and the other ways of **GENERATING IDEAS** covered in this book. Take some time to think about the ideas you come up with.

- *Don't wait until the last minute.* Some students say they do better under the pressure of a deadline. Don't believe it! It's *always* better to give yourself time to think, to explore ideas, to "sleep on" assignments that first stump you.

- *Take risks!* Explore questions and topics that you haven't thought about before. Try out methods you haven't used previously. Challenge yourself to come up with ten ideas. Or twenty.

- *Ask questions.* And remember that there's no such thing as a dumb question.

Persist

Sometimes the key to success is simply sticking to the task at hand: ignoring distractions, hanging in there, forgetting frustration, getting the work done even in the face of setbacks and failures. Here's some advice from actress and singer Julie Andrews: "Perseverance is failing 19 times and succeeding the 20th."

293–95 ○
19–20 ✳
16–18

- *Don't quit.* Assume that you can complete the task, and make up your mind to do it. If you're reading a book that seems hopelessly confusing or over your head, for example, keep at it until it starts to make sense. Reread, **OUTLINE CHAPTERS**, **SUMMARIZE**, **ANNOTATE**, and do whatever else you need to do to understand it.

- *Remember that sometimes you'll encounter setbacks* — and that the goal (a passing grade, a degree, a job) is still reachable if you keep trying. Those who play video games know that failing is an inherent part of playing them; the same is true of many other things as well.

- *Make a plan and establish a schedule,* and stick to.
- *Break large projects into smaller goals.* Especially with assignments that call for a huge amount of work, approach it in stages: focus on getting through the next chapter, the next draft, the next whatever. It may be good to "keep your eyes on the prize," but it's usually best to take it one step at a time.
- *When you're working on several assignments, tackle the hardest ones first.* Work on them when you're fresh and your mind is clear.
- *If you don't understand something, ask for clarification.* Better to admit to confusion than to act as if you know something when you don't.
- *Ask for help when you need it.* Teachers are usually happy to help students during office hours or by appointment, before or after class, or over email. Get to know your teachers: they're there to help you.
- *Take advantage of whatever help is available* at your school's writing center or learning center and in class. An important part of being persistent is getting help when you need it.

Reflect

Pay attention to the ways you work and make decisions. Reflect on the ways you think and on how you think about the world. This kind of "meta-cognitive" thinking is one of the most important habits of mind, and it's one that will continue to serve you well throughout your life.

- *Figure out when you are most efficient* and do your best work — and try to schedule your work accordingly.
- *Pay attention to what you're reading and how you're doing it.* Think about why you're reading x, and use **READING STRATEGIES** appropriate to your purpose. If you lose the thread of an explanation or argument, figure out where you got lost and why.

❋ 10–32

- *After completing an assignment, reflect in writing* on what you did well, what problems you had, and how you solved them (or not). What would you do differently next time — or if you had more time? You'll find prompts for "Taking Stock of Your Work" at the end of Chapters 10–13 that can help.

- *Troubleshoot.* Pay attention to bumps in the road as you encounter them. Try to understand what caused the problem, what you did to solve it, how successful you were and why.

- *Try to focus on your achievements, what you can do,* rather than on what you may not be able to do or to do as well as you'd like.

Take Responsibility

In one way or another, all the habits of mind discussed above involve taking responsibility for your own actions. It may be tempting to blame others or society or bad luck for problems in your academic life, but the more you take ownership of your own learning, the more control you have over the results. Some ways you can enhance your sense of responsibility and demonstrate it include these:

- *Acknowledge that how much you learn and what grades you get depend mostly on you.* Teachers often say that they don't *give* grades, students *earn* grades — an important difference.

- *Treat school as you do a job,* one for which you must show up on time, perform tasks at a certain level of competence, and meet deadlines. In college, where your time is mostly unstructured, you have to become your own boss. So attend class regularly, follow instructions, and turn in assignments on time.

- *Get organized.* Maintain a calendar so you know what's due when. Create a schedule for your day that includes time for class, studying, working, and personal activities. Develop a system for organizing your written work and notes for each course you're taking. Learn where to find the materials you need to do your classwork.

478–95
496–99

- *Use research sources responsibly.* QUOTE, PARAPHRASE, and SUMMARIZE the work of others accurately and DOCUMENT it correctly. Give appropriate credit to those whose ideas and words you are using.

academic literacies | rhetorical situations | genres | processes | strategies | research MLA / APA | media / design | readings | handbook

Rhetorical Situations

Whenever we write, whether it's a text to a friend or a toast for a wedding, an English essay or a résumé, we face some kind of rhetorical situation. We have a PURPOSE, a certain AUDIENCE, a particular STANCE, a GENRE, and a MEDIUM to consider—and often as not a DESIGN. All are important elements that we need to think about carefully. The following chapters offer brief discussions of those elements of the rhetorical situation, along with questions that can help you make the choices you need to as you write. See also the GENRE chapters for guidelines for considering your rhetorical situation in each of these specific kinds of writing.

Rhetorical Situations

Purpose 5

All writing has a purpose. We write to explore our thoughts and emotions, to express ourselves, to entertain; we write to record words and events, to communicate with others, to try to persuade others to believe as we do or to behave in certain ways. In fact, we often have several purposes at the same time. We may write an essay in which we try to explain something to an audience, but at the same time we may be trying to persuade that audience of something. Look, for example, at this passage from a 2012 *New York Times* op-ed essay by economist and editorial columnist Paul Krugman about social and economic trends among "the traditional working-class family" — declining rates of marriage and of male participation in the labor force and increasing numbers of out-of-wedlock births. Krugman asserts that the primary reason for those statistics is a "drastic reduction in the work opportunities available to less-educated men":

> Most of the numbers you see about income trends in America focus on households rather than individuals, which makes sense for some purposes. But when you see a modest rise in incomes for the lower tiers of the income distribution, you have to realize that all — yes, all — of this rise comes from the women, both because more women are in the paid labor force and because women's wages aren't as much below male wages as they used to be.
>
> For lower-education working men, however, it has been all negative. Adjusted for inflation, entry-level wages of male high school graduates have fallen 23 percent since 1973. Meanwhile, employment benefits have collapsed. In 1980, 65 percent of recent high-school graduates working in the private sector had health benefits, but, by 2009, that was down to 29 percent.
>
> So we have become a society in which less-educated men have great difficulty finding jobs with decent wages and good benefits.
>
> —Paul Krugman, "Money and Morals"

academic literacies

rhetorical situations

genres

processes

strategies

research MLA / APA

media / design

readings

handbook

Krugman is reporting information here, outlining how the earnings and benefits of less-educated men have dropped over the last forty years. He is also making an argument, that these economic setbacks are the cause of the social ills among working-class Americans and not, as some would have it, the result of them. (Krugman, writing for a newspaper, is also using a style — including dashes, contractions, and other informal elements — that strives to be engaging while it informs and argues.)

Even though our purposes may be many, knowing our primary reason for writing can help us shape that writing and understand how to proceed with it. Our purpose can determine the genre we choose, our audience, even the way we design what we write.

Identify your purpose. While a piece of writing often has many purposes, a writer usually focuses on one. When you get an assignment or see a need to write, ask yourself what the primary purpose of the writing task is: to entertain? to inform? to persuade? to demonstrate your knowledge or your writing ability? What are your own goals? What are your audience's expectations, and do they affect the way you define your purpose?

Thinking about Purpose

- *What do you want your audience to do, think, or feel?* How will your readers use what you tell them?

- *What does this writing task call on you to do?* Do you need to show that you have mastered certain content or skills? Do you have an assignment that specifies a particular **STRATEGY** or **GENRE** — to compare two things, perhaps, or to argue a position?

- *What are the best ways to achieve your purpose?* What **STANCE** should you take? Should you write in a particular genre? Do you have a choice of **MEDIUM**, and does your text require any special format or **DESIGN** elements?

333 ◆
71 ▲
64–67 ■
591 ▢

Audience 6

Who will read (or hear) what you are writing? A seemingly obvious but crucially important question. Your audience affects your writing in various ways. Consider a piece of writing as simple as a text from a mother to her son:

Pls. take chicken out to thaw and feed Annye. Remember Dr. Wong at 4.

On the surface, this brief note is a straightforward reminder to do three things. But in fact it is a complex message filled with compressed information for a specific audience. The writer (the mother) counts on the reader (her son) to know a lot that can be left unsaid. She expects that he knows that the chicken is in the freezer and needs to thaw in time to be cooked for dinner; she knows that he knows who Annye is (a pet?), what he or she is fed, and how much; she assumes that he knows who (and where) Dr. Wong is. She doesn't need to spell out any of that because she knows what her son knows and what he needs to know — and in her text she can be brief. She understands her audience. Think how different such a reminder would be were it written to another audience — a babysitter, perhaps, or a friend helping out while Mom is out of town.

What you write, how much you write, how you phrase it, even your choice of **GENRE** (memo, essay, email, note, speech) — all are influenced by the audience you envision. And your audience will interpret your writing according to their own expectations and experiences, not yours.

61–63

When you are a student, your audience is most often your teachers, so you need to be aware of their expectations and know the conventions (rules, often unstated) for writing in specific academic fields. You may make statements that seem obvious to you, not realizing that your instructors may consider them assertions that must be proved with evidence of one sort or another. Or you may write more or less formally than teachers expect. Understanding your audience's expectations — by asking outright, by reading materials in your field of study, by trial and error — is important to your success as a college writer.

This point is worth dwelling on. You are probably reading this textbook for a writing course. As a student, you will be expected to produce essays with few or no errors. If you correspond with family, friends, or coworkers using email and texts, you may question such standards; after all, many of the messages you get in these contexts are not grammatically perfect. But in a writing class, the instructor needs to see your best work. Whatever the rhetorical situation, your writing must meet the expectations of your audience.

Identify your audience.   Audiences may be defined as *known*, *multiple*, or *unknown*. *Known audiences* can include people with whom you're familiar as well as people you don't know personally but whose needs and expectations you do know. You yourself are a known, familiar audience, and you write to and for yourself often. Class notes, to-do lists, reminders, and journals are all written primarily for an audience of one: you. For that reason, they are often in shorthand, full of references and code that you alone understand.

Other known, familiar audiences include anyone you actually know — friends, relatives, teachers, classmates — and whose needs and expectations you understand. You can also know what certain readers want and need, even if you've never met them personally, if you write for them within a specific shared context. Such a known audience might include PC gamers who read cheat codes that you have posted on the internet for beating a game; you don't know those people, but you know roughly what they know about the game and what they need to know, and you know how to write about it in ways they will understand.

You often have to write for *multiple audiences*. Business memos or reports may be written initially for a supervisor, but he or she may pass them along to others. Grant proposals may be reviewed by four to six levels of readers — each, of course, with its own expectations and perspectives.

academic literacies   rhetorical situations   genres   processes   strategies   research MLA / APA   media / design   readings   handbook

Even writing for a class might involve multiple audiences: your instructor and your classmates.

Unknown audiences can be the most difficult to address since you can't be sure what they know, what they need to know, how they'll react. Such an audience could be your downstairs neighbor, with whom you've chatted occasionally in the laundry room. How will she respond to your letter asking her to sponsor you in an upcoming charity walk? Another unknown audience — perhaps surprisingly — might be many of your instructors, who want — and expect! — you to write in ways that are new to you. While you can benefit from analyzing any audience, you need to think most carefully about those you don't know.

Thinking about Audience

- *Whom do you want to reach?* To whom are you writing (or speaking)?

- *What is your audience's background — their education and life experiences?* It may be important for you to know, for example, whether your readers attended college, fought in a war, or have young children.

- *What are their interests?* What do they like? What motivates them? What do they care about?

- *Is there any demographic information that you should keep in mind?* Consider whether race, gender, sexual orientation, disabilities, occupation, religious beliefs, economic status, and so on should affect what or how you write. For example, writers for *Men's Health*, *InStyle*, and *Out* must consider the particular interests of each magazine's readers.

- *What political circumstances may affect their reading?* What attitudes — opinions, special interests, biases — may affect the way your audience reads your piece? Are your readers conservative, liberal, or middle of the road? Politics may take many other forms as well — retirees on a fixed income may object to increased school taxes, so a letter arguing for such an increase would need to appeal to them differently than would a similar letter sent to parents of young children.

- *What does your audience already know — or believe — about your topic? What do you need to tell them? What is the best way to do so?* Those retirees who oppose school taxes already know that taxes are a burden for them; they may need to know why schools are justified in asking for more money every few years. A good way to explain this may be with a bar graph showing how property values benefit from good schools with adequate funding. Consider which **STRATEGIES** will be effective — narrative, comparison, something else?

  329 ◆

- *What's your relationship with your audience, and how should it affect your language and tone?* Do you know them, or not? Are they friends? colleagues? mentors? adversaries? strangers? Will they likely share your **STANCE**? In general, you need to write more formally when you're addressing readers you don't know, and you may address friends and colleagues more informally than you would a boss.

  64–67 ▧

- *What does your audience need and expect from you?* Your history professor, for example, may need to know how well you can discuss the economy of the late Middle Ages in order to assess your learning; he may expect you to write a carefully reasoned argument, drawing conclusions from various sources, with a readily identifiable thesis in the first paragraph. Your boss, on the other hand, may need an informal email that briefly lists your sales contacts for the day; she may expect that you list the contacts in the order in which you saw them, that you clearly identify each one, and that you briefly say how well each contact went. What **GENRE** is most appropriate?

  71 ▲

- *What kind of response do you want?* Do you want readers to believe or do something? to accept as valid your information on a topic? to understand why an experience you once had matters to you?

  591 ☐

- *How can you best appeal to your audience?* Is there a particular **MEDIUM** that will best reach them? Are there any **DESIGN** requirements? (Elderly readers may need larger type, for instance.)

Genres are kinds of writing. Letters, profiles, reports, position papers, poems, blog posts, instructions, parodies — even jokes — are genres. For example, here is the beginning of a **PROFILE** of a mechanic who repairs a specific kind of automobile:

224–34

> Her business card reads Shirley Barnes, M.D., and she's a doctor, all right — a Metropolitan Doctor. Her passion is the Nash Metropolitan, the little car produced by Austin of England for American Motors between 1954 and 1962. Barnes is a legend among southern California Met lovers — an icon, a beacon, and a font of useful knowledge and freely offered opinions.

A profile offers a written portrait of someone or something that informs and sometimes entertains, often examining its subject from a particular angle — in this case, as a female mechanic who fixes Nash Metropolitans. While the language in this example is informal and lively ("she's a doctor, all right"), the focus is on the subject, Shirley Barnes, "M.D." If this same excerpt were presented as a poem, however, the new genre would change our reading:

> Her business card reads
> Shirley Barnes, M.D.,
> and she's a doctor, all right
> — a Metropolitan Doctor.
> Her passion is the Nash Metropolitan,
> the little car produced by Austin of England
> for American Motors between 1954 and 1962.
> Barnes is a legend
> among southern California Met lovers
> — an icon,

a beacon,

and a font of useful knowledge and

freely offered opinions.

The content hasn't changed, but the different presentation invites us to read not only to learn about Shirley Barnes but also to explore the significance of the words and phrases on each line, to read for deeper meaning and greater appreciation of language. The genre thus determines how we read and how we interpret what we read.

Genres help us write by establishing features for conveying certain kinds of content. They give readers clues about what sort of information they're likely to find and so help them figure out how to read ("This article begins with an abstract, so it's probably a scholarly source" or "Thank goodness! I found the instructions for editing videos on my phone"). At the same time, genres are flexible; writers often tweak the features or combine elements of different genres to achieve a particular purpose or connect with an audience in a particular way. Genres also change as writers' needs and available technologies change. For example, computers have enabled us to add audio and video content to texts that once could appear only on paper.

Identify your genre. Does your writing situation call for a certain 71 ▲ **GENRE**? A memo? A report? A proposal? A letter? Some situations may 265–72 call for **MIXING GENRES**. Academic assignments generally specify the genre ("take a position," "analyze the text"), but if not, see Chapter 24 for help 273–78 ▲ **CHOOSING GENRES** — or ask your instructor.

Thinking about Genre

- *How does your genre affect what content you can or should include?* Objective information? Researched source material? Your own opinions? Personal experience? A mix?

329 ◆ - *Does your genre call for any specific* **STRATEGIES**? Profiles, for example, usually include some narration; lab reports often explain a process.

academic literacies | rhetorical situations | genres | processes | strategies | research MLA / APA | media / design | readings | handbook

- *Does your genre require a certain organization?* **PROPOSALS**, for instance, usually need to show a problem exists before offering a solution. Some genres leave room for choice. Business letters delivering good news might be organized differently than those making sales pitches.

235–44

- *Does your genre affect your tone?* An abstract of a scholarly paper calls for a different **TONE** than a memoir. Should your words sound serious and scholarly? brisk and to the point? objective? opinionated? Sometimes your genre affects the way you communicate your **STANCE**.

65

64–67

- *Does the genre require formal (or informal) language?* A letter to the mother of a friend asking for a summer job in her bookstore calls for more formal language than does an email to the friend thanking him for the lead.

- *Do you have a choice of medium?* Some genres call for print; others for an electronic medium. Sometimes you have a choice: a résumé, for instance, can be printed to bring to an interview, or it may be downloaded or emailed. Some teachers want reports turned in on paper; others prefer that they be emailed or posted in the class course management system. If you're not sure what **MEDIUM** you can use, ask.

591

- *Does your genre have any design requirements?* Some genres call for paragraphs; others require lists. Some require certain kinds of fonts — you wouldn't use **Impact** for a personal narrative, nor would you likely use chiller for an invitation to Grandma's sixty-fifth birthday party. Different genres call for different **DESIGN** elements.

591

8 Stance

Whenever you write, you have a certain stance, an attitude toward your topic. The way you express that stance affects the way you come across to your audience as a writer and a person. This email from a college student to his father, for example, shows a thoughtful, reasonable stance for a carefully researched argument:

> Hi Dad,
> I'll get right to the point: I'd like to buy a car. I saved over $4,500 from working this summer, and I've found three different cars that I can get for under $3,000. That'll leave me $1,400 to cover the insurance. I can park in Lot J, over behind Monte Hall, for $75 for both semesters. And I can earn gas and repair money by upping my hours at the cafeteria. It won't cost you any more, and if I have a car, you won't have to come and pick me up when I want to come home. May I buy it?
> Love,
> Michael

While such a stance can't guarantee that Dad will give permission, it's more likely to produce results than this version:

> Hi Dad,
> I'm buying a car. A guy in my Western Civ course has a cool Nissan he wants to get rid of. I've got $4,500 saved from working this summer, it's mine, and I'm going to use it to get some wheels. Mom said you'd freak if I did, but I want this car. OK?
> Michael

The writer of the first email respects his reader and offers reasoned arguments and evidence of research to convince him that buying a car is an action that will benefit them both. The writer of the second, by contrast, seems impulsive, ready to buy the first car that comes along, and defiant —

he's picking a fight. Each email reflects a certain stance that shows the writer as a certain kind of person dealing with a topic in a certain way and establishing a certain relationship with his audience.

Identify your stance. What is your attitude toward your topic? Objective? Critical? Curious? Opinionated? Passionate? Indifferent? Your stance may be affected by your relationship to your **AUDIENCE**. How do you want them to see you? As a colleague sharing information? As a good student showing what you can do? As an advocate for a position? Often your stance is affected by your **GENRE**: for example, lab reports require an objective, unemotional stance that emphasizes the content and minimizes the writer's own attitudes. Memoir, by comparison, allows you to reveal your feelings about your topic. Your stance is also affected by your **PURPOSE**, as the two emails about cars show. Your stance in a piece written to entertain will likely differ from the stance you'd adopt to persuade.

57–60

▲ 71

55–56

You communicate (or downplay) your stance through your tone — through the words you use and other ways your text expresses an attitude toward your subject and audience. For example, in an academic essay you would state your position directly — "the *Real Housewives* series reflects the values of American society today" — a confident, authoritative tone. In contrast, using qualifiers like "might" or "I think" can give your writing a wishy-washy, uncertain tone: "I think the *Real Housewives* series might reflect some of the values of American society today." The following paragraph, from an essay analyzing a text, has a sarcastic tone that might be appropriate for a comment on a blog post but that isn't right for an academic essay:

> In "Just Be Nice," Stephen M. Carter complains about a boy who wore his pants too low, showing his underwear. Is that really something people should worry about? We have wars raging and terrorism happening every day, and he wants to talk about how inconsiderate it is for someone to wear his pants too low? If by that boy pulling his pants up, the world would be a better place and peace would break out in the Middle East, I'm sure everyone would buy a belt.

This writer clearly thinks Carter's complaint is trivial in comparison with the larger issues of the day, but her sarcastic tone belittles Carter's argument instead of answering it with a serious counterargument. Like every other element of writing, your tone must be appropriate for your rhetorical situation.

Just as you likely alter what you say depending on whether you're speaking to a boss, an instructor, a parent, or a good friend, so you need to make similar adjustments as a writer. It's a question of appropriateness: we behave in certain ways in various social situations, and writing is a social situation. You might sign an email to a friend with an XO, but in an email to your supervisor you'll likely sign off with a "Many thanks" or "Sincerely." To write well, you need to write with integrity, to say as much as possible what you wish to say; yet you also must understand that in writing, as in speaking, your stance and tone need to suit your purpose, your relationship to your audience, the way in which you wish your audience to perceive you, and your medium.

In writing as in other aspects of life, the Golden Rule applies: "Do unto audiences as you would have them do unto you." Address readers respectfully if you want them to respond to your words with respect.

Thinking about Stance

- *What is your stance, and how does it relate to your purpose for writing?* If you feel strongly about your topic and are writing an argument that tries to persuade your audience to feel the same way, your stance and your **PURPOSE** fit naturally together. But suppose you are writing about the same topic with a different purpose — to demonstrate the depth of your knowledge about the topic, for example, or your ability to consider it in a detached, objective way. You will need to adjust your stance to meet the demands of this different purpose.

- *How should your stance be reflected in your tone?* Can your tone grow directly out of your stance, or do you need to "tone down" your attitude toward the topic or take a different tone altogether? Do you want to be seen as reasonable? angry? thoughtful? gentle? funny? ironic? If you're writing about something you want to be seen as taking very

55–56 ■

seriously, be sure that your language and even your font reflect that seriousness. Check your writing for words that reflect the tone you want to convey — and for ones that do not (and revise as necessary).

- *How is your stance likely to be received by your audience?* Your tone and especially the attitude it projects toward your **AUDIENCE** will affect how they react to the content of what you say.

57–60

- *Should you openly discuss your stance?* Do you want or need to announce your own perspective on your topic? Will doing so help you reach your audience, or would it be better not to say directly where you're coming from?

9 Media/Design

In its broadest sense, a medium is a go-between: a way for information to be conveyed from one person to another. We communicate through many media, verbal and nonverbal: our bodies (we catch someone's eye, wave, nod); our voices (we whisper, talk, shout, groan); and various technologies, including handwriting, print, telephone, radio, CD, film, and computer.

Each medium has unique characteristics that influence both what and how we communicate. As an example, consider this message: "I haven't told you this before, but I love you." Most of the time, we communicate such a message in person, using the medium of voice (with, presumably, help from eye contact and touch). A phone call will do, though most of us would think it a poor second choice, and a handwritten letter or note would be acceptable, if necessary. Few of us would break such news on a website, with a tweet, or during a radio call-in program.

By contrast, imagine whispering the following sentence in a darkened room: "By the last decades of the nineteenth century, the territorial expansion of the United States had left almost all Indians confined to reservations." That sentence starts a chapter in a history textbook, and it would be strange indeed to whisper it into someone's ear. It is appropriate, however, in the textbook, in print or in an e-book, or on a *PowerPoint* slide accompanying an oral presentation.

As you can see, we can often choose among various media depending on our purpose and audience. In addition, we can often combine media to create **MULTIMEDIA** texts. And different media allow us to use different ways or modes of expressing meaning, from words to images to sound to hyperlinks, that can be combined into **MULTIMODAL** formats.

No matter the medium or media, a text's design affects the way it is received and understood. A typed letter on official letterhead sends a different message than the same words handwritten on pastel stationery. Classic type

595

academic literacies · rhetorical situations · genres · processes · strategies · research MLA / APA · media / design · readings · handbook

sends a different message than *flowery italics*. Some genres and media (and audiences) demand **PHOTOS**, **DIAGRAMS**, or color. Some information is easier to explain — and read — in the form of a **PIE CHART** or a **BAR GRAPH** than in the form of a paragraph. Some reports and documents are so long and complex that they need to be divided into sections, which are then best labeled with **HEADINGS**. These are some of the elements to consider when you are thinking about how to design what you write.

□ 609–11

□ 604–5

Identify your media and design needs.   Does your writing situation call for a certain medium and design? A printed essay? An oral report with visual aids? A blog? A podcast? Academic assignments often assume a particular medium and design, but if you're unsure about your options or the degree of flexibility you have, check with your instructor.

Thinking about Media

- *What medium are you using* — print? spoken? electronic? a combination? — and how does it affect the way you will create your text? A printed résumé is usually no more than one page long; a scannable résumé sent via email has no length limits. An oral presentation should contain detailed information; accompanying slides should provide only an outline.

- *How does your medium affect your organization and* **STRATEGIES**? Long paragraphs are fine on paper but don't work well on the web. On presentation slides, phrases or keywords work better than sentences. In print, you need to define unfamiliar terms; on the web, you can sometimes just add a link to a definition found elsewhere.

◆ 329

- *How does your medium affect your language?* Some print documents require a more formal voice than spoken media; email and texting often invite greater informality.

- *How does your medium affect what modes of expression you use?* Should your text include photos, graphics, audio or video files, or links? Do you need slides, handouts, or other visuals to accompany an oral presentation?

Thinking about Design

53 ■

- *What's the appropriate look for your* RHETORICAL SITUATION? Should your text look serious? whimsical? personal? something else? What design elements will suit your audience, purpose, stance, genre, and medium?

- *What elements need to be designed?* Is there any information you would like to highlight by putting it in a box? Are there any key terms that should be boldfaced? Do you need navigation buttons? How should you indicate links?

- *What font(s) are appropriate* to your audience, purpose, stance, genre, and medium?

607–15 □
57–60 ■

- *Are you including any* VISUALS? Should you? Will your AUDIENCE expect or need any? Is there any information in your text that would be easier to understand as a chart or graph? If you need to include video or audio clips, how should the links be presented?

61–63 ■
69

- *Should you include headings?* Would they help you organize your materials and help readers follow the text? Does your GENRE or MEDIUM require them?

MLA 500–548 ●
APA 549–89 ●

- *Should you use a specific format?* MLA? APA?

part 3

Genres

When we make a shopping list, we automatically write each item we need in a single column. When we email a friend, we begin with a salutation: "Hi, Brian." Whether we are writing a letter, a résumé, or a proposal, we know generally what it should contain and what it should look like because we are familiar with each of those genres. Genres are kinds of writing, and texts in any given genre share goals and features—a proposal, for instance, generally starts out by identifying a problem and then suggests a certain solution. The chapters in this part provide guidelines for writing in thirteen common academic genres. First come detailed chapters on four genres often assigned in writing classes—LITERACY NARRATIVES, TEXTUAL ANALYSES, REPORTS, and ARGUMENTS— followed by brief chapters on NINE OTHER GENRES and two on MIXING and CHOOSING GENRES.

Genres

Writing a Literacy Narrative **10**

Narratives are stories, and we read and tell them for many different purposes. Parents read their children bedtime stories as an evening ritual. College applicants write about significant moments in their lives. In *psychology* courses, you may write a personal narrative to illustrate how individuals' stories inform the study of behavior. In *education* courses, you may share stories of your teaching experiences. And in *computer science* courses, you may write programming narratives to develop programming skills.

This chapter provides detailed guidelines for writing a specific kind of narrative: a literacy narrative, in which a writer explores his or her experiences with reading, writing, or both. We'll begin with three good examples, the first annotated to point out the key features found in most literacy narratives.

EMILY VALLOWE

Write or Wrong Identity

Emily Vallowe wrote this literacy narrative for a writing class at the University of Mary Washington in Virginia. In it, she explores her lifelong identity as a writer — and her doubts about that identity.

I'm sitting in the woods with a bunch of Catholic people I just met yesterday. Suddenly, they ask me to name one of the talents God has given me. I panic for a split second and then breathe an internal sigh of relief. I tell them I'm a writer. As the group leaders move on to question someone else, I sit trying to mentally catch my breath. It will take a moment before the terror leaves my forearms, chest, and stomach,

Attention-getting opening.

academic literacies · rhetorical situations · genres · processes · strategies · research MLA / APA · media / design · readings · handbook

but I tell myself that I have nothing to fear. I am a writer. Yes, I most definitely am a writer. *Now breathe,* I tell myself . . . *and suppress that horrifying suspicion that you are actually not a writer at all.*

The retreat that prepared me for my eighth-grade confirmation was not the first time I found myself pulling out the old "I'm a writer" card and wondering whether I was worthy enough to carry this sacred card in the wallet of my identity. Such things happen to people with identity crises.

Clearly described details.

In kindergarten I wrote about thirty books. They were each about five pages long, with one sentence and a picture on each page. They were held together with three staples on the left side or top and had construction paper covers with the book's title and the phrase "By Emily Vallowe" written out in neat kindergarten-teacher handwriting. My mom still has all of these books in a box at the bottom of her closet.

One day at the very end of the school year, my kindergarten teacher took me to meet my future first-grade teacher, Mrs. Meadows. I got to make a special trip to meet her because I had been absent on the day the rest of the kindergarteners had gone to meet their future teachers. Mrs. Meadows's classroom was big and blue and different from the kindergarten class, complete with bigger, different kids (I think Mrs. Meadows had been teaching third or fourth graders that year, so her students were much older than I was). During this visit, Mrs. Meadows showed me a special writing desk, complete with a small, old-fashioned desk lamp (with a lamp shade and everything). I'm not sure if I understood why she was showing me this writing area. She may have said that she'd heard good things about me.

Vallowe traces her identity as a writer through her life.

This handful of images is all I can remember about the most   5 significant event in my writing life. I'm not sure why I connect the memory of my kindergarten books with the image of me sitting in Mrs. Meadows's old classroom (for by the time I had her she was in a room on the opposite side of the school). I guess I don't even know exactly when this major event happened. Was it kindergarten? First grade? Somewhere in between? All I know is that some event occurred in early elementary school that made me want to be a writer. I don't even clearly remember what this event was, but it is something that has actively affected me for the fourteen years since then.

I have wanted to be a writer my entire life — or at least that's what I tell people. Looking back, I don't know if I ever *wanted* to be a writer. The idea might never have even occurred to me. Yet somehow I was marked as a writer. My teachers must have seen something in my writing that impressed them and clued me in on it. Teachers like to recognize kids for their strengths, and at the age of five, I probably started to notice that different kids were good at different things: Bobby was good at t-ball; Sally was good at drawing; Jenny could run really fast. I was probably starting to panic at the thought that I might not be good at anything — and then a teacher came along and told me I was good at writing. Someone gave me a compliment, and I ran with it. I declared myself to be a writer and have clung to this writer identity ever since.

There are certain drawbacks to clinging to one unchanging iden-tity since the age of five. Constant panic is one of these drawbacks. It is a strange feeling to grow up defining yourself as something when you don't know if that something is actually true. By the time I got to middle school, I could no longer remember having become a writer; I had just always been one — and had been one without any proof that I deserved to be called one. By the age of ten, I was facing a seasoned writer's terror of "am I any good?!" and this terror has followed me throughout my entire life since then. Every writing assignment I ever had was a test — a test to see if I was a real writer, to prove myself to teachers, to classmates, to myself. I approached every writing assign-ment thinking, "I am supposed to be good at this," not "I am going to try to make this good," and such an attitude is not a healthy way to approach anything.

Ongoing discussion of the central issue: is she a writer or not?

It doesn't help that if I am a writer, I am a very slow one. I can't sit down and instantly write something beautiful like some people I know can. I have been fortunate to go to school with some very smart classmates, some of whom can whip out a great piece of writing in minutes. I still find these people threatening. If they are faster than I am, does that make them better writers than I am? *I thought I was supposed to be "the writer"!*

My obsession with being "the" writer stems from my under-standing of what it means to be "the" anything. My childhood was marked by a belief in many abstract absolutes that I am only now allowing to crumble. I was born in Chicago (and was thus the fourth generation of my family to live there), but I grew up in northern Virginia. I came to look down on my Virginia surroundings because I had been taught to view Chicago as this great Mecca — the world's most amazing city to which I must someday return, and to which all other places on earth pale in comparison. Throughout my childhood, I gathered that Chicago is a real city in which average people live and which has an economy historically based in shipping and manufacturing; Washington, D.C., on the other hand, where my dad works, has a population that includes a bizarre mix of impoverished people and the most influential leaders and diplomats in the world — and so manufactures nothing but political power. People in Chicago know how to deal with snow; Virginians panic at the *possibility* of snow. Chicago rests on soil that is so fertile it's *black*; Virginia does not even have soil — it has reddish clay suitable for growing nothing except tobacco. Even Chicago's tap water tastes amazing; D.C.'s tap water is poisoned with lead. I grew up thinking that every aspect of Chicago was perfect — so perfect that Chicago became glorious to the point of abstraction. No other city could compare, and after a while I forgot *why* no other city could compare. I just knew that Chicago was "the" city . . . and that if "the" city exists, there must also be an abstract "the" everything.

Vallowe examines the roots of her identity as a writer — and why she questions that identity.

I grew up with this and many other abstract ideals that I would 10 defend against my friends' attacks . . . until I learned that they were just abstractions — and so was I. My writing identity was just another ideal, an absolute that I clung to without any basis in fact. I used to use writing as an easy way to define myself on those over-simplistic surveys teachers always asked us to fill out in elementary and middle school — the surveys that assumed that someone could know all about me simply by finding out my favorite color, my favorite TV show, or my hobbies. I used to casually throw out the "I'm a writer" card just to get these silly surveys over with. "I'm a writer" was just an easy answer to the complicated question, "Who are you?" I always thought the surveys avoided asking this question, but maybe I was the one avoiding it. For years, I had been defining myself as "the writer" without really pondering what this writer identity meant. Is a writer simply someone who writes all the time? Well, I often went through long stretches in which I did not write anything, so this definition did not seem to suit me. Is a writer someone who is good at writing? Well, I've already mentioned that I've been having "am I any good?!" thoughts

academic literacies · rhetorical situations · genres · processes · strategies · research MLA / APA · media / design · readings · handbook

since elementary school, so this definition didn't seem to fit me, either. I was identifying myself as "the writer" as an abstraction, without any just cause to do so.

The funny thing is that I recognized my writing identity as an abstract ideal before I recognized any of the other ideals I was clinging to, but that didn't make the situation any better. It is one thing to learn that dead people have been voting in Chicago elections for decades, and so perhaps Chicago isn't the perfect city, but what happens when the absolute ideal is you? More important, what would happen if *this* absolute were to crumble? It was terrifying to think that I might discover that I was not a writer because to not be a writer was to suddenly be nothing. If a writer was the only thing that I had ever been, what would happen if writing was a lie? I would vanish. Looking back, the logical part of my brain tells me that, if I am not a writer, I am still plenty of other things: I am a Catholic; I am a Vallowe; people tell me that I have other good qualities. But when facing these horrifying spells of writer's doubt, my brain doesn't see these other things. I am driven only by the fear of nothingness and the thought that I have to be a writer because I'm not good at anything else.

Am I really not good at anything else? I used to blame this entire writer's complex on whoever it was that told me I was a writer. If that person hadn't channeled this burdensome identity into me, I might never have expected great literary things from myself, and life would have been easier. I had these thoughts until one day in high school I mentioned something to my mom about the fact that I'd been writing since I was five years old. My mom corrected me by saying that I'd been writing since I was three years old. At the age of three I couldn't even physically form letters, but apparently I would dictate stories to my mom on a regular basis. My mom explained to me how I would run to her and say, "Mommy, Mommy, write my story for me!"

This new information was both comforting and unsettling. On one hand, it was a great relief to know that I had been a writer all along — that I would have been a writer even if no one had told me that I was one. On the other hand, the knowledge that I had been a writer all along drove me into an entirely new realm of panic.

I've been a writer my entire life?

WHAT?!

She continues to explore her identity as a writer.

15

I've been a writer since I was three? Three? *Three* years old: How is that even possible? I didn't know it was possible to be anything at age three, let alone the thing that might define me for my entire life.

I have been taught that each person has a vocation — a calling that he or she must use to spread God's love to others. Yet I've also assumed that one must go on some sort of journey to figure out what this vocation is. If I found my vocation at the age of three, have I skipped this journey? And if I've skipped the journey, does that mean that the vocation isn't real? Or am I just really lucky for having found my vocation so early? Was I really born a writer? Was I born to do one thing and will I do that one thing for my entire life? Can anything be that consistent? That simple? And if I am living out some divine vocation, is that any comfort at all? If I am channeling some divine being in my writing, and everything I write comes from some outside source, where does that leave me? Am I nothing even if I am a writer?

This questioning has not led me to any comforting conclusions. I still wonder if my writer identity has been thrust upon me, and what it means to have someone else determine who I am. If I am a writer, then I am someone who passionately seeks originality — someone who gets pleasure from inventing entire fictional worlds. Yet if someone — either a teacher or a divine being — is channeling an identity into me, then I am no more original than the characters that I create in my fiction. If my identity is not original, then this identity is not real, and if I am not real . . . I can't even finish this sentence.

I don't know if I really wrote thirty books in kindergarten. It might have been twenty — or fifteen — or ten — or five. I might have made up that part about the special writing desk in Mrs. Meadows's old classroom. I don't know if God predestined me to write masterpieces or if a teacher just casually mentioned that I wrote well and I completely overreacted to the compliment. Questioning my identity as "the writer" has led me to new levels of fear and uncertainty, but this questioning is not going to stop. Even if I one day sit, withered and gray, with a Nobel Prize for Literature proudly displayed on my desk as I try to crank out one last novel at the age of ninety-two, my thoughts will probably drift back to Mrs. Meadows and those books I wrote in kindergarten. In my old age, I still might not understand my writer identity,

Ending refers back to the opening anecdote.

Conclusion is tentative (since the end of the story is decades in the future).

but maybe by that point, I will have written a novel about a character with an identity crisis — and maybe the character will have come
through all right.

*In this literacy narrative, Vallowe reflects on the origins of her identity as a
writer: her early teachers, her parents, God, herself. The significance of her story
lies in her inability to settle on any one of these possibilities.*

MARJORIE AGOSÍN

Always Living in Spanish: Recovering the Familiar, through Language

*Marjorie Agosín, a Spanish professor at Wellesley College, wrote this literacy
narrative for* Poets & Writers *magazine in 1999. Originally written in Spanish, it tells of Agosín's Chilean childhood and her continuing connection to the
Spanish language.*

In the evenings in the northern hemisphere, I repeat the ancient ritual
that I observed as a child in the southern hemisphere: going out while
the night is still warm and trying to recognize the stars as it begins to
grow dark silently. In the sky of my country, Chile, that long and wide
stretch of land that the poets blessed and dictators abused, I could
easily name the stars: the three Marias, the Southern Cross, and the
three Lilies, names of beloved and courageous women.

But here in the United States, where I have lived since I was a
young girl, the solitude of exile makes me feel that so little is mine,
that not even the sky has the same constellations, the trees and the
fauna the same names or sounds, or the rubbish the same smell. How
does one recover the familiar? How does one name the unfamiliar?
How can one be another or live in a foreign language? These are the
dilemmas of one who writes in Spanish and lives in translation.

Since my earliest childhood in Chile I lived with the tempos and
the melodies of a multiplicity of tongues: German, Yiddish, Russian,
Turkish, and many Latin songs. Because everyone was from somewhere

else, my relatives laughed, sang, and fought in a Babylon of languages. Spanish was reserved for matters of extreme seriousness, for commercial transactions, or for illnesses, but everyone's mother tongue was always associated with the memory of spaces inhabited in the past: the shtetl, the flowering and vast Vienna avenues, the minarets of Turkey, and the Ladino whispers of Toledo. When my paternal grandmother sang old songs in Turkish, her voice and body assumed the passion of one who was there in the city of Istanbul, gazing by turns toward the west and the east.

Destiny and the always ambiguous nature of history continued my family's enforced migration, and because of it I, too, became one who had to live and speak in translation. The disappearances, torture, and clandestine deaths in my country in the early seventies drove us to the United States, that other America that looked with suspicion at those who did not speak English and especially those who came from the supposedly uncivilized regions of Latin America. I had left a dangerous place that was my home, only to arrive in a dangerous place that was not: a high school in the small town of Athens, Georgia, where my poor English and my accent were the cause of ridicule and insult. The only way I could recover my usurped country and my Chilean childhood was by continuing to write in Spanish, the same way my grandparents had sung in their own tongues in diasporic sites.

The new and learned English language did not fit with the visceral 5 emotions and themes that my poetry contained, but by writing in Spanish I could recover fragrances, spoken rhythms, and the passion of my own identity. Daily I felt the need to translate myself for the strangers living all around me, to tell them why we were in Georgia, why we are different, why we had fled, why my accent was so thick, and why I did not look Hispanic. Only at night, writing poems in Spanish, could I return to my senses, and soothe my own sorrow over what I had left behind.

This is how I became a Chilean poet who wrote in Spanish and lived in the southern United States. And then, one day, a poem of mine was translated and published in the English language. Finally, for the first time since I had left Chile, I felt I didn't have to explain myself. My poem, expressed in another language, spoke for itself . . . and for me.

Sometimes the austere sounds of English help me bear the solitude of knowing that I am foreign and so far away from those about whom

academic literacies   rhetorical situations   genres   processes   strategies   research MLA / APA   media / design   readings   handbook

I write. I must admit I would like more opportunities to read in Spanish to people whose language and culture is also mine, to join in our common heritage and in the feast of our sounds. I would also like readers of English to understand the beauty of the spoken word in Spanish, that constant flow of oxytonic and paraoxytonic syllables (*Vérde qué té quiéro vérde*),* the joy of writing — of dancing — in another language. I believe that many exiles share the unresolvable torment of not being able to live in the language of their childhood.

I miss that undulating and sensuous language of mine, those baroque descriptions, the sense of being and feeling that Spanish gives me. It is perhaps for this reason that I have chosen and will always choose to write in Spanish. Nothing else from my childhood world remains. My country seems to be frozen in gestures of silence and oblivion. My relatives have died, and I have grown up not knowing a young generation of cousins and nieces and nephews. Many of my friends disappeared, others were tortured, and the most fortunate, like me, became guardians of memory. For us, to write in Spanish is to always be in active pursuit of memory. I seek to recapture a world lost to me on that sorrowful afternoon when the blue electric sky and the Andean cordillera bade me farewell. On that, my last Chilean day, I carried under my arm my innocence recorded in a little blue notebook I kept even then. Gradually that diary filled with memoranda, poems written in free verse, descriptions of dreams and of the thresholds of my house surrounded by cherry trees and gardenias. To write in Spanish is for me a gesture of survival. And because of translation, my memory has now become a part of the memory of many others.

Translators are not traitors, as the proverb says, but rather splendid friends in this great human community of language.

Agosín's narrative uses vivid detail to bring her childhood in Chile to life for her readers. Her love for her homeland and its people is clear, as is the significance of her narrative — with her childhood home gone, to write in Spanish is a "gesture of survival."

---

*"*Vérde qué té quiéro vérde*" ("Green, how I want you, green"): the opening line of a famous Spanish poem that demonstrates the interplay of words with the main stress on the final syllable (oxytonic) and those with the main stress on the next-to-last syllable (paroxytonic) in Spanish. [Editor's note]

SHANNON NICHOLS

"Proficiency"

In the following literacy narrative, Shannon Nichols, a student at Wright State University, describes her experience taking the standardized writing proficiency test that high school students in Ohio must pass to graduate. She wrote this essay for a college writing course, where her audience included her classmates and instructor.

The first time I took the ninth-grade proficiency test was in March of eighth grade. The test ultimately determines whether students may receive a high school diploma. After months of preparation and anxiety, the pressure was on. Throughout my elementary and middle school years, I was a strong student, always on the honor roll. I never had a GPA below 3.0. I was smart, and I knew it. That is, until I got the results of the proficiency test.

Although the test was challenging, covering reading, writing, math, and citizenship, I was sure I had passed every part. To my surprise, I did pass every part—except writing. "Writing! Yeah right! How did I manage to fail writing, and by half a point, no less?" I thought to myself in disbelief. Seeing my test results brought tears to my eyes. I honestly could not believe it. To make matters worse, most of my classmates, including some who were barely passing eighth-grade English, passed that part.

Until that time, I loved writing just as much as I loved math. It was one of my strengths. I was good at it, and I enjoyed it. If anything, I thought I might fail citizenship. How could I have screwed up writing? I surely spelled every word correctly, used good grammar, and even used big words in the proper context. How could I have failed?

Finally I got over it and decided it was no big deal. Surely I would pass the next time. In my honors English class I worked diligently, passing with an A. By October I'd be ready to conquer that writing test. Well, guess what? I failed the test again, again with only 4.5 of the 5 points needed to pass. That time I did cry, and even went to my English teacher, Mrs. Brown, and asked, "How can I get A's in all my English classes but fail the writing part of the proficiency test twice?" She couldn't answer my question. Even my friends and classmates were confused. I felt like a failure. I had disappointed my family and seriously let myself down. Worst of all, I still couldn't figure out what I was doing wrong.

academic literacies   rhetorical situations   genres   processes   strategies   research MLA / APA   media / design   readings   handbook

I decided to quit trying so hard. Apparently — I told myself — the people grading the tests didn't have the slightest clue about what constituted good writing. I continued to excel in class and passed the test on the third try. But I never again felt the same love of reading and writing.

This experience showed me just how differently my writing could be judged by various readers. Obviously all my English teachers and many others enjoyed or at least appreciated my writing. A poem I wrote was put on television once. I must have been a pretty good writer. Unfortunately the graders of the ninth-grade proficiency test didn't feel the same, and when students fail the test, the state of Ohio doesn't offer any explanation.

After I failed the test the first time, I began to hate writing, and I started to doubt myself. I doubted my ability and the ideas I wrote about. Failing the second time made things worse, so perhaps to protect myself from my doubts, I stopped taking English seriously. Perhaps because of that lack of seriousness, I earned a 2 on the Advanced Placement English Exam, barely passed the twelfth-grade proficiency test, and was placed in developmental writing in college. I wish I knew why I failed that test because then I might have written what was expected on the second try, maintained my enthusiasm for writing, and continued to do well.

Nichols's narrative focuses on her emotional reaction to failing a test that she should have passed easily. The contrast between her demonstrated writing ability and her repeated failures creates a tension that captures readers' attention. We want to know what will happen to her.

For four more literacy narratives, see CHAPTER 59.

Key Features / Literacy Narratives

A well-told story. As with most narratives, those about literacy often set up some sort of situation that needs to be resolved. That need for resolution makes readers want to keep reading. We want to know whether Nichols ultimately will pass the proficiency test. Some literacy narratives simply explore the role that reading or writing played at some time in someone's life — assuming, perhaps, that learning to read or write is a challenge to be met.

Vivid detail.   Details can bring a narrative to life for readers by giving them vivid mental sensations of the sights, sounds, smells, tastes, and textures of the world in which your story takes place. The details you use when describing something can help readers picture places, people, and events; dialogue can help them hear what is being said. We get a picture of Agosín's Chilean childhood when she writes of the "blue electric sky" and her "little blue notebook" in which she described her "house surrounded by cherry trees and gardenias." Similarly, we can picture and hear Vallowe as a little girl running to her mother and saying, "Mommy, Mommy, write my story for me!"

Some indication of the narrative's significance.   By definition, a literacy narrative tells something the writer remembers about learning to read or write. In addition, the writer needs to make clear why the incident matters to him or her. You may reveal its significance in various ways. Nichols does it when she says she no longer loves to read or write. Agosín points out that she writes in Spanish because "nothing else from my childhood world remains. . . . To write in Spanish is for me a gesture of survival." The trick is to avoid tacking a brief statement about your narrative's significance onto the end as if it were a kind of moral of the story. Vallowe's narrative would be less effective if, instead of questioning her identity as a writer from several perspectives, she had simply said, "I became a writer at the age of three."

A GUIDE TO WRITING LITERACY NARRATIVES

Choosing a Topic

In general, it's a good idea to focus on a single event that took place during a relatively brief period of time. For example:

- any early memory about writing or reading that you recall vividly
- someone who taught you to read or write

- a book or other text that has been significant for you in some way
- an event at school that was related to reading or writing and that you found interesting, humorous, or embarrassing
- a writing or reading task that you found (or still find) especially difficult or challenging
- a memento that represents an important moment in your literacy development (perhaps the start of a **LITERACY PORTFOLIO**)

◯ 326–27

- the origins of your current attitudes about writing or reading
- learning to text, learning to write email appropriately, creating and maintaining a *Facebook* page or blog

Make a list of possible topics, and then choose one that you think will be interesting to you and to others — and that you're willing to share with others. If several seem promising, try them out on a friend or classmate. Or just choose one and see where it leads; you can switch to another if need be. If you have trouble coming up with a topic, try **FREEWRITING**, **LISTING**, **CLUSTERING**, or **LOOPING**.

◯ 289–92

Considering the Rhetorical Situation

PURPOSE   Why do you want to tell this story? To share a memory with others? To fulfill an assignment? To teach a lesson? To explore your past learning? Think about the reasons for your choice and how they will shape what you write.

▮ 55–56

AUDIENCE   Are your readers likely to have had similar experiences? Would they tell similar stories? How much explaining will you have to do to help them understand your narrative? Can you assume that they will share your attitudes toward your story, or will you have to work at making them see your perspective? How much about your life are you willing to share with this audience?

▮ 57–60

64–67
STANCE   What attitude do you want to project? Affectionate? Neutral? Critical? Do you wish to be sincere? serious? humorously detached? self-critical? self-effacing? something else? How do you want your readers to see you?

68–70
MEDIA/DESIGN   Will your narrative be in print? presented orally? online? Should you use photos, tables, graphs, or video or audio clips? Is there a font that conveys the right tone? Do you need headings?

Generating Ideas and Text

Good literacy narratives share certain elements that make them interesting and compelling for readers. Remember that your goals are to tell the story as clearly and vividly as you can and to convey the meaning the incident has for you today. Start by thinking about what you already know about writing a literacy narrative. Then write out what you remember about the setting of your narrative and those involved, perhaps trying out some of the methods in the chapter on **GENERATING IDEAS AND TEXT**. You may also want to **INTERVIEW** a teacher or parent who figures in your narrative.

289–92
463–64

Explore what you already know about writing a literacy narrative. Think about recent occasions when you've had to narrate a story, either orally or in writing, in school or out. Take a few moments to think about a couple of those occasions, especially ones involving your reading, writing, or learning to do something. Why and to whom were you telling these stories? How successful do you think your narratives were? What aspects of telling the story did you feel most confident about or do especially well? What could you have done better? What do you still need to learn about writing a literacy narrative?

Describe the setting. Where does your narrative take place? List the places where your story unfolds. For each place, write informally for a few minutes, **DESCRIBING** what you remember:

399–407

- *What do you see?* If you're inside, what color are the walls? What's hanging on them? What can you see out any windows? What else do you see? Books? Lined paper? Red ink? Are there people? places to sit? a desk or a table?
- *What do you hear?* A radiator hissing? Leaves rustling? The wind howling? Rain? Someone reading aloud? Shouts? Cheers? Children playing? Music? The chime of a text arriving on your phone?
- *What do you smell?* Sweat? Perfume? Incense? Food cooking?
- *How and what do you feel?* Nervous? Happy? Cold? Hot? A scratchy wool sweater? Tight shoes? Rough wood on a bench?
- *What do you taste?* Gum? Mints? Graham crackers? Juice? Coffee?

Think about the key people. Narratives include people whose actions play an important role in the story. In your literacy narrative, you are probably one of those people. A good way to develop your understanding of the people in your narrative is to write about them:

- *Describe each person in a paragraph or so.* What do the people look like? How do they dress? How do they speak? Quickly? Slowly? With an accent? Do they speak clearly, or do they mumble? Do they use any distinctive words or phrases? You might begin by describing their movements, their posture, their bearing, their facial expressions. Do they have a distinctive scent?
- *Recall (or imagine) some characteristic dialogue.* A good way to bring people to life and move a story along is with **DIALOGUE**, to let readers hear them rather than just hearing about them. Try writing six to ten lines of dialogue between two people in your narrative. If you can't remember an actual conversation, make up one that could have happened. (After all, you are telling the story, and you get to decide how it is to be told.) Try to remember (and write down) some of the characteristic words or phrases that the people in your narrative used.

408–13

Write about "what happened." At the heart of every good **NARRATIVE** is the answer to the question "What happened?" The action in a literacy

419–27

narrative may be as dramatic as winning a spelling bee or as subtle as a conversation between two friends; both contain action, movement, or change that the narrative tries to capture for readers. A good story dramatizes the action. Try **SUMMARIZING** the action in your narrative in a paragraph—try to capture what happened. Use active and specific verbs (*pondered, shouted, laughed*) to describe the action as vividly as possible.

486–87

Consider the significance of the narrative. You need to make clear the ways in which any event you are writing about is significant for you now. Write a page or so about the meaning it has for you. How did it change or otherwise affect you? What aspects of your life now can you trace to that event? How might your life have been different if this event had not happened or had turned out differently? Why does this story matter to you?

Ways of Organizing a Literacy Narrative

293–94

Start by **OUTLINING** the main events in your narrative. Then think about how you want to tell the story. Don't assume that the only way to tell your story is just as it happened. That's one way—starting at the beginning of the action and continuing to the end. But you could also start in the middle—or even at the end. Shannon Nichols, for example, could have begun her narrative by telling how she finally passed the proficiency test and then gone back to tell about the times she tried to pass it, even as she was an A student in an honors English class. Several ways of organizing a narrative follow.

[Chronologically, from beginning to end]

Introduce the story. → Describe the setting and people. → Tell what happened. → Say how the story was resolved. → Say something about the significance.

academic literacies | rhetorical situations | genres | processes | strategies | research MLA / APA | media / design | readings | handbook

[Beginning in the middle]

| Start in the middle of the action, giving enough information to let readers know what was happening. | → | Fill in details: setting, people, specific actions. | → | Make clear how the situation was resolved. | → | Say something about the significance. |

[Beginning at the end]

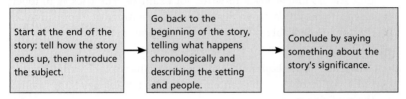

| Start at the end of the story: tell how the story ends up, then introduce the subject. | → | Go back to the beginning of the story, telling what happens chronologically and describing the setting and people. | → | Conclude by saying something about the story's significance. |

Writing Out a Draft

Once you have generated ideas and thought about how you want to organize your narrative, it's time to begin **DRAFTING**. Do this quickly—try to write a complete draft in one sitting, concentrating on getting the story on paper or screen and on putting in as much detail as you can. Some writers find it helpful to work on the beginning or ending first. Others write out the main event first and then draft the beginning and ending.

298–300

Draft a **BEGINNING**. A good narrative grabs readers' attention right from the start. Here are some ways of beginning:

331–39

- *Jump right in.* Sometimes you may want to get to the main action as quickly as possible. Nichols, for example, begins as she takes the ninth-grade proficiency test for the first time.

- *Describe the context.* You may want to provide background information at the start of your narrative, as Vallowe does with an anecdote exposing her fears that she may not be who she thinks she is.

- *Describe the setting, especially if it's important to the narrative.* Agosín begins by describing the constellations in her native Chile.

339–42 **Draft an ENDING.** Think about what you want readers to read last. An effective ending helps them understand the meaning of your narrative. Here are some possibilities:

- *End where your story ends.* It's up to you to decide where a narrative ends. Vallowe ends far in the future, in her imagined old age.

- *Say something about the significance of your narrative.* Nichols observes that she no longer loves to write, for example. The trick is to touch upon the narrative's significance without stating it too directly, like the moral of a fable. Vallowe and Agosín both explore the meaning of their experiences over several paragraphs.

- *Refer back to the beginning.* Vallowe refers back to her kindergarten writing; Nichols ends by contemplating the negative effects of failing the proficiency test.

- *End on a surprising note.* Agosín catches our attention when she tells us of the deaths and disappearances of her friends and relatives.

344–45 **Come up with a title.** A good **TITLE** indicates something about the subject of your narrative—and makes readers want to take a look. Nichols's title, "'Proficiency,'" is also her subject; her use of quote marks around this word calls its meaning into question in a way that might make readers wonder — and read on. Vallowe focuses on the significance of her narrative: "Write or Wrong Identity." Agosín makes her title an expression of her sense of identity: "Always Living in Spanish."

Considering Matters of Design

You'll probably write your narrative in paragraph form, but think about the information you're presenting and how you can design it to enhance your story and appeal to your audience.

- What would be an appropriate **FONT**? Something serious, like Times Roman? Something whimsical, like *Comic Sans*? Something else?

601–2

- Would it help your readers if you added **HEADINGS** in order to divide your narrative into shorter sections?

604–5

- Would photographs or other **VISUALS** show details better than you can describe them with words alone? If you're writing about learning to read, for example, you might scan in an image of one of the first books you read. Or if your topic is learning to write, you could include something you wrote. You could even include a video or audio recording. Would your narrative best be conveyed as a multimodal composition that combines written text, images, and video or audio?

607–15

Getting Response and Revising

The following questions can help you study your draft with a critical eye. **GETTING RESPONSE** from others is always good, and these questions can guide their reading, too. Make sure they know your purpose and audience.

306–7

- Do the title and first few sentences make readers want to read on? If not, how else might you begin?
- Is the sequence of events in the narrative clear? Does it flow, and are there effective transitions? Does the narrative get sidetracked at any point?
- Is anything confusing?
- Is there enough detail, and is it interesting? Will readers be able to imagine the setting? Can they picture the characters and sense what they're like? Would it help to add some dialogue so that readers can "hear" them?
- Are visuals used effectively and integrated smoothly with the written text? If there are no visuals, would using some strengthen the narrative?
- Have you made the narrative meaningful enough for readers so that they wonder and care about what will happen?

- Do you narrate any actions clearly? vividly? Does the action keep readers engaged?
- Is the significance of the narrative clear?
- Is the ending satisfying? What are readers left thinking?

307–10 The preceding questions should identify aspects of your narrative you need to work on. When it's time to **REVISE**, make sure your text appeals to your audience and achieves your purpose as successfully as possible.

Editing and Proofreading

313–16 Readers equate correctness with competence. Once you've revised your draft, follow these guidelines for **EDITING** a narrative:

419–27
349
- Make sure events are **NARRATED** in a clear order and include appropriate time markers, **TRANSITIONS**, and summary phrases to link the parts and show the passing of time.

HB-39
- Be careful that **VERB TENSES ARE CONSISTENT** throughout. If you start your narrative in the past tense ("he *taught* me how to use a computer"), be careful not to switch to the present ("So I *look* at him and *say* . . . ") along the way.

HB-12–14
- Check to see that **VERB TENSES** correctly indicate when an action took place. If one action took place before another action in the past, for example, you should use the past perfect tense: "I forgot to dot my i's, a mistake I *had made* many times before."

408–13
- Punctuate **DIALOGUE** correctly. Whenever someone speaks, surround the speech with quotation marks ("No way," I said). Periods and commas go inside quotation marks; exclamation points and question marks go inside if they're part of the quotation, outside if they're part of the whole sentence:

  INSIDE　Opening the door, Ms. Cordell announced, "Pop quiz!"
  OUTSIDE　It wasn't my intention to announce "I hate to read"!

316–17
- **PROOFREAD** your finished narrative carefully before turning it in.

Taking Stock of Your Work

- How well do you think you told the story?
- What did you do especially well?
- What could still be improved?
- How did you go about coming up with ideas and generating text?
- How did you go about drafting your narrative?
- Did you use photographs or any other visual or audio elements? What did they add? Can you think of such elements you might have used?
- How did others' responses influence your writing?
- What would you do differently next time?

IF YOU NEED MORE HELP

See also **MEMOIRS** (Chapter 18), a kind of narrative that focuses more generally on a significant event from your past, and **REFLECTIONS** (Chapter 21), a kind of essay for thinking about a topic in writing. See Chapter 32 if you are required to submit your literacy narrative as part of a writing **PORTFOLIO**.

▲ 216–23
245–52

● 318–28

11 Analyzing Texts

Both the *Huffington Post* and *National Review Online* cover the same events, but each one interprets them differently. All toothpaste ads claim to make teeth "the whitest." The Environmental Protection Agency is a guardian of America's air, water, and soil — or an unconstitutional impediment to economic growth, depending on which politician is speaking. Those are but three examples that demonstrate why we need to be careful, analytical readers of magazines, newspapers, blogs, websites, ads, political documents, even textbooks.

Text is commonly thought of as words, as a piece of writing. In the academic world, however, text can include not only writing but images — photographs, illustrations, videos, films — and even sculptures, buildings, and music and other sounds. And many texts combine words, images, and sounds. We are constantly bombarded with texts: on the web, in print, on signs and billboards, even on our clothing. Not only does text convey information, but it also influences how and what we think. We need to read, then, to understand not only what texts say but also how they say it and how they try to persuade or influence what we think.

Because understanding how texts say what they say and achieve their effects is so crucial, assignments in many disciplines ask you to analyze texts. You may be asked to analyze candidates' speeches in a *political science* course or to analyze the imagery in a poem for a *literature* class. In a *statistics* course, you might analyze a set of data — a numerical text — to find the standard deviation from the mean.

This chapter offers detailed guidelines for writing an essay that closely examines a text both for what it says and for how it does so, with the goal of demonstrating for readers how — and how well — the text achieves its effects. We'll begin with three good examples, the first annotated to point out the key features found in most textual analyses.

academic literacies   rhetorical situations   genres   processes   strategies   research MLA / APA   media / design   readings   handbook

HANNAH BERRY

The Fashion Industry: Free to Be an Individual

Hannah Berry wrote this analysis of two visual texts, shoe ads, for a first-year writing course at Wright State University.

As young women, we have always been told through the medium of advertisement that we must use certain products to make ourselves beautiful. For decades, ads for things like soap, makeup, and mouthwash have established a sort of misplaced control over our lives, telling us what will make us attractive and what will not. Recently, however, a new generation of advertisement has emerged in the fashion industry, one that cleverly equates the products shown in the ads with the quest for confident individuality. Ads such as the two for Clarks and Sorel discussed below encourage us to break free from the standard beauty mold and be ourselves; using mostly imagery, they remind us that being unique is the true origin of beauty.

The first ad promotes Clarks fashion as band geek chic, quite literally raising a unique personality onto a pedestal, with the subject poised on a decorative stone platform as shown in fig. 1. Photographed in standing profile, this quirky-looking young woman is doing what she loves — playing some kind of trumpet — and looks great doing it. She is wearing her hair in a French twist with a strand tucked behind her ear, as if she recently moved it out of her face to play the music she loves without distraction. The downturn of her nose points to the short gray-black dress that stops several inches above her knees but covers her chest and shoulders modestly, with a collar situated at the base of her neck and sleeves that reach for her elbows. The dress is plain, but it is a perfect fit for the personality implied in the photo. Set against the background of a light-tan wall, the model leans back slightly as if supporting the weight of her instrument. Her right knee is bent while her left knee remains straight. The positioning of her legs not only accentuates her unbalanced posture but also points out the pair of simple brown pumps that complete the look. She wears the shoes with a pair of socks in a much darker shade of brown pulled up around her shins. Around her ankles are sandy-colored rings of shaggy fabric that are most likely attached to the socks, giving the whole outfit a sense of nerdy flair. Her expression is a simple mix of calm and concentration. It's as if the photographer happened to take the picture while she was practicing for a school recital.

Attention to the context of the ads Berry will analyze.

Clear thesis.

Detailed description of the first text.

Illustrations are labeled in MLA format.

Fig. 1. Clarks ad shows a band geek doing what she loves (Clarks).

Clarks has taken what looks like your average high school student and dressed her in an outfit that speaks to her own distinctive character and talents. The image sparks the idea that her beauty comes from an internal base of secure self-confidence and moves outward to infuse her physical appearance and sense of style. This ad urges us to celebrate individuality with the right look. Using an image alone, Clarks advertises its products with the simple promise that they will support you in doing what you love and keep you original.

Analysis of the first text.

Taking a narrower perspective on originality, the ad for Sorel boots shown in fig. 2 dramatizes the idea that spontaneity is key to a distinctive personal identity. This abstract idea is depicted in a vividly concrete way, using the featured fur-topped boots as a base for encouraging a bold sense of self. The ad dares us to break free from the mold of society and do something "fearless" (Sorel). It shows us a dark-haired, red-lipped woman sitting in a formal French upholstered chair in a dark-blue, elaborately paneled parlor. An expression of triumph and mischief adorns her sultry visage. She's wearing a revealing short white dress that overlaps slightly around her chest and falls strategically over her hips so that large portions of her upper thighs are visible. Feathers in autumn colors cover her shoulders, and a gold belt accentuates her waist. Next to her is a polished wood table supporting a lighted candle, a small glass vase of pink and white flowers, and a black-and-white-patterned orb. There is a dormant, ornate fireplace to her left. But what makes this scene extraordinary is what seems to have taken place moments before the picture was taken. One of the young woman's feet, clad in the devil-red black-laced boots being advertised, rests defiantly on top of the shattered remains of a crystal chandelier. In her right hand, the woman holds an old-looking shotgun with her forefinger still resting on the trigger.

Description of the second text.

Speculation about the story behind the image.

In Sorel's explosive ad, it is apparent that the woman not only shot down the ceiling fixture but also has no regrets about doing so. Her white dress represents a sort of purity and innocence that is completely contradicted by the way she wears it — and by the boots. They gave her the power to shoot down the chandelier, the push she needed to give in to a long-held desire that perhaps she couldn't have indulged in without the extra help. They symbolize her liberty to decide to be herself and do what she wants. Along with the white dress, the formal decor represents the bounds that society tells her she must fit into — but that she decides

Analysis of the second text.

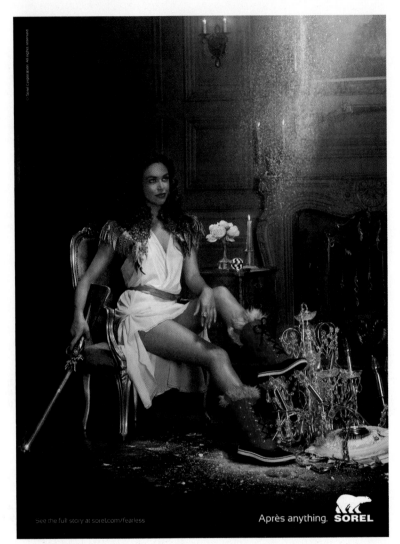

See the full story at sorel.com/fearless

Après anything. SOREL

Fig. 2. Sorel ad flaunts devil-red boots worn by a fearless woman with a shotgun (Sorel).

academic literacies
rhetorical situations
genres
processes
strategies
research MLA / APA
media / design
readings
handbook

to take a potshot at instead. Focusing on the beauty of inner power, not just the power of outer beauty, this Sorel ad punctuates its bold visual statement with a single verbal phrase: "Après anything" (Sorel). In the French language, the word *après* means "after." So, the ad suggests, no matter what outrageous or outlandish deed you do, the Sorel boots will be there for you, suitable for slipping into afterward like a negligee.

With these pioneering fashion ads that celebrate blowing your own horn or shooting up fancy French lighting fixtures for fun, young women are told to accessorize their inner beauty with articles of clothing geared toward their distinctive individual desires. "You don't have to just try to be beautiful in the ways other women do," they say; "you can strike out on your own, and our products will help you do it." The extent to which women will respond to these messages remains to be seen, but certainly the ads themselves achieve a strikingly different look. Whether celebrating individual talents or random acts of defiance in our everyday lives, they dare us to accessorize our personalities.

Conclusion ties together the strands of the analysis.

Works Cited

Clarks. Advertisement. *Lucky*, Sept. 2011, p. 55.
Sorel. Advertisement. *Lucky*, Sept. 2011, p. 65.

Berry summarizes each ad clearly and focuses her analysis on a theme running through both ads: that clothing is an expression of one's individuality. She describes patterns of images in both ads as evidence.

DANIELLE ALLEN

Our Declaration

Danielle Allen is a political philosopher who teaches at the Institute for Advanced Study in Princeton, New Jersey. This analysis is a chapter from her book Our Declaration: A Reading of the Declaration of Independence in Defense of Equality.

There's something quite startling about the phrase "We hold these truths to be self-evident." Perhaps it can be made visible most easily with a comparison.

The Catholic Church, too, is committed to a set of truths. At every mass priest and parishioners together recite a list of their beliefs called the *Credo*. One version, called the Apostles' Creed, starts like this: "I believe in God, the Father almighty, creator of heaven and earth. I believe in Jesus Christ, his only son and Lord." Each section begins with the words "I believe," and that's why this recitation is called the *Credo*. Latin, "credo" simply means "I believe."

The Declaration launches its list of truths altogether differently. Jefferson and his colleagues do not say, "I believe," or even "we believe," that all men are created equal. Instead, they say, "We hold these truths to be self-evident," and then they give us a set of either three or five truths, depending on how you count.

What's the difference between "We believe" and "We hold these truths to be self-evident"? In the Catholic *Credo*, when one says, "I believe," the basis for that belief is God's revealed word. In contrast, when Jefferson and his colleagues say, "We hold these truths to be self-evident," they are claiming to know the truths thanks to their own powers of perception and reasoning. These truths are self-evident, and so humans can grasp and hold them without any external or divine assistance.

In order to understand what "We hold these truths to be self-evident" really means, then, it is important to know what "self-evident" means. 5

Sometimes people take it to mean that we can instantly understand an idea, but that's not really right. It's true that sometimes the idea of self-evidence is used for things that we simply perceive. For instance, when I look out my window I immediately perceive that the world includes things like trees and flowers. If outside my window there are many different kinds of tree — hickory and maple and oak, for instance — when I look at them, I nonetheless rapidly perceive that they are all the same kind of thing. That many different kinds of a particular sort of growing thing are all trees is self-evident. We can call this self-evidence from sense perception.

The immediacy of perception, though, is not the same as instantly understanding an idea. And, in fact, to call a proposition self-evident is not at all to say that you will instantly get it. It means instead that if you look into the proposition, if you entertain it, if you reflect upon it, you will inevitably come to affirm it. All the evidence that you need in order to believe the proposition exists within the proposition itself.

This second kind of self-evidence comes not from perception but from logic and how language works.

For instance, we define a chair as an object with a seat and some structure of legs to hold that seat up; and the artifact serves the purpose of having someone sit on it. Then, if I say that a chair is for sitting on, I am expressing a self-evident truth based only on the definition of a chair. Of course a chair is for sitting on! That is how I've defined the word, after all. That's a pretty trivial example of self-evidence. If that were all there were to the idea of self-evidence, it wouldn't be very interesting.

So here is where matters get more interesting: one can string together more than one kind of self-evident proposition — let's call them "premises" — in order to lead to a new piece of knowledge, a conclusion, which will also count as self-evident, since it has been deduced from a few basic self-evident premises.

Aristotle called this method of stringing together valid premises to yield a self-evident conclusion, a syllogism. Above, I said that "syllogism" is a technical word. Here is a basic example:

FIRST PREMISE: *Bill Gates is a human being.*
SECOND PREMISE: *All human beings are mortal.*
CONCLUSION: *Bill Gates is mortal.*

This is a bit like math. We can use a Venn diagram to show how the syllogism works. Venn diagrams represent sets of things and how they overlap, and the argument of a syllogism can be thought of as expressing facts about sets and their members. Bill Gates is in the set of human beings. And the set of human beings is entirely contained within the set of mortals. It follows that Bill Gates is in the set of mortals. The validity of this syllogism becomes self-evident when those facts are represented as in this Venn diagram:

Now, in this syllogism, our two premises are both self-evident truths based on sense perception. We know Bill Gates is a human being by looking at and listening to him. As to the idea that human beings are mortal, we know that human beings die by seeing it happen all around us and never seeing a counterexample. Then we take these two

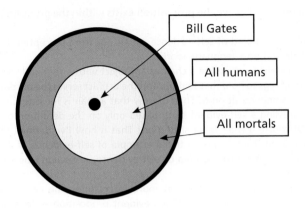

premises, each self-evident through sense perception, and generate a third self-evident proposition, in this case a conclusion, through deduction. From the two premises, we can deduce the certain conclusion that Bill Gates will die.

The Declaration introduces a similar kind of argument when it says, "We hold these truths to be self-evident." At first glance, it looks as if we just have three separate self-evident truths. But if we look closer, we notice that our truths also represent an argument with two premises, which are true from sense perception, and a conclusion that is deduced from them.

Here's how it works.

After the Declaration says, "We hold these truths to be self-evident," the text proceeds to identify three truths: one about human beings, one about government, and one about revolution. The truth about human beings, though, is a three-part truth.

It is self-evidently true:

> that all men are created equal, that they are endowed by their Creator with certain unalienable Rights, that among these are Life, Liberty and the pursuit of Happiness.

15

How do these three claims make a single truth? Human beings are equal in all acquiring the same rights at the moment of their creation. From the moment of their emergence as living beings, human beings seek to survive, to be free from domination, and to be happy. This is something we simply observe about human beings. For that matter, we observe it about other animals, too. For instance, I've never seen a cat that didn't want to survive, to be free, and to be happy.

Then, with the next truth, we come to the difference between human beings and animals. The Declaration says, it is self-evidently true

—*That to secure these rights, Governments are instituted among Men, deriving their just powers from the consent of the governed.*

This is a truly salient point. The signers are saying that, in contrast to the animal kingdom, the world of human beings is indeed full of kingdoms and other kinds of governments. The so-called animal kingdom is a kingdom only metaphorically. There are no governments among animals. Animals have social hierarchies, and they have their own methods for seeking their survival, freedom, and happiness, but human beings use politics. Human beings display self-conscious thought about social organization, and politics is the activity that flows from that self-consciousness about power. Again, this is simply a matter of observation. From the beginning of time to the present day, human beings have formed governments. Human beings have done this just as regularly as birds build nests.

Then the Declaration puts these first two truths together. Since 20 human beings seek their own survival, freedom, and happiness, and since they have a special tool for doing so — namely, the ability to form governments — it makes sense for them to stick with any particular version of that tool, any particular government, only if it's doing the work it's been built to do.

Compare it to a bird with a nest. What's the point of a bird's staying in a nest if it turns out that the nest has been built out of material inimical or poisonous to the bird? What's the use, in other words, of having a government, if it doesn't serve the purposes of protecting life, liberty, and the pursuit of happiness for which governments are set up in the first place?

The Declaration puts it this way: It is self-evidently true

— *That whenever any Form of Government becomes destructive of these ends, it is the Right of the People to alter or to abolish it, and to institute new Government, laying its foundation on such principles and organizing its powers in such form, as to them shall seem most likely to effect their Safety and Happiness.*

From the facts, first, that people are simply wired, as are all animals, to seek their survival, freedom, and happiness, and, second, that human beings use governments as their central instrument for protecting their life, liberty, and pursuit of happiness, we can deduce that people have a right to change governments that aren't working for them.

This makes an argument that goes like this:

PREMISE 1:   All people have rights to life, liberty, and the pursuit of happiness.

PREMISE 2:   Properly constituted government is necessary to their securing their rights

CONCLUSION: All people have a right to a properly constituted government.

In fact, a philosopher would say that a premise is missing from that argument and that the full formally valid syllogism would look like this: 25

PREMISE 1:   All people have rights to life, liberty, and the pursuit of happiness.

PREMISE 2:   Properly constituted government is necessary to their securing these rights.

PREMISE 3:   [All people have a right to whatever is necessary to secure what they have a right to].

CONCLUSION: All people have a right to a properly constituted government.

Politicians often craft maxims simply by dropping out pieces of their argument. With the missing premise inserted, the Declaration's truths fit together almost like the pieces of a mathematical equation; we intuitively feel the puzzle pieces snap together. That is how self-evidence should feel.

Allen's analysis focuses on the Declaration's second sentence, unpacking its logic through a careful examination of its key term, "self-evident," and explaining how the rest of the sentence forms a syllogism that "snaps together." She looks carefully at every word, restricting her analysis here to a very brief part of the text — but provides insights that illuminate the whole document.

SAM ANDERSON

Just One More Game . . . : Angry Birds, Farmville, and Other Hyperaddictive Stupid Games

Journalist and critic Sam Anderson analyzes the lure of video games in this essay, which appeared in print in the New York Times Sunday Magazine *and simultaneously online at* nytimes.com*. In addition to the text reproduced here, the online version, available via* wwnorton.com/write/fieldguidelinks*, includes illustrations, a simulation of the online game Kick Ass, and personal narratives of Anderson's video gaming experiences.*

In 1989, as communism was beginning to crumble across Eastern Europe, just a few months before protesters started pecking away at the Berlin Wall, the Japanese game-making giant Nintendo reached across the world to unleash upon America its own version of freedom. The new product was the Game Boy — a hand-held, battery-powered plastic slab that promised to set gamers loose, after all those decades of sweaty bondage, from the tyranny of rec rooms and pizza parlors and arcades.

The unit came bundled with a single cartridge: *Tetris*, a simple but addictive puzzle game whose goal was to rotate falling blocks — over and over and over and over and over and over and over — in order to build the most efficient possible walls. (Well, it was complicated. You were both building walls and not building walls; if you built them right, the walls disappeared, thereby ceasing to be walls.) This turned out to be a perfect symbiosis of game and platform. *Tetris*'s graphics were simple enough to work on the Game Boy's small gray-scale screen; its motion was slow enough not to blur; its action was a repetitive, storyless puzzle that could be picked up, with no loss of potency, at any moment, in any situation. The pairing went on to sell more than 70 million copies, spreading the freedom of compulsive wall-building into every breakfast nook and bank line in the country.

And so a tradition was born: a tradition I am going to call (half descriptively, half out of revenge for all the hours I've lost to them) "stupid games." In the nearly 30 years since *Tetris*'s invention — and especially over the last five, with the rise of smartphones — *Tetris* and its offspring (*Angry Birds*, *Bejeweled*, *Fruit Ninja*, etc.) have colonized our pockets and our brains and shifted the entire economic model of the video-game industry. Today we are living, for better and worse, in a world of stupid games.

Game-studies scholars (there are such things) like to point out that games tend to reflect the societies in which they are created and played. Monopoly, for instance, makes perfect sense as a product of the 1930s — it allowed anyone, in the middle of the Depression, to play at being a tycoon. Risk, released in the 1950s, is a stunningly literal expression of cold-war realpolitik. Twister is the translation, onto a game board, of the mid-1960s sexual revolution. One critic called it "sex in a box."

Tetris was invented exactly when and where you would expect — in a Soviet computer lab in 1984 — and its game play reflects this origin. The enemy in *Tetris* is not some identifiable villain (Donkey Kong, Mike Tyson, Carmen Sandiego) but a faceless, ceaseless, reasonless force that threatens constantly to overwhelm you, a churning production of blocks against which your only defense is a repetitive, meaningless sorting. It is bureaucracy in pure form, busywork with no aim or end, impossible to avoid or escape. And the game's final insult is that it annihilates free will. Despite its obvious futility, somehow we can't make ourselves stop rotating blocks. *Tetris*, like all the stupid games it spawned, forces us to choose to punish ourselves.

In 2009, 25 years after the invention of *Tetris*, a nearly bankrupt Finnish company called Rovio hit upon a similarly perfect fusion of game and device: *Angry Birds*. The game involves launching peevish birds at green pigs hiding inside flimsy structures. Its basic mechanism — using your index finger to pull back a slingshot, over and over and over and over and over and over and over — was the perfect use of the new technology of the touch screen: simple enough to lure a suddenly immense new market of casual gamers, satisfying enough to hook them.

5

academic literacies   rhetorical situations   genres   processes   strategies   research MLA / APA   media / design   readings   handbook

Within months, *Angry Birds* became the most popular game on the iPhone, then spread across every other available platform. Today it has been downloaded, in its various forms, more than 700 million times. It has also inspired a disturbingly robust merchandising empire: films, T-shirts, novelty slippers, even plans for *Angry Birds* "activity parks" featuring play equipment for kids. For months, a sign outside my local auto-repair shop promised, "Free *Angry Birds* pen with service." The game's latest iteration, *Angry Birds Space*, appeared a couple weeks ago with a promotional push from Wal-Mart, T-Mobile, National Geographic Books, MTV and NASA. (There was an announcement on the International Space Station.) *Angry Birds*, it seems, is our *Tetris*: the string of digital prayer beads that our entire culture can twiddle in moments of rapture or anxiety — economic, political or existential. . . .

Humans have always played stupid games. Dice are older than recorded history. Ancient Egyptians played a board game called Senet, which archaeologists believe was something like sacred backgammon. We have rock-paper-scissors, tick-tack-toe, checkers, dominoes and solitaire — small, abstract games in which sets of simple rules play out in increasingly complex scenarios. (Chess, you might say, is the king of stupid games: the tide line where stupid games meet genius.)

But pre-*Tetris* games were different in a primal way. They required human opponents or at least equipment — the manipulation of three-dimensional objects in space. When you sat down to play them, chances were you meant to sit down and play them.

Stupid games, on the other hand, are rarely occasions in themselves. They are designed to push their way through the cracks of other occasions. We play them incidentally, ambivalently, compulsively, almost accidentally. They're less an activity in our day than a blank space in our day; less a pursuit than a distraction from other pursuits. You glance down to check your calendar and suddenly it's 40 minutes later and there's only one level left before you jump to the next stage, so you might as well just launch another bird. . . .

Then, in 2007, the iPhone appeared. Games were much easier to develop and easier to distribute through Apple's app store. Instead of just passing their work around to one another on blogs, independent game designers suddenly had a way to reach everyone — not just hardcore gamers, but their mothers, their mailmen and their college professors. Consumers who never would have put a quarter into an arcade or even set eyes on an Xbox 360 were now carrying a sophisticated game console with them, all the time, in their pockets or their purses.

This had a profound impact on game design. In the era of consoles, most games were designed to come to life on a stationary piece of furniture — a television or a desktop computer. The games were built accordingly, around long narratives (quests, wars, the rise and fall of civilizations) that could be explored comfortably while sitting cross-legged on a living-room carpet.

Smartphone games are built on a very different model. The iPhone's screen is roughly the size of a playing card; it responds not to the fast-twitch button combos of a controller but to more intuitive and intimate motions: poking, pinching, tapping, tickling. This has encouraged a very different kind of game: Tetris-like little puzzles, broken into discrete bits, designed to be played anywhere, in any context, without a manual, by any level of player. (Charles Pratt, a researcher in New York University's Game Center, refers to such games as "knitting games.") You could argue that these are *pure* games: perfectly designed minisystems engineered to take us directly to the core of gaming pleasure without the distraction of narrative. The *Angry Birds* creators like to compare their game with *Super Mario Brothers*. But the first and simplest level of *Super Mario Brothers* takes about a minute and a half to finish. The first level of *Angry Birds* takes around 10 seconds. . . .

There are people who see the proliferation of stupid games as a good thing. In fact, they believe that games may be the answer to all of humanity's problems. In her book *Reality Is Broken*, Jane McGonigal argues that play is possibly the best, healthiest, most productive activity a human can undertake — a gateway to our ideal psychological state. Games aren't an escape from reality, McGonigal contends, they are an optimal form of engaging it. In fact, if we could just find a way to impose game mechanics on top of everyday life, humans would be infinitely better off. We might even use these approaches to help solve real-world problems like obesity, education and government abuse. Some proponents point to successful examples of games applied to everyday life: Weight Watchers and frequent-flier miles, for example.

Corporations, of course, have been using similar strategies for 15 decades, hooking consumers on products by giving them constant small victories for spending money (think of the old Monopoly game promotion at McDonald's). The buzzword for this is "gamification" and the ubiquity of computers and smartphones has only supercharged these tendencies. Gartner, a technology research firm, predicted last year that, in the near future, "a gamified service for consumer-goods marketing and customer retention will become as important as Facebook, eBay or Amazon." Companies have already used online games to sneakily advertise sugary cereals directly to children.

Although there is a certain utopian appeal to McGonigal's "games for change" model, I worry about the dystopic potential of gamification. Instead of just bombarding us with jingles, corporations will be able to inject their messages directly into our minds with ads disguised as games. Gamification seeks to turn the world into one giant chore chart covered with achievement stickers — the kind of thing parents design for their children — though it raises the potentially terrifying question of who the parents are. This, I fear, is the dystopian future of stupid games: amoral corporations hiring teams of behavioral psychologists to laser-target our addiction cycles for profit. . . .

[Game designer Frank] Lantz seemed undisturbed by the dark side of stupid games, like addiction or cynical corporate hijacking. He said that real games are far too fragile and complex to be engineered by corporations and that their appeal goes much deeper than reward schedules. "It's as hard to make a really good game as it is to make a really good movie or opera or hat," he told me. "Sure, there's mathematics to it, but it's also a piece of culture. The type of game you play is also a part of how you think about yourself as a person. There's no formula that's going to solve that equation. It's impossible, because it's infinitely deep and wonderful."

As for my nightmare vision of a world splintered by addiction to stupid games, Lantz had a different perspective. He said that he liked to think *Drop7* [a game Lantz designed that combines elements of *Tetris* and Sudoku] was not only addictive but also, on some level, about addiction. Games, he told me, are like "homebrew neuroscience" — "a little digital drug you can use to run experiments on your own brain." Part of the point of letting them seduce you, as Lantz sees it, is to come out the other side a more interesting and self-aware person; more conscious of your habits, weaknesses, desires and strengths. "It's like heroin that is abstracted or compressed or stylized," he said. "It gives you a window into your brain that doesn't crush your brain."

I tried to think about what — if anything — I had learned from this window into my brain. Like their spiritual forefather, *Tetris*, most stupid games are about walls: building them, scaling them, knocking them down. Walls made of numbers, walls made of digital bricks, walls with green pigs hiding behind them. They're like miniature boot camps of containment. Ultimately, I realized, these games are also about a more subtle and mysterious form of wall-building: the internal walls we build to compartmentalize our time, our attention, our lives. The legendary game designer Sid Meier once defined a game as, simply, "a series of interesting choices." Maybe that's the secret genius of stupid games: they force us to make a series of interesting choices about what matters, moment to moment, in our lives. . . .

Anderson describes Tetris *and other games clearly and outlines their relationship to older "stupid games." He interprets the "gamification" of American culture positively and provides evidence from experts as well as the games themselves, including the playable online* Kick Ass *game, to support his interpretation.*

 For four more textual analyses, see CHAPTER 60.

Key Features / Textual Analysis

A summary or description of the text. Your readers may not know the text you are analyzing, so you need to include it or tell them about it before you analyze it. Allen's text, the Declaration of Independence, is well known, so she assumes that her readers already know its first sentences. Texts that are not so well known require a more detailed summary or description. For example, Berry includes the ads she analyzes and also describes them in detail.

Attention to the context. Texts don't exist in isolation: they are influenced by and contribute to ongoing conversations, controversies, debates, and cultural trends. To understand a particular text, you need to understand its larger context. Anderson begins by offering a brief history of handheld video games, and Berry places shoe ads into the context of fashion advertising.

A clear interpretation or judgment. Your goal in analyzing a text is to lead readers through careful examination of the text to some kind of interpretation or reasoned judgment, sometimes announced clearly in a thesis statement. When you interpret something, you explain what you think it means, as Berry does when she argues that the two ads suggest that our clothing choices enhance our individuality. She might instead have chosen to judge the effectiveness of the ads, perhaps noting that they promise the impossible: uniqueness through mass-produced clothing. Anderson judges "stupid games" to be positive, as "they force us to make a series of interesting choices about what matters, moment to moment, in our lives."

Reasonable support for your conclusions. Written analysis of a text is generally supported by evidence from the text itself and sometimes from other sources as well. The writer might support his or her interpretation by quoting words or passages from a verbal text or referring to images in a visual text. Allen, for example, interprets the term "self-evident" by referring to formal logic, Venn diagrams, and the Catholic *Credo*. Berry examines patterns of both language and images in her analysis of two ads. Anderson quotes expert game designers to support his thesis. Note that the support you offer for your interpretation need only be "reasonable" — there is never only one way to interpret something.

A GUIDE TO WRITING TEXTUAL ANALYSES

Choosing a Text to Analyze

Most of the time, you will be assigned a text or a type of text to analyze: a poem in a literature class, the work of a political philosopher in a political science class, a speech in a history or communications course, a painting or sculpture in an art class, a piece of music in a music theory course. If you must choose a text to analyze, look for one that suits the demands of the assignment—one that is neither too large or complex to analyze thoroughly (a Dickens novel or a Beethoven symphony is probably too big) nor too brief or limited to generate sufficient material (a ten-second TV news brief or a paragraph from *Moneyball* would probably be too small). You might also choose to analyze three or four texts by examining elements common to all. Be sure you understand what the assignment asks you to do, and ask your instructor for clarification if you're not sure.

Considering the Rhetorical Situation

55–56 **PURPOSE**   Why are you analyzing this text? To demonstrate that you understand it? To show how its argument works — or doesn't? Or are you using the text as a way to make some other point?

57–60 **AUDIENCE**   Are your readers likely to know your text? How much detail will you need to supply?

64–67 **STANCE**   What interests you (or not) about your text? Why? What do you know or believe about it, and how will your own beliefs affect your analysis?

68–70 **MEDIA / DESIGN**   Will your analysis appear in print? on the web? How will your medium affect your analysis? If you are analyzing a visual text, you will probably need to include an image of it.

Generating Ideas and Text

In analyzing a written text, your goal is to understand what it says, how it works, and what it means. To do so, you may find it helpful to follow a certain sequence: read, respond, summarize, analyze, and draw conclusions from your analysis.

Read to see what the text says.   Start by reading carefully, to get a sense of what it says. This means first skimming to **PREVIEW THE TEXT**, rereading

12–13
16–18 for the main ideas, then questioning and **ANNOTATING**.

14   Consider your **INITIAL RESPONSE**. Once you have a sense of what the text says, what do you think? What's your reaction to the argument, the

✳ academic literacies
■ rhetorical situations
▲ genres
○ processes
◆ strategies
● research MLA / APA
□ media / design
▶ readings
⟋ handbook

tone, the language, the images? Do you find the text difficult? puzzling? Do you agree with what the writer says? disagree? agree *and* disagree? Your reaction to a text can color your analysis, so start by thinking about how you react — and why. Consider both your intellectual and any emotional reactions. Identify places in the text that trigger or account for those reactions. If you think that you have no particular reaction or response, try to articulate why. Whatever your response, think about what accounts for it.

Next, consolidate your understanding of the text by **SUMMARIZING** what it says in your own words. You may find it helpful to **OUTLINE** its main ideas. For instance, Allen carefully maps out the parts of the syllogism at the heart of her analysis.

● 486–87
○ 293–95

Decide what you want to analyze. Having read the text carefully, think about what you find most interesting or intriguing and why. Does the argument interest you? its logic? its attempt to create an emotional response? its reliance on the writer's credibility or reputation? its use of design to achieve its aims? its context? Does the text's language, imagery, or structure intrigue you? something else? You might begin your analysis by exploring what attracted your notice.

Think about the larger context. All texts are part of larger conversations with other texts that have dealt with the same topic. An essay arguing for handgun trigger locks is part of an ongoing conversation about gun control, which is itself part of a conversation on individual rights and responsibilities. Academic texts include documentation in part to weave in voices from the conversation. And, in fact, any time you're reading to learn, you're probably reading for some larger context. Whatever your reading goals, being aware of that larger context can help you better understand what you're reading. Here are some specific aspects of the text to pay attention to:

- *Who else cares about this topic?* Especially when you're reading in order to learn about a topic, the texts you read will often reveal which people or groups are part of the conversation — and might be sources of further reading. For example, an essay describing the formation of Mammoth Cave could be of interest to geologists, spelunkers, travel writers, or tourists. If you're reading such an essay while doing research on the cave, you should consider how the audience addressed determines the nature of the information provided — and its suitability as a source for your research.

- *Ideas.* Does the text refer to any concepts or ideas that give you some sense that it's part of a larger conversation? An argument on airport security measures, for example, is part of larger conversations about government response to terrorism, the limits of freedom in a democracy, and the possibilities of using technology to detect weapons and explosives, among others.

- *Terms.* Is there any terminology or specialized language that reflects the writer's allegiance to a particular group or academic discipline? If you run across words like *false consciousness, ideology,* and *hegemony,* for example, you might guess the text was written by a Marxist scholar.

- *Citations.* Whom does the writer cite? Do the other writers have a particular academic specialty, belong to an identifiable intellectual school, share similar political leanings? If an article on politics cites Michael Moore and Barbara Ehrenreich in support of its argument, you might assume the writer holds liberal opinions; if it cites Rush Limbaugh and Sean Hannity, the writer is likely a conservative.

Write a brief paragraph describing the larger context surrounding the text and how that context affects your understanding of the text.

Consider what you know about the writer. What you know about the person who created a text can influence your understanding of it. His or her CREDENTIALS, other work, reputation, stance, and beliefs are all useful windows into understanding a text. You may need to conduct an online search to find information on the writer. Then write a sentence or two summarizing what you know about the writer and how that information affects your understanding of the text.

470

Study how the text works. Written texts are made up of various components, including words, sentences, paragraphs, headings, lists, punctuation — and sometimes images as well. Look for patterns in the way these components are used and try to decide what those patterns reveal about the text. How do they affect its message? See the sections on **THINKING ABOUT HOW THE TEXT WORKS** and **IDENTIFYING PATTERNS** for specific guidelines on examining patterns this way. Then write a sentence or two describing the patterns you've discovered and how they contribute to what the text says.

20–22
28–29

Analyze the argument.   Every text makes an argument and provides some kind of support for it. An important part of understanding any text is to recognize its argument — what the writer wants the audience to believe, feel, or do. Here are some questions you'll want to consider when you analyze an argument:

- *What is the claim?*   What is the main point the writer is trying to make? Is there a clearly stated **THESIS**, or is the thesis merely implied? Is it appropriately qualified?

345–47

- *What support does the writer offer for the claim?*   What **REASONS** are given to support the claim? What **EVIDENCE** backs up those reasons? Facts? Statistics? Examples? Testimonials by authorities? Anecdotes or stories? Are the reasons and evidence appropriate, plausible, and sufficient? Are you convinced by them? If not, why not?

358–59

- *How does the writer appeal to readers?*   Does he or she appeal to your **EMOTIONS**? rely on **LOGIC**? try to establish **COMMON GROUND**? demonstrate **CREDIBILITY**?

370
356–67
367
367–69
369

- *How evenhandedly does the writer present the argument?*   Is there any mention of **COUNTERARGUMENTS**? If so, how does the writer deal with them? By refuting them? By acknowledging them and responding to them reasonably? Does the writer treat other arguments respectfully? dismissively?

- *Does the writer use any logical **FALLACIES**?*   Are the arguments or beliefs of others distorted or exaggerated? Is the logic faulty?

370–72

- *What authorities or other sources of outside information does the writer use?* How are they used? How credible are they? Are they in any way biased or otherwise unreliable? Are they current?

- *How does the writer address you as the reader?* Does the writer assume that readers know something about what is being discussed? Does his or her language include you or exclude you? (Hint: If you see the word *we*, do you feel included?) Do you sense that you and the writer share any beliefs or attitudes? If the writer is not writing to you, what audience is the target? How do you know?

Then write a brief paragraph summarizing the argument the text makes and the main way the writer argues it, along with your reactions to or questions about that argument.

In analyzing a visual text, your goal is to understand its intended effect on viewers as well as its actual effect, the ways it creates that effect, and its relationship to other texts. If the visual text accompanies a written one, you need to understand how the texts work together to convey a message or make an argument.

Describe the text. Your first job is to examine the image carefully. Focus on specific details; given the increasing use of *Photoshop* and other digital image manipulation tools, you can usually assume that every detail in the image is intentional. Ask yourself these questions:

- What kind of image is it? Does it stand alone, or is it part of a group? Are there typical features of this kind of image that it includes — or lacks?

- What does the image show? What stands out? What is in the background? Are some parts of the image grouped together or connected? Or set apart from one another?

- As you look at the image, does the content seem far away, close up, or in between? Are you level with it, looking down from above, or looking up from below? What is the effect of your viewing position?

- Does the image tell or suggest a story, about what has happened (as in Berry's ad for Sorel shoes) or is about to happen?

academic literacies · rhetorical situations · genres · processes · strategies · research MLA / APA · media / design · readings · handbook

- Does the image allude to or refer to anything else? For example, the Starbucks logo features the image of a Siren, the mythical beings who lured sailors to their doom.

Explore your response.   Images, particularly those in advertisements, are often trying to persuade us to buy something or to feel, think, or behave a certain way. News photographs and online videos also try to evoke **EMOTIONAL** responses, from horror over murdered innocents to amuse-ment at cute kittens. Think about your response:

◆ 370

- How does the image make you feel? What emotional response, if any, does the image make you feel? Sympathy? Concern? Anger? Happiness? Contentment? Something else?

- What does the image lead you to think about? What connections does it have to things in your life, in the news, in your knowledge of the world?

- Do the image and any words accompanying seem to be trying to per-suade you to think or do something? Do they do so directly, such as by pointing out the virtues of a product (Buick Encore: "Sized to Fit Your Life")? Or indirectly, by setting a tone or establishing a mood (the Clarks shoe ad that Berry analyzes)?

- Does the **GENRE** affect your response? For example, do you expect to laugh at a comic? feel empathy with victims of a tragedy in a photo accompanying a news story? find a satirical editorial cartoon offensive?

▲ 71

Consider the context.   Like written texts, visual texts are part of larger conversations with other texts that have dealt with the same topic or used similar imagery. This editorial cartoon on global warming, for example, is part of an ongoing conversation about climate change and the role our lifestyles play in it:

Consider what you know about the artist or sponsor. Editorial cartoons, like the one above, are usually signed, and information about the artist and his or her other work is usually readily available on the Web. Many commercials and advertisements, however, are created by ad agencies, so the organization or company that sponsored or posted the image should be identified and researched. How does that information affect your understanding of the text?

Decide on a focus for your analysis. What do you find most interesting about the text, and why? Its details and the way they work together (or not)? The argument it makes? The way it uses images to appeal to its audience? The emotional response it evokes? The way any words and images work together to deliver a message? These are just some ways of thinking about a visual text, ones that can help you find a focus.

However you choose to focus your analysis, it should be limited in scope so that you can zero in on the details of the visual you're analyzing. Here, for example, is an excerpt from an essay by an art historian responding to a statement made by President Barack Obama that manufacturing skills may be worth more than a degree in art history.

> *"I promise you, folks can make a lot more potentially with skilled manufacturing or the trades than they might with an art history degree."* President Barack Obama

> Charged with interrogating this quote from the president, I Google "Obama art history." I click on the first result, a video from CNN, in which the quote is introduced by a gray-haired man in a dark and serious suit, standing in front of a bank of monitors in a digitally created nonspace. The camera cuts from this man to President Obama, who stands in shirtsleeves, his tie slightly loosened. His undershirt is visible through his buttondown under the intense light from what I assume is the work-day sun.

> Behind him is a crowd of men and women in more casual clothing, some wearing sweatshirts that have the name of a union printed across them. Their presence creates a spectrum of skin tones. Each person was clearly vetted for visual effect, as were the president's and the newscaster's costumes, the size of their flag lapel pins, the shape of the microphones they speak into, and the angle of the light on their faces. The president makes the comment in question, immediately declares his love for art history, and says that he doesn't want to get a bunch of angry emails from art historians. The crowd behind him laughs and the clip cuts off abruptly.

> A click away, I find a digitized copy of a handwritten note from President Obama, apologizing to an angry art history professor who emailed him to complain about his comments. The card on which the note is written is plain, undecorated save for two lines of text printed in a conservative, serif font in a shade of blue that is just on the vibrant side of navy — THE WHITE HOUSE — and under it in smaller letters,

WASHINGTON. Its tasteful, minimal aesthetic pulls double duty, meant to convey both populist efficiency (note the absence of gold gilding) and stern superiority (you know where Washington is, right?). It sets up a productive contrast with the friendliness of the president's own handwriting, particularly his looping signature, soft on the outside with a strong slash through the middle.

Like the video of the president's speech, it is a screen-scale tour de force of political imagecraft, certainly produced with the full knowledge that it would be digitized and go viral, at least among a particular demographic.

—Joel Parsons, "Richness in the Eye of the Beholder"

Parsons begins by describing the images — Obama's clothing, the people standing behind him, the letterhead on his note card, his "looping

President Obama speaking at a General Electric plant in Waukesha, Wisconsin, 2014.

THE WHITE HOUSE
WASHINGTON

Ann —

Let me apologize for my off-the-cuff remarks. I was making a point about the jobs market, not the value of art history. As it so happens, art history was one of my favorite subjects in high school, and it has helped me take in a great deal of joy in my life that

I might otherwise have missed.

So please pass on my apology for the glib remark to the entire department, and understand that I was trying to encourage young people who may not be predisposed to a four year college experience to be open to technical training that can lead them to an honorable career.

Sincerely,

Obama's apology note to Ann Johns, art history professor at the University of Texas at Austin.

signature" — followed by an analysis of how every aspect of the video and the note card was "certainly produced with the full knowledge that it would be digitized and go viral." Notice as well that Parsons's analysis focuses more on the visual aspects of the video and note card than on what was said or written. And in a part of his essay not shown here, he notes that his analysis is grounded in "tools . . . he learned in a first-year art history course" — a not-so-subtle response to what President Obama said.

Coming Up with a Thesis

355–73

When you analyze a text, you are basically **ARGUING** that the text should be read or seen in a certain way. Once you've studied the text thoroughly, you need to identify your analytical goal: do you want to show that the text has a certain meaning? uses certain techniques to achieve its purposes? tries to influence its audience in particular ways? relates to some larger context in some significant manner? should be taken seriously — or not? 345–47 something else? Come up with a tentative **THESIS** to guide your thinking and analyzing — but be aware that your thesis may change as you continue to work.

Ways of Organizing a Textual Analysis

293–95

Examine the information you have to see how it supports or complicates your thesis. Look for clusters of related information that you can use to structure an **OUTLINE**. Your analysis might be structured in at least two ways. You might, as Anderson does, discuss patterns, elements, or themes that run through the text. Alternatively, you might analyze each text or section of text separately, as Berry does. Following are graphic representations of some ways of organizing a textual analysis.

academic literacies   rhetorical situations   genres   processes   strategies   research MLA / APA   media / design   readings   handbook

[Thematically]

[Part by part, or text by text]

[Spatially, as the text is likely to be experienced by viewers]

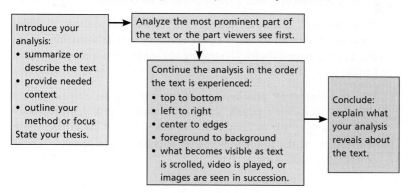

Writing Out a Draft

In drafting your analysis, your goal should be to integrate the various parts into a smoothly flowing, logically organized essay. However, it's easy to get bogged down in the details. Consider writing one section of the analysis first, then another and another until you've drafted the entire middle; then draft your beginning and ending. Alternatively, start by summarizing the text and moving from there to your analysis and then to your ending. However you do it, you need to support your analysis with evidence: from the text itself (as Berry's analysis of advertisements does), or from **RESEARCH** on the larger context of the text (as Allen does), or by incorporating various experts' views of your subject (as Anderson does).

433

331–38

Draft a BEGINNING. The beginning of an essay that analyzes a text generally has several tasks: to introduce or summarize the text for your readers, to offer any necessary information on the larger context, and to present your thesis.

486–87

- *Summarize or describe the text.* If the text is one your readers don't know, you need to **SUMMARIZE** or **DESCRIBE** it early on to show that you understand it fully. For example, Berry begins each analysis of a shoe advertisement with a description of its content.

- *Show the text.* If you're analyzing a visual text online, consider starting off with an image, a video, or a link to it or something similar, as Anderson does by illustrating his essay with a playable video game.

- *Provide a context for your analysis.* If there is a larger context that is significant for your analysis, you might mention it in your introduction. Allen does this by comparing the Declaration's statement about self-evident truths to the statements of belief in the Apostles' Creed of the Catholic Church.

- *State your* **THESIS**. Berry ends her first paragraph by stating her thesis explicitly: These ads "for Clarks and Sorel. . . encourage us to break free from the standard beauty mold and be ourselves; using mostly imagery, they remind us that being unique is the true origin of beauty." 345–47

Draft an **ENDING**. Think about what you want your readers to take away from your analysis, and end by getting them to focus on those thoughts. 338–42

- *Restate your thesis — and say why it matters.* Berry, for example, ends by asserting that the ads she examines invite women to "be ourselves" by "accessoriz[ing] our personalities."
- *Explain what your analysis reveals.* Your analysis should tell your readers something about the way the text works or about what it means or says. Allen, for example, concludes by noting that "the Declaration's truths fit together almost like the pieces of a mathematical equation; we intuitively feel the puzzle pieces snap together. That is how self-evidence should feel."

Come up with a **TITLE**. A good title indicates something about the subject of your analysis — and makes readers want to see what you have to say about it. Berry's title provides a preview of her thesis that the ads she is analyzing are selling a vision of clothing as a vehicle for being unique, while Anderson's title tells us that his topic is video games while enticing us to read on with provocative language like "hyperaddictive" and "stupid." 344–45

Considering Matters of Design

- If you cite written text as evidence, be sure to set long quotations and **DOCUMENTATION** according to the style you're using. 496–99

604–5

- If your essay is lengthy, consider whether **HEADINGS** would make your analysis easier for readers to follow.

- If you're analyzing a visual text, include a copy of the image and a caption identifying it.

- If you're submitting your essay electronically, provide links to whatever text you are analyzing.

- If you're analyzing an image or a screen shot, consider annotating elements of it right on the image.

Getting Response and Revising

306–7

The following questions can help you and others study your draft with a critical eye. Make sure that anyone you ask to read and **RESPOND** to your text knows your purpose and audience.

- Is the beginning effective? Does it make a reader want to continue?

- Does the introduction provide an overview of your analysis? Is your thesis clear?

- Is the text described or summarized clearly and sufficiently?

- Is the analysis well organized and easy to follow? Do the parts fit together coherently? Does it read like an essay rather than a collection of separate bits of analysis?

- Does each part of the analysis relate to and support the thesis?

- Is anything confusing or in need of more explanation?

- Are all quotations accurate and correctly documented?

- Is it clear how the analysis leads to the interpretation? Is there adequate evidence to support the interpretation?

- Does the ending make clear what your analysis shows?

Then it's time to **REVISE**. Make sure your text appeals to your audience and think hard about whether it will achieve your purpose.

307–10

Editing and Proofreading

Readers equate correctness with competence. Once you've revised your draft, edit carefully:

- Is your **THESIS** clearly stated?

345–47

- Check all **QUOTATIONS**, **PARAPHRASES**, and **SUMMARIES** for accuracy and form. Be sure that each has the required **DOCUMENTATION**.

478–90
496–99

- Make sure that your analysis flows clearly from one point to the next and that you use **TRANSITIONS** to help readers move through your text.

349

- **PROOFREAD** your finished analysis carefully before turning it in.

316–17

Taking Stock of Your Work

Take stock of what you've written and learned by writing out answers to these questions:

- How did you go about analyzing the text? What methods did you use — and which ones were most helpful?
- How did you go about drafting your essay?
- How well did you organize your written analysis? What, if anything, could you do to make it easier to read?
- Did you provide sufficient evidence to support your analysis?
- What did you do especially well?
- What could still be improved?
- Did you include any visuals, and if so, what did they add? Could you have shown the same thing with words?

- How did other readers' responses influence your writing?
- What would you do differently next time?
- Are you pleased with your analysis? What did it teach you about the text you analyzed? Did it make you want to study more works by the same writer or artist?

IF YOU NEED MORE HELP

See Chapter 28 for guidelines on **DRAFTING**, Chapter 29 on **ASSESSING YOUR OWN WRITING**, Chapter 30 on **GETTING RESPONSE AND REVISING**, and Chapter 31 on **EDITING AND PROOFREADING**. See Chapter 32 if you are required to submit your analysis in a writing **PORTFOLIO**. See Chapter 56 for help **USING VISUALS**.

298–300
301–5
306–12
313–17
318–28
607–15

Reporting Information **12**

Many kinds of writing report information. Newspapers report on local and world events; textbooks give information about biology, history, writing; websites provide information about products (*jcrew.com*), people (*pharrellwilliams.com*), institutions (*smithsonian.org*). We write out a lot of information ourselves, from a note we post on our door saying we've gone to choir practice to a text we send to tell a friend where to meet us for dinner and how to get there.

College assignments often call for reporting information as well. In a *history* class, you may be assigned to report what you've learned about the state of U.S. relations with Japan just before the bombing of Pearl Harbor. A *biology* course may require you to report the effects of an experiment in which plants are deprived of sunlight for different periods of time. In a *nursing* class, you may have to report the changes in a patient's symptoms after the administration of a particular drug.

This chapter focuses on reports that are written to inform readers about a particular topic. Very often this kind of writing calls for some kind of research: you need to know your subject in order to report on it! When you write to report information, you are the expert. We'll begin with three good examples, the first annotated to show the key features found in most reports.

MICHAELA CULLINGTON

Does Texting Affect Writing?

This essay by a student at Marywood University was published in Young Scholars in Writing, *a journal of undergraduate writing published by the University of Missouri–Kansas City.*

It's taking over our lives. We can do it almost anywhere — walking to class, waiting in line at the grocery store, or hanging out at home. It's quick, easy, and convenient. It has become a concern of doctors, parents, and teachers alike. What is it? It's texting!

Text messaging — or texting, as it's more commonly called — is the process of sending and receiving typed messages via a cellular phone. It is a common means of communication among teenagers and is even becoming popular in the business world because it allows quick messages to be sent without people having to commit to a telephone conversation. A person is able to say what is needed, and the other person will receive the information and respond when it's convenient to do so.

Definitions of key terms.

In order to more quickly type what they are trying to say, many people use abbreviations instead of words. The language created by these abbreviations is called textspeak. Some people believe that using these abbreviations is hindering the writing abilities of students, and others argue that texting is actually having a positive effect on writing. In fact, it seems likely that texting has no significant effect on student writing.

Here's the thesis.

Concerns about Textspeak

A September 2008 article in *USA Today* entitled "Texting, Testing Destroys Kids' Writing Style" summarizes many of the most common complaints about the effect of texting. It states that according to the National Center for Education Statistics, only 25% of high school seniors are "proficient" writers. The article quotes Jacquie Ream, a former teacher and author of *K.I.S.S.— Keep It Short and Simple*, a guide for writing more effectively. Ream states, "[W]e have a whole generation being raised without communication skills." She blames the use of acronyms and shorthand in text messages for students' inability to spell and ultimately to write well. Ream also points out that students struggle to convey emotion in their writing because, as she states, in text messages "emotions are always sideways smiley faces."

Analysis of causes and effects.

This debate became prominent after some teachers began to believe they were seeing a decline in the writing abilities of their students. Many attributed this perceived decline to the increasing popularity of text messaging and its use of abbreviations. Naomi Baron, a linguistics professor at American University, blames texting for what she sees as the fact that "so much of American society has become sloppy and laissez faire about   5 the mechanics of writing" ("Should"). Teachers report finding "2" for "to," "gr8" for "great," "dat" for "that," and "wut" for "what," among other examples of textspeak, in their students' writing. A Minnesota teacher of the seventh and ninth grades says that she has to spend extra time in class editing papers and must "explicitly" remind her students that it is not acceptable to use text slang and abbreviations in writing (Walsh). Another English teacher believes that text language has become "second nature" to her students (Carey); they are so used to it that they do not even catch themselves doing it.

Many also complain that because texting does not stress the importance of punctuation, students are neglecting it in their formal writing. Teachers say that their students are forgetting commas, apostrophes, and even capital letters to begin sentences. Another complaint is that text messages lack emotion. Many argue that texts lack feeling because of their tendency to be short, brief, and to the point. Because students are not able to communicate emotion effectively through texts, some teachers worry, they may lose the ability to do so in writing.

To get a more personal perspective on the question of how teachers perceive texting to be influencing student writing, I interviewed two of my former high school teachers — my junior-year English teacher and my senior-year theology teacher. Both teachers stress the importance of writing in their courses. They maintain that they notice text abbreviations in their students' writing often. To correct this problem, they point it out when it occurs and take points off for its use. They also remind their students to use proper sentence structure and complete sentences. The English teacher says that she believes texting inhibits good writing — it reinforces simplistic writing that may be acceptable for conversation but is "not so good for critical thinking or analysis." She suggests that texting tends to generate topic sentences without emphasizing the following explanation. According to these teachers, then, texting is inhibiting good writing. However, their evidence is limited, based on just a few personal experiences rather than on a significant amount of research.

Responses to Concerns about Textspeak

In response to these complaints that texting is having a negative impact on student writing, others insist that texting should be viewed as beneficial because it provides students with motivation to write, practice in specific writing skills, and an opportunity to gain confidence in their writing. For example, Betty Sternberg and her coauthors argue that texting is a good way to motivate students: teens enjoy texting, and if they frequently write through texts, they will be more motivated to write formally. Texting also helps to spark students' creativity, these authors argue, because they are always coming up with new ways to express their ideas (417).

In addition, because they are engaging in written communication rather than oral speech, texting teens learn how to convey their message to a reader in as few words as possible. In his book *Txtng: The Gr8 Db8*, David Crystal discusses a study that concludes that texting actually helps foster "the ability to summarize and express oneself concisely" in writing (168). Furthermore, Crystal explains that texting actually helps people to "sharpen their diplomatic skills . . . [because] it allows more time to formulate their thoughts and express them carefully" (168). One language arts teacher from Minnesota believes that texting helps students develop their own "individual voice" (qtd. in Walsh). Perfecting such a voice allows the writer to offer personal insights and express feelings that will interest and engage readers.

Synthesis of various sources of information. Quotations are introduced with signal phrases.

Supporters of texting also argue that it not only teaches elements 10 of writing but provides extra practice to those who struggle with the conventions of writing. As Crystal points out, children who struggle with literacy will not choose to use a technology that requires them to do something that is difficult for them. However, if they do choose to text, the experience will help them "overcome their awkwardness and develop their social and communication skills" (*Txtng* 171). Shirley Holm, a junior high school teacher, describes texting as a "comfortable form of communication" (qtd. in Walsh). Teenagers are used to texting, enjoy doing so, and as a result are always writing. Through this experience of writing in ways they enjoy, they can learn to take pleasure in writing formally. If students are continually writing in some form, they will eventually develop better skills.

Furthermore, those who favor texting explain that with practice comes the confidence and courage to try new things, which some observers believe they are seeing happen with writing as a result of texting. Teenagers have, for example, created an entirely new language — one that uses abbreviations and symbols instead of words, does not require punctuation, and uses short, incomplete phrases throughout the entire conversation. It's a way of speaking that is a language in and of itself. Crystal, among others, sees this "language evolution" as a positive effect of texting; he seems, in fact, fascinated that teenagers are capable of creating such a phenomenon, which he describes as the "latest manifestation of the human ability" (*Txtng* 175). David Warlick, a teacher and author of books about technology in the classroom, would agree with Crystal. He believes students should be given credit for "inventing a new language ideal for communicating in a high-tech world" (qtd. in Carey).

Methods

I decided to conduct my own research into this controversy. I wanted to get different, more personal, perspectives on the issue. First, I surveyed seven students on their opinions about the impact of texting on writing. Second, I questioned two high school teachers, as noted above. Finally, in an effort to compare what students are actually doing to people's perceptions of what they are doing, I analyzed student writing samples for instances of textspeak.[1]

To let students speak for themselves, I created a list of questions for seven high school and college students, some of my closest and most reliable friends. Although the number of respondents was small, I could trust my knowledge of them to help me interpret their responses. In addition, these students are very different from one another, and I believed their differences would allow for a wide array of thoughts and opinions on the issue. I was thus confident in the reliability and diversity of their answers but was cautious not to make too many assumptions because of the small sample size.

I asked the students how long they had been texting; how often they texted; what types of abbreviations they used most and how often they used them; and whether they noticed themselves using any type of textspeak in their formal writing. In analyzing their responses, I looked for commonalities to help me draw conclusions about the students' texting habits and if/how they believed their writing was affected.

I created a list of questions for teachers similar to the one for the students and asked two of my high school teachers to provide their input. I asked if they had noticed their students using textspeak in their writing assignments and, if so, how they dealt with it. I also asked if they believed texting had a positive or negative effect on writing. Next, I asked if they were texters themselves. And, finally, I solicited their

Firsthand research: interviews and survey.

15

opinions on what they believed should be done to prevent teens from using text abbreviations and other textspeak in their writing.

I was surprised at how different the students' replies and opinions were from the teachers'. I decided to find out for myself whose impressions were more accurate by comparing some students' actual writing with students' and teachers' perceptions of that writing. To do this I looked at twenty samples of student writing — end-of-semester research arguments written in two first-year college writing courses with different instructors. The topics varied from increased airport security after September 11 to the weapons of the Vietnam War to autism, and lengths ranged from eight to ten pages. To analyze the papers for the presence of textspeak, I looked closely for use of abbreviations and other common slang terms, especially those usages which the students had stated in their surveys were most common. These included "hbu" ("How about you?"); "gtg" ("Got to go"); and "cuz" ("because"). I also looked for the numbers 2 and 4 used instead of the words "to" and "for."

Comparison and contrast.

Discussion of Findings

My research suggests that texting actually has a minimal effect on student writing. It showed that students do not believe textspeak is appropriate in formal writing assignments. They recognize the difference between texting friends and writing formally and know what is appropriate in each situation. This was proven true in the student samples, in which no examples of textspeak were used. Many experts would agree that there is no harm in textspeak, as long as students continue to be taught and reminded that occasions where formal language is expected are not the place for it. As Crystal explains, the purpose of the abbreviations used in text messages is not to replace language but rather to make quick communications shorter and easier, since in a standard text message, the texter is allowed only 160 characters for a communication ("Texting" 81).

Dennis Baron, an English and linguistics professor at the University of Illinois, has done much research on the effect of technology on writing, and his findings are aligned with those of my own study. In his book *A Better Pencil: Readers, Writers, and the Digital Revolution,* he concludes that students do not use textspeak in their writing. In fact, he suggests students do not even use abbreviations in their text messages very often. Baron says that college students have "put away such

Summary and quotations of sources.

academic literacies   rhetorical situations   genres   processes   strategies   research MLA / APA   media / design   readings   handbook

childish things, and many of them had already abandoned such signs of middle-school immaturity in high school" (qtd. in Golden).

In surveying the high school and college students, I found that most have been texting for a few years, usually starting around ninth grade. The students said they generally text between thirty and a hundred messages every day but use abbreviations only occasionally, with the most common being "lol" ("Laugh out loud"), "gtg" ("Got to go"), "hbu" ("How about you?"), "cuz" ("because"), and "jk" ("Just kidding"). None of them believed texting abbreviations were acceptable in formal writing. In fact, research has found that most students report that they do not use textspeak in formal writing. As one Minnesota high school student says, "[T]here is a time and a place for everything," and formal writing is not the place for communicating the way she would if she were texting her friends (qtd. in Walsh). Another student admits that in writing for school she sometimes finds herself using these abbreviations. However, she notices and corrects them before handing in her final paper (Carey). One teacher reports that, despite texting, her students' "formal writing remains solid." She occasionally sees an abbreviation; however, it is in informal, "warm-up" writing. She believes that what students do in everyday writing is up to them as long as they use standard English in formal writing (qtd. in Walsh).

Summary of survey results with quotations.

Also supporting my own research findings are those from a study which took place at a midwestern research university. This study involved eighty-six students who were taking an Introduction to Education course at the university. The participants were asked to complete a questionnaire that included questions about their texting habits, the spelling instruction they had received, and their proficiency at spelling. They also took a standardized spelling test. Before starting the study, the researchers had hypothesized that texting and the use of abbreviations would have a negative impact on the spelling abilities of the students. However, they found that the results did not support their hypothesis. The researchers did note that text messaging is continuing to increase in popularity; therefore, this issue should continue to be examined (Shaw et al.).

20

Summary of research that supports her own.

I myself am a frequent texter. I chat with my friends from home every day through texting. I also use texting to communicate with my school friends, perhaps to discuss what time we are going to meet for dinner or to ask quick questions about homework. According to my cell phone bill, I send and receive around 6,400 texts a month. In the messages I send, I

Pertinent personal experience.

rarely notice myself using abbreviations. The only time I use them is if I do not have time to write out the complete phrase. However, sometimes I find it more time-consuming to try to figure out how to abbreviate something so that my message will still be comprehensible.

Since I rarely use abbreviations in my texting, I never use them in my formal writing. I know that they are unacceptable and that it would make me look unintelligent if I included acronyms and symbols instead of proper and formal language. I also have not noticed an effect on my spelling as a result of texting. I am confident in my spelling abilities, and even when I use an abbreviation, I know how to spell the word(s) it stands for.

Conclusion: summary of research and restatement of claim.

On the basis of my own research, expert research, and personal observations, I can confidently state that texting is not interfering with students' use of standard written English and has no effect on their writing abilities in general. It is interesting to look at the dynamics of the arguments over these issues. Teachers and parents who claim that they are seeing a decline in the writing abilities of their students and children mainly support the negative-impact argument. Other teachers and researchers suggest that texting provides a way for teens to practice writing in a casual setting and thus helps prepare them to write formally. Experts and students themselves, however, report that they see no effect, positive or negative. Anecdotal experiences should not overshadow the actual evidence.

Note

1. All participants in the study have given permission for their responses to be published.

Works Cited

Baron, Dennis. *A Better Pencil: Readers, Writers, and the Digital Revolution.* Oxford UP, 2009.

Carey, Bridget. "The Rise of Text, Instant Messaging Vernacular Slips into Schoolwork." *Miami Herald,* 6 Mar. 2007, *Academic OneFile,* search.ebscohost.com/login.aspx?.direct=true&db=edsgao&AN=edsgcl.160190230&site=eds-live. Accessed 27 Oct. 2009.

Crystal, David. "Texting." *ELT Journal*, vol. 62, no. 1, Jan. 2008, pp. 77-83. *Academic OneFile,* search.ebscohost.com/login.aspx?direct=true&db=edsgao&AN=edsgcl.177163353&site=eds-live. Accessed 8 Nov. 2009.

———. *Txtng: The Gr8 Db8*. Oxford UP, 2008.

academic literacies   rhetorical situations   genres   processes   strategies   research MLA / APA   media / design   readings   handbook

Golden, Serena. Rev. of *A Better Pencil*. *Inside Higher Ed*, 18 Sept. 2009, insidehighered.com/news/2009/09/18/barron. Accessed 9 Nov. 2009.

Shaw, Donita M., et al. "An Exploratory Investigation into the Relationship between Text Messaging and Spelling." *New England Reading Association Journal*, vol. 43, no. 1, pp. 57-62. *EBSCO Discovery Service for Marywood University*, search.ebscohost.com/login.aspx?direct=true&db=edb&AN=25648081&site=eds-live. Accessed 8 Nov. 2009.

"Should We Worry or LOL?" *NEA Today*, Mar. 2004, p. 12. *ProQuest*, search.proquest.com/docview/198894194?accountid=42654. Accessed 27 Oct. 2009.

Sternberg, Betty, et al. "Enhancing Adolescent Literacy Achievement through Integration of Technology in the Classroom." *Reading Research Quarterly*, vol. 42, no. 3, July-Sept. 2007, pp. 416-20. *ProQuest*, search.proquest.com/docview/212128056?accountid=42654. Accessed 8 Nov. 2009.

"Texting, Testing Destroys Kids' Writing Style." *USA Today Magazine*, vol. 137, no. 2760, Sept. 2008, p. 8. *ProQuest*, search.proquest.com/docview/214595644?accountid=42654. Accessed 9 Nov. 2009.

Walsh, James. "Txt Msgs Creep in2 class; Some Say That's gr8." *McClatchy-Tribune News Service*, 23 Oct. 2007. *ProQuest*, search.proquest.com/docview/456879133?accountid=42654. Accessed 27 Oct. 2009.

Cullington's essay examines whether or not texting affects students' writing. Her information is based on both published scholarship and a small survey of students and teachers.

JAMES FALLOWS

Throwing Like a Girl

In the following report for the Atlantic, *national correspondent James Fallows explores the art of throwing a baseball and the misconceptions that lead to the phrase "throwing like a girl."*

Most people remember the 1994 baseball season for the way it ended — with a strike rather than a World Series. I keep thinking about the way it began. On opening day, April 4, Bill Clinton went to Cleveland and, like many Presidents before him, threw out a ceremonial first pitch. That same day Hillary Rodham Clinton went to Chicago and, like no First Lady before her, also threw out a first ball, at a Cubs game in Wrigley Field.

The next day photos of the Clintons in action appeared in newspapers around the country. Many papers, including *The New York Times* and *The Washington Post*, chose the same two photos to run. The one of Bill Clinton showed him wearing an Indians cap and warm-up jacket. The President, throwing lefty, had turned his shoulders sideways to the plate in preparation for delivery. He was bringing the ball forward from behind his head in a clean-looking throwing action as the photo was snapped. Hillary Clinton was pictured wearing a dark jacket, a scarf, and an oversized Cubs hat. In preparation for her throw she was standing directly facing the plate. A right-hander, she had the elbow of her throwing arm pointed out in front of her. Her forearm was tilted back, toward her shoulder. The ball rested on her upturned palm. As the picture was taken, she was in the middle of an action that can only be described as throwing like a girl.

The phrase "throwing like a girl" has become an embattled and offensive one. Feminists smart at its implication that to do something "like a girl" is to do it the wrong way. Recently, on the heels of the O. J. Simpson case, a book appeared in which the phrase was used to help explain why male athletes, especially football players, were involved in so many assaults against women. Having been trained (like most American boys) to dread the accusation of doing anything "like a girl," athletes were said to grow into the assumption that women were valueless, and natural prey.

Hillary and Bill Clinton throw the first ball at two games in 1994.

I grant the justice of such complaints. I am attuned to the hurt caused by similar broad-brush stereotypes when they apply to groups I belong to — "dancing like a white man," for instance, or "speaking foreign languages like an American," or "thinking like a Washingtonian."

Still, whatever we want to call it, the difference between the two Clintons in what they were doing that day is real, and it is instantly recognizable. And since seeing those photos I have been wondering, Why, exactly, do so many women throw "like a girl"? If the motion were easy to change, presumably a woman as motivated and self-possessed as Hillary Clinton would have changed it. (According to her press secretary, Lisa Caputo, Mrs. Clinton spent the weekend before opening day tossing a ball in the Rose Garden with her husband, for practice.) Presumably, too, the answer to the question cannot be anything quite as simple as, Because they *are* girls. 5

A surprising number of people think that there is a structural difference between male and female arms or shoulders — in the famous "rotator cuff," perhaps — that dictates different throwing motions. "It's in the shoulder joint," a well-educated woman told me recently. "They're hinged differently." Someday researchers may find evidence to support a biological theory of throwing actions. For now, what you'll hear if you ask an orthopedist, an anatomist, or (especially) the coach of a women's softball team is that there is no structural reason why men and women should throw in different ways. This point will be obvious to any male who grew up around girls who liked to play baseball and became good at it. It should be obvious on a larger scale this summer, in broadcasts of the Olympic Games. This year [1996], for the first time, women's fast-pitch softball teams will compete in the Olympics. Although the pitchers in these games will deliver the ball underhand, viewers will see female shortstops, center fielders, catchers, and so on pegging the ball to one another at speeds few male viewers could match.

Even women's tennis is a constant if indirect reminder that men's and women's shoulders are "hinged" the same way. The serving motion in tennis is like a throw — but more difficult, because it must be coordinated with the toss of the tennis ball. The men in professional tennis serve harder than the women, because they are bigger and stronger. But women pros serve harder than most male amateurs have ever done, and the service motion for good players is the same for men and women alike. There is no expectation in college or pro tennis that because of their anatomy female players must "serve like a girl." "I know many women who can throw a lot harder and better than the normal male," says Linda Wells, the coach of the highly successful women's softball team at Arizona State University. "It's not gender that makes the difference in how they throw."

At a superficial level it's easy to tick off the traits of an awkward-looking throw. The fundamental mistake is the one Mrs. Clinton appeared to be making in the photo: trying to throw a ball with your body facing the target, rather than rotating your shoulders and hips ninety degrees away from the target and then swinging them around in order to accelerate the ball. A throw looks bad if your elbow is lower than your shoulder as your arm comes forward (unless you're throwing sidearm). A throw looks really bad if, as the ball leaves your hand, your wrist is "inside your elbow"—that is, your elbow joint is bent in such a way that your forearm angles back toward your body and your wrist is closer to your head than your elbow is. Slow-motion film of big-league pitchers shows that when they release the ball, the throwing arm is fully extended and straight from shoulder to wrist. The combination of these three elements—head-on stance, dropped elbow, and wrist inside the elbow—mechanically dictates a pushing rather than a hurling motion, creating the familiar pattern of "throwing like a girl."

It is surprisingly hard to find in the literature of baseball a deeper explanation of the mechanics of good and bad throws. Tom Seaver's pitching for the Mets and the White Sox got him into the Hall of Fame, but his book *The Art of Pitching* is full of bromides that hardly clarify the process of throwing, even if they might mean something to accomplished pitchers. His chapter "The Absolutes of Pitching Mechanics," for instance, lays out these four unhelpful principles: "Keep the Front Leg Flexible!" "Rub Up the Baseball!" "Hide the Baseball!" "Get It Out, Get It Up!" (The fourth refers to the need to get the ball out of the glove and into the throwing hand in a quick motion.)

A variety of other instructional documents, from *Little League's Official How-to-Play Baseball Book* to *Softball for Girls & Women*, mainly reveal the difficulty of finding words to describe a simple motor activity that everyone can recognize. The challenge, I suppose, is like that of writing a manual on how to ride a bike, or how to kiss. Indeed, the most useful description I've found of the mechanics of throwing comes from a man whose specialty is another sport: Vic Braden made

10

his name as a tennis coach, but he has attempted to analyze the physics of a wide variety of sports so that they all will be easier to teach.

Braden says that an effective throw involves connecting a series of links in a "kinetic chain." The kinetic chain, which is Braden's tool for analyzing most sporting activity, operates on a principle like that of crack-the-whip. Momentum builds up in one part of the body. When that part is suddenly stopped, as the end of the "whip" is stopped in crack-the-whip, the momentum is transferred to and concentrated in the next link in the chain. A good throw uses six links of chain, Braden says. The first two links involve the lower body, from feet to waist. The first motion of a throw (after the body has been rotated away from the target) is to rotate the legs and hips back in the direction of the throw, building up momentum as large muscles move body mass. Then those links stop—a pitcher stops turning his hips once they face the plate— and the momentum is transferred to the next link. This is the torso, from waist to shoulders, and since its mass is less than that of the legs, momentum makes it rotate faster than the hips and legs did. The torso stops when it is facing the plate, and the momentum is transferred to the next link—the upper arm. As the upper arm comes past the head, it stops moving forward, and the momentum goes into the final links—the forearm and wrist, which snap forward at tremendous speed.

This may sound arcane and jerkily mechanical, but it makes perfect sense when one sees Braden's slow-mo movies of pitchers in action. And it explains why people do, or don't, learn how to throw. The implication of Braden's analysis is that throwing is a perfectly natural action (millions and millions of people can do it), but not at all innate. A successful throw involves an intricate series of actions coordinated among muscle groups, as each link of the chain is timed to interact with the next. Like bike riding or skating, it can be learned by anyone—male or female. No one starts out knowing how to ride a bike or throw a ball. Everyone has to learn.

Fallows describes in detail what distinguishes a successful baseball throw from an awkward-looking one, concluding with the point that throwing a baseball effectively is a learned activity. He draws on various sources—including a women's softball coach, a tennis coach, and his own observations—to support his claim. Notice how he establishes the context for his essay by focusing on the differences between the stances of the Clintons when photographed throwing a baseball.

JON MARCUS

The Reason College Costs More than You Think

Writing online for Time *in 2014, Hechinger Report editor Jon Marcus examines the length of time students take to graduate and how that affects the cost of getting a degree.*

When Alex Nichols started as a freshman at the University of Mississippi, he felt sure he'd earn his bachelor's degree in four years. Five years later, and Nichols is back on the Oxford, Mississippi, campus for what he hopes is truly his final semester.

"There are a lot more students staying another semester or another year than I thought there would be when I got here," Nichols says. "I meet people once a week who say, 'Yes, I'm a second-year senior,' or, 'I've been here for five years.'"

They're likely as surprised as Nichols still to be toiling away in school.

The Lyceum, the oldest building at the University of Mississippi.

Nearly nine out of 10 freshmen think they'll earn their bachelor's degrees within the traditional four years, according to a nationwide survey conducted by the Higher Education Research Institute at UCLA. But the U.S. Department of Education reports that fewer than half that many actually will. And about 45 percent won't have finished even after six years.

That means the annual cost of college, a source of so much anxiety 5 for families and students, often overlooks the enormous additional expense of the extra time it will actually take to graduate.

"It's a huge inconvenience," says Nichols, whose college career has been prolonged for the common reason that he changed majors and took courses he ended up not needing. His athletic scholarship — Nichols was a middle-distance runner on the cross-country team — ran out after four years. "I had to get some financial help from my parents."

The average added cost of just one extra year at a four-year public university is $63,718 in tuition, fees, books, and living expenses, plus lost wages each of those many students could have been earning had they finished on time, according to the advocacy group Complete College America.

A separate report by the Los Angeles-based Campaign for College Opportunity finds that the average student at a California State University campus who takes six years instead of four to earn a bachelor's degree will spend an additional $58,000 and earn $52,900 less over their lifetimes than a student who graduates on time, for a total loss of $110,900.

"The cost of college isn't just what students and their families pay in tuition or fees," says Michele Siqueiros, the organization's executive director. "It's also about time. That's the hidden cost of a college education."

So hidden that most families still unknowingly plan on four years 10 for a bachelor's degree, says Sylvia Hurtado, director of the Higher Education Research Institute at UCLA.

Although the institute does not poll parents in its annual survey, "that high percentage of freshmen [who are confident they'll finish in four years] is probably reflecting their parents' expectation — 'This is costing me a lot, so you're going to be out in four years.' So the students think, 'Sure, why not?' I don't think the parents even initially entertain or plan for six years or some possible outcome like that."

Yet many students almost immediately doom themselves to taking longer, since they register for fewer courses than they need to stay on track. Surveys of incoming freshmen in California and Indiana who said they expected to graduate in four years found that half signed up for fewer courses than they'd needed to meet that goal, according to a new report by the higher-education consulting firm HCM Strategists.

It's not entirely the students' fault.

More than half of community-college students are slowed down by having to retake subjects such as math and reading that they should have learned in high school, says Complete College America. And at some schools, budget cuts have made it difficult to register for the courses students do need to take. Two-thirds of students at one California State University campus weren't able to get into their required courses, according to a 2010 study by the University of California's Civil Rights Project.

Most state financial-aid programs, meanwhile, cover only four years. "They do not fund a fifth or sixth year," says Stan Jones, president of Complete College America and a former Indiana commissioner of higher education. "And by that time the parents' resources and the students' resources have run out. So that fifth year is where you borrow."   15

Students at the most elite colleges and universities tend not to have this problem, which means that schools with some of the highest annual tuition can turn out to be relative bargains. These schools "would have a revolt if their students had to go a fifth year," Jones says. "But that recognition has really not hit the public sector yet, about the hidden cost of that extra year."

Policymakers urge speeding students through remedial classes more quickly, adding more sections of required courses so students can get in when they need them, and encouraging students to take 15 credits per semester instead of the typical 12.

Change won't come soon enough for Nichols, who is determined that it won't take more than one extra semester to finish his degree in integrated marketing communications.

"That's time you're wasting," he says, "that you could be out making money."

Marcus combines information from various research institutes, advocacy groups, surveys, and academic sources to support his argument. His statistics are given

academic literacies   rhetorical situations   genres   processes   strategies   research MLA / APA   media / design   readings   handbook

a human face by quotations from a student who is taking longer to graduate than he expected.

For four more reports, see CHAPTER 61.

Key Features / Reports

A tightly focused topic. The goal of this kind of writing is to inform readers about something without digressing—and without, in general, bringing in the writer's own opinions. All three examples focus on a particular topic—texting, throwing a baseball, and the cost of college — and present information about the topics evenhandedly.

Accurate, well-researched information. Reports usually require some research. The kind of research depends on the topic. Library research to locate scholarly sources may be necessary for some topics—Cullington, for example, uses various sources available through her library's database. Other topics may require field research—interviews, observations, and so on. Fallows interviewed two coaches in addition to reading several books on pitching baseballs.

Synthesis of ideas. Reports do more than present lists of unconnected facts; they **SYNTHESIZE IDEAS** by showing patterns in and relationships among the information presented. Marcus compares undergraduate students' expectations of finishing college in four years with statistics showing that more than half will take longer. Fallows combines observations of women pitching baseballs and serving tennis balls to refute claims that their arms are structured differently from men's.

473–77

Various writing strategies. Presenting information usually requires various organizing patterns—defining, comparing, classifying, explaining processes, analyzing causes and effects, and so on. Fallows explains the process governing throwing a baseball and classifies different ways of throwing. Marcus analyzes the financial effects of delaying graduation, and Cullington analyzes the effects (or lack of effects) of texting on students' writing ability.

Clear definitions.   Reports need to provide clear definitions of any key terms that their audience may not know. Cullington defines both *texting* and *textspeak*. Fallows defines several pitching terms, such as *inside your elbow*.

Appropriate design.   Reports often combine paragraphs with information presented in lists, tables, diagrams, and other illustrations. When you're presenting information, you need to think carefully about how to design it—numerical data, for instance, can be easier to understand and remember in a table than in a paragraph. Often a photograph can bring a subject to life, as do the photos on page 138, which accompany "Throwing Like a Girl." The caption provides important information that is explained more fully in the essay itself. Online reports offer the possibility of video and audio clips as well as links to source materials and more detailed information.

A GUIDE TO WRITING REPORTS

Choosing a Topic

Whether you get to choose your topic or are working with an assigned one, see if you can approach the topic from an angle that interests you.

If you get to choose.   What interests you? What do you wish you knew more about? The possible topics for informational reports are limitless, but the topics that you're most likely to write well on are those that engage you. They may be academic in nature or reflect your personal interests or both. If you're not sure where to begin, here are some places to start:

- an intriguing technology: hybrid cars, touchscreens, tooth whiteners
- sports: soccer, snowboarding, ultimate Frisbee, basketball
- an important world event: the Arab Spring, the fall of Rome, the Black Death

- a historical period: the African diaspora, the Middle Ages, the Ming dynasty, the Great Depression
- a common object: hoodies, gel pens, mascara, Post-it notes
- a significant environmental issue: melting Arctic ice, deer overpopulation, mercury and the fish supply
- the arts: hip-hop, outsider art, the Crystal Bridges Museum of American Art, Savion Glover, Mary Cassatt

LIST a few possibilities, and then choose one that you'd like to know more about—and that your audience might find interesting, too. You might start out by phrasing your topic as a question that your research will attempt to answer. For example:

290–91

> How is *Google* different from *Yahoo!*?
>
> How was the Great Pyramid constructed?
>
> What kind of training do football referees receive?

If your topic is assigned.   If your assignment is broad—"Explain some aspect of the U.S. government"—try focusing on a more limited topic within the larger topic: federalism, majority rule, political parties, states' rights. Even if an assignment seems to offer little flexibility — "Explain the physics of roller coasters" — your task is to decide how to research the topic—and sometimes even narrow topics can be shaped to fit your own interests and those of your audience.

Considering the Rhetorical Situation

PURPOSE	Why are you presenting this information? To teach readers about the subject? To demonstrate your research and writing skills? For some other reason?	55–56
AUDIENCE	Who will read this report? What do they already know about the topic? What background information do they	57–60

need in order to understand it? Will you need to define any terms? What do they want or need to know about the topic? Why should they care about it? How can you attract their interest?

64–67 ■

STANCE What is your own attitude toward your subject? What interests you most about it? What about it seems important?

68–70 ■

MEDIA / DESIGN What medium are you using? What is the best way to present the information? Will it all be in paragraph form, or is there information that is best presented as a chart, table, or infographic? Do you need headings? Would diagrams, photographs, or other illustrations help you explain the information?

Generating Ideas and Text

Good reports share certain features that make them useful and interesting to readers. Remember that your goal is to present information clearly and accurately. Start by exploring your topic.

289–92 ◯

Explore what you already know about your topic. Write out whatever you know or want to know about your topic, perhaps by **FREEWRITING**, **LISTING**, or **CLUSTERING**. Why are you interested in this topic? What questions do you have about it? Such questions can help you decide what you'd like to focus on and how you need to direct your research efforts.

Narrow your topic. To write a good report, you need to narrow your focus—and to narrow your focus, you need to know a fair amount about your subject. If you are assigned to write on a subject like biodiversity, for example, you need to know what it is, what the key issues are, and so on. If you do, you can simply list or brainstorm possibilities, choose one, and start your research. If you don't know much about the subject, though, you need to do some research to discover focused, workable top-ics. This research may shape your thinking and change your focus. Start with **SOURCES** that can give you a general sense of the subject, such as a *Wikipedia* entry, a magazine article, a website, perhaps an interview with an expert. Your goal at this point is simply to find out what issues your topic might include and then to focus your efforts on an aspect of the topic you will be able to cover.

445–68

Come up with a tentative thesis. Once you narrow your topic, write out a statement that explains what you plan to report or explain. A good **THESIS** is potentially interesting (to you and your readers) and limits your topic enough to make it manageable. Fallows phrases his thesis as a question: "Why, exactly, do so many women throw 'like a girl'?" Cullington frames her thesis in relation to the context surrounding her topic: "Some people believe that using these abbreviations is hindering the writing abilities of students, and others argue that texting is actually having a positive effect on writing. In fact, it seems likely that texting has no significant effect on student writing." At this point, however, you need only a tentative thesis that will help focus any research you do.

345–47

Do any necessary research, and revise your thesis. To focus your research efforts, **OUTLINE** the aspects of your topic that you expect to dis-cuss. Identify any aspects that require additional research and **DEVELOP A RESEARCH PLAN**. Expect to revise your outline as you do your research, since more information will be available for some aspects of your topic than others, some may prove irrelevant to your topic, and some may turn out to be more than you need. You'll need to revisit your tentative thesis once you've done any research, to finalize your statement.

293–94
435–44

Ways of Organizing a Report

Reports can be organized in various ways. Here are three common orga-nizational structures.

[Reports on topics that are unfamiliar to readers]

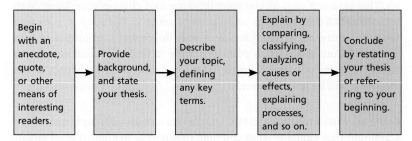

Begin with an anecdote, quote, or other means of interesting readers. → Provide background, and state your thesis. → Describe your topic, defining any key terms. → Explain by comparing, classifying, analyzing causes or effects, explaining processes, and so on. → Conclude by restating your thesis or referring to your beginning.

[Reports on events]

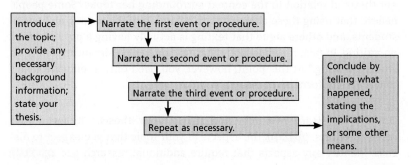

Introduce the topic; provide any necessary background information; state your thesis. → Narrate the first event or procedure. ↓ Narrate the second event or procedure. ↓ Narrate the third event or procedure. ↓ Repeat as necessary. → Conclude by telling what happened, stating the implications, or some other means.

[Reports that compare and contrast]

Introduce the topic; provide any necessary background information; state your thesis. → Describe one item. ↓ Describe the other items, using the same structure used to describe the first. → Conclude by restating your thesis.

academic literacies · rhetorical situations · genres · processes · strategies · research MLA / APA · media / design · readings · handbook

Many reports use a combination of organizational structures; don't be afraid to use whatever method of organization best suits your material and your purpose.

Writing Out a Draft

Once you have generated ideas and thought about how you want to organize your report, it's time to start **DRAFTING**. Do this quickly—try to write a complete draft in one sitting, concentrating on getting the report on paper or screen and on putting in as much detail as you can.

298–300

Writing that reports information often calls for certain writing strategies. The report on throwing a baseball, for example, **EXPLAINS THE PROCESS** of throwing, whereas the report on college costs **ANALYZES THE EFFECTS** of delaying college graduation. When you're reporting on a topic your readers aren't familiar with, you may wish to **COMPARE** it with something more familiar; you can find useful advice on these and other writing strategies in Part 5 of this book.

414–18
350–54

380–87

Draft a BEGINNING. Essays that report information often need to begin in a way that will get your audience interested in the topic. Here are a few ways of beginning:

331–38

- *Simply state your thesis.* Cullington states her thesis about texting after only a brief introduction. Opening with a thesis works well when you can assume your readers have enough familiarity with your topic that you don't need to give much detailed background information.

- *Start with something that will provoke readers' interest.* Marcus's report begins with an anecdote about a college student.

- *Begin with an illustrative example.* Fallows uses the contrasting photographs of the Clintons throwing baseballs as a way of defining "throwing like a girl."

Draft an ENDING. Think about what you want your readers to read last. An effective ending leaves them thinking about your topic.

338–42

- *Summarize your main points.* This is a good way to end when you've presented several key points you want readers to remember. Cullington ends this way, summarizing the debate about texting's effects and the results of her research.

- *Point out the implications of your report.* Cullington ends by affirming the importance of researched evidence when drawing conclusions not only about texting but in general.

- *Frame your report by referring to its introduction.* Marcus begins and ends his report by quoting the same student.

- *Tell what happened.* If you are reporting on an event, you could conclude by telling how it turns out.

Come up with a title. You'll want a title that tells readers something about your subject—and makes them want to know more. Cullington's title, "Does Texting Affect Writing?," is a straightforward description of what's to come. Marcus suggests that his essay will disclose the reason college costs more than you think—but doesn't tell us in the title. See the chapter on **GUIDING YOUR READER** for tips on coming up with titles that are informative and enticing enough to make readers wish to read on.

344–49

Considering Matters of Design

You'll probably write the main text of your report in paragraph form, but think about what kind of information you're presenting and how you can design and format it to make it as easy as possible for your readers to understand. You might ask yourself these questions:

601–2

- What is an appropriate **FONT**? Something serious like Times Roman, something traditional like Courier, something else?

604–5

- Would it help your readers if you divided your report into shorter sections and added **HEADINGS**?

603

- Is there any information that would be easier to follow in a **LIST**?

academic literacies · rhetorical situations · genres · processes · strategies · research MLA / APA · media / design · readings · handbook

- Could any of your information be summarized in a **TABLE** or **FIGURE**?

609–11

- Do you have any data that readers would more easily understand in the form of a bar **GRAPH**, line graph, or pie chart?

609–11

- Would **ILLUSTRATIONS** (diagrams, photos, drawings, and so on), video or audio clips, or links help you explain anything in your report?

607–15

Getting Response and Revising

The following questions can help you study your draft with a critical eye. **GETTING RESPONSE** from others is always good, and these questions can guide their reading, too. Make sure they know your purpose and audience.

306–7

- Do the title and opening sentences get readers' interest? If not, how might they do so?

- What information does this text provide, and for what purpose?

- Does the introduction explain why this information is being presented? Does it place the topic in a larger context?

- Are all key terms defined that need to be?

- Do you have any questions? Where might more explanation or an example help you understand something better?

- Is any information presented visually, with a chart, graph, table, drawing, or photograph? If so, is it clear how the illustration relates to the written text? Is there any text that would be more easily understood if it were presented visually?

- Is any information presented through digital media, such as hyperlinks, video clips, or audio files? If so, is the relation of these elements to the written text made clear? Would any aspect of the report be clearer if presented using such elements?

- Does the organization help make sense of the information? Does the text include description, comparison, or any other writing strategies? Does the topic or rhetorical situation call for any particular strategies that should be added?

487–90

- If the report cites any sources, are they quoted, paraphrased, or summarized effectively (and with appropriate documentation)? Is information from sources introduced with **SIGNAL PHRASES**?

- Does the report end in a satisfying way? What are readers left thinking?

307–10

These questions should identify aspects of your report you need to work on. When it's time to **REVISE**, make sure your report appeals to your audience and achieves your purpose as successfully as possible.

Editing and Proofreading

313–16

Readers equate correctness with the writer's competence. Once you've revised your draft, follow these guidelines for **EDITING** a report:

HB-29–34

- Check your use of key terms. Repeating key words is acceptable in reports; using synonyms for unfamiliar words may confuse readers, while the repetition of key words or the use of clearly identified **PRONOUNS** for them can be genuinely helpful.

349

- Check to be sure you have **TRANSITIONS** where you need them.

604–5

- If you have included **HEADINGS**, make sure they're parallel in structure and consistent in design.

607–15

- Make sure that any photos or other **ILLUSTRATIONS** have captions, that charts and graphs have headings—and that all are referred to in the main text. Use white space as necessary to separate sections of your report and to highlight graphic elements.

496–99

- Check any **DOCUMENTATION** to see that it follows the appropriate style without mistakes.

316–17

- **PROOFREAD** and spell-check your report carefully.

Taking Stock of Your Work

- How well did you convey the information? Is it complete enough for your audience's needs?

- What strategies did you rely on, and how did they help you achieve your purpose?
- How well did you organize the report?
- How did you go about researching the information for this piece?
- How did you go about drafting this piece?
- Did you use any tables, graphs, diagrams, photographs, illustrations, or other graphics effectively?
- How did others' responses influence your writing?
- What did you do especially well?
- What could still be improved?
- What would you do differently next time?

IF YOU NEED MORE HELP

See Chapter 32 if you are required to submit your report in a writing **PORTFOLIO**.
See also Chapter 14 on **ABSTRACTS** if your report requires one; and Chapter 19 on **PROFILES**, a report based on firsthand research.

● 318–28
▲ 183–87
224–34

13 Arguing a Position

Everything we say or do presents some kind of argument, takes some kind of position. Often we take overt positions: "Everyone in the United States is entitled to affordable health care." "The university needs to offer more language courses." "Photoshopped images should carry disclosure notices." But arguments can be less direct and specific as well, from yellow ribbons that honor U.S. troops to a yellow smiley face, which might be said to argue for a good day.

In college course work, you are constantly called on to argue positions: in an *English* class, you may argue for a certain interpretation of a poem; in a *business* course, you may argue for the merits of a flat tax; in a *linguistics* class, you may argue that English is now a global language. All of those positions are arguable—people of goodwill can agree or disagree with them and present reasons and evidence to support their positions.

This chapter provides guidelines for writing an essay that argues a position. We'll begin with three good examples, the first one annotated to point out key features of this kind of writing.

JOANNA MacKAY

Organ Sales Will Save Lives

In this essay, written for a class on ethics and politics in science, MIT student Joanna MacKay argues that the sale of human organs should be legal.

Clear and
arguable position.

There are thousands of people dying to buy a kidney and thousands of people dying to sell a kidney. It seems a match made in heaven. So why are we standing in the way? Governments should not ban the sale of human organs; they should regulate it. Lives should not be wasted; they should be saved.

156

academic literacies   rhetorical situations   genres   processes   strategies   research MLA / APA   media / design   readings   handbook

About 350,000 Americans suffer from end-stage renal disease, a state of kidney disorder so advanced that the organ stops functioning altogether. There are no miracle drugs that can revive a failed kidney, leaving dialysis and kidney transplantation as the only possible treatments (McDonnell and Mallon, pars. 2 and 3).

Dialysis is harsh, expensive, and, worst of all, only temporary. Acting as an artificial kidney, dialysis mechanically filters the blood of a patient. It works, but not well. With treatment sessions lasting three hours, several times a week, those dependent on dialysis are, in a sense, shackled to a machine for the rest of their lives. Adding excessive stress to the body, dialysis causes patients to feel increasingly faint and tired, usually keeping them from work and other normal activities.

Kidney transplantation, on the other hand, is the closest thing to a cure that anyone could hope for. Today the procedure is both safe and reliable, causing few complications. With better technology for confirming tissue matches and new anti-rejection drugs, the surgery is relatively simple.

But those hoping for a new kidney have high hopes indeed. In the year 2000 alone, 2,583 Americans died while waiting for a kidney transplant; worldwide the number of deaths is around 50,000 (Finkel 27). With the sale of organs outlawed in almost every country, the number of living donors willing to part with a kidney for free is small. When no family member is a suitable candidate for donation, the patient is placed on a deceased donors list, relying on the organs from people dying of old age or accidents. The list is long. With over 60,000 people in line in the United States alone, the average wait for a cadaverous kidney is ten long years.

Necessary background information.

Daunted by the low odds, some have turned to an alternative solution: purchasing kidneys on the black market. For about $150,000, they can buy a fresh kidney from a healthy, living donor. There are no lines, no waits. Arranged through a broker, the entire procedure is carefully planned out. The buyer, seller, surgeons, and nurses are flown to a predetermined hospital in a foreign country. The operations are performed, and then all are flown back to their respective homes. There is no follow-up, no paperwork to sign (Finkel 27).

The illegal kidney trade is attractive not only because of the promptness but also because of the chance at a living donor. An organ from a cadaver will most likely be old or damaged, estimated to function for about ten years at most. A kidney from a living donor can last over twice as long. Once a person's transplanted cadaverous kidney stops functioning, he or she must get back on the donor list, this time probably at the end of the line. A transplanted living kidney, however, could last a person a lifetime.

While there may seem to be a shortage of kidneys, in reality there is a surplus. In third-world countries, there are people willing to do anything for money. In such extreme poverty these people barely have enough to eat, living in shacks and sleeping on dirt floors. Eager to pay off debts, they line up at hospitals, willing to sell a kidney for about $1,000. The money will go toward food and clothing, or perhaps to pay for a family member's medical operation (Goyal et al. 1590–91). Whatever the case, these people need the money.

There is certainly a risk in donating a kidney, but this risk is not great enough to be outlawed. Millions of people take risks to their health every day for money, or simply for enjoyment. As explained in *The Lancet*, "If the rich are free to engage in dangerous sports for pleasure, or dangerous jobs for high pay, it is difficult to see why the poor who take the lesser risk of kidney selling for greater rewards . . . should be thought so misguided as to need saving from themselves" (Radcliffe-Richards et al. 1951). Studies have shown that a person can live a healthy life with only one kidney. While these studies might not apply to the poor living under strenuous conditions in unsanitary environments, the risk is still theirs to take. These people have decided that their best hope for money is to sell a kidney. How can we deny them the best opportunity they have?

Some agree with Pope John Paul II that the selling of organs is morally wrong and violates "the dignity of the human person" (qtd. in Finkel 26), but this is a belief professed by healthy and affluent individuals. Are we sure that the peasants of third-world countries agree? The morals we hold are not absolute truths. We have the responsibility to protect and help those less fortunate, but we cannot let our own ideals cloud the issues at hand.

In a legal kidney transplant, everybody gains except the donor. The doctors and nurses are paid for the operation, the patient receives a new kidney, but the donor receives nothing. Sure, the donor will have the warm, uplifting feeling associated with helping a fellow human being, but this is not enough reward for most people to part with a

Reason (donors need the money) supported by evidence.

Counterargument (donating a kidney is risky) acknowledged.

Counterargument (selling organs is wrong) acknowledged.

Reason (altruism is not enough) supported by evidence.

10

piece of themselves. In an ideal world, the average person would be altruistic enough to donate a kidney with nothing expected in return. The real world, however, is run by money. We pay men for donating sperm, and we pay women for donating ova, yet we expect others to give away an entire organ for no compensation. If the sale of organs were allowed, people would have a greater incentive to help save the life of a stranger.

While many argue that legalizing the sale of organs will exploit the poorer people of third-world countries, the truth of the matter is that this is already the case. Even with the threat of a $50,000 fine and five years in prison (Finkel 26), the current ban has not been successful in preventing illegal kidney transplants. The kidneys of the poor are still benefiting only the rich. While the sellers do receive most of the money promised, the sum is too small to have any real impact on their financial situation. A study in India discovered that in the long run, organ sellers suffer. In the illegal kidney trade, nobody has the interests of the seller at heart. After selling a kidney, their state of living actually worsens. While the $1,000 pays off one debt, it is not enough to relieve the donor of the extreme poverty that placed him in debt in the first place (Goyal et al. 1591).

These impoverished people do not need stricter and harsher penalties against organ selling to protect them, but quite the opposite. If the sale of organs were made legal, it could be regulated and closely monitored by the government and other responsible organizations. Under a regulated system, education would be incorporated into the application process. Before deciding to donate a kidney, the seller should know the details of the operation and any hazards involved. Only with an understanding of the long-term physical health risks can a person make an informed decision (Radcliffe-Richards et al. 1951).

Regulation would ensure that the seller is fairly compensated. In the illegal kidney trade, surgeons collect most of the buyer's money in return for putting their careers on the line. The brokers arranging the procedure also receive a modest cut, typically around ten percent. If the entire practice were legalized, more of the money could be directed toward the person who needs it most, the seller. By eliminating the middleman and allowing the doctors to settle for lower prices, a regulated system would benefit all those in need of a kidney, both rich

Counterargument (poor people are exploited) acknowledged.

Reason (regulating organ sales would lead to better decisions).

Reason (fairness to sellers) followed by evidence.

and poor. According to Finkel, the money that would otherwise be spent on dialysis treatment could not only cover the charge of a kidney transplant at no cost to the recipient, but also reward the donor with as much as $25,000 (32). This money could go a long way for people living in the poverty of third-world countries.

Critics fear that controlling the lawful sale of organs would be too difficult, but could it be any more difficult than controlling the unlawful sale of organs? Governments have tried to eradicate the kidney market for decades to no avail. Maybe it is time to try something else. When "desperately wanted goods" are made illegal, history has shown that there is more opportunity for corruption and exploitation than if those goods were allowed (Radcliffe-Richards et al. 1951). (Just look at the effects of the prohibition of alcohol, for example.) Legalization of organ sales would give governments the authority and the opportunity to closely monitor these live kidney operations.

Regulation would also protect the buyers. Because of the need for secrecy, the current illegal method of obtaining a kidney has no contracts and, therefore, no guarantees. Since what they are doing is illegal, the buyers have nobody to turn to if something goes wrong. There is nobody to point the finger at, nobody to sue. While those participating in the kidney market are breaking the law, they have no other choice. Without a new kidney, end-stage renal disease will soon kill them. Desperate to survive, they are forced to take the only offer available. It seems immoral to first deny them the opportunity of a new kidney and then to leave them stranded at the mercy of the black market. Without laws regulating live kidney transplants, these people are subject to possibly hazardous procedures. Instead of turning our backs, we have the power to ensure that these operations are done safely and efficiently for both the recipient and the donor.

Those suffering from end-stage renal disease would do anything for the chance at a new kidney, take any risk or pay any price. There are other people so poor that the sale of a kidney is worth the profit. Try to tell someone that he has to die from kidney failure because selling a kidney is morally wrong. Then turn around and try to tell another person that he has to remain in poverty for that same reason. In matters of life and death, our stances on moral issues must be reevaluated. If legalized and regulated, the sale of human organs would save lives. Is it moral to sentence thousands to unnecessary deaths?

Counterargument (controlling organ sales would be difficult) acknowledged.

Reason (fairness to buyers) supported by examples.

Concludes by asking a question for readers to consider.

15

Works Cited

Finkel, Michael. "This Little Kidney Went to Market." *The New York Times Magazine,* 27 May 2001, pp. 26+.

Goyal, Madhav, et al. "Economic and Health Consequences of Selling a Kidney in India." *Journal of the American Medical Association,* vol. 288, 2002, pp. 1589–92.

McDonnell, Michael B., and William K. Mallon. "Kidney Transplant." *eMedicine Health,* 18 Aug. 2008, www.emedicinehealth.com/articles/24500-1.asp. Accessed 30 Nov. 2008.

Radcliffe-Richards, J., et al. "The Case for Allowing Kidney Sales." *The Lancet,* vol. 351, no. 9120, 27 June 1998, pp. 1950-52.

MacKay clearly states her position at the beginning of her text: "Governments should not ban the sale of human organs; they should regulate it." Her argument appeals to her readers' sense of fairness; when kidney sales are legalized and regulated, both sellers and buyers will benefit from the transaction. She uses MLA style to document her sources.

NICHOLAS KRISTOF

Our Blind Spot about Guns

In this essay, which first appeared in the New York Times *in 2014, columnist Nicholas Kristof argues that if guns and their owners were regulated in the same way that cars and their drivers are, thousands of lives could be saved each year.*

If we had the same auto fatality rate today that we had in 1921, by my calculations we would have 715,000 Americans dying annually in vehicle accidents.

Instead, we've reduced the fatality rate by more than 95 percent — not by confiscating cars, but by regulating them and their drivers sensibly.

We could have said, "Cars don't kill people. People kill people," and there would have been an element of truth to that. Many accidents are a result of alcohol consumption, speeding, road rage or driver distraction. Or we could have said, "It's pointless because even if you regulate cars, then people will just run each other down with bicycles," and that, too, would have been partly true.

Yet, instead, we built a system that protects us from ourselves. This saves hundreds of thousands of lives a year and is a model of what we should do with guns in America.

Whenever I write about the need for sensible regulation of guns, some readers jeer: *Cars kill people, too, so why not ban cars? Why are you so hypocritical as to try to take away guns from law-abiding people when you don't seize cars?*

That question is a reflection of our national blind spot about guns. The truth is that we regulate cars quite intelligently, instituting evidence-based measures to reduce fatalities. Yet the gun lobby is too strong, or our politicians too craven, to do the same for guns. So guns and cars now each kill more than 30,000 in America every year.

One constraint, the argument goes, is the Second Amendment. Yet the paradox is that a bit more than a century ago, there was no universally recognized individual right to bear arms in the United States, but there was widely believed to be a "right to travel" that allowed people to drive cars without regulation.

A court struck down an early attempt to require driver's licenses, and initial attempts to set speed limits or register vehicles were met with resistance and ridicule. When authorities in New York City sought in 1899 to ban horseless carriages in the parks, the idea was lambasted in the *New York Times* as "devoid of merit" and "impossible to maintain."

Yet, over time, it became increasingly obvious that cars were killing and maiming people, as well as scaring horses and causing accidents. As a distinguished former congressman, Robert Cousins, put it in 1910: "Pedestrians are menaced every minute of the days and nights by a wanton recklessness of speed, crippling and killing people at a rate that is appalling."

Courts and editorial writers alike saw the carnage and agreed that something must be done. By the 1920s, courts routinely accepted driver's license requirements, car registration and other safety measures.

That continued in recent decades with requirements of seatbelts and air bags, padded dashboards and better bumpers. We cracked down on drunken drivers and instituted graduated licensing for young people, while also improving road engineering to reduce accidents. The upshot is that there is now just over 1 car fatality per 100 million miles driven.

Yet as we've learned to treat cars intelligently, we've gone in the opposite direction with guns. In his terrific new book, *The Second Amendment: A Biography,* Michael Waldman, the president of the Brennan Center for Justice at the New York University School of Law, notes that "gun control laws were ubiquitous" in the nineteenth century. Visitors to Wichita, Kansas, for example, were required to check their revolvers at police headquarters.

And Dodge City, symbol of the Wild West? A photo shows a sign on the main street in 1879 warning: "The Carrying of Fire Arms Strictly Prohibited."

Dodge City, Kansas, 1878. The sign reads, "The Carrying of Fire Arms strictly prohibited."

The National Rifle Association supported reasonable gun control for most of its history and didn't even oppose the landmark Gun Control Act of 1968. But, since then, most attempts at safety regulation have stalled or gone backward, and that makes the example of cars instructive.

"We didn't ban cars, or send black helicopters to confiscate them," notes Waldman. "We made cars safer: air bags, seatbelts, increasing the drinking age, lowering the speed limit. There are similar technological and behavioral fixes that can ease the toll of gun violence, from expanded background checks to trigger locks to smart guns that recognize a thumbprint, just like my iPhone does." 15

Some of these should be doable. A Quinnipiac poll this month found 92 percent support for background checks for all gun buyers.

These steps won't eliminate gun deaths any more than seatbelts eliminate auto deaths. But if a combination of measures could reduce the toll by one-third, that would be 10,000 lives saved every year.

A century ago, we reacted to deaths and injuries from unregulated vehicles by imposing sensible safety measures that have saved hundreds of thousands of lives a year. Why can't we ask politicians to be just as rational about guns?

Kristof argues that because regulating cars has made them much safer, guns should be regulated similarly. He supports his argument with data on fatality rates and the history of automobile and gun regulation in the United States.

ANDREW LEONARD

Black Friday: Consumerism Minus Civilization

This essay arguing that advertising for day-after-Thanksgiving sales has gone too far first appeared on Salon, where it includes several videos and links to other websites, which are underlined in this text. The online version may be accessed via wwnorton.com/write/fieldguidelinks.

Here's a Thanksgiving recipe guaranteed to deliver a nervous breakdown impervious to even the most bleeding-edge psychopharmaceutical wonder drug. Go to *YouTube*, search for "Black Friday

Grown men scream at Justin Bieber in the Macy's Black Friday ad.

commercials," start watching, and then, once you've sated yourself on grown men screaming at Justin Bieber, remakes of Rebecca Black's "Friday," and, most distressingly, the continuing adventures of the Crazy Target Lady, ask yourself this question:

What does it all mean?

I stared into this heart of retail panic darkness, and the more I clicked and pondered, the more confused — (mind-boggled? fascinated? flabbergasted?) — I became. The Crazy Target Lady, so proud of her OCD — obsessive Christmas disorder — is not funny. She's scary. She's why people trample each other to death. She is wrong.

There is a point in our culture beyond which camp and kitsch no longer make the least ironic sense, where consumerism loses its last mooring to civilization, where even seemingly legitimate protest devolves into farce. That point is Black Friday.

Let me be clear. I am not opposed to vigorous sprees of retail 5 spending. For the sake of the U.S. economy, I would love to see a robust Christmas shopping season and I plan to do my part. I find the notion that we should "occupy Black Friday" and withhold our consumer dollars as a way of hitting back at the 1 percent just nutty. Voluntarily subtracting demand from the economy hurts *us*. A general consumer strike would result in more layoffs and pay cuts and bankruptcies and foreclosures. Sure, Wal-Mart would take a hit, but so would Wal-Mart employees.

But there's also a point where healthy consumerism becomes out-of-control marketing-driven commodity fetishism, and when we find ourselves checking our smartphones for last minute online deals while standing in line for a chain store opening at midnight on Thanksgiving, we are clearly too far gone. That's insanity.

And corporate America knows this. The retail moguls are counting on it. They are outright encouraging it — and role-modeling the appropriate behavior for us. The Crazy Target Lady is not a joke. Watch her cannibalize her gingerbread man, or strategize her reverse psychology shopping techniques, or show off her shopping utility belt: You cannot avoid the dual conclusion that a) she is not a healthy woman, and b) she is *America*. She might be a lunatic, but it's a culturally approved lunacy — the kind that keeps the American engine of capitalism all stoked up. The message that keeps getting blasted across my TV is that we should all be more like her — doing our patriotic duty to boost

The Crazy Target Lady models her shopping utility belt.

fourth-quarter retail sales. Sure, you can laugh at her. But then get in line and keep your credit card handy.

But, of course, the big story of this year's Black Friday has been the welcome news that at least some subsection of the population of the United States has come to the realization that it's time to step back from the brink. The budding protests against the decision by some of the country's biggest retailers — Target, Macy's, Best Buy, Kohl's — to move the start of their Black Friday sales to midnight Thanksgiving, or even earlier, is laudable.

The nearly 200,000 signatures on part-time Target employee Anthony Hardwick's petition to "Save Thanksgiving" is proof that both employees and customers of Target are beginning to see this endless race by retailers to one-up each other as dehumanizing and ridiculous. What does a Target employee forced to go to work at 11 p.m. on Thanksgiving have to give thanks for?

(Although, even here, in the protest arena, it's hard to know what 10 to make of the "Respect the Bird" campaign hosted at AllRecipes.com

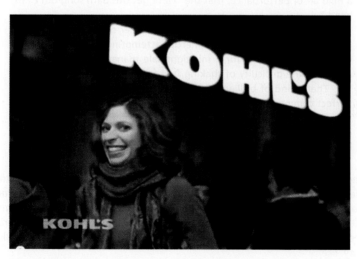

The "Friday" parody used in the Kohl's campaign.

that mixes pledges to "take back Thanksgiving" with KitchenAid mixer promotions and ads for pop-up turkey timers. Even the protests are inseparable from consumerist mania.)

The chains are lamely defending their move as a response to forces beyond their control:

"As that is the busiest shopping day of the year, it is imperative that we be competitive," said Anahita Cameron, a Target human resources director, in a statement quoted by the *L.A. Times*. "Our guests have expressed that they would prefer to kick off their holiday shopping by heading out after their holiday celebrations rather than getting up in the middle of the night."

Guests? Pre-programmed automatons would be more accurate. I am undoubtedly reading too much into the "Black Friday" parody of Rebecca Black's "Friday" currently touting the midnight Thanksgiving sale at Kohl's, but there is an awfully revealing moment at the very end of the ad.

After the perky Stepford-wife shopper sings joyfully about how she's "been in line since yesterday" and how everybody's going to Kohl's at "midnight, midnight" the ad ends with her observing, with a mild air of perturbance, that she "can't get this darn song out of my head."

Ladies and gentlemen, there's your winner of the 2011 award for honesty in advertising. A commercial attempting to brainwash consumers into lining up for a midnight sale manages also to explicitly reference the difficulty of shaking free from mindless jingles. 15

That's kind of brilliant. But also very wrong. Which makes it the perfect commercial for summing up the culture-wide psychotic spasm that is Black Friday. Stay home Thanksgiving night. Go shopping after getting a full night's rest. Sure, you might miss a sale or two. But you'll be a better human being.

For four more arguments, see CHAPTER 62.

Leonard's claim, that Black Friday represents "out-of-control marketing-driven commodity fetishism" or, more concisely, "insanity," is vividly illustrated by several videos of commercials that provide both background information and evidence for his argument. He acknowledges the need for "vigorous sprees of retail spending" while decrying the "psychotic spasm that is Black Friday."

Key Features / Arguments

A clear and arguable position. At the heart of every argument is a claim with which people may reasonably disagree. Some claims are not arguable because they're completely subjective, matters of taste or opinion ("I hate sauerkraut"), because they are a matter of fact ("The first *Star Wars* movie came out in 1977"), or because they are based on belief or faith ("There is life after death"). To be arguable, a position must reflect one of at least two points of view, making reasoned argument necessary: Guns should (or should not) be regulated; selling human organs should be legal (or illegal). In college writing, you will often argue not that a position is correct but that it is plausible—that it is reasonable, supportable, and worthy of being taken seriously.

Necessary background information. Sometimes we need to provide some background on a topic we are arguing so that readers can understand what is being argued. MacKay establishes the need for kidney donors before launching her argument for legalizing the selling of organs; Kristof describes the history of automobile regulation.

Good reasons. By itself, a position does not make an argument; the argument comes when a writer offers reasons to back up the position. There are many kinds of good reasons. Kristof makes his argument by comparing cars to guns. MacKay bases her argument in favor of legalizing the sale of human organs on the grounds that doing so would save more lives, that impoverished people should be able to make risky choices, and that regulation would protect such people who currently sell their organs on the black market as well as desperate buyers.

Convincing evidence. Once you've given reasons for your position, you then need to offer evidence for your reasons: facts, statistics, expert testimony, anecdotal evidence, case studies, textual evidence. All three arguments use a mix of these types of evidence. MacKay cites statistics about Americans who die from renal failure to support her argument for legalizing organ sales; Kristof shows how regulating cars led to dramatic decreases in driving deaths and injuries. Leonard presents several videos to demonstrate how excessive Black Friday advertising has become.

Appeals to readers' values.　Effective arguers try to appeal to readers' values and emotions. MacKay appeals to basic values of compassion and fairness. These are deeply held values that we may not think about very much and as a result may see as common ground we share with the writers. And some of MacKay's evidence appeals to emotion—her descriptions of people dying from kidney disease and of poor people selling their organs are likely to evoke an emotional response in many readers.

A trustworthy tone.　Arguments can stand or fall on the way readers perceive the writer. Very simply, readers need to trust the person who's making the argument. One way of winning this trust is by demonstrating that you know what you're talking about. Kristof offers plenty of facts to show his knowledge of the history of automotive regulation — and he does so in a self-assured tone. There are many other ways of establishing yourself (and your argument) as trustworthy — by showing that you have some experience with your subject, that you're fair, and of course that you're honest. Occasionally, an outraged tone such as Leonard's is appropriate, especially when it is tempered by good reasons and qualified as he does in noting that he is "undoubtedly reading too much into the Kohl's . . . parody."

Careful consideration of other positions.　No matter how reasonable and careful we are in arguing our positions, others may disagree or offer counterarguments. We need to consider those other views and to acknowledge and, if possible, refute them in our written arguments. MacKay, for example, acknowledges that some believe that selling organs is unethical, but she counters that it's usually healthy, affluent people who say this — not people who need either an organ or the money they could get by selling one.

A GUIDE TO WRITING ARGUMENTS

Choosing a Topic

A fully developed argument requires significant work and time, so choosing a topic in which you're interested is very important. Students often find that widely debated topics such as "animal rights" or "abortion" can be difficult to write on because they don't feel any personal connection to them. Better topics include those that

- interest you right now
- are focused but not too narrowly
- have some personal connection to your life

One good way to **GENERATE IDEAS** for a topic that meets those three criteria is to explore your own roles in life.

289–97

Start with your roles in life. Make four columns with the headings "Personal," "Family," "Public," and "School." Then **LIST** the roles you play that relate to it. Here is a list one student wrote:

290–91

Personal	Family	Public	School
gamer	son	voter	college student
dog owner	younger	homeless-shelter	work-study
old-car owner	brother	volunteer	employee
male	grandson	American	dorm resident
white		resident	primary-education
middle class		of Texas	major

Identify issues that interest you. Think, then, about issues or controversies that may concern you as a member of one or more of those groups. For instance, as a primary-education major, this student cares about the controversy over whether teachers' jobs should be focused on preparing kids for high-stakes standardized tests. As a college student, he cares about the costs of a college education. Issues that stem from these subjects could include the following: Should student progress be measured by standardized tests? Should college cost less than it does?

Pick four or five of the roles you list. In five or ten minutes, identify issues that concern or affect you as a member of each of those roles. It might help to word each issue as a question starting with *Should*.

Frame your topic as a problem.   Most position papers address issues that are subjects of ongoing debate—their solutions aren't easy, and people disagree on which ones are best. Posing your topic as a problem can help you think about the topic, find an issue that's suitable to write about, and find a clear focus for your essay.

For example, if you wanted to write an argument on the lack of student parking at your school, you could frame your topic as one of several problems: What causes the parking shortage? Why are the university's parking garages and lots limited in their capacity? What might alleviate the shortage?

Choose one issue to write about.   Remember that the issue should be interesting to you and have some connection to your life. It is a tentative choice; if you find later that you have trouble writing about it, simply go back to your list of roles or issues and choose another.

Considering the Rhetorical Situation

55–56 **PURPOSE**   Do you want to persuade your audience to do something? Change their minds? Consider alternative views? Accept your position as plausible — see that you have thought carefully about an issue and researched it appropriately?

57–60 **AUDIENCE**   Who is your intended audience? What do they likely know and believe about this issue? How personal is it for them? To what extent are they likely to agree or disagree with you — and with one another? Why? What common ground can you find with them?

academic literacies　　rhetorical situations　　genres　　processes　　strategies　　research MLA / APA　　media / design　　readings　　handbook

STANCE What's your attitude toward your topic, and why? How do you want your audience to perceive your attitude? How do you want your audience to perceive you? As an authority on your topic? As someone much like them? As calm? reasonable? impassioned or angry? something else?

64–67

MEDIA/DESIGN What media will you use, and how do your media affect your argument? Does your print or online argument call for photos or charts? If you're giving an oral presentation, should you put your reasons and support on slides? If you're writing electronically, should you include audio or video evidence or links to counterarguments or your sources?

68–70

Generating Ideas and Text

Most essays that successfully argue a position share certain features that make them interesting and persuasive. Remember that your goal is to stake out a position and convince your readers that it is plausible.

Explore what you already know about the issue. Write out whatever you know about the issue by **FREEWRITING** or as a **LIST** or **OUTLINE**. Why are you interested in this topic? What is your position on it at this point, and why? What aspect do you think you'd like to focus on? Where do you need to focus your research efforts? This activity can help you discover what more you need to learn. Chances are you'll need to learn a lot more about the issue before you even decide what position to take.

289–291

293–94

Do some research. At this point, try to get an overview. Start with one **GENERAL SOURCE** of information that will give you a sense of the ins and outs of your issue, one that isn't overtly biased. *The atlantic.com*, *Time.com*, *Slate*, and other online newspapers and magazines can be good starting points on current issues. For some issues, you may need to **INTERVIEW** an expert. For example, one student who wanted to write about chemical

455–56

463–64

abuse of animals at 4-H competitions interviewed an experienced show competitor. Use your overview source to find out the main questions raised about your issue and to get some idea about the various ways in which you might argue it.

Explore the issue strategically.   Most issues may be argued from many different perspectives. You'll probably have some sense of the different views that exist on your issue, but you should explore multiple perspectives before deciding on your position. The following methods are good ways of exploring issues:

- As a matter of **DEFINITION**. What is it? How should it be defined? How can *organic* or *genetically modified food* be defined? How do proponents of *organic food* define it—and how do they define *genetically modified food*? How do advocates of *genetically modified food* define it—and how do they define *organic food*? Considering such definitions is one way to identify different perspectives on the topic.

- As a matter of **CLASSIFICATION**. Can the issue be divided into categories? Are there different kinds of, or different ways of, producing organic foods and genetically modified foods? Do different categories suggest particular positions or perhaps a way of supporting a certain position? Are there other ways of categorizing foods?

- As a matter of **COMPARISON**. Is one subject being considered better than another? Is organic food healthier or safer than genetically modified food? Is genetically modified food healthier or safer than organic? Is the answer somewhere in the middle?

- As a matter of **PROCESS**. Should somebody do something? What? Should people buy and eat more organic food? More genetically modified food? Should they buy and eat some of each?

Reconsider whether the issue can be argued.   Is this issue worth discussing? Why is it important to you and to others? What difference will it make if one position or another prevails? Is it **ARGUABLE**? At this point, you want to be sure that your topic is worth arguing about.

Draft a thesis. Having explored the possibilities, decide your position, and write it out as a complete sentence. For example:

> Parents should be required to have their children vaccinated.
>
> Pod-based coffeemakers should be banned.
>
> Genetically modified foods should be permitted in the United States.

Qualify your thesis. Rather than taking a strict pro or con position, in most cases you'll want to **QUALIFY YOUR POSITION** — in certain circumstances, with certain conditions, with these limitations, and so on. This is not to say that we should settle, give in, sell out; rather, it is to say that our position may not be the only "correct" one and that other positions may be valid as well. **QUALIFYING YOUR THESIS** also makes your topic manageable by limiting it. For example:

357

345–47

> Parents should be required to have their children vaccinated, with only medical exemptions allowed.
>
> Pod-based coffeemakers should be banned unless the pods are recyclable.
>
> Genetically modified foods should be permitted in the United States if they are clearly labeled as such.

Come up with good reasons. Once you have a thesis, you need to come up with good **REASONS** to convince your readers that it's plausible. Write out your position, and then list several reasons. For instance, if your thesis is that pod-based coffeemakers should be banned, two of your reasons might be:

358–59

> The pods cannot be recycled.
>
> Other methods of making coffee are more environmentally sound.

Think about which reasons are best for your purposes. Which seem the most persuasive? Which are most likely to be accepted by your audience? Which seem to matter the most now? If your list of reasons is short or you think you'll have trouble developing them enough to write an appropriate essay, this is a good time to rethink your topic — before you've invested too much time in it.

359–67 ◆

Develop support for your reasons. Next you have to come up with **EVIDENCE** to support your reasons: facts, statistics, examples, testimony by authorities and experts, anecdotal evidence, scenarios, case studies and observation, and textual evidence. For some topics, you may want or need to use evidence in visual form like photos, graphs, and charts; online, you could also use video or audio evidence and links to evidence in other websites.

What counts as evidence varies across audiences. Statistical evidence may be required in certain disciplines but not in others; anecdotes may be accepted as evidence in some courses but not in engineering. Some audiences will be persuaded by emotional appeals while others will not. For example, if you argue that foods produced from genetically modified organisms (GMOs) should be allowed to be sold because they're safe, you could support that reason with *facts*: GMOs are tested thoroughly by three separate U.S. government agencies. Or you could support it with *statistics*: A study of 29 years of data on livestock fed GMO feed found that GMO-fed cattle had no adverse health effects. *Expert testimony* might include R. E. Goodman of the Department of Food Science and Technology at the University of Nebraska–Lincoln, who writes that "there is an absence of proof of harm to consumers from commercially available GMOs."

Identify other positions. Now think about positions other than yours and the reasons people are likely to give for those positions. Be careful to represent their points of view as accurately and fairly as you can. Then decide whether you need to acknowledge or to refute each position.

368–69 ◆

Acknowledging other positions. Some positions can't be refuted but are too important to ignore, so you need to **ACKNOWLEDGE** concerns and objections they raise to show that you've considered other perspectives. For example, in an essay arguing that vacations are necessary to maintain good health, medical writer Alina Tugend acknowledges that "in some cases, these trips — particularly with entire families in tow — can be stressful in their own way. The joys of a holiday can also include lugging around a ridiculous amount of paraphernalia, jet-lagged children sobbing on airplanes, hotels that looked wonderful on the Web but are in reality next to a construction site." Tugend's acknowledgment moderates her position and makes her argument appear more reasonable.

Refuting other positions. State the position as clearly and as fairly as you can, and then **REFUTE** it by showing why you believe it is wrong. Perhaps the reasoning is faulty or the supporting evidence inadequate. Acknowledge the merits of the position, if any, but emphasize its short-comings. Avoid the **FALLACY** of attacking the person holding the position or bringing up a competing position that no one seriously entertains.

◆ 369

◆ 370–72

Ways of Organizing an Argument

Readers need to be able to follow the reasoning of your argument from beginning to end; your task is to lead them from point to point as you build your case. Sometimes you'll want to give all the reasons for your argument first, followed by discussion of any other positions. Alternatively, you might discuss each reason and any opposing arguments together.

[Reasons to support your argument, followed by opposing arguments]

[Reason/opposing argument, reason/opposing argument]

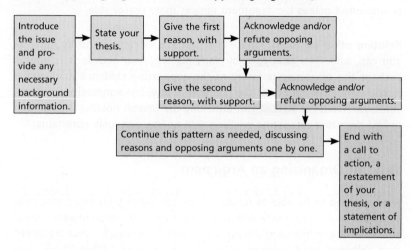

Consider carefully the order in which you discuss your reasons. Usually what comes last makes the strongest impression on readers and what comes in the middle the least impression, so you might want to put your most important or strongest reasons first and last.

Writing Out a Draft

298–300 ○

Once you have generated ideas, done some research, and thought about how you want to organize your argument, it's time to start **DRAFTING**. Your goal in the initial draft is to develop your argument — you can fill in support and transitions as you revise. You may want to write your first draft in one sitting, so that you can develop your reasoning from beginning to end. Or you may write the main argument first and the introduction and conclusion after you've drafted the body of the essay; many writers find that beginning and ending an essay are the hardest tasks they face. Here is some advice on how you might **BEGIN AND END** your argument:

◆ 331–43

Draft a beginning. There are various ways to begin an argument essay, depending on your audience and purpose. Here are a few suggestions:

- *Offer background information.* You may need to give your readers information to help them understand your position. MacKay outlines the extent of kidney failure in the United States and the limits of dialysis as treatment.

- *Define a key term.* You may need to show how you're using certain keywords. MacKay, for example, defines *end-stage renal disease* as "a state of kidney disorder so advanced that the organ stops functioning altogether," a **DEFINITION** that is central to her argument.

◆ 388–98

- *Begin with something that will get readers' attention.* MacKay begins emphatically: "There are thousands of people dying to buy a kidney and thousands of people dying to sell a kidney . . . So why are we standing in the way?" Leonard offers still photos from two commercials and links to two more available online.

- *Explain the context for your position.* All arguments are part of a larger, ongoing conversation, so you might begin by showing how your position fits into the arguments others have made. Kristof places his argument about guns in the **CONTEXT** of government regulation of other dangerous technologies.

▲ 110

Draft an ending. Your conclusion is the chance to wrap up your argument in such a way that readers will remember what you've said. Here are a few ways of concluding an argument essay:

- *Summarize your main points.* Especially when you've presented a complex argument, it can help readers to **SUMMARIZE** your main point. MacKay sums up her argument with the sentence "If legalized and regulated, the sale of human organs would save lives."

● 486–87

- *Call for action*. Kristof does this by asking politicians to consider "sensible safety measures." Leonard presents an alternative to Black Friday's excesses: "Stay home Thanksgiving night. Go shopping after getting a full night's rest."
- *Frame your argument by referring to the introduction.* MacKay does this when she ends by reiterating that selling organs benefits both seller and buyer.

Come up with a title.   Most often you'll want your title to tell readers something about your topic—and to make them want to read on. MacKay's "Organ Sales Will Save Lives" tells us both her topic and position. Kristof's title, "Our Blind Spot about Guns," entices us to find out what that blind spot is. See the chapter on **GUIDING YOUR READER** for more advice on composing a good title.

344–49

Considering Matters of Design

You'll probably write the main text of your argument in paragraph form, but think about what kind of information you're presenting and how you can design it to make your argument as easy as possible for your readers to understand. Think also about whether any visual or audio elements would be more persuasive than written words.

601–2
- What would be an appropriate **FONT**? Something serious like Times Roman? Something traditional like Courier? Something else?
604–5
- Would it help your readers if you divided your argument into shorter sections and added **HEADINGS**?
603
- If you're making several points, would they be easier to follow if you set them off in a **LIST**?
609–11
- Do you have any supporting evidence that would be easier to understand in the form of a bar **GRAPH**, line graph, or pie chart?
607–15
- Would **ILLUSTRATIONS**—photos, diagrams, or drawings—add support for your argument? Online, would video, audio, or links help?

academic literacies | rhetorical situations | genres | processes | strategies | research MLA / APA | media / design | readings | handbook

Getting Response and Revising

At this point you need to look at your draft closely, and if possible **GET RESPONSE** from others as well. Following are some questions for looking at an argument with a critical eye.

○ 306–7

- Is there sufficient background or context?
- Have you defined terms to avoid misunderstandings?
- Is the thesis clear and appropriately qualified?
- Are the reasons plausible?
- Is there enough evidence to support these reasons? Will readers accept the evidence as valid and sufficient?
- Can readers follow the steps in your reasoning?
- Have you considered potential objections or other positions? Are there any others that should be addressed?
- Have you cited enough sources, and are these sources credible?
- Are source materials documented carefully and completely, with in-text citations and a works cited or references section?
- Are any visuals or links that are included used effectively and integrated smoothly with the rest of the text? If there are no visuals or links, would using some strengthen the argument?

Next it's time to **REVISE**, to make sure your argument offers convincing evidence, appeals to readers' values, and achieves your purpose.

○ 307–10

Editing and Proofreading

Readers equate correctness with competence. Once you've revised your draft, follow these guidelines for **EDITING** an argument:

○ 313–16

- Check to see that your tone is appropriate and consistent throughout, reflects your **STANCE** accurately, and enhances the argument you're making.

■ 64–67

- Be sure readers will be able to follow the argument; check to see you've provided **TRANSITIONS** and summary statements where necessary.

349

- Make sure you've smoothly integrated **QUOTATIONS**, **PARAPHRASES**, and **SUMMARIES** from source material into your writing and **DOCUMENTED** them accurately.

478–90
496–99

- Look for phrases such as "I think" or "I feel" and delete them; your essay itself expresses your opinion.

- Make sure that **ILLUSTRATIONS** have captions and that charts and graphs have headings—and that all are referred to in the main text.

607–15

- If you're writing online, make sure all your links work.

- **PROOFREAD** and spell-check your essay carefully.

316–17

Taking Stock of Your Work

Take stock of what you've written by writing out answers to these questions:

- What did you do well in this piece?
- What could still be improved?
- How did you go about researching your topic?
- How did others' responses influence your writing?
- How did you go about drafting this piece?
- Did you use visual elements (tables, graphs, diagrams, photographs), audio elements, or links effectively? If not, would they have helped?
- What would you do differently next time?
- What have you learned about your writing ability from writing this piece? What do you need to work on in the future?

> **IF YOU NEED MORE HELP**
>
> See Chapter 32 if you are required to submit your argument as part of a writing **PORTFOLIO**. See also Chapter 11 on **ANALYZING A TEXT**, Chapter 16 on **EVALUATIONS**, and Chapter 20 on **PROPOSALS** for advice on writing those specific types of arguments.

318–28
94–128
197–205
235–44

Abstracts 14

Abstracts are summaries written to give readers the gist of a **REPORT** or presentation. Sometimes they are published in conference proceedings or databases. In courses in the *sciences, social sciences*, and *engineering*, you may be asked to create abstracts of your proposed projects and completed reports and essays. Abstracts are brief, typically 100–200 words, sometimes even shorter. Three common kinds are *informative abstracts, descriptive abstracts*, and *proposal abstracts*.

▲ 129–55

INFORMATIVE ABSTRACTS

Informative abstracts state in one paragraph the essence of a whole paper about a study or a research project. That one paragraph must mention all the main points or parts of the paper: a description of the study or project, its methods, the results, and the conclusions. Here is an example of the abstract accompanying a seven-page essay that appeared in the *Journal of Clinical Psychology*:

> The relationship between boredom proneness and health-symptom reporting was examined. Undergraduate students ($N = 200$) completed the Boredom Proneness Scale and the Hopkins Symptom Checklist. A multiple analysis of covariance indicated that individuals with high boredom-proneness total scores reported significantly higher ratings on all five subscales of the Hopkins Symptom Checklist (Obsessive–Compulsive, Somatization, Anxiety, Interpersonal Sensitivity, and Depression). The results suggest that boredom proneness may be an important element to consider when assessing symptom reporting. Implications for determining the effects of boredom proneness on

psychological- and physical-health symptoms, as well as the application in clinical settings, are discussed.

— Jennifer Sommers and Stephen J. Vodanovich,
"Boredom Proneness"

The first sentence states the nature of the study being reported. The next summarizes the method used to investigate the problem, and the following one gives the results: students who, according to specific tests, are more likely to be bored are also more likely to have certain medical or psychological symptoms. The last two sentences indicate that the paper discusses those results and examines the conclusion and its implications.

DESCRIPTIVE ABSTRACTS

Descriptive abstracts are usually much briefer than informative abstracts and provide much less information. Rather than summarizing the entire paper, a descriptive abstract functions more as a teaser, providing a quick overview that invites the reader to read the whole. Descriptive abstracts usually do not give or discuss results or set out the conclusion or its implications. A descriptive abstract of the boredom-proneness essay might simply include the first sentence from the informative abstract plus a final sentence of its own:

The relationship between boredom proneness and health-symptom reporting was examined. The findings and their application in clinical settings are discussed.

PROPOSAL ABSTRACTS

Proposal abstracts contain the same basic information as informative abstracts, but their purpose is very different. You prepare proposal abstracts to persuade someone to let you write on a topic, pursue a project, conduct an experiment, or present a paper at a scholarly conference. This kind of abstract is not written to introduce a longer piece but rather to stand alone, and often the abstract is written before the paper itself. Titles and other aspects of the proposal deliberately reflect the theme of the proposed work, and you may use the future tense, rather than the past, to describe work not yet completed. Here is a possible proposal for doing research on boredom:

> Undergraduate students will complete the Boredom Proneness Scale and the Hopkins Symptom Checklist. A multiple analysis of covariance will be performed to determine the relationship between boredom-proneness total scores and ratings on the five subscales of the Hopkins Symptom Checklist (Obsessive–Compulsive, Somatization, Anxiety, Interpersonal Sensitivity, and Depression).

Key Features / Abstracts

A summary of basic information. An informative abstract includes enough information to substitute for the report itself, a descriptive abstract offers only enough information to let the audience decide whether to read further, and a proposal abstract gives an overview of the planned work.

Objective description. Abstracts present information on the contents of a report or a proposed study; they do not present arguments about or personal perspectives on those contents. The informative abstract on boredom proneness, for example, offers only a tentative conclusion: "The results *suggest* that boredom proneness *may* be an important element to consider."

Brevity. Although the length of abstracts may vary, journals and organizations often restrict them to 120–200 words — meaning you must carefully select and edit your words.

A BRIEF GUIDE TO WRITING ABSTRACTS

Considering the Rhetorical Situation

PURPOSE   Are you giving a brief but thorough overview of a completed study? only enough information to create interest? a proposal for a planned study or presentation?

55–56

55–56
AUDIENCE   For whom are you writing this abstract? What information about your project will your readers need?

64–67
STANCE   Whatever your stance in the longer work, your abstract must be objective.

68–70
MEDIA / DESIGN   How will you set your abstract off from the rest of the text? If you are publishing it online, should it be on a separate page? What format do your readers expect?

Generating Ideas and Text

Write the paper first, the abstract last.   You can then use the finished work as the guide for the abstract, which should follow the same basic structure. *Exception:* You may need to write a proposal abstract months before the work it describes will be complete.

345–47
Copy and paste key statements.   If you've already written the work, highlight your **THESIS**, objective, or purpose; basic information on your methods; your results; and your conclusion. Copy and paste those sentences into a new document to create a rough version of your abstract.

486–87
Pare down the rough abstract.   **SUMMARIZE** the key ideas in the document, editing out any nonessential words and details. In your first sentence, introduce the overall scope of your study. Also include any other information that seems crucial to understanding your paper. Avoid phrases that add unnecessary words, such as "It is concluded that." In general, you probably won't want to use "I"; an abstract should cover ideas, not say what you think or will do.

Conform to any requirements.   In general, an informative abstract should be at most 10 percent as long as the original and no longer than the maximum length allowed. Descriptive abstracts should be shorter still, and proposal abstracts should conform to the requirements of the organization calling for the proposal.

Ways of Organizing an Abstract

[An informative abstract]

[A descriptive abstract]

[A proposal abstract]

IF YOU NEED MORE HELP

See Chapter 28 for guidelines on **DRAFTING**, Chapter 29 on **ASSESSING YOUR OWN WRITING**, Chapter 30 on **GETTING RESPONSE AND REVISING**, and Chapter 31 on **EDITING AND PROOFREADING**.

298–300
301–5
313–17

15 Annotated Bibliographies

Annotated bibliographies describe, give publication information for, and sometimes evaluate each work on a list of sources. When we do research, we may consult annotated bibliographies to evaluate potential sources. In some college courses, you may be assigned to create annotated bibliographies to weigh the potential usefulness of sources and to document your search efforts so that teachers can assess your ability to find, describe, and evaluate sources. There are two kinds of annotations, *descriptive* and *evaluative*; both may be brief, consisting only of phrases, or more formal, consisting of sentences and paragraphs. Sometimes an annotated bibliography is introduced by a short statement explaining its scope.

Descriptive annotations simply summarize the contents of each work, without comment or evaluation. They may be very short, just long enough to capture the flavor of the work, like the examples in the following excerpt from a bibliography of books and articles on teen films, published in the *Journal of Popular Film and Television*.

MICHAEL BENTON, MARK DOLAN, AND REBECCA ZISCH

Teen Film$

In the introduction to his book *The Road to Romance and Ruin*, Jon Lewis points out that over half of the world's population is currently under the age of twenty. This rather startling fact should be enough to make most Hollywood producers drool when they think of the potential profits from a target movie audience. Attracting the largest demographic group is, after all, the quickest way to box-office success. In fact, almost from its beginning, the film industry has recognized the importance of the teenaged audience, with characters such as Andy Hardy and locales such as Ridgemont High and the 'hood.

Beyond the assumption that teen films are geared exclusively toward teenagers, however, film researchers should keep in mind that people of all ages have attended and still attend teen films. Popular films about adolescents are also expressions of larger cultural currents. Studying the films is important for understanding an era's common beliefs about its teenaged population within a broader pattern of general cultural preoccupations.

This selected bibliography is intended both to serve and to stimulate interest in the teen film genre. It provides a research tool for those who are studying teen films and their cultural implications. Unfortunately, however, in the process of compiling this list we quickly realized that it was impossible to be genuinely comprehensive or to satisfy every interest.

Doherty, Thomas. *Teenagers and Teenpics: The Juvenilization of American Movies in the 1950s*. Unwin Hyman, 1988. Historical discussion of the identification of teenagers as a targeted film market.

Foster, Harold M. "Film in the Classroom: Coping with 'Teenpics.'" *English Journal*, vol. 76, no. 3, Mar. 1987, pp. 86-88. Evaluation of the potential of using teen films such as *Sixteen Candles*, *The Karate Kid*, *Risky Business*, *The Flamingo Kid*, and *The Breakfast Club* to instruct adolescents on the difference between film as communication and film as exploitation.

Washington, Michael, and Marvin J. Berlowitz. "Blaxploitation Films and High School Youth: Swat Superfly." *Jump Cut*, vol. 9, Oct.-Dec. 1975, pp. 23-24. Marxist reaction to the trend of youth-oriented black action films. Article seeks to illuminate the negative influences the films have on high school students by pointing out the false ideas about education, morality, and the black family espoused by the heroes in the films.

These annotations are purely descriptive; the authors express none of their own opinions. They describe works as "historical" or "Marxist" but do not indicate whether they're "good." The bibliography entries are documented in MLA style.

Evaluative annotations offer opinions on a source as well as describe it. They are often helpful in assessing how useful a source will be for your own writing. The following evaluative annotations are from a bibliography by Jessica Ann Olson, a student at Wright State University.

JESSICA ANN OLSON

Global Warming

Gore, Al. *An Inconvenient Truth: The Planetary Emergency of Global Warming and What We Can Do about It.* Rodale, 2006.

This publication, which is based on Gore's slide show on global warming, stresses the urgency of the global warming crisis. It centers on how the atmosphere is very thin and how greenhouse gases such as carbon dioxide are making it thicker. The thicker atmosphere traps more infrared radiation, causing warming of the Earth. Gore argues that carbon dioxide, which is created by burning fossil fuels, cutting down forests, and producing cement, accounts for eighty percent of greenhouse gas emissions. He includes several examples of problems caused by global warming. Penguins and polar bears are at risk because the glaciers they call home are quickly melting. Coral reefs are being bleached and destroyed when their inhabitants overheat and leave. Global warming is now affecting people's lives as well. For example, the highways in Alaska are only frozen enough to be driven on fewer than eighty days of the year. In China and elsewhere, record-setting floods and droughts are taking place. Hurricanes are on the rise. This source's goal is to inform its audience about the ongoing global warming crisis and to inspire change across the world. It is useful because it relies on scientific data that can be referred to easily and it provides a solid foundation for me to build on. For example, it explains how carbon dioxide is produced and how it is currently affecting plants and animals. This evidence could potentially help my research on how humans are biologically affected by global warming. It will also help me structure my essay, using its general information to lead into the specifics of my topic. For example, I could introduce the issue by explaining the thinness of the atmosphere and the effect of greenhouse gases, then focus on carbon dioxide and its effects on organisms.

Parmesan, Camille, and Hector Galbraith. "Executive Summary." *Observed Impacts of Global Climate Change in the U.S.,* Pew Center on Global

academic literacies • rhetorical situations • genres • processes • strategies • research MLA / APA • media / design • readings • handbook

Climate Change, Nov. 2004, c2es.org/docUploads/final_ObsImpact. pdf. Accessed 17 Jan. 2007.

This report summarizes recent scientific findings that document the impact changes in the climate have had on the distribution of plants and animals in the United States and on how they interact within their communities. For example, it explains how a shift has taken place in the blooming period for plants and the breeding period for animals caused by global warming. Because of changes in their geographic range, species may interact differently, possibly resulting in population declines. For example, the red fox is now found in areas dominated by the arctic fox and is threatening its survival. The report stresses that such shifts can harm the world's biodiversity. Plants and animals that are rare now face extinction. The annual cycle of carbon dioxide levels in the atmosphere has also changed, largely due to the lengthening of the growing season, affecting basic ecosystem processes. I did not find this report as helpful as other sources because its information is based only on observations made in the United States. The information appears reliable, though, because it is based on scientific evidence. This essay will be helpful to my essay because it focuses on how plants and animals are currently affected, such as their shifting communities and how they are clashing. I could use this to explain human changes by providing evidence of what is happening to other species. This source will not be as helpful in explaining the climate's effects on human biological function in particular, but it will provide some framework. For example, I could explain how the plants that help convert carbon dioxide into oxygen are being harmed and relate that to how the humans will suffer the consequences.

These annotations not only describe the sources in detail, but also evaluate their usefulness for the writer's own project. They show that the writer understands the content of the sources and can relate it to her own anticipated needs as a researcher and writer.

Key Features / Annotated Bibliographies

A statement of scope. Sometimes you need or are asked to provide a brief introductory statement to explain what you're covering. The authors of the bibliography on teen films introduce their bibliography with three paragraphs establishing a context for the bibliography and announcing their purpose for compiling it.

Complete bibliographic information. Provide all the information about each source using one documentation system (MLA, APA, or another one) so that you, your readers, or other researchers will be able to find the source easily. It's a good idea to include sources' URLs or **PERMALINKS** to make accessing online sources easier.

443

A concise description of the work. A good annotation describes each item as carefully and objectively as possible, giving accurate information and showing that you understand the source. These qualities will help to build authority—for you as a writer and for your annotations.

Relevant commentary. If you write an evaluative bibliography, your comments should be relevant to your purpose and audience. The best way to achieve relevance is to consider what questions a potential reader might have about each source: What are the main points of the source? What is its argument? How current and reliable is it? Will the source be helpful for your project?

Consistent presentation. All annotations should follow a consistent pattern: if one is written in complete sentences, they should all be. Each annotation in the teen films bibliography, for example, begins with a phrase (not a complete sentence) characterizing the work.

A BRIEF GUIDE TO WRITING ANNOTATED BIBLIOGRAPHIES

Considering the Rhetorical Situation

55–56

PURPOSE Will your bibliography need to demonstrate the depth or breadth of your research? Will your readers actually track down and use your sources? Do you need or want to convince readers that your sources are good?

AUDIENCE	For whom are you compiling this bibliography? What does your audience need to know about each source?	■ 57–60
STANCE	Are you presenting yourself as an objective describer or evaluator? Or are you expressing a particular point of view toward the sources you evaluate?	■ 64–67
MEDIA / DESIGN	If you are publishing the bibliography electronically, will you provide links from each annotation to the source itself? Online or off, should you distinguish the bibliographic information from the annotation by using a different font?	■ 68–70

Generating Ideas and Text

Decide what sources to include. You may be tempted to include in a bibliography every source you find or look at. A better strategy is to include only those sources that you or your readers may find potentially useful in researching your topic. For an academic bibliography, you need to consider the qualities in the list below. Some of these qualities should not rule a source in or out; they simply raise issues you need to think about.

- *Appropriateness.* Is this source relevant to your topic? Is it a primary source or a secondary source? Is it aimed at an appropriate audience? General or specialized? Elementary, advanced, or somewhere in between?

- *Credibility.* Is the author reputable? Is the publication, publishing company, or sponsor of the site reputable? Do the ideas more or less agree with those in other sources you've read?

- *Balance.* Does the source present enough evidence for its assertions? Does it show any particular bias? Does it present countering arguments fairly?

- *Timeliness.* Is the source recent enough? Does it reflect current thinking or research about the subject?

If you need help **FINDING SOURCES**, see Chapter 46.

● 445–68

Compile a list of works to annotate. Give the sources themselves in whatever documentation style is required; see the guidelines for **MLA** and **APA** styles in Chapters 52 and 53.

MLA 500–548 ●
APA 549–89

Determine what kind of bibliography you need to write. Descriptive or evaluative? Will your annotations be in the form of phrases? complete sentences? paragraphs? The form will shape your reading and note taking. If you're writing a descriptive bibliography, your reading goal will be just to understand and capture the writer's message as clearly as possible. If you're writing an evaluative bibliography, you will also need to assess the source as you read in order to include your own opinions of it.

Read carefully.   To write an annotation, you must understand the source's argument, but when you are writing an annotated bibliography as part of a **PROPOSAL**, you may have neither the time nor the need to read the whole text. Here's a way of quickly determining whether a source is likely to serve your needs:

235–44 ▲

- Check the publisher or sponsor (university press? scholarly journal? popular magazine? website sponsored by a reputable organization?).

- Read the preface (of a book), abstract (of a scholarly article), introduction (of an article in a nonscholarly magazine or a website).

- Skim the table of contents or the headings.

- Read the parts that relate specifically to your topic.

Research the writer, if necessary. If you are required to indicate the writer's credentials, you may need to do additional research. You may find information by typing the writer's name into a search engine or looking up the writer in *Contemporary Authors*. In any case, information about the writer should take up no more than one sentence in your annotation.

399–407 ◆

Summarize the work in a sentence or two.   **DESCRIBE** it as objectively as possible: even if you are writing an evaluative annotation, you can evaluate the central point of a work better by stating it clearly first. *If you're writing a descriptive annotation, you're done.*

Establish criteria for evaluating sources. If you're **EVALUATING** sources for a project, you'll need to evaluate them in terms of their usefulness for your project, their **STANCE**, and their overall credibility.

469–72

64–67

Write a brief evaluation of the source. If you can generalize about the worth of the entire work, fine. You may find, however, that some parts are useful while others are not, and what you write should reflect that mix.

Be consistent—in content, sentence structure, and format.

- **Content.** Try to provide about the same amount of information for each entry. If you're evaluating, don't evaluate some sources and just describe others.

- **Sentence structure.** Use the same style throughout—**COMPLETE SEN-TENCES**, brief phrases, or a mix.

HB-4–7

- **Format.** Use one documentation style throughout; use a consistent **FONT** for each element in each entry—for example, italicize or underline all book titles.

601–2

Ways of Organizing an Annotated Bibliography

Depending on their purpose, annotated bibliographies may or may not include an introduction. Most annotated bibliographies cover a single topic and so are organized alphabetically by author's or editor's last name. When a work lacks a named author, alphabetize it by the first important word in its title. Consult the documentation system you're using for additional details about alphabetizing works appropriately.

State scope. → List first alphabetical entry, and annotate it. → List second alphabetical entry, and annotate it. → List third alphabetical entry, and annotate it. ⇢ List final alphabetical entry, and annotate it.

Sometimes an annotated bibliography needs to be organized into several subject areas (or genres, periods, or some other category); if so, the entries are listed alphabetically within each category. For example, a bibliography about terrorism breaks down into subjects such as "Global Terrorism" and "Weapons of Mass Destruction."

[Multicategory bibliography]

298–300
301–5
306–12
313–17
318–28

IF YOU NEED MORE HELP

See Chapter 28 for guidelines on **DRAFTING**, Chapter 29 on **ASSESSING YOUR OWN WRITING**, Chapter 30 on **GETTING RESPONSE AND REVISING**, and Chapter 31 on **EDITING AND PROOFREADING**. See Chapter 32 if you are required to submit your bibliography in a writing **PORTFOLIO**.

Evaluations 16

ConsumerReports.org evaluates cars and laundry detergents. The *Princeton Review* and *U.S. News & World Report* evaluate colleges and universities. You probably consult such sources to make decisions, and you probably evaluate things all the time—when you recommend a film (or not) or a teacher (ditto). An evaluation is at bottom a judgment; you judge something according to certain criteria, supporting your judgment with reasons and evidence. You need to give your reasons for evaluating it as you do because often your evaluation will affect your audience's actions: they must see this movie, needn't bother with this book, should be sure to have the Caesar salad at this restaurant, and so on.

In college courses, students in *literature, film, drama,* and *art* classes may be assigned to evaluate poems, fiction, movies, plays, and art works,

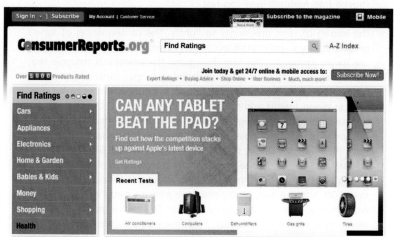

ConsumerReports.org uses lab testing to support the evaluations it publishes.

and those in *business* and *political science* classes may be asked to evaluate advertising or political campaigns or plans for business or public-policy initiatives. In a review that follows, written for a first-year writing class at Wright State University, Ali Heinekamp offers her evaluation of the film *Juno.*

ALI HEINEKAMP

Juno: Not Just Another Teen Movie

It all starts with a chair, where Juno (Ellen Page) has unprotected sex with her best friend Bleeker (Michael Cera). Several weeks later, she's at a convenience store, buying a pregnancy test. Only sixteen, Juno faces the terrifying task of telling her parents that she is pregnant. With their support, Juno moves forward in her decision to give birth and give the child to Mark (Jason Bateman) and Vanessa (Jennifer Garner), a wealthy and seemingly perfect married couple looking to adopt. Although the situations *Juno*'s characters find themselves in and their dialogue may be criticized as unrealistic, the film, written by Diablo Cody and directed by Jason Reitman, successfully portrays the emotions of a teen being shoved into maturity way too fast.

Much of the time, *Juno* seems unrealistic because it seems to treat the impact of teen pregnancy so lightly. The consequences of Juno's pregnancy are sugar-coated to such an extent that in many cases, they are barely apparent. The film downplays the emotional struggle that a pregnant woman would feel in deciding to give birth and then put that child up for adoption, and it ignores the discomforts of pregnancy, such as mood swings and nausea.

Likewise, *Juno*'s dialogue is too good to be true—funny and clever, but unrealistic. For example, Juno tells Mark and Vanessa "If I could just have the thing and give it to you now, I totally would. But I'm guessing it looks probably like a sea monkey right now, and we should let it get a little cuter." At another point, talking about her absent mother, Juno says, "Oh, and she inexplicably mails me a cactus every Valentine's Day. And I'm like, 'Thanks a heap, coyote ugly. This cactus-gram stings even worse than your abandonment.' " As funny as they are, the creatively quirky one-liners often go a bit too far, detracting from both the gravity of Juno's situation and the film's believability.

academic literacies   rhetorical situations   genres   processes   strategies   research MLA / APA   media / design   readings   handbook

Ellen Page as Juno.

But although the situations and dialogue are unrealistic, the emotional heart of the movie is believable—and moving. Despite the movie's lack of realism in portraying her pregnancy, Juno's vulnerability transforms her character and situation into something much more believable. Juno mentions at various times that her classmates stare at her stomach and talk about her behind her back, but initially she seems unconcerned with the negative attention. This façade falls apart, however, when Juno accuses Bleeker, the baby's father, of being ashamed of the fact that he and Juno have had sex. The strong front she is putting up drops when she bursts out, "At least you don't have to have the evidence under your sweater." This break in Juno's strength reveals her vulnerability and makes her character relatable and believable.

The juxtaposition of Juno's teenage quirks and the adult situation she's in also reminds us of her youth and vulnerability. As a result of the adult situation Juno finds herself in and her generally stoic demeanor, it's easy to see her as a young adult. But the film fills each scene with visual reminders that Juno is just a kid being forced into situations beyond her maturity level. At a convenience store, Juno buys a pregnancy test along with a licorice rope. She calls Women Now, an abortion clinic, on a phone that looks like a hamburger. And while she is giving birth, she wears long, brightly striped socks. These subtle visual cues help us remember the reality of Juno's position as both physically an adult and emotionally an adolescent.

While the dialogue is too clever to be realistic, in the end it's carried by the movie's heart. Scott Tobias from the entertainment website *The A.V. Club* says it best when he writes that the colorful dialogue is often "too ostentatious for its own good, but the film's sincerity is what ultimately carries it across." In fact, intensely emotional scenes are marked by their *lack* of witty dialogue. For example, when Juno runs into Vanessa at the mall, Vanessa, reluctantly at first, kneels down to talk to the baby through Juno's stomach. Vanessa's diction while talking to the baby is so simple, so expected. She simply starts with, "Hi baby, it's me. It's Vanessa," and then continues, "I can't wait to meet you." This simple, everyday statement stands out in comparison to the rest of the well-crafted, humorous script. For her part, Juno simply stares admiringly at Vanessa. She doesn't have to say anything to transform the scene into a powerful one. Another scene in which the dialogue stops being clever is the one in which Juno and Bleeker lie side by side in a hospital bed after Juno has given birth, Juno in tears and Bleeker lost in thought. They don't need to say anything for us to feel their pain at the realization that although the pregnancy is over, it will never truly be in the past. The absence of dialogue in scenes such as these actually contributes to their power. We finally see more than stoicism and sarcasm from Juno: we see caring and fear, which are feelings most would expect of a pregnant teen.

There has been much concern among critics that as a pregnant teenager, Juno doesn't present a good role model for teen girls. Worrying that teens may look up to Juno so much that being pregnant becomes "cool," Dana Stevens writes in *Slate*, "Let's hope that the teenage girls of America don't cast their condoms to the wind in hopes of becoming as cool as 16-year-old Juno MacGuff." But it is not Juno's pregnancy that makes her cool: it is her ability to overcome the difficult obstacles thrown at her, and that strength does make her a good role model. Another critic, Lisa Schwarzbaum from *Entertainment Weekly*, feels that the movie might have been more realistic had Juno chosen to go through with an abortion. It's true that Juno may have chosen the more difficult answer to a teen pregnancy, but she is far from alone in her decision. Perhaps Schwarzbaum underestimates teens in thinking that they would not be able to cope with the emotionally difficult situation Juno chooses. Again, in her strength, Juno is a role model for young women.

Although *Juno* is a comedy filled with improbable situations, exaggerations, and wit, its genuine emotion allows us to connect with and relate to the film. The reality of the characters' emotions in controversial and serious situations allows *Juno* to transcend its own genre. It reaches depths of emotion that are unusual for teenage comedies, proving that *Juno* is not just another teen movie.

Works Cited

Juno. Written by Diablo Cody, directed by Jason Reitman, performance by Ellen Page, Michael Cera, Jennifer Garner, and Jason Bateman. Fox Searchlight, 2007.

Schwarzbaum, Lisa. Review of *Juno. Entertainment Weekly*, 9 Jan. 2008, www.ew.com/article/2008/01/09/juno. Accessed 14 Apr. 2008.

Stevens, Dana. "Superpregnant: How *Juno* Is *Knocked Up* from the Girl's Point of View." Review of *Juno. Slate*, 5 Dec. 2007, www.slate.com/articles/arts/movies/2007/12/superpregnant.html. Accessed 12 Apr. 2008.

Tobias, Scott. Review of *Juno. The A.V. Club*, 6 Dec. 2007, www.avclub.com/review/juno-3171. Accessed 13 Apr. 2008.

Heinekamp quickly summarizes Juno's plot and then evaluates the film according to clearly stated criteria. She responds to several reviewers' comments, joining the critical conversation about the film, and documents her sources in MLA style.

For four more evaluations, see CHAPTER 63.

Key Features / Evaluations

A concise description of the subject. You should include just enough information to let readers who may not be familiar with your subject understand what it is; the goal is to evaluate, not summarize. Depending on your topic and medium, some of this information may be in visual or audio form. Heinekamp briefly describes *Juno's* main plot points in her first paragraph, only providing what readers need to understand the context of her evaluation.

Clearly defined criteria. You need to determine clear criteria as the basis for your judgment. In reviews or other evaluations written for a broad audience, you can integrate the criteria into the discussion as reasons for your assessment, as Heinekamp does in her evaluation of *Juno*. In more formal evaluations, you may need to announce your criteria explicitly. Heinekamp evaluates the film based on the power of its emotion and the realism of its situations, characters, and dialogue.

A knowledgeable discussion of the subject.   To evaluate something credibly, you need to show that you know it yourself and that you've researched what other authoritative sources say. Heinekamp cites many examples from *Juno*, showing her knowledge of the film. She also cites reviews from three internet sources, showing that she's researched others' views as well.

A balanced and fair assessment.   An evaluation is centered on a judgment. Heinekamp concedes that *Juno*'s situations and dialogue are unrealistic, but she says it nevertheless "reaches depths of emotion that are unusual for teenage comedies." It is important that any judgment be balanced and fair. Seldom is something all good or all bad. A fair evaluation need not be all positive or all negative; it may acknowledge both strengths and weaknesses. For example, a movie's soundtrack may be wonderful while the plot is not. Heinekamp criticizes *Juno*'s too-witty dialogue and unrealistic situations, even as she appreciates its heart.

Well-supported reasons.   You need to argue for your judgment, providing reasons and evidence that might include visual and audio as well as verbal material. Heinekamp gives several reasons for her positive assessment of *Juno*—the believability of its characters, the intensely emotional scenes, the strength of the main character as a role model—and she supports these reasons with many quotations and examples from the film.

A BRIEF GUIDE TO WRITING EVALUATIONS

Choosing Something to Evaluate

You can more effectively evaluate a limited subject than a broad one: review certain dishes at a local restaurant rather than the entire menu; review one film or episode rather than all the films by Alfred Hitchcock

academic literacies | rhetorical situations | genres | processes | strategies | research MLA / APA | media / design | readings | handbook

or all sixty-two *Breaking Bad* episodes. The more specific and focused your subject, the better you can write about it.

Considering the Rhetorical Situation

PURPOSE   Are you writing to affect your audience's opinion of a subject? to help others decide what to see, do, or buy? to demonstrate your expertise in a field?

55–56

AUDIENCE   To whom are you writing? What will your audience already know about the subject? What will they expect to learn from your evaluation of it? Are they likely to agree with you or not?

57–60

STANCE   What is your attitude toward the subject, and how will you show that you have evaluated it fairly and appropriately? Think about the tone you want to use: should it be reasonable? passionate? critical?

64–67

MEDIA / DESIGN   How will you deliver your evaluation? In print? Electronically? As a speech? Can you show images or audio or video clips? If you're submitting your text for publication, are there any format requirements?

68–70

Generating Ideas and Text

Explore what you already know. **FREEWRITE** to answer the following questions: What do you know about this subject or subjects like it? What are your initial or gut feelings, and why do you feel as you do? How does this subject reflect or affect your basic values or beliefs? How have others evaluated subjects like this?

289–90

Identify criteria.   Make a list of criteria you think should be used to evaluate your subject. Think about which criteria will likely be important to your **AUDIENCE**. You might find **CUBING** and **QUESTIONING** to be useful processes for thinking about your criteria.

57–60
292–93

Evaluate your subject.　Study your subject closely to determine to what extent it meets each of your criteria. You may want to list your criteria and take notes related to each one, or you may develop a rating scale for each criterion to help stay focused on it. Come up with a tentative judgment.

380–87

Compare your subject with others.　Often, evaluating something involves **COMPARING AND CONTRASTING** it with similar things. We judge movies in comparison with the other movies we've seen and french fries with the other fries we've tasted. Sometimes those comparisons can be made informally. For other evaluations, you may have to do research—to try on several pairs of jeans before buying any, for example—to see how your subject compares.

345–47

State your judgment as a tentative thesis statement.　Your **THESIS STATEMENT** should be one that addresses both pros and cons. "*Hawaii Five-O* is fun to watch despite its stilted dialogue." "Of the five sport-utility vehicles tested, the Toyota 4Runner emerged as the best in comfort, power, and durability, though not in styling or cargo capacity." Both of these examples offer a judgment but qualify it according to the writer's criteria.

Anticipate other opinions.　I think Will Ferrell is a comic genius whose movies are first-rate. You think Will Ferrell is a terrible actor who makes awful movies. How can I write a review of his latest film that you will at least consider? One way is by **ACKNOWLEDGING** other opinions—and **REFUTING** those opinions as best I can. I may not persuade you to see Ferrell's next film, but I can at least demonstrate that by certain criteria he should be appreciated. You may need to **RESEARCH** how others have evaluated your subject.

368
369
433

Identify and support your reasons.　Write out all the **REASONS** you can think of that will convince your audience to accept your judgment. Review your list to identify the most convincing or important reasons. Then review how well your subject meets your criteria and decide how best to **SUPPORT** your reasons: through examples, authoritative opinions, statistics, visual or audio evidence, or something else.

358–59

359–67

academic literacies　　rhetorical situations　　genres　　processes　　strategies　　research MLA / APA　　media / design　　readings　　handbook

Ways of Organizing an Evaluation

Evaluations are usually organized in one of two ways. One way is to introduce what's being evaluated, followed by your judgment, discussing your criteria along the way. This is a useful strategy if your audience may not be familiar with your subject.

[Start with your subject]

Describe what you're evaluating. → State your judgment. → Provide reasons and evidence, discussing criteria as you apply them. → Acknowledge objections or other opinions. → Restate your overall judgment.

You might also start by identifying your criteria and then follow with a discussion of how well your subject meets those criteria. This strategy foregrounds the process by which you reached your conclusions.

[Start with your criteria]

Identify criteria for evaluation. → Describe what you're evaluating. → Evaluate it against each of your criteria, one at a time, adding potential objections or other opinions in relation to each criterion. → State your overall judgment.

IF YOU NEED MORE HELP

See Chapter 28 for guidelines on **DRAFTING**, Chapter 29 on **ASSESSING YOUR OWN WRITING**, Chapter 30 on **GETTING RESPONSE AND REVISING**, and Chapter 31 on **EDITING AND PROOFREADING**. See Chapter 32 if you are required to submit your report in a writing **PORTFOLIO**.

298–300
301–5
306–12
313–17
318–28

17 Literary Analyses

Literary analyses are essays that examine literary texts closely to understand their messages, interpret their meanings, appreciate their techniques, or understand their historical or social contexts. Such texts traditionally include novels, short stories, poems, and plays but may also include films, TV shows, videogames, music, and comics. You might read *Macbeth* and notice that Shakespeare's play contains a pattern of images of blood. You could explore the distinctive point of view in Ambrose Bierce's story "An Occurrence at Owl Creek Bridge." Or you could point out the differences between Stephen King's *The Shining* and Stanley Kubrick's screenplay based on that novel. In all these cases, you use specific analytical techniques to go below the surface of the work to deepen your understanding of how it works and what it means.

You may be assigned to analyze works of literature in courses in *English, film, drama,* and many other subjects. Here is a sonnet by the nineteenth-century English Romantic poet Percy Bysshe Shelley, followed by a student's analysis of it written for a literature course at Wright State University.

PERCY BYSSHE SHELLEY

Sonnet: "Lift not the painted veil which those who live"

Lift not the painted veil which those who live
Call Life: though unreal shapes be pictured there,
And it but mimic all we would believe
With colours idly spread, —behind, lurk Fear
And Hope, twin Destinies; who ever weave   5

academic literacies · rhetorical situations · genres · processes · strategies · research MLA / APA · media / design · readings · handbook

Their shadows, o'er the chasm, sightless and drear.
I knew one who had lifted it —he sought,
For his lost heart was tender, things to love,
But found them not, alas! nor was there aught
The world contains, the which he could approve. 10
Through the unheeding many he did move,
A splendour among shadows, a bright blot
Upon this gloomy scene, a Spirit that strove
For truth, and like the Preacher found it not.

STEPHANIE HUFF

Metaphor and Society in Shelley's "Sonnet"

In his sonnet "Lift not the painted veil which those who live," Percy Bysshe Shelley introduces us to a bleak world that exists behind veils and shadows. We see that although fear and hope both exist, truth is dishearteningly absent. This absence of truth is exactly what Shelley chooses to address as he uses metaphors of grim distortion and radiant incandescence to expose the counterfeit nature of our world.

The speaker of Shelley's poem presents bold assertions about the nature of our society. In the opening lines of the poem, he warns the reader, "Lift not the painted veil which those who live / Call Life" (lines 1–2). Here, the "painted veil" serves as a grim metaphor for life. More specifically, the speaker equates the veil with what people like to *call* life. In this sense, the speaker asserts that what we believe to be pure reality is actually nothing more than a covering that masks what really lies beneath. Truth is covered by a veil of falsehood and is made opaque with the paint of people's lies.

This painted veil does not completely obstruct our view but rather distorts what we can see. All that can be viewed through it are "unreal shapes" (2) that metaphorically represent the people that make up this counterfeit society. These shapes are not to be taken for truth. They are unreal, twisted, deformed figures of humanity, people full of falsities and misrepresentations.

Most people, however, do not realize that the shapes and images seen through the veil are distorted because all they know of life is the veil —this life we see as reality only "mimic[s] all we would believe" (3), using "colours idly spread" (4) to create pictures that bear little resemblance to that which they claim to portray. All pure truths are covered up and painted over until they are mere mockeries. The lies that cloak the truth are not even carefully constructed, but are created idly, with little attention to detail. The paint is not applied carefully but merely spread across the top. This idea of spreading brings to mind images of paint slopped on so heavily that the truth beneath becomes nearly impossible to find. Even the metaphor of color suggests only superficial beauty —"idly spread" (4) —rather than any sort of pure beauty that could penetrate the surface of appearances.

What really lies behind this facade are fear and hope, both of which "weave / Their shadows, o'er the chasm, sightless and drear" (5–6). These two realities are never truly seen or experienced, though. They exist only as shadows. Just as shadows appear only at certain times of day, cast only sham images of what they reflect, and are paid little attention, so too do these emotions of hope and fear appear only as brief, ignored imitations of themselves when they enter the artificiality of this chasmlike world. Peering into a chasm, one cannot hope to make out what lies at the bottom. At best one could perhaps make out shadows and even that cannot be done with any certainty as to true appearance. The world is so large, so caught up in itself and its counterfeit ways, that it can no longer see even the simple truths of hope and fear. Individuals and civilizations have become sightless, dreary, and as enormously empty as a chasm.

This chasm does not include *all* people, however, as we are introduced to one individual, in line 7, who is trying to bring to light whatever truth may yet remain. This one person, who defies the rest of the world, is portrayed with metaphors of light, clearly standing out among the dark representations of the rest of mankind. He is first presented to us as possessing a "lost heart" (8) and seeking things to love. It is important that the first metaphor applied to him be a heart because this is the organ with which we associate love, passion, and purity. We associate it with brightness of the soul, making it the most radiant spot of the body. He is then described as a "splendour among shadows" (12), his purity and truth brilliantly shining through the darkness of the majority's falsehood. Finally, he is equated with "a bright blot / Upon this gloomy scene" (12–13), his own bright blaze of authenticity burning in stark contrast to the murky phoniness of the rest of the world.

These metaphors of light are few, however, in comparison to those of grim distortion. So, too, are this one individual's radiance and zeal too little to alter the warped darkness they temporarily pierce. This one person, though bright, is not bright enough to light up the rest of civilization and create real change. The light simply confirms the dark falsity that comprises the rest of the world. Shelley gives us one flame of hope, only to reveal to us what little chance it has under the suffocating veil. Both the metaphors of grim distortion and those of radiant incandescence work together in this poem to highlight the world's counterfeit nature.

Huff focuses her analysis on patterns in Shelley's imagery. In addition, she pays careful attention to individual words and to how, as the poem unfolds, they create a certain meaning. That meaning is her interpretation.

For two more literary analyses, see CHAPTER 64.

Key Features / Literary Analyses

An arguable thesis. A literary analysis is a form of argument; you are arguing that your analysis of a literary work is valid. Your thesis, then, should be arguable, as Huff's is: "[Shelley] uses metaphors of grim distortion and radiant incandescence to expose the counterfeit nature of our world." A mere summary —"Shelley writes about a person who sees reality and seeks love but never finds it" —would not be arguable and therefore is not a good thesis.

Careful attention to the language of the text. The key to analyzing a text is looking carefully at the language, which is the foundation of its meaning. Specific words, images, metaphors—these are where analysis begins. You may also bring in contextual information, such as cultural, historical, or biographical facts, or you may refer to similar texts. But the words, phrases, and sentences that make up the text you are analyzing are your primary source when dealing with texts. That's what literature teachers mean by "close reading": reading with the assumption that every word of a text is meaningful.

Attention to patterns or themes. Literary analyses are usually built on evidence of meaningful patterns or themes within a text or among several texts. These patterns and themes reveal meaning. In Shelley's poem, images of light and shadow and artifice and reality create patterns of meaning, while the poem's many half rhymes (*live / believe, love / approve*) create patterns of sound that may contribute to the overall meaning.

A clear interpretation.   A literary analysis demonstrates the plausibility of its thesis by using evidence from the text and, sometimes, relevant contextual evidence to explain how the language and patterns found there support a particular interpretation. When you write a literary analysis, you show readers one way the text may be read and understood; that is your interpretation.

MLA style.   Literary analyses usually follow MLA style. Even though Huff's essay has no works-cited list, it refers to line numbers using MLA style.

A BRIEF GUIDE TO WRITING LITERARY ANALYSES

Considering the Rhetorical Situation

55–56

PURPOSE   What do you need to do? Show that you have examined the text carefully? Offer your own interpretation? Demonstrate a particular analytical technique? Or some combination? If you're responding to an assignment, does it specify what you need to do?

57–60

AUDIENCE   What do you need to do to convince your readers that your interpretation is plausible and based on sound analysis? Can you assume that readers are already familiar with the text you are analyzing, or do you need to tell them about it?

64–67

STANCE   How can you see your subject through interested, curious eyes—and then step back in order to see what your observations might *mean*?

MEDIA/DESIGN   Will your analysis focus on an essentially verbal text or one that has significant visual content, such as a graphic novel? Will you need to show visual elements in your analysis? Will it be delivered in a print, spoken, or electronic medium? Are you required to follow MLA or some other style?

68–70

Generating Ideas and Text

Look at your assignment.   Does it specify a particular kind of analysis? Does it ask you to consider a particular theme? To use any specific critical approaches? Look for any terms that tell you what to do, words like *analyze*, *compare*, *interpret*, and so on.

Study the text with a critical eye.   When we read a literary work, we often come away with a reaction to it: we like it, we hate it, it made us cry or laugh, it perplexed us. That may be a good starting point for a literary analysis, but to write about literature you need to go beyond initial reactions, to think about **HOW THE TEXT WORKS**: What does it *say*, and what does it *do*? What elements make up this text? How do those elements work together or fail to work together? Does this text lead you to think or feel a certain way? How does it fit into a particular context (of history, culture, technology, genre, and so on)?

✳ 20–22

Choose a method for analyzing the text.   There are various ways to analyze your subject. Three common focuses are on the text itself, on your own experience reading it, and on other cultural, historical, or literary contexts.

- *The text itself.* Trace the development and expression of themes, characters, and language through the work. How do they help to create the overall meaning, tone, or effect for which you're arguing? To do this, you might look at the text as a whole, something you can understand from all angles at once. You could also pick out parts from the beginning, middle, and end as needed to make your case, **DEFINING**

◆ 388–98

399–407
419–27

key terms, **DESCRIBING** characters and settings, and **NARRATING** key scenes. Huff's essay about the Shelley sonnet offers a text-based analysis that looks at patterns of images in the poem. You might also examine the same theme in several different works.

- *Your own response as a reader.* Explore the way the text affects you or develops meanings as you read through it from beginning to end. By doing such a close reading, you're slowing down the process to notice how one element of the text leads you to expect something, confirming earlier suspicions or surprises. You build your analysis on your experience of reading the text—as if you were pretending to drive somewhere for the first time, though in reality you know the way intimately. By closely examining the language of the text as you experience it, you explore how it leads you to a set of responses, both intellectual and emotional. If you were responding in this way to the Shelley poem, you might discuss how its first lines suggest that while life is an illusion, a veil, one might pull it aside and glimpse reality, however "drear."

427

- *Context.* Analyze the text as part of some **LARGER CONTEXT**—as part of a certain time or place in history or as an expression of a certain culture (how does this text relate to the time and place of its creation?), as one of many other texts like it, a representative of a genre (how is this text like or unlike others of its kind? how does it use, play with, or flout the conventions of the genre?). A context-based approach to the Shelley poem might look at Shelley's own philosophical and religious views and how they may have influenced the poem's characterization of the world we experience as illusory, a "veil."

Read the work more than once.   Reading literature, watching films, or listening to speeches is like driving to a new destination: the first time you go, you need to concentrate on getting there; on subsequent trips, you can see other aspects—the scenery, the curve of the road, other possible routes—that you couldn't pay attention to earlier. When you experience a piece of literature for the first time, you usually focus on the story, the plot, the overall meaning. By experiencing it repeatedly, you can see how its effects are achieved, what the pieces are and how they fit together, where different patterns emerge, how the author crafted the work.

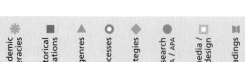

academic literacies · rhetorical situations · genres · processes · strategies · research MLA / APA · media / design · readings · handbook

To analyze a literary work, then, plan to read it more than once, with the assumption that every part of the text is there for a reason. Focus on details, even on a single detail that shows up more than once: Why is it there? What can it mean? How does it affect our experience of reading or studying the text? Also, look for anomalies, details that *don't* fit the patterns: Why are they part of the text? What can they mean? How do they affect the experience of the text? See the **READING IN ACADEMIC CONTEXTS** chapter for several different methods for reading a text.

10–32

Compose a strong thesis.   The **THESIS** of a literary analysis should be specific, limited, and open to potential disagreement. In addition, it should be analytical, not evaluative: avoid thesis statements that make overall judgments, such as a reviewer might do: "Virginia Woolf's *The Waves* is a failed experiment in narrative" or "No one has equaled the achievement of *The Lego Movie*." Rather, offer a way of seeing the text: "The choice presented in Robert Frost's 'The Road Not Taken' ultimately makes no difference"; "The plot of *The Lego Movie* reflects contemporary American media culture."

345–47

Read the text carefully.   When you analyze a text, you need to find specific, brief passages that support your interpretation. Then you should interpret those passages in terms of their language, their context, or your reaction to them as a reader. To find such passages, you must read the text closely, questioning it as you go, asking, for example:

- What language provides evidence to support your thesis?
- What does each word (phrase, passage) mean exactly?
- Why does the writer choose *this* language, *these* words? What are the implications or connotations of the language? If the language is dense or difficult, why might the writer have written it that way?
- What images or metaphors are used? What is their effect on the meaning?
- What patterns of language, imagery, or plot do you see? If something is repeated, what significance does the repetition have?
- How does each word, phrase, or passage relate to what precedes and follows it?

- How does the experience of reading the text affect its meaning?

10–32 ✳

- What words, phrases, or passages connect to a larger **CONTEXT**? What language demonstrates that this work reflects or is affected by that context?
- How do these various elements of language, image, and pattern support your interpretation?

Your analysis should focus on analyzing and interpreting your subject, not simply summarizing or paraphrasing it. Many literary analyses

380–87 ◆

also use the strategy of **COMPARING** two or more works.

Find evidence to support your interpretation.   The parts of the text you examine in your close reading become the evidence you use to support your interpretation. Some think that we're all entitled to our own opinions about literature. And indeed we are. But when writing a literary analysis, we're entitled only to our own *well-supported* and *well-argued* opinions.

355–73 ◆

When you analyze a text, you must treat it like any other **ARGUMENT**: you need to discuss how the text creates an effect or expresses a theme,

359–67 ◆

and then you have to show **EVIDENCE** from the text—significant plot or structural elements; important characters; patterns of language, imagery, or action—to back up your argument.

Pay attention to matters of style.   Literary analyses have certain conventions for using pronouns and verbs.

- In informal papers, it's okay to use the first person: "I believe Frost's narrator has little basis for claiming that one road is 'less traveled.'" In more formal essays, make assertions directly; claim authority to make statements about the text: "Frost's narrator has no basis for claiming that one road is 'less traveled.'"

HB-12–14 ◹

- Discuss textual features in the **PRESENT TENSE** even if quotations from the text are in another tense: "When Nick finds Gatsby's body floating in the pool, he says very little about it: 'the laden mattress moved irregularly down the pool.'" Describe the historical context of

HB-12–14 ◹

the setting in the **PAST TENSE**: "In the 1920s, such estates as Gatsby's were rare."

Cite and document sources appropriately. Use **MLA** citation and documentation style unless told otherwise. Format **QUOTATIONS** properly, and use **SIGNAL PHRASES** to introduce quoted material.

● MLA 500–548
480–83
487–90

Think about format and design. Brief essays do not require **HEADINGS**; text divisions are usually marked by **TRANSITIONS** between paragraphs. In longer papers, though, headings can be helpful.

▢ 604–5
◆ 349

Organizing a Literary Analysis

[Of a single text]

[Comparing two texts]

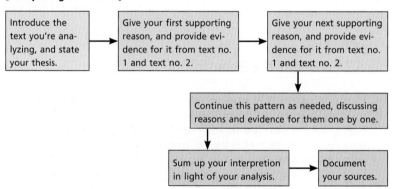

IF YOU NEED MORE HELP

See Chapter 28 for guidelines on **DRAFTING**, Chapter 29 on **ASSESSING YOUR OWN WRITING**, Chapter 30 on **GETTING RESPONSE AND REVISING**, and Chapter 31 on **EDITING AND PROOFREADING**. See Chapter 32 if you are required to submit your analysis in a writing **PORTFOLIO**.

○ 298–300
301–5
306–12
313–17
318–28

18 Memoirs

We write memoirs to explore our past—about shopping for a party dress with Grandma, or driving a car for the first time, or breaking up with our first love. Memoirs focus on events and people and places that are important to us. We usually have two goals when we write a memoir: to capture an important moment and to convey something about its significance for us. You may be asked to write memoirs or personal reflections that include memoirs in *psychology*, *education*, and *English* courses. The following example is from Pulitzer Prize–winning journalist Rick Bragg's autobiography, *All Over but the Shoutin'*. Bragg grew up in Alabama, and in this memoir he recalls when, as a teenager, he paid a final visit to his dying father.

RICK BRAGG

All Over but the Shoutin'

He was living in a little house in Jacksonville, Alabama, a college and mill town that was the closest urban center—with its stoplights and a high school and two supermarkets—to the country roads we roamed in our raggedy cars. He lived in the mill village, in one of those houses the mills subsidized for their workers, back when companies still did things like that. It was not much of a place, but better than anything we had ever lived in as a family. I knocked and a voice like an old woman's, punctuated with a cough that sounded like it came from deep in the guts, told me to come on in, it ain't locked.

It was dark inside, but light enough to see what looked like a bundle of quilts on the corner of a sofa. Deep inside them was a ghost of a man, his hair and beard long and going dirty gray, his face pale and cut with deep grooves. I knew I was in the right house because my daddy's only

academic literacies · rhetorical situations · genres · processes · strategies · research MLA / APA · media / design · readings · handbook

real possessions, a velvet-covered board pinned with medals, sat inside a glass cabinet on a table. But this couldn't be him.

He coughed again, spit into a can and struggled to his feet, but stopped somewhere short of standing straight up, as if a stoop was all he could manage. "Hey, Cotton Top," he said, and then I knew. My daddy, who was supposed to be a still-young man, looked like the walking dead, not just old but damaged, poisoned, used up, crumpled up and thrown in a corner to die. I thought that the man I would see would be the trim, swaggering, high-toned little rooster of a man who stared back at me from the pages of my mother's photo album, the young soldier clowning around in Korea, the arrow-straight, good-looking boy who posed beside my mother back before the fields and mop handle and the rest of it took her looks. The man I remembered had always dressed nice even when there was no cornmeal left, whose black hair always shone with oil, whose chin, even when it wobbled from the beer, was always angled up, high.

I thought he would greet me with that strong voice that sounded so fine when he laughed and so evil when, slurred by a quart of corn likker, he whirled through the house and cried and shrieked, tormented by things we could not see or even imagine. I thought he would be the man and monster of my childhood. But that man was as dead as a man could be, and this was what remained, like when a snake sheds its skin and leaves a dry and brittle husk of itself hanging in the Johnson grass.

"It's all over but the shoutin' now, ain't it, boy," he said, and when 5 he let the quilt slide from his shoulders I saw how he had wasted away, how the bones seemed to poke out of his clothes, and I could see how it killed his pride to look this way, unclean, and he looked away from me for a moment, ashamed.

He made a halfhearted try to shake my hand but had a coughing fit again that lasted a minute, coughing up his life, his lungs, and after that I did not want to touch him. I stared at the tops of my sneakers, ashamed to look at his face. He had a dark streak in his beard below his lip, and I wondered why, because he had never liked snuff. Now I know it was blood.

I remember much of what he had to say that day. When you don't see someone for eight, nine years, when you see that person's life red on their lips and know that you will never see them beyond this day, you listen close, even if what you want most of all is to run away.

"Your momma, she alright?" he said.

I said I reckon so.

"The other boys? They alright?"   10

I said I reckon so.

Then he was quiet for a minute, as if trying to find the words to a question to which he did not really want an answer.

"They ain't never come to see me. How come?"

I remember thinking, fool, why do you think? But I just choked down my words, and in doing so I gave up the only real chance I would ever have to accuse him, to attack him with the facts of his own sorry nature and the price it had cost us all. The opportunity hung perfectly still in the air in front of my face and fists, and I held my temper and let it float on by. I could have no more challenged him, berated him, hurt him, than I could have kicked some three-legged dog. Life had kicked his ass pretty good.

"How come?"   15

I just shrugged.

For the next few hours—unless I was mistaken, having never had one before—he tried to be my father. Between coughing and long pauses when he fought for air to generate his words, he asked me if I liked school, if I had ever gotten any better at math, the one thing that just flat evaded me. He asked me if I ever got even with the boy who blacked my eye ten years ago, and nodded his head, approvingly, as I described how I followed him into the boys' bathroom and knocked his dick string up to his watch pocket, and would have dunked his head in the urinal if the aging principal, Mr. Hand, had not had to pee and caught me dragging him across the concrete floor.

He asked me about basketball and baseball, said he had heard I had a good game against Cedar Springs, and I said pretty good, but it was two years ago, anyway. He asked if I had a girlfriend and I said, "One," and he said, "Just one?" For the slimmest of seconds he almost grinned and the young, swaggering man peeked through, but disappeared again in the disease that cloaked him. He talked and talked and never said a word, at least not the words I wanted.

He never said he was sorry.

He never said he wished things had turned out different.   20

He never acted like he did anything wrong.

Part of it, I know, was culture. Men did not talk about their feelings in his hard world. I did not expect, even for a second, that he would bare his soul. All I wanted was a simple acknowledgment that he was wrong, or at least too drunk to notice that he left his pretty wife and sons alone again and again, with no food, no money, no way to get any, short of begging, because when she tried to find work he yelled, screamed, refused. No, I didn't expect much.

After a while he motioned for me to follow him into a back room where he had my present, and I planned to take it and run. He handed me a long, thin box, and inside was a brand-new, well-oiled Remington .22 rifle. He said he had bought it some time back, just kept forgetting to give it to me. It was a fine gun, and for a moment we were just like anybody else in the culture of that place, where a father's gift of a gun to his son is a rite. He said, with absolute seriousness, not to shoot my brothers.

I thanked him and made to leave, but he stopped me with a hand on my arm and said wait, that ain't all, that he had some other things for me. He motioned to three big cardboard egg cartons stacked against one wall.

Inside was the only treasure I truly have ever known.   25

I had grown up in a house in which there were only two books, the King James Bible and the spring seed catalog. But here, in these boxes, were dozens of hardback copies of everything from Mark Twain to Sir Arthur Conan Doyle. There was a water-damaged Faulkner, and the nearly complete set of Edgar Rice Burroughs's *Tarzan*. There was poetry and trash, Zane Grey's *Riders of the Purple Sage,* and a paper-back with two naked women on the cover. There was a tiny, old copy of *Arabian Nights,* threadbare Hardy Boys, and one Hemingway. He had bought most of them at a yard sale, by the box or pound, and some at a flea market. He did not even know what he was giving me, did not recognize most of the writers. "Your momma said you still liked to read," he said.

There was Shakespeare. My father did not know who he was, exactly, but he had heard the name. He wanted them because they were pretty, because they were wrapped in fake leather, because they looked like rich folks' books. I do not love Shakespeare, but I still have those books. I would not trade them for a gold monkey.

"They's maybe some dirty books in there, by mistake, but I know you ain't interested in them, so just throw 'em away," he said. "Or at

least, throw 'em away before your momma sees 'em." And then I swear
to God he winked.

I guess my heart should have broken then, and maybe it did, a
little. I guess I should have done something, anything, besides mumble "Thank you, Daddy." I guess that would have been fine, would
not have betrayed in some way my mother, my brothers, myself. But
I just stood there, trapped somewhere between my long-standing,
comfortable hatred, and what might have been forgiveness. I am
trapped there still.

For four more memoirs, see CHAPTER 65.

Bragg's memoir illustrates all the features that make a memoir good: how the
son and father react to each other creates the kind of suspense that keeps us
reading; vivid details and rich dialogue bring the scene to life. His later reflec-
tions make the significance of that final meeting very clear.

Key Features / Memoirs

A good story.   Your memoir should be interesting, to yourself and others.
It need not be about a world-shaking event, but your topic—and how you
write about it—should interest your readers. At the center of most good
stories stands a conflict or question to be resolved. The most compelling
memoirs feature some sort of situation or problem that needs resolution.
That need for resolution is another name for suspense. It's what makes
us want to keep reading.

Vivid details.   Details bring a memoir to life by giving readers mental
images of the sights, sounds, smells, tastes, and textures of the world in
which your story takes place. The goal is to show as well as tell, to take
readers there. When Bragg describes a "voice like an old woman's, punctuated with a cough that sounded like it came from deep in the guts," we can
hear his dying father ourselves. A memoir is more than simply a report of
what happened; it uses vivid details and dialogue to bring the events of
the past to life, much as good fiction brings to life events that the writer
makes up or embellishes. Depending on your topic and medium, you may
want to provide some of the details in audio or visual form.

academic literacies   rhetorical situations   genres   processes   strategies   research MLA / APA   media / design   readings   handbook

Clear significance. Memories of the past are filtered through our view from the present: we pick out some moments in our lives as significant, some as more important or vivid than others. Over time, our interpretations change, and our memories themselves change.

A good memoir conveys something about the significance of its subject. As a writer, you need to reveal something about what the incident means to you. You don't, however, want to simply announce the significance as if you're tacking on the moral of the story. Bragg tells us that he's "trapped between [his] long-standing, comfortable hatred, and what might have been forgiveness," but he doesn't come right out and say that's why the incident is so important to him.

A BRIEF GUIDE TO WRITING MEMOIRS

Choosing an Event to Write About

LIST several events or incidents from your past that you consider significant in some way. They do not have to be earthshaking; indeed, they may involve a quiet moment that only you see as important—a brief encounter with a remarkable person, a visit to a special place, a memorable achievement (or failure), something that makes you laugh whenever you think about it. Writing about events that happened at least a few years ago is often easier than writing about recent events because you can more easily step back and see those events with a clear perspective. To choose the event that you will write about, consider how well you can recall what happened, how interesting it will be to readers, and whether you want to share it with an audience.

○ 290–91

Considering the Rhetorical Situation

PURPOSE   What is the importance of the memory you are trying to convey? How will this story help you understand yourself and your readers understand you, as you were then and as you are now?

■ 55–56

57–60 **AUDIENCE**   Who are your readers? Why will they care about your memoir? What do you want them to think of you after reading it? How can you help them understand your experience?

64–67 **STANCE**   What impression do you want to give, and how can your words contribute to that impression? What tone do you want to project? Sincere? Serious? Humorous? Detached? Self-critical?

68–70 **MEDIA / DESIGN**   Will your memoir be a print document? A speech? Will it be posted on a website? Can you include photographs, audio or video clips, or other visual texts?

Generating Ideas and Text

Think about what happened.   Take a few minutes to write out an account of the incident: **WHAT** happened, **WHERE** it took place, **WHO** else was involved, what was said, how you feel about it, and so on. Can you identify any tension or conflict that will make for a compelling story? If not, you might want to rethink your topic.

292–93

Consider its significance.   Why do you still remember this event? What effect has it had on your life? What makes you want to tell someone else about it? Does it say anything about you? What about it might interest someone else? If you have trouble answering these questions, you should probably find another topic. But in general, once you have defined the significance of the incident, you can be sure you have a story to tell—and a reason for telling it.

Think about the details.   The best memoirs connect with readers by giving them a sense of what it was like to be there, leading them to experience in words and images what the writer experienced in life. Spend some time **DESCRIBING** the incident, writing what you see, hear, smell, touch, and taste when you envision it. Do you have any photos or memorabilia or

399–407

other **VISUAL** materials you might include in your memoir? Try writing out **DIALOGUE**, things that were said (or, if you can't recall exactly, things that might have been said). Look at what you come up with—is there detail enough to bring the scene to life? Anything that might be called vivid? If you don't have enough detail, you might reconsider whether you recall enough about the incident to write about it. If you have trouble coming up with plenty of detail, try **FREEWRITING**, **LISTING**, or **LOOPING**.

607–15
408–13
289–91

Ways of Organizing Memoirs

[Tell about the event from beginning to end]

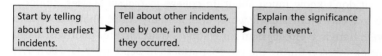

[Start at the end and tell how the event came about]

IF YOU NEED MORE HELP

See Chapter 28 for guidelines on **DRAFTING**, Chapter 29 on **ASSESSING YOUR OWN WRITING**, Chapter 30 on **GETTING RESPONSE AND REVISING**, and Chapter 31 on **EDITING AND PROOFREADING**. See Chapter 32 if you are required to submit your memoir in a writing **PORTFOLIO**.

298–300
301–5
306–12
313–17
318–28

19 Profiles

Profiles are written portraits—of people, places, events, or other things. We find profiles of celebrities, travel destinations, and offbeat festivals in magazines and newspapers, on radio and TV. A profile presents a subject in an entertaining way that conveys its significance, showing us something or someone that we may not have known existed or that we see every day but don't know much about. In college *journalism* classes, students learn to create profiles using words and, in many cases, photos and video as well. Here is a profile of an Air National Guard fighter pilot who faced a suicide mission during the terrorist attacks of September 11, 2001. The writer, Steve Hendrix, writes for the *Washington Post*, where this essay originally appeared.

STEVE HENDRIX

F-16 Pilot Was Ready to Give Her Life on Sept. 11

Late in the morning of the Tuesday that changed everything, Lt. Heather "Lucky" Penney was on a runway at Andrews Air Force Base and ready to fly. She had her hand on the throttle of an F-16 and she had her orders: Bring down United Airlines Flight 93. The day's fourth hijacked airliner seemed to be hurtling toward Washington. Penney, one of the first two combat pilots in the air that morning, was told to stop it.

The one thing she didn't have as she roared into the crystalline sky was live ammunition. Or missiles. Or anything at all to throw at a hostile aircraft.

Except her own plane. So that was the plan.

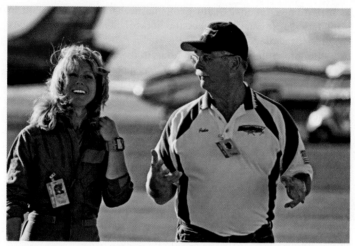

Penney was to stop Flight 93 — by crashing her own plane into it.

Because the surprise attacks were unfolding, in that innocent age, faster than they could arm war planes, Penney and her commanding officer went up to fly their jets straight into a Boeing 757.

"We wouldn't be shooting it down. We'd be ramming the aircraft," 5 Penney recalls of her charge that day. "I would essentially be a kamikaze pilot."

For years, Penney, one of the first generation of female combat pilots in the country, gave no interviews about her experiences on September 11 (which included, eventually, escorting Air Force One back into Washington's suddenly highly restricted airspace).

But 10 years later, she is reflecting on one of the lesser-told tales of that endlessly examined morning: how the first counterpunch the U.S. military prepared to throw at the attackers was effectively a suicide mission.

"We had to protect the airspace any way we could," she said last week in her office at Lockheed Martin, where she is a director in the F-35 program.

Penney, now a major but still a petite blonde with a Colgate grin, is no longer a combat flier. She flew two tours in Iraq and she serves as a part-time National Guard pilot, mostly hauling VIPs around in a military Gulfstream. She takes the stick of her own vintage 1941 Taylorcraft tail-dragger whenever she can.

But none of her thousands of hours in the air quite compare with   10
the urgent rush of launching on what was supposed to be a one-way flight to a midair collision.

First of her kind

She was a rookie in the autumn of 2001, the first female F-16 pilot they'd ever had at the 121st Fighter Squadron of the D.C. Air National Guard. She had grown up smelling jet fuel. Her father flew jets in Vietnam and still races them. Penney got her pilot's license when she was a literature major at Purdue. She planned to be a teacher. But during a graduate program in American studies, Congress opened up combat aviation to women and Penney was nearly first in line.

"I signed up immediately," she says. "I wanted to be a fighter pilot like my dad."

On that Tuesday, they had just finished two weeks of air combat training in Nevada. They were sitting around a briefing table when someone looked in to say a plane had hit the World Trade Center in New York. When it happened once, they assumed it was some yahoo in a Cessna. When it happened again, they knew it was war.

But the surprise was complete. In the monumental confusion of those first hours, it was impossible to get clear orders. Nothing was ready. The jets were still equipped with dummy bullets from the training mission.

As remarkable as it seems now, there were no armed aircraft stand-   15
ing by and no system in place to scramble them over Washington. Before that morning, all eyes were looking outward, still scanning the old Cold War threat paths for planes and missiles coming over the polar ice cap.

"There was no perceived threat at the time, especially one coming from the homeland like that," says Col. George Degnon, vice commander of the 113th Wing at Andrews. "It was a little bit of a helpless feeling, but we did everything humanly possible to get the aircraft armed and in the air. It was amazing to see people react."

Things are different today, Degnon says. At least two "hot-cocked" planes are ready at all times, their pilots never more than yards from the cockpit.

A third plane hit the Pentagon, and almost at once came word that a fourth plane could be on the way, maybe more. The jets would be armed within an hour, but somebody had to fly now, weapons or no weapons.

"Lucky, you're coming with me," barked Col. Marc Sasseville.

They were gearing up in the pre-flight life-support area when 20 Sasseville, struggling into his flight suit, met her eye.

"I'm going to go for the cockpit," Sasseville said.

She replied without hesitating.

"I'll take the tail."

It was a plan. And a pact.

"Let's go!"

Penney had never scrambled a jet before. Normally the pre-flight is a 25 half-hour or so of methodical checks. She automatically started going down the list.

"Lucky, what are you doing? Get your butt up there and let's go!" Sasseville shouted.

She climbed in, rushed to power up the engines, screamed for her ground crew to pull the chocks. The crew chief still had his headphones plugged into the fuselage as she nudged the throttle forward. He ran along pulling safety pins from the jet as it moved forward.

She muttered a fighter pilot's prayer — "God, don't let me [expletive] up" — and followed Sasseville into the sky.

They screamed over the smoldering Pentagon, heading north-west at more than 400 mph, flying low and scanning the clear horizon. Her commander had time to think about the best place to hit the enemy.

"We don't train to bring down airliners," said Sasseville, now sta- 30 tioned at the Pentagon. "If you just hit the engine, it could still glide and you could guide it to a target. My thought was the cockpit or the wing."

He also thought about his ejection seat. Would there be an instant just before impact?

"I was hoping to do both at the same time," he says. "It probably wasn't going to work, but that's what I was hoping."

Penney worried about missing the target if she tried to bail out.

"If you eject and your jet soars through without impact ..." she trails off, the thought of failing more dreadful than the thought of dying.

But she didn't have to die. She didn't have to knock down an air- 35 liner full of kids and salesmen and girlfriends. They did that themselves.

It would be hours before Penney and Sasseville learned that United 93 had already gone down in Pennsylvania, an insurrection by hostages willing to do just what the two Guard pilots had been willing to do: Anything. And everything.

"The real heroes are the passengers on Flight 93 who were willing to sacrifice themselves," Penney says. "I was just an accidental witness to history."

She and Sasseville flew the rest of the day, clearing the airspace, escorting the president, looking down onto a city that would soon be sending them to war.

She's a single mom of two girls now. She still loves to fly. And she still thinks often of that extraordinary ride down the runway a decade ago.

"I genuinely believed that was going to be the last time I took 40 off," she says. "If we did it right, this would be it."

For four more profiles, see CHAPTER 66.

This profile focuses on Lt. Heather "Lucky" Penney's role in responding to the attempted attack on Washington, D.C. The writer engages our interest first by recounting Penney's orders to stop Flight 93 — and then by revealing that Penney would have to do so by flying her fighter plane into the airliner. The rest of the profile shows how she and her commander came to be in that situation and how it played out.

Key Features / Profiles

An interesting subject. The subject may be something unusual, or it may be something ordinary shown in an intriguing way. You might profile an interesting person (like Heather "Lucky" Penney), a place (like the cockpit of an F-16), or an event (like scrambling a fighter plane on a suicide mission).

academic literacies · rhetorical situations · genres · processes · strategies · research MLA / APA · media / design · readings · handbook

Any necessary background. A profile usually includes just enough information to let readers know something about the subject's larger context. Hendrix tells us how Penney became a fighter pilot and that she is still involved in aviation but leaves out other details about her life that don't matter for this profile.

An interesting angle. A good profile captures its subject from a particular angle. Sometimes finding an angle will be fairly easy because your topic — like preparing to fly a plane into a terrorist-controlled airliner — is offbeat enough to be interesting in and of itself. Other topics, though, may require you to find a particular aspect that you can focus on. For example, a profile of a person might focus on the important work the person does or a challenging hobby he or she pursues; it would likely ignore aspects of the person's life that don't relate to that angle.

A firsthand account. Whether you are writing about a person, place, or event, you need to spend time observing and interacting with your subject. With a person, interacting means watching and conversing. Journalists tell us that "following the guy around," getting your subject to do something and talk about it at the same time, yields excellent material for a profile. When one writer met Theodor Geisel (Dr. Seuss) before profiling him, she asked him not only to talk about his characters but also to draw one—resulting in an illustration for her profile. With a place or event, interacting may mean visiting and participating, although sometimes you may gather even more information by playing the role of the silent observer.

Engaging details. You need to include details that bring your subject to life. These may include *specific information* ("The crew chief still had his headphones plugged into the fuselage as she nudged the throttle forward."); *sensory images* ("she roared into the crystalline sky"); *figurative language* ("She had grown up smelling jet fuel."); *dialogue* ("'I'm going to go for the cockpit,' Sasseville said. . . . 'I'll take the tail.'"); and *anecdotes* ("They were sitting around a briefing table when someone looked in to say a plane had hit the World Trade Center in New York"). Choose details that show rather than tell — that let your audience see and hear your subject rather than merely read an abstract description of it. Sometimes you may let them see and hear it literally, by including *photographs* or *video and audio clips*. And be sure all the details create some *dominant impression* of your subject: the impression that we get out of this profile, for example, is of a modest but heroic woman willing to sacrifice her life to protect her country.

A BRIEF GUIDE TO WRITING PROFILES

Choosing a Suitable Subject

A person, a place, an event—whatever you choose, make sure it's something that arouses your curiosity and that you're not too familiar with. Knowing your subject too well can blind you to interesting details. **LIST** five to ten interesting subjects that you can experience firsthand. Obviously, you can't profile a person who won't be interviewed or a place or activity that can't be observed. So before you commit to a topic, make sure you'll be able to carry out firsthand research and not find out too late that the people you need to interview aren't willing or that places you need to visit are off-limits.

290–91 ○

Considering the Rhetorical Situation

55–56 ■

PURPOSE

Why are you writing the profile? What angle will best achieve your purpose? How can you inform *and engage* your audience?

57–60 ■

AUDIENCE

Who is your audience? How familiar are they with your subject? What expectations of your profile might they have? What background information or definitions do you need to provide? How interested will they be—and how can you get their interest?

STANCE What view of your subject do you expect to present? Sympathetic? Critical? Sarcastic? Will you strive for a carefully balanced perspective?

64–67

MEDIA / DESIGN Will your profile be a print document? electronic? an oral presentation? Can (and should) you include images or any other visuals? Will it be recorded as an audio file or multimodal text?

68–70

Generating Ideas and Text

Explore what you already know about your subject. Why do you find this subject interesting? What do you know about it now? What do you expect to find out about it from your research? What preconceived ideas about or emotional reactions to this subject do you have? Why do you have them? It may be helpful to try some of the activities in the chapter on **GENERATING IDEAS AND TEXT**.

289–97

Visit your subject. If you're writing about an amusement park, go there; if you're profiling the man who runs the carousel, make an appointment to meet and interview him. Get to know your subject—if you profile Ben and Jerry, sample the ice cream! Take photos or videos if there's anything you might want to show visually in your profile. Find helpful hints for **OBSERVING** and **INTERVIEWING** in the chapter on finding sources.

463–66

If you're planning to interview someone, prepare questions. Hendrix likely asked Heather Penney questions like "What led you to become a fighter pilot?" "How long does a pre-flight check normally take?"

Do additional research. You may be able to write a profile based entirely on your field research. You may, though, need to do some library or web **RESEARCH** as well, to deepen your understanding, get a different perspective, or fill in gaps. Often the people you interview can help you find sources

433

Research can lead you to more than just text sources. These photos of Heather Penney and Marc Sasseville were found with a Google search.

of additional information; so can the sponsors of events and those in charge of places. To learn more about a city park, for instance, contact the government office that maintains it. Download any good photos of your subject that you find online (such as the photos of Heather Penney and Marc Sasseville), both to refer to as you write and to illustrate your profile.

Analyze your findings. Look for patterns, images, recurring ideas or phrases, and engaging details. Look for contrasts or discrepancies: between a subject's words and actions, between the appearance of a place and what goes on there, between your expectations and your research findings. Hendrix probably expected Penney to be an enthusiastic pilot but may not have expected that she had gotten her pilot's license while still an undergraduate literature major. You may find the advice in the **READING IN ACADEMIC CONTEXTS** chapter helpful here.

Come up with an angle. What's most memorable about your subject? What most interests you? What will interest your audience? Hendrix focuses on a woman who was one of the first female F-16 pilots and one of two pilots ready to undertake a suicide mission. Sometimes you'll know your angle from the start; other times you'll need to look further into your topic. You might try **CLUSTERING**, **CUBING**, **FREEWRITING**, and **LOOPING**, activities that will help you look at your topic from many different angles.

289–92

Note details that support your angle. Use your angle to focus your research and generate text. Try **DESCRIBING** your subject as clearly as you can, **COMPARING** your subject with other subjects of its sort, writing **DIALOGUE** that captures your subject. Hendrix, for instance, describes Heather Penney as "a petite blonde with a Colgate grin," providing details that help us see his subject, and he quotes Penney to give a sense of her attitude toward her experience: "We had to protect the airspace any way we could." Engaging details will bring your subject to life for your audience. Together, these details should create a dominant impression of your subject.

399–407
380–87
408–13

Ways of Organizing a Profile

[As a narrative]

One common way to organize a profile is by **NARRATING**. For example, if you are profiling a chess championship, you may write about it chronologically, creating suspense as you move from start to finish. The profile of Heather Penney's flight is organized this way.

419–27

| Introduce your subject and your angle on it; provide any necessary background. | → | Tell about various incidents or characteristics, one by one, that bring your subject to life. | → | Conclude by stating your overall impression—with an anecdote, a quote, a summary comment, or some other ending. |

[As a description]

Sometimes you may organize a profile by **DESCRIBING** — a person or a place, for instance.

399–407

Introduce your subject and your angle on it, providing any necessary background.

→ Present details that create some dominant impression of your subject:
- sensory details
- examples
- dialogue
- anecdotes
- *and so on*

→ State your overall impression, offering a final anecdote or quote or finishing a description begun earlier.

IF YOU NEED MORE HELP

298–300
301–5
306–12
313–17
318–28

See Chapter 28 for guidelines on **DRAFTING**, Chapter 29 on **ASSESSING YOUR OWN WRITING**, Chapter 30 on **GETTING RESPONSE AND REVISING**, and Chapter 31 on **EDITING AND PROOFREADING**. See Chapter 32 if you are required to submit your analysis in a writing **PORTFOLIO**.

academic literacies · rhetorical situations · genres · processes · strategies · research MLA / APA · media / design · readings · handbook

Proposals **20**

Proposals are part of our personal lives: lovers propose marriage, friends propose sharing dinner and a movie, you offer to pay half the cost of a car and insurance if your parents will pay the other half. They are also part of our academic and professional lives: student leaders lobby for lights on bike paths. *Musicians, artists, writers,* and *educators* apply for grants. Researchers in all fields of the *humanities, social sciences, sciences,* and *technology* seek funding for their projects. In business, contractors bid on building projects and companies and freelancers solicit work from potential clients. These are all examples of proposals, ideas put forward for consideration that say, "Here is a solution to a problem" or "This is what ought to be done." For example, here is a proposal for reducing the costs of college textbooks, written by an accounting professor at the University of Texas who is chairman of the university's Co-op Bookstore and himself a textbook author.

MICHAEL GRANOF

Course Requirement: Extortion

By now, entering college students and their parents have been warned: textbooks are outrageously expensive. Few textbooks for semester-long courses retail for less than $120, and those for science and math courses typically approach $180. Contrast this with the $20 to $30 cost of most hardcover best sellers and other trade books.

Perhaps these students and their parents can take comfort in knowing that the federal government empathizes with them, and in an attempt to ease their pain Congress asked its Advisory Committee on Student Financial Assistance to suggest a cure for the problem. Unfortunately, though, the committee has proposed a remedy that would only worsen the problem.

The committee's report, released in May, mainly proposes strengthening the market for used textbooks—by encouraging college bookstores to guarantee that they will buy back textbooks, establishing online book swaps among students, and urging faculty to avoid switching textbooks from one semester to the next. The fatal flaw in that proposal (and similar ones made by many state legislatures) is that used books are the cause of, not the cure for, high textbook prices.

Yet there is a way to lighten the load for students in their budgets, if not their backpacks. With small modifications to the institutional arrangements between universities, publishers, and students, textbook costs could be reduced—and these changes could be made without government intervention.

Today the used-book market is exceedingly well organized and efficient. Campus bookstores buy back not only the books that will be used at their university the next semester but also those that will not. Those that are no longer on their lists of required books they resell to national wholesalers, which in turn sell them to college bookstores on campuses where they will be required. This means that even if a text is being adopted for the first time at a particular college, there is almost certain to be an ample supply of used copies.

As a result, publishers have the chance to sell a book to only one of the multiple students who eventually use it. Hence, publishers must cover their costs and make their profit in the first semester their books are sold— before used copies swamp the market. That's why the prices are so high.

As might be expected, publishers do what they can to undermine the used-book market, principally by coming out with new editions every three or four years. To be sure, in rapidly changing fields like biology and physics, the new editions may be academically defensible. But in areas like algebra and calculus, they are nothing more than a transparent attempt to ensure premature textbook obsolescence. Publishers also try to discourage students from buying used books by bundling the text with extra materials like workbooks and CDs that are not reusable and therefore cannot be passed from one student to another.

The system could be much improved if, first of all, colleges and publishers would acknowledge that textbooks are more akin to

5

academic literacies   rhetorical situations   genres   processes   strategies   research MLA / APA   media / design   readings   handbook

computer software than to trade books. A textbook's value, like that of a software program, is not in its physical form, but rather in its intellectual content. Therefore, just as software companies typically "site license" to colleges, so should textbook publishers.

Here's how it would work: A teacher would pick a textbook, and the college would pay a negotiated fee to the publisher based on the number of students enrolled in the class. If there were 50 students in the class, for example, the fee might be $15 per student, or $750 for the semester. If the text were used for ten semesters, the publisher would ultimately receive a total of $150 ($15 × 10) for each student enrolled in the course, or as much as $7,500.

In other words, the publisher would have a stream of revenue for as long as the text was in use. Presumably, the university would pass on this fee to the students, just as it does the cost of laboratory supplies and computer software. But the students would pay much less than the $900 a semester they now typically pay for textbooks.

Once the university had paid the license fee, each student would have the option of using the text in electronic format or paying more to purchase a hard copy through the usual channels. The publisher could set the price of hard copies low enough to cover only its production and distribution costs plus a small profit, because it would be covering most of its costs and making most of its profit by way of the license fees. The hard copies could then be resold to other students or back to the bookstore, but that would be of little concern to the publisher.

A further benefit of this approach is that it would not affect the way courses are taught. The same cannot be said for other recommendations from the Congressional committee and from state legislatures, like placing teaching materials on electronic reserve, urging faculty to adopt cheaper "no frills" textbooks, and assigning mainly electronic textbooks. While each of these suggestions may have merit, they force faculty to weigh students' academic interests against their fiscal concerns and encourage them to rely less on new textbooks.

Neither colleges nor publishers are known for their cutting-edge innovations. But if they could slightly change the way they do business, they would make a substantial dent in the cost of higher education and provide a real benefit to students and their parents.

For four more proposals, see CHAPTER 67.

This proposal clearly defines the problem—some textbooks cost a lot—and explains why. It proposes a solution to the problem of high textbook prices and offers reasons why this solution will work better than others. Its tone is reasonable and measured, yet decisive.

Key Features / Proposals

A well-defined problem.   Some problems are self-evident and relatively simple, and you would not need much persuasive power to make people act—as with the problem "This university discards too much paper." While some people might see nothing wrong with throwing paper away, most are likely to agree that recycling is a good thing. Other issues are controversial: some people see them as problems while others do not, such as this one: "Motorcycle riders who do not wear helmets risk serious injury and raise health-care costs for everyone." Some motorcyclists believe that wearing or not wearing a helmet should be a personal choice; you would have to present arguments to convince your readers that not wearing a helmet is indeed a problem needing a solution. Any written proposal must establish at the outset that there is a problem—and that it's serious enough to require a solution. For some topics, visual or audio evidence of the problem may be helpful.

A recommended solution.   Once you have defined the problem, you need to describe the solution you are suggesting and to explain it in enough detail for readers to understand what you are proposing. Again, photographs, diagrams, or other visuals may help. Sometimes you might suggest several solutions, weigh their merits, and choose the best one.

A convincing argument for your proposed solution.   You need to convince readers that your solution is feasible—and that it is the best way to solve the problem. Sometimes you'll want to explain in detail how your proposed solution would work. See, for example, how the textbook proposal details the way a licensing system would operate. Visuals may strengthen this part of your argument as well.

academic literacies · rhetorical situations · genres · processes · strategies · research MLA / APA · media / design · readings · handbook

Granof's proposal for reducing textbook prices via licensing fees might benefit from a photograph like this one, which provides a comparison of other approaches to the problem.

A response to anticipated questions. You may need to consider any questions readers may have about your proposal—and to show how its advantages outweigh any disadvantages. Had the textbook proposal been written for college budget officers, it would have needed to anticipate and answer questions about the costs of implementing the proposed solution.

A call to action. The goal of a proposal is to persuade readers to accept your proposed solution. This solution may include asking readers to take action.

An appropriate tone. Since you're trying to persuade readers to act, your tone is important—readers will always react better to a reasonable, respectful presentation than to anger or self-righteousness.

A BRIEF GUIDE TO WRITING PROPOSALS

Deciding on a Topic

Choose a problem that can be solved. Complex, large problems, such as poverty, hunger, or terrorism, usually require complex, large solutions. Most of the time, focusing on a smaller problem or a limited aspect of a large problem will yield a more manageable proposal. Rather than tackling the problem of world poverty, for example, think about the problem faced by people in your community who have lost jobs and need help until they find employment.

Considering the Rhetorical Situation

55–56

PURPOSE Do you have a stake in a particular solution, or do you simply want to eliminate the problem by whatever solution might be adopted?

57–60

AUDIENCE Do your readers share your view of the problem as a serious one needing a solution? Are they likely to be open to possible solutions or resistant? Do they have the authority to carry out a proposed solution?

64–67

STANCE How can you show your audience that your proposal is reasonable and should be taken seriously? How can you demonstrate your own authority and credibility?

68–70

MEDIA / DESIGN How will you deliver your proposal? In print? Electronically? As a speech? Would visuals, or video or audio clips help support your proposal?

Generating Ideas and Text

Explore potential solutions to the problem. Many problems can be solved in more than one way, and you need to show your readers that

academic literacies   rhetorical situations   genres   processes   strategies   research MLA / APA   media / design   readings   handbook

you've examined several potential solutions. You may develop solutions on your own; more often, though, you'll need to do **RESEARCH** to see how others have solved — or tried to solve — similar problems. Don't settle on a single solution too quickly — you'll need to **COMPARE** the advantages and disadvantages of several solutions in order to argue convincingly for one.

433

380–87

Decide on the most desirable solution(s).   One solution may be head and shoulders above others — but be open to rejecting all the possible solutions on your list and starting over if you need to, or to combining two or more potential solutions in order to come up with an acceptable fix.

Think about why your solution is the best one.   Why did you choose your solution? Why will it work better than others? What has to be done to enact it? What will it cost? What makes you think it can be done? Writing out answers to these questions will help you argue for your solution: to show that you have carefully and objectively outlined a problem, analyzed the potential solutions, weighed their merits, and determined the reasons the solution you propose is the best.

Ways of Organizing a Proposal

You can organize a proposal in various ways, but always you will begin by establishing that there is a problem. You may then identify several possible solutions before recommending one of them or a combination of several. Sometimes, however, you might discuss only a single solution.

[Several possible solutions]

[A single solution]

TOPIC PROPOSALS

188–96 ▲ Instructors often ask students to write topic proposals to ensure that their topics are appropriate or manageable. Some instructors may also ask for an **ANNOTATED BIBLIOGRAPHY** showing that appropriate sources of information are available—more evidence that the project can be carried out. Here a first-year student proposes a topic for an assignment in a writing course in which she has been asked to take a position on a global issue.

JENNIFER CHURCH

Biodiversity Loss and Its Effect on Medicine

The loss of biodiversity—the variety of organisms found in the world—is affecting the world every day. Some scientists estimate that we are losing approximately one hundred species per day and that more than a quarter of all species may vanish within fifty years. I recently had the issue of biodiversity loss brought to my attention in a biological sciences course that I am taking this quarter. I have found myself interested in and intrigued by the subject and have found an abundance of information both in books and on the Internet.

In this paper, I will argue that it is crucial for people to stop this rapid loss of our world's biodiversity. Humans are the number-one cause of biodiversity loss in the world. Whether through pollution or toxins, we play a crucial role in the extinction of many different species. For example, 80 percent of the world's medicine comes from biological species and their habitats. One medicine vanishing due to biodiversity loss is TAXOL. Found in the Wollemi pine tree, TAXOL is one of the most promising drugs for the treatment of ovarian and breast cancer. If the Wollemi pine tree becomes extinct, we will lose this potential cure.

I will concentrate primarily on biodiversity and its effects on the medical field. If we keep destroying the earth's biodiversity at the current rate, we may lose many opportunities to develop medicines we need to survive. The majority of my information will be found on the Internet, because there are many reliable Web sites from all around the world that address the issue of biodiversity loss and medicine.

Church defines and narrows her topic (from biodiversity loss to the impact of that loss on medicine), discusses her interest, outlines her argument, and discusses her research strategy. Her goal is to convince her instructor that she has a realistic writing project and a clear plan.

Key Features / Topic Proposals

You'll need to explain what you want to write about, why you want to explore it, and what you'll do with your topic. Unless your instructor has additional requirements, here are the features to include:

A concise discussion of the subject.   Topic proposals generally open with a brief discussion of the subject, outlining any important areas of controversy or debate associated with it and clarifying the extent of the writer's current knowledge of it. In its first two paragraphs, Church's proposal includes a concise statement of the topic she wishes to address.

A clear statement of your intended focus.   State what aspect of the topic you intend to write on as clearly as you can, narrowing your focus appropriately. Church does so by stating her intended topic—loss of biodiversity—and then showing how she will focus on the importance of biodiversity to the medical field.

A rationale for choosing the topic. Tell your instructor why this topic interests you and why you want to write about it. Church both states what made her interested in her topic and hints at a practical reason for choosing it: plenty of information is available.

Mention of resources. To show your instructor that you can achieve your goal, you need to identify the available research materials.

298–300 ○
301–5
306–12
313–17
318–28

> **IF YOU NEED MORE HELP**
>
> See Chapter 28 for guidelines on **DRAFTING**, Chapter 29 on **ASSESSING YOUR OWN WRITING**, Chapter 30 on **GETTING RESPONSE AND REVISING**, and Chapter 31 on **EDITING AND PROOFREADING**. See Chapter 32 if you are required to submit your proposal in a writing **PORTFOLIO**.

✳ academic literacies
▪ rhetorical situations
▲ genres
○ processes
◆ strategies
● research MLA / APA
▢ media / design
▮ readings
▨ handbook

Sometimes we write essays just to think about something—to speculate, ponder, probe; to play with an idea, develop a thought; or simply to share something. Reflective essays are our attempt to think something through by writing about it and to share our thinking with others. If such essays make an argument, it is about things we care or think about more than about what we believe to be "true." In college, you might be asked in courses across the curriculum to write formal or informal reflections in the form of essays, journals, design reports, or learning logs. Have a look at one example of a reflection by Jonathan Safran Foer, a novelist who lives in Brooklyn. This essay originally appeared on the Op-Ed page of the *New York Times*.

JONATHAN SAFRAN FOER

My Life as a Dog

For the last twenty years, New York City parks without designated dog runs have permitted dogs to be off-leash from 9 p.m. to 9 a.m. Because of recent complaints from the Juniper Park Civic Association in Queens, the issue has been revisited. On December 5, the Board of Health will vote on the future of off-leash hours.

Retrievers in elevators, Pomeranians on No. 6 trains, bull mastiffs crossing the Brooklyn Bridge . . . it is easy to forget just how strange it is that dogs live in New York in the first place. It is about as unlikely a place for dogs as one could imagine, and yet 1.4 million of them are among us. Why do we keep them in our apartments and houses, always at some expense and inconvenience? Is it even possible, in a city, to provide a good life for a dog, and what is a "good life"? Does the health board's vote matter in ways other than the most obvious?

I adopted George (a Great Dane / Lab / pit / greyhound / ridgeback / whatever mix — a.k.a. Brooklyn shorthair) because I thought it would be fun. As it turns out, she is a major pain an awful lot of the time.

She mounts guests, eats my son's toys (and occasionally tries to eat my son), is obsessed with squirrels, lunges at skateboarders and Hasids,* has the savant-like ability to find her way between the camera lens and subject of every photo taken in her vicinity, backs her tush into the least interested person in the room, digs up the freshly planted, scratches the newly bought, licks the about-to-be-served, and occasionally relieves herself on the wrong side of the front door. Her head is resting on my foot as I type this. I love her.

Our various struggles — to communicate, to recognize and accommodate each other's desires, simply to coexist — force me to interact with something, or rather someone, entirely "other." George can respond to a handful of words, but our relationship takes place almost entirely outside of language. She seems to have thoughts and emotions, desires and fears. Sometimes I think I understand them; often I don't. She is a mystery to me. And I must be one to her.

Of course our relationship is not always a struggle. My morning walk with George is very often the highlight of my day — when I have my best thoughts, when I most appreciate both nature and the city, and in a deeper sense, life itself. Our hour together is a bit of compensation for the burdens of civilization: business attire, email, money, etiquette, walls, and artificial lighting. It is even a kind of compensation for language. Why does watching a dog be a dog fill one with happiness? And why does it make one feel, in the best sense of the word, human?

It is children, very often, who want dogs. In a recent study, when asked to name the ten most important "individuals" in their lives, 7- and 10-year-olds included two pets on average. In another study, 42 percent of 5-year-olds spontaneously mentioned their pets when asked, "Whom do you turn to when you are feeling, sad, angry, happy, or wanting to share a secret?" Just about every children's book in my local bookstore has an animal for its hero. But then, only a few feet away in the cookbook section, just about every cookbook includes

5

———————————

*Hasids: a Jewish sect whose members dress distinctively. [Editor's note]

academic literacies   rhetorical situations   genres   processes   strategies   research MLA / APA   media / design   readings   handbook

recipes for cooking animals. Is there a more illuminating illustration of our paradoxical relationship with the nonhuman world?

In the course of our lives, we move from a warm and benevolent relationship with animals (learning responsibility through caring for our pets, stroking and confiding in them) to a cruel one (virtually all animals raised for meat in this country are factory farmed—they spend their lives in confinement, dosed with antibiotics and other drugs).

How do you explain this? Is our kindness replaced with cruelty? I don't think so. I think in part it's because the older we get, the less exposure we have to animals. And nothing facilitates indifference or forgetfulness so much as distance. In this sense, dogs and cats have been very lucky: they are the only animals we are intimately exposed to daily.

Folk parental wisdom and behavioral studies alike generally view 10 the relationships children have with companion animals as beneficial. But one does not have to be a child to learn from a pet. It is precisely my frustrations with George, and the inconveniences she creates, that reinforce in me how much compromise is necessary to share space with other beings.

The practical arguments against off-leash hours are easily refuted. One doesn't have to be an animal scientist to know that the more a dog is able to exercise its "dogness"—to run and play, to socialize with other dogs—the happier it will be. Happy dogs, like happy people, tend not to be aggressive. In the years that dogs have been allowed to run free in city parks, dog bites have decreased 90 percent. But there is another argument that is not so easy to respond to: some people just don't want to be inconvenienced by dogs. Giving dogs space necessarily takes away space from humans.

We have been having this latter debate, in different forms, for ages. Again and again we are confronted with the reality—some might say the problem—of sharing our space with other living things, be they dogs, trees, fish, or penguins. Dogs in the park are a present example of something that is often too abstracted or far away to gain our consideration.

The very existence of parks is a response to this debate: earlier New Yorkers had the foresight to recognize that if we did not carve out places for nature in our cities, there would be no nature. It was recently estimated that Central Park's real estate would be worth more than

$500 billion. Which is to say we are half a trillion dollars inconvenienced by trees and grass. But we do not think of it as an inconvenience. We think of it as balance.

Living on a planet of fixed size requires compromise, and while we are the only party capable of negotiating, we are not the only party at the table. We've never claimed more, and we've never had less. There has never been less clean air or water, fewer fish or mature trees. If we are not simply ignoring the situation, we keep hoping for (and expecting) a technological solution that will erase our destruction, while allowing us to continue to live without compromise. Maybe zoos will be an adequate replacement for wild animals in natural habitats. Maybe we will be able to recreate the Amazon somewhere else. Maybe one day we will be able to genetically engineer dogs that do not wish to run free. Maybe. But will those futures make us feel, in the best sense of the word, human?

I have been taking George to Prospect Park twice a day for more 15 than three years, but her running is still a revelation to me. Effortlessly, joyfully, she runs quite a bit faster than the fastest human on the planet. And faster, I've come to realize, than the other dogs in the park. George might well be the fastest land animal in Brooklyn. Once or twice every morning, for no obvious reason, she'll tear into a full sprint. Other dog owners can't help but watch her. Every now and then someone will cheer her on. It is something to behold.

A vote regarding off-leash hours for dogs sparks Foer's reflection on the relationship between dogs and humans. He begins by thinking about his relationship with his own dog, then goes on to consider the paradoxical nature of our treatment of animals in general. From there, he moves into a larger discussion of the compromises we make to "share space with other beings." Finally, he brings his reflection back to the personal, describing the joy of watching his dog be herself, off-leash.

■ For four more reflections, see CHAPTER 68.

Key Features / Reflections

A topic that intrigues you. A reflective essay has a dual purpose: to ponder something you find interesting or puzzling and to share your thoughts

academic literacies   rhetorical situations   genres   processes   strategies   research MLA / APA   media / design   readings   handbook

with an audience. Your topic may be anything that interests you. You might write about someone you have never met and are curious about, an object or occurrence that makes you think, a place where you feel comfortable or safe. Your goal is to explore the meaning that the person, object, event, or place has for you in a way that will interest others. One way to do that is by making connections between your personal experience and more general ones that readers may share. Foer writes about his experience with his dog, but in so doing he raises questions and offers insights about the way everyone relates to others, human and nonhuman alike.

Some kind of structure.   A reflective essay can be structured in many ways, but it needs to *be* structured. It may seem to wander, but all its paths and ideas should relate, one way or another. The challenge is to keep your readers' interest as you explore your topic and to leave readers satisfied that the journey was pleasurable, interesting, and profitable. Foer brings his essay full circle, introducing the vote on the off-leash law in his opening, then considering our complex relationship with dogs, and, after suggesting some of the compromises we make to share our world with other nonhuman living things, closing with an indelible image of the joy that freedom from a leash brings.

Specific details.   You'll need to provide specific details to help readers understand and connect with your subject, especially if it's an abstract or unfamiliar one. Foer offers a wealth of details about his dog: "She mounts guests, eats my son's toys (and occasionally tries to eat my son), is obsessed by squirrels, lunges at skateboarders and Hasids." Anecdotes can bring your subject to life: "Once or twice every morning, for no obvious reason, she'll tear into a full sprint. Other dog owners can't help but watch her. Every now and then someone will cheer her on." Reflections may be about causes, such as why dogs make us feel more human; comparisons, such as when Foer compares animals as pets and as food; and examples: "virtually all animals raised for meat in this country are factory farmed." Photographs or other visuals may help provide details as well as set a certain tone for a reflection, as discussed below.

A questioning, speculative tone. In a reflective essay, you are working toward answers, not providing them neatly organized and ready for consumption. So your tone is usually tentative and open, demonstrating a willingness to entertain, accept, and reject various ideas as your essay progresses from beginning to end. Foer achieves this tone by looking at people's relationships with dogs from several different perspectives as well as by asking questions for which he provides no direct answers.

A BRIEF GUIDE TO WRITING REFLECTIONS

Deciding on a Topic

Choose a subject you want to explore. Write a list of things that you think about, wonder about, find puzzling or annoying. They may be big things — life, relationships — or little things — quirks of certain people's behavior, curious objects, everyday events. Try **CLUSTERING** one or more of those things, or begin by **FREEWRITING** to see what comes to mind as you write.

291–92 ○
289–90

Considering the Rhetorical Situation

55–56 ■

PURPOSE   What's your goal in writing this essay? To introduce a topic that interests you? Entertain? Provoke readers to think about something? What aspects of your subject do you want to ponder and reflect on?

57–60 ■

AUDIENCE   Who is the audience? How familiar are they with your subject? How will you introduce it in a way that will interest them?

64–67 ■

STANCE   What is your attitude toward the topic you plan to explore? Questioning? Playful? Critical? Curious? Something else?

MEDIA / DESIGN Will your essay be a print document? an oral presentation? Will it be posted on a website or blog? Would it help to include any visuals or video or audio files?

68–70

Generating Ideas and Text

Explore your subject in detail. Reflections often include descriptive details. Foer, for example, **DESCRIBES** the many ways he encounters dogs in New York: "Retrievers in elevators, Pomeranians on No. 6 trains, bull mastiffs crossing the Brooklyn Bridge." Those details provide a base for the speculations to come. You may also make your point by **DEFINING**, **COMPARING**, even **CLASSIFYING**. Virtually any organizing pattern will help you explore your subject.

399–407

388–98
380–87
374–79

Back away. Ask yourself why your subject matters: why is it important or intriguing or significant? You may try **LISTING** or **OUTLINING** possibilities, or you may want to start **DRAFTING** to see where the writing takes your thinking. Your goal is to think on screen (or paper) about your subject, to play with its possibilities.

290–91
293–95
296–97

Think about how to keep readers with you. Reflections may seem loose or unstructured, but they must be carefully crafted so that readers can follow your train of thought. It's a good idea to sketch out a rough **THESIS** to help focus your thoughts. You may not include the thesis in the essay itself, but every part of the essay should in some way relate to it.

345–47

Ways of Organizing a Reflective Essay

Reflective essays may be organized in many ways because they mimic the way we think, associating one idea with another in ways that make sense but do not necessarily form a "logical" progression. In general, you might consider organizing a reflection using this overall strategy:

Another way to organize this type of essay is as a series of brief reflections that together create an overall impression:

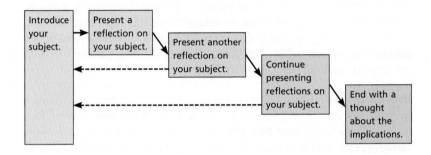

298–300 ◐
301–5
306–12
313–17
318–28

IF YOU NEED MORE HELP

See Chapter 28 for guidelines on **DRAFTING**, Chapter 29 on **ASSESSING YOUR OWN WRITING**, Chapter 30 on **GETTING RESPONSE AND REVISING**, and Chapter 31 on **EDITING AND PROOFREADING**. See Chapter 32 if you are required to submit your reflection in a writing **PORTFOLIO**.

Résumés and Job Letters

Résumés summarize our education, work experience, and other accomplishments for prospective employers. Application letters introduce us to those employers. When you send a letter and résumé applying for a job, you are making an argument for why that employer should want to meet you and perhaps hire you. In a way, the two texts together serve as an advertisement selling your talents and abilities to someone who likely has to sift through many applications to decide whom to invite for an interview. That's why résumés and application letters require a level of care that few other documents do. In the same way, sending a thank-you letter following an interview completes your presentation of yourself to potential employers. Résumés, application letters, and thank-you letters are obviously very different genres—yet they share one common purpose and are done for the same audience. Thus, they are presented together in this chapter.

Social Media and Job Hunting

Social media have become important aspects of finding a job, for both good and ill. In fact, over half of all employers always search for job applicants' online profiles — and in many cases, those profiles lower the applicants' chances of being hired. So it's important to create or revise your profiles on *Facebook, LinkedIn,* and *Twitter,* the three most-searched social media sites, as well as other sites. Emphasize any volunteer or charity work you do, and highlight potential qualifications for and interest in the kind of work you want. Make sure your profiles contain no profanity or references to your sexual activity, or use of alcohol, guns, or illegal drugs—and proofread your posts for grammar and spelling. Your photos of yourself should project a professional image, too. Also, Google yourself to see what a search reveals about you.

You can also use social media to improve your job search. Read the descriptions of positions you would like to have, looking for keywords that describe what employers want in such employees; then use those keywords in your profiles. Also, join *LinkedIn* groups related to your desired job or industry to stay current with the conversations in those fields; then follow the companies where you'd like to work, as new job opportunities are sometimes posted there before they appear in other places.

RÉSUMÉS

A résumé is one of a job seeker's most important tools. If done well, a résumé not only tells potential employers about your education and work history, it says a lot about your attention to detail, writing skills, and professionalism. Taking the time to craft an excellent résumé, then, is time well spent. Here's an example, a résumé written by a college student applying for an internship before his senior year.

Samuel Praeger •············· *name in boldface*
28 Murphy Lane
Springfield, OH 45399
937-555-2640
spraeger22@webmail.com

OBJECTIVE	To obtain an internship with a public relations firm •··········	*objective tailored to specific job sought*
EDUCATION Fall 2012–present	Wittenberg University, Springfield, OH • BA in Psychology expected in May 2016 • Minor in East Asian Studies	
EXPERIENCE 2014–present	Department of Psychology, Wittenberg University •········· *Research Assistant* • Collect and analyze data • Interview research participants	*work experience in reverse chronological order*
Summer 2014	Landis and Landis Public Relations, Springfield, OH *Events Coordinator* • Organized local charity events • Coordinated database of potential donors • Produced two radio spots for event promotion	
Summers 2012, 2013	Springfield Aquatic Club, Springfield, OH *Assistant Swim Coach* • Instructed children ages 5–18 in competitive swimming	
HONORS 2015	Psi Chi National Honor Society in Psychology	
2013–2015	Community Service Scholarship, Wittenberg University	
ACTIVITIES	Varsity Swim Team; Ronald McDonald House Fund-raiser	
SKILLS	Microsoft Office; SPSS for Windows; Prezi; fluent in Japanese	
REFERENCES	Available upon request •··········	*format to fill entire page*

Samuel Praeger's résumé is arranged chronologically, and because he was looking for work in a certain field, the résumé is targeted, focusing on his related work and skills and leaving out any references to high school (that he is in college allows readers to assume graduation from high school) or his past job as a house painter, which is not relevant. He describes his work responsibilities using action verbs to highlight what he actually did—produced, instructed, *and so on*.

Key Features / Résumés

A structure that suits your goals and experience. There are conventional ways of organizing a résumé but no one right way. You can organize a résumé chronologically or functionally, and it can be targeted or not. A *chronological résumé* is the most general, listing pretty much all your academic and work experience from the most recent to the earliest. A *targeted résumé* will generally announce the specific goal up top, just beneath your name, and will offer information selectively, showing only the experience and skills relevant to your goal. A *functional résumé* is organized around various kinds of experience and is not chronological. You might write a functional résumé if you wish to demonstrate a lot of experience in more than one area and perhaps if you wish to downplay dates.

Succinct. A résumé should almost always be short—one page if at all possible. Entries should be parallel but do not need to be written in complete sentences—"Produced two radio spots," for instance, rather than "I produced two radio spots." Use action verbs ("instructed," "produced") to emphasize what you accomplished.

A design that highlights key information. It's important for a résumé to look good and to be easy to skim; typography, white space, and alignment matter. Your name should be bold at the top. Major sections should be labeled with headings, all of which should be in one slightly larger or bolder font. And you need to surround each section and the text as a whole with adequate white space to make the parts easy to read—and to make the entire document look professional.

academic literacies | rhetorical situations | genres | processes | strategies | research MLA / APA | media / design | readings | handbook

A BRIEF GUIDE TO WRITING RÉSUMÉS

Considering the Rhetorical Situation

PURPOSE   Are you seeking a job? an internship? some other position? How will the position for which you're applying affect what you include on your résumé?   55–56

AUDIENCE   What sort of employee is the company or organization seeking? What experience and qualities will the person doing the hiring be looking for?   57–60

STANCE   What personal and professional qualities do you want to convey? Think about how you want to come across — as eager? polite? serious? ambitious?— and choose your words accordingly.   64–67

MEDIA/DESIGN   Are you planning to send your résumé and letter as PDFs? on paper? as an email attachment? Whatever your medium, be sure both documents are formatted appropriately and proofread carefully.   68–70

Generating Ideas and Text for a Résumé

Define your objective.   Are you looking for a particular job for which you should create a targeted résumé? Are you preparing a generic chronological résumé to use in a search for work of any kind? Defining your objective as specifically as possible helps you decide on the form the résumé will take and the information it will include.

Consider how you want to present yourself.   Begin by gathering the information you will need to include. As you work through the steps of putting your résumé together, think about the method of organization that works best for your purpose — chronological, targeted, or functional.

- *Contact information.* At the top of your résumé, list your full name, a permanent address (rather than your school address), a permanent telephone number with area code, and your email address (which should sound professional; addresses like hotbabe334@gmail.com do not make a good first impression on potential employers).

- **Your education.** Start with the most recent: degree, major, college attended, and minor (if any). You may want to list your GPA (if it's over 3.0) and any academic honors you've received. If you don't have much work experience, list education first.

- **Your work experience.** As with education, list your most recent job first and work backward. Include job title, organization name, city and state, start and end dates, and responsibilities. Describe them in terms of your duties and accomplishments. If you have extensive work experience in the area in which you're applying, list that first.

- **Community service, volunteer, and charitable activities.** Many high school students are required to perform community service, and many students participate in various volunteer activities that benefit others. List what you've done, and think about the skills and aptitudes that participation helped you develop or demonstrate.

- **Other activities, interests, and abilities.** What do you do for fun? What skills do your leisure activities require? (For example, if you play a sport, you probably have a good grasp of the value of teamwork. You should describe your skills in a way that an employer might find useful.)

Choose references.   Whether you list references on your résumé or offer to provide them on request, ask people to serve as references for you before you send out a résumé. It's a good idea to provide each reference with a one-page summary of relevant information about you (for example, give professors a list of courses you took with them, including the grades you earned and the titles of papers you wrote).

Choose your words carefully.   Remember, your résumé is a sales document—you're trying to present yourself as someone worth a second look. Focus on your achievements, using action verbs that say what you've done. Be honest—employers expect truthfulness, and embellishing the truth can cause you to lose a job later.

Consider key design elements. Make sure your résumé is centered on the page and that it looks clean and clear. It's usually best to use a single, simple **FONT** (Times New Roman is a good one) throughout and to print on white paper. Use bold type and bullets to make the résumé easy to read, and limit it to no more—and no less—than one full page.

601–2

Edit and proofread carefully. Your résumé must be perfect. Show it to others, and proofread again. You don't want even one typo or other error.

Send the résumé as a PDF. PDFs look the same on all devices, whereas *Word* or other formats may not. Make sure potential employers see your résumé as you intended.

Ways of Organizing a Résumé

If you don't have much work experience or if you've just gone back to school to train for a new career, put education before work experience; if you have extensive work experience in the area in which you're applying, list work before education.

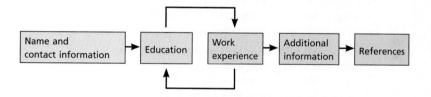

APPLICATION AND THANK-YOU LETTERS

The application letter argues that the writer should be taken seriously as a candidate for a job or some other opportunity. Generally, it is sent together with a résumé, so it doesn't need to give that much information. It does, however, have to make a favorable impression: the way it's written and presented can get you in for an interview—or not. On pages 260 and 261

Application Letter

equal space at top and bottom of page, all text aligning at left margin

street address
city, state ZIP
date

28 Murphy Lane
Springfield, OH 45399
May 19, 2015

line space

recipient's name and title, organization, address

Barbara Jeremiah, President
Jeremiah Enterprises
44322 Commerce Way
Worthington, OH 45322

line space

salutation, with a colon

Dear Ms. Jeremiah:

position identified

I am writing to apply for the public relations internship advertised in the Sunday, May 15, *Columbus Dispatch*. The success of your company makes me eager to work with you and learn from you.

line space between paragraphs

match between experience and job description

My grasp of public relations goes beyond the theories I have learned in the classroom. I worked last summer at Landis and Landis, the Springfield public relations firm, where I was responsible for organizing two charity events that drew over two hundred potential donors each. Since your internship focuses on public relations, my experience in the field will allow me to make a contribution to your company's public relations team.

availability

I will be available to begin any time after May 23, when the spring term at Wittenberg ends. I enclose my résumé, which provides detailed information about my background. I will phone this week to see if I might arrange an interview.

line space

closing

Sincerely,

4 lines space for signature

Samuel Praeger

sender's name, typed

Samuel Praeger

Thank-You Email

line space

Dear Ms. Jeremiah: ●·· salutation, with a colon

Thank you for the opportunity to meet with you yesterday. I enjoyed talking with you and meeting the people who work with you, and I continue to be very interested in becoming an intern with Jeremiah Enterprises. ●···· thanks and confirmation of interest

line space between paragraphs

As we discussed, I worked with a public relations firm last summer, and since then I have completed three courses in marketing and public relations that relate directly to the work I would be doing as an intern. ●···· brief review of qualifications

invitation for further contact

I have attached a list of references, as you requested. If you need any more information, please do not hesitate to contact me by email at spraeger22@webmail.com or by phone at 937-555-2640. Thanks again; ●···· attachments

repeat thanks I hope to hear from you soon.

line space

Sincerely, ●··· closing
Samuel Praeger

is an application letter that Samuel Praeger wrote seeking a position at the end of his junior year. Praeger tailored his letter to one specific reader at a specific organization. The letter cites details, showing that it is not a generic application letter being sent to many possible employers. Rather, it identifies a particular position—the public relations internship—and stresses the fit between Praeger's credentials and the position. Praeger also states his availability. Send a thank-you email to each person who interviewed you within twenty-four hours of the interview; follow up by mailing a printed note that follows the same format as the application letter. Doing so is a way of showing appreciation for the interview and restating your interest in the position. It also shows that you have good manners and understand proper business etiquette. On the previous page is an email Samuel Praeger sent to the person who interviewed him for an internship, thanking the interviewer for her time and the opportunity to meet her, indicating his interest in the position, and reiterating his qualifications.

Key Features / Application and Thank-You Letters

A succinct indication of your qualifications.   In an application letter, you need to make clear why you're interested in the position or the organization—and at the same time give some sense of why the person you're writing to should at least want to meet you. In a thank-you letter, you should remind the interviewer of your qualifications.

A reasonable and pleasing tone.   When writing application and thank-you letters, you need to go beyond simply stating your accomplishments or saying thank you. Through your words, you need to demonstrate that you will be the kind of employee the organization wants. Presentation is also important—your letter should be neat and error-free.

A conventional, businesslike format.   Application and thank-you letters typically follow a prescribed format. The most common is the block format shown in the examples. It includes the writer's address, the date, the recipient's name and address, a salutation, the message, a closing, and a signature.

A BRIEF GUIDE TO WRITING JOB LETTERS

Generating Ideas and Text for Application and Thank-You Letters

Focus.   Application and thank-you letters are not personal and should not be chatty. Keep them focused: when you're applying for a position, include only information relevant to the position. Don't make your audience wade through irrelevant side issues. Stay on topic.

academic literacies rhetorical situations genres processes strategies research MLA / APA media / design readings handbook

State the reason for the letter. Unlike essays, which develop a thesis over several paragraphs, or emails, which announce their topic in a subject line, letters need to explicitly introduce their reason for being written, usually in the first paragraph. When you're applying for something or thanking someone, say so in the first sentence: "I am writing to apply for the Margaret Branscomb Peabody Scholarship for students majoring in veterinary science." "Thank you for meeting with me."

Think of your letter as an argument. When you're asking for a job, you're making an **ARGUMENT**. You're making a claim—that you're qualified for a certain position—and you need to support your claim with reasons and evidence. Praeger, for example, cites his education and his work experience—and he offers to supply references who will support his application.

◆ 355–73

Choose an appropriate salutation. If you know the person's name and title, use it: "Dear Professor Turnigan." If you don't know the person's title, one good solution is to address him or her by first and last name: "Dear Julia Turnigan." If, as sometimes happens, you must write to an unknown reader, your options include "To Whom It May Concern" and the more old fashioned "Dear Sir or Madam." Another option in such situations might be to omit the salutation completely and instead use a subject line, for example: "Subject: Public Relations Internship Application." Whenever possible, though, write to a specific person; research or contact the organization and find out whom to write to. Once you've had an interview, write to your interviewer.

Proofread. Few writing situations demand greater perfection than professional letters—especially job letters. Employers receive dozens, sometimes hundreds, of applications, and often can't look at them all. Typos, grammar errors, and other forms of sloppiness prejudice readers against applicants: they're likely to think that if this applicant can't take the time and care to **PROOFREAD**, how badly does he or she want this position? To compete, strive for perfection.

○ 316–17

Ways of Organizing an Application or Thank-You Letter

Application and thank-you letters should both follow a conventional organization, though you might vary the details somewhat. Here are two standard organizations:

[Application letter]

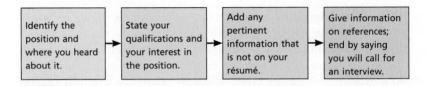

| Identify the position and where you heard about it. | → | State your qualifications and your interest in the position. | → | Add any pertinent information that is not on your résumé. | → | Give information on references; end by saying you will call for an interview. |

[Thank-you letter]

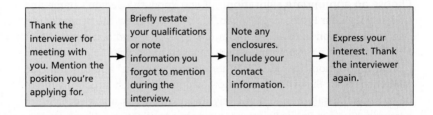

| Thank the interviewer for meeting with you. Mention the position you're applying for. | → | Briefly restate your qualifications or note information you forgot to mention during the interview. | → | Note any enclosures. Include your contact information. | → | Express your interest. Thank the interviewer again. |

IF YOU NEED MORE HELP

See Chapter 28 for guidelines on **DRAFTING**, Chapter 29 on **ASSESSING YOUR OWN WRITING**, Chapter 30 on **GETTING RESPONSE AND REVISING**, and Chapter 31 on **EDITING AND PROOFREADING**.

298–300
301–5
306–12
313–17

academic literacies · rhetorical situations · genres · processes · strategies · research MLA / APA · media / design · readings · handbook

Musicians regularly mix genres, blending, for instance, reggae, hip-hop, and jazz to create a unique sound. Like musicians, writers often combine different genres in a single text. An **EVALUATION** of mining practices might include a **PROFILE** of a coal company CEO. A **PROPOSAL** to start a neighborhood watch might begin with a **REPORT** on crime in the area. Here's a column that mixes genres, written by Anna Quindlen for *Newsweek* magazine in 2007.

▲ 197–205
224–34
235–44
129–55

ANNA QUINDLEN

Write for Your Life

The new movie *Freedom Writers* isn't entirely about the themes the trailers suggest. It isn't only about gang warfare and racial tensions and tolerance. It isn't only about the difference one good teacher can make in the life of one messed-up kid. *Freedom Writers* is about the power of writing in the lives of ordinary people. That's a lesson everyone needs. The movie, and the book from which it was taken, track the education of a young teacher named Erin Gruwell, who shows up shiny-new to face a class of what are called, in pedagogical jargon, "at risk" students. It's a mixed bag of Latino, Asian, and black teenagers with one feckless white kid thrown in. They ignore, belittle, and dismiss her as she proffers lesson plans and reading materials seriously out of step with the homelessness, drug use, and violence that are the stuff of their precarious existences.

And then one day, she gives them all marbled composition books and the assignment to write their lives, ungraded, unjudged, and the world breaks open.

Textual analysis

265

"My probation officer thinks he's slick; he swears he's an expert on gangs."

"Sorry, diary, I was going to try not to do it tonight, but the little baggy of white powder is calling my name."

"If you pull up my shirtsleeves and look at my arms, you will see   5 black and blue marks."

"The words 'Eviction Notice' stopped me dead in my tracks."

"When I was younger, they would lock me up in the closet because they wanted to get high and beat up on each other."

Ms. G, as the kids called her, embraced a concept that has been lost in modern life: writing can make pain tolerable, confusion clearer and the self stronger.

How is it, at a time when clarity and strength go begging, that we have moved so far from everyday prose? Social critics might trace this back to the demise of letter writing. The details of housekeeping and child rearing, the rigors of war and work, advice to friends and family: none was slated for publication. They were communications that gave shape to life by describing it for others.

Report

But as the letter fell out of favor and education became pro-   10 fessionalized, with its goal less the expansion of the mind than the acquisition of a job, writing began to be seen largely as the purview of writers. Writing at work also became so stylistically removed from the story of our lives that the two seemed to have nothing in common. Corporate prose conformed to an equation: information × polysyllabic words + tortured syntax = aren't you impressed?

And in the age of the telephone most communication became evanescent, gone into thin air no matter how important or heartfelt. Think of all those people inside the World Trade Center saying goodbye by phone. If only, in the blizzard of paper that followed the collapse of the buildings, a letter had fallen from the sky for every family member and friend, something to hold on to, something to read and reread. Something real. Words on paper confer a kind of immortality. Wouldn't all of us love to have a journal, a memoir, a letter, from those we have loved and lost? Shouldn't all of us leave a bit of that behind?

Reflection

The age of technology has both revived the use of writing and provided ever more reasons for its spiritual solace. Emails are letters, after all, more lasting than phone calls, even if many of them r 2 cursory 4 u.

And the physical isolation they and other arms-length cyber-advances create makes talking to yourself more important than ever. That's also what writing is: not just a legacy, but therapy. As the novelist Don DeLillo once said, "Writing is a form of personal freedom. It frees us from the mass identity we see in the making all around us. In the end, writers will write not to be outlaw heroes of some underculture but mainly to save themselves, to survive as individuals."

That's exactly what Gruwell was after when she got the kids in her class writing, in a program that's since been duplicated at other schools. Salvation and survival for teenagers whose chances of either seemed negligible. "Growing up, I always assumed I would either drop out of school or get pregnant," one student wrote. "So when Ms. G started talking about college, it was like a foreign language to me." Maybe that's the moment when that Latina girl began to speak that foreign language, when she wrote those words down. Today she has a college degree.

Argument

One of the texts Erin Gruwell assigned was *The Diary of a Young Girl* by Anne Frank. A student who balked at reading a book about someone so different, so remote, went on to write: "At the end of the book, I was so mad that Anne died, because as she was dying, a part of me was dying with her." Of course Anne never dreamed her diary would be published, much less read by millions of people after her death at the hands of the Nazis. She wrote it for the same reason the kids who called themselves Freedom Writers wrote in those composition books: to make sense of themselves. That's not just for writers. That's for people.

Quindlen argues that writing helps us understand ourselves and our world. She uses several genres to help advance her argument—textual analysis of the film Freedom Writers, *a brief report on the decline of letter writing, and a reflection on the technologies we use to write. Together, these genres help her develop her argument that writing helps us "make sense of [our]selves."*

📖 For four more multigenre texts, see CHAPTER 69.

Key Features / Texts That Mix Genres

One primary genre.   Your writing situation will often call for a certain genre that is appropriate for your purpose—an argument, a proposal, a report, a textual analysis, and so forth. Additional genres then play supporting roles. Quindlen's essay, for example, primarily argues a position and mixes in other genres, including report and reflection, to elaborate her argument and bring it to life.

A clear focus. A text that mixes genres approaches the topic several different ways, but each genre must contribute to your main point. One genre may serve as the introduction, and others may be woven throughout the text in other ways, but all must address some aspect of the topic and support the central claim. Quindlen's analysis of the film *Freedom Writers*, for example, supports her claim that writing is one way we learn about ourselves.

Careful organization. A text that combines several genres requires careful organization — the various genres must fit together neatly and clearly. Quindlen opens by analyzing the theme of *Freedom Writers*, noting that it's about "the power of writing in the lives of ordinary people." She then switches genres, reporting on how "we have moved so far from everyday prose" and then reflecting on the consequences of that move.

Clear transitions. When a text includes several genres, those genres need to be connected in some way. Transitions do that, and in so doing, they help readers make their way through the text. Transitions may include words such as "in addition" and "however," and they may also consist of phrases that sum up an idea and move it forward. See, for example, how Quindlen ends one paragraph by quoting Don DeLillo as saying that writers write "to save themselves, to survive as individuals" and then begins the next paragraph by referring to DeLillo's words, saying "That's exactly what Gruwell was after."

Some Typical Ways of Mixing Genres

It's possible to mix almost any genres together. Following are some of the most commonly mixed genres and how they combine with other genres.

Memoirs. Sometimes a personal anecdote can help support an **ARGUMENT** or enhance a **REPORT**. Stories from your personal experience can help readers understand your motivations for arguing a certain position and can enhance your credibility as a writer.

▲ 156–82
129–55

Profiles. One way to bring a **REPORT** on an abstract topic to life is to include a profile of a person, place, or event. For example, if you were writing a report for your boss on the need to hire more sales representatives, including a profile of one salesperson's typical day might drive home the point that your sales force is stretched too thin.

▲ 129–55

Textual analyses. You might need to analyze a speech or other document as part of an **ARGUMENT**, especially on a historical or political topic. For instance, you might analyze speeches by Abraham Lincoln and Jefferson Davis if you're writing about the causes of the Civil War, or an advertisement for e-cigarettes if you're making an argument about teen smoking.

▲ 156–82

Evaluations. You might include an evaluation of something when you write a **PROPOSAL** about it. For example, if you were writing a proposal for additional student parking on your campus, you would need to evaluate the current parking facilities to discuss their inadequacy.

▲ 235–44

A BRIEF GUIDE TO WRITING TEXTS THAT MIX GENRES

Considering the Rhetorical Situation

PURPOSE | Why are you writing this text? To inform? persuade? entertain? explore an idea? something else? What genres will help you achieve your purpose?

■ 55–56

AUDIENCE | Who are your readers? Which genres will help these readers understand your point? Will starting with a memoir or profile draw them in? Will some analysis help them

■ 57–60

understand the topic? Will a profile make the topic less abstract or make them more sympathetic to your claim?

GENRE   What is your primary genre? What other genres might support that primary genre?

61-63

STANCE   What is your stance on your topic—objective? opinionated? something else? Will including a textual analysis or report help you establish an objective or analytical tone? Will some reflection or a brief memoir show your personal connection to your topic?

64-67

MEDIA / DESIGN   Will your text be an electronic or a print document? an oral presentation? Will it be published on a blog or other website? Should you include illustrations? audio or video clips? Do you need to present any information that would be best shown in a chart or graph?

68-70

Generating Ideas and Text

Identify your primary genre.   If you're writing in response to an assignment, does it specify a particular genre? Look for key verbs that name specific genres — for example, *analyze, argue, evaluate,* and so on. Be aware that other verbs imply certain genres: *explain, summarize, review,* and *describe* ask for a report; *argue, prove,* and *justify* signal that you need to argue a position; and *evaluate* and *propose* specify evaluations and proposals.

    If the choice of genre is up to you, consider your **PURPOSE** and **AUDIENCE** carefully to determine what genre is most appropriate. Consult the appropriate genre chapter to identify the key features of your primary genre and to generate ideas and text.

55-56
57-60

Determine if other genres would be helpful.   As you write a draft, you may identify a need — for a beginning that grabs readers' attention, for a satisfying ending, for ways to make an abstract concept more concrete or to help in analyzing something. At this point, you may want to try mixing

academic literacies | rhetorical situations | genres | processes | strategies | research MLA / APA | media / design | readings | handbook

one or more genres within your draft. Determine what genre will help you achieve your purpose and consult the appropriate genre chapter for advice on writing in that genre. Remember, however, that you're mixing genres into your draft to support and enhance it—so your supporting genres may not be as developed as complete texts in that genre would be and may not include all the key features. For example, if you include a brief memoir as part of an argument, it should include a good story and vivid details—but its significance may well be stated as part of the argument rather than revealed through the storytelling itself.

Integrate the genres. Your goal is to create a focused, unified, coherent text. So you need to make sure that your genres work together to achieve that goal. Make sure that each genre fulfills a purpose within the text—for example, that a textual analysis within an argument provides evidence to support your claim, or that the profile you include in a report provides a clear illustration of the larger subject. Also, use TRANSITIONS to help readers move from section to section in your text.

349

Multigenre Projects

Sometimes a collection of texts can together represent an experience or advance an argument. For example, you might document a trip to the Grand Canyon in an album that contains journal entries written during the trip, photographs, a map of northern Arizona showing the canyon, postcards, an essay on the geology of the canyon, and a souvenir coin stamped with an image of the canyon. Each represents a different way of experiencing the Grand Canyon, and together they offer a multifaceted way to understand your trip.

You might also write in several different genres on the same topic. If you begin by ARGUING that the government should provide universal health care, for example, writing a MEMOIR about a time you were ill could help you explore a personal connection to the topic. Composing a PROFILE of a doctor might give you new insights into the issue, and writing a PROPOSAL for how universal health care could work might direct

355–73
216–23
224–34
235–44

you to potential solutions. You could assemble all these texts in a folder, with a title page and table of contents so that readers can see how it all fits together — or you could create an online multimodal text, combining text, images, video, sound, and links to other sites.

IF YOU NEED MORE HELP

See Chapter 28 for guidelines on **DRAFTING**, Chapter 29 on **ASSESSING YOUR OWN WRITING**, Chapter 33 on **BEGINNING AND ENDING**, and Chapter 34 on **GUIDING YOUR READER**.

298–300
301–5
331–43
344–49

Choosing Genres 24

Write an essay responding to one of the course readings. Show how James Joyce uses financial and economic imagery in "Araby." Explore the various policies adopted toward the use of marijuana. Much of the time, your college writing assignments will specify a particular genre, but sometimes — as these examples suggest — they won't. Vague verbs like *discuss* or *explore* may leave you wondering exactly what your instructor expects. This chapter will help you decide what genre(s) to use when an assignment doesn't tell you what to do.

Recognizing Which Genres Are Required

LITERACY NARRATIVE   A personal account of how you learned to read or write or to make meaning through words, pictures, music, or other means. If you're assigned to explore your development as a writer or reader or to describe how you came to be interested in a particular subject or career, you'll likely need to write a literacy narrative or a variation on one. Some terms that might signal a literacy narrative: *describe a learning experience, tell how you learned, trace your development, write a story.*

▲ 73–93

TEXTUAL ANALYSIS or **LITERARY ANALYSIS**   A careful examination of a text both for what it says and for how it says it, with the goal of demonstrating the ways the text achieves certain effects. If your assignment calls on you to look at a nonfiction text to see not only what it says but how it works, you likely need to write a textual analysis. If the text is a short story, novel, poem, or play, you probably need to write a literary analysis. If you are analyzing a text or texts in multiple media, you might choose either genre

▲ 94–128
206–15

or mix the two. Some terms that might signal that a textual or literary analysis is being asked for: *analyze, examine, explicate, read closely, interpret.*

129–55 ◸

REPORT A presentation of information as objectively as possible to inform readers about a subject. If your task is to research a topic and then tell your audience in a balanced, neutral way what you know about it, your goal is probably to write a report. Some terms that might signal that a report is being asked for: *define, describe, explain, inform, observe, record, report, show.*

156–82 ◸

POSITION PAPER or **ARGUMENT** Writing that asserts a belief or claim about an issue — usually stated as a thesis — and supports it with reasons and various kinds of evidence. Some terms that might signal that your instructor wants you to take a position or argue for or against something: *agree or disagree, argue, claim, criticize, defend, justify, position paper, prove.*

183–87 ◸
486–87 ●

ABSTRACT or **SUMMARY** A condensation of a text into a briefer version that conveys the main points of the original. If your assignment is to reduce a text, either someone else's or your own, into a single paragraph or so, one of these genres is called for. A summary usually either stands on its own or is inserted within a larger text you're writing; an abstract is a condensation of a text you've written yourself, and you write it either to submit the text for publication or to serve as an introduction to the text. Some terms that might signal that an abstract or summary is expected: *abridge, boil down, compress, condense, recap, summarize.*

188–96 ◸

ANNOTATED BIBLIOGRAPHY A genre that includes an overview of published research and scholarship on a topic. Assignments asking you to list potential sources on a topic with complete publication information for and descriptions or evaluations of each one are likely asking for annotated bibliographies. Some terms that might signal that an annotated bibliography is expected: *an annotated list, list and comment on, list and describe, list and evaluate, list sources.*

197–205 ◸

EVALUATION Writing that makes a judgment about something — a source, poem, film, restaurant, whatever — based on certain criteria. If your instructor asks you to say whether or not you like something or whether it's a good or bad example of a category or better or worse than something else, an evaluation is likely being called for. Some terms that might signal that an evaluation is expected: *assess, critique, evaluate, judge, recommend, review*.

MEMOIR   A genre of writing that focuses on something significant in your past. If you're asked to explore an important moment or event in your life, you're probably being asked to write a memoir. Some terms that likely signal that a memoir is desired: *autobiography, chronicle, narrate, a significant personal memory, a story drawn from your experience*.

▲ 216–23

PROFILE   A type of writing that presents a person, place, or event from an interesting angle in an engaging way and is based on firsthand field research. If your instructor assigns you the task of portraying a subject in a way that is both informative and entertaining, you're likely being asked to write a profile. Some terms that might indicate that a profile is being asked for: *angle, describe, dominant impression, interview, observe, report on*.

▲ 224–34

PROPOSAL   Writing that argues for a particular solution to a problem or suggests some action — or that makes a case for pursuing a certain project. Some terms that might indicate a proposal: *argue for [a solution or action], propose, put forward, recommend*.

▲ 235–44

REFLECTION   A genre of writing that presents a writer's thoughtful, personal exploration of a subject. If your assignment calls on you to think in writing about something or to play with ideas, you are likely being asked to write a reflection. Some terms that may mean that a reflection is called for: *consider, explore, ponder, probe, reflect, speculate*.

▲ 245–52

Dealing with Ambiguous Assignments

Sometimes even the key term in an assignment doesn't indicate clearly which genre is wanted, so you need to read such an assignment especially carefully. A first step might be to consider whether it's asking for a report or an argument. For example, here are two sample assignments:

> Discuss ways in which the invention of gas and incandescent lighting significantly changed people's daily lives in the nineteenth century.
>
> Discuss why Willy Loman in *Death of a Salesman* is, or is not, a tragic hero.

Both assignments use the word *discuss*, but in very different ways. The first may be simply be requesting an informative, researched report: the thesis — new forms of lighting significantly changed people's daily lives in various ways — is already given, and you may be simply expected to research and explain what some of these changes were. It's also possible, though, that this assignment is asking you to make an argument about which of these changes were the most significant ones.

In contrast, *discuss* in the second assignment is much more open-ended. It does not lead to a particular thesis but is more clearly asking you to present an argument: to choose a position (Willy Loman is a tragic hero; Willy Loman is *not* a tragic hero; even, possibly, Willy Loman *is and is not* a tragic hero) and to marshal reasons and evidence from the play to support your position. A clue that an argument is being asked for lies in the way the assignment offers a choice of paths.

Other potentially ambiguous words in assignments are *show* and *explore*, both of which could lead in many directions. If after a careful reading of the entire assignment you still aren't sure what it's asking for, ask your instructor to clarify the appropriate genre or genres.

Mixing Genres

Genres are seldom "pure" — a pure argument, a pure memoir, a pure literary analysis. Most of the writing we read and produce mixes genres to meet the needs of the writer's purpose and audience. For example, writing that **TAKES A POSITION** rarely jumps into the argument immediately. Instead, it may include several paragraphs in which the context for the disputed position is explained or information crucial to the audience's understanding is reported. Sometimes that **REPORT** will be introduced by

156–82 △

129–55 △

academic literacies ✳ | rhetorical situations ■ | genres ▲ | processes ○ | strategies ◆ | research MLA / APA ● | media / design ☐ | readings ◗◖ | handbook ▨

a brief **MEMOIR** that makes the topic personal to the writer and so less abstract. And the argument itself may well do much more than simply take a position — it may **EVALUATE** alternatives and end with a **PROPOSAL**, and even include genres in other media, such as a video clip **PROFILING** the subject of the argument.

216–23
197–205
235–44
224–34

A decision about whether to mix genres or not should depend primarily on your purpose and audience. If doing so would help you achieve your goal, and you are not restricted to a particular genre, then combining genres is appropriate. Be creative — but not to the extent that you confuse or annoy readers who expect, say, a straightforward academic report. And if you are required to write using a single genre, then you must find ways of making it suit your purpose.

Considering the Rhetorical Situation

If you're still unsure which genre or combination of genres you should use, try exploring your rhetorical situation by answering some or all of the following questions:

PURPOSE   Why are you writing? What do you hope to achieve? What genre(s) do writers typically use to achieve this purpose? Where might you find examples of these genres? What alternatives to these genres are available?

55–56

AUDIENCE   To whom are you writing? How do members of this audience typically communicate with one another? What information do they typically include, and what do they omit? How much information or explanation will they need? Will they expect you to cite the work of others?

57–60

GENRE   What will your audience expect? Which ones do they use themselves in similar situations?

61–63

STANCE   What stance do you wish to project — and what stances are acceptable for your audience and purpose? What is

64–67

your relationship with your audience? Are you writing as an equal, a student, an interested or concerned outsider, something else? What tone is appropriate — objective, impassioned, respectful, informal, something else? What genre(s) will allow you to express that tone?

68–70 ■

MEDIA / DESIGN   What media are typically used to communicate in this situation, and do these media suggest or encourage a particular genre? If so, does the genre require a particular design or format? Are charts, graphs, photos, or other visual elements typically included?

part 4

Processes

To create anything, we generally break the work down into a series of steps. We follow a recipe (or the directions on a box) to bake a cake; we break a song down into different parts and the music into various chords to arrange a piece of music. So it is when we write. We rely on various processes to get from a blank screen or page to a finished product. The chapters that follow offer advice on some of these processes—from WRITING AS INQUIRY and GENERATING IDEAS to DRAFTING to GETTING RESPONSE to EDITING to COMPILING A PORTFOLIO, and more.

Processes

Writing as Inquiry 25

Sometimes we write to say what we think. Other times, however, we write in order to figure out what we think. Much of the writing you do in college will be the latter. Even as you learn to write, you will be writing to learn. This chapter is about writing with a spirit of inquiry — approaching writing projects with curiosity, moving beyond the familiar, keeping your eyes open, tackling issues that don't have easy answers. It's about starting with questions and going from there — and taking risks. As Mark Twain once said, "Sail away from the safe harbor. . . . Explore. Dream. Discover." This chapter offers strategies for doing just that with your writing.

Starting with Questions

The most important thing is to start with questions — with what you don't know rather than with what you do know. Your goal is to learn about your subject and then to learn more. If you're writing about a topic you know well, you want to expand on what you already know. In academic writing, good topics arise from important questions, issues, and problems that are already being discussed. As a writer, you need to find out what's being said about your topic and then see your writing as a way of entering that larger conversation.

So start with questions, and don't expect to find easy answers. If there were easy answers, there would be no reason for discussion — or for you to write. For purposes of inquiry, the best questions can't be answered by looking in a reference book. Instead, they are ones that help you explore what you think — and why. As it happens, many of the strategies in this book can help you ask questions of this kind. Following are some questions to get you started.

academic literacies | rhetorical situations | genres | processes | strategies | research MLA / APA | media / design | readings | handbook

388–98 **How can it be DEFINED?**　What is it, and what does it do? Look it up in a dictionary; check *Wikipedia*. Remember, though, that these are only starting points. How *else* can it be defined? What more is there to know about it? If your topic is being debated, chances are that its very definition is subject to debate. If, for instance, you're writing about gay marriage, how you define marriage will affect how you approach the topic.

399–407 **How can it be DESCRIBED?**　What details should you include? From what vantage point should you describe your topic? If, for example, your topic were the physiological effects of running a marathon, what would those effects be — on the lungs, heart muscles, nerves, brain, and so on? How would you describe the physical experience of running over twenty-six miles from the runner's point of view?

414–18 **How can it be EXPLAINED?**　What does it do? How does it work? If you were investigating the use of performance-enhancing drugs by athletes, for example, what exactly is the effect of these drugs? What makes them dangerous — and are they always dangerous or only in certain conditions? Why are they illegal — and should they be illegal?

380–87 **What can it be COMPARED with?**　Again using performance-enhancing drugs by athletes as an example, how does taking such supplements compare with wearing high-tech footwear or uniforms? Does such a comparison make you see taking steroids or other performance-enhancing drugs in a new light?

350–54 **What may have CAUSED it? What might be its EFFECTS?**　Who or what does it affect? What causes cerebral palsy in children, for example? What are its symptoms? If children with cerebral palsy are not treated, what might be the consequences?

375–79 **How can it be CLASSIFIED?**　Is it a topic or issue that can be placed into categories of similar topics or issues? What categories can it be placed into? Are there legal and illegal performance-enhancing supplements (human growth hormone and steroids, for instance), and what's the difference? Are some safe and others less safe? Classifying your topic in this way can help you consider its complexities.

How can it be ANALYZED?   What parts can the topic be divided into? For example, if you were exploring the health effects of cell phone use, you might ask what evidence suggests that cell phone radiation causes cancer? What cancers are associated with cell phone use? What do medical experts and phone manufacturers say? How can cell phone users reduce their risk?

▲ 94–128

How can it be interpreted?   What does it really mean? How do you interpret it, and how does your interpretation differ from others? What evidence supports your interpretation, and what argues against it? Imagine you were exploring the topic of sports injuries among young women. Do these injuries reflect a larger cultural preoccupation with competition? a desire to win college scholarships? something else?

What expectations does it raise?   What will happen next? What makes you think so? If this happens, how will it affect those involved? For instance, will the governing bodies of professional sports require more testing of athletes' blood, urine, and hair than they do now? Will such tests be unfair to athletes taking drugs for legitimate medical needs?

What are the different POSITIONS on it?   What controversies or disagreements exist, and what evidence is offered for the various positions? What else might be said? Are there any groups or individuals who seem especially authoritative? If so, you might want to explore what they have said.

▲ 156–82

What are your own feelings about it?   What interests you about the topic? How much do you already know about it? For example, if you're an athlete, how do you feel about competing against others who may have taken supplements? If a friend has problems with drugs, do those problems affect your thinking about drugs in sports? How do you react to what others say about the topic? What else do you want to find out?

Are there other ways to think about it?   Is what seems true in this case also true in others? How can you apply this subject in another situation? Will what works in another situation also work here? What do you have to do to adapt it? Imagine you were writing about traffic fatalities. If replacing stop signs with roundabouts or traffic circles reduced traffic fatalities in England, could doing so also reduce accidents in the United States?

292–93 ◐

You can also start with the journalist's **QUESTIONS**: *Who? What? When? Where? Why? How?* Asking questions from these various perspectives can help you deepen your understanding of your topic by leading you to see it from many angles.

Keeping a Journal

295–96 ◐

One way to get into the habit of using writing as a tool for inquiry is to keep a **JOURNAL**. You can use a journal to record your observations, reactions, whatever you wish. Some writers find journals especially useful places to articulate questions or speculations. You may be assigned by teachers to do certain work in a journal, but in general, you can use a journal to write for yourself. Note your ideas, speculate, digress — go wherever your thoughts lead you.

Keeping a Blog

618–19 ▢

You may also wish to explore issues or other ideas online in the form of a **BLOG**. Most blogs have a comments section that allows others to read and respond to what you write, leading to potentially fruitful discussions. You can also include links to other websites, helping you connect various strands of thought and research. The blogs of others, along with online discussion forums and groups, may also be useful sources of opinion on your topic, but keep in mind that they probably aren't authoritative research sources. There are a number of search engines that can help you find blog posts related to specific topics, including *Google Blog Search, Ask,* and *IceRocket.* You can create your own blog on sites such as *Blogger, Tumblr, Svbtle,* or *WordPress.*

Collaborating 26

Whether you're working in a face-to-face group, posting on an online discussion board or class *Facebook* page, or exchanging drafts with a classmate for peer review, you likely spend a lot of time collaborating with others on writing tasks. Even if you do much of your writing sitting alone at a computer, you probably get help from others at various stages in the writing process — and provide help as well. The fact is that two heads can be better than one — and learning to work well with a team is as important as anything else you'll learn in college. This chapter offers some guidelines for collaborating successfully with other writers.

Some Ground Rules for Face-to-Face Group Work

- Make sure everyone is facing everyone else and is physically part of the group. Doing that makes a real difference in the quality of the interactions — think how much better conversation works when you're sitting around a table than it does when you're sitting in a row.

- Thoughtfulness, respect, and tact are key, since most writers (as you know) are sensitive and need to be able to trust those commenting on their work. Respond to the contributions of others as you would like others to respond to yours.

- Each meeting needs an agenda — and careful attention paid to time. Appoint one person as timekeeper to make sure all necessary work gets done in the available time.

- Appoint another person to be group leader or facilitator. That person needs to make sure everyone gets a chance to speak, no one dominates the discussion, and the group stays on task.

- Appoint a member of the group to keep a record of the group's discussion, jotting down the major points as they come up and afterward writing a **SUMMARY** of the discussion that the group members then approve.

486–87

Online Collaboration

Sometimes you'll need or want to work with one or more people online. Working together online offers many advantages, including the ability to collaborate without being in the same place at the same time. Nonetheless, it also presents some challenges that differ from those of face-to-face group work. When sharing writing or collaborating with others online in other ways, consider the following suggestions:

- As with all online communication, remember that you need to choose your words carefully to avoid inadvertently hurting someone's feelings. Without facial expressions, gestures, and other forms of body language and without tone of voice, your words carry all the weight.

57–60

- Remember that the **AUDIENCE** for what you write may well extend beyond your group — your work might be forwarded to others, so there is no telling who else might read it.

- Decide as a group how best to deal with the logistics of exchanging drafts and comments. You can cut and paste text directly into email, send it as an attachment to a message, or post it to your class course management system site or a file-sharing site like *Dropbox* or *Google Docs*. You may need to use a combination of methods, depending on each group member's access to equipment and software. In any case, name your files carefully so that everyone knows which version to use.

Group Writing Projects

Creating a document with a team is common in business and professional work and in some academic fields as well. Here are some tips for making collaboration of this kind work well:

- *Define the task as clearly as possible.* Make sure everyone understands and agrees with the stated goals.
- *Divide the task into parts.* Decide which parts can be done by individuals, which can be done by a subgroup, and which need to be done by everyone together.
- *Assign each group member certain tasks.* Try to match tasks to each person's skills and interests and to divide the work equally.
- *Establish a deadline for each task.* Allow time for unforeseen problems before the project deadline.
- *Try to accommodate everyone's style of working.* Some people value discussion; others want to get right down to the writing. There's no best way to get work done; everyone needs to be conscious that his or her way is not the only way.
- *Work for consensus — not necessarily total agreement.* Everyone needs to agree that the plan to get the writing accomplished is doable and appropriate — if not exactly the way you would do the project if you were working alone.
- *Make sure everyone performs.* In some situations, your instructor may help, but in others the group itself may have to develop a way to make sure that the work gets done well and fairly. During the course of the project, it's sometimes helpful for each group member to write an assessment both of the group's work and of individual members' contributions.

Writing Conferences

Conferences with instructors or writing tutors can be an especially helpful kind of collaboration. These one-on-one sessions often offer the most strongly focused assistance you can get — and truly valuable instruction. Here are some tips for making the most of conference time:

- *Come prepared.* Bring all necessary materials, including the draft you'll be discussing, your notes, any outlines — and, of course, any questions.

- *Be prompt.* Your instructor or tutor has set aside a block of time for you, and once that time is up, there's likely to be another student writer waiting.

- *Listen carefully, discuss your work seriously, and try not to be defensive.* Your instructor or tutor is only trying to help you produce the best piece possible. If you sense that your work is being misunderstood, explain what you're trying to say. Don't get angry! If a sympathetic reader who's trying to help can't understand what you mean, maybe you haven't conveyed your meaning well enough.

- *Take notes.* During the conference, jot down keywords and suggestions. Immediately afterward, flesh out your notes so you'll have a complete record of what was said.

- *Reflect on the conference.* Afterward, think about what you learned. What do you have to do now? Create a plan for revising or doing further work, and write out questions you will ask at your next conference.

academic literacies

rhetorical situations

genres

processes

strategies

research MLA / APA

media / design

readings

handbook

All good writing revolves around ideas. Whether you're writing a job-application letter, a sonnet, or an essay, you'll always spend time and effort generating ideas. Some writers can come up with a topic, put their thoughts in order, and flesh out their arguments in their heads; but most of us need to write out our ideas, play with them, tease them out, and examine them from some distance and from multiple perspectives. This chapter offers activities that can help you do just that. *Freewriting*, *looping*, *listing*, and *clustering* can help you explore what you know about a subject; *cubing* and *questioning* nudge you to consider a subject in new ways; and *outlining*, *letter writing*, *journal keeping*, and *discovery drafting* offer ways to generate a text.

Freewriting

An informal method of exploring a subject by writing about it, freewriting ("writing freely") can help you generate ideas and come up with materials for your draft. Here's how to do it:

1. Write as quickly as you can without stopping for 5 to 10 minutes (or until you fill a screen or page).
2. If you have a subject to explore, write it at the top and then start writing about it, but if you stray, don't worry — just keep writing. If you don't have a subject yet, just start writing and don't stop until the time is up. If you can't think of anything to say, write that ("I can't think of anything to say") again and again until you do — and you will!
3. Once the time is up, read over what you've written, and underline or highlight passages that interest you.

4. Write some more, starting with one of those underlined or highlighted passages as your new topic. Repeat the process until you've come up with a usable topic.

Looping

Looping is a more focused version of freewriting; it can help you explore what you know about a subject. You stop, reflect on what you've written, and then write again, developing your understanding in the process. It's good for clarifying your knowledge and understanding of a subject and finding a focus. Here's what you do:

1. Write for 5 to 10 minutes on whatever you know about your subject. This is your first loop.

2. Read over what you wrote, and then write a single sentence summarizing the most important or interesting idea. You might try completing one of these sentences: "I guess what I was trying to say was . . . " or "What surprises me most in reading what I wrote is . . ." This will be the start of another loop.

3. Write again for 5 to 10 minutes, using your summary sentence as your beginning and your focus. Again, read what you've written, and then write a sentence capturing the most important idea — in a third loop.

Keep going until you have enough understanding of your topic to be able to decide on a tentative focus — something you can write about.

Listing

Some writers find it useful to keep lists of ideas that occur to them while they are thinking about a topic. Follow these steps:

1. Write a list of potential ideas about a topic. Don't try to limit your list — include anything that interests you.

academic literacies | rhetorical situations | genres | processes | strategies | research MLA / APA | media / design | readings | handbook

2. Look for relationships among the items on your list: what patterns do you see? If other ideas occur to you, add them to the list.

3. Arrange the items in an order that makes sense for your purpose and can serve as the beginning of an outline for your writing.

Clustering or Mapping Ideas

Clustering (also called idea mapping) is a way of generating and connecting ideas visually. It's useful for seeing how various ideas relate to one another and for developing subtopics. The technique is simple:

1. Write your topic in the middle of a sheet of paper and circle it.

2. Write ideas relating to that topic around it, circle them, and connect them to the central circle.

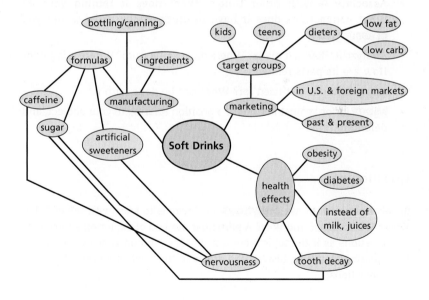

3. Write down examples, facts, or other details relating to each idea, and join them to the appropriate circles.

4. Keep going until you can't think of anything else relating to your topic.

You should end up with various ideas about your topic, and the clusters will allow you to see how they relate to one another. In the example cluster on the topic of "soft drinks" from page 291, note how some ideas link not only to the main topic or related topics but also to other ideas.

Cubing

A cube has six sides. You can examine a topic as you might a cube, looking at it in these six ways:

399–407
- **DESCRIBE** it. What's its color? shape? age? size? What's it made of?

380–87
- **COMPARE** it to something else. What is it similar to or different from?

374–79
- Associate it with other things. What does it remind you of? What connections does it have to other things? How would you **CLASSIFY** it?

- Analyze it. How is it made? Where did it come from? Where is it going? How are its parts related?

- Apply it. What is it used for? What can be done with it?

156–82
- **ARGUE** for or against it. Choose a position relating to your subject, and defend it.

Questioning

281–84
It's always useful to ask **QUESTIONS**. One way is to start with *What? Who? When? Where? How?* and *Why?* A particular method of exploring a topic is to ask questions as if the topic were a play. This method is especially useful for exploring literature, history, the arts, and the social sciences. Start with these questions:

- *What?* What happens? How is it similar to or different from other actions?
- *Who?* Who are the actors? Who are the participants, and who are the spectators? How do the actors affect the action, and how are they affected by it?
- *When?* When does the action take place? How often does it happen? What happens before, after, or at the same time? Would it be different at another time? Does the time have historical significance?
- *Where?* What is the setting? What is the situation, and what makes it significant?
- *How?* How does the action occur? What are the steps in the process? What techniques are required? What equipment is needed?
- *Why?* Why did this happen? What are the actors' motives? What end does the action serve?

Using Genre Features

Genres typically include particular kinds of information and organize it in particular ways. One way to generate ideas and text, then, is to identify the key features of the genre in which you're writing and use them to guide you as you write. Of course, you may alter the genre's features or combine two or more genres in order to achieve your purpose, but the overall shape and content of the genre can give you a way to develop and organize your ideas and research.

Outlining

You may create an *informal outline* by simply listing your ideas and numbering them in the order in which you want to write about them. You might prefer to make a *working outline*, to show the hierarchy of relationships among your ideas. While still informal, a working outline distinguishes your main ideas and your support, often through simple indentation:

> First main idea
>> Supporting evidence or detail
>> Supporting evidence or detail
>
> Second main idea
>> Supporting evidence or detail
>> Supporting evidence or detail

A *formal outline* shows the hierarchy of your ideas through a system of indenting, numbering, and lettering. Remember that when you divide a point into more specific subpoints, you should have at least two of them — you can't divide something into only one part. Also, try to keep items at each level parallel in structure. Formal outlines work this way:

> Thesis statement
> I. First reason
>> A. Supporting evidence
>>> 1. Detail of evidence
>>> 2. Detail of evidence
>> B. Supporting evidence
> II. Another reason

Here is a formal outline of the research report by Carolyn Stonehill on pages 579–89, "It's in Our Genes," that shows how she organized it:

> I. Introduction: Reasons for choosing mates
> II. Women
>> A. Experience long pregnancy, childbirth risks, and infant dependence
>> B. Are attracted to signs of resources and protective ability
> III. Men
>> A. Need mates with reproductive fitness
>> B. Are attracted to signs of health and youth

    IV. Possible objections to biological theory of selection
       A. Role of culture
          1. Media influence on selection standards
          2. Unclear relation between cause and effect
       B. Role of species-specific development
          1. Symbolic thought as unique human quality
          2. Impossibility of inherited preferences
    V. Conclusion: Dominant influence of ancestral strategies

Writing out a formal outline can be helpful when you're dealing with a complex subject; as you revise your drafts, though, be flexible and ready to change your outline as your understanding of your topic develops.

Letter Writing

Sometimes the prospect of writing a report or essay can be intimidating. You may find that simply explaining your topic to someone will help you get started. In that case, write a letter or email to someone you know — your best friend, a parent or grandparent, a sibling — in which you discuss your subject. Explain it in terms that your reader can understand. Use the unsent letter to rehearse your topic; make it a kind of rough draft that you can then revise and develop to suit your actual audience.

Keeping a Journal

Some writers find that writing in a journal helps them generate ideas. Making note of your ideas, thoughts, feelings, or the events of your day can provide a wealth of topics, and a journal can also be a good place to explore what you think and why you think as you do.

Journals are private — you are the only audience — so you can feel free to write whatever comes to mind. And you can do more than write.

If you choose a paper journal, doodle or draw in it, and keep clippings or scraps of paper between the pages; if you keep your journal on a computer, copy and paste interesting images or text you find online. Whatever form your journal takes, feel free to play with its contents, and don't worry about errors or grammar. The goal is to generate ideas; let yourself wander without censoring yourself or fretting that your writing is incorrect or incomplete or incoherent. That's okay.

289–90 ◉
290–91
292

One measure of the success of journaling and other personal writing is length: journal entries, **FREEWRITING**, **LISTING**, **CUBING**, and other types of informal writing are like warm-up exercises to limber you up and get you thinking. If you don't give them enough time and space, they may not do what you want them to. Often, students' best insights appear at the end of their journal entries. Had they stopped before that point, they would never have had those good ideas.

After you've written several journal entries, one way to study the ideas in them is to highlight useful patterns in different colors. For example, journal entries usually include some questioning and speculating, as well as summarizing and paraphrasing. Try color-coding each of these, sentence by sentence, phrase by phrase: yellow for summaries or paraphrases, green for questions, blue for speculations. Do any colors dominate? If, for example, your entries are mostly yellow, you may be restating the course content or quoting from the textbook too much and perhaps need to ask more questions. If you're generating ideas for an essay, you might assign colors to ideas or themes to see which ones are the most promising.

Discovery Drafting

Some writers do best by jumping in and writing. Here are the steps to take if you're ready to write a preliminary **DRAFT**:

298–300 ◉

1. Write your draft quickly, in one sitting if possible.

2. Assume that you are writing to discover what you want to say and how you need to say it — and that you will make substantial revisions in a later part of the process.

3. Don't worry about grammatical or factual correctness — if you can't think of a word, leave a blank space to fill in later. If you're unsure of a date or spelling, put a question mark in parentheses as a reminder to check it later. Just write.

IF YOU NEED MORE HELP

See each of the GENRE chapters for specific strategies for generating text in each genre.

▲ 71

28 Drafting

At some point, you need to write out a draft. By the time you begin drafting, you've probably written quite a bit — in the form of notes, lists, outlines, and other kinds of informal writing. This chapter offers some hints on how to write a draft — and reminds you that as you draft, you may well need to get more information, rethink some aspect of your work, or follow new ideas that occur to you as you write.

Establishing a Schedule with Deadlines

Don't wait until the last minute to write. Computers crash, printers jam. Life intervenes in unpredictable ways. You increase your chances of success immensely by setting and meeting **DEADLINES**: Research done by ___; rough draft done by ___; revisions done by ___; final draft edited, proofread, and submitted by ___. How much time you need varies with each writing task — but trying to compress everything into twenty-four or forty-eight hours before the deadline is asking for trouble.

435–36

Getting Comfortable

When are you at your best? When do you have your best ideas? For major writing projects, consider establishing a schedule that lets you write when you stand the best chance of doing good work. Schedule breaks for exercise and snacks. Find a good place to write, a place where you've got a good surface on which to spread out your materials, good lighting, a comfortable chair, and the right tools (computer, pen, paper) for the job. Often, however, we must make do: you may have to do your drafting in a busy computer lab or classroom. The trick is to make yourself as comfortable as you can manage. Sort out what you *need* from what you *prefer*.

academic literacies | rhetorical situations | genres | processes | strategies | research MLA / APA | media / design | readings | handbook

Starting to Write

All of the above advice notwithstanding, don't worry so much about the trappings of your writing situation that you don't get around to writing. Write. Start by **FREEWRITING**, start with a first sentence, start with awful writing that you know you'll discard later — but write. That's what gets you warmed up and going.

◉ 289–90

Write quickly in spurts.   Write quickly with the goal of writing a complete draft, or a complete section of a longer draft, in one sitting. If you need to stop in the middle, make some notes about where you were headed when you stopped so that you can easily pick up your train of thought when you begin again.

Break down your writing task into small segments.   Big projects can be intimidating. But you can always write one section or, if need be, one paragraph or even a single sentence — and then another and another. It's a little like dieting. If I think I need to lose twenty pounds, I get discouraged and head for the doughnuts; but if I decide that I'll lose one pound and I lose it, well, I'll lose another — *that* I can do.

Expect surprises.   Writing is a form of thinking; the words you write lead you down certain roads and away from others. You may end up somewhere you didn't anticipate. Sometimes that can be a good thing — but sometimes you can write yourself into a dead end or out onto a tangent. Just know that this is natural, part of every writer's experience, and it's okay to double back or follow a new path that opens up before you.

Expect to write more than one draft.   A first sentence, first page, or first draft represents your attempt to organize into words your thoughts, ideas, feelings, research findings, and more. It's likely that some of that first try will not achieve your goals. That's okay — having writing on screen or on paper that you can change, add to, and cut means you're part of the way there. As you revise, you can fill in gaps and improve your writing and thinking.

Dealing with Writer's Block

You may sit down to write but find that you can't — nothing occurs to you; your mind is blank. Don't panic; here are some ways to get started writing again:

- Think of the assignment as a problem to be solved. Try to capture that problem in a single sentence: "How do I explain the context for my topic?" "What is the best way to organize my argument?" "What am I trying to do in the conclusion?"

- Start early and break the writing task into small segments drafted over several days. Waiting until the night before an assignment is due can create panic — and writer's block

- Stop trying: take a walk, take a shower, do something else. Come back in a half hour, refreshed.

289–91 ◉
- Open a new document on your computer or get a fresh piece of paper and **FREEWRITE**, or try **LOOPING** or **LISTING**. What are you trying to say? Just let whatever comes come — you may write yourself out of your box.

- If you usually write on your computer, turn it off, get out paper and pencil, and write by hand.

291–92 ◉
- Try a graphic approach: try **CLUSTERING**, or draw a chart of what you want to say; draw a picture; doodle.

433 ●
- Do some **RESEARCH** on your topic to see what others have said about it.

306–7 ◉
- Talk to someone about what you are trying to do. If there's a writing center at your school, talk to a tutor: **GET RESPONSE**. If there's no one to talk to, talk to yourself. It's the act of talking — using your mouth instead of your hands — that can free you up.

IF YOU NEED MORE HELP

289–97 ◉
301–5
306–12
See the chapter on **GENERATING IDEAS AND TEXT** if you find you need more material. And once you have a draft, see the chapters on **ASSESSING YOUR OWN WRITING** and **GETTING RESPONSE AND REVISING** for help evaluating your draft.

In school and out, our work is continually assessed by others. Teachers determine whether our writing is strong or weak; supervisors decide whether we merit raises or promotions; even friends and relatives size up in various ways the things we do. As writers, we need to assess our own work — to step back and see it with a critical eye. By developing standards of our own and being conscious of the standards others use, we can assess — and shape — our writing, making sure it does what we want it to do. This chapter will help you assess your own written work.

What we write for others must stand on its own because we usually aren't present when it is read — we rarely get to explain to readers why we did what we did and what it means. So we need to make our writing as clear as we can before we submit, post, display, or publish it. It's a good idea to assess your writing in two stages, first considering how well it meets the needs of your particular rhetorical situation, then studying the text itself to check its focus, argument, organization, and clarity. Sometimes some simple questions can get you started:

What works?
What still needs work?
Where do I need to say more (or less)?

Considering the Rhetorical Situation

PURPOSE   What is your purpose for writing? If you have multiple purposes, list them, and then note which ones are the most important. How well does your draft achieve your purpose(s)? If you're writing for an assignment, what are

55–56

the requirements of the assignment, and does your draft meet those requirements?

57–60 **AUDIENCE**   To whom are you writing? What do those readers need and expect, as far as you can tell? Does your draft answer their needs? Do you define any terms and explain any concepts they won't know?

61–63 **GENRE**   What is the genre, and what are the key features of that genre? Does your draft include each of those features? If not, is there a good reason?

64–67 **STANCE**   Is your attitude toward your topic and your audience clear? Does your language project the personality and tone that you want?

68–70 **MEDIA/DESIGN**   What medium (print? spoken? electronic?) or combination of media is your text intended for, and how well does your writing suit it? How well does the design of the text suit your purpose and audience? Does it meet any requirements of the genre or of the assignment, if you're writing for one?

Examining the Text Itself

Look carefully at your text to see how well it says what you want it to say. Start with its focus, and then examine its reasons and evidence, organization, and clarity, in that order. If your writing lacks focus, the revising you'll do to sharpen the focus is likely to change everything else; if it needs more reasons and evidence, the organization may well change.

Consider your focus.   Your writing should have a clear point, and every part of the writing should support that point. Here are some questions that can help you see if your draft is adequately focused:

345–47 • What is your **THESIS**? Even if it is not stated directly, you should be able to summarize it for yourself in a single sentence.

academic literacies   rhetorical situations   genres   processes   strategies   research MLA / APA   media / design   readings   handbook

- Is your thesis narrow or broad enough to suit the needs and expectations of your audience?
- How does the **BEGINNING** focus attention on your thesis or main point?   331–38
- Does each paragraph support or develop that point? Do any paragraphs or sentences stray from your focus?
- Does the **ENDING** leave readers thinking about your main point? Is there another way of concluding the essay that would sharpen your focus?   338–42

Consider the support you provide for your argument. Your writing needs to give readers enough information to understand your points, follow your argument, and see the logic of your thinking. How much information is enough will vary according to your audience. If they already know a lot about your subject or are likely to agree with your point of view, you may need to give less detail. If, however, they are unfamiliar with your topic or are skeptical about your views, you will probably need to provide much more.

- What **REASONS** and **EVIDENCE** do you give to support your thesis? Where might more information be helpful? If you're writing online, could you provide links to it?   358–67
- What key terms and concepts do you **DEFINE**? Are there any other terms your readers might need to have explained? Could you do so by providing links?   388–98
- Where might you include more **DESCRIPTION** or other detail?   399–407
- Do you make any **COMPARISONS**? Especially if your readers will not be familiar with your topic, it can help to compare it with something more familiar.   380–87
- If you include **NARRATIVE**, how is it relevant to your point?   419–27
- See Part 5 for other useful **STRATEGIES**.   329

Consider the organization.   As a writer, you need to lead readers through your text, carefully structuring your material so that they will be able to follow your argument.

- Analyze the structure by **OUTLINING** it. An informal outline will do since you mainly need to see the parts, not the details.

293–95

- Is your text complete? Does your genre require an **ABSTRACT**, a **WORKS-CITED LIST**, or any other elements?

578
510–37

- What **TRANSITIONS** help readers move from idea to idea and paragraph to paragraph? Do you need more?

349

- If there are no **HEADINGS**, would adding them help orient readers?

604–5

Check for clarity. Nothing else matters if readers can't understand what you write. Following are some questions that can help you see whether your meaning is clear and your text is easy to read:

- Does your **TITLE** announce the subject of your text and give some sense of what you have to say? If not, would a more direct title strengthen your argument?

344–45

- Do you state your **THESIS** directly? If not, will readers easily understand what your main point is? Try stating your thesis outright, and see if it makes your argument easier to follow.

345–47

- Does your **BEGINNING** tell readers what they need to understand your text, and does your **ENDING** help them make sense of what they've just read?

331–38
338–42

- How does each paragraph relate to the ones before and after? Are those relationships clear — or do you need to add **TRANSITIONS**?

349

- Do you vary your sentences? If all the sentences are roughly the same length or follow the same subject-verb-object pattern, your text probably lacks any clear emphasis and might even be difficult to read.

- Are **VISUALS** clearly labeled, positioned near the text they relate to, and referred to clearly in the text?

607–15

- If you introduce materials from other sources, have you clearly distinguished **QUOTED**, **PARAPHRASED**, or **SUMMARIZED** ideas from your own?

478–90

- Do you **DEFINE** all the words that your readers may not know?

388–98

academic literacies · rhetorical situations · genres · processes · strategies · research MLA / APA · media / design · readings · handbook

- Does your punctuation make your writing more clear or less? Incorrect punctuation can make writing difficult to follow or, worse, change the meaning from what you intended. As a best-selling punctuation manual reminds us, there's a considerable difference between "eats, shoots, and leaves" and "eats shoots and leaves."

Thinking about Your Process

Your growth as a writer depends on how well you understand what you do when you write so that you can build on good habits. After you finish a writing project, considering the following questions can help you see the process that led to its creation — and find ways to improve the process next time.

- How would you tell the story of your thinking? Try writing these sentences: "When I first began with my topic, I thought _____. But as I did some thinking, writing, and research about the topic, my ideas changed and I thought _____."
- At some point in your writing, did you have to choose between two or more alternatives? What were they, and how did you choose?
- What was the most difficult problem you faced while writing? How did you go about trying to solve it?
- Whose advice did you seek while researching, organizing, drafting, revising, and editing? What advice did you take, and what did you ignore? Why?

Assessing a Body of Your Work

If you are required to submit a portfolio of your writing as part of a class, you will likely need to write a letter or essay that introduces the portfolio's contents and describes the processes that you used to create them and that **ASSESSES THE WRITING IN YOUR PORTFOLIO**. See Chapter 32 for detailed advice and a good example of a portfolio self-assessment.

◉ 322–25

30 Getting Response and Revising

If we want to learn to play a song on the guitar, we play it over and over again until we get it right. If we play basketball or baseball, we likely spend hours shooting foul shots or practicing a swing. Writing works the same way. Making meaning clear can be tricky, and you should plan on revising and, if need be, rewriting in order to get it right. When we speak with someone face-to-face or on the phone or text a friend, we can get immediate response and restate or adjust our message if we've been misunderstood. In most other situations when we write, that immediate response is missing, so we need to seek out responses from readers to help us revise. This chapter includes a list of things for those readers to consider, along with various strategies for subsequent revising and rewriting.

Getting Response

Sometimes the most helpful eyes belong to others: readers you trust, including trained writing-center tutors. They can often point out problems (and strengths) that you simply cannot see in your own work. Ask your readers to consider the specific elements in the list below, but don't restrict them to those elements. Caution: if a reader says nothing about any of these elements, don't be too quick to assume that you needn't think about them yourself.

344–45 • What did you think when you first saw the **TITLE**? Is it interesting? informative? appropriate? Will it attract other readers' attention?

331–38 • Does the **BEGINNING** grab your attention? If so, how does it do so? Does it give enough information about the topic? offer necessary background information? How else might the piece begin?

345–47 • Is there a clear **THESIS**? What is it?

academic literacies   rhetorical situations   genres   processes   strategies   research MLA / APA   media / design   readings   handbook

- Is there sufficient **SUPPORT** for the thesis? Is there anywhere you'd like to have more detail? Is the supporting material sufficiently **DOCUMENTED**?

  356–67
  496–99

- Does the text have a clear pattern of organization? Does each part relate to the thesis? Does each part follow from the one preceding it? Was the text easy to follow? How might the organization be improved?

- Is the **ENDING** satisfying? What did it leave you thinking? How else might the piece end?

  338–42

- Can you tell the writer's **STANCE** or attitude toward the subject and audience? What words convey that attitude? Is it consistent throughout?

  64–67

- How well does the text meet the needs and expectations of its **AUDIENCE**? Where might readers need more information, guidance, or clarification? How well does it achieve its **PURPOSE**? Does every part of the text help achieve the purpose? Could anything be cut? Should anything be added? Does the text meet the requirements of its **GENRE**? Should anything be added, deleted, or changed to meet those requirements?

  57–60
  55–56
  61–63

Revising

Once you have studied your draft with a critical eye and, if possible, gotten responses from other readers, it's time to revise. Major changes may be necessary, and you may need to generate new material or do some rewriting. But assume that your draft is good raw material that you can revise to achieve your purposes. Revision should take place on several levels, from global (whole-text issues) to particular (the details). Work on your draft in that order, starting with the elements that are global in nature and gradually moving to smaller, more particular aspects. This allows you to use your time most efficiently and take care of bigger issues first. In fact, as you deal with the larger aspects of your writing, many of the smaller ones will be taken care of along the way.

Give yourself time to revise. When you have a due date, set deadlines for yourself that will give you time — preferably several days but as much as your schedule permits — to work on the text before it has to be delivered.

Also, get some distance. Often when you're immersed in a project, you can't see the big picture because you're so busy creating it. If you can, get away from your writing for a while and think about something else. When you return to it, you're more likely to see it freshly. If there's not time to put a draft away for several days or more, even letting it sit overnight or for a few hours can help.

As you revise, assume that nothing is sacred. Bring a critical eye to all parts of a draft, not only to those parts pointed out by your reviewers. Content, organization, sentence patterns, individual words—all are subject to improvement. Be aware that a change in one part of the text may require changes in other parts.

At the same time, don't waste energy struggling with writing that simply doesn't work; you can always discard it. Look for the parts of your draft that do work — the parts that match your purpose and say what you want to say. Focus your efforts on those bright spots, expanding and developing them.

345–47
55–56
293–95

Revise to sharpen your focus. Examine your **THESIS** to make sure it matches your **PURPOSE** as you now understand it. Read each paragraph to ensure that it contributes to your main point; you may find it helpful to **OUTLINE** your draft to help you see all the parts. One way to do this is to highlight one sentence in each paragraph that expresses the paragraph's main idea. Then copy and paste the highlighted sentences into a new document. Does one state the thesis of the entire essay? Do the rest relate to the thesis? Are they in the best order? If not, you need to either modify the parts of the draft that don't advance your thesis or revise your thesis to reflect your draft's focus and to rearrange your points so they advance your discussion more effectively.

331–42

Read your **BEGINNING AND ENDING** carefully; make sure that the first paragraphs introduce your topic and provide any needed contextual information and that the final paragraphs provide a satisfying conclusion.

Revise to strengthen the argument. If readers find some of your claims unconvincing, you need to provide more information or more support. You may need to define terms you've assumed they will understand, offer additional examples, or provide more detail by describing, explaining

academic literacies | rhetorical situations | genres | processes | strategies | research MLA / APA | media / design | readings | handbook

processes, adding dialogue, or using some other **STRATEGIES**. Make sure you show as well as tell — and don't forget that you might need to do so literally, with visuals like photos, graphs, or charts. You might try freewriting, clustering, or other ways of **GENERATING IDEAS AND TEXT**. If you need to provide additional evidence, you might need to do additional **RESEARCH**.

◆ 329

◉ 289–97
● 433

Revise to improve the organization.   If you've outlined your draft, number each paragraph, and make sure each one follows from the one before. If anything seems out of place, move it, or if necessary, cut it completely. Check to see if you've included appropriate **TRANSITIONS** or **HEADINGS** to help readers move through the text, and add them as needed. Check to make sure your text meets readers' expectations of the **GENRE** you're writing in.

◆ 349

☐ 604–5

■ 61–63

Revise for clarity.   Be sure readers will be able to understand what you're saying. Look closely at your **TITLE** to be sure it gives a sense of what the text is about and at your **THESIS**: will readers recognize your main point? If you don't state a thesis directly, consider whether you should. Provide any necessary background information and **DEFINE** any key terms. Make sure you've integrated any **QUOTATIONS**, **PARAPHRASES**, or **SUMMARIES** into your text smoothly. Are all paragraphs focused around one main point? Do the sentences in each paragraph contribute to that point? Finally, consider whether there are any data that would be more clearly presented in a **CHART**, **TABLE**, or **GRAPH**.

◆ 344–45
345–47

◆ 388–98
● 478–90

☐ 609–11

One way to test whether your text is clear is to switch audiences: write what you're trying to express as if you were talking to an eight-year-old. Your final draft probably won't be written that way, but the act of explaining your ideas to a young audience or readers who know nothing about your topic can help you discover any points that may be unclear.

Read and reread — and reread.   Take some advice from writing theorist Donald Murray:

> Nonwriters confront a writing problem and look away from the text to rules and principles and textbooks and handbooks and models. Writers look at the text, knowing that the text itself will reveal what needs to be done and what should not yet be done or may never be done.

> The writer reads and rereads and rereads, standing far back and reading quickly from a distance, moving in close and reading slowly line by line, reading again and again, knowing that the answers to all writing problems lie within the evolving text.
>
> — Donald Murray, *A Writer Teaches Writing*

Rewriting

Some writers find it useful to try rewriting a draft in various ways or from various perspectives just to explore possibilities. Try it! If you find that your original plan works best for your purpose, fine. But you may find that another way will work better. Especially if you're not completely satisfied with your draft, consider the following ways of rewriting. Experiment with your rhetorical situation:

- Rewrite your draft from different points of view, through the eyes of different people perhaps or through the eyes of an animal or even from the perspective of an object. See how the text changes (in the information it presents, its perspective, its voice).

57–60 ■
- Rewrite for a different **AUDIENCE**. How might an email detailing a recent car accident be written to a friend, an insurance agent, a parent?

64–67 ■
- Rewrite in a different **TONE**. If the first draft was temperate and judicious, be extreme; if it was polite, be more direct. If the first draft was in standard English, rewrite it more informally.

61–63 ■
68–70 ■
- Rewrite the draft in a different **GENRE** or **MEDIUM**. Rewrite an essay as a letter, story, poem, speech, comic strip, *PowerPoint* presentation. Which genre and medium work best to reach your intended audience and achieve your purpose?

Ways of rewriting a narrative

408–13 ◆
- Rewrite one scene completely in **DIALOGUE**.
- Start at the end of the story and work back to the beginning, or start in the middle and fill in the beginning as you work toward the end.

Ways of rewriting a textual analysis

- **COMPARE** the text you're analyzing with another text (which may be in a completely different genre — film, TV, song lyrics, computer games, poetry, fiction, whatever). 380–87

- Write a parody of the text you're analyzing. Be as silly and as funny as you can while maintaining the structure of the original text. Alternatively, write a parody of your analysis, using evidence from the text to support an outrageous analysis.

Ways of rewriting a report

- Rewrite for a different **AUDIENCE**. For example, explain a concept to your grandparents; describe the subject of a profile to a visitor from another planet. 57–60

- Be silly. Rewrite the draft as if for *The Daily Show* or the *Onion*, or rewrite it as if it were written by Bart Simpson.

Ways of rewriting an argument

- Rewrite taking another **POSITION**. Argue as forcefully for that position as you did for your actual one, acknowledging and refuting your original position. Alternatively, write a rebuttal to your first draft from the perspective of someone with different beliefs. 156–82

- Rewrite your draft as a **STORY**—make it real in the lives of specific individuals. (For example, if you were writing about abortion rights, you could write a story about a young pregnant woman trying to decide what she believes and what to do.) Or rewrite the argument as a fable or parable. 419–27

- Rewrite the draft as a letter responding to a hostile reader, trying at least to make him or her understand what you have to say.

- Rewrite the draft as an angry letter to someone or as a table-thumping dinner-with-the-relatives discussion. Write from the most extreme position possible.

115–16

- Write an **ANALYSIS** of the topic of your argument in which you identify, as carefully and as neutrally as you can, the various positions people hold on the issue.

Once you've rewritten a draft in any of these ways, see whether there's anything you can use. Read each draft, considering how it might help you achieve your purpose, reach your audience, convey your stance. Revise your actual draft to incorporate anything you think will make your text more effective, whether it's other genres or a different perspective.

academic literacies

rhetorical situations

genres

processes

strategies

research MLA / APA

media / design

readings

handbook

Editing and Proofreading 31

Your ability to produce clear, error-free writing shows something about your ability as a writer and also leads readers to make assumptions about your intellect, your work habits, even your character. Readers of job-application letters and résumés, for example, may reject applications if they contain a single error, for no other reason than it's an easy way to narrow the field of potential candidates. In addition, they may well assume that applicants who present themselves sloppily in an application will do sloppy work on the job. This is all to say that you should edit and proofread your work carefully.

Editing

Editing is the stage when you work on the details of your paragraphs, sentences, words, and punctuation to make your writing as clear, precise, correct — and effective — as possible. Your goal is not to achieve "perfection" (whatever that may be) so much as to make your writing as effective as possible for your particular purpose and audience. Check a good writing handbook for detailed advice, but the following guidelines can help you check your drafts systematically for some common errors with paragraphs, sentences, and words.

Editing paragraphs

- Does each paragraph focus on one point? Does it have a **TOPIC SENTENCE** 347–48 that announces that point, and if so, where is it located? If it's not the first sentence, should it be? If there's no clear topic sentence, should there be one?

- Does every sentence relate to the main point of the paragraph? If any sentences do not, should they be deleted, moved, or revised?

329
- Is there enough detail to develop the paragraph's main point? How is the point developed — with narrative? definition? some other **STRATEGY**?

- Where have you placed the most important information—at the beginning? the end? in the middle? The most emphatic spot is at the end, so in general that's where to put information you want readers to remember. The second most emphatic spot is at the beginning.

- Are any paragraphs especially long or short? Consider breaking long paragraphs if there's a logical place to do so—maybe an extended example should be in its own paragraph, for instance. If you have paragraphs of only a sentence or two, see if you can add to them or combine them with another paragraph, unless you're using a brief paragraph to provide emphasis.

349
- Check the way your paragraphs fit together. Does each one follow smoothly from the one before? Do you need to add any **TRANSITIONS**?

331–38
- Does the **BEGINNING** paragraph catch readers' attention? In what other ways might you begin your text?

338–42
- Does the final paragraph provide a satisfactory **ENDING**? How else might you conclude your text?

Editing sentences

HB-4
- Is each sentence **COMPLETE**? Does it have someone or something (the subject) performing some sort of action or expressing a state of being (the verb)? Does each sentence begin with a capital letter and **END** with a period, question mark, or exclamation point?

HB-84–86

HB-19
- Check your use of the **PASSIVE VOICE**. Although there are some rhetorical situations in which the passive voice ("The emperor was assassinated by an anarchist") is more appropriate than the active voice ("An anarchist assassinated the emperor") because you want to emphasize an action rather than who performed it, you'll do well to edit it out unless you have a good reason for using it.

academic literacies · rhetorical situations · genres · processes · strategies · research MLA / APA · media / design · readings · handbook

- Check for **PARALLELISM**. Items in a list or series should be parallel in form — all nouns (lions, tigers, bears), all verbs (hopped, skipped, jumped), all clauses (he came, he saw, he conquered), and so on.

  HB-34–37

- Do many of your sentences begin with **IT** or **THERE**? Too often these words make your writing wordy and vague or even conceal needed information. Why write "There are reasons we voted for him" when you can say "We had reasons to vote for him"?

  HB-59

- Are your sentences varied? If they all start with the subject or are the same length, your writing might be dull and maybe even hard to read. Try varying your sentence openings by adding **TRANSITIONS**, introductory phrases or clauses. Vary sentence lengths by adding detail to some or combining some sentences.

  349

- Make sure you've used **COMMAS** correctly. Is there a comma after each introductory element? ("After the lead singer quit, the group nearly disbanded. However, they then produced a string of hits.") Do commas set off nonrestrictive elements — parts that aren't needed to understand the sentence? ("The books I read in middle school, like the Harry Potter series, became longer and more challenging.") Are compound sentences connected with a comma? ("I'll eat broccoli steamed, but I prefer it roasted.")

  HB-77–83

Editing words

- Are you sure of the meaning of every word? Use a dictionary; be sure to look up words whose meanings you're not sure about. And remember your audience — do you use any terms they'll need to have defined?

- Is any of your language too **GENERAL** or vague? Why write that you competed in a race, for example, if you could say you ran the 4 × 200 relay?

  HB-45

- What about the **TONE**? If your stance is serious (or humorous or critical or something else), make sure that your words all convey that attitude.

  65

- Do any pronouns have vague or unclear **ANTECEDENTS**? If you use "he" or "they" or "it" or "these," will readers know whom or what the words refer to?

  HB-31

- Have you used any **CLICHÉS** — expressions that are used so frequently that they are no longer fresh? "Live and let live," avoiding something

  HB-43–44

"like the plague," and similar expressions are so predictable that your writing will almost always be better off without them.

HB-66–68

- Be careful with **LANGUAGE THAT REFERS TO OTHERS**. Make sure that your words do not stereotype any individual or group. Mention age, gender, race, religion, sexual orientation, and so on only if they are relevant to your subject. When referring to an ethnic group, make every effort to use the terms members of the group prefer.

HB-67–68

- Edit out language that might be considered sexist. Do you say "he" when you mean **"HE AND SHE"**? Have you used words like *manpower* or *policeman* to refer to people who may be female? If so, substitute less gendered words such as *personnel* or *police officer*. Do your words reflect any gender stereotypes—for example, that all engineers are male, or all nurses female? If you mention someone's gender, is it even necessary? If not, eliminate the unneeded words.

HB-44

- How many of your verbs are forms of **BE** and **DO**? If you rely too much on these words, try replacing them with more specific verbs. Why write "She did a proposal for" when you could say "She proposed"?

HB-54

- Do you ever confuse **ITS** and **IT'S**? Use *it's* when you mean *it is* or *it has*. Use *its* when you mean *belonging to it*.

Proofreading

Proofreading is the final stage of the writing process, the point where you clean up your work to present it to your readers. Proofreading is like checking your appearance in a mirror before going into a job interview: being neat and well groomed looms large in creating a good first impression, and the same principle applies to writing. Misspelled words, missing pages, mixed-up fonts, and other lapses send a negative message about your work—and about you. Most readers excuse an occasional error, but by and large readers are an intolerant bunch: too many errors will lead them to declare your writing—and maybe your thinking—flawed. There goes your credibility. So proofread your final draft with care to ensure that your message is taken as seriously as you want it to be.

academic literacies · rhetorical situations · genres · processes · strategies · research MLA / APA · media / design · readings · handbook

Up to this point, you've been told *not* to read individual words on the page and instead to read for meaning. Proofreading demands the opposite: you must slow down your reading so that you can see every word, every punctuation mark.

- Use your computer's grammar checker and spelling checker, but only as a first step, and know that they're not very reliable. Computer programs don't read writing; instead, they rely on formulas and banks of words, so what they flag (or don't flag) as mistakes may or may not be accurate. If you were to write, "my brother was diagnosed with a leaning disorder," *leaning* would not be flagged as misspelled because it is a word, even though it's the wrong word in that sentence.

- To keep your eyes from jumping ahead, place a ruler or piece of paper under each line as you read. Use your finger or a pencil as a pointer.

- Some writers find it helpful to read the text one sentence at a time, beginning with the last sentence and working backward.

- Read your text out loud to yourself—or better, to others, who may *hear* problems you can't see. Alternatively, have someone else read your text aloud to you while you follow along on the screen or page.

- Ask someone else to read your text. The more important the writing is, the more important this step is.

- If you find a mistake after you've printed out your text and are unable to print out a corrected version, make the change as neatly as possible in pencil or pen.

32 Compiling a Portfolio

Artists maintain portfolios of their work to show gallery owners, collectors, and other potential buyers. Money managers work with investment portfolios of stocks, bonds, and various mutual funds. And often as part of a writing class, student writers compile portfolios of their work. As with a portfolio of paintings or drawings, a portfolio of writing includes a writer's best work and, sometimes, preliminary and revised drafts of that work, along with a statement by the writer articulating why he or she considers it good. The *why* is as important as the work, for it provides you with an occasion for assessing your overall strengths and weaknesses as a writer. This chapter offers guidelines to help you compile both a *writing portfolio* and a *literacy portfolio*, a project that writing students are sometimes asked to complete as part of a literacy narrative.

Considering the Rhetorical Situation

As with the writing you put in a portfolio, the portfolio itself is generally intended for a particular audience but could serve a number of different purposes. It's a good idea, then, to consider these and the other elements of your rhetorical situation when you begin to compile a portfolio.

<table>
<tr><td>55–56 ■</td><td>PURPOSE</td><td>Why are you creating this portfolio? To show your learning? To create a record of your writing? As the basis for a grade in a course? To organize your research? To explore your literacy? For something else?</td></tr>
<tr><td>57–60 ■</td><td>AUDIENCE</td><td>Who will read your portfolio? What will your readers expect it to contain? How can you help them understand the context or occasion for each piece of writing you include?</td></tr>
</table>

academic literacies   rhetorical situations   genres   processes   strategies   research MLA / APA   media / design   readings   handbook

GENRE   What genres of writing should the portfolio contain?   61–63
Do you want to demonstrate your ability to write one
particular type of writing or in a variety of genres? Will
your introduction to or assessment of the portfolio be
in the form of a letter or an essay?

STANCE   How do you want to portray yourself in this portfolio?   64–67
What items should you include to create this impres-
sion? What stance do you want to take in your written
assessment of its contents? Thoughtful? Enthusiastic?
Something else?

MEDIA / DESIGN   Will your portfolio be in print? Or will it be electronic?   68–70
Will it include multiple media? Whichever medium you
use, how can you help readers navigate its contents?
What design elements will be most appropriate to your
purpose and medium?

A WRITING PORTFOLIO

What to Include

A portfolio developed for a writing course typically contains examples of
your best work in that course, including any notes, outlines, preliminary
drafts, and so on, along with your own assessment of your performance
in the course. You might include any of the following items:

- freewriting, outlines, and other work you did to generate ideas
- drafts, rough and revised
- in-class writing assignments
- source material—copies of articles and online sources, observation
  notes, interview transcripts, and other evidence of your research
- tests and quizzes

- responses to your drafts
- conference notes, error logs, lecture notes, other course materials
- electronic material including visuals, blogs, and multimedia texts
- reflections on your work

What you include will vary depending on what your instructor asks for. You may be asked to include three or four of your best papers or every-thing you've written. You may also be asked to show work in several different genres. In any case, you will usually need to choose, and to do that you will need to have criteria for making your choices. Don't base your decision solely on grades (unless grades are one criterion); your portfolio should reflect *your* assessment of your work, not your instructor's. What do you think is your best work? your most interest-ing work? your most ambitious work? Whatever criteria you use, you are the judge.

Organizing a Portfolio

Your instructor may provide explicit guidelines for organizing your portfolio. If not, here are some guidelines. If you set up a way to organize your writing at the start of the course, you'll be able to keep track of it through-out the course, making your job at term's end much easier. Remember that your portfolio presents you as a writer, presumably at your best. It should be neat, well organized, and easy to navigate.

Paper portfolios.   Choose something in which to gather your work. You might use a two-pocket folder, a three-ring binder, or a file folder, or you may need a box, basket, or some other container to accommodate bulky or odd-shaped items.

Label everything. Label each piece at the top of the first page, specify-ing the assignment, the draft, and the date: "Proposal, Draft 1, 9/12/12"; "Text Analysis, Final Draft, 10/10/12"; "Portfolio Self-Assessment, Final Draft, 12/11/12"; and so on. Write this information neatly on the page,

academic literacies · rhetorical situations · genres · processes · strategies · research MLA / APA · media / design · readings · handbook

or put it on a Post-it note. For each assignment, arrange your materials chronologically, with your earliest material (freewriting, for example) on the bottom, and each successive item (source materials, say, then your outline, then your first draft, and so on) on top of the last, ending with your final draft on top. That way readers can see how your writing changed from draft to draft.

Electronic portfolios. You might also create an electronic portfolio, or e-portfolio, that includes a homepage with links to your portfolio's contents. There are several tools that can help you create an e-portfolio:

- *Online tools.* Several websites, including *Weebly* and *Wix*, offer free tools to help you create a preformatted e-portfolio. For example, *GoogleSites* provides templates you can use to build an e-portfolio, uploading documents, images, and videos from your computer.

- *Blogging tools.* You can create an e-portfolio using a blogging platform, like *Tumblr* or *WordPress*, which allows you to upload files and create a network of linked pages. Readers can then comment on your e-portfolio, just as they might on your blog entries.

- *Wikis.* Wiki-based e-portfolios differ from blog-based ones in the level of interactivity they allow. In addition to commenting, readers may — if you allow them — make changes and add information. *PBworks* is one free provider, as is *WikiSpaces*.

- *Courseware.* Your school may use a learning platform, such as *Blackboard, Desire2Learn,* or *Moodle,* that allows you to create an e-portfolio of your work.

It's also possible to create an electronic portfolio using word processing, spreadsheet, or presentation software. The programs available for your use and the requirements for publishing your portfolio vary from school to school and instructor to instructor; ask your instructor or your school's help desk for assistance (and see Chapter 57 on **WRITING ONLINE** for general guidance).

616–24

Assessing Your Portfolio

An important part of your portfolio is your written self-assessment of your work. This is an opportunity to assess your work with a critical eye and to think about what you're most proud of, what you most enjoyed doing, what you want to improve. It's your chance to think about and say what you've learned during the class. Some instructors may ask you to write out your assessment in essay form, as an additional sample of your writing; others will want you to put it in letter form, which usually allows for a more relaxed and personal tone. Whatever form it takes, your statement should cover the following ground:

- *An evaluation of each piece of writing in the portfolio.* Consider both strengths and weaknesses, and give examples from your writing to support what you say. What would you change if you had more time? Which is your favorite piece, and why? your least favorite?

- *An assessment of your overall writing performance.* What do you do well? What still needs improvement? What do you *want* your work to say about you? What *does* your work say about you?

- *A discussion of how the writing you did in this course has affected your development as a writer.* How does the writing in your portfolio compare with writing you did in the past? What do you know now that you didn't know before? What can you do that you couldn't do before?

- *A description of your writing habits and process.* What do you usually do? How well does it work? What techniques seem to help you most, and why? Which seem less helpful? Cite passages from your drafts that support your conclusions.

- *An analysis of your performance in the course.* How did you spend your time? Did you collaborate with others? Did you have any conferences with your instructor? Did you visit the writing center? Consider how these or any other activities contributed to your success.

A Sample Self-Assessment

Here is a self-assessment written by Nathaniel Cooney as part of his portfolio for his first-year writing class at Wright State University.

2 June 2016

Dear Reader,

It is my hope that in reading this letter you will gain an understanding of the projects contained in this portfolio. I enclose three works that I have submitted for an introductory writing class at Wright State University, English 102, Writing in Academic Discourse: an informative report, an argument paper, and a genre project based largely on the content of the argument paper. I selected the topics of these works for two reasons: First, they address issues that I believe to be relevant in terms of both the intended audience (peers and instructors of the course) and the times when they were published. Second, they speak to issues that are important to me personally. Below I present general descriptions of the works, along with my review of their strengths and weaknesses.

My purpose in writing the informative report "Higher Standards in Education Are Taking Their Toll on Students" was to present a subject in a factual manner and to support it with well-documented research. My intent was not to argue a point. However, because I chose a narrowly focused topic and chose information to support a thesis, the report tends to favor one side of the issue over the other. Because as a student I have a personal stake in the changing standards in the formal education system, I chose to research recent changes in higher education and their effects on students. Specifically, I examine students' struggles to reach a standard that seems to be moving further and further beyond their grasp.

I believe that this paper could be improved in two areas. The first is a bias that I think exists because I am a student presenting information from the point of view of a student. It is my hope, however, that my inclusion of unbiased sources lessens this problem somewhat and, furthermore, that it presents the reader with a fair and accurate collection of facts and examples that supports the thesis. My second area of concern is the overall balance in the paper between outside sources supporting my own thoughts and outside sources supporting opposing points of view. Rereading the paper, I notice many places where I may have worked too hard to include sources that support my ideas.

The second paper, "Protecting Animals That Serve," is an argument intended not only to take a clear position on an issue but also to argue for that position and convince the reader that it is a valid one. That issue is the need for legislation guaranteeing that certain rights of service animals be protected. I am blind and use a guide dog. Thus, this issue is especially important to me. During the few months that I have had him, my guide dog has already encountered a number of situations where intentional or negligent treatment by others has put him in danger. At the time I was writing the paper, a bill was being written in the Ohio House of Representatives that, if passed, would protect service animals and establish consequences for those who violated the law. The purpose of the paper, therefore, was to present the reader with information about service animals, establish the need for the legislation in Ohio and nationwide, and argue for passage of such legislation.

I think that the best parts of my argument are the introduction and the conclusion. In particular, I think that the conclusion does a good job of not only bringing together the various points but also conveying the significance of the issue for me and for others. In contrast, I think that the area most in need of further attention is the body of the paper. While I think the content is strong, I believe the overall organization could be improved. The connections between ideas are unclear in places, particularly in the section that acknowledges opposing viewpoints. This may be due in part to the fact that I had difficulty understanding the reasoning behind the opposing argument.

The argument paper served as a starting point for the genre project, for which the assignment was to revise one paper written for this class in a different genre. My genre project consists of a poster and a brochure. As it was for the argument paper, my

academic literacies   rhetorical situations   genres   processes   strategies   research MLA / APA   media / design   readings   handbook

primary goal was to convince my audience of the importance of a particular issue and viewpoint—specifically, to convince my audience to support House Bill 369, the bill being introduced in the Ohio legislature that would create laws to protect the rights of service animals in the state.

Perhaps both the greatest strength and the greatest weakness of the genre project is my use of graphics. Because of my blindness, I was limited in my use of some graphics. Nevertheless, the pictures were carefully selected to capture the attention of readers and, in part, to appeal to their emotions as they viewed and reflected on the material.

I put a great deal of time, effort, and personal reflection into each project. While I am hesitant to say that they are finished and while I am dissatisfied with some of the finer points, I am satisfied with the overall outcome of this collection of works. Viewing it as a collection, I am also reminded that writing is an evolving process and that even if these works never become exactly what I envisioned them to be, they stand as reflections of my thoughts at a particular time in my life. In that respect, they need not be anything but what they already are, because what they are is a product of who I was when I wrote them. I hope that you find the papers interesting and informative and that as you read them, you, too, may realize their significance.

Respectfully,

Nathaniel J. Cooney

Nathaniel J. Cooney

Enclosures (3)

Cooney describes each of the works he includes and considers their strengths and weaknesses, citing examples from his texts to support his assessment.

A LITERACY PORTFOLIO

As a writing student, you may be asked to think back to the time when you first learned to read and write or to remember significant books or other texts you've read, and perhaps to put together a portfolio that chronicles your development as a reader and writer. You may also be asked to put together a literacy portfolio to accompany a **LITERACY NARRATIVE**.

71–93

What you include in such a portfolio will vary depending on what you've kept over the years and what your family has kept. You may have all of your favorite books, stories you dictated to a preschool teacher, notebooks in which you practiced writing the alphabet. Or you may have almost nothing. What you have or don't have is unimportant in the end: what's important is that you gather what you can and arrange it in a way that shows how you think about your development and growth as a literate person. What have been your experiences with reading and writing? What's your earliest memory of learning to write? If you love to read, what led you to love it? Who was most responsible for shaping your writing ability? Those are some of the questions you'll ask if you write a literacy narrative. You might also compile a literacy portfolio as a good way to generate ideas and text for that assignment.

What to Include in a Literacy Portfolio

- school papers
- drawings and doodles from preschool
- favorite books
- photographs you've taken
- drawings
- poems
- letters
- journals and diaries
- lists
- reading records or logs

- electronic texts you've created
- marriage vows
- speeches you've given
- awards you've received

Organizing a Literacy Portfolio

You may wish to organize your material chronologically, but there are other methods of organization to consider as well. For example, you might group items according to where they were written (at home, at school, at work), by genre (stories, poems, essays, letters, notes), or even by purpose (pleasure, school, work, church, and so on). Arrange your portfolio in the way that best conveys who you are as a literate person. Label each item you include, perhaps with a Post-it note, to identify what it is, when it was written or read, and why you've included it in your portfolio. Or you might create an e-portfolio, scanning print items to include in it with electronic items.

Reflecting on Your Literacy Portfolio

- Why did you choose each item?
- Is anything missing? Are there any other important materials that should be here?
- Why is the portfolio organized as it is?
- What does the portfolio show about your development as a reader and writer?
- What patterns do you see? Are there any common themes you've read or written about? Any techniques you rely on? Any notable changes over time?
- What are the most significant items, and why?

part 5

Strategies

Whenever we write, we draw on many different strategies to articulate what we have to say. We may DEFINE
key terms, DESCRIBE people or places, and EXPLAIN how
something is done. We may COMPARE one thing
to another. Sometimes we may choose a pertinent story
to NARRATE, and we may even want to include some
DIALOGUE. The chapters that follow offer advice on how
to use these and OTHER BASIC STRATEGIES for developing
and organizing the texts you write.

Strategies

Beginning and Ending 33

Whenever we pick up something to read, we generally start by looking at the first few words or sentences to see if they grab our attention, and based on them we decide whether to keep reading. Beginnings, then, are important, both attracting readers and giving them some information about what's to come. When we get to the end of a text, we expect to be left with a sense of closure, of satisfaction—that the story is complete, our questions have been answered, the argument has been made. So endings are important, too. This chapter offers advice on how to write beginnings and endings.

Beginning

How you begin depends on your **RHETORICAL SITUATION**, especially your purpose and audience. Academic audiences generally expect your introduction to establish context, explaining how the text fits into some larger conversation, addresses certain questions, or explores an aspect of the subject. Most introductions also offer a brief description of the text's content, often in the form of a thesis statement. The following opening of an essay on the effect of texting on student writing does all of this:

■ 53

> It's taking over our lives. We can do it almost anywhere—walking to class, waiting in line at the grocery store, or hanging out at home. It's quick, easy, and convenient. It has become a concern of doctors, parents, and teachers alike. What is it? It's texting!
>
> Text messaging—or texting, as it's more commonly called—is the process of sending and receiving typed messages via a cellular phone. It is a common means of communication among teenagers and is even becoming popular in the business world because it allows quick messages

academic literacies · rhetorical situations · genres · processes · strategies · research MLA / APA · media / design · readings · handbook

to be sent without people having to commit to a telephone conversation. A person is able to say what is needed, and the other person will receive the information and respond when it's convenient to do so.

In order to more quickly type what they are trying to say, many people use abbreviations instead of words. The language created by these abbreviations is called textspeak. Some people believe that using these abbreviations is hindering the writing abilities of students, and others argue that texting is actually having a positive effect on writing. In fact, it seems likely that texting has no significant effect on student writing. —Michaela Cullington, "Does Texting Affect Writing?"

If you're writing for a nonacademic audience or genre—for a newspaper or a website, for example—your introduction may need to entice your readers to read on by connecting your text to their interests through shared experiences, anecdotes, or some other attention-getting device. Cynthia Bass, writing a newspaper article about the Gettysburg Address on its 135th anniversary, connects that date—the day her audience would read it—to Lincoln's address. She then develops the rationale for thinking about the speech and introduces her specific topic: debates about the writing and delivery of the Gettysburg Address:

November 19 is the 135th anniversary of the Gettysburg Address. On that day in 1863, with the Civil War only half over and the worst yet to come, Abraham Lincoln delivered a speech now universally regarded as both the most important oration in U.S. history and the best explanation—"government of the people, by the people, for the people"—of why this nation exists.

We would expect the history of an event so monumental as the Gettysburg Address to be well established. The truth is just the opposite. The only thing scholars agree on is that the speech is short—only ten sentences—and that it took Lincoln under five minutes to stand up, deliver it, and sit back down.

Everything else—when Lincoln wrote it, where he wrote it, how quickly he wrote it, how he was invited, how the audience reacted—has been open to debate since the moment the words left his mouth.

—Cynthia Bass, "Gettysburg Address: Two Versions"

Ways of Beginning

Explain the larger context of your topic. Most essays are part of an ongoing conversation, so you might begin by outlining the context of the subject to which your writing responds. An essay exploring the "emotional climate" of the United States after Barack Obama became president begins by describing the national moods during some of his predecessors' administrations:

> Every president plays a symbolic, almost mythological role that's hard to talk about, much less quantify—it's like trying to grab a ball of mercury. I'm not referring to using the bully pulpit to shape the national agenda but to the way that the president, as America's most inescapably powerful figure, colors the emotional climate of the country. John Kennedy and Ronald Reagan did this affirmatively, expressing ideals that shaped the whole culture. Setting a buoyant tone, they didn't just change movies, music, and television; they changed attitudes. Other presidents did the same, only unpleasantly. Richard Nixon created a mood of angry paranoia, Jimmy Carter one of dreary defeatism, and George W. Bush, especially in that seemingly endless second term, managed to do both at once.
>
> —John Powers, "Dreams from My President"

State your thesis. Sometimes the best beginning is a clear **THESIS** stating your position, like the following statement in an essay arguing that fairy tales and nursery rhymes introduce us to "the rudiments and the humanness of engineering": 345–47

> We are all engineers of sorts, for we all have the principles of machines and structures in our bones. We have learned to hold our bodies against the forces of nature as surely as we have learned to walk. We calculate the paths of our arms and legs with the computer of our brain, and we catch baseballs and footballs with more dependability than the most advanced weapons systems intercept missiles. We may wonder if human evolution may not have been the greatest engineering feat of all time. And though many of us forget how much we once knew about the principles and practices of engineering, the nursery rhymes and fairy tales of our youth preserve the evidence that we did know quite a bit.
>
> —Henry Petroski, "Falling Down Is Part of Growing Up"

Forecast your organization. You might begin by briefly outlining the way in which you will organize your text. The following example from a scholarly paper on the role of immigrants in the U.S. labor market offers background on the subject and describes the points that the writer's analysis will discuss:

> Debates about illegal immigration, border security, skill levels of workers, unemployment, job growth and competition, and entrepreneurship all rely, to some extent, on perceptions of immigrants' role in the U.S. labor market. These views are often shaped as much by politics and emotion as by facts.
>
> To better frame these debates, this short analysis provides data on immigrants in the labor force at the current time of slowed immigration, high unemployment, and low job growth and highlights eight industries where immigrants are especially vital. How large a share of the labor force are they and how does that vary by particular industry? How do immigrants compare to native-born workers in their educational attainment and occupational profiles?
>
> The answers matter because our economy is dependent on immigrant labor now and for the future. The U.S. population is aging rapidly as the baby boom cohort enters old age and retirement. As a result, the labor force will increasingly depend upon immigrants and their children to replace current workers and fill new jobs. This analysis puts a spotlight on immigrant workers to examine their basic trends in the labor force and how these workers fit into specific industries and occupations of interest.
>
> —Audrey Singer, "Immigrant Workers in the U.S. Labor Force"

Offer background information. If your readers may not know as much as you do about your topic, giving them information to help them understand your position can be important, as David Guterson does in an essay on the Mall of America:

> Last April, on a visit to the new Mall of America near Minneapolis, I carried with me the public-relations press kit provided for the benefit of reporters. It included an assortment of "fun facts" about the mall: 140,000 hot dogs sold each week, 10,000 permanent jobs, 44 escalators and 17 elevators, 12,750 parking places, 13,300 short tons of steel, $1 million in cash disbursed weekly from 8 automatic-teller machines.

The rotunda of the Mall of America.

> Opened in the summer of 1992, the mall was built on the 78-acre site of the former Metropolitan Stadium, a five-minute drive from the Minneapolis–St. Paul International Airport. With 4.2 million square feet of floor space—including twenty-two times the retail footage of the average American shopping center—the Mall of America was "the largest fully enclosed combination retail and family entertainment complex in the United States."
>
> —David Guterson, "Enclosed. Encyclopedic. Endured. One Week at the Mall of America"

Visuals can also help provide context. For example, this essay on the Mall of America might have included a photo like the one on the preceding page to convey the size of the structure.

Define key terms or concepts.   The success of an argument often hinges on how key terms are **DEFINED**. You may wish to provide definitions up front, as an advocacy website, *Health Care without Harm*, does in a report on the hazards of fragrances in health-care facilities:

388–98

> To many people, the word "fragrance" means something that smells nice, such as perfume. We don't often stop to think that scents are chemicals. Fragrance chemicals are organic compounds that volatilize, or vaporize into the air—that's why we can smell them. They are added to products to give them a scent or to mask the odor of other ingredients. The volatile organic chemicals (VOCs) emitted by fragrance products can contribute to poor indoor air quality (IAQ) and are associated with a variety of adverse health effects.
>
> —"Fragrances," *Health Care without Harm*

Connect your subject to your readers' interests or values.   You'll always want to establish common ground with your readers, and sometimes you may wish to do so immediately, in your introduction, as in this example:

> We all want to feel safe. Most Americans lock their doors at night, lock their cars in parking lots, try to park near buildings or under lights, and wear seat belts. Many invest in expensive security systems, carry pepper spray or a stun gun, keep guns in their homes, or take self-defense classes. Obviously, safety and security are important issues in American life.
>
> —Andy McDonie, "Airport Security: What Price Safety?"

academic literacies   rhetorical situations   genres   processes   strategies   research MLA / APA   media / design   readings   handbook

Start with something that will provoke readers' interest. Anna Quindlen opens an essay on feminism with the following eye-opening assertion:

> Let's use the F word here. People say it's inappropriate, offensive, that it puts people off. But it seems to me it's the best way to begin, when it's simultaneously devalued and invaluable.
> Feminist. Feminist, feminist, feminist.
>
> —Anna Quindlen, "Still Needing the F Word"

Start with an anecdote. Sometimes a brief **NARRATIVE** helps bring a topic to life for readers. See, for example, how an essay on the dozens, a type of verbal contest played by some African Americans, begins:

◆ 419–27

> Alfred Wright, a nineteen-year-old whose manhood was at stake on Longwood Avenue in the South Bronx, looked fairly calm as another teenager called him Chicken Head and compared his mother to Shamu the whale.
> He fingered the gold chain around his thin neck while listening to a detailed complaint about his sister's sexual abilities. Then he slowly took the toothpick out of his mouth; the jeering crowd of young men quieted as he pointed at his accuser.
> "He was so ugly when he was born," Wright said, "the doctor smacked his mom instead of him."
>
> —John Tierney, "Playing the Dozens"

Ask a question. Instead of a thesis statement, you might open with a question about the topic your text will explore, as this study of the status of women in science does:

> Are women's minds different from men's minds? In spite of the women's movement, the age-old debate centering around this question continues. We are surrounded by evidence of de facto differences between men's and women's intellects—in the problems that interest them, in the ways they try to solve those problems, and in the professions they choose. Even though it has become fashionable to view such differences as environmental in origin, the temptation to seek an explanation in terms of innate differences remains a powerful one.
>
> —Evelyn Fox Keller, "Women in Science: A Social Analysis"

Jump right in.   Occasionally you may wish to start as close to the key action as possible. See how one writer jumps right into his profile of a blues concert:

> Long Tongue, the Blues Merchant, strolls onstage. His guitar rides side-saddle against his hip. The drummer slides onto the tripod seat behind the drums, adjusts the high-hat cymbal, and runs a quick, off-beat tattoo on the tom-tom, then relaxes. The bass player plugs into the amplifier, checks the settings on the control panel, and nods his okay. Three horn players stand off to one side, clustered, lurking like brilliant sorcerer-wizards waiting to do magic with their musical instruments.
>
> —Jerome Washington, "The Blues Merchant"

Ending

Endings are important because they're the last words readers read. How you end a text will depend in part on your **RHETORICAL SITUATION**. You may end by wrapping up loose ends, or you may wish to give readers something to think about. Some endings do both, as Cynthia Bass does in a report on the debate over the Gettysburg Address. In her two final paragraphs, she first summarizes the debate and then shows its implications:

> What's most interesting about the Lincoln-as-loser and Lincoln-as-winner versions is how they marshal the same facts to prove different points. The invitation asks Lincoln to deliver "a few appropriate remarks." Whether this is a putdown or a reflection of the protocol of the time depends on the "spin"—an expression the highly politicized Lincoln would have readily understood—which the scholar places on it.
>
> These diverse histories should not in any way diminish the power or beauty of Lincoln's words. However, they should remind us that history, even the history of something as deeply respected as the Gettysburg Address, is seldom simple or clear. This reminder is especially useful today as we watch expert witnesses, in an effort to divine what the founders meant by "high crimes and misdemeanors," club one another with conflicting interpretations of the same events, the same words, the same precedents, and the same laws.
>
> —Cynthia Bass, "Gettysburg Address: Two Versions"

Bass summarizes the dispute about Lincoln's address and then moves on to discuss the role of scholars in interpreting historical events. Writing during the Clinton impeachment hearings, she concludes by pointing out the way in which expert government witnesses often offer conflicting interpretations of events to suit their own needs. The ending combines several strategies to bring various strands of her essay together, leaving readers to interpret her final words themselves.

Ways of Ending

Restate your main point. Sometimes you'll simply **SUMMARIZE** your central idea, as in this example from an essay arguing that we have no "inner" self and that we should be judged by our actions alone:

486–87

> The inner man is a fantasy. If it helps you to identify with one, by all means, do so; preserve it, cherish it, embrace it, but do not present it to others for evaluation or consideration, for excuse or exculpation, or, for that matter, for punishment or disapproval.
>   Like any fantasy, it serves your purposes alone. It has no standing in the real world which we share with each other. Those character traits, those attitudes, that behavior—that strange and alien stuff sticking out all over you—*that's the real you!*
>
> —Willard Gaylin, "What You See Is the Real You"

Discuss the implications of your argument. The following conclusion of an essay on the development of Post-it notes leads readers to consider how failure sometimes leads to innovation:

> Post-it notes provide but one example of a technological artifact that has evolved from a perceived failure of existing artifacts to function without frustrating. Again, it is not that form follows function but, rather, that the form of one thing follows from the failure of another thing to function as we would like. Whether it be bookmarks that fail to stay in place or taped-on notes that fail to leave a once-nice surface clean and intact, their failure and perceived failure is what leads to the true evolution of artifacts. That the perception of failure may take

centuries to develop, as in the case of loose bookmarks, does not reduce the importance of the principle in shaping our world.

—Henry Petroski, "Little Things Can Mean a Lot"

419–27 ◆ **End with an anecdote,** maybe finishing a NARRATIVE that was begun earlier in your text or adding one that illustrates the point you are making. See how Sarah Vowell uses a story to end an essay on students' need to examine news reporting critically:

> I looked at Joanne McGlynn's syllabus for her media studies course, the one she handed out at the beginning of the year, stating the goals of the class. By the end of the year, she hoped her students would be better able to challenge everything from novels to newscasts, that they would come to identify just who is telling a story and how that person's point of view affects the story being told. I'm going to go out on a limb here and say that this lesson has been learned. In fact, just recently, a student came up to McGlynn and told her something all teachers dream of hearing. The girl told the teacher that she was listening to the radio, singing along with her favorite song, and halfway through the sing-along she stopped and asked herself, "What am I singing? What do these words mean? What are they trying to tell me?" And then, this young citizen of the republic jokingly complained, "I can't even turn on the radio without thinking anymore."

> —Sarah Vowell, "Democracy and Things Like That"

Refer to the beginning. One way to bring closure to a text is to bring up something discussed in the beginning; often the reference adds to or even changes the original meaning. For example, Amy Tan opens an essay on her Chinese mother's English by establishing herself as a writer and lover of language who uses many versions of English in her writing:

> I am not a scholar of English or literature. I cannot give you much more than personal opinions on the English language and its variations in this country or others.
>
> I am a writer. And by that definition, I am someone who has always loved language. I am fascinated by language in daily life. I spend a

academic literacies

rhetorical situations

genres

processes

strategies

research MLA / APA

media / design

readings

handbook

great deal of my time thinking about the power of language — the way it can evoke an emotion, a visual image, a complex idea, or a simple truth. Language is the tool of my trade. And I use them all — all the Englishes I grew up with.

At the end of her essay, Tan repeats this phrase, but now she describes language not in terms of its power to evoke emotions, images, and ideas but in its power to evoke "the essence" of her mother. When she began to write fiction, she says,

> [I] decided I should envision a reader for the stories I would write. And the reader I decided upon was my mother, because these were stories about mothers. So with this reader in mind — and in fact she did read my early drafts — I began to write stories using all the Englishes I grew up with: the English I spoke to my mother, which for lack of a better term might be described as "simple"; the English she used with me, which for lack of a better term might be described as "broken"; my translation of her Chinese, which could certainly be described as "watered down"; and what I imagined to be her translation of her Chinese if she could speak in perfect English, her internal language, and for that I sought to preserve the essence, but neither an English nor a Chinese structure. I wanted to capture what language ability tests can never reveal: her intent, her passion, her imagery, the rhythms of her speech and the nature of her thoughts.
>
> —Amy Tan, "Mother Tongue"

Note how Tan not only repeats "all the Englishes I grew up with" but also provides parallel lists of what those Englishes can do for her: "evoke an emotion, a visual image, a complex idea, or a simple truth," on the one hand, and, on the other, capture her mother's "intent, her passion, her imagery, the rhythms of her speech and the nature of her thoughts."

Propose some action, as in the following conclusion of a report on the consequences of binge drinking among college students:

> The scope of the problem makes immediate results of any interventions highly unlikely. Colleges need to be committed to large-scale and long-term behavior-change strategies, including referral of alcohol abusers

to appropriate treatment. Frequent binge drinkers on college campuses are similar to other alcohol abusers elsewhere in their tendency to deny that they have a problem. Indeed, their youth, the visibility of others who drink the same way, and the shelter of the college community may make them less likely to recognize the problem. In addition to addressing the health problems of alcohol abusers, a major effort should address the large group of students who are not binge drinkers on campus who are adversely affected by the alcohol-related behavior of binge drinkers.

—Henry Wechsler et al., "Health and Behavioral Consequences of Binge Drinking in College: A National Survey of Students at 140 Campuses"

Considering the Rhetorical Situation

As a writer or speaker, think about the message that you want to articulate, the audience you want to reach, and the larger context you are writing in.

55–56 **PURPOSE** Your purpose will affect the way you begin and end. If you're trying to persuade readers to do something, you may want to open by clearly stating your thesis and end by calling for a specific action.

57–60 **AUDIENCE** Who do you want to reach, and how does that affect the way you begin and end? You may want to open with an intriguing fact or anecdote to entice your audience to read a profile, for instance, whereas readers of a report may expect it to conclude with a summary of your findings.

61–63 **GENRE** Does your genre require a certain type of beginning or ending? Arguments, for example, often provide a statement of the thesis near the beginning; proposals typically end with a call for some solution.

64–67 **STANCE** What is your stance, and can your beginning and ending help you convey that stance? For example, beginning an argument on the distribution of AIDS medications to underdeveloped countries with an anecdote may demonstrate concern for the human costs of the disease, whereas starting with a statistical analysis may suggest the stance of a careful researcher. Ending a proposal by weighing the advantages and disadvantages of the solution you propose may make you seem reasonable.

MEDIA / DESIGN   Your medium may affect the way you begin and end. A web text, for instance, may open with a homepage listing a menu of the site—and giving readers a choice of where they will begin. With a print text, you get to decide how it will begin and end.

68–70

IF YOU NEED MORE HELP

See also the guides to writing in Chapters 10–13 for ways of beginning and ending a **LITERACY NARRATIVE**, an essay **ANALYZING TEXT**, a **REPORT**, or an **ARGUMENT**.

89–90
124–25
151–52
179–80

34 Guiding Your Reader

Traffic lights, street signs, and lines on the road help drivers find their way. Readers need similar guidance—to know, for example, whether they're reading a report or an argument, an evaluation or a proposal. They also need to know what to expect: What will the report be about? What perspective will it offer? What will this paragraph cover? What about the next one? How do the two paragraphs relate to each other?

When you write, then, you need to provide cues to help your readers navigate your text and understand the points you're trying to make. This chapter offers advice on guiding your reader and, specifically, on using *titles*, *thesis statements*, *topic sentences*, and *transitions*.

Titles

A title serves various purposes, naming a text and providing clues to the content. It also helps readers decide whether they want to read further, so it's worth your while to come up with a title that attracts interest. Some titles include subtitles. You generally have considerable freedom in choosing a title, but always you'll want to consider the **RHETORICAL SITUATION** to be sure your title serves your purpose and appeals to the audience you want to reach.

Some titles simply announce the subject of the text:

"Black Men and Public Space"
The Pencil
"Why Colleges Shower Their Students with A's"
"Does Texting Affect Writing?"

344

Some titles provoke readers or otherwise entice them to read:

> "Kill 'Em! Crush 'Em! Eat 'Em Raw!"
> "Thank God for the Atom Bomb"
> "What Are Homosexuals For?"

Sometimes writers add a subtitle to explain or illuminate the title:

> *Aria: Memoir of a Bilingual Childhood*
> "It's in Our Genes: The Biological Basis of Human Mating Behavior"
> "From Realism to Virtual Reality: Images of America's Wars"

Sometimes when you're starting to write, you'll think of a title that helps you generate ideas and write. More often, though, a title is one of the last things you'll write, when you know what you've written and can craft a suitable name for your text.

Thesis Statements

A thesis identifies the topic of your text along with the claim you are making about it. A good thesis helps readers understand an essay. Working to create a sharp thesis can help you focus both your thinking and your writing. Here are three steps for moving from a topic to a thesis statement:

1. State your topic as a question. You may have an idea for a topic, such as "gasoline prices," "analysis of 'real women' ad campaigns," or "famine." Those may be good topics, but they're not thesis statements, primarily because none of them actually makes a statement. A good way to begin moving from topic to thesis statement is to turn your topic into a question:

> What causes fluctuations in gasoline prices?
>
> Are ads picturing "real women" who aren't models effective?
>
> What can be done to prevent famine in Africa?

2. Then turn your question into a position. A thesis statement is an assertion—it takes a stand or makes a claim. Whether you're writing a report or an argument, you are saying, "This is the way I see . . . ," "My research shows . . . ," or "This is what I believe about . . ." Your thesis statement announces your position on the question you are raising about your topic, so a relatively easy way of establishing a thesis is to answer your own question:

> Gasoline prices fluctuate for several reasons.

> Ads picturing "real women" instead of models are effective because women can easily identify with them.

> The most recent famine in Somalia could have been avoided if certain measures had been taken.

3. Narrow your thesis. A good thesis is specific, guiding you as you write and showing your audience exactly what your essay will cover. The preceding thesis statements need to be qualified and focused—they need to be made more specific. For example:

> Gasoline prices fluctuate because of production procedures, consumer demand, international politics, and oil companies' policies.

> Dove's "Campaign for Self-Esteem" and Cover Girl's ads featuring Queen Latifah work because consumers can identify with the women's bodies and admire their confidence in displaying them.

> The 2012 famine in Somalia could have been avoided if farmers had received training in more effective methods and had had access to certain technology and if other nations had provided more aid more quickly.

281–84

A good way to narrow a thesis is to ask **QUESTIONS** about it: Why do gasoline prices fluctuate? How could the Somalia famine have been avoided? The answers will help you craft a narrow, focused thesis.

4. Qualify your thesis. Sometimes you want to make a strong argument and to state your thesis bluntly. Often, however, you need to acknowledge that your assertions may be challenged or may not be unconditionally true. In those cases, consider limiting the scope of your thesis by adding to it such terms as *may*, *probably*, *apparently*, *very likely*, *sometimes*, and *often*.

academic literacies | rhetorical situations | genres | processes | strategies | research MLA / APA | media / design | readings | handbook

Gasoline prices *very likely* fluctuate because of production procedures, consumer demand, international politics, and oil companies' policies.

Dove's and Cover Girl's ad campaigns featuring "real women" *may* work because consumers can identify with the women's bodies and admire their confidence in displaying them.

The 2012 famine in Somalia could *probably* have been avoided if farmers had received training in more effective methods and had had access to certain technology and if other nations had provided more aid more quickly.

Thesis statements are typically positioned at or near the end of a text's introduction, to let readers know at the outset what is being claimed and what the text will be aiming to prove. A thesis doesn't necessarily forecast your organization, which may be more complex than the thesis itself. For example, Carolyn Stonehill's research paper, "It's in Our Genes: The Biological Basis of Human Mating Behavior," contains this thesis statement:

While cultural values and messages clearly play a part in the process of mate selection, the genetic and psychological predispositions developed by our ancestors play the biggest role in determining to whom we are attracted.

However, the paper that follows includes sections on "Women's Need to Find a Capable Mate" and "Men's Need to Find a Healthy Mate," in which the "genetic and psychological predispositions" are discussed, followed by sections titled "The Influence of the Media on Mate Selection" and "If Not Media, Then What?" discussing "cultural values and messages." The paper delivers what the thesis includes without following the order in which the thesis presents the topics.

Topic Sentences

Just as a thesis statement announces the topic and position of an essay, a topic sentence states the subject and focus of a paragraph. Good paragraphs focus on a single point, which is summarized in a topic sentence. Usually, but not always, the topic sentence begins the paragraph:

Graduating from high school or college is an exciting, occasionally even traumatic event. Your identity changes as you move from being a high school teenager to a university student or a worker; your connection to home loosens as you attend school elsewhere, move to a place of your own, or simply exercise your right to stay out later. You suddenly find yourself doing different things, thinking different thoughts, fretting about different matters. As recent high school graduate T. J. Devoe puts it, "I wasn't really scared, but having this vast range of opportunity made me uneasy. I didn't know *what* was gonna happen." Jenny Petrow, in describing her first year out of college, observes, "It's a tough year. It was for all my friends."

—Sydney Lewis, *Help Wanted: Tales from the First Job Front*

Sometimes the topic sentence may come at the end of the paragraph or even at the end of the preceding paragraph, depending on the way the paragraphs relate to one another. Other times a topic sentence will summarize or restate a point made in the previous paragraph, helping readers understand what they've just read as they move on to the next point. See how the linguist Deborah Tannen does this in the first paragraphs of an article on differences in men's and women's conversational styles:

I was addressing a small gathering in a suburban Virginia living room — a women's group that had invited men to join them. Throughout the evening, one man had been particularly talkative, frequently offering ideas and anecdotes, while his wife sat silently beside him on the couch. Toward the end of the evening, I commented that women frequently complain that their husbands don't talk to them. This man quickly concurred. He gestured toward his wife and said, "She's the talker in our family." The room burst into laughter; the man looked puzzled and hurt. "It's true," he explained. "When I come home from work I have nothing to say. If she didn't keep the conversation going, we'd spend the whole evening in silence."

This episode crystallizes the irony that although American men tend to talk more than women in public situations, they often talk less at home. And this pattern is wreaking havoc with marriage.

—Deborah Tannen, "Sex, Lies, and Conversation:
Why Is It So Hard for Men and Women to Talk to Each Other?"

academic literacies · rhetorical situations · genres · processes · strategies · research MLA / APA · media / design · readings · handbook

Transitions

Transitions help readers move from thought to thought—from sentence to sentence, paragraph to paragraph. You are likely to use a number of transitions as you draft; when you're **EDITING**, you should make a point of checking transitions. Here are some common ones:

313–16

- *To signal causes and effects:* accordingly, as a result, because, consequently, hence, so, then, therefore, thus
- *To signal comparisons:* also, in the same way, like, likewise, similarly
- *To signal changes in direction or expectations:* although, but, even though, however, in contrast, instead, nevertheless, nonetheless, on the contrary, on the one hand . . . on the other hand, still, yet
- *To signal examples:* for example, for instance, indeed, in fact, such as
- *To signal sequences or similarities:* again; also; and; and then; besides; finally; furthermore; last; moreover; next; too; first, second, third, etc.
- *To signal time relations:* after, as soon as, at first, at the same time, before, eventually, finally, immediately, later, meanwhile, next, simultaneously, so far, soon, then, thereafter
- *To signal a summary or conclusion:* as a result, as we have seen, finally, in a word, in any event, in brief, in conclusion, in other words, in short, in the end, in the final analysis, on the whole, therefore, thus, to summarize

---

IF YOU NEED MORE HELP

See also Chapter 56 on **USING VISUALS, INCORPORATING SOUND** for ways of creating visual signals for your readers.

607–15

35 Analyzing Causes and Effects

Analyzing causes helps us think about why something happened, whereas thinking about effects helps us consider what might happen. When we hear a noise in the night, we want to know what caused it. Children poke sticks into holes to see what will happen. Researchers try to understand the causes of diseases. Writers often have occasion to consider causes or effects as part of a larger topic or sometimes as a main focus: in a **PROPOSAL**, we might consider the effects of reducing tuition or the causes of recent tuition increases; in a **MEMOIR**, we might explore why the person we had a date with failed to show up.

Usually we can only speculate about *probable* causes or *likely* effects. In writing about causes and effects, then, we are generally **ARGUING** for those we consider plausible, not proven. This chapter will help you analyze causes and effects in writing—and to do so in a way that suits your rhetorical situation.

235–44
216–23

355–73

Determining Plausible Causes and Effects

What causes ozone depletion? Sleeplessness? Obesity? And what are their effects? Those are of course large, complex topics, but whenever you have reason to ask why something happened or what could happen, there will likely be several possible causes and just as many predictable effects. There may be obvious causes, though often they will be less important than others that are harder to recognize. (Eating too much may be an obvious cause of being overweight, but *why* people eat too much has several less obvious causes: portion size, advertising, lifestyle, and physiological disorders are only a few possibilities.) Similarly, short-term effects are often less important than long-term ones. (A stomachache may be an

academic literacies

rhetorical situations

genres

processes

strategies

research MLA / APA

media / design

readings

handbook

effect of eating too much candy, but the chemical imbalance that can result from consuming too much sugar is a much more serious effect.)

LISTING, **CLUSTERING**, and **OUTLINING** are useful processes for analyzing causes. And at times you might need to do some **RESEARCH** to identify possible causes or effects and to find evidence to support your analysis. When you've identified potential causes and effects, you need to analyze them. Which causes and effects are primary? Which seem to be secondary? Which are most relevant to your **PURPOSE** and are likely to convince your **AUDIENCE**? You will probably have to choose from several possible causes and effects for your analysis because you won't want or need to include all of them.

290–95
433
55–56
57–60

Arguing for Causes or Effects

Once you've identified several possible causes or predictable effects, you need to **ARGUE** that some are more plausible than others. You must provide convincing support for your argument because you usually cannot *prove* that x causes y or that y will be caused by z; you can only show, with good reasons and appropriate evidence, that x is *likely* to cause y or that y will *likely* follow from z. See, for example, how an essay on the psychological basis for risk taking speculates about two potential causes for the popularity of extreme sports:

355–73

> Studies now indicate that the inclination to take high risks may be hardwired into the brain, intimately linked to arousal and pleasure mechanisms, and may offer such a thrill that it functions like an addiction. The tendency probably affects one in five people, mostly young males, and declines with age. It may ensure our survival, even spur our evolution as individuals and as a species. Risk taking probably bestowed a crucial evolutionary advantage, inciting the fighting and foraging of the hunter-gatherer. . . .
>
> As psychologist Salvadore Maddi, PhD, of the University of California at Davis warns, "High-risk takers may have a hard time deriving meaning and purpose from everyday life." Indeed, this peculiar form of dissatisfaction could help explain the explosion of high-risk sports in America and other postindustrial Western nations. In unstable cultures, such as those at war or suffering poverty, people rarely seek

out additional thrills. But in a rich and safety-obsessed country like America, land of guardrails, seat belts, and personal-injury lawsuits, everyday life may have become too safe, predictable, and boring for those programmed for risk taking. —Paul Roberts, "Risk"

Roberts suggests that genetics is one likely cause of extreme sports and that an American obsession with safety is perhaps a cause of their growing popularity. Notice, however, that he presents these as likely or possible, not certain, by choosing his words carefully: "studies now *indicate*"; "the inclination to take high risks *may* be hardwired"; "[r]isk taking *probably* bestowed a crucial evolutionary advantage"; "this . . . dissatisfaction *could help* explain." Like Roberts, you will almost always need to qualify what you say about causes and effects—to say that something *could explain* (rather than saying it "explains") or that it *suggests* (rather than "shows"). Causes and effects can seldom be proved definitively, so you need to acknowledge that your argument is not the last word on the subject.

Ways of Organizing an Analysis of Causes and Effects

Your analysis of causes and effects may be part of a proposal or some other genre of writing, or you may write a text whose central purpose is to analyze causes or speculate about effects. While there are many ways to organize an analysis of causes and effects, three common ways are to state a cause and then discuss its effects, to state an effect and then discuss its causes, and to identify a chain of causes and effects.

Identify a cause and then discuss its effects.   If you were writing about climate change, you might first show that many scientists fear it will have several effects, including more violent storms, the extinction of various kinds of plants, and elevated sea levels.

academic literacies　rhetorical situations　genres　processes　strategies　research MLA / APA　media / design　readings　handbook

Identify an effect and then trace its causes. If you were writing about school violence, for example, you might argue that it is a result of sloppy dress, informal teacher-student relationships, low academic standards, and disregard for rules.

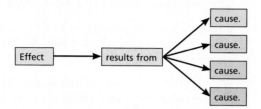

Identify a chain of causes and effects. You may sometimes discuss a chain of causes and effects. If you were writing about the right to privacy, for example, you might consider the case of Megan's law. A convicted child molester raped and murdered a girl named Megan; the crime caused New Jersey legislators to pass the so-called Megan's law (an effect), which requires that convicted sex offenders be publicly identified. As more states enacted versions of Megan's law, concern for the rights of those who are identified developed—the effect became a cause of further effects.

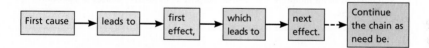

Considering the Rhetorical Situation

As a writer or speaker, you need to think about the message that you want to articulate, the audience you want to reach, and the larger context you are writing in.

PURPOSE Your main purpose may be to analyze the causes and effects of something. But sometimes you'll have another goal that calls for such analysis — a business report, for

55–56

example, might need to explain what caused a decline in sales.

57–60 **AUDIENCE** Who is your intended audience, and how will analyzing causes help you reach them? Do you need to tell them why some event happened or what effects resulted?

61–63 **GENRE** Does your genre require you to analyze causes? Proposals, for example, often need to consider the effects of a proposed solution.

64–67 **STANCE** What is your stance, and could analyzing causes or effects show that stance? Could it help demonstrate your seriousness or show that your conclusions are reasonable?

68–70 **MEDIA / DESIGN** You can rely on words to analyze causes, but sometimes a drawing will help readers *see* how causes lead to effects.

IF YOU NEED MORE HELP

279 See also the **PROCESSES** chapters for help generating ideas, drafting, and so on if you need to write an entire text whose purpose is to analyze causes or speculate about effects.

Arguing 36

Football fans argue about who's better, Eli or Peyton Manning. Political candidates argue that they have the most experience or best judgment. A toilet paper ad argues that "you deserve a little luxury in your life, and so does your bottom." As you likely realize, we are surrounded by arguments, and much of the work you do as a college student requires you to read and write arguments. When you write a **LITERARY ANALYSIS**, for instance, you argue for a particular interpretation. In a **PROPOSAL**, you argue for a particular solution to a problem. Even a **PROFILE** argues that a subject should be seen in a certain way. This chapter offers advice on some of the key elements of making an argument, from developing an arguable thesis and identifying good reasons and evidence that supports those reasons to building common ground and dealing with viewpoints other than your own.

206–15
235–44
224–34

Reasons for Arguing

We argue for many reasons, and they often overlap: to convince others that our position on a subject is reasonable, to influence the way they think about a subject, to persuade them to change their point of view or to take some sort of action. In fact, many composition scholars and teachers believe that all writing makes an argument.

As a student, you'll be called upon to make arguments continually: when you participate in class discussions, when you take an essay exam, when you post a comment to an online discussion or a blog. In all these instances, you are adding your opinions to some larger conversation, arguing for what you believe—and why.

Arguing Logically: Claims, Reasons, and Evidence

The basic building blocks of argument are claims, reasons, and evidence that supports those reasons. Using these building blocks, we can construct a strong logical argument.

Claims.   Good arguments are based on arguable claims—statements that reasonable people may disagree about. Certain kinds of statements cannot be argued:

- *Verifiable statements of fact.* Most of the time, there's no point in arguing about facts like "The earth is round" or "George H. W. Bush was America's forty-first president." Such statements contain no controversy, no potential opposition—and so no interest for an audience. However, you might argue about the basis of a fact. For example, until recently it was a fact that our solar system had nine planets, but when further discoveries led to a change in the definition of *planet*, Pluto no longer qualified.

- *Issues of faith or belief.* By definition, matters of faith cannot be proven or refuted. If you believe in reincarnation or don't believe there is an afterlife, there's no way I can convince you otherwise. However, in a philosophy or religion course you may be asked to argue, for example, whether or not the universe must have a cause.

- *Matters of simple opinion or personal taste.* If you think cargo pants are ugly, no amount of arguing will convince you to think otherwise. If you own every Taylor Swift CD and think she's the greatest singer ever, you won't convince your Nirvana-loving parents to like her, too. If matters of taste are based on identifiable criteria, though, they may be argued in an **EVALUATION**, where "Tom Cruise is a terrible actor" is more than just your opinion—it's an assertion you can support with evidence.

197–205 ▲

You may begin with an opinion: "I think wearing a helmet makes riding a bike more dangerous, not less." As it stands, that statement can't be considered a claim—it needs to be made more reasonable and informed. To do that, you might reframe it as a question—"Do bike riders who wear helmets get injured more often than those who don't?"—that may be answered as you do research and start to write. Your opinion or question should lead you to an arguable claim, however, one that could be challenged by another thoughtful person. In this case, for example, your research might lead you to a focused, qualified claim: *Contrary to common sense, wearing a helmet while riding a bicycle increases the chances of injury, at least to adult riders.*

Qualifying a claim. According to an old saying, there are two sides to every story. Much of the time, though, arguments don't sort themselves neatly into two sides, pro and con. No matter what your topic, your argument will rarely be a simple matter of being for or against; in most cases, you'll want to qualify your claim—that it is true in certain circumstances, with certain conditions, with these limitations, and so on. Qualifying your claim shows that you're reasonable and also makes your topic more manageable by limiting it. The following questions can help you qualify your claim.

- *Can it be true in some circumstances or at some times but not others?* For example, freedom of speech should generally be unrestricted, but individuals can sue for slander or libel.

- *Can it be true only with certain conditions?* For instance, cell phones and computer monitors should be recycled, but only by licensed, domestic recyclers.

- *Can it be true for some groups or individuals but not others?* For example, nearly everyone should follow a low-carb diet, but some people, such as diabetics, should avoid it.

SOME WORDS FOR QUALIFYING A CLAIM

sometimes	nearly	it seems/seemingly
rarely	usually	some
in some cases	more or less	perhaps
often	for the most part	possibly
routinely	in many cases	in most cases

Drafting a thesis statement. Once your claim is focused and appropriately qualified, it can form the core of your essay's **THESIS STATEMENT**, which announces your position and forecasts the path your argument will follow. For example, here is the opening paragraph of an essay by the

345–47

executive director of the National Congress of American Indians arguing that the remains of Native Americans should be treated with the same respect given to others. The author outlines the context of her argument and then presents her thesis (here, in italics):

> What if museums, universities and government agencies could put your dead relatives on display or keep them in boxes to be cut up and otherwise studied? What if you believed that the spirits of the dead could not rest until their human remains were placed in a sacred area? The ordinary American would say there ought to be a law—and there is, for ordinary Americans. *The problem for American Indians is that there are too many laws of the kind that make us the archeological property of the United States and too few of the kind that protect us from such insults.* —Susan Shown Harjo, "Last Rites for Indian Dead: Treating Remains Like Artifacts Is Intolerable"

Reasons. Your claim must be supported by reasons that your audience will accept. A reason can usually be linked to a claim with the word *because*:

CLAIM	+	*BECAUSE*	+	REASON
College students should strive to graduate		*because*		they will earn far more over their lifetimes than those who do not.

Keep in mind that you likely have a further reason, a rule or principle that underlies the reason you link directly to your claim. In this argument, the underlying reason is that isolation from other people is bad. If your audience doesn't accept that principle, you may have to back it up with further reasons or evidence.

To come up with good reasons, start by stating your position and then answering the question *why?*

CLAIM: College students should strive to graduate. *Why?*

REASON: (Because) They will earn far more over their lifetimes than those who do not. *Why?*

UNDERLYING REASON: The economy values college graduates and pays them more.

As you can see, this exercise can continue indefinitely as the underlying reasons grow more and more general and abstract. You can do the same with other positions:

CLAIM: Smoking should be banned. *Why?*

REASON: (Because) It is harmful to smokers and also to nonsmokers.

UNDERLYING REASON: People should be protected from harmful substances.

Evidence. Evidence to support your reasons can come from various sources. In fact, you may need to use several kinds of evidence to persuade your audience that your claim is true. Some of the most common types of evidence include facts, statistics, examples, authorities, anecdotes, scenarios, case studies, textual evidence, and visuals.

Facts are ideas that are proven to be true. Facts can include observations or scholarly research (your own or someone else's), but they need to be accepted as true. If your audience accepts the facts you present, they can be powerful means of persuasion. For example, an essay on junk email offers these facts to demonstrate the seasonal nature of spam:

> The flow of spam is often seasonal. It slows in the spring, and then, in the month that technology specialists call "black September"—when hundreds of thousands of students return to college, many armed with new computers and access to fast Internet connections—the levels rise sharply.
>
> —Michael Specter, "Damn Spam"

Specter offers this fact with only a general reference to its origin ("technology specialists"), but given what most people know—or think they know—about college students, it rings true. A citation from a study published by a "technology specialist" would offer even greater credibility.

Statistics are numerical data, usually produced through research, surveys, or polls. Statistics should be relevant to your argument, as current as possible, accurate, and from a reliable source. An argument advocating that Americans should eat less meat presents these data to support the writer's contention that we eat far too much of it:

Americans are downing close to 200 pounds of meat, poultry, and fish per capita per year (dairy and eggs are separate, and hardly insignificant), an increase of 50 pounds per person from 50 years ago. We each consume something like 110 grams of protein a day, about twice the federal government's recommended allowance; of that, about 75 grams come from animal protein. (The recommended level is itself considered by many dietary experts to be higher than it needs to be.) It's likely that most of us would do just fine on around 30 grams of protein a day, virtually all of it from plant sources.

—Mark Bittman, "Rethinking the Meat-Guzzler"

Bittman's statistics demonstrate the extent to which Americans have increased their meat consumption over the last half century, the proportion of our diets that comes from meat, and, by comparison, how much protein our bodies require—and summarize the heart of his argument in stark numeric terms.

Examples are specific instances that illustrate general statements. In a book on life after dark in Europe, a historian offers several examples to demonstrate his point that three hundred years ago, night—without artificial lighting—was treacherous:

Even sure-footed natives on a dark night could misjudge the lay of the land, stumbling into a ditch or off a precipice. In Aberdeenshire, a fifteen-year-old girl died in 1739 after straying from her customary path through a churchyard and tumbling into a newly dug grave. The Yorkshireman Arthur Jessop, returning from a neighbor's home on a cold December evening, fell into a stone pit after losing his bearings.

—A. Roger Ekirch, *At Day's Close: Night in Times Past*

Ekirch illustrates his point and makes it come alive for readers by citing two specific individuals' fates.

Authorities are experts on your subject. To be useful, authorities must be reputable, trustworthy, and qualified to address the subject. You should 469–72 **EVALUATE** any authorities you consult carefully to be sure they have the credentials necessary for readers to take them seriously. When you cite

academic literacies · rhetorical situations · genres · processes · strategies · research MLA / APA · media / design · readings · handbook

experts, you should clearly identify them and the origins of their authority in a **SIGNAL PHRASE**, as does the author of an argument that deforested land can be reclaimed:

487–90

> Reed Funk, professor of plant biology at Rutgers University, believes that the vast areas of deforested land can be used to grow millions of genetically improved trees for food, mostly nuts, and for fuel. Funk sees nuts used to supplement meat as a source of high-quality protein in developing-country diets.
>
> —Lester R. Brown, *Plan B 2.0: Rescuing a Planet under Stress and a Civilization in Trouble*

Brown cites Funk, an expert on plant biology, to support his argument that humans need to rethink the global economy in order to create a sustainable world. Without the information on Funk's credentials, though, readers would have no reason to take his proposal seriously.

Anecdotes are brief **NARRATIVES** that your audience will find believable and that contribute directly to your argument. Anecdotes may come from your personal experience or the experiences of others. In an essay arguing that it's understandable when athletes give in to the temptation to use performance-enhancing drugs, sports blogger William Moller uses an anecdote to show that the need to perform can outweigh the potential negative consequences of using drugs:

419–27

> I spent my high school years at a boarding school hidden among the apple orchards of Massachusetts. Known for a spartan philosophy regarding the adolescent need for sleep, the school worked us to the bone, regularly slamming us with six hours of homework. I pulled a lot more all-nighters (of the scholastic sort) in my years there than I ever did in college. When we weren't in class, the library, study hall, or formal sit-down meals, we were likely found on a sports field. We also had school on Saturday, beginning at 8 a.m. just like every other non-Sunday morning.
>
> Adding kindling to the fire, the students were not your laid-back types; everyone wanted that spot at the top of the class, and social life was rife with competition. The type A's that fill the investment banking,

legal, and political worlds — those are the kids I spent my high school years with.

And so it was that midway through my sophomore year, I found myself on my third all-nighter in a row, attempting to memorize historically significant pieces of art out of E. H. Gombrich's *The Story of Art*. I had finished a calculus exam the day before, and the day before that had been devoted to world history. And on that one cold night in February, I had had enough. I had hit that point where you've had so little sleep over such a long time that you start seeing spots, as if you'd been staring at a bright light for too long. The grade I would compete for the next day suddenly slipped in importance, and I began daydreaming about how easy the real world would be compared to the hell I was going through.

But there was hope. A friend who I was taking occasional study breaks with read the story in the bags beneath my eyes, in the slump of my shoulders, the nervous drumming of my fingers on the chair as we sipped flat, warm Coke in the common room. My personal *deus ex machina*,* he handed me a small white pill.

I was very innocent. I matured way after most of my peers, and was probably best known for being the kid who took all the soprano solos away from the girls in the choir as a first-year student. I don't think I had ever been buzzed, much less drunk. I'd certainly never smoked a cigarette. And knowing full well that what I was doing could be nothing better than against the rules (and less importantly, illegal) I did what I felt I needed to do, to accomplish what was demanded of me. And it worked. I woke up and regained focus like nothing I'd ever experienced. Unfortunately, it also came with serious side effects: I was a hypersensitized, stuffed-up, sweaty, wide-eyed mess, but I studied until the birds started chirping. And I aced my test.

Later I found out the pill was Ritalin, and it was classified as a class 3 drug.† I did it again, too — only a handful of times, as the side effects were so awful. But every time it was still illegal, still against

---

Deus ex machina: In ancient Greek and Roman drama, a god introduced into the plot to resolve complications.

†*Class 3 drug:* Drug that is illegal to possess without a prescription.

the rules. And as emphasized above, I was much more worried about the scholastic consequences if I were discovered abusing a prescription drug than the fact that I was breaking the law. Though I was using it in a far different manner than the baseball players who would later get caught with it in their systems, it was still very clearly a "performance-enhancing drug."

Just like every other person on this planet, I was giving in to the incentive scheme that was presented to me. The negative of doing poorly on the test was far greater than the negative of getting caught, discounted by the anesthetic of low probability.

—William Moller, "We, the Public,
Place the Best Athletes on Pedestals"

Moller uses this anecdote to demonstrate the truth of his argument, that given the choice between "breaking the rules and breaking my grades" or "getting an edge" in professional sports, just about everyone will choose to break the rules.

Scenarios are hypothetical situations. Like anecdotes, "what if" scenarios can help you describe the possible effects of particular actions or offer new ways of looking at a particular state of affairs. For example, a mathematician presents this lighthearted scenario about Santa Claus in a tongue-in-cheek argument that Christmas is (almost) pure magic:

Let's assume that Santa only visits those who are children in the eyes of the law, that is, those under the age of 18. There are roughly 2 billion such individuals in the world. However, Santa started his annual activities long before diversity and equal opportunity became issues, and as a result he doesn't handle Muslim, Hindu, Jewish and Buddhist children. That reduces his workload significantly to a mere 15% of the total, namely 378 million. However, the crucial figure is not the number of children but the number of homes Santa has to visit. According to the most recent census data, the average size of a family in the world is 3.5 children per household. Thus, Santa has to visit 108,000,000 individual homes. (Of course, as everyone knows, Santa only visits good children, but we can surely assume that, on an average, at least one child of the 3.5 in each home meets that criterion.)

—Keith Devlin, "The Mathematics of Christmas"

Devlin uses this scenario, as part of his mathematical analysis of Santa's yearly task, to help demonstrate that Christmas is indeed magical—because if you do the math, it's clear that Santa's task is physically impossible.

Case studies and observations feature detailed reporting about a subject. Case studies are in-depth, systematic examinations of an occasion, a person, or a group. For example, in arguing that class differences exist in the United States, sociologist Gregory Mantsios presents studies of three "typical" Americans to show "enormous class differences" in their lifestyles.

Observations offer detailed descriptions of a subject. Here's an observation of the emergence of a desert stream that flows only at night:

At about 5:30 water came out of the ground. It did not spew up, but slowly escaped into the surrounding sand and small rocks. The wet circle grew until water became visible. Then it bubbled out like a small fountain and the creek began.

—Craig Childs, *The Secret Knowledge of Water*

Childs presents this and other observations in a book that argues (among other things) that even in harsh, arid deserts, water exists, and knowing where to find it can mean the difference between life and death.

478–90 **Textual evidence** includes QUOTATIONS, PARAPHRASES, and SUMMARIES. Usually, the relevance of textual evidence must be stated directly, as excerpts from a text may carry several potential meanings. For example, here is an excerpt from a student essay analyzing the function of the raft in *Huckleberry Finn* as "a platform on which the resolution of conflicts is made possible":

[T]he scenes where Jim and Huck are in consensus on the raft contain the moments in which they are most relaxed. For instance, in chapter twelve of the novel, Huck, after escaping capture from Jackson's Island, calls the rafting life "solemn" and articulates their experience as living "pretty high" (Twain 75–76). Likewise, subsequent to escaping the unresolved feud between the Grangerfords and Shepherdsons in chapter eighteen, Huck is unquestionably at ease on the raft: "I was powerful glad to get away from the feuds. . . . We said there warn't no home like a raft, after all. Other places do seem so cramped up and smothery, but a raft don't. You feel mighty free and easy and comfortable on a raft" (Twain 134).

—Dave Nichols, "'Less All Be Friends': Rafts as Negotiating Platforms in Twain's *Huckleberry Finn*"

Huck's own words support Nichols's claim that he can relax on a raft. Nichols strengthens his claim by quoting evidence from two separate pages, suggesting that Huck's opinion of rafts pervades the novel.

Visuals can be a useful way of presenting evidence. Remember, though, that charts, graphs, photos, drawings, and other **VISUAL TEXTS** seldom speak for themselves and thus must be explained in your text. Below, for example, is a photograph of a poster carried by demonstrators at the 2008 Beijing Summer Olympics, protesting China's treatment of Tibetans.

607–15

If you were to use this photo in an essay, you would need to explain that the poster combines the image of a protester standing before a tank during the 1989 Tiananmen Square uprising with the Olympic logo, making clear to your readers that the protesters are likening China's treatment of Tibetans to its brutal actions in the past. Similarly, the poster for a recycling campaign below uses an American flag made from household waste to argue that recycling is patriotic.

Choosing appropriate evidence. The kinds of evidence you provide to support your argument depends on your RHETORICAL SITUATION. If your purpose is, for example, to convince readers to accept the need for a proposed solution, you'd be likely to include facts, statistics, and anecdotes. If you're writing for an academic audience, you'd be less likely to rely on anecdotes, preferring authorities, textual evidence, statistics, and case studies instead. And even within academic communities different disciplines and genres may focus primarily on different kinds of evidence. If you're not sure what counts as appropriate evidence, ask your instructor for guidance.

■ 53

Convincing Readers You're Trustworthy

For your argument to be convincing, you need to establish your own credibility with readers—to demonstrate your knowledge about your topic, to show that you and your readers share some common ground, and to show yourself to be evenhanded in the way you present your argument.

Building common ground. One important element of gaining readers' trust is to identify some common ground, some values you and your audience share. For example, to introduce a book arguing for the compatibility of science and religion, author Chet Raymo offers some common memories:

> Like most children, I was raised on miracles. Cows that jump over the moon; a jolly fat man that visits every house in the world in a single night; mice and ducks that talk; little engines that huff and puff and say, "I think I can"; geese that lay golden eggs. This lively exercise of credulity on the part of children is good practice for what follows—for believing in the miracle stories of traditional religion, yes, but also for the practice of poetry or science.
>
> —Chet Raymo, *Skeptics and True Believers: The Exhilarating Connection between Science and Religion*

Raymo presents childhood stories and myths that are part of many people's shared experiences to help readers find a connection between two realms that are often seen as opposed.

Incorporating other viewpoints. To show that you have carefully considered the viewpoints of others, including those who may agree or disagree with you, you should incorporate those viewpoints into your argument by acknowledging, accommodating, or refuting them.

Acknowledging other viewpoints. One essential part of establishing your credibility is to acknowledge that there are viewpoints different from yours and to represent them fairly and accurately. Rather than weakening your argument, acknowledging possible objections to your position shows that you've thought about and researched your topic thoroughly. For example, in an essay about his experience growing up homosexual, writer Andrew Sullivan admits that not every young gay man or woman has the same experience:

> I should add that many young lesbians and homosexuals seem to have had a much easier time of it. For many, the question of sexual identity was not a critical factor in their life choices or vocation, or even a factor at all.   —Andrew Sullivan, "What Is a Homosexual?"

In response to a reasonable objection, Sullivan qualifies his assertions, making his own stance appear to be reasonable.

Accommodating other viewpoints. You may be tempted to ignore views you don't agree with, but in fact it's important to demonstrate that you are aware of them and have considered them carefully. You may find yourself conceding that opposing views have some merit and qualifying your claim or even making them part of your own argument. See, for example, how a philosopher arguing that torture is sometimes "not merely permissible but morally mandatory" addresses a major objection to his position:

> The most powerful argument against using torture as a punishment or to secure confessions is that such practices disregard the rights of the individual. Well, if the individual is all that important—and he is— it is correspondingly important to protect the rights of individuals threatened by terrorists. If life is so valuable that it must never be

taken, the lives of the innocents must be saved even at the price of hurting the one who endangers them.

—Michael Levin, "The Case for Torture"

Levin acknowledges his critics' argument that the individual is indeed important but then asserts that if the life of one person is important, the lives of many people must be even more important. In effect, he uses an opposing argument to advance his own.

Refuting other viewpoints. Often you may need to refute other arguments and make a case for why you believe they are wrong. Are the values underlying the argument questionable? Is the reasoning flawed? Is the evidence inadequate or faulty? For example, an essay arguing for the elimination of college athletics scholarships includes this refutation:

> Some argue that eliminating athletics scholarships would deny opportunity and limit access for many students, most notably black athletes. The question is, access to what? The fields of competition or an opportunity to earn a meaningful degree? With the six-year graduation rates of black basketball players hovering in the high 30-percent range, and black football players in the high 40-percent range, despite years of "academic reform," earning an athletics scholarship under the current system is little more than a chance to play sports.   —John R. Gerdy, "For True Reform, Athletics Scholarships Must Go"

Gerdy bases his refutation on statistics showing that for more than half of African American college athletes, the opportunity to earn a degree by playing a sport is an illusion.

When you incorporate differing viewpoints, be careful to avoid the **FALLACIES** of attacking the person making the argument or refuting a competing position that no one seriously entertains. It is also important that you not distort or exaggerate opposing viewpoints. If *your* argument is to be persuasive, other arguments should be represented fairly.

370–72

Appealing to Readers' Emotions

Logic and facts, even when presented by someone who seems reasonable and trustworthy, may not be enough to persuade readers. Many successful arguments include an emotional component that appeals to readers' hearts as well as to their minds. Advertising often works by appealing to its audience's emotions, as in this paragraph from a Volvo ad:

> Choosing a car is about the comfort and safety of your passengers, most especially your children. That's why we ensure Volvo's safety research examines how we can make our cars safer for everyone who travels in them — from adults to teenagers, children to babies. Even those who aren't even born yet.   —*Volvo.com*

This ad plays on the fear that children — or a pregnant mother — may be injured or killed in an automobile accident.

Keep in mind that emotional appeals can make readers feel as though they are being manipulated and, consequently, less likely to accept an argument. For most kinds of academic writing, use emotional appeals sparingly.

Checking for Fallacies

Fallacies are arguments that involve faulty reasoning. It's important to avoid fallacies in your writing because they often seem plausible but are usually unfair or inaccurate and make reasonable discussion difficult. Here are some of the most common fallacies:

- **Ad hominem** arguments attack someone's character rather than address the issues. (*Ad hominem* is Latin for "to the man.") It is an especially common fallacy in political discourse and elsewhere: "Jack Turner has no business talking about the way we run things in this city. He's just another flaky liberal." Whether or not Turner is a "flaky liberal" has no bearing on the worth of his argument about "the way we run things in this city"; insulting one's opponents isn't an argument against their positions.

- **Bandwagon appeals** argue that because others think or do something, we should, too. For example, an advertisement for a rifle association suggests that "67 percent of voters support laws permitting concealed weapons. You should, too." It assumes that readers want to be part of the group and implies that an opinion that is popular must be correct.

- **Begging the question** is a circular argument. It assumes as a given what is trying to be proved, essentially supporting an assertion with the assertion itself. Consider this statement: "Affirmative action can never be fair or just because you cannot remedy one injustice by committing another." This statement begs the question because to prove that affirmative action is unjust, it assumes that it is an injustice.

- **Either-or** arguments, also called *false dilemmas*, are oversimplifications that assert there can be only two possible positions on a complex issue. For example, "Those who oppose our actions in this war are enemies of freedom" inaccurately assumes that if someone opposes the war in question, he or she opposes freedom. In fact, people might have many other reasons for opposing the war.

- **False analogies** compare things that resemble each other in some ways but not in the most important respects — for example, "Trees pollute the air just as much as cars and trucks do." Although it's true that plants emit hydrocarbons, and hydrocarbons are a component of smog, they also produce oxygen, whereas motor vehicles emit gases that combine with hydrocarbons to form smog. Vehicles pollute the air; trees provide the air that vehicles' emissions pollute.

- **Faulty causality,** also known as *post hoc, ergo propter hoc* (Latin for "after this, therefore because of this"), assumes that because one event followed another, the first event caused the second—for example, "Legalizing same-sex marriage in Sweden led to a decline in the marriage rate of opposite-sex couples." The statement contains no evidence to show that the first event caused the second.

- **Straw man** arguments misrepresent an opposing position to make it ridiculous or extreme and thus easy to refute, rather than dealing with the actual position. For example, if someone argues that funding for food stamps should be cut, a straw man response would be, "You want the poor to starve," transforming a proposal to cut a specific program into an exaggerated argument that the proposer hasn't made.

- *Hasty generalizations* are conclusions based on insufficient or inappropriately qualified evidence. This summary of a research study is a good example: "Twenty randomly chosen residents of Brooklyn, New York, were asked whether they found graffiti tags offensive; fourteen said yes, five said no, and one had no opinion. Therefore, 70 percent of Brooklyn residents find tagging offensive." In Brooklyn, a part of New York City with a population of over two million, twenty residents is far too small a group from which to draw meaningful conclusions. To be able to generalize, the researcher would have had to survey a much greater percentage of Brooklyn's population.

- *Slippery slope* arguments assert that one event will inevitably lead to another, often cataclysmic event without presenting evidence that such a chain of causes and effects will in fact take place. Here's an example: "If the state legislature passes this 2 percent tax increase, it won't be long before all the corporations in the state move to other states and leave thousands unemployed." According to this argument, if taxes are raised, the state's economy will be ruined—not a likely scenario, given the size of the proposed increase.

Considering the Rhetorical Situation

To argue effectively, you need to think about the message that you want to articulate, the audience you want to persuade, the effect of your stance, and the larger context you are writing in.

55–56   **PURPOSE**   What do you want your audience to do? To think a certain way? To take a certain action? To change their minds? To consider alternative views to their current ones? To accept your position as plausible? To see that you have thought carefully about an issue and researched it appropriately?

academic literacies   rhetorical situations   genres   processes   strategies   research MLA / APA   media / design   readings   handbook

AUDIENCE   Who is your intended audience? What do they likely know and believe about your topic? How personal is it for them? To what extent are they likely to agree or disagree with you? Why? What common ground can you find with them? How should you incorporate other viewpoints they have? What kind of evidence are they likely to accept?

57–60

GENRE   What genre will help you achieve your purpose? A position paper? An evaluation? A review? A proposal? An analysis?

61–63

STANCE   What's your attitude toward your topic, and why? What strategies will help you to convey that stance? How do you want your audience to perceive you? As an authority on your topic? As someone much like them? As calm? reasonable? impassioned or angry? something else?

64–67

MEDIA / DESIGN   What media will you use, and how do your media affect your argument? If you're writing on paper, does your argument call for photos or charts? If you're giving an oral presentation, should you put your reasons and support on slides? If you're writing online, should you add links to sites representing other positions or containing evidence that supports your position?

68–70

37 Classifying and Dividing

Classification and division are ways of organizing information: various items may be classified according to their similarities, or a single topic may be divided into parts. We might classify different kinds of flowers as annuals or perennials, for example, and classify the perennials further as dahlias, daisies, roses, and peonies. We might also divide a flower garden into distinct areas: for herbs, flowers, and vegetables.

Writers often use classification and division as ways of developing and organizing material. This book, for instance, classifies comparison, definition, description, and several other common ways of thinking and writing as strategies. It divides the information it provides about writing into seven parts: "Rhetorical Situations," "Genres," "Processes," and so on. Each part further divides its material into various chapters. Even if you never write a book, you will have occasion to classify and divide material in **ANNOTATED BIBLIOGRAPHIES**, essays **ANALYZING TEXTS**, and other kinds of writing. This chapter offers advice for classifying and dividing information for various writing purposes—and in a way that suits your own rhetorical situation.

188–96
94–128

Classifying

When we classify something, we group it with similar things. A linguist would classify French and Spanish and Italian as Romance languages, for example—and Russian, Polish, and Bulgarian as Slavic languages. In a hilarious (if totally phony) news story from the *Onion* about a church bake sale, the writer classifies the activities observed there as examples of the seven deadly sins:

academic literacies · rhetorical situations · genres · processes · strategies · research MLA / APA · media / design · readings · handbook

GADSDEN, AL—The seven deadly sins—avarice, sloth, envy, lust, gluttony, pride, and wrath—were all committed Sunday during the twice-annual bake sale at St. Mary's of the Immaculate Conception Church.

—"All Seven Deadly Sins Committed at Church Bake Sale," *The Onion*

The article goes on to categorize the participants' behavior in terms of the sins, describing one parishioner who commits the sin of pride by bragging about her cookies and others who commit the sin of envy by envying the popularity of the prideful parishioner's baked goods (the consumption of which leads to the sin of gluttony). In all, the article notes, "347 individual acts of sin were committed at the bake sale," and every one of them can be classified as one of the seven deadly sins.

Dividing

As a writing strategy, division is a way of breaking something into parts—and a way of making the information easy for readers to follow and understand. See how this example about children's ways of nagging divides their tactics into seven categories:

James U. McNeal, a professor of marketing at Texas A&M University, is considered America's leading authority on marketing to children. In his book *Kids as Customers* (1992), McNeal provides marketers with a thorough analysis of "children's requesting styles and appeals." He [divides] juvenile nagging tactics into seven major categories. A *pleading* nag is one accompanied by repetitions of words like "please" or "mom, mom, mom." A *persistent* nag involves constant requests for the coveted product and may include the phrase "I'm gonna ask just one more time." *Forceful* nags are extremely pushy and may include subtle threats, like "Well, then, I'll go and ask Dad." *Demonstrative* nags are the most high risk, often characterized by full-blown tantrums in public places, breath holding, tears, a refusal to leave the store. *Sugar-coated* nags promise affection in return for a purchase and may rely on seemingly heartfelt declarations, like "You're the best dad in the world." *Threatening* nags are youthful forms of blackmail, vows of eternal hatred and of running away if something isn't bought. *Pity* nags claim the child will be heartbroken, teased, or socially stunted if the parent refuses to buy a certain item. "All of these appeals and styles may be used in combination," McNeal's research has discovered, "but kids tend to stick to one or two of each that prove most effective . . . for their own parents."

> —Eric Schlosser, *Fast Food Nation:*
> *The Dark Side of the All-American Meal*

Here the writer announces the division scheme of "seven major categories." Then he names each tactic and describes how it works. And notice the italics: each nagging tactic is italicized, making it easy to recognize and follow. Take away the italics, and the divisions would be less visible.

Creating Clear and Distinct Categories

When you classify or divide, you need to create clear and distinct categories. If you're writing about music, you might divide it on the basis of the genre (hip-hop, rock, classical, gospel), artist (male or female, group or solo), or instruments (violins, trumpets, bongos, guitars). These categories must be distinct, so that no information overlaps or fits into more than one category, and they must include every member of the group you're discussing. The simpler the criteria for selecting the categories, the better. The nagging categories in the example from *Fast Food Nation* are based on only one criterion: a child's verbal behavior.

Sometimes you may want to highlight your categories visually to make them easier to follow. Eric Schlosser does that by italicizing each category: the *pleading* nag, the *persistent* nag, the *forceful* nag, and so on. Other **DESIGN** elements—bulleted lists, pie charts, tables, images—might also prove useful.

597–606

See, for instance, how *The World of Caffeine* authors Bennett Alan Weinberg and Bonnie K. Bealer use a two-column list to show what they say are the differing cultural connotations of coffee and tea:

academic literacies · rhetorical situations · genres · processes · strategies · research MLA / APA · media / design · readings · handbook

Coffee Aspect	Tea Aspect
Male	Female
Boisterous	Decorous
Indulgence	Temperance
Hardheaded	Romantic
Topology	Geometry
Heidegger	Carnap
Beethoven	Mozart
Libertarian	Statist
Promiscuous	Pure

—Bennett Alan Weinberg and Bonnie K. Bealer,
The World of Caffeine

Sometimes you might show categories visually, as in this website promoting Michigan apples. Each of the sixteen varieties grown in Michigan is pictured, and its taste, uses, and texture are described.

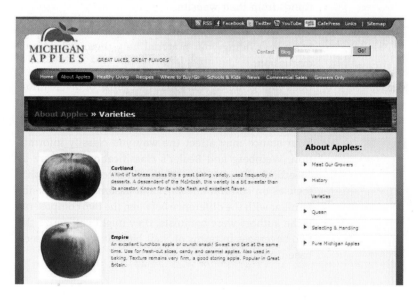

The photographs allow us to see the differences among the varieties at a glance. The varieties are arranged alphabetically but could have been arranged by color, flavor (sweet or tart), or whether they are best for baking or eating raw.

Considering the Rhetorical Situation

As a writer or speaker, you need to think about the message that you want to articulate, the audience you want to reach, and the larger context you are writing in.

55–56　**PURPOSE**　Your purpose for writing will affect how you classify or divide information. Weinberg and Bealer classify coffee as "boisterous" and tea as "decorous" to help readers understand the cultural styles the two beverages represent, whereas J. Crew might divide sweaters into cashmere, wool, and cotton to help shoppers find and buy things from their website.

57–60　**AUDIENCE**　What audience do you want to reach, and will classifying or dividing your material help them follow your discussion?

61–63　**GENRE**　Does your genre call for you to categorize or divide information? A long report might need to be divided into sections, for instance.

64–67　**STANCE**　Your stance may affect the way you classify information. Weinberg and Bealer's classification of coffee as "Beethoven" and tea as "Mozart" reflects a stance that focuses on cultural analysis (and assumes an audience familiar with the difference between the two composers). If the authors were botanists, they might categorize the two beverages in terms of their biological origins ("seed based" and "leaf based").

MEDIA/DESIGN You can classify or divide in paragraph form, but sometimes a pie chart or list will show the categories better.

68–70

IF YOU NEED MORE HELP

See also **CLUSTERING**, **CUBING**, and **LOOPING**, three methods of generating ideas
discussed in Chapter 30 that can be especially helpful for classifying material. And
see all the **PROCESSES** chapters for guidelines on drafting, revising, and so on if
you need to write a classification essay.

290–92

279

38 Comparing and Contrasting

Comparing things looks at their similarities; contrasting them focuses on their differences. It's a kind of thinking that comes naturally and that we do constantly—for example, comparing Houston with Dallas, iPhones with Androids, or three paintings by Renoir. And once we start comparing, we generally find ourselves contrasting—Houston and Dallas have differences as well as similarities.

235–44 ▲
197–205

As a student, you'll often be asked to compare and contrast paintings or poems or other things. As a writer, you'll have cause to compare and contrast in most kinds of writing. In a **PROPOSAL**, for instance, you will need to compare your solution with other possible solutions; or in an **EVALUATION**, such as a movie review, you might contrast the film you're reviewing with some other film. This chapter offers advice on ways of comparing and contrasting things for various writing purposes and for your own rhetorical situations.

Most of the time, we compare obviously similar things: cars we might purchase, three competing political candidates, two versions of a film. Occasionally, however, we might compare things that are less obviously similar. See how John McMurtry, an ex–football player, compares football with war in an essay arguing that the attraction football holds for spectators is based in part on its potential for violence and injury:

> The family resemblance between football and war is, indeed, striking. Their languages are similar: "field general," "long bomb," "blitz," "take a shot," "front line," "pursuit," "good hit," "the draft," and so on. Their principles and practices are alike: mass hysteria, the art of intimidation, absolute command and total obedience, territorial aggression, censorship, inflated insignia and propaganda, blackboard maneuvers and strategies, drills, uniforms, marching bands, and training

camps. And the virtues they celebrate are almost identical: hyper-aggressiveness, coolness under fire, and suicidal bravery.

—John McMurtry, "Kill 'Em! Crush 'Em! Eat 'Em Raw!"

McMurtry's comparison helps focus readers' attention on what he's arguing about football in part because it's somewhat unexpected. But the more unlikely the comparison, the more you might be accused of comparing apples and oranges. It's important, therefore, that the things we compare be legitimately compared—as is the case in the following comparison of the health of the world's richest and poorest people:

World Health Organization (WHO) data indicate that roughly 1.2 billion people are undernourished, underweight, and often hungry. At the same time, roughly 1.2 billion people are overnourished and overweight, most of them suffering from excessive caloric intake and exercise deprivation. So while 1 billion people worry whether they will eat, another billion should worry about eating too much.

Disease patterns also reflect the widening gap. The billion poorest suffer mostly from infectious diseases—malaria, tuberculosis, dysentery, and AIDS. Malnutrition leaves infants and small children even more vulnerable to such infectious diseases. Unsafe drinking water takes a heavier toll on those with hunger-weakened immune systems, resulting in millions of fatalities each year. In contrast, among the billion at the top of the global economic scale, it is diseases related to aging and lifestyle excesses, including obesity, smoking, diets rich in fat and sugar, and exercise deprivation, that cause most deaths.

—Lester R. Brown, *Plan B 2.0: Rescuing a Planet under Stress and a Civilization in Trouble*

While the two groups of roughly a billion people each undoubtedly have similarities, this selection from a book arguing for global action on the environment focuses on the stark contrasts.

Two Ways of Comparing and Contrasting

Comparisons and contrasts may be organized in two basic ways: block and point by point.

The block method. One way is to discuss separately each item you're comparing, giving all the information about one item and then all the information about the next item. A report on Seattle and Vancouver, for example, compares the firearm regulations in each city using a paragraph about Seattle and then a paragraph about Vancouver:

> Although similar in many ways, Seattle and Vancouver differ markedly in their approaches to the regulation of firearms. In Seattle, handguns may be purchased legally for self-defense in the street or at home. After a thirty-day waiting period, a permit can be obtained to carry a handgun as a concealed weapon. The recreational use of handguns is minimally restricted.
>
> In Vancouver, self-defense is not considered a valid or legal reason to purchase a handgun. Concealed weapons are not permitted. Recreational uses of handguns (such as target shooting and collecting) are regulated by the province, and the purchase of a handgun requires a restricted-weapons permit. A permit to carry a weapon must also be obtained in order to transport a handgun, and these weapons can be discharged only at a licensed shooting club. Handguns can be transported by car, but only if they are stored in the trunk in a locked box.
>
> —John Henry Sloan et al., "Handgun Regulations, Crime,
> Assaults, and Homicide: A Tale of Two Cities"

The point-by-point method. The other way to compare things is to focus on specific points of comparison. In this paragraph, humorist David Sedaris compares his childhood with his partner's, discussing corresponding aspects of the childhoods one at a time:

> Certain events are parallel, but compared with Hugh's, my childhood was unspeakably dull. When I was seven years old, my family moved to North Carolina. When he was seven years old, Hugh's family moved to the Congo. We had a collie and a house cat. They had a monkey and two horses named Charlie Brown and Satan. I threw stones at stop signs. Hugh threw stones at crocodiles. The verbs are the same, but he definitely wins the prize when it comes to nouns and objects. An eventful day for my mother might have involved a trip to the dry cleaner or a conversation with the potato-chip deliveryman. Asked

one ordinary Congo afternoon what she'd done with her day, Hugh's mother answered that she and a fellow member of the Ladies' Club had visited a leper colony on the outskirts of Kinshasa.

—David Sedaris, "Remembering My Childhood on the Continent of Africa"

Using Graphs and Images to Present Comparisons

Some comparisons can be easier to understand if they're presented visually, as a **CHART**, **GRAPH**, or **ILLUSTRATION**. For example, this excerpt from a chart from the *Huffington Post* shows the results of various opinion polls about Americans' identification with a political party in April and May 2012; it allows readers to compare not only percentages of Republicans, Democrats, and Independents but also differences in results among the polls. (In the third column, pop-up links explain that "Pop." means "Population," "A" means "adults," "RV" means "registered voters," and "LV" means "likely voters.")

607–15

Pollster	Dates	Pop.	Democrat	Independent	Republican	Undecided
AP-GfK	5/3–5/7	1,004 A	31	46	22	1
DailyKos/SEIU/ PPP (D)	5/3–5/6	1,000 RV	38	26	35	—
NBC/WSJ	4/13–4/17	800 A	30	42	24	4
CBS/Times	4/13–4/17	957 A	34	36	30	—
Ipsos/Reuters	4/12–4/15	1,044 A	29	49	22	—

—*Huffington Post*

The following bar graph, from an economics textbook, compares the incomes of various professions in the United States, both with one another and with the average U.S. income (defined as 100 percent). Again, it would be possible to write out this information in a paragraph—but it is much easier to understand it this way:

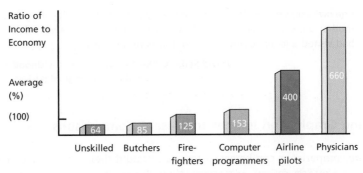

Ratio of Income to Economy

Average (%)

(100)

Unskilled: 64
Butchers: 85
Firefighters: 125
Computer programmers: 153
Airline pilots: 400
Physicians: 660

—Joseph E. Stiglitz, *Economics*

Sometimes photographs can make a comparison. The two photos below show an area of Japan before and after the 2011 tsunami.

Ishinomaki Prefecture before the 2011 tsunami (top) and *after the storm (bottom).*

Using Figurative Language to Make Comparisons

Another way we make comparisons is with figurative language: words and phrases used in a nonliteral way to help readers see a point. Three kinds of figurative language that make comparisons are similes, metaphors, and analogies. When Robert Burns wrote that his love was "like a red, red rose," he was comparing his love with a rose and evoking an image — in this case, a simile — that helps us understand his feelings for her. A simile makes a comparison using *like* or *as*. In the following example, from an article in the food section of the *New York Times*, a restaurant critic uses several similes (underlined) to help us visualize an unusual food dish:

> Once upon a time, possibly at a lodge in Wyoming, possibly at a butcher shop in Maurice, Louisiana, or maybe even at a plantation in South Carolina, an enterprising cook decided to take a boned chicken, a boned duck, and a boned turkey, stuff them one inside the other <u>like Russian dolls</u>, and roast them. He called his masterpiece turducken. . . .
>
> A well-prepared turducken is a marvelous treat, a free-form poultry terrine layered with flavorful stuffing and moistened with duck fat. When it's assembled, it looks <u>like a turkey</u> and it roasts <u>like a turkey</u>, but when you go to carve it, you can slice through it <u>like a loaf of bread</u>. In each slice you get a little bit of everything: white meat from the breast; dark meat from the legs, duck, carrots, bits of sausage, bread, herbs, juices, and chicken, too.
>
> —Amanda Hesser, "Turkey Finds Its Inner Duck (and Chicken)"

Metaphors make comparisons without such connecting words as *like* or *as*. See how desert ecologist Craig Childs uses a metaphor to help us understand the nature of water during a flood in the Grand Canyon:

> Water splashed off the desert and ran all over the surface, looking for the quickest way down. It was too swift for the ground to absorb. When water flows like this, it will not be clean tap water. It will be <u>a gravy of debris</u>, snatching everything it finds.
>
> —Craig Childs, *The Secret Knowledge of Water*

Calling the water "a gravy of debris" allows us to see the murky liquid as it streams through the canyon.

Analogies are extended similes or metaphors that compare something unfamiliar with something more familiar. Arguing that corporations should not patent parts of DNA whose function isn't yet clear, a genetics professor uses the familiar image of a library to explain an unfamiliar concept:

> It's like having a library of books and randomly tearing pages out. You may know which books the pages came from but that doesn't tell you much about them.　　—Peter Goodfellow, quoted in John Vidal and
> John Carvel, "Lambs to the Gene Market"

Sometimes analogies are used for humorous effect as well as to make a point, as in this passage from a critique of history textbooks:

> Another history text—this one for fifth grade—begins with the story of how Henry B. Gonzalez, who is a member of Congress from Texas, learned about his own nationality. When he was ten years old, his teacher told him he was an American because he was born in the United States. His grandmother, however, said, "The cat was born in the oven. Does that make him bread?"
>
> —Frances FitzGerald, *America Revised:*
> *History Schoolbooks in the Twentieth Century*

The grandmother's question shows how an intentionally ridiculous analogy can be a source of humor—and can make a point memorably.

Considering the Rhetorical Situation

As a writer or speaker, you need to think about the message that you want to articulate, the audience you want to reach, and the larger context you are writing in.

55–56 **PURPOSE** Sometimes your main purpose for writing will be to compare two or more things. Other times, you may want to compare several things for some other purpose—to compare your views with those of others in an argument essay or to compare one text with another as you analyze them.

academic literacies　rhetorical situations　genres　processes　strategies　research MLA / APA　media / design　readings　handbook

AUDIENCE   Who is your audience, and will comparing your topic with a more familiar one help them to follow your discussion?

57–60

GENRE   Does your genre require you to compare something? Evaluations often include comparisons—one book to another in a review, or ten different cell phones in *Consumer Reports*.

61–63

STANCE   Your stance may affect any comparisons you make. How you compare two things—evenhandedly, or clearly favoring one over the other, for example—will reflect your stance.

64–67

MEDIA / DESIGN   Some things you will want to compare with words alone (lines from two poems, for instance), but sometimes you may wish to make comparisons visually (two images juxtaposed on a page, or several numbers plotted on a line graph).

68–70

IF YOU NEED MORE HELP

See **LOOPING** and **CUBING**, two methods of generating ideas discussed in Chapter 27 that can be especially helpful for comparing and contrasting. If you're writing an essay whose purpose is to compare two or more things, see also the **PROCESSES** chapters for help drafting, revising, and so on.

290–92
279

39 Defining

Defining something says what it is—and what it is not. A terrier, for example, is a kind of dog. A fox terrier is a small dog now generally kept as a pet but once used by hunters to dig for foxes. Happiness is a jelly donut, at least according to Homer Simpson. All of those are definitions. As writers, we need to define any terms our readers may not know. And sometimes you'll want to stipulate your own definition of a word in order to set the terms of an **ARGUMENT**—as Homer Simpson does with a definition that's not found in any dictionary. This chapter details strategies for using definitions in your writing to suit your own rhetorical situations.

355–73

Formal Definitions

Sometimes to make sure readers understand you, you will need to provide a formal definition. If you are using a technical term that readers are unlikely to know or if you are using a term in a specific way, you need to say then and there what the word means. The word *mutual*, for example, has several dictionary meanings:

> **mu•tu•al . . .**
>
> **1a:** directed by each toward the other or the others <*mutual* affection> **b:** having the same feelings one for the other <they had long been *mutual* enemies> **c:** shared in common <enjoying their *mutual* hobby> **d:** joint
> **2:** characterized by intimacy
> **3:** of or relating to a plan whereby the members of an organization share in the profits and expenses; *specifically*: of, relating to, or taking the form of an insurance method in which the policyholders constitute the members of the insuring company   —*Merriam-Webster.com*

academic literacies   rhetorical situations   genres   processes   strategies   research MLA / APA   media / design   readings   handbook

The first two meanings are commonly understood and probably require no definition. But if you were to use *mutual* in the third sense, it might—depending on your audience. A general audience would probably need the definition; an audience from the insurance industry would not. A website that gives basic financial advice to an audience of non-specialists, for instance, offers a specific definition of the term *mutual fund*:

> *Mutual funds* are financial intermediaries. They are companies set up to receive your money and then, having received it, to make investments with the money.
>
> —Bill Barker, "A Grand, Comprehensive Overview to Mutual Funds Investing"

But even writers in specialized fields routinely provide formal definitions to make sure their readers understand the way they are using certain words. See how two writers define the word *stock* as it pertains to their respective (and very different) fields:

> Stocks are the basis for sauces and soups and important flavoring agents for braises. Admittedly, stock making is time consuming, but the extra effort yields great dividends.
>
> —Tom Colicchio, *Think Like a Chef*

> Want to own part of a business without having to show up at its office every day? Or ever? Stock is the vehicle of choice for those who do. Dating back to the Dutch mutual stock corporations of the sixteenth century, the modern stock market exists as a way for entrepreneurs to finance businesses using money collected from investors. In return for ponying up the dough to finance the company, the investor becomes a part owner of the company. That ownership is represented by stock—specialized financial "securities," or financial instruments, that are "secured" by a claim on the assets and profits of a company.
>
> —"Investing Basics: Stocks," *The Motley Fool*

To write a formal definition

- Use words that readers are likely to be familiar with.
- Don't use the word being defined in the definition.

- Begin with the word being defined; include the general category to which the term belongs and the attributes that make it different from the others in that category.

For example:

Term	General Category	Distinguishing Attributes
Stock is	a specialized financial "security"	that is "secured" by a claim.
Photosynthesis is	a process	by which plants use sunlight to create energy.
Astronomers are	scientists	who study celestial objects and phenomena.
Zach Galifianakis,	a comedian,	has acted in several films, including *The Hangover* and *The Campaign.*

Note that the category and distinguishing attributes cannot be stated too broadly; if they were, the definition would be too vague to be useful. It wouldn't be helpful in most circumstances, for example, to say, "Zach Galifianakis is a man who has acted" or "Photosynthesis is something having to do with plants."

Extended Definitions

Sometimes you need to provide a more detailed definition. Extended definitions may be several sentences long or several paragraphs long and may include pictures or diagrams. Sometimes an entire essay is devoted to defining a difficult or important concept. Here is one writer's extended definition of *meme*:

> Richard Dawkins first came up with the idea of a meme in his 1976 book *The Selfish Gene*. Essentially, memes are ideas that evolve according to the same principles that govern biological evolution. Think about all the ideas that you have in your head right now. They are all memes,

academic literacies rhetorical situations genres processes strategies research MLA / APA media / design readings handbook

and they all came from somewhere. Some of them will have come from friends and some will have come from the internet or television. Examples of memes are musical tunes, jokes, trends, fashions, catch phrases, and car designs. Now, the memes that inhabit your mind are in competition with all the other memes in the *memepool* (the collection of all existing memes). This means that they are all competing to get themselves copied into other people's minds. Some of these memes do quite well. Every time you whistle your favorite tune or utter a useful catch phrase, you are facilitating the spread of those memes. Every time you wear something that is "in fashion" you are helping the idea of that fashion enter other people's minds. Consider the first four notes of Beethoven's 5th symphony, or the "Happy Birthday" song. These are ideas that inhabit our minds and have been very successful at replicating. Not only have these memes found their way into literally millions of minds, they have also managed to leave copies of themselves on paper, in books, on audiotape, on compact disks, and in computer hard-drives.

There is a limited amount of memetic storage space on this planet, so only the best memes manage to implant themselves. Memes that are good at replicating tend to leave more copies of themselves in minds and in other mediums such as books. Memes that are not so good at replicating tend to die out. We can imagine what sorts of memes have become extinct. Ancient songs that were once sung and never written down are one example. Another example is the many stories that were once told but have since slipped into oblivion.

—Brent Silby, "What Is a Meme?"

That definition includes a description of the basic features and behavior of memes, examples of them, and the origin of the term. We can assume that it's written for a general audience, one that doesn't know anything about memes.

Abstract concepts often require extended definitions because by nature they are more complicated to define. There are many ways of writing an extended definition, depending in part on the term being defined and on your audience and purpose. The following examples show some of the methods that can be used for composing extended definitions of *democracy*.

Explore the word's origins.   Where did the word come from? When did it first come into use? In the following example, from an essay considering what democracy means in the twenty-first century, the writer started by looking at the word's first known use in English. Though it's from an essay written for a first-year writing course and thus for a fairly general audience, it's a definition that might pique any audience's interest:

> According to the *Oxford English Dictionary*, the term *democracy* first appeared in English in a thirteenth-century translation of Aristotle's works—specifically, in his *Politics*, where he stated that the "underlying principle of democracy is freedom" and that "it is customary to say that only in democracies do men have a share in freedom, for that is what every democracy makes its aim." By the sixteenth century, the word was used much as it is now. One writer in 1586, for instance, defined it in this way: "where free and poore men being the greater number, are lords of the estate."
>
> —Susanna Mejía, "What Does Democracy Mean Now?"

Here's another example, this one written for a scholarly audience, from an essay about women, participation, democracy, and the information age:

> The very word *citizenship* carries with it a connotation of place, a "citizen" being, literally, the inhabitant of a city. Over the years the word has, of course, accumulated a number of associated meanings . . . and the word has come to stand in for such concepts as participation, equality, and democracy. The fact that the concept of locality is deeply embedded in the word *citizen* suggests that it is also fundamental to our current understanding of these other, more apparently abstract words.
>
> In Western thought, the concepts of citizenship, equality, and democracy are closely interlinked and can be traced back to a common source, in Athens in the fifth century B.C. Perhaps it is no accident that it was the same culture which also gave us, in its theater, the concept of the unity of time and space. The Greek city-state has been represented for centuries as the ideal model of democracy, with free and equal access for all citizens to decision making. Leaving aside, for the moment, the question of who was included, and who excluded from this notion of citizenship, we can see that the sense of place is fundamental to this model. Entitlement to participate in the democratic process is circumscribed by geography; it is the inhabitants of the

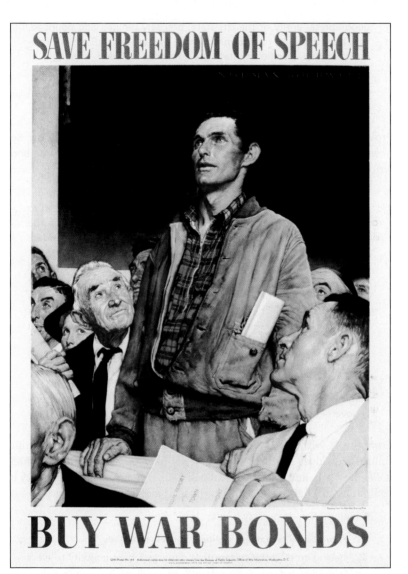

Norman Rockwell's 1943 painting Freedom of Speech *presents a visual definition of democracy: a citizen stands to speak at a public meeting while his fellow citizens listen attentively.*

geographical entity of the city-state, precisely defined and bounded, who have the rights to citizenship. Those who are not defined as inhabitants of that specific city-state are explicitly excluded, although, of course, they may have the right to citizenship elsewhere.

—Ursula Huws, "Women, Participation, and
Democracy in the Information Society"

Provide details.   What are its characteristics? What is it made of? See how a historian explores the basic characteristics of democracy in a book written for an audience of historians:

As a historian I am naturally disposed to be satisfied with the meaning which, in the history of politics, men have commonly attributed to the word—a meaning, needless to say, which derives partly from the experience and partly from the aspirations of mankind. So regarded, the term *democracy* refers primarily to a form of government, and it has always meant government by the many as opposed to government by the one—government by the people as opposed to government by a tyrant, a dictator, or an absolute monarch. . . . Since the Greeks first used the term, the essential test of democratic government has always been this: the source of political authority must be and remain in the people and not in the ruler. A democratic government has always meant one in which the citizens, or a sufficient number of them to represent more or less effectively the common will, freely act from time to time, and according to established forms, to appoint or recall the magistrates and to enact or revoke the laws by which the community is governed.   —Carl Becker, *Modern Democracy*

Compare it with other words.   How is this concept like other similar things? How does it differ? What is it *not* like? **COMPARE AND CONTRAST** it. See how a political science textbook defines a *majoritarian democracy* by comparing its characteristics with those of a *consensual democracy*:

380–87

A majoritarian democracy is one

1. having only two major political parties, not many

2. having an electoral system that requires a bare majority to elect one clear winner in an election, as opposed to a proportional

academic literacies   rhetorical situations   genres   processes   strategies   research MLA / APA   media / design   readings   handbook

electoral system that distributes seats to political parties according to the rough share of votes received in the election

3. a strong executive (president or prime minister) and cabinet that together are largely independent of the legislature when it comes to exercising the executive's constitutional duties, in contrast to an executive and cabinet that are politically controlled by the parties in the legislature and therefore unable to exercise much influence when proposing policy initiatives.

—Benjamin Ginsberg, Theodore J. Lowi, and Margaret Weir,
We the People: An Introduction to American Politics

And here's an example in which democracy is contrasted with various other forms of governments of the past:

Caesar's power derived from a popular mandate, conveyed through established republican forms, but that did not make his government any the less a dictatorship. Napoleon called his government a democratic republic, but no one, least of all Napoleon himself, doubted that he had destroyed the last vestiges of the democratic republic.

—Carl Becker, *Modern Democracy*

Give examples. See how the essayist E. B. White defines democracy by giving some everyday examples of considerate behavior, humility, and civic participation—all things he suggests constitute democracy:

It is the line that forms on the right. It is the don't in "don't shove." It is the hole in the stuffed shirt through which the sawdust slowly trickles; it is the dent in the high hat. Democracy is the recurrent suspicion that more than half of the people are right more than half of the time. . . . Democracy is a letter to the editor.   —E. B. White, "Democracy"

White's definition is elegant because he uses examples that his readers will know. His characteristics—metaphors, really—define democracy not as a conceptual way of governing but as an everyday part of American life.

374–79 ◆

Classify it. Often it is useful to divide or **CLASSIFY** a term. The ways in which democracy unfolds are complex enough to warrant entire textbooks, of course, but the following definition, from a political science textbook, divides democracy into two kinds, representative and direct:

> A system of government that gives citizens a regular opportunity to elect the top government officials is usually called a representative democracy or republic. A system that permits citizens to vote directly on laws and policies is often called a direct democracy. At the national level, America is a representative democracy in which citizens select government officials but do not vote on legislation. Some states, however, have provisions for direct legislation through popular referendum. For example, California voters in 1995 decided to bar undocumented immigrants from receiving some state services.
>
> —Benjamin Ginsberg, Theodore J. Lowi, and Margaret Weir,
> *We the People: An Introduction to American Politics*

Stipulative Definitions

Sometimes a writer will stipulate a certain definition, essentially saying, "This is how I'm defining x." Such definitions are not usually found in a dictionary—and at the same time are central to the argument the writer is making. Here is one example, from an essay by Toni Morrison. Describing a scene from a film in which a newly arrived Greek immigrant, working as a shoe shiner in Grand Central Terminal, chases away an African American competitor, Morrison calls the scene an example of "race talk," a concept she then goes on to define:

> This is race talk, the explicit insertion into everyday life of racial signs and symbols that have no meaning other than pressing African Americans to the lowest level of the racial hierarchy. Popular culture, shaped by film, theater, advertising, the press, television, and literature, is heavily engaged in race talk. It participates freely in this most enduring and efficient rite of passage into American culture: negative appraisals of the native-born black population. Only when the lesson

academic literacies rhetorical situations genres processes strategies research MLA / APA media / design readings handbook

of racial estrangement is learned is assimilation complete. Whatever the lived experience of immigrants with African Americans—pleasant, beneficial, or bruising—the rhetorical experience renders blacks as noncitizens, already discredited outlaws.

All immigrants fight for jobs and space, and who is there to fight but those who have both? As in the fishing ground struggle between Texas and Vietnamese shrimpers, they displace what and whom they can. Although U.S. history is awash in labor battles, political fights and property wars among all religious and ethnic groups, their struggles are persistently framed as struggles between recent arrivals and blacks. In race talk the move into mainstream America always means buying into the notion of American blacks as the real aliens. Whatever the ethnicity or nationality of the immigrant, his nemesis is understood to be African American.   —Toni Morrison, "On the Backs of Blacks"

The following example is from a book review of Nancy L. Rosenblum's *Membership and Morals: The Personal Uses of Pluralism in America*, published in the *American Prospect*, a magazine for readers interested in political analysis. In it a Stanford law professor outlines a definition of "the democracy of everyday life":

Democracy, in this understanding of it, means simply treating people as equals, disregarding social standing, avoiding attitudes of either deference or superiority, making allowances for others' weaknesses, and resisting the temptation to respond to perceived slights. It also means protesting everyday instances of arbitrariness and unfairness—from the rudeness of the bakery clerk to the sexism of the car dealer or the racism of those who vandalize the home of the first black neighbors on the block.   —Kathleen M. Sullivan, "Defining Democracy Down"

Considering the Rhetorical Situation

As a writer or speaker, you need to think about the message that you want to articulate, the audience you want to reach, and the larger context you are writing in.

PURPOSE   Your purpose for writing will affect any definitions you include. Would writing an extended definition help you explain something? Would stipulating definitions of key terms help you shape an argument? Could an offbeat definition help you entertain your readers?

AUDIENCE   What audience do you want to reach, and are there any terms your readers are unlikely to know (and therefore need to be defined)? Are there terms they might understand differently from the way you're defining them?

GENRE   Does your genre require you to define terms? Chances are that if you're reporting information you'll need to define some terms, and some arguments rest on the way you define key terms.

STANCE   What is your stance, and do you need to define key terms to show that stance clearly? How you define *fetus*, for example, is likely to reveal your stance on abortion.

MEDIA/DESIGN   Your medium will affect the form your definitions take. In a print text, you will need to define terms in your text; if you're giving a speech or presentation, you might also provide images of important terms and their definitions. In an electronic text, you may be able to define terms by linking to an online dictionary definition.

IF YOU NEED MORE HELP

See also the **PROCESSES** chapters for help generating ideas, drafting, revising, and so on if you are writing a whole essay dedicated to defining a term or concept.

---

academic literacies   rhetorical situations   genres   processes   strategies   research MLA / APA   media / design   readings   handbook

Describing **40**

When we describe something, we indicate what it looks like — and some-times how it sounds, feels, smells, and tastes. Descriptive details are a way of showing rather than telling, of helping readers see (or hear, smell, and so on) what we're writing about — that the sky is blue, that Miss Havisham is wearing an old yellowed wedding gown, that the chemicals in the beaker have reacted and smell like rotten eggs. You'll have occasion to describe things in most of the writing you do — from describing a favorite hat in a **MEMOIR** to detailing a chemical reaction in a lab report. This chapter will help you work with description — and, in particular, help you think about the use of *detail*, about *objectivity and subjectivity*, about *vantage point*, about creating a clear *dominant impression*, and about using description to fit your rhetorical situation.

▲ 216–23

Detail

The goal of using details is to be as specific as possible, providing infor-mation that will help your audience imagine the subject or make sense of it. See, for example, how Nancy Mairs, an author with multiple sclerosis, describes the disease in clear, specific terms:

> During its course, which is unpredictable and uncontrollable, one may lose vision, hearing, speech, the ability to walk, control of bladder and/ or bowels, strength in any or all extremities, sensitivity to touch, vibra-tion, and/or pain, potency, coordination of movements — the list of pos-sibilities is lengthy and, yes, horrifying. One may also lose one's sense of humor. That's the easiest to lose and the hardest to survive without.
>
> In the past ten years, I have sustained some of these losses. Char-acteristic of MS are sudden attacks, called exacerbations, followed by

> remissions, and these I have not had. Instead, my disease has been slowly progressive. My left leg is now so weak that I walk with the aid of a brace and a cane, and for distances I use an Amigo, a variation on the electric wheelchair that looks rather like an electrified kiddie car. I no longer have much use of my left hand. Now my right side is weakening as well. I still have the blurred spot in my right eye. Overall, though, I've been lucky so far. —Nancy Mairs, "On Being a Cripple"

Mairs's gruesome list demonstrates, through *specific details*, how the disease affects sufferers generally and her in particular. We know far more after reading this text than we do from the following more general description, from a National Multiple Sclerosis Society brochure:

> Multiple sclerosis is a chronic, unpredictable disease of the central nervous system (the brain, optic nerves, and spinal cord). It is thought to be an autoimmune disorder. This means the immune system incorrectly attacks the person's healthy tissue.
>
> MS can cause blurred vision, loss of balance, poor coordination, slurred speech, tremors, numbness, extreme fatigue, problems with memory and concentration, paralysis, and blindness. These problems may be permanent, or they may come and go.
>
> —National Multiple Sclerosis Society, *Just the Facts*

Specific details are also more effective than labels, which give little meaningful information. Instead of saying that someone is a "moron" or "really smart," it's better to give details so that readers can understand the reasons behind the label: what does this person *do* or *say* that makes him or her deserve this label? See, for example, how the writer of a news story about shopping on the day after Thanksgiving opens with a description of a happy shopper:

> Last Friday afternoon, the day ritualized consumerism is traditionally at its most frenetic, Alexx Balcuns twirled in front of a full-length mirror at the Ritz Thrift Shop on West Fifty-seventh Street as if inhabited by the soul of Eva Gabor in *Green Acres*. Ms. Balcuns was languishing in a $795 dyed-mink parka her grandmother had just bought her. Ms. Balcuns is six.
>
> —Ginia Bellafante, "Staying Warm and Fuzzy during Uncertain Times"

academic literacies   rhetorical situations   genres   processes   strategies   research MLA / APA   media / design   readings   handbook

The writer might simply have said, "A spoiled child admired herself in the mirror." Instead, she shows her subject twirling and "languishing" in a "$795 dyed-mink parka" and seemingly possessed by the soul of the actress Eva Gabor—all details that create a far more vivid description.

Sensory details help readers imagine sounds, odors, tastes, and physical sensations in addition to sights. In the following example, writer Scott Russell Sanders recalls sawing wood as a child. Note how visual details, odors, and even the physical sense of being picked up by his father mingle to form a vivid scene:

> As the saw teeth bit down, the wood released its smell, each kind with its own fragrance, oak or walnut or cherry or pine—usually pine because it was the softest, easiest for a child to work. No matter how weathered and gray the board, no matter how warped and cracked, inside there was this smell waiting, as of something freshly baked. I gathered every smidgen of sawdust and stored it away in coffee cans, which I kept in a drawer of the workbench. When I did not feel like hammering nails I would dump my sawdust on the concrete floor of the garage and landscape it into highways and farms and towns, running miniature cars and trucks along miniature roads. Looming as huge as a colossus, my father worked over and around me, now and again bending down to inspect my work, careful not to trample my creations. It was a landscape that smelled dizzyingly of wood. Even after a bath my skin would carry the smell, and so would my father's hair, when he lifted me for a bedtime hug.
>
> —Scott Russell Sanders, *The Paradise of Bombs*

Whenever you describe something, you'll select from many possible details you might use. Simply put, to exhaust all the details available to describe something is impossible—and would exhaust your readers as well. To focus your description, you'll need to determine the kinds of details appropriate for your subject. They will vary, depending on your **PURPOSE**. See, for example, how the details might differ in three different genres:

55–56

- For a **MEMOIR** about an event, you might choose details that are significant for you, that evoke the sights, sounds, and other sensations that give meaning to your event.

216–23

224–34 ▲

- *For a* **PROFILE**, you're likely to select details that will reinforce the dominant impression you want to give, that portray the event from the perspective you want readers to see.

- *For a lab report,* you need to give certain specifics—what equipment was used, what procedures were followed, what exactly were the results.

Deciding on a focus for your description can help you see it better, as you'll look for details that contribute to that focus.

Objectivity and Subjectivity

Descriptions can be written with objectivity, with subjectivity, or with a mixture of both. Objective descriptions attempt to be uncolored by personal opinion or emotion. Police reports and much news writing aim to describe events objectively; scientific writing strives for objectivity in describing laboratory procedures and results. See, for example, the following objective account of what happened at the World Trade Center on September 11, 2001:

> **World Trade Center Disaster—Tuesday, September 11, 2001**
>
> On Tuesday, September 11, 2001, at 8:45 a.m. New York local time, One World Trade Center, the north tower, was hit by a hijacked 767 commercial jet airplane loaded with fuel for a transcontinental flight. Two World Trade Center, the south tower, was hit by a similar hijacked jet eighteen minutes later, at 9:03 a.m. (In separate but related attacks, the Pentagon building near Washington, D.C., was hit by a hijacked 757 at 9:43 a.m., and at 10:10 a.m. a fourth hijacked jetliner crashed in Pennsylvania.) The south tower, WTC 2, which had been hit second, was the first to suffer a complete structural collapse, at 10:05 a.m., 62 minutes after being hit itself, 80 minutes after the first impact. The north tower, WTC 1, then also collapsed, at 10:29 a.m., 104 minutes after being hit. WTC 7, a substantial forty-seven-story office building in its own right, built in 1987, was damaged by the collapsing towers, caught fire, and later in the afternoon also totally collapsed.
>
> —"World Trade Center," *GreatBuildings.com*

academic literacies | rhetorical situations | genres | processes | strategies | research MLA / APA | media / design | readings | handbook

Subjective descriptions, on the other hand, allow the writer's opinions and emotions to come through. A house can be described as comfortable, with a lived-in look, or as rundown and in need of a paint job and a new roof. Here's a subjective description of the planes striking the World Trade Center, as told by a woman watching from a nearby building:

> Incredulously, while looking out [the] window at the damage and carnage the first plane had inflicted, I saw the second plane abruptly come into my right field of vision and deliberately, with shimmering intention, thunder full-force into the south tower. It was so close, so low, so huge and fast, so intent on its target that I swear to you, I swear to you, I felt the vengeance and rage emanating from the plane.
>
> —Debra Fontaine, "Witnessing"

Vantage Point

Sometimes you'll want or need to describe something from a certain vantage point. Where you locate yourself in relation to what you're describing will determine what you can perceive (and so describe) and what you can't. You may describe your subject from a *stationary vantage point*, from which you (and your readers) see your subject from one angle only, as if you were a camera. This description of one of three photographs that captured a woman's death records only what the camera saw from one angle at one particular moment:

> The first showed some people on a fire escape—a fireman, a woman and a child. The fireman had a nice strong jaw and looked very brave. The woman was holding the child. Smoke was pouring from the building behind them. A rescue ladder was approaching, just a few feet away, and the fireman had one arm around the woman and one arm reaching out toward the ladder.
>
> —Nora Ephron, "The Boston Photographs"

By contrast, this description of a drive to an Italian villa uses a *moving vantage point*; the writer recounts what he saw as he passed through a gate in a city wall, moving from city to country:

La Pietra—"the stone"—is situated one mile from the Porta San Gallo, an entry to the Old City of Florence. You drive there along the Via Bolognese, twisting past modern apartment blocks, until you come to a gate, which swings open—and there you are, at the upper end of a long lane of cypresses facing a great ocher palazzo; with olive groves spreading out on both sides over an expanse of fifty-seven acres. There's something almost comically wonderful about the effect: here, the city, with its winding avenue; there, on the other side of a wall, the country, fertile and gray green.   —James Traub, "Italian Hours"

The description of quarries in the following section uses *multiple vantage points* to capture the quarries from many perspectives.

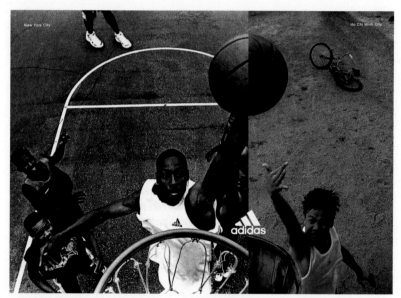

This ad for Adidas sports apparel combines photos of two basketball games, one in New York City and one in Ho Chi Minh City, to show the universality of the game. Both photos use a stationary vantage point, looking down on the court from above the backboard.

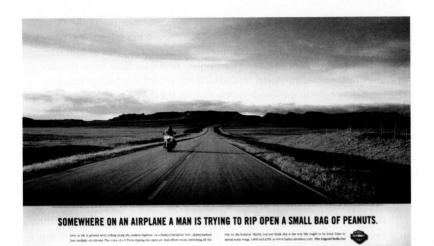

SOMEWHERE ON AN AIRPLANE A MAN IS TRYING TO RIP OPEN A SMALL BAG OF PEANUTS.

The visual image of vast sky and desert in this Harley-Davidson motorcycle ad creates a dominant impression of spaciousness and freedom that contrasts with the written text to argue that riding on a Harley is far better than sitting on a cramped airplane.

Dominant Impression

With any description, your aim is to create some dominant impression—the overall feeling that the individual details add up to. The dominant impression may be implied, growing out of the details themselves. For example, Scott Russell Sanders's memory of the smell of sawdust creates a dominant impression of warmth and comfort: the "fragrance . . . as of something freshly baked," sawdust "stored . . . away in coffee cans," a young boy "lifted . . . for a bedtime hug." Sometimes, though, a writer will state the dominant impression directly, in addition to creating it with details. In an essay about Indiana limestone quarries, Sanders makes the dominant impression clear from the start: "they are battlefields."

> The quarries will not be domesticated. They are not backyard pools; they are battlefields. Each quarry is an arena where violent struggles have taken place between machines and planet, between human ingenuity and brute

resisting stone, between mind and matter. Waste rock litters the floor and brim like rubble in a bombed city. The ragged pits might have been the basements of vanished skyscrapers. Stones weighing tens of tons lean against one another at precarious angles, as if they have been thrown there by some gigantic strength and have not yet finished falling. Wrecked machinery hulks in the weeds, grimly rusting, the cogs and wheels, twisted rails, battered engine housings, trackless bulldozers and burst boilers like junk from an armored regiment. Everywhere the ledges are scarred from drills, as if from an artillery barrage or machine-gun strafing. Stumbling onto one of these abandoned quarries and gazing at the ruins, you might be left wondering who had won the battle, men or stone.

—Scott Russell Sanders, *The Paradise of Bombs*

The rest of his description, full of more figurative language ("like rubble in a bombed city," "like junk from an armored regiment," "as if from an artillery barrage or machine-gun strafing") reinforces the direct "they are battlefields" statement.

Organizing Descriptions

You can organize descriptions in many ways. When your description is primarily visual, you will probably organize it spatially: from left to right, top to bottom, outside to inside. One variation on this approach is to begin with the most significant or noteworthy feature and move outward from that center, as Ephron does. Or you may create a chronological description of objects as you move past or through them in space, as Traub does in his description of his drive. You might even pile up details to create a dominant impression, as Sanders and Mairs do, especially if your description draws on senses besides vision.

Considering the Rhetorical Situation

As a writer or speaker, you need to think about the message that you want to articulate, the audience you want to reach, and the larger context you are writing in.

academic literacies   rhetorical situations   genres   processes   strategies   research MLA / APA   media / design   readings   handbook

PURPOSE   Your purpose may affect the way you use description. If you're arguing that a government should intervene in another country's civil war, for example, describing the anguish of refugees from that war could make your argument more persuasive. If you're analyzing a painting, you will likely need to describe it.   55–56

AUDIENCE   Who is your audience, and will they need detailed description to understand the points you wish to make?   57–60

GENRE   Does your genre require description? A lab report generally calls for you to describe materials and results; a memoir about grandma should probably describe her— her smile, her dress, her apple pie.   61–63

STANCE   The way you describe things can help you convey your stance. For example, the details you choose can show you to be objective (or not), careful or casual.   64–67

MEDIA/DESIGN   Your medium will affect the form your description can take. In a print or spoken text, you will likely rely on words, though you may also include visuals. In an electronic text, you can easily provide links to visuals as well as audio clips and so may need fewer words of your own.   68–70

IF YOU NEED MORE HELP

See also **FREEWRITING**, **CUBING**, and **LISTING**, three methods of generating ideas that can be especially helpful for developing detailed descriptions. Sometimes you may be assigned to write a whole essay describing something: see the **PROCESSES** chapters for help drafting, revising, and so on.   289–97
279

41 Dialogue

216–23
224–34
206–15
156–82

Dialogue is a way of including people's own words in a text, letting readers hear those people's voices—not just what you say about them. **MEMOIRS** and **PROFILES** often include dialogue, and many other genres do as well: **LITERARY ANALYSES** often quote dialogue from the texts they analyze, and essays **ARGUING A POSITION** might quote an authoritative source as support for a claim. This chapter provides brief guidelines for the conventions of paragraphing and punctuating dialogue and offers some good examples of how you can use dialogue most effectively to suit your own rhetorical situations.

Why Add Dialogue?

Dialogue is a way of bringing in voices other than your own, of showing people and scenes rather than just telling about them. It can add color and texture to your writing, making it memorable. Most important, however, dialogue should be more than just colorful or interesting. It needs to contribute to your rhetorical purpose, to support the point you're making. See how dialogue is used in the following excerpt from a magazine profile of the Mall of America, how it gives us a sense of the place that the journalist's own words could not provide:

> Two pubescent girls in retainers and braces sat beside me sipping coffees topped with whipped cream and chocolate sprinkles, their shopping bags gathered tightly around their legs, their eyes fixed on the passing crowds. They came, they said, from Shakopee—"It's no-where," one of them explained. The megamall, she added, was "a buzz at first, but now it seems pretty normal. 'Cept my parents are like Twenty Questions every time I want to come here. 'Specially since the shooting."

academic literacies · rhetorical situations · genres · processes · strategies · research MLA / APA · media / design · readings · handbook

> On a Sunday night, she elaborated, three people had been wounded when shots were fired in a dispute over a San Jose Sharks jacket. "In the *mall*," her friend reminded me. "Right here at megamall. A shooting."
> "It's like nowhere's safe," the first added.
>
> —David Guterson, "Enclosed. Encyclopedic. Endured.
> One Week at the Mall of America"

Of course it was the writer who decided whom and what to quote, and Guterson deliberately chose words that capture the young shoppers' speech patterns, quoting fragments ("In the *mall*. . . . Right here at megamall. A shooting"), slang ("a buzz at first," "my parents are like Twenty Questions"), even contractions ("'cept," "'specially").

Integrating Dialogue into Your Writing

There are certain conventions for punctuating and paragraphing dialogue:

- *Punctuating.* Enclose each speaker's words in quotation marks, and put any end punctuation—periods, question marks, and exclamation marks—inside the closing quotation mark. Whether you're transcribing words you heard or making them up, you will sometimes need to add punctuation to reflect the rhythm and sound of the speech. In the last sentence of the example below, see how Chang-Rae Lee adds a comma after *well* and italicizes *practice* to show intonation—and attitude.
- *Paragraphing.* When you're writing dialogue that includes more than one speaker, start a new paragraph each time the speaker changes.
- *Signal phrases.* Sometimes you'll need to introduce dialogue with SIGNAL PHRASES—"I said," "she asked," and so on—to make clear who is speaking. At times, however, the speaker will be clear enough, and you won't need any signal phrases.

487–90

Here is a conversation between a mother and her son that illustrates each of the conventions for punctuating and paragraphing dialogue:

> "Whom do I talk to?" she said. She would mostly speak to me in Korean, and I would answer back in English.

"The bank manager, who else?"

"What do I say?"

"Whatever you want to say."

"Don't speak to me like that!" she cried.

"It's just that you should be able to do it yourself," I said.

"You know how I feel about this!"

"Well, maybe then you should consider it *practice*," I answered lightly, using the Korean word to make sure she understood.

—Chang-Rae Lee, "Coming Home Again"

Interviews

Interviews are a kind of dialogue, with different conventions for punctuation. When you're transcribing an interview, give each speaker's name each time he or she speaks, starting a new line but not indenting, and do not use quotation marks. Here is an excerpt from a National Public Radio interview that Audie Cornish conducted with writer Susan Cain:

> **Audie Cornish:** In the 1940s and '50s, the message to most Americans was, don't be shy. And in the era of reality television, Twitter and relentless self-promotion, it seems that cultural mandate is in overdrive.
>
> A new book tells the story of how things came to be this way, and it's called *Quiet: The Power of Introverts in a World that Can't Stop Talking*. The author is Susan Cain, and she joins us from the NPR studios in New York to talk more about it. Welcome, Susan.
>
> **Susan Cain:** Thank you. It's such a pleasure to be here, Audie.
>
> **Cornish:** Well, we're happy to have you. And to start out — I think we should get this on the record — do you consider yourself an introvert or an extrovert?
>
> **Cain:** Oh, I definitely consider myself an introvert, and that was part of the fuel for me to write the book.
>
> **Cornish:** And what's the difference between being an introvert versus being shy? I mean, what's your definition?
>
> **Cain:** So introversion is really about having a preference for lower-stimulation environments — so just a preference for quiet, for less noise, for less action — whereas extroverts really crave more stimulation

in order to feel at their best. And what's important to understand about this is that many people believe that introversion is about being antisocial. And that's really a misperception because actually, it's just that introverts are differently social. So they would prefer to have, you know, a glass of wine with a close friend as opposed to going to a loud party full of strangers.

Now shyness, on the other hand, is about a fear of negative social judgment. So you can be introverted without having that particular fear at all, and you can be shy but also be an extrovert.

Cornish: And in the book, you say that there's a spectrum. So if some people are listening and they think, well, I, too, like a glass of wine and a party. It's like we all have these tendencies.

Cain: Yeah, yeah. That's an important thing. And, in fact, Carl Jung, the psychologist who first popularized these terms all the way back in the 1920s — even he said there's no such thing as a pure introvert or a pure extrovert, and he said such a man would be in a lunatic asylum.

Cornish: That makes me worry because I took your test in the book and I'm like, 90 percent extroverted, basically.

[*soundbite of laughter*]

Cornish: Now, you mentioned going back into the history. And I want to talk more about that because I was really fascinated by how you showed how this extrovert ideal — you call it — came to be. When did being introverted move from being a character trait to being looked at as a problem?

Cain: Yeah. What I found is, to some extent, we've always had an admiration for extroversion in our culture. But the extrovert ideal really came to play at the turn of the 20th century, when we had the rise of big business. And so suddenly, people were flocking to the cities, and they were needing to prove themselves in big corporations — at job interviews and on sales calls.

And so at that moment in time, we moved from what cultural historians call a culture of character to a culture of personality. So during the culture of character, what was important was the good deeds that you performed when nobody was looking. You know, Abraham Lincoln is the embodiment of the culture of character, and people celebrated him back then for being a man who did not offend by superiority.

But at the turn of the century, when we moved into this culture of personality, suddenly, what was admired was to be magnetic and charismatic. And then at the same time, we suddenly had the rise of movies and movie stars. And movie stars, of course, were the embodiment of what it meant to be a charismatic figure. And so part of people's fascination with these movie stars was for what they could learn from them, and bring with them to their own jobs.

—"Quiet, Please: Unleashing 'The Power of Introverts'"

In preparing the interview transcript for publication, NPR had to add punctuation, which of course was not part of the oral conversation, and probably deleted pauses and verbal expressions such as *um* and *uh*. At the same time, the editor kept informal constructions, such as incomplete sentences, which are typical answers to questions ("Yeah.") to maintain the oral flavor of the interview and to reflect Cain's voice.

Considering the Rhetorical Situation

As a writer or speaker, you need to think about the message that you want to articulate, the audience you want to reach, and the larger context of your writing.

55–56 ■ **PURPOSE** Your purpose will affect any use of dialogue. Dialogue can help bring a profile to life and make it memorable. Interviews with experts or firsthand witnesses can add credibility to a report or argument.

57–60 ■ **AUDIENCE** Whom do you want to reach, and will dialogue help? Sometimes actual dialogue can help readers hear human voices behind facts or reason.

61–63 ■ **GENRE** Does your genre require dialogue? If you're evaluating or analyzing a literary work, for instance, you may wish to include dialogue from that work. If you're writing a profile of a person or event, dialogue can help you bring your subject to life. Similarly, an interview with an expert can add credibility to a report or argument.

academic literacies   rhetorical situations   genres   processes   strategies   research MLA / APA   media / design   readings   handbook

STANCE What is your stance, and can dialogue help you communicate that stance? For example, excerpts of an interview may allow you to challenge someone's views and make your own views clear.

64–67

MEDIA / DESIGN Your medium will affect the way you present dialogue. In a print text, you will present dialogue through written words. In an oral or electronic text, you might include actual recorded dialogue.

68–70

IF YOU NEED MORE HELP

See also the guidelines on **INTERVIEWING EXPERTS** for advice on setting up and recording interviews and those on **QUOTING, PARAPHRASING,** and **SUMMARIZING** for help deciding how to integrate dialogue into your text.

463–64
478–90

42 Explaining Processes

When you explain a process, you tell how something is (or was) done—how a bill becomes a law, how an embryo develops—or you tell someone how to do something—how to throw a curve ball, how to write a memoir. This chapter focuses on those two kinds of explanations, offering examples and guidelines for explaining a process in a way that works for your rhetorical situation.

Explaining a Process Clearly

Whether the process is simple or complex, you'll need to identify its key stages or steps and explain them one by one, in order. The sequence matters because it allows readers to follow your explanation; it is especially important when you're explaining a process that others are going to follow. Most often you'll explain a process chronologically, from start to finish. **TRANSITIONS**—words like *first*, *next*, *then*, and so on—are often necessary, therefore, to show readers how the stages of a process relate to one another and to indicate time sequences. Finally, you'll find that verbs matter; they indicate the actions that take place at each stage of the process.

349

Explaining How Something Is Done

All processes consist of steps, and when you explain how something is done, you describe each step, generally in order, from first to last. Here, for

academic literacies

rhetorical situations

genres

processes

strategies

research MLA / APA

media / design

readings

handbook

example, is an explanation of how French fries are made, from an essay published in the *New Yorker*:

> Fast-food French fries are made from a baking potato like an Idaho russet, or any other variety that is mealy, or starchy, rather than waxy. The potatoes are harvested, cured, washed, peeled, sliced, and then blanched—cooked enough so that the insides have a fluffy texture but not so much that the fry gets soft and breaks. Blanching is followed by drying, and drying by a thirty-second deep fry, to give the potatoes a crisp shell. Then the fries are frozen until the moment of service, when they are deep-fried again, this time for somewhere around three minutes. Depending on the fast-food chain involved, there are other steps interspersed in this process. McDonald's fries, for example, are briefly dipped in a sugar solution, which gives them their golden-brown color; Burger King fries are dipped in a starch batter, which is what gives those fries their distinctive hard shell and audible crunch. But the result is similar. The potato that is first harvested in the field is roughly 80 percent water. The process of creating a French fry consists, essentially, of removing as much of that water as possible—through blanching, drying, and deep-frying—and replacing it with fat.
>
> —Malcolm Gladwell, "The Trouble with Fries"

Gladwell clearly explains the process of making French fries, showing us the specific steps—how the potatoes "are harvested, cured, washed, peeled, sliced," and so on—and using clear transitions—"followed by," "then," "until," "when"—and action verbs to show the sequence. His last sentence makes his stance clear, pointing out that the process of creating a French fry consists of removing as much of a potato's water as possible "and replacing it with fat."

Explaining How to Do Something

In explaining how to do something, you are giving instruction so that others can follow the process themselves. See how Martha Stewart explains the process of making French fries. She starts by listing the ingredients and then describes the steps:

4 medium baking potatoes
2 tablespoons olive oil
$1^1/_2$ teaspoons salt
$^1/_4$ teaspoon freshly ground pepper
malt vinegar (optional)

1. Heat oven to 400 degrees. Place a heavy baking sheet in the oven. Scrub and rinse the potatoes well, and then cut them lengthwise into $^1/_2$-inch-wide batons. Place the potato batons in a medium bowl, and toss them with the olive oil, salt, and pepper.

2. When baking sheet is hot, about 15 minutes, remove from the oven. Place prepared potatoes on the baking sheet in a single layer. Return to oven, and bake until potatoes are golden on the bottom, about 30 minutes. Turn potatoes over, and continue cooking until golden all over, about 15 minutes more. Serve immediately.

—Martha Stewart, *Favorite Comfort Food*

Coming from Martha Stewart, the explanation leaves out no details, giving a clear sequence of steps and descriptive verbs that tell us exactly what to do: "heat," "place," "scrub and rinse," and so on. After she gives the recipe, she even goes on to explain the process of *serving* the fries—"Serve these French fries with a bowl of malt vinegar"—and reminds us that "they are also delicious dipped in spicy mustard, mayonnaise, and, of course, ketchup."

Explaining a Process Visually

607–15 Some processes are best explained **VISUALLY**, with diagrams or photographs. See, for example, how a blogger explains one process of shaping dough into a bagel—giving the details in words and then showing us in photos how to do it:

Roll each portion into a ball and place on prepared baking sheet. Cover with a damp towel and let rest for 20 minutes.

Roll balls into 6- to 7-inch ropes. If the dough resists, just let it rest for a few minutes and try rolling it again.

Wrap the dough around your palm and the back of your hand, overlapping the ends by an inch or two.

Press the overlapping edges against the countertop, rolling the bagel back and forth to seal the seam.

Place bagels back on baking sheet and cover with plastic wrap that has been coated with cooking spray.

—Maggie Lauer, *The Other Side of Fifty*

Considering the Rhetorical Situation

As always, you need to think about the message that you want to articulate, the audience you want to reach, and the larger context you are writing in.

55–56 **PURPOSE** Your purpose for writing will affect the way you explain a process. If you're arguing that we should avoid eating fast food, you might explain the process by which chicken nuggets are made. But to give information about how to fry chicken, you would explain the process quite differently.

57–60 **AUDIENCE** Whom are you trying to reach, and will you need to provide any special background information or to interest them in the process before you explain it?

61–63 **GENRE** Does your genre require you to explain a process? In a lab report, for example, you'll need to explain processes used in the experiment. You might want to explain a process in a profile of an activity or a proposal for a solution.

64–67 **STANCE** If you're giving practical directions for doing something, you'll want to take a straightforward "do this, then do that" perspective. If you're writing to entertain, you need to take a clever or amusing stance.

68–70 **MEDIA/DESIGN** Your medium will affect the way you explain a process. In a print text, you can use both words and images. On the web, you may have the option of showing an animation of the process as well.

IF YOU NEED MORE HELP

224–34 ▲
419–27 ◆
279 ○
See also **PROFILES** if you are writing about an activity that needs to be explained. See **NARRATING** for more advice on organizing an explanation chronologically. Sometimes you may be assigned to write a whole essay or report that explains a process; see **PROCESSES** for help drafting, revising, and so on.

---

academic literacies   rhetorical situations   genres   processes   strategies   research MLA / APA   media / design   readings   handbook

Narrating 43

Narratives are stories. As a writing strategy, a good narrative can lend support to most kinds of writing—in a **POSITION PAPER** arguing for Title IX compliance, for example, you might include a brief narrative about an Olympic sprinter who might never have had an opportunity to compete on a track-and-field team without Title IX. Or you can bring a **PROFILE** of a favorite coach to life with an anecdote about a pep talk he or she once gave before a championship track meet. Whatever your larger writing purpose, you need to make sure that any narratives you add support that purpose—they should not be inserted simply to tell an interesting story. You'll also need to compose them carefully—to put them in a clear *sequence*, include *pertinent detail*, and make sure they are appropriate to your particular rhetorical situation.

▲ 156–82

▲ 224–34

Sequencing

When we write a narrative, we arrange events in a particular sequence. Writers typically sequence narratives in chronological order, reverse chronological order, or as a flashback.

Use chronological order. Often you may tell the story chronologically, starting at the beginning of an event and working through to the end, as Maya Angelou does in this brief narrative from an essay about her high school graduation:

> The school band struck up a march and all classes filed in as had been rehearsed. We stood in front of our seats, as assigned, and on a signal from the choir director, we sat. No sooner had this been accomplished

419

than the band started to play the national anthem. We rose again and sang the song, after which we recited the pledge of allegiance. We remained standing for a brief minute before the choir director and the principal signaled to us, rather desperately I thought, to take our seats. —Maya Angelou, "Graduation"

Use reverse chronological order. You may also begin with the final action and work back to the first, as Aldo Leopold does in this narrative about cutting down a tree:

> Now our saw bites into the 1890s, called gay by those whose eyes turn cityward rather than landward. We cut 1899, when the last passenger pigeon collided with a charge of shot near Babcock, two counties to the north; we cut 1898, when a dry fall, followed by a snowless winter, froze the soil seven feet deep and killed the apple trees; 1897, another drouth year, when another forestry commission came into being; 1896, when 25,000 prairie chickens were shipped to market from the village of Spooner alone; 1895, another year of fires; 1894, another drouth year; and 1893, the year of "the Bluebird Storm," when a March blizzard reduced the migrating bluebirds to near zero.
>
> —Aldo Leopold, *A Sand County Almanac*

253–64 ▲

RÉSUMÉS are one genre where we generally use reverse chronological order, listing the most recent jobs or degrees first and then working backward. Notice, too, that we usually write these as narratives—telling what we have done rather than just naming positions we have held:

Sept. 2014–present	*Student worker*, Department of Information Management, Central State University, Wilberforce, OH. Compile data and format reports using Excel, Word, and university database.
June–Sept. 2014	*Intern*, QuestPro Corporation, West Louisville, KY. Assisted in development of software.
Sept. 2013–June 2014	*Bagger*, Ace Groceries, Elba, KY. Bagged customers' purchases.

Use a flashback. You can sometimes put a flashback in the middle of a narrative, to tell about an incident that illuminates the larger narrative. Terry Tempest Williams does this in an essay about the startling incidence of breast cancer in her family: she recalls a dinnertime conversation with her father right after her mother's death from cancer, when she learned for the first time what caused all of the cancer in her family:

> Over dessert, I shared a recurring dream of mine. I told my father that for years, as long as I could remember, I saw this flash of light in the night in the desert. That this image had so permeated my being, I could not venture south without seeing it again, on the horizon, illuminating buttes and mesas.
>
> "You did see it," he said.
>
> "Saw what?" I asked, a bit tentative.
>
> "The bomb. The cloud. We were driving home from Riverside, California. You were sitting on your mother's lap. She was pregnant. In fact, I remember the date, September 7, 1957. We had just gotten out of the Service. We were driving north, past Las Vegas. It was an hour or so before dawn, when this explosion went off. We not only heard it, but felt it. I thought the oil tanker in front of us had blown up. We pulled over and suddenly, rising from the desert floor, we saw it, clearly, this golden-stemmed cloud, the mushroom. The sky seemed to vibrate with an eerie pink glow. Within a few minutes, a light ash was raining on the car."
>
> I stared at my father. This was new information to me.
>
> —Terry Tempest Williams, "The Clan of the One-Breasted Women"

Williams could have simply announced this information as a fact—but see how much more powerful it is when told in narrative form.

Use time markers. Time markers help readers follow a sequence of events. The most obvious time markers are those that simply label the time, as the narrative entries in a diary, journal, or log might. For example, here is the final part of the narrative kept in a diary by a doomed Antarctic explorer:

WEDNESDAY, MARCH 21: Got within eleven miles of depot. Monday night; had to lay up all yesterday in severe blizzard. Today forlorn hope, Wilson and Bowers going to depot for fuel.

MARCH 22 and 23: Blizzard bad as ever—Wilson and Bowers unable to start—tomorrow last chance—no fuel and only one or two [days] of food left—must be near the end. Have decided it shall be natural—we shall march for the depot with or without our effects and die in our tracks.

THURSDAY, MARCH 29: Since the 21st we have had a continuous gale from W.S.W. and S.W. We had fuel to make two cups of tea apiece and bare food for two days on the 20th. Every day we have been ready to start for our depot eleven miles away, but outside the door of the tent it remains a scene of whirling drift. I do not think we can hope for any better things now. We shall stick it out to the end, but we are getting weaker, of course, and the end cannot be far. It seems a pity, but I do not think I can write more. . . .

Last Entry: For God's sake look after our people.

—Robert F. Scott, *Scott's Last Expedition: The Journals*

More often you will integrate time markers into the prose itself, as is done in this narrative about a woman preparing and delivering meals to workers at a cotton gin:

She made her plans meticulously and in secret. <u>One early evening</u> to see if she was ready, she placed stones in two five-gallon pails and carried them three miles to the cotton gin. She rested a little, and then, discarding some rocks, she walked in the darkness to the sawmill five miles farther along the dirt road. <u>On her way back</u> to her little house and her babies, she dumped the remaining rocks along the path.

<u>That same night</u> she worked into the early hours boiling chicken and frying ham. She made dough and filled the rolled-out pastry with meat. <u>At last</u> she went to sleep.

<u>The next morning</u> she left her house carrying the meat pies, lard, an iron brazier, and coals for a fire. <u>Just before lunch</u> she appeared in an empty lot behind the cotton gin. <u>As the dinner noon bell rang</u>, she

dropped the savors into boiling fat, and the aroma rose and floated over to the workers who spilled out of the gin, covered with white lint, looking like specters.

—Maya Angelou, *Wouldn't Take Nothing for My Journey Now*

Use transitions. Another way to help readers follow a narrative is with TRANSITIONS, words like *first, then, meanwhile, at last,* and so on. See how the following paragraphs from Langston Hughes's classic essay about meeting Jesus use transitions (and time markers) to advance the action:

◆ 349

> Suddenly the whole room broke into a sea of shouting, as they saw me rise. Waves of rejoicing swept the place. Women leaped in the air. My aunt threw her arms around me. The minister took me by the hand and led me to the platform.
>
> When things quieted down, in a hushed silence, punctuated by a few ecstatic "Amens," all the new young lambs were blessed in the name of God. Then joyous singing filled the room. That night, for the last time in my life but one—for I was a big boy twelve years old—I cried. —Langston Hughes, "Salvation"

Including Pertinent Detail

When you include a narrative in your writing, you must decide which details you need—and which ones you don't need. For example, you don't want to include so much detail that the narrative distracts the reader from the larger text. You must also decide whether you need to include any background, to set the stage for the narrative. The amount of detail you include depends on your audience and purpose: How much detail does your audience need? How much detail do you need to make your meaning clear? In an essay on the suspicion African American men often face when walking at night, a journalist deliberately presents a story without setting the stage at all:

> My first victim was a woman—white, well dressed, probably in her late twenties. I came upon her late one evening on a deserted street

in Hyde Park, a relatively affluent neighborhood in an otherwise mean, impoverished section of Chicago. As I swung onto the avenue behind her, there seemed to be a discreet, uninflammatory distance between us. Not so. She cast back a worried glance. To her, the youngish black man—a broad six feet two inches with a beard and billowing hair, both hands shoved into the pockets of a bulky military jacket—seemed menacingly close. After a few more quick glimpses, she picked up her pace and was soon running in earnest. Within seconds she disappeared into a cross street.　　—Brent Staples, "Black Men and Public Space"

Words like *victim* and phrases like "came upon her" lead us to assume the narrator is scary and perhaps dangerous. We don't know why he is walking on the deserted street because he hasn't told us: he simply begins with the moment he and the woman encounter each other. For his purposes, that's all the audience needs to know at first, and details of his physical appearance that explain the woman's response come later, after he tells us about the encounter. Had he given us those details at the outset, the narrative would not have been nearly so effective. In a way, Staples lets the story sneak up on us, as the woman apparently felt he had on her.

Other times you'll need to provide more background information, as an MIT professor does when she uses an anecdote to introduce an essay about young children's experiences with electronic toys. First the writer tells us a little about Merlin, the computer tic-tac-toe game that the children in her anecdote play with. As you'll see, the anecdote would be hard to follow without the introduction:

Among the first generation of computational objects was Merlin, which challenged children to games of tic-tac-toe. For children who had only played games with human opponents, reaction to this object was intense. For example, while Merlin followed an optimal strategy for winning tic-tac-toe most of the time, it was programmed to make a slip every once in a while. So when children discovered strategies that allowed them to win and then tried these strategies a second time, they usually would not work. The machine gave the impression of not being "dumb enough" to let down its defenses twice. Robert, seven, playing with his friends on the beach, watched his friend Craig perform the "winning trick," but when he tried it, Merlin did not slip up and the game ended in a draw. Robert, confused and frustrated, threw Merlin into the sand and said, "Cheater. I hope your brains break." He was overheard by Craig and Greg, aged six and eight, who salvaged the by-now very sandy toy and took it upon themselves to set Robert straight. "Merlin doesn't know if it cheats," says Craig. "It doesn't know if you break it, Robert. It's not alive." Greg adds, "It's smart enough to make the right kinds of noises. But it doesn't really know if it loses. And when it cheats, it don't even know it's cheating." Jenny, six, interrupts with disdain: "Greg, to cheat you have to know you are cheating. Knowing is part of cheating."

—Sherry Turkle, "Cuddling Up to Cyborg Babies"

Opening and Closing with Narratives

Narratives are often useful as **BEGINNINGS** to essays and other kinds of writing. Everyone likes a good story, so an interesting or pithy narrative can be a good way to get your audience's attention. In the following introductory paragraph, a historian tells a gruesome but gripping story to attract our attention to a subject that might not otherwise merit our interest, bubonic plague:

331–38

In October 1347, two months after the fall of Calais, Genoese trading ships put into the harbor of Messina in Sicily with dead and dying men at the oars. The ships had come from the Black Sea port of Caffa (now Feodosiya) in the Crimea, where the Genoese maintained a trading post. The diseased sailors showed strange black swellings about the size of an egg or an apple in the armpits and groin. The swellings oozed blood and pus and were followed by spreading boils and black blotches on the skin from internal bleeding. The sick suffered severe pain and died quickly, within five days of the first symptoms. As the disease spread, other symptoms of continuous fever and spitting of blood appeared instead of the swellings or buboes. These victims coughed and sweated heavily and died even more quickly, within three days or less, sometimes in twenty-four hours. In both types everything that issued from the body—breath, sweat, blood from the buboes and lungs, bloody urine, and blood-blackened excrement—smelled foul. Depression and despair accompanied the physical symptoms, and before the end "death is seen seated on the face."

—Barbara Tuchman, "This Is the End of the World: The Black Death"

Imagine how different the preceding paragraph would be if it weren't in the form of a narrative. Imagine, for example, that Tuchman began by defining bubonic plague. Would that have gotten your interest? The piece was written for a general audience; how might it have been different if it had been written for scientists? Would they need (or appreciate) the story told here?

338–42 Narrative can be a good way of **ENDING** a text, too, by winding up a discussion with an illustration of the main point. Here, for instance, is a concluding paragraph from an essay on American values and Las Vegas weddings.

I sat next to one . . . wedding party in a Strip restaurant the last time I was in Las Vegas. The marriage had just taken place; the bride still wore her dress, the mother her corsage. A bored waiter poured out a few swallows of pink champagne ("on the house") for everyone but the bride, who was too young to be served. "You'll need something with more kick than that," the bride's father said with heavy jocularity to his new son-in-law; the ritual jokes about the wedding night had a certain Panglossian character, since the bride was clearly several months pregnant. Another round of pink champagne, this time not on the house, and the bride began to cry. "It was just as nice," she sobbed, "as I hoped and dreamed it would be."

—Joan Didion, "Marrying Absurd"

No doubt Didion makes her points about American values clearly and cogently in the essay. But concluding with this story lets us *see* (and hear) what she is saying about Las Vegas wedding chapels, which sell " 'niceness,' the facsimile of proper ritual, to children who do not know how else to find it, how to make the arrangements, how to do it 'right.'"

academic literacies | rhetorical situations | genres | processes | strategies | research MLA / APA | media / design | readings | handbook

Considering the Rhetorical Situation

As a writer or speaker, you need to think about the message that you want to articulate, the audience you want to reach, and the larger context you are writing in.

PURPOSE
Your purpose will affect the way you use narrative. For example, in an essay about seat belt laws, you might tell about the painful rehabilitation of a teenager who was not wearing a seat belt and was injured in an accident in order to persuade readers that seat belt use should be mandatory.

■ 55–56

AUDIENCE
Whom do you want to reach, and do you have an anecdote or other narrative that will help them understand your topic or persuade them that your argument has merit?

■ 57–60

GENRE
Does your genre require you to include narrative? A memoir about an important event might be primarily narrative, whereas a reflection about an event might focus more on the significance of the event than on what happened.

■ 61–63

STANCE
What is your stance, and do you have any stories that would help you convey that stance? A funny story, for example, can help create a humorous stance.

■ 64–67

MEDIA / DESIGN
In a print or spoken text, you will likely be limited to brief narratives, perhaps illustrated with photos or other images. In an electronic text, you might have the option of linking to full-length narratives or visuals available on the web.

■ 68–70

IF YOU NEED MORE HELP

See also the **PROCESSES** chapters if you are assigned to write a narrative essay and need help drafting, revising, and so on. Two special kinds of narratives are **LAB REPORTS** (which use narrative to describe the steps in an experiment from beginning to end) and **RÉSUMÉS** (which essentially tell the story of the work we've done, at school and on the job).

◗ 279

Glossary

▲ 253–64

44 Taking Essay Exams

Essay exams present writers with special challenges. You must write quickly, on a topic presented to you on the spot, to show your instructor what you know about a specific body of information. This chapter offers advice on how to take essay exams.

Considering the Rhetorical Situation

<table>
<tr><td>55–56</td><td>**PURPOSE**</td><td>In an essay exam, your purpose is to show that you have mastered certain material and that you can analyze and apply it in an essay. You may need to make an argument or simply to convey information on a topic.</td></tr>
<tr><td>57–60</td><td>**AUDIENCE**</td><td>Will your course instructor be reading your exam, or a TA? Sometimes standardized tests are read by groups of trained readers. What specific criteria will your audience use to evaluate your writing?</td></tr>
<tr><td>61–63</td><td>**GENRE**</td><td>Does the essay question specify or suggest a certain genre? In a literature course, you may need to write a compelling literary analysis of a passage. In a history course, you may need to write an argument for the significance of a key historical event. In an economics course, you may need to contrast the economies of the North and South before the Civil War. If the essay question doesn't specify a genre, look for keywords such as *argue*, *evaluate*, or *explain*, which point to a certain genre.</td></tr>
<tr><td>64–67</td><td>**STANCE**</td><td>In an essay exam, your stance is usually unemotional, thoughtful, and critical.</td></tr>
</table>

academic literacies · rhetorical situations · genres · processes · strategies · research MLA / APA · media / design · readings · handbook

MEDIA / DESIGN Since essay exams are usually handwritten on lined paper or in an exam booklet, legible handwriting is a must.

68–70

Analyzing Essay Questions

Essay questions usually include key verbs that specify the kind of writing you'll need to do—argue a position, compare two texts, and so on. Following are some of the most common kinds of writing you'll be asked to do on an essay exam.

- *Analyze:* Break an idea, theory, text, or event into its parts and examine them. For example, a world history exam might ask you to **ANALYZE** European imperialism's effect on Africa in the late nineteenth century, and discuss how Africans responded.

94–128

- *Apply:* Consider how an idea or concept might work out in practice. For instance, a film studies exam might ask you to apply the concept of auteurism—a theory of film that sees the director as the primary creator, whose body of work reflects a distinct personal style—to two films by Clint Eastwood. An economics exam might ask you to apply the concept of opportunity costs to a certain supplied scenario.

- *Argue/prove/justify:* Offer reasons and evidence to support a position. A philosophy exam, for example, might ask you to **ARGUE** whether or not all stereotypes contain a "kernel of truth" and whether believing a stereotype is ever justified.

355–73

- *Classify:* Group something into categories. For example, a marketing exam might ask you to **CLASSIFY** shoppers in categories based on their purchasing behavior, motives, attitudes, or lifestyle patterns.

374–79

- *Compare/contrast:* Explore the similarities and/or differences between two or more things. An economics exam, for example, might ask you to **COMPARE** the effectiveness of patents and tax incentives in encouraging technological advances.

380–87

94–128
197–205
- *Critique:* **ANALYZE** and **EVALUATE** a text or argument, considering its strengths and weaknesses. For instance, an evolutionary biology exam might ask you to critique John Maynard Smith's assertion that "scientific theories say nothing about what is right but only about what is possible" in the context of the theory of evolution.

388–98
- *Define:* Explain what a word or phrase means. An art history exam, for example, might ask you to **DEFINE** negative space and discuss the way various artists use it in their work.

399–407
- *Describe:* Tell about the important characteristics or features of something. For example, a sociology exam might ask you to **DESCRIBE** Erving Goffman's theory of the presentation of self in ordinary life, focusing on roles, props, and setting.

197–205
- *Evaluate:* Determine something's significance or value. A drama exam, for example, might ask you to **EVALUATE** the setting, lighting, and costumes in a filmed production of *Macbeth*.

- *Explain:* Provide reasons and examples to clarify an idea, argument, or event. For instance, a rhetoric exam might ask you to explain the structure of the African American sermon and discuss its use in writings of Frederick Douglass and Martin Luther King Jr.

486–87
- *Summarize/review:* Give the major points of a text or idea. A political science exam, for example, might ask you to **SUMMARIZE** John Stuart Mill's concept of utilitarianism and its relation to freedom of speech.

- *Trace:* Explain a sequence of ideas or order of events. For instance, a geography exam might ask you to trace the patterns of international migration since 1970 and discuss how these patterns differ from those of the period between 1870 and World War I.

Some Guidelines for Taking Essay Exams

Before the exam

16–18
- *Read* over your class notes and course texts strategically, **ANNOTATING** them to keep track of details you'll want to remember.

academic literacies   rhetorical situations   genres   processes   strategies   research MLA / APA   media / design   readings   handbook

- *Collaborate* by forming a **STUDY GROUP** to help one another master the course content.

285–86

- *Review* key ideas, events, terms, and themes. Look for common themes and **CONNECTIONS** in lecture notes, class discussions, and any readings—they'll lead you to important ideas.

473–75

- *Ask* your instructor about the form the exam will take: how long it will be, what kind of questions will be on it, how it will be evaluated, and so on. Working with a study group, write questions you think your instructor might ask, and then answer the questions together.

- *Warm up* just before the exam by **FREEWRITING** for ten minutes or so to gather your thoughts.

289–90

During the exam

- *Scan the questions* to determine how much each part of the test counts and how much time you should spend on it. For example, if one essay is worth 50 points and two others are worth 25 points each, you'll want to spend half your time on the 50-point question.

- *Read over* the entire test before answering any questions. Start with the question you feel most confident answering, which may or may not be the first question on the test.

- *Don't panic.* Sometimes when students first read an essay question, their minds go blank, but after a few moments they start to recall the information they need.

- *Plan.* Although you won't have much time for revising or editing, you still need to plan and allow yourself time to make some last-minute changes before you turn in the exam. So apportion your time. For a three-question essay test in a two-hour test period, you might divide your time like this:

Total Exam Time—120 minutes
Generating ideas—20 minutes (6–7 minutes per question)
Drafting—85 minutes (45 for the 50-point question,
                        20 for each 25-point question)
Revising, editing, proofreading—15 minutes

Knowing that you have built in time at the end of the exam period can help you remain calm as you write, as you can use that time to fill in gaps or reconsider answers you feel unsure about.

• *Jot down the main ideas* you need to cover in answering the question on scratch paper or on the cover of your exam book, number those ideas in the order you think makes sense—and you have an outline for your essay. If you're worried about time, plan to write the most important parts of your answers early on. If you don't complete your answer, refer your instructor to your outline to show where you were headed.

• *Turn the essay question into your introduction,* like this:

> *Question:* How did the outcomes of World War II differ from those of World War I?

> *Introduction:* The outcomes of World War II differed from those of World War I in three major ways: World War II affected more of the world and its people than World War I, distinctions between citizens and soldiers were eroded, and the war's brutality made it impossible for Europe to continue to claim cultural superiority over other cultures.

358–67 ◆

• *State your thesis explicitly,* provide **REASONS** and **EVIDENCE** to support your thesis, and use transitions to move logically from one idea to the next. Restate your main point in your conclusion. You don't want to give what one professor calls a "garbage truck answer," dumping everything you know into a blue book and expecting the instructor to sort it all out.

• *Write on every other line* and only on one side of each page so that you'll have room to make additions or corrections. If you're typing on a computer, double space.

• *If you have time left, go over your exam,* looking for ideas that need elaboration as well as for grammatical and punctuation errors.

After the exam. If your instructor doesn't return your exam, consider asking for a conference to go over your work so you can learn what you did well and where you need to improve—important knowledge to take with you into your next exam.

Doing Research

We do research all the time, for many different reasons. We search the web for information about a new computer, ask friends about the best place to get coffee, try on several pairs of jeans before deciding which ones to buy. You have no doubt done your share of library research before now, and you probably have visited a number of schools' websites before deciding which college you wanted to attend. Research, in other words, is something you do every day. The following chapters offer advice on the kind of research you'll need to do for your academic work and, in particular, for research projects.

Doing Research

Developing a Research Plan **45**

When you need to do research, it's sometimes tempting to jump in and start looking for information right away. To do research well, however — to find appropriate sources and use them wisely — you need to work systematically. You need a research plan. This chapter will help you establish such a plan and then get started.

Establishing a Schedule

Doing research is complex and time-consuming, so it's good to establish a schedule for yourself. Research-based writing projects usually require you to come up with a topic (or to analyze the requirements of an assigned topic) and then come up with a research question to guide your research efforts. Once you do some serious, focused research to find the information you need, you'll be ready to turn your research question into a tentative thesis and sketch out a rough outline. After doing whatever additional research you need to fill in your outline, you'll write a draft — and get some response to that draft. Perhaps you'll need to do additional research before revising. Finally, you'll need edit and proofread. And so you'll want to start by creating a timeline for getting all this work done, perhaps using the form on the next page.

Getting Started

Once you have a schedule, you can get started. The sections that follow offer advice on considering your rhetorical situation, coming up with a topic, and doing preliminary research; developing a research question, a

academic literacies   rhetorical situations   genres   processes   strategies   research MLA / APA   media / design   readings   handbook

Scheduling a Research Project

Complete by:

Analyze your rhetorical situation.   _____

Choose a possible topic or analyze the assignment.   _____

Plan a research strategy and do
    preliminary research.   _____

Come up with a research question.   _____

Schedule interviews and other field research.   _____

Find sources.   _____

Read sources and take notes.   _____

Do any field research.   _____

Come up with a tentative thesis and outline.   _____

Write a draft.   _____

Get response.   _____

Do any additional research.   _____

Revise.   _____

Prepare a list of works cited.   _____

Edit.   _____

Proofread the final draft.   _____

Submit the final draft.

tentative thesis, and a rough outline; and creating a working bibliography and keeping track of your sources. The chapters that follow offer guidelines for **FINDING SOURCES**, **EVALUATING SOURCES**, and **SYNTHESIZING IDEAS**.

445–68
469–72
473–77

Considering the Rhetorical Situation

As with any writing task, you need to start by considering your purpose, your audience, and the rest of your rhetorical situation:

academic literacies   rhetorical situations   genres   processes   strategies   research MLA / APA   media / design   readings   handbook

PURPOSE Is this project part of an assignment—and if so, does it specify any one purpose? If not, what is your broad purpose? To inform? argue? analyze? a combination? 55–56

AUDIENCE To whom are you writing? What does your audience likely know about your topic, and is there any background information you'll need to provide? What opinions or attitudes do your readers likely hold? What kinds of evidence will they find persuasive? How do you want them to respond to your writing? 57–60

GENRE Are you writing to report on something? to compose a profile? to make a proposal? an argument? What are the requirements of your genre in terms of the number and kind of sources you must use? 61–63

STANCE What is your attitude toward your topic? What accounts for your attitude? How do you want to come across? Curious? Critical? Positive? Something else? 64–67

MEDIA / DESIGN What medium or media will you use? Print? Spoken? Electronic? Will you need to create any charts, photographs, video, presentation software slides, or other visuals? 68–70

Coming Up with a Topic

If you need to choose a topic, consider your interests as they relate to the course for which you're writing. What do you want to learn about? What do you have questions about? What topics from the course have you found intriguing? What community, national, or global issues do you care about?

If your topic is assigned, you need to make sure you understand exactly what it asks you to do. Read the assignment carefully, looking for keywords: does it ask you to **ANALYZE**, **COMPARE**, **EVALUATE**, **SUMMARIZE**, or **ARGUE**? If the assignment offers broad guidelines but allows you to choose within them, identify the requirements and the range of possible topics and define your topic within those constraints. 94–128
380–87
197–205
486–87
355–73

For example, in an American history course, your instructor might ask you to "discuss social effects of the Civil War." Potential but broad topics might include poverty among Confederate soldiers or former slaveholders, the migration of members of those groups to Mexico or Northern cities, the establishment of independent African American churches, or the spread of the Ku Klux Klan—to name only a few of the possibilities.

Narrow the topic.   As you consider possible topics, look for ways to narrow your topic's focus to make it specific enough to discuss in depth. For example:

> **Too general:** fracking
>
> **Still too general:** fracking and the environment
>
> **Better:** the potential environmental effects of extracting natural gas through the process of hydraulic fracturing, or fracking

If you limit your topic, you can address it with specific information that you'll be more easily able to find and manage. In addition, a limited topic will be more likely to interest your audience than a broad topic that forces you to use abstract, general statements. For example, it's much harder to write well about "the environment" than it is to address a topic that explores a single environmental issue.

Think about what you know about your topic.   Chances are you already know something about your topic, and articulating that knowledge can help you see possible ways to focus your topic or come up with potential 289–92 sources of information. FREEWRITING, LISTING, CLUSTERING, and LOOPING are all good ways of tapping your knowledge of your topic. Consider where you might find information about it: Have you read about it in a textbook? heard stories about it on the news? visited websites focused on it? Do you know anyone who knows about this topic?

Consulting with Librarians and Doing Preliminary Research

Consulting with a reference librarian at your school and doing some preliminary research in the library can save you time in the long run. Reference librarians can direct you to the best scholarly sources for your topic and help you focus your topic by determining appropriate search terms and **KEYWORDS** — significant words that appear in the title, abstract, or text of potential sources and that you can use to search for information on your topic in library catalogs, in databases, and on the web. These librarians can also help you choose the most appropriate reference works, sources that provide general overviews of the scholarship in a field. General internet searches can be time-consuming, as they often result in thousands of possible sites — too many to weed out efficiently, either by revising your search terms or by going through the sites themselves, many of which are unreliable. Library databases, on the other hand, include only sources that already have been selected by experts, and searches in them usually present manageable numbers of results.

● 452–55

Wikipedia can often serve as a jumping-off point for preliminary research, but since its entries are written and edited by people who may not have expertise in the subject, it is not considered a reliable academic source. Specialized encyclopedias, however, usually present subjects in much greater depth and provide more scholarly references that might suggest starting points for your research. Even if you know a lot about a subject, doing preliminary research can open you to new ways of seeing and approaching it, increasing your options for developing and narrowing your topic.

Coming Up with a Research Question

Once you've surveyed the territory of your topic, you'll likely find that your understanding of the topic has become broader and deeper. You may find that your interests have changed and your research has led to surprises and additional research. That's okay: as a result of exploring avenues you hadn't anticipated, you may well come up with a better topic than the one you'd started with. At some point, though, you need to develop a research question—a specific question that you will then work to answer through your research.

53 ■

To write a research question, review your analysis of the **RHETORICAL SITUATION**, to remind yourself of any time constraints or length considerations. Generate a list of questions beginning with *What? When? Where? Who? How? Why? Would? Could?* and *Should?* Here, for example, are some questions about the tentative topic "the potential environmental effects of extracting natural gas through the process of hydraulic fracturing, or fracking":

What are the environmental effects of fracking?

When was fracking introduced as a way to produce natural gas?

Where is fracking done, and how does this affect the surrounding people and environment?

Who will benefit from increased fracking?

How much energy does fracking use?

Why do some environmental groups oppose fracking?

Would other methods of extracting natural gas be safer?

Could fracking cause earthquakes?

Should fracking be expanded, regulated, or banned?

Select one question from your list that you find interesting and that suits your rhetorical situation. Use the question to guide your research.

Drafting a Tentative Thesis

345–47 ◆

Once your research has led you to a possible answer to your research question, try formulating that answer as a tentative **THESIS**. You need not be committed to the thesis; in fact, you should not be. The object of your research should be to learn about your topic, not to find information that simply supports what you already think you believe. Your tentative thesis may (and probably will) change as you learn more about your subject, consider the many points of view on it, and reconsider your topic and, perhaps, your goal: what you originally planned to be an argument for considering other points of view may become a call to action. However tentative, a thesis allows you to move forward by clarifying your purpose for doing research. Here are some tentative thesis statements on the topic of fracking:

academic literacies   rhetorical situations   genres   processes   strategies   research MLA / APA   media / design   readings   handbook

Fracking is a likely cause of earthquakes in otherwise seismically stable regions of the country.

The federal government should strictly regulate the production of natural gas by fracking.

Fracking can greatly increase our supplies of natural gas, but other methods of producing energy should still be pursued.

As with a research question, a tentative thesis should guide your research efforts—but be ready to revise it as you learn still more about your topic. Research should be a process of **INQUIRY** in which you approach your topic with an open mind, ready to learn and possibly change. If you hold too tightly to a tentative thesis, you risk focusing only on evidence that supports your view, making your writing biased and unconvincing.

O 281–84

Creating a Rough Outline

After you've created a tentative thesis, write out a rough **OUTLINE** for your research project. Your outline can be a simple list of topics you want to explore, something that will help you structure your research efforts and organize your notes and other materials. As you read your sources, you can use your outline to keep track of what you need to find and where the information you do find fits into your argument. Then you'll be able to see if you've covered all the ideas you intended to explore—or whether you need to rethink the categories on your outline.

O 293–95

Keeping a Working Bibliography

A working bibliography is a record of all the sources you consult. You should keep such a record so that you can find sources easily when you need them and then cite any that you use. Your library likely offers tools to store source information you find in its databases and catalog, and software such as *Zotero* can also help you save, manage, and cite your sources.

Information for a Working Bibliography

FOR A BOOK

Library call number
Author(s) or editor(s)
Title and subtitle
Publication information: city, publisher, year of publication
Other information: edition, volume number, translator, and so on
If your source is an essay in a collection, include its author, title, and page numbers.

FOR A SOURCE FROM A DATABASE

Publication information for the source, as listed above
Name of database
DOI (digital object identifier) or URL of original source, such as the periodical in which an article was published. (for APA style)
Stable URL or permalink for database
Date you accessed source

FOR AN ARTICLE IN A PRINT PERIODICAL

Author(s)
Title and subtitle
Name of periodical
Volume number, issue number, date
Page numbers

FOR A WEB SOURCE

URL
Author(s) or editor(s) if available
Name of site
Sponsor of site
Date site was first posted or last updated
Date you accessed site
If the source is an article or book reprinted on the web, include its title, the title and publication information of the periodical or book, where it was first published, and any page numbers.

academic literacies | rhetorical situations | genres | processes | strategies | research MLA / APA | media / design | readings | handbook

You may find it useful to print out bibliographical data you find useful or to keep your working bibliography on index cards or in a notebook. However you decide to compile your working bibliography, include all the information you'll need later to document any sources you use; follow the **DOCUMENTATION** style you'll use when you write so that you won't need to go back to your sources to find the information. Some databases make this step easy by preparing rough-draft citations in several styles that you can copy, paste, and edit.

496–99

On the previous page is most of the basic information you'll want to include for each source in your working bibliography. Go to wwnorton.com/write/fieldguide for templates you can use to keep track of this information.

Keeping Track of Your Sources

- *Staple together photocopies and printouts.* It's easy for individual pages to get shuffled or lost on a desk or in a backpack. Keep a stapler handy, and fasten pages together as soon as you copy them or print them out.

- *Bookmark web sources* or save them using a free bookmark management tool. For database sources, use the DOI or stable URL, permalink, or document URL (the terms used by databases vary) — not the URL in the "Address" or "Location" box in your browser, which will expire after you end your online session.

- *Label everything.* Label your copies with the source's author and title.

- *Highlight sections you plan to use.* When you sit down to draft, your goal will be to find what you need quickly, so as soon as you decide you might use a source, highlight the paragraphs or sentences that you think you'll use. If your instructor wants copies of your sources to see how you used them, you've got them ready. If you're using PDF copies, you can highlight or add notes using *Adobe Reader*.

- *Use your rough outline to keep track of what you've got.* In the margin of each highlighted section, write the number or letter of the outline division to which the section corresponds. (It's a good idea to write it in the same place consistently so you can flip through a stack of copies and easily see what you've got.) Alternatively, attach sticky notes to each copy, using a different color for each main heading in your outline.

- *Keep everything in an online folder, file folder, or box.* Keep everything related to your research in one place. If you create online subfolders or create folders that correspond to your rough outline, you'll be able to organize your material, at least tentatively. And if you highlight, label, and use sticky notes, your material will be even better organized, making writing a draft easier. The folder or box will also serve you well if you are required to create a portfolio that includes your research notes, copies of sources, and drafts.

- *Use a reference management system.* Web-based reference or citation management systems allow you to create and organize a personal database of resources. You can import references from databases to a personal account, organize them, and draft citations in various formats. *RefWorks, EndNote, Mendeley, CiteULike,* and *Zotero* are five such systems; check with your librarian to see what system your library supports, or search online, as several of them are available for free. Be aware, though, that the citations generated are often inaccurate and need to be checked carefully for content and format. So treat them as rough drafts and plan to edit them.

IF YOU NEED MORE HELP

445–68
469–72

See the guidelines on **FINDING SOURCES** once you're ready to move on to in-depth research and those on **EVALUATING SOURCES** for help thinking critically about the sources you find.

---

academic literacies | rhetorical situations | genres | processes | strategies | research MLA / APA | media / design | readings | handbook

Finding Sources

To analyze media coverage of the 2012 Democratic National Convention, you examine news stories and blogs published at the time. To write an essay interpreting a poem by Maya Angelou, you study the poem and read several critical interpretations in literary journals. To write a report on career opportunities in psychology, you interview a graduate of your university who is working in a psychology clinic. In each of these cases, you go beyond your own knowledge to consult additional sources of information.

This chapter offers guidelines for locating a range of sources—print and online, general and specialized, published and firsthand. Keep in mind that as you do research, finding and **EVALUATING SOURCES** are two activities that usually take place simultaneously. So this chapter and the next one go hand in hand.

469–72

Kinds of Sources

Primary and secondary sources. Your research will likely lead you to both primary and secondary sources. *Primary sources* include historical documents, literary works, eyewitness accounts, field reports, diaries, letters, and lab studies, as well as any original research you do through interviews, observation, experiments, or surveys. *Secondary sources* include scholarly books and articles, reviews, biographies, textbooks, and other works that interpret or discuss primary sources. Novels and films are primary sources; articles interpreting them are secondary sources. The Declaration of Independence is a primary historical document; a historian's description of the events surrounding the Declaration's writing is secondary. A published report of scientific findings is primary; a critique of that report is secondary.

Whether a work is considered primary or secondary sometimes depends on your topic and purpose. If you're analyzing a poem, a critic's article interpreting the poem is a secondary source—but if you're investigating that critic's work, the article would be a primary source for your own study and interpretation.

Secondary sources are often useful because they can help you understand and evaluate primary source material. Whenever possible, however, you should find and use primary sources, because secondary sources can distort or misrepresent the information in primary sources. For example, a seemingly reputable secondary source describing the 1948 presidential election asserted that the *New York Times* ran a headline reading, "Thomas E. Dewey's Election as President Is a Foregone Conclusion." But the actual article was titled "Talk Is Now Turning to the Dewey Cabinet," and it began by noting "[the] *popular view that* Gov. Thomas E. Dewey's election as President is a foregone conclusion." Here the secondary source got not only the headline wrong but also distorted the source's intended meaning by leaving out an important phrase. Your research should be as accurate and reliable as it can be; using primary sources whenever you can helps ensure that it is.

Scholarly and popular sources. Scholarly sources are written by academic experts or scholars in a particular discipline and are *peer-reviewed* — evaluated by other experts in the same discipline for their factual accuracy and lack of bias. They are also written largely *for* experts in a discipline, as a means of sharing research, insights, and in-depth analysis with one another; that's why they must meet high standards of accuracy and objectivity and adhere to the discipline's accepted research methods, including its style for documenting sources. Scholarly articles are usually published in academic journals; scholarly books may be published by university presses or by other academically focused publishers.

Popular sources include just about all other online and print publications, from websites to magazines to books written for nonspecialists. These sources generally explain or provide opinion on current events or topics of general interest; when they discuss scholarly research, they tend to simplify the concepts and facts, providing definitions, narratives, and examples to make them understandable to nonspecialist audiences. They are often written by journalists or other professional writers who may specialize in a particular area but who report or comment on the scholarship of others rather than doing any themselves. Their most important difference from scholarly sources is that popular sources are not reviewed by other experts in the field being discussed, although editors or fact-checkers review the writing before it's published.

In most of your college courses, you'll be expected to rely primarily on scholarly sources rather than popular ones. However, if you're writing about a very current topic or need to provide background information on a topic, a mix of scholarly and popular sources may be appropriate. To see how scholarly and popular sources differ in appearance, look at the Documentation Map for scholarly journals (p. 516) and at the illustrations on pages 448–49. Here's a guide to determining whether or not a potential source is scholarly:

IDENTIFYING SCHOLARLY SOURCES: WHAT TO LOOK FOR

- *Author.* Look for the author's scholarly credentials, including his or her affiliations with academic or other research-oriented institutions.

- *Peer review.* Look for a list of reviewers at the front of the journal or on the journal's or publisher's website. If you don't find one, the source is probably not peer-reviewed.

- *Source citations.* Look for a detailed list of works cited or references at the end of the source and citations either parenthetically within the text or in footnotes or endnotes. (Popular sources may include a reference list but seldom cite sources within the text, except in signal phrases.)

Scholarly Source

Published in an academic journal.

Includes an abstract.

Cites academic research with consistent documentation style.

Describes research methods, includes numerical data.

Multiple authors who are academics.

Includes complete references list.

J Res Pers. Author manuscript; available in PMC 2011 August 1.
Published in final edited form as:
J Res Pers. 2010 August 1; 44(4): 478–484.
doi: 10.1016/j.jrp.2010.06.001

PMCID: PMC2918908
NIHMSID: NIHMS216233

Sounds like a Narcissist: Behavioral Manifestations of Narcissism in Everyday Life

Nicholas S. Holtzman, Simine Vazire, and Matthias R. Mehl
Author information ► Copyright and License information ►

See other articles in PMC that cite the published article.

Abstract

Little is known about narcissists' everyday behavior. The goal of this study was to describe how narcissism is manifested in everyday life. Using the Electronically Activated Recorder (EAR), we obtained naturalistic behavior from participants' everyday lives. The results suggest that the defining characteristics of narcissism that have been established from questionnaire and laboratory-based studies are borne out in narcissists' day-to-day behaviors. Narcissists do indeed behave in more extraverted and less agreeable ways than non-narcissists, skip class more (among narcissists high in exploitativeness/entitlement only), and use more sexual language. Furthermore, we found that the link between narcissism and disagreeable behavior is strengthened when controlling for self-esteem, thus extending prior questionnaire-based findings (Paulhus, Robins, Trzesniewski & Tracy, 2004) to observed, real-world behavior.

Keywords: narcissism, behavior, personality traits, sexual behavior, language use

Narcissists love attention. Lucky for them, they have recently received a considerable amount of it from academic psychologists, especially in laboratory settings (e.g., Back, Schmukle, & Egloff, 2010; Bushman & Baumeister, 1998; Campbell, Foster, & Finkel, 2002; Miller et al., 2009). This laboratory research has led to several wide-reaching theories about why narcissists do what they do (Holtzman & Strube, 2010a; Morf & Rhodewalt, 2001; Twenge & Campbell, 2009; Vazire & Funder, 2006). Despite all this attention from researchers, however, we still know little about what narcissists actually do in their everyday lives. The aim of this paper is to help create an empirical basis for a more complete understanding of narcissism by exploring behavioral manifestations of narcissism in everyday life. Thus, we intend to answer a simple, yet largely unanswered question: What do narcissists do on a day-to-day basis?

Method

Participants

Participants were 80 undergraduate students at the University of Texas at Austin (79 provided valid EAR data), recruited mainly from introductory psychology courses and by flyers in the psychology department. The sample was 54% female, and the ethnic composition of the sample was 65% White, 21% Asian, 11% Latino, and 3% of another ethnicity. Participants ranged from 18 to 24 years old ($M = 18.7$, $SD = 1.4$). Participants were compensated $50. Data from this sample were also reported in Vazire and Mehl (2008), where further information can be found about the study.

Narcissistic Personality Inventory (NPI)

The NPI is a 40-item test of narcissism that is reliable and well-validated (Raskin & Terry, 1988). The items on this forced-choice test contain pairs of statements such as "Sometimes I tell good stories" (non-narcissistic) versus "Everybody likes to hear my stories" (narcissistic). In our study, the NPI exhibited good reliability (α = .83). As seen in Table 1, we also calculated means and reliabilities for four facets (Emmons, 1987).

Table 1
Means, Standard Deviations, Gender-Differences, and Reliabilities
for the NPI and NPI Facets

Contributor Information

Nicholas S. Holtzman, Washington University in St. Louis.

Simine Vazire, Washington University in St. Louis.

Matthias R. Mehl, University of Arizona.

References

1. Back MD, Schmukle SC, Egloff B. Why are narcissists so charming at first sight? Decoding the narcissism-popularity link at zero acquaintance. Journal of Personality and Social Psychology. 2010;98:132–145. [PubMed]
2. Baumeister RF, Vohs KD, Funder DC. Psychology as the science of self-reports and finger movements: Whatever happened to actual behavior? Perspectives on Psychological Science. 2007;2:396–403.

Formats:
Article | PubReader | ePub (beta) | PDF (338K)

Related citations in PubMed
Impulsivity and the self-defeating behavior of narcissists. [Pers Soc Psychol Rev. 2006]
Why are narcissists so charming at first sight? Decoding the narcissism-popularity link at zero acquai [J Pers Soc Psychol. 2010]
The performance of narcissists rises and falls with perceived opportunity for glory. [J Pers Soc Psychol. 2002]
An empirical typology of narcissism and mental health in late adolescence. [J Adolesc. 2006]
Animal models of obsessive-compulsive disorder: rationale to understanding psychobiology and [Psychiatr Clin North Am 2006]
See reviews...
See all...

Cited by other articles in PMC
Evidence for the criterion validity and clinical utility of the Pathological Narcissism Inventory [Assessment 2012]
See all...

Links
MedGen
PubMed

Recent activity
Turn Off Clear
Sounds like a Narcissist: Behavioral Manifestations of Narcissism in Everyday Li...   PMC
See more...

Does self-love lead to love for others? A story of narcissistic game playing. [J Pers Soc Psychol. 2002]
Interpersonal and intrapsychic adaptiveness of trait self-enhancement: a mixed blessing? [J Pers Soc Psychol. 1998]

Knowing me, knowing you: the accuracy and unique predictive validity of self-ratings and other-ratin [J Pers Soc Psychol. 2008]

A principal-components analysis of the Narcissistic Personality Inventory and further evidence of its [J Pers Soc Psychol. 1988]
Narcissism: theory and measurement. [J Pers Soc Psychol. 1987]

PubReader format: click here to try

 academic literacies
 rhetorical situations
 genres
 processes
 strategies
 research MLA / APA
 media / design
readings
handbook

Popular Source

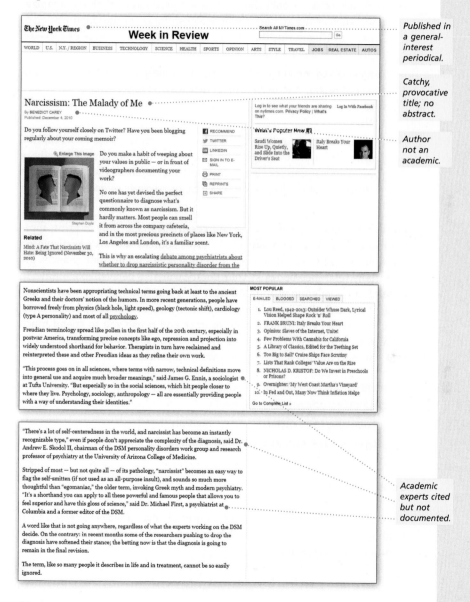

Published in a general-interest periodical.

Catchy, provocative title; no abstract.

Author not an academic.

Academic experts cited but not documented.

- *Publisher.* Look for publishers that are professional scholarly organizations, such as the Modern Language Association or the Organization of American Historians, that are affiliated with universities or colleges, or that have a stated academic mission.

- *Language and content.* Look for abstracts (one-paragraph summaries of the contents) at the beginning of articles and for technical or specialized language and concepts that readers are assumed to be familiar with.

- *Other clues.* Look for little or no advertising on websites or within the journal; for a plain design with few or no illustrations, especially in print sources; and for listing in academic databases when you limit your search to *academic, peer-reviewed,* or *scholarly sources.*

Print and online sources.　Some sources are available only in print; some are available only online. But many print sources are also available on the web. You'll find print sources in your school's library, but chances are that many reference books in your library will also be available online. In general, for academic writing it's best to try to find most of your online sources through the library's website rather than commercial search sites, which may lead you to unreliable sources and cause you to spend much more time sorting and narrowing search results. This chapter discusses four paths to finding sources you'll want to consult:

455–57
457–58
459–61
462–63

REFERENCE WORKS, for encyclopedias, bibliographies, and the like

THE LIBRARY CATALOG, for books

INDEXES AND DATABASES, for periodicals

SEARCH SITES AND SUBJECT DIRECTORIES, for material on the web

Searching in Academic Libraries

College and university libraries typically offer several ways to search their holdings. Take a look at this search box, from the homepage of the Houston Community College libraries:

academic literacies · rhetorical situations · genres · processes · strategies · research MLA / APA · media / design · readings · handbook

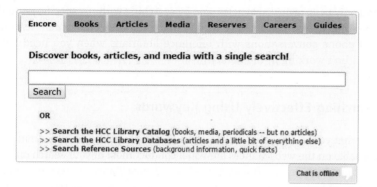

This box allows you to search through all the library's holdings at once an option that may be a good way to get started. You may already know, though, that you need to focus your search on one type of source, such as scholarly articles, leading you to choose the Articles tab.

This box lets you shape and limit your search in several ways: by selecting a specific database, by choosing to search only for full-text articles and only peer-reviewed articles, and by searching within a specific journal. The Chat button can be very useful; many libraries offer email, texting, and phone conversations with reference librarians when you need help but aren't working in the library.

Searching Effectively Using Keywords

Whether you're searching for books, articles in periodicals, or other material available on the web, chances are you'll conduct most of your search online. Most materials produced since the 1980s and most library catalogs are online, and most periodical articles can be found by searching electronic indexes and databases. In each case, you can search for authors, titles, or subjects.

To search online, you'll need to come up with keywords. The key to searching efficiently is to use keywords and combinations of them that will focus your searches on the information you need — but not too much of it. Often you'll start out with one general keyword that will yield far too many results; then you'll need to switch to more specific terms or combinations (*homeopathy* instead of *medicine* or *secondary education Japan* instead of *education Japan*).

Other times your keyword search won't yield enough sources; then you'll need to use broader terms or combinations (*education Japan* instead of *secondary education Japan*) or substitute synonyms (*home remedy* instead of *folk medicine*). Sometimes you'll need to learn terms used in academic disciplines or earlier in history for things you know by other names, such as *myocardial infarction* rather than *heart attack* or *the Great War* instead of *World War I*. Or look through the sources that turn up in response to other terms to see what keywords you might use in subsequent searches. Searching requires flexibility, in the words you use and the methods you try.

Finding keywords using word clouds. One way to find keywords to help you narrow and focus your topic is to create a word cloud, a visual representation of words used in a text; the more often a word is used, the larger it looks in the word cloud. Several websites, including *Tagxedo*, *Wordle*, and *TagCrowd*, let you create word clouds. Examining a word cloud created from an article in a reference work may help you see what terms are used to discuss your topic — and may help you see new possible ways to narrow it. Here, for example, is a word cloud derived from an article in *Scientific American* discussing fracking. Many of the terms — *fracking, water, gas, wells, drilling* — are just what you'd expect. However, some terms — *Ingraffea, Marcellus, cementing* — may be unfamiliar and lead to additional possibilities for research. For instance, *Ingraffea* refers to an expert on fracking whose publications might be worth examining, while *cementing* refers to an important and controversial aspect of the hydraulic fracturing process.

Finding keywords using databases.   Once you've begun searching for and finding possible sources, you can expand your list of possible keywords by skimming the "detailed record" or "metadata" page for any scholarly articles you find, where full bibliographic information on the source may be found. A search for *fracking* resulted in this source:

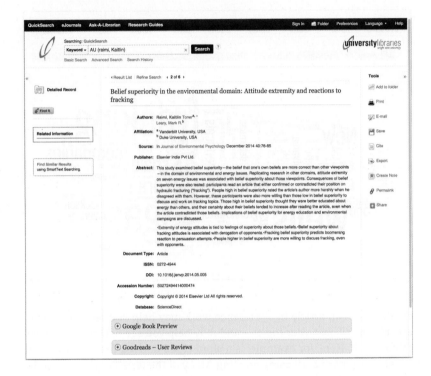

Note the list of author-supplied keywords, which offers options for narrowing and focusing your topic. Each keyword is a link, so simply clicking on it will produce a new list of sources.

Advanced keyword searching.   Most search sites have "advanced search" options that will help you focus your research. Some allow you to ask questions in conversational language: *What did Thomas Jefferson write about slavery?* Others allow you to focus your search by using specific words or symbols. Here are some of the most common ones:

academic literacies · rhetorical situations · genres · processes · strategies · research MLA / APA · media / design · readings · handbook

- Type quotation marks around words to search for an exact phrase—"Thomas Jefferson."

- Type AND to specify that more than one keyword must appear in sources: Jefferson AND Adams. Some search engines require a plus sign instead: +Jefferson +Adams.

- Type OR if you're looking for sources that include any of several terms: Jefferson OR Adams OR Madison.

- Type NOT to find sources *without* a certain word: Jefferson NOT Adams. Some search engines call for a minus sign (actually, a hyphen) instead: +Jefferson –Adams.

- Type an asterisk to search for words in different form. For example, teach* will yield sources containing *teacher* and *teaching*.

Reference Works

The reference section of your school's library is the place to find encyclopedias, dictionaries, atlases, almanacs, bibliographies, and other reference works in print. Many of these sources are also online and can be accessed from any computer that is connected to the internet. Others are available only in the library. Remember, though, that whether in print or online, reference works are only a starting point, a place where you can get an overview of your topic.

General reference works.   Consult encyclopedias for general background information on a subject, dictionaries for definitions of words, atlases for maps and geographic data, and almanacs for statistics and other data on current events. These are some works you might consult:

The New Encyclopaedia Britannica

The Columbia Encyclopedia

Webster's Third New International Dictionary

Oxford English Dictionary

National Geographic Atlas of the World

Statistical Abstract of the United States

The World Almanac and Book of Facts

Caution: *Wikipedia* is a popular online research tool, but since anyone can edit its entries, you can't be certain of its accuracy. Use it for general overviews, but look elsewhere — including *Wikipedia*'s own references and citations — for authoritative sources.

Specialized reference works.　You can also go to specialized reference works, which provide in-depth information on a single field or topic. These may also include authoritative bibliographies, leading you to more specific works. A reference librarian can refer you to specialized encyclopedias in particular fields, but good places to start are online collections of many topic-specific reference works that offer overviews of a topic, place it in a larger context, and sometimes provide links to potential academic sources. Collections that are available through libraries include the following:

> *CQ Researcher* offers in-depth reports on topics in education, health, the environment, criminal justice, international affairs, technology, the economy, and social trends. Each report gives an overview of a particular topic, outlines of the differing positions on it, and a bibliography of resources on it.

> *Gale Virtual Reference Library* (*GVRL*) offers thousands of full-text specialized encyclopedias, almanacs, articles, and ebooks.

> *Oxford Reference Online* contains hundreds of dictionaries, encyclopedias, and other reference works on a wide variety of subjects, as well as timelines with links to each item mentioned on each timeline.

> *SAGE Reference Online* includes many encyclopedias and handbooks on topics in the social sciences.

Bibliographies.　Bibliographies provide an overview of what has been published on a topic, listing published works along with the information you'll need to find each work. Some are annotated with brief summaries of each work's contents. You'll find bibliographies at the end of scholarly articles and books, and you can also find book-length bibliographies, both

academic literacies　rhetorical situations　genres　processes　strategies　research MLA / APA　media / design　readings　handbook

in the reference section of your library and online. Check with a reference librarian for bibliographies on your research topic.

Books / Searching the Library Catalog

The library catalog is your primary source for finding books. Almost all library catalogs are computerized and can be accessed through the library's website. You can search by author, title, subject, or keyword. The image below shows the result of a keyword search for material on art in Nazi Germany. This search of the library's catalog revealed forty items — print books, ebooks, and video recordings — on the topic; to access information on each one, the researcher must simply click on the title or thumbnail image. The image on the next page shows detailed information for one source: bibliographic data about author, title, and publication; related subject headings (which may lead to other useful materials in the library)—and more. Library catalogs also supply a call number, which identifies the book's location on the library's shelves.

Results of a keyword search for material on art in Nazi Germany.

Detailed information about one of the books located with a keyword search.

Ebooks / Finding Books Online

Many books in the library catalog are available online. Some may be down-loaded to a tablet or mobile device. In addition, thousands of classic works that are in the public domain — no longer protected by copyright — may be read online. *Bartleby*, *Google Books*, *Open Library*, and *Project Gutenberg* are four collections of public-domain works. Here are some other sources of ebooks:

> *Hathi Trust Digital Library* offers access to millions of ebooks, about a third of them in the public domain, contributed by university libraries.
>
> *Internet Archive* includes millions of ebooks as well as audio, moving images, a live music archive, and the Way Back Machine, which archives historical webpages.
>
> The *Gale Virtual Reference Library (GVRL)*, *Oxford Scholarship Online*, and *SAGE Reference Online* all contain large ebook collections.

Periodicals / Searching Indexes and Databases

To find journal, magazine, and newspaper articles, you will need to search periodical indexes and databases. Indexes provide listings of articles organized by topics; many databases provide the full texts. Some indexes are in print and can be found in the reference section of the library; most are online. Some databases are available for free; most of the more authoritative ones, however, are available only by subscription and so must be accessed through a library.

Many databases now include not only scholarly articles but also dissertations, theses, book chapters, book reviews, and conference proceedings. Dissertations and theses are formal works of scholarship done as requirements for graduate degrees; book reviews offer critical evaluations of scholarly and popular books; and conference proceedings are papers presented, usually orally, at scholarly meetings.

When you access a source through a database, the URL or link address is different each time you log in, so if you want to return to a source, look for a *stable URL*, *permalink*, or *document URL* option and choose it to copy and paste into your list of sources.

General indexes and databases. A reference librarian can help you determine which databases will be most helpful to you, but here are some useful ones:

Academic Search Complete is a multidisciplinary index and database containing the full text of articles in thousands of journals and indexing of even more, with abstracts of their articles.

EBSCOhost provides interlinked databases of abstracts and full-text articles from a variety of periodicals.

FirstSearch offers access to millions of full-text, full-image articles in dozens of databases covering many disciplines.

InfoTrac offers millions of full-text articles in a broad spectrum of disciplines and on a wide variety of topics from thousands of scholarly and popular periodicals, including the *New York Times*.

JSTOR archives scanned copies of entire publication runs of scholarly journals in many disciplines, but it does not include current issues of the journals.

LexisNexis contains full-text publications and articles from a large number of sources—newspapers, business and legal resources, medical texts, and reference sources such as *The World Almanac* and the Roper public opinion polls.

ProQuest Central provides access to full-text articles from thousands of books, scholarly journals, conference papers, magazines, newspapers, blogs, podcasts, and websites and a large collection of dissertations and theses.

Single-subject indexes and databases.   The following are just a sample of what's available; check with a reference librarian for indexes and databases in the subject you're researching.

America: History and Life indexes scholarly literature on the history and culture of the United States and Canada.

BIOSIS Previews provides abstracts and indexes for thousands of sources on a wide variety of biological and medical topics.

ERIC is the U.S. Department of Education's Educational Resource Information Center database. It includes hundreds of journal titles as well as conference papers, technical reports, and other resources on education.

Historical Abstracts includes abstracts of articles on the history of the world, excluding the United States and Canada, since 1450.

Humanities International Index contains bibliographic references to more than 2,000 journals dealing with the humanities.

MLA International Bibliography indexes scholarly articles on modern languages, literature, folklore, and linguistics.

PsycINFO indexes scholarly literature in a number of disciplines relating to the behavioral sciences and mental health.

PubMed includes millions of citations for biomedical literature, many with links to full-text content.

Print indexes.   You may need to consult print indexes to find articles published before the 1980s. Here are six useful ones:

academic literacies   rhetorical situations   genres   processes   strategies   research MLA / APA   media / design   readings   handbook

The Readers' Guide to Periodical Literature (print, 1900–; online, 1983–)

InfoTrac Magazine Index (print, 1988–; online, 1973–)

The New York Times Index (print and online, 1851–)

Humanities Index (print, 1974–; online, 1984–)

Social Sciences Index (print, 1974–; online, 1983–)

General Science Index (print, 1978–; online, 1984–)

Images, Sound, and More

Your library likely subscribes to various databases that allow you to find and download video, audio, and image files. Here is a sampling:

AP Images provides access to photographs taken for the Associated Press, the cooperative agency of thousands of newspapers and radio and television stations worldwide.

ArtStor provides images in the arts, architecture, humanities, and sciences.

Dance in Video offers hundreds of videos of dance productions and documentaries on dance.

Education in Video includes thousands of videos of teaching demonstrations, lectures, documentaries, and footage of students and teachers in their classrooms.

Naxos Music Library contains more than 100,000 classical, jazz, and world music recordings, as well as libretti and synopses of hundreds of operas and other background information.

Theatre in Video provides videos of more than 250 performances of plays and more than 100 film documentaries.

The following indexes and databases are freely available on the internet:

ipl2, the Internet Public Library, is a searchable, annotated subject directory of thousands of websites selected and evaluated by librarians for their usefulness to users of public libraries.

The WWW Virtual Library is a catalog of websites on a wide range of subjects, compiled by volunteers with expertise in particular subject areas.

CSA Discovery Guides provide comprehensive information on current issues in the arts and humanities, natural sciences, social sciences, and technology, with an overview of each subject, key citations with abstracts, and links to websites.

The Voice of the Shuttle, or *VOS,* offers information on subjects in the humanities, organized to mirror "the way the humanities are organized for research and teaching as well as the way they are adapting to social, cultural, and technological changes."

The Library of Congress offers online access to information on a wide range of subjects, including academic subjects, as well as prints, photographs, and government documents.

JURIST is a university-based online gateway to authoritative legal instruction, information, scholarship, and news.

Searching the Web

The web provides access to countless sites containing information posted by governments, educational institutions, organizations, businesses, and individuals. Such websites are different from other sources — including the kinds of online sources you access through indexes and databases — in two key ways: (1) their content varies greatly in its reliability and (2) they are not stable: what you see on a site today may be different (or gone) tomorrow. Anyone who wants to can post material on the web, so you need to evaluate carefully what you find there to eliminate sources that are not current, lack credibility, or are primarily advertisements or promotional in nature.

Because it is so vast and dynamic, finding what you need on the web for academic writing can be a challenge. The primary way of finding information on the web is with a search site. You may find the most suitable results for academic writing by using *Google Scholar,* a search site that finds scholarly literature, including peer-reviewed papers, technical reports, and abstracts. Here are other ways of searching the web:

- *Keyword searches. Google, Yahoo!, Bing,* and most other search sites all scan the web looking for keywords that you specify.

- **Subject directories.** *Google*, *Yahoo!*, and some other search sites offer directories that arrange information by topics, much like a library cataloging system. Such directories allow you to broaden or narrow your search if you need to — for example, a search for "birds" can be broadened to "animals" or narrowed to "blue-footed booby."

- **Metasearches.** *Yippy*, *Dogpile*, and *ZapMeta* are metasearch sites that allow you to use several search engines simultaneously. They are best for searching broadly; use a single search site for the most precise results.

- **Twitter searches.** In addition to *Twitter* Search, you can find *Twitter* content through search sites such as *Twazzup* and *Topsy*.

Each search site and metasearch site has its own protocols for searching; most have an "advanced search" option that will help you search more productively. Remember, though, that you need to be careful about **EVALUATING SOURCES** that you find on the web because the web is unregulated and no one independently verifies the information posted on its sites.

469–72

Doing Field Research

Sometimes you'll need to do your own research, to go beyond the information you find in published sources and gather data by doing field research. Three kinds of field research you might want to consider are interviews, observations, and questionnaires.

Interviewing experts.   Some kinds of writing — a profile of a living person, for instance — almost require that you conduct an interview. And sometimes you may just need to find information that you haven't been able to find in published sources. To get firsthand information on the experience of serving as a soldier in Afghanistan, you might interview your cousin who served a tour of duty there; to find current research on pesticide residues in food, you might need to interview a toxicologist. Whatever your goal, you can conduct interviews in person, using video-calling software such as *Skype* or *FaceTime*, by telephone, through email, or by mail. In general, you will want to use interviews to find information you can't find elsewhere. Below is some advice on planning and conducting an interview.

Before the interview

55–56 ▨

1. Once you identify someone you want to interview, email or phone to ask the person, stating your **PURPOSE** for the interview and what you hope to learn.
2. Once you've set up an appointment, send a note or email confirming the time and place. If you wish to record the interview, be sure to ask for permission to do so. If you plan to conduct the interview by mail or email, state when you will send your questions.
3. Write out questions. Plan questions that invite extended response and supporting details: "What accounts for the recent spike in gasoline prices?" forces an explanation, whereas "Is the recent spike in gas prices a direct result of global politics?" is likely to elicit only a yes or a no.

At the interview

4. Record the full name of the person you interview, along with the date, time, and place of the interview; you'll need this information to cite and document the interview accurately.
5. Take notes, even if you are recording the interview.
6. Keep track of time: don't take more than you agreed to beforehand unless both of you agree to keep talking. End by thanking your subject and offering to provide a copy of your final product.

After the interview

7. Flesh out your notes with details as soon as possible after the interview, while you still remember them. What did you learn? What surprised you? Summarize both the interviewee's words and your impressions.
8. Make sure you've reproduced quotations from the interview accurately and fairly. Avoid editing quotations in ways that distort the speaker's intended meaning.
9. Be sure to send a thank-you note or email.

academic literacies · rhetorical situations · genres · processes · strategies · research MLA / APA · media / design · readings · handbook

Observation. Some writing projects are based on information you get by observing something. For a sociology report, you may observe how students behave in large lectures. For an education course, you may observe one child's progress as a writer over a period of time. The following advice can help you conduct observations.

Before observing

1. Think about your research PURPOSE: What are you looking for? What do you expect to find? How will your presence as an observer affect what you observe? What do you plan to do with what you find?

2. If necessary, set up an appointment. You may need to ask permission of the people you wish to observe and of your school as well. (Check with your instructor about your school's policy in this area.) Be honest and open about your goals and intentions; college students doing research assignments are often welcomed where others may not be.

55–56

While observing

3. If you're taking notes on paper, you may want to divide each page down the middle vertically and write only on the left side of the page, reserving the right side for information you will fill in later. If you're using a laptop, you can set up two columns or a split screen.

4. Note descriptive details about the setting. What do you see? What do you hear? Do you smell anything? Get down details about color, shape, size, sound, and so on. Consider photographing or making a sketch of what you see.

5. Who is there, and what are they doing? DESCRIBE what they look like, and make notes about what they say. Note any significant demographic details—about gender, race, occupation, age, dress, and so on.

399–407

6. What is happening? Who's doing what? What's being said? Make note of these kinds of NARRATIVE details.

419–27

After observing

7. As soon as possible after you complete your observations, use the right side of your notes to fill in gaps and include additional details.

94–128 ▲

8. **ANALYZE** your notes, looking for patterns. Did some things appear or happen more than once? Did anything stand out? surprise or puzzle you? What did you learn?

Questionnaires and surveys. Various kinds of questionnaires and surveys can provide information or opinions from a large number of people. For a political science course, you might conduct a survey to ask students who they plan to vote for. Or, for a marketing course, you might distribute a questionnaire asking what they think about an advertising campaign. The advice in this section will help you create useful questionnaires and surveys.

Define your goal. The goal of a questionnaire or survey should be limited and focused, so that every question will contribute to your research question. Also, people are more likely to respond to a brief, focused survey.

Define your sample. A survey gets responses from a representative sample of the whole group. The answers to these questions will help you define that sample:

1. Who should answer the questions? The people you contact should represent the whole population. For example, if you want to survey undergraduate students at your school, your sample should reflect your school's enrollment in terms of gender, year, major, age, ethnicity, and so forth as closely as possible.
2. How many people make up a representative sample? In general, the larger your sample, the more the answers will reflect those of the whole group. But if your population is small—200 students in a history course, for example—your sample must include a large percentage of that group.

Decide on a medium. Will you ask the questions face-to-face? over the phone? on a website such as *SurveyMonkey*? by mail? by email? Face-to-face questions work best for simple surveys or for gathering impersonal information. You're more likely to get responses to more personal questions with printed or online questionnaires, which should be neat and easy to read. Phone interviews may require well-thought-out scripts that anticipate possible answers and make it easy to record these answers.

Design good questions. The way you ask questions will determine the usefulness of the answers you get, so take care to write questions that are clear and unambiguous. Here are some typical question types:

- *Multiple-choice*

  What is your current age?

  ____ 15–20   ____ 21–25   ____ 26–30   ____ 31–35   ____ Other

- *Rating scale*

  How would you rate the service at the campus bookstore?

  ____ Excellent   ____ Good   ____ Fair   ____ Poor

- *Agreement scale*

  How much do you agree with the following statements?

	Strongly Agree	Agree	Disagree	Strongly Disagree
The bookstore has sufficient numbers of textbooks available.	❐	❐	❐	❐

	Strongly Agree	Agree	Disagree	Strongly Disagree
Staff at the bookstore are knowledgeable.	❐	❐	❐	❐
Staff at the bookstore are courteous.	❐	❐	❐	❐

- *Open-ended*

  How often do you visit the campus bookstore?

  How can the campus bookstore improve its service?

Include all potential alternatives when phrasing questions to avoid biasing the answers. And make sure each question addresses only one issue — for example, "bookstore staff are knowledgeable and courteous" could lead to the response "knowledgeable, agree; courteous, disagree."

When arranging questions, place easier ones at the beginning and harder ones near the end (but if the questions seem to fall into a different natural order, follow it). Make sure each question asks for information you will need—if a question isn't absolutely necessary, omit it.

Include an introduction. Start by stating your survey's purpose and how the results will be used. It's also a good idea to offer an estimate of the time needed to complete the questions. Remind participants of your deadline.

Test the survey or questionnaire. Make sure your questions elicit the kinds of answers you need by asking three or four people who are part of your target population to answer them. They can help you find unclear instructions, questions that aren't clear or that lack sufficient alternatives, or other problems that you should correct to make sure your results are useful. But if you change the questionnaire as a result of their responses, don't include their answers in your total.

469–72
478–80

> **IF YOU NEED MORE HELP**
>
> See **EVALUATING SOURCES** for help determining their usefulness. See also Chapter 49 for help **TAKING NOTES** on your sources.

Evaluating Sources **47**

Searching the *Health Source* database for information on the incidence of meningitis among college students, you find seventeen articles. A *Google* search on the same topic produces over 10,000 hits. How do you decide which sources to read? This chapter presents advice on evaluating sources—first to determine whether a source might be useful for your purposes and is worth looking at more closely and then to read with a critical eye the ones you choose.

Considering Whether a Source Might Be Useful

Think about your **PURPOSE**. Are you trying to persuade readers to believe or do something? to inform them about something? If the former, it will be especially important to find sources representing various positions; if the latter, you may need sources that are more factual or informative. Reconsider your **AUDIENCE**. What kinds of sources will they find persuasive? If you're writing for readers in a particular field, what counts as evidence in that field? Following are some questions that can help you judge whether a possible source you've found deserves your time and attention:

55–56

57–60

446–48

- *Is it reliable?* Is it **SCHOLARLY**? peer-reviewed? published in a reputable journal or magazine, or by a reputable publisher? Did you find it in a library database? on the web? Evaluating web-based texts may require more work than using results from library databases. But whatever kind of search you do, skim the results quickly to evaluate their reliability.

- *Is it relevant?* How does the source relate to your purpose? What will it add to your work? Look at the title and at any introductory material— a preface, abstract, or introduction—to see what the source covers.

- **What are the author's credentials?** How is the author qualified to write on the subject? Is he or she associated with a particular position on the issue? See whether the source mentions other works this author has written. In any case, you might do a web search to see what else you can learn about him or her.

64–67

- **What is the STANCE?** Consider whether a source covers various perspectives or advocates one particular point of view. Does its title suggest a certain slant? If it's online, you might check to see whether it includes links to other sites and, if so, what their perspectives are. You'll want to consult sources with a variety of viewpoints.

- **Who is the publisher or sponsor?** If it's a book, what kind of company published it; if an article, what kind of periodical did it appear in? Books published by university presses and articles in scholarly journals are reviewed by experts before they are published. Books and articles written for the general public typically do not undergo rigorous review—and they may lack the kind of in-depth discussion that is useful for research.

  If the source is online, is the site maintained by an organization? an interest group? a government agency? an individual? Look for clues in the URL: *edu* is used mostly by colleges and universities, *gov* by government agencies, *org* by nonprofit organizations, *mil* by the military, and *com* by commercial organizations. Evaluate the publisher's or sponsor's motives: to present information even-handedly? to promote a certain point of view, belief, or position? to sell something?

- **What is the level?** Can you understand the material? Texts written for a general audience might be easier to understand but not authoritative enough for academic work. Texts written for scholars will be more authoritative but may be hard to comprehend.

- **When was it published?** See when books and articles were published. Check to see when online sources were created and last updated. (If the site lists no date, see if links to other sites still work.) Recent does not necessarily mean better — some topics may require very current information whereas others may call for older sources.

- **Is it available?** Is it a source you can get hold of? If it's a book and your school's library doesn't have it, can you get it through interlibrary loan?

- **Does it include other useful information?** Is there a bibliography that might lead you to other sources? How current are the sources it cites?

Once you've decided that a source should be examined more closely, use the following questions to give it critical scrutiny.

Reading Sources with a Critical Eye

- **What ARGUMENTS does the author make?** Does the author present a number of different positions, or does he or she argue for a particular position? Do you need to **ANALYZE THE ARGUMENT**? ▲ 156–82　✳ 29–30

- **How persuasive do you find the argument?** What reasons and evidence does the author provide in support of any position(s)? Are there citations or links — and if so, are they credible? Is any evidence presented without citations? Do you find any of the author's assumptions questionable? How thoroughly does he or she consider opposing arguments?

- **What is the author's STANCE?** Does the author strive for objectivity, or does the content or language reveal a particular bias? Does the author consider opposing views and treat them fairly? ■ 64–67

- **Do you recognize ideas you've run across in other sources?** Does the source leave out any information or perspective that other sources include — or include any that other sources leave out?

- **Does this source support or challenge your own position—or does it do both?** Does it support your thesis? Offer a different argument altogether? Does it represent a position you may need to **ACKNOWLEDGE** or **REFUTE**? Don't reject a source just because it challenges your views; your sources should reflect a variety of views on your topic, showing that you've considered the subject thoroughly. ▲ 176　▲ 177

- **What can you tell about the intended AUDIENCE and PURPOSE?** Is the author writing to a general audience, to a subset of that audience, to ■ 57–60　55–56 specialists in a particular field? Are you a member of that audience? If not, does that affect the way you interpret what you read? Is the main purpose to inform readers about a topic or to argue a certain point?

478–90
491–95

> **IF YOU NEED MORE HELP**
>
> See **QUOTING, PARAPHRASING, AND SUMMARIZING** for help in taking notes on your sources and deciding how to use them in your writing. See also **ACKNOWL-EDGING SOURCES, AVOIDING PLAGIARISM** for advice on giving credit to the sources you use.

academic literacies | rhetorical situations | genres | processes | strategies | research MLA / APA | media / design | readings | handbook

Synthesizing Ideas 48

To **ANALYZE** the works of a poet, you show how she uses similar images in three different poems to explore a recurring concept. To solve a crime, a detective studies several eyewitness accounts to figure out who did it. To trace the history of photojournalism, a professor **COMPARES** the uses of photography during the Civil War and during the Vietnam War. These are all cases where someone *synthesizes*—brings together material from two or more sources in order to generate new information or to support a new perspective. When you do research, you need to go beyond what your sources say; you need to use what they say to inspire and support *what you want to say*. This chapter focuses on how to synthesize ideas you find in other sources as the basis for your own ideas.

94–128

380–87

Reading for Patterns and Connections

Your task as a writer is to find as much information as you can on your topic—and then to sift through all that you have found to determine and support what you yourself will write. In other words, you'll need to synthesize ideas and information from the sources you've consulted to figure out first what arguments *you* want to make and then to provide support for those arguments.

When you synthesize, you group similar bits of information together, looking for patterns or themes or trends and trying to identify the key points. For example, in researching the effectiveness of the SAT writing exam, you find several sources showing that scores correlate directly with length and that a majority of U.S. colleges and universities have decided not to count the results of the test in their admission decisions. You can infer from that pattern of research results that the test is not yet seen as an effective measure of writing ability. Here are some tips for reading to identify patterns and connections:

- Read all your sources with an open mind. Withhold judgment, even of sources that seem wrong-headed or implausible. Don't jump to conclusions.

486–87

- Take notes and write a brief **SUMMARY** of each source to help you see relationships, patterns, and connections among your sources. Take notes on your own thoughts, too.

- Pay attention to your first reactions. You'll likely have many ideas to work with, but your first thoughts can often lead somewhere that you will find interesting. Try **FREEWRITING**, **CLUSTERING**, or **LISTING** to see where they lead. How do these thoughts and ideas relate to your topic? Where might they fit into your rough **OUTLINE**?

289–92
293–95

- Try to think creatively, and pay attention to thoughts that flicker at the edge of your consciousness, as they may well be productive.

- Be playful. Good ideas sometimes come when we let our guard down or take ideas to extremes just to see where they lead.

Ask yourself these questions about your sources:

- What sources make the strongest arguments? What makes them so strong?

- Do some arguments recur in several sources?

- Which arguments do you agree with? disagree with? Of those you disagree with, which ones seem strong enough that you need to **ACKNOWLEDGE** them in your text?

368

- Are there any disagreements among your sources?

- Are there any themes you see in more than one source?

- Are any data—facts, statistics, examples—or experts cited in more than one source?

- Do several of your sources use the same terms? Do they use the terms similarly, or do they use them in different ways?

- What have you learned about your topic? How have your sources affected your thinking on your topic? Do you need to adjust your **THESIS**? If so, how?

◆ 345–47

- Have you discovered new questions you need to investigate?

- Keep in mind your **RHETORICAL SITUATION** — have you found the information you need that will achieve your purpose, appeal to your audience, and suit your genre and medium?

■ 53

What is likely to emerge from this questioning is a combination of big ideas, including new ways of understanding your topic and insights into recent scholarship about it, and smaller ones, such as how two sources agree with each other but not completely and how the information in one source supports or undercuts the argument of another. These ideas and insights will become the basis for your own ideas and for what *you* have to say about the topic.

Synthesizing Ideas Using Notes

You may find that identifying connections among your sources is easier if you examine them together rather than reading them one by one. For example, taking notes on note cards and then laying the cards out on a desk or table (or on the floor) lets you see passages that seem related. Doing the same with photocopies or printouts of your sources can help you identify similarities as well.

In doing research for an essay arguing that the sale of assault weapons should be banned, you might find several sources that address the scope of U.S. citizens' right to bear arms. On the next page are notes taken on three such sources: Joe Klein, a journalist writing in *Time.com*; Antonin Scalia, a U.S. Supreme Court justice, quoted in an online news article; and Drew Westen, a professor of psychology writing in a blog sponsored by the *New York Times*. Though the writers hold very different views, juxtaposing these notes and highlighting certain passages shows a common thread running through the sources. In this example, all three sources might be used to support the thesis that restrictions on the owning of weapons — but not an outright ban — are both constitutional and necessary.

Source 1

Limits of gun ownership

Although the U. S. Constitution includes the right to bear arms, that right is not absolute. "No American has the right to own a stealth bomber or a nuclear weapon. Armor-piercing bullets are forbidden. The question is where you draw a reasonable bright line."
—Klein, "How the Gun Won" — quote

Source 4

Limits of gun ownership

Supreme Court Justice Antonin M. Scalia has noted that when the Constitution was written and ratified, some weapons were barred. So limitations could be put on owning some weapons, as long as the limits are consistent with those in force in 1789.
—Scalia, quoted in Woods — paraphrase

Source 3

Limits of gun ownership

Westen's "message consulting" research has shown that Americans are ambivalent about guns but react very positively to a statement of principle that includes both the right to own guns and restrictions on their ownership, such as prohibiting large ammunition clips and requiring all gun purchasers to undergo background checks for criminal behavior or mental illness.
—Westen — paraphrase

Synthesizing Information to Support Your Own Ideas

If you're doing research to write a **REPORT**, your own ideas will be communicated primarily through which information you decide to include from the sources you cite and how you organize that information. If you're writing a **TEXTUAL ANALYSIS**, your synthesis may focus on the themes, techniques, or other patterns you find. If you're writing a research-based **ARGUMENT**, on the other hand, your synthesis of sources must support the position you take in that argument. No matter what your genre, the challenge is to synthesize information from your research to develop ideas about your topic and then to support those ideas.

▲ 129–55

▲ 94–128

▲ 156–82

Entering the Conversation

As you read and think about your topic, you will come to an understanding of the concepts, interpretations, and controversies relating to your topic — and you'll become aware that there's a larger conversation going on. When you begin to find connections among your sources, you will begin to see your own place in that conversation, to discover your own ideas and your own stance on your topic. This is the exciting part of a research project, for when you write out your own ideas on the topic, you will find yourself entering that conversation. Remember that your **STANCE** as an author needs to be clear: simply stringing together the words and ideas of others isn't enough. You need to show readers *how* your source materials relate to one another and to your thesis.

■ 64–67

> **IF YOU NEED MORE HELP**
> See Chapter 49, **QUOTING, PARAPHRASING, AND SUMMARIZING**, for help in integrating source materials into your own text. See also Chapter 50 on **ACKNOWL-EDGING SOURCES, AVOIDING PLAGIARISM** for advice on giving credit to the sources you cite.

● 478–90

491–95

49 Quoting, Paraphrasing, and Summarizing

In an oral presentation about the rhetoric of Abraham Lincoln, you quote a memorable line from the Gettysburg Address. For an essay on the Tet Offensive in the Vietnam War, you paraphrase arguments made by several commentators and summarize some key debates about that war. When you work with the ideas and words of others, you need to clearly distinguish those ideas and words from your own and give credit to their authors. This chapter will help you with the specifics of quoting, paraphrasing, and summarizing source materials that you use in your writing.

Taking Notes

When you find material you think will be useful, take careful notes. How do you determine how much to record? You need to write down enough information so that when you refer to it later, you will be reminded of its main points and have a precise record of where it comes from.

- *Use a computer file, note cards, or a notebook,* labeling each entry with the information that will allow you to keep track of where it comes from—author, title, and the pages or the URL (or DOI [digital object identifier]). You needn't write down full bibliographic information (you can abbreviate the author's name and title) since you'll include that information in your WORKING BIBLIOGRAPHY.

441–43 ●

- *Take notes in your own words, and use your own sentence patterns.* If you make a note that is a detailed PARAPHRASE, label it as such so that you'll know to provide appropriate DOCUMENTATION if you use it.

483–86 ●
496–99

478

- *If you find wording that you'd like to quote,* be sure to enclose it in quotation marks to distinguish your source's words from your own. Double-check your notes to be sure any quoted material is accurately quoted—and that you haven't accidentally **PLAGIARIZED** your sources.

491–95

- *Label each note with a number to identify the source and a subject heading* to relate the note to a subject, supporting point, or other element in your essay. Doing this will help you to sort your notes easily and match them up with your rough outline. Restrict each note to a single subject.

Here are a few examples of one writer's notes on a source discussing synthetic dyes, bladder cancer, and the use of animals to determine what causes cancers. Each note includes a subject heading and brief source information and identifies whether the source is quoted or paraphrased.

Source 3

<u>Synthetic dyes</u>

The first synthetic dye was mauve, invented in 1854 and derived from coal. Like other coal-derived dyes, it contained aromatic amines.
Steingraber, "Pesticides," 976 —paraphrase

Source 3

<u>Synthetic dyes & cancer</u>

Bladder cancer was common among textile workers who used dyes. Steingraber: "By the beginning of the twentieth century, bladder cancer rates among this group of workers had skyrocketed."
Steingraber, "Pesticides," 976 — paraphrase and quote

> **Source 3**
>
> Synthetic dyes & cancer
>
> In 1938, Wilhelm Hueper exposed dogs to aromatic amines
> and showed that the chemical caused bladder cancer.
> Steingraber, "Pesticides," 976 —paraphrase

Deciding Whether to Quote, Paraphrase, or Summarize

298–300 ○
480–83 ●
483–86 ●
486–87 ●

When it comes time to **DRAFT**, you'll need to decide *how* to use any source you want to include—in other words, whether to quote, paraphrase, or summarize it. You might follow this rule of thumb: **QUOTE** texts when the wording is worth repeating or makes a point so well that no rewording will do it justice, when you want to cite the exact words of a known authority on your topic, when an authority's opinions challenge or disagree with those of others, or when the source is one you want to emphasize. **PARAPHRASE** sources that are not worth quoting but contain details you need to include. **SUMMARIZE** longer passages whose main points are important but whose details are not.

Quoting

Quoting a source is a way of weaving someone else's exact words into your text. You need to reproduce the source exactly, though you can modify it to omit unnecessary details (with ellipses) or to make it fit smoothly into your text (with brackets). You also need to distinguish quoted material from your own by enclosing short quotations in quotation marks, setting off
487–90 ●
longer quotes as a block, and using appropriate **SIGNAL PHRASES**.

Incorporate short quotations into your text, enclosed in quotation marks.
MLA 500–548 ●
If you are following **MLA STYLE**, short quotations are defined as four typed

academic literacies · rhetorical situations · genres · processes · strategies · research MLA / APA · media / design · readings · handbook

lines or fewer; if using **APA STYLE**, as below, short means fewer than forty words.

APA 549–89

> Gerald Graff (2003) has argued that colleges make the intellectual life seem more opaque than it needs to be, leaving many students with "the misconception that the life of the mind is a secret society for which only an elite few qualify" (p. 1).

If you are quoting three lines or fewer of poetry, run them in with your text, enclosed in quotation marks. Separate lines with slashes, leaving one space on each side of the slashes.

> Emma Lazarus almost speaks for the Statue of Liberty with the words inscribed on its pedestal: "Give me your tired, your poor, / Your huddled masses yearning to breathe free, / The wretched refuse of your teeming shore" (58).

Set off long quotations block style.   If you are using MLA style, set off quotations of five or more typed lines by indenting the quote one-half inch (or five spaces) from the left margin. If you are using APA style, indent quotations of forty or more words one-half inch (or five spaces) from the left margin. In either case, do not use quotation marks, and put any parenthetical documentation *after* any end punctuation.

> Nonprofit organizations such as Oxfam and Habitat for Humanity rely on visual representations of the poor. What better way to get our attention, asks rhetorician Diana George:
>
>> In a culture saturated by the image, how else do we convince Americans that—despite the prosperity they see all around them—there is real need out there? The solution for most nonprofits has been to show the despair. To do that they must represent poverty as something that can be seen and easily recognized: fallen down shacks and trashed out public housing, broken windows, dilapidated porches, barefoot kids with stringy hair, emaciated old women and men staring out at the camera with empty eyes. (210)

If you are quoting four or more lines of poetry, they need to be set off block style in the same way.

Indicate any omissions with ellipses. You may sometimes delete words from a quotation that are unnecessary for your point. Insert three ellipsis marks (leaving a space before the first and after the last one) to indicate the deletion. If you omit a sentence or more in the middle of a quotation, put a period before the three ellipsis dots. Be careful not to distort the source's meaning, however.

> Faigley points out that Gore's "Information Superhighway" metaphor "associated the economic prosperity of the 1950s and . . . 1960s facilitated by new highways with the potential for vast . . . commerce to be conducted over the Internet" (253).

> According to Welch, "Television is more acoustic than visual. . . . One can turn one's gaze away from the television, but one cannot turn one's ears from it without leaving the area where the monitor leaks its aural signals into every corner" (102).

Indicate additions or changes with brackets. Sometimes you'll need to change or add words in a quotation — to make the quotation fit grammatically within your sentence, for example, or to add a comment. In the following example, the writer changes the passage "one of our goals" to clarify the meaning of "our."

> Writing about the dwindling attention among some composition scholars to the actual teaching of writing, Susan Miller notes that "few discussions of writing pedagogy take it for granted that one of [writing teachers'] goals is to teach how to write" (480).

Here's an example of brackets used to add explanatory words to a quotation:

> Barbosa observes that Buarque's lyrics have long included "many a metaphor of *saudades* [yearning] so characteristic of *fado* music" (207).

Use punctuation correctly with quotations. When you incorporate a quotation into your text, you have to think about the end punctuation in the quoted material and also about any punctuation you need to add when you insert the quote into your own sentence.

Periods and commas. Put periods or commas *inside* closing quotation marks, except when you have parenthetical documentation at the end, in which case you put the period or comma after the parentheses.

> "Country music," Tichi says, "is a crucial and vital part of the American identity" (23).

After long quotations set off block style with no quotation marks, however, the period goes *before* the documentation, as in the example on page 481.

Question marks and exclamation points. These go *inside* closing quotation marks if they are part of the quoted material but *outside* when they are not. If there's parenthetical documentation at the end of the quotation, any punctuation that's part of your sentence comes after it.

> Speaking at a Fourth of July celebration in 1852, Frederick Douglass asked, "What have I, or those I represent, to do with your national independence?" (35).

> Who can argue with W. Charisse Goodman's observation that media images persuade women that "thinness equals happiness and fulfillment" (53)?

Colons and semicolons. These always go *outside* closing quotation marks.

> It's hard to argue with W. Charisse Goodman's observation that media images persuade women that "thinness equals happiness and fulfillment"; nevertheless, American women today are more overweight than ever (53).

Paraphrasing

When you paraphrase, you restate information from a source in your own words, using your own sentence structures. Paraphrase when the source material is important but the original wording is not. Because it includes all the main points of the source, a paraphrase is usually about the same length as the original.

Here is a paragraph about synthetic dyes and cancer, followed by two paraphrases of it that demonstrate some of the challenges of paraphrasing:

ORIGINAL SOURCE

In 1938, in a series of now-classic experiments, exposure to synthetic dyes derived from coal and belonging to a class of chemicals called aromatic amines was shown to cause bladder cancer in dogs. These results helped explain why bladder cancers had become so prevalent among dyestuffs workers. With the invention of mauve in 1854, synthetic dyes began replacing natural plant-based dyes in the coloring of cloth and leather. By the beginning of the twentieth century, bladder cancer rates among this group of workers had skyrocketed, and the dog experiments helped unravel this mystery. The International Labor Organization did not wait for the results of these animal tests, however, and in 1921 declared certain aromatic amines to be human carcinogens. Decades later, these dogs provided a lead in understanding why tire-industry workers, as well as machinists and metalworkers, also began falling victim to bladder cancer: aromatic amines had been added to rubbers and cutting oils to serve as accelerants and antirust agents.

—Sandra Steingraber, "Pesticides, Animals, and Humans"

The following paraphrase borrows too much of the language of the original or changes it only slightly, as the highlighted words and phrases show:

UNACCEPTABLE PARAPHRASE: WORDING TOO CLOSE

Now-classic experiments in 1938 showed that when dogs were exposed to aromatic amines, chemicals used in synthetic dyes derived from coal, they developed bladder cancer. Similar cancers were prevalent among dyestuffs workers, and these experiments helped to explain why. Mauve, a synthetic dye, was invented in 1854, after which cloth and leather manufacturers replaced most of the natural plant-based dyes with synthetic dyes. By the early twentieth century, this group of workers had skyrocketing rates of bladder cancer, a mystery the dog experiments helped to unravel. As early as 1921, though, before the test results proved the connection, the International Labor Organization had labeled certain aromatic amines carcinogenic. Even so, decades later many metalworkers, machinists, and tire-industry workers began developing bladder cancer. The animal tests helped researchers understand that rubbers and cutting oils contained aromatic amines as accelerants and antirust agents (Steingraber 976).

The next paraphrase uses original language but follows the sentence structure of Steingraber's text too closely:

UNACCEPTABLE PARAPHRASE: SENTENCE STRUCTURE TOO CLOSE

In 1938, several pathbreaking experiments showed that being exposed to synthetic dyes that are made from coal and belong to a type of chemicals called aromatic amines caused dogs to get bladder cancer. These results helped researchers identify why cancers of the bladder had become so common among textile workers who worked with dyes. With the development of mauve in 1854, synthetic dyes began to be used instead of dyes based on plants in the dyeing of leather and cloth. By the end of the nineteenth century, rates of bladder cancer among these workers had increased dramatically, and the experiments using dogs helped clear up this oddity. The International Labor Organization anticipated the results of these tests on animals, though, and in 1921 labeled some aromatic amines carcinogenic. Years later these experiments with dogs helped researchers explain why workers in the tire industry, as well as metalworkers and machinists, also started dying of bladder cancer: aromatic amines had been put into rubbers and cutting oils as rust inhibitors and accelerants (Steingraber 976).

Patchwriting, a third form of unacceptable paraphrase, combines the other two. Composition researcher Rebecca Moore Howard defines it as "copying from a source text and then deleting some words, altering grammatical structures, or plugging in one-for-one synonym-substitutes." Here is a patchwrite of the first two sentences of the original source: (The source's exact words are shaded in yellow; paraphrases are in blue.)

PATCHWRITE

Scientists have known for a long time that chemicals in the environment can cause cancer. For example, in 1938, in a series of important experiments, being exposed to synthetic dyes made out of coal and belonging to a kind of chemicals called aromatic amines was shown to cause dogs to develop bladder cancer. These experiments explain why this type of cancer had become so common among workers who handled dyes.

Here is an acceptable paraphrase of the entire passage:

ACCEPTABLE PARAPHRASE

Biologist Sandra Steingraber explains that pathbreaking experiments in 1938 demonstrated that dogs exposed to aromatic amines (chemicals used in coal-derived synthetic dyes) developed cancers of the bladder that were similar to cancers common among dyers in the textile industry. After mauve, the first synthetic dye, was invented in 1854, leather and cloth manufacturers replaced most natural dyes made from plants with synthetic dyes, and by the early 1900s textile workers had very high rates of bladder cancer. The experiments with dogs proved the connection, but years before, in 1921, the International Labor Organization had labeled some aromatic amines carcinogenic. Even so, years later many metal-workers, machinists, and workers in the tire industry started to develop unusually high rates of bladder cancer. The experiments with dogs helped researchers understand that the cancers were caused by aromatic amines used in cutting oils to inhibit rust and in rubbers as accelerants (976).

Some guidelines for paraphrasing

- *Use your own words and sentence structure.* It is acceptable to use some words from the original, but as much as possible, the phrasing and sentence structures should be your own.

487–90 ⬤

- *Introduce paraphrased text with* SIGNAL PHRASES.

- *Put in quotation marks any of the source's original phrasing that you use.*

- *Indicate the source.* Although the wording may be yours, the ideas and information come from another source; be sure to name the author

MLA 503–37 ⬤
APA 552–75
491–95

and include DOCUMENTATION to avoid the possibility of PLAGIARISM.

Summarizing

A summary states the main ideas in a source concisely and in your own words. Unlike a paraphrase, a summary does *not* present all the details, and it is generally as brief as possible. Summaries may boil down an entire

academic literacies · rhetorical situations · genres · processes · strategies · research MLA / APA · media / design · readings · handbook

book or essay into a single sentence, or they may take a paragraph or more to present the main ideas. Here, for example, is a one-sentence summary of the Steingraber paragraph:

> Steingraber explains that experiments with dogs demonstrated that aromatic amines, chemicals used in synthetic dyes, cutting oils, and rubber, cause bladder cancer (976).

In the context of an essay, the summary might take this form:

> Medical researchers have long relied on experiments using animals to expand understanding of the causes of disease. For example, biologist and ecologist Sandra Steingraber notes that in the second half of the nineteenth century, the rate of bladder cancer soared among textile workers. According to Steingraber, experiments with dogs demonstrated that synthetic chemicals in dyes used to color the textiles caused the cancer (976).

Some guidelines for summarizing

- *Include only the main ideas; leave out the details.* A summary should include just enough information to give the reader the gist of the original. It is always much shorter than the original, sometimes even as brief as one sentence.

- *Use your own words.* If you quote phrasing from the original, enclose the phrase in quotation marks.

- *Indicate the source.* Although the wording may be yours, the ideas and information come from another source. Name the author, either in a signal phrase or parentheses, and include an appropriate **IN-TEXT CITATION** to avoid the possibility of **PLAGIARISM**.

MLA 503–9

APA 552–75

491–95

Introducing Source Materials Using Signal Phrases

You need to introduce quotations, paraphrases, and summaries clearly, usually letting readers know who the author is—and, if need be, something about his or her credentials. Consider this sentence:

> Professor and textbook author Elaine Tyler May argues that many high school history books are too bland to interest young readers (531).

The beginning ("Professor and textbook author Elaine Tyler May argues") functions as a *signal phrase*, telling readers who is making the assertion and why she has the authority to speak on the topic—and making clear that everything between the signal phrase and the parenthetical citation comes from that source. Since the signal phrase names the author, the parenthetical citation includes only the page number; had the author not been identified in the signal phrase, she would have been named in the parentheses:

> Even some textbook authors believe that many high school history books are too bland to interest young readers (May 531).

MLA and APA have different conventions for constructing signal phrases. In MLA, the language you use in a signal phrase can be neutral — like *X says* or *Y thinks* or *according to Z*. Or it can suggest something about the **STANCE**—the source's or your own. The example above referring to the textbook author uses the verb *argues*, suggesting that what she says is open to dispute (or that the writer believes it is). How would it change your understanding if the signal verb were *observes* or *suggests*?

In addition to the names of sources' authors, signal phrases often give readers information about institutional affiliations and positions authors have, their academic or professional specialties, and any other information that lets readers judge the credibility of the sources. You should craft each signal phrase you use so as to highlight the credentials of the author. Here are some examples:

> A study done by Anthony M. Armocida, professor of psychology at Duke University, showed that . . .

The signal phrase identifies the source's author, his professional position, and his university affiliation, emphasizing his title.

> Science writer Isaac McDougal argues that . . .

This phrase acknowledges that the source's author may not have scholarly credentials but is a published writer; it's a useful construction if the source doesn't provide much information about the writer.

academic literacies · rhetorical situations · genres · processes · strategies · research MLA / APA · media / design · readings · handbook

Writing in *Psychology Today*, Amanda Chao-Fitz notes that . . .

This is the sort of signal phrase you use if you have no information on the author; you establish credibility on the basis of the publication in which the source appears.

If you're writing using APA style, signal phrases are typically briefer, giving only the author's last name and the date of publication:

According to Benzinger (2010), . . .

Quartucci (2011) observed that . . .

SOME COMMON SIGNAL VERBS

acknowledges	claims	disagrees	observes
admits	comments	disputes	points out
advises	concludes	emphasizes	reasons
agrees	concurs	grants	rejects
argues	confirms	illustrates	reports
asserts	contends	implies	responds
believes	declares	insists	suggests
charges	denies	notes	thinks

Verb tenses.   MLA and APA also have different conventions regarding the tenses of verbs in signal phrases. MLA requires present-tense verbs (*writes, asserts, notes*) in signal phrases to introduce a work you are quoting, paraphrasing, or summarizing.

In *Poor Richard's Almanack*, Benjamin Franklin notes, "He that cannot obey, cannot command" (739).

If, however, you are referring to the act of writing or saying something rather than simply quoting someone's words, you might not use the present tense. The writer of the following sentence focuses on the year in which the source was written—therefore, the verb is necessarily in the past tense:

> Back in 1941, Kenneth Burke <u>wrote</u> that "the ethical values of work are in its application of the competitive equipment to cooperative ends" (316).

If you are following APA style, use the past tense or present-perfect tense to introduce sources composed in the past.

> Dowdall, Crawford, and Wechsler (1998) <u>observed</u> that women attending women's colleges are less likely to engage in binge drinking than are women who attend coeducational colleges (p. 713).

APA requires the present tense, however, to discuss the results of an experiment or to explain conclusions that are generally agreed on.

> The findings of this study <u>suggest</u> that excessive drinking has serious consequences for college students and their institutions.

> The authors of numerous studies <u>agree</u> that smoking and drinking among adolescents are associated with lower academic achievement.

IF YOU NEED MORE HELP

See Chaper 50 for help **ACKNOWLEDGING SOURCES** and giving credit to the sources you use. See also the **SAMPLE RESEARCH PAPERS** to see how sources are cited in MLA and APA styles. And see Chapter 3 if you're writing a **SUMMARY/RESPONSE** essay.

491–95 ●
MLA 539–48 ●
APA 578–89
33–44 ✳

 academic literacies   rhetorical situations   genres   processes   strategies   research MLA / APA   media / design   readings   handbook

Acknowledging Sources, **50**
Avoiding Plagiarism

Whenever you do research-based writing, you find yourself entering a conversation—reading what many others have had to say about your topic, figuring out what you yourself think, and then putting what you think in writing—"putting in your oar," as the rhetorician Kenneth Burke once wrote. As a writer, you need to *acknowledge* any words and ideas that come from others—to give credit where credit is due, to recognize the various authorities and many perspectives you have considered, to show readers where they can find your sources, and to situate your own arguments in the ongoing conversation. Using other people's words and ideas without acknowledgment is *plagiarism,* a serious academic and ethical offense. This chapter will show you how to acknowledge the materials you use and avoid plagiarism.

Acknowledging Sources

When you insert in your text information that you've obtained from others, your reader needs to know where your source's words or ideas begin and end. Therefore, you should usually introduce a source by naming the author in a **SIGNAL PHRASE** and then provide brief **DOCUMENTATION** of the specific material from the source in a parenthetical reference following the material. (Sometimes you can put the author's name in the parenthetical reference as well.) You need only brief documentation of the source here, since your readers will find full bibliographic information about it in your list of **WORKS CITED** or **REFERENCES** .

487–90
MLA 503–9
APA 552–56

MLA 510–38
APA 557–75

Sources that need acknowledgment. You almost always need to acknowledge any information that you get from a specific source. Material you should acknowledge includes the following:

- *Direct quotations.* Unless they are well known (see p. 494 for some examples), any quotations from another source must be enclosed in quotation marks, cited with brief bibliographic information in parentheses, and usually introduced with a signal phrase that tells who wrote or said it and provides necessary contextual information, as in the following sentence:

  > In a dissenting opinion on the issue of racial preferences in college admissions, Supreme Court justice Ruth Bader Ginsburg argues, "The stain of generations of racial oppression is still visible in our society, and the determination to hasten its removal remains vital" (*Gratz v. Bollinger*).

- *Arguable statements and information that may not be common knowledge.* If you state something about which there is disagreement or for which arguments can be made, cite the source of your statement. If in doubt about whether you need to give the source of an assertion, provide it. As part of an essay on "fake news" programs, for example, you might make the following assertion:

  > The satire of *The Daily Show* complements the conservative bias of FOX News, since both have abandoned the stance of objectivity maintained by mainstream news sources, contends Michael Hoyt, executive editor of the *Columbia Journalism Review* (43).

Others might argue with the contention that the FOX News Channel offers biased reports of the news, so the source of this assertion needs to be acknowledged. In the same essay, you might present information that should be cited because it's not widely known, as in this example:

> According to a report by the Pew Research Center, 12 percent of Americans under thirty got information about the 2012 presidential campaign primarily from "fake news" and comedy shows like *The Daily Show* and *Saturday Night Live* (2).

academic literacies   rhetorical situations   genres   processes   strategies   research MLA / APA   media / design   readings   handbook

- *The opinions and assertions of others.* When you present the ideas, opinions, and assertions of others, cite the source. You may have rewritten the concept in your own words, but the ideas were generated by someone else and must be acknowledged, as they are here:

  > David Boonin, writing in the *Journal of Social Philosophy*, asserts that, logically, laws banning marriage between people of different races are not discriminatory since everyone of each race is affected equally by them. Laws banning same-sex unions are discriminatory, however, since they apply only to people with a certain sexual orientation (256).

- *Any information that you didn't generate yourself.* If you did not do the research or compile the data yourself, cite your source. This goes for interviews, statistics, graphs, charts, visuals, photographs—anything you use that you did not create. If you create a chart using data from another source, you need to cite that source.

- *Collaboration with and help from others.* In many of your courses and in work situations, you'll be called on to work with others. You may get help with your writing at your school's writing center or from fellow students in your writing courses. Acknowledging such collaboration or assistance, in a brief informational note, is a way of giving credit—and saying thank you. See guidelines for writing notes in the **MLA** and **APA** sections of this book.

MLA 509–10

APA 557

Sources that don't need acknowledgment.   Widely available information and common knowledge do not require acknowledgment. What constitutes common knowledge may not be clear, however. When in doubt, provide a citation, or ask your instructor whether the information needs to be cited. You generally do not need to cite the following:

- *Information that most readers are likely to know.* You don't need to acknowledge information that is widely known or commonly accepted as fact. For example, in a literary analysis, you wouldn't cite a source saying that Harriet Beecher Stowe wrote *Uncle Tom's Cabin*; you can assume your readers already know that. On the other hand, you should cite the source from which you got the information that the book was first published in installments in a magazine and then, with revisions, in book form, because that information isn't common knowledge. As you do research in areas you're not familiar with, be aware that what constitutes common knowledge isn't always clear; the history of the novel's publication would be known to Stowe scholars and would likely need no acknowledgment in an essay written for them. In this case, too, if you aren't sure whether to acknowledge information, do so.

- *Information and documents that are widely available.* If a piece of information appears in several sources or reference works or if a document has been published widely, you needn't cite a source for it. For example, the date when astronauts Neil Armstrong and Buzz Aldrin landed a spacecraft on the moon can be found in any number of reference works. Similarly, the Declaration of Independence and the Gettysburg Address are reprinted in thousands of sources, so the ones where you found them need no citation.

- *Well-known quotations.* These include such famous quotations as Lady Macbeth's "Out, damned spot!" and John F. Kennedy's "Ask not what your country can do for you; ask what you can do for your country." Be sure, however, that the quotation is correct. Winston Churchill is said to have told a class of schoolchildren, "Never, ever, ever, ever, ever, ever, ever give up. Never give up. Never give up. Never give up." His actual words, however, are much different and begin "Never give in."

- *Material that you created or gathered yourself.* You need not cite photographs that you took, graphs that you composed based on your own findings, or data from an experiment or survey that you conducted—though you should make sure readers know that the work is yours.

A good rule of thumb: *when in doubt, cite your source.* You're unlikely to be criticized for citing too much—but you may invite charges of plagiarism by citing too little.

Avoiding Plagiarism

When you use the words or ideas of others, you need to acknowledge who and where the material came from; if you don't credit those sources, you

academic literacies · rhetorical situations · genres · processes · strategies · research MLA / APA · media / design · readings · handbook

are guilty of plagiarism. Plagiarism is often committed unintentionally — as when a writer paraphrases someone else's ideas in language that is too close to the original. It is essential, therefore, to know what constitutes plagiarism: (1) using another writer's words or ideas without acknowledging the source, (2) using another writer's exact words without quotation marks, and (3) paraphrasing or summarizing someone else's ideas using language or sentence structures that are too close to theirs.

To avoid plagiarizing, take careful **NOTES** as you do your research, clearly labeling as quotations any words you quote directly and being careful to use your own phrasing and sentence structures in paraphrases and summaries. Be sure you know what source material you must **DOCUMENT**, and give credit to your sources, both in the text and in a list of **REFERENCES** or **WORKS CITED**.

● 475–76

● 496–99
● APA 557–75
● MLA 510–38

Be aware that it's easy to plagiarize inadvertently when you're working with online sources, such as full-text articles, that you've downloaded or cut and pasted into your notes. Keep careful track of these materials, since saving copies of your sources is so easy. Later, be sure to check your draft against the original sources to make sure your quotations are accurately worded — and take care, too, to include quotation marks and document the source correctly. Copying online material right into a document you are writing and forgetting to put quotation marks around it or to document it (or both) is all too easy to do. You must acknowledge information you find on the web just as you must acknowledge all other source materials.

And you must recognize that plagiarism has consequences. Scholars' work will be discredited if it too closely resembles another's. Journalists found to have plagiarized lose their jobs, and students routinely fail courses or are dismissed from their school when they are caught cheating—all too often by submitting as their own essays that they have purchased from online "research" sites. If you're having trouble completing an assignment, seek assistance. Talk with your instructor, or if your school has a writing center, go there for advice on all aspects of your writing, including acknowledging sources and avoiding plagiarism.

51 Documentation

In everyday life, we are generally aware of our sources: "I read it on Megan McArdle's blog." "Amber told me it's your birthday." "If you don't believe me, ask Mom." Saying how we know what we know and where we got our information is part of establishing our credibility and persuading others to take what we say seriously.

The goal of a research project is to study a topic, combining what we learn from sources with our own thinking and then composing a written text. When we write up the results of a research project, we cite the sources we use, usually by quoting, paraphrasing, or summarizing, and we acknowledge those sources, telling readers where the ideas came from. The information we give about sources is called documentation, and we provide it not only to establish our credibility as researchers and writers but also so that our readers, if they wish to, can find the sources themselves.

Understanding Documentation Styles

The Norton Field Guide covers the documentation styles of the Modern Language Association (MLA) and the American Psychological Association (APA). MLA style is used chiefly in the humanities; APA is used mainly in the social sciences. Both are two-part systems, consisting of (1) brief in-text parenthetical documentation for quotations, paraphrases, or summaries and (2) more-detailed documentation in a list of sources at the end of the text. MLA and APA require that the end-of-text documentation provide the following basic information about each source you cite:

- author, editor, or creator of the source
- title of source (and of publication or site where it appears)
- place of publication (for print sources; APA only)
- name of publisher
- date of publication
- retrieval information (for online sources)

MLA and APA are by no means the only documentation styles. Many other publishers and organizations have their own style, among them the University of Chicago Press and the Council of Science Editors. We focus on MLA and APA here because those are styles that college students are often required to use. On the following page are examples of how the two parts—the brief parenthetical documentation in your text and the more detailed information at the end—correspond in each of these systems.

The examples here and throughout this book are color-coded to help you see the crucial parts of each citation: brown for author and editor, yellow for title, and gray for publication information: place of publication, name of publisher, date of publication, page number(s), and so on.

As the examples of in-text documentation show, in either MLA or APA style you should name the author either in a signal phrase or in parentheses following the source information. But there are several differences between the two styles in the details of the documentation. In MLA, the author's full name is used in a signal phrase; in APA, only the last name is used. In APA, the abbreviation *p.* is used with the page number, which is provided only for a direct quotation; in MLA, a page number (if there is one) is always given, but with no abbreviation before it. Finally, in APA the date of publication always appears just after the author's name.

Comparing the MLA and APA styles of listing works cited or references also reveals some differences: MLA includes an author's first name while APA gives only initials; MLA puts the date near the end while APA places it right after the author's name; APA requires the place of publication while MLA usually does not; MLA capitalizes most of the words in a book's title and subtitle while APA capitalizes only the first words and proper nouns and proper adjectives in each.

MLA Style

IN-TEXT DOCUMENTATION

As Lester Faigley puts it, "The world has become a bazaar from which to shop for an individual 'lifestyle' " (12).

As one observer suggests, "The world has become a bazaar from which to shop for an individual 'lifestyle' " (Faigley 12).

WORKS-CITED DOCUMENTATION

Faigley, Lester. *Fragments of Rationality: Postmodernity and the Subject of Composition.* U of Pittsburgh P, 1992.

APA Style

IN-TEXT DOCUMENTATION

As Faigley (1992) suggested, "The world has become a bazaar from which to shop for an individual 'lifestyle'" (p. 12).

As one observer has noted, "The world has become a bazaar from which to shop for an individual 'lifestyle'" (Faigley, 1992, p. 12).

REFERENCE-LIST DOCUMENTATION

Faigley, L. (1992). *Fragments of rationality: Postmodernity and the subject of composition.* Pittsburgh, PA: University of Pittsburgh Press.

author   title   publication

Some of these differences are related to the nature of the academic fields in which the two styles are used. In humanities disciplines, the authorship of a text is emphasized, so both first and last names are included in MLA documentation. Scholarship in those fields may be several years old but still current, so the publication date doesn't appear in the in-text citation. In APA style, as in many documentation styles used in the sciences, education, and engineering, emphasis is placed on the date of publication because in these fields, more recent research is usually preferred over older studies. However, although the elements are arranged differently, both MLA and APA — and other documentation styles as well — require similar information about author, title, and publication.

52 MLA Style

MLA style calls for (1) brief in-text documentation and (2) complete bibliographic information in a list of works cited at the end of your text. The models and examples in this chapter draw on the eighth edition of the *MLA Handbook*, published by the Modern Language Association in 2016. For additional information, visit style.mla.org.

A DIRECTORY TO MLA STYLE

Formatting a Research Paper   538

Sample Research Paper   539

Throughout this chapter, you'll find models and examples that are color coded to help you see how writers include source information in their texts and in their lists of works cited: tan for author, editor, translator, and other contributors; yellow for titles; gray for publication information—date of publication, page number(s) or other location information, and so on.

IN-TEXT DOCUMENTATION

Brief documentation in your text makes clear to your reader what you took from a source and where in the source you found the information.

In your text, you have three options for citing a source: **QUOTING**, **PARAPHRASING**, and **SUMMARIZING**. As you cite each source, you will need to decide whether or not to name the author in a signal phrase—"as Toni Morrison writes"—or in parentheses—"(Morrison 24)."

478–90

The first examples below show basic in-text documentation of a work by one author. Variations on those examples follow. The examples illustrate the MLA style of using quotation marks around titles of short works and italicizing titles of long works.

1. AUTHOR NAMED IN A SIGNAL PHRASE

If you mention the author in a **SIGNAL PHRASE**, put only the page number(s) in parentheses. Do not write *page* or *p*.

487–90

> McCullough describes John Adams's hands as those of someone used to manual labor (18).

2. AUTHOR NAMED IN PARENTHESES

If you do not mention the author in a signal phrase, put his or her last name in parentheses along with the page number(s). Do not use punctuation between the name and the page number(s).

> Adams is said to have had "the hands of a man accustomed to pruning his own trees, cutting his own hay, and splitting his own firewood" (McCullough 18).

Whether you use a signal phrase and parentheses or parentheses only, try to put the parenthetical documentation at the end of the sentence or as close as possible to the material you've cited—without awkwardly interrupting the sentence. Notice that in the example above, the parenthetical reference comes after the closing quotation marks but before the period at the end of the sentence.

3. TWO OR MORE WORKS BY THE SAME AUTHOR

If you cite multiple works by one author, include the title of the work you are citing either in the signal phrase or in parentheses. Give the full title if it's brief; otherwise, give a short version.

> Kaplan insists that understanding power in the Near East requires "Western leaders who know when to intervene, and do so without illusions" (*Eastward* 330).

Put a comma between author and title if both are in the parentheses.

> Understanding power in the Near East requires "Western leaders who know when to intervene, and do so without illusions" (Kaplan, *Eastward* 330).

4. AUTHORS WITH THE SAME LAST NAME

Give the author's first and last names in any signal phrase, or add the author's first initial in the parenthetical reference.

author   title   publication

Imaginative applies not only to modern literature but also to writing of all periods, whereas *magical* is often used in writing about Arthurian romances (A. Wilson 25).

5. TWO OR MORE AUTHORS

For a work with two authors, name both, either in a signal phrase or in parentheses.

> Carlson and Ventura's stated goal is to introduce Julio Cortázar, Marjorie Agosín, and other Latin American writers to an audience of English-speaking adolescents (v).

For a work by three or more authors, name the first author followed by *et al.*

> One popular survey of American literature breaks the contents into sixteen thematic groupings (Anderson et al. A19-24).

6. ORGANIZATION OR GOVERNMENT AS AUTHOR

Acknowledge the organization either in a signal phrase or in parentheses. It's acceptable to shorten long names.

> The US government can be direct when it wants to be. For example, it sternly warns, "If you are overpaid, we will recover any payments not due you" (Social Security Administration 12).

7. AUTHOR UNKNOWN

If you don't know the author, use the work's title or a shortened version of the title in the parenthetical reference.

> A powerful editorial in last week's paper asserts that healthy liver donor Mike Hurewitz died because of "frightening" faulty postoperative care ("Every Patient's Nightmare").

8. LITERARY WORKS

When referring to literary works that are available in many different editions, give the page numbers from the edition you are using, followed by information that will let readers of any edition locate the text you are citing.

NOVELS. Give the page and chapter number, separated by a semicolon.

> In *Pride and Prejudice*, Mrs. Bennet shows no warmth toward Jane and Elizabeth when they return from Netherfield (105; ch. 12).

VERSE PLAYS. Give act, scene, and line numbers, separated with periods.

> Macbeth continues the vision theme when he says, "Thou hast no speculation in those eyes / Which thou dost glare with" (3.3.96-97).

POEMS. Give the part and the line numbers (separated by periods). If a poem has only line numbers, use the word *line(s)* only in the first reference.

> Whitman sets up not only opposing adjectives but also opposing nouns in "Song of Myself" when he says, "I am of old and young, of the foolish as much as the wise, / . . . a child as well as a man" (16.330-32).

> One description of the mere in *Beowulf* is "not a pleasant place" (line 1372). Later, it is labeled "the awful place" (1378).

9. WORK IN AN ANTHOLOGY

Name the author(s) of the work, not the editor of the anthology—either in a signal phrase or in parentheses.

> "It is the teapots that truly shock," according to Cynthia Ozick in her essay on teapots as metaphor (70).

> In *In Short: A Collection of Creative Nonfiction*, readers will find both an essay on Scottish tea (Hiestand) and a piece on teapots as metaphors (Ozick).

10. ENCYCLOPEDIA OR DICTIONARY

Acknowledge an entry in an encyclopedia or dictionary by giving the author's name, if available. For an entry without an author, give the entry's title in parentheses. If entries are arranged alphabetically, no page number is needed.

> According to *Funk & Wagnall's New World Encyclopedia*, early in his
> career Kubrick's main source of income came from "hustling chess
> games in Washington Square Park" ("Kubrick, Stanley").

11. LEGAL AND HISTORICAL DOCUMENTS

For legal cases and acts of law, name the case or act in a signal phrase or in parentheses. Italicize the name of a legal case.

> In 2005, the Supreme Court confirmed in *MGM Studios, Inc. v. Grokster,*
> *Ltd.* that peer-to-peer file sharing is copyright infringement.

Do not italicize the titles of laws, acts, or well-known historical documents such as the Declaration of Independence. Give the title and any relevant articles and sections in parentheses. It's fine to use common abbreviations such as *art.* or *sec.* and to abbreviate well-known titles.

> The president is also granted the right to make recess appointments
> (US Const., art. 2, sec. 2).

12. SACRED TEXT

When citing a sacred text such as the Bible or the Qur'an for the first time, give the title of the edition, and in parentheses give the book, chapter, and verse (or their equivalent), separated by periods. MLA recommends abbreviating the names of the books of the Bible in parenthetical references. Later citations from the same edition do not have to repeat its title.

> The wording from *The New English Bible* follows: "In the beginning of
> creation, when God made heaven and earth, the earth was without form
> and void, with darkness over the face of the abyss, and a mighty wind
> that swept over the surface of the waters" (Gen. 1.1-2).

13. MULTIVOLUME WORK

If you cite more than one volume of a multivolume work, each time you cite one of the volumes, give the volume *and* the page number(s) in parentheses, separated by a colon and a space.

> Sandburg concludes with the following sentence about those paying last
> respects to Lincoln: "All day long and through the night the unbroken
> line moved, the home town having its farewell" (4: 413).

If your works cited list includes only a single volume of a multivolume work, give just the page number in parentheses.

14. TWO OR MORE WORKS CITED TOGETHER

If you're citing two or more works closely together, you will sometimes need to provide a parenthetical reference for each one.

> Tanner (7) and Smith (viii) have looked at works from a cultural perspective.

If you include both in the same parentheses, separate the references with a semicolon.

> Critics have looked at both *Pride and Prejudice* and *Frankenstein* from
> a cultural perspective (Tanner 7; Smith viii).

15. SOURCE QUOTED IN ANOTHER SOURCE

When you are quoting text that you found quoted in another source, use the abbreviation *qtd. in* in the parenthetical reference.

> Charlotte Brontë wrote to G. H. Lewes: "Why do you like Miss Austen so
> very much? I am puzzled on that point" (qtd. in Tanner 7).

16. WORK WITHOUT PAGE NUMBERS

For works without page numbers, including many online sources, identify the source using the author or other information either in a signal phrase or in parentheses.

author   title   publication

> Studies show that music training helps children to be better at multitasking later in life ("Hearing the Music").

If the source has chapter, paragraph, or section numbers, use them with the abbreviations *ch., par.,* or *sec.*: ("Hearing the Music," par. 2). Alternatively, you can refer to a heading on a screen to help readers locate text.

> Under the heading "The Impact of the Railroad," Rawls notes that the transcontinental railroad was called an iron horse and a greedy octopus.

For an audio or a video recording, give the hours, minutes, and seconds (separated by colons) as shown on the player: (00:05-08:30).

17. AN ENTIRE WORK OR A ONE-PAGE ARTICLE

If you cite an entire work rather than a part of it, or if you cite a single-page article, there's no need to include page numbers.

> Throughout life, John Adams strove to succeed (McCullough).

NOTES

Sometimes you may need to give information that doesn't fit into the text itself —to thank people who helped you, to provide additional details, to refer readers to other sources, or to add comments about sources. Such information can be given in a *footnote* (at the bottom of the page) or an *endnote* (on a separate page with the heading *Notes* just before your works cited list). Put a superscript number at the appropriate point in your text, signaling to readers to look for the note with the corresponding number. If you have multiple notes, number them consecutively throughout your paper.

TEXT

> This essay will argue that small liberal arts colleges should not recruit athletes and, more specifically, that giving student athletes preferential treatment undermines the larger educational goals.[1]

NOTE

1. I want to thank all those who have contributed to my thinking on this topic, especially my classmates and my teacher Marian Johnson.

LIST OF WORKS CITED

A works cited list provides full bibliographic information for every source cited in your text. See page 539 for guidelines on formatting this list and page 547 for a sample works cited list.

Core Elements

The new MLA style provides a list of "core elements" for documenting sources, advising writers to list as many of them as possible in the order that MLA specifies. We've used these general principles to provide templates and examples for documenting 53 kinds of sources college writers most often need to cite, and the following general guidelines for how to treat each of the core elements.

AUTHORS AND OTHER CONTRIBUTORS

- If there is one author, list the name last name first: Morrison, Toni.

- If there are two authors, list the first author last name first and the second one first name first: Lunsford, Andrea, and Lisa Ede. Put their names in the order given in the work.

- If there are three or more authors, give the first author's name followed by *et al.*: Rose, Mike, et al.

- Include any middle names or initials: Heath, Shirley Brice; Toklas, Alice B.

- If you're citing an editor, translator, or others who are not authors, specify their role. For works with multiple contributors, put the one whose work you wish to highlight before the title, and list any others you want to mention after the title. For contributors named before the title, put the label after the name: Fincher, David, director. For

author   title   publication

those named after the title, specify their role first: directed by David Fincher.

TITLES

- Include any subtitles and capitalize all the words in titles and subtitles except for articles (*a, an, the*), prepositions (*to, at, from,* and so on), and coordinating conjunctions (*and, but, for, or, nor, yet*)—unless they are the first or last word of a title or subtitle.
- Italicize the titles of books, periodicals, and other long whole works (*Pride and Prejudice, Wired*), even if they are part of a larger work.
- Enclose in quotation marks the titles of short works and sources that are part of larger works: "Letter from Birmingham Jail."
- To document a source that has no title, describe it without italics or quotation marks: Letter to the author, Review of doo wop concert.

PUBLICATION INFORMATION

- Write publishers' names in full, but omit words like *Company* or *Inc.*
- For university presses, use *U* for "University" and *P* for "Press": Princeton UP, U of California P.

DATES

- Whether to give just the year or to include the month and day depends on the source. Give the full date that you find there.
- For books, give the year of publication: 1948. If a book lists more than one date, use the most recent one.
- Periodicals may be published annually, monthly, seasonally, weekly, or daily. Give the full date that you find in the periodical: 2011, Apr. 2011, Spring 2011, 16 Apr. 2011.
- Abbreviate the months except for May, June, and July: Jan., Feb., Mar., Apr., Aug., Sept., Oct., Nov., Dec.
- Because online sources often change or even disappear, provide the date on which you accessed them: Accessed 6 June 2015.

- If an online source includes the time when it was posted or modified, include the time along with the date: 18 Oct. 2005, 9:20 a.m.

LOCATION

- For most print articles and other short works, help readers locate the source by giving a page number or range of pages: p. 24, pp. 24-35. For those that are not on consecutive pages, give the first page number with a plus sign: pp. 24+.
- For online sources, give the URL, omitting *http://* or *https://*. If a source has a permalink, give that.
- For sources found in a database, give the DOI for any that have one. Otherwise, give the URL.
- For physical objects that you find in a museum, archive, or some other place, give the name of the place and its city: Menil Collection, Houston. Omit the city if it's part of the place's name: Boston Public Library.
- For performances or other live presentations, name the venue and its city: Mark Taper Forum, Los Angeles. Omit the city if it's part of the place's name: Berkeley Repertory Theatre.

PUNCTUATION

- Use a period after the author name(s) that start an entry (Morrison, Toni.) and the title of the source you're documenting (*Beloved*.)
- Use a comma between the author's last and first names: Morrison, Toni.
- Sometimes you'll need to provide information about more than one work for a single source—for instance, when you cite an article from a periodical that you access through a database. MLA refers to the periodical and database (or any other entity that holds a source) as "containers." Use commas between elements within each container and put a period at the end of each container. For example:

> Semuels, Alana. "The Future Will Be Quiet." *The Atlantic,* Apr. 2016,
>
>   pp. 19-20. *ProQuest,* search.proquest.com/docview/
>
>   1777443553?accountid+42654. Accessed 5 Apr. 2016.

author   title   publication

The guidelines below should help you document kinds of sources you're likely to use. The first section shows how to acknowledge authors and other contributors and applies to all kinds of sources—print, online, or others. Later sections show how to treat titles, publication information, location, and access information for many specific kinds of sources. In general, provide as much information as possible for each source—enough to tell readers how to find a source if they wish to access it themselves.

Authors and Other Contributors

When you name authors and other contributors in your citations, you are crediting them for their work and letting readers know who's in on the conversation. The following guidelines for citing authors and other contributors apply to all sources you cite: in print, online, or in some other media.

1. ONE AUTHOR

> Author's Last Name, First Name. *Title.* Publisher, Date.

> Anderson, Curtis. *The Long Tail: Why the Future of Business Is Selling Less of More.* Hyperion, 2006.

2. TWO AUTHORS

> 1st Author's Last Name, First Name, and 2nd Author's First and Last Names. *Title.* Publisher, Date.

> Lunsford, Andrea, and Lisa Ede. *Singular Texts/Plural Authors: Perspectives on Collaborative Writing.* Southern Illinois UP, 1990.

3. THREE OR MORE AUTHORS

> 1st Author's Last Name, First Name, et al. *Title.* Publisher, Date.

> Sebranek, Patrick, et al. *Writers INC: A Guide to Writing, Thinking, and Learning.* Write Source, 1990.

4. TWO OR MORE WORKS BY THE SAME AUTHOR

Give the author's name in the first entry, and then use three hyphens in the author slot for each of the subsequent works, listing them alphabetically by the first important word of each title.

> Author's Last Name, First Name. *Title That Comes First Alphabetically.*
> Publisher, Date.
>
> - - -. *Title That Comes Next Alphabetically.* Publisher, Date.
>
> Kaplan, Robert D. *The Coming Anarchy: Shattering the Dreams of the
> Post Cold War.* Random House, 2000.
>
> - - -. *Eastward to Tartary: Travels in the Balkans, the Middle East, and the
> Caucasus.* Random House, 2000.

5. AUTHOR AND EDITOR OR TRANSLATOR

> Author's Last Name, First Name. *Title.* Role by First and Last Names,
> Publisher, Date.
>
> Austen, Jane. *Emma.* Edited by Stephen M. Parrish, W. W. Norton, 2000.
>
> Dostoevsky, Fyodor. *Crime and Punishment.* Translated by Richard Pevear
> and Larissa Volokhonsky, Vintage Books, 1993.

Start with the editor or translator if you are focusing on their contribution rather than the author's.

> Pevear, Richard, and Larissa Volokhonsky, translators. *Crime and
> Punishment.* By Fyodor Dostoevsky, Vintage Books, 1993.

6. NO AUTHOR OR EDITOR

When there's no known author or editor, start with the title.

> *The Turner Collection in the Clore Gallery.* Tate Publications, 1987.
>
> "Being Invisible Closer to Reality." *The Atlanta Journal-Constitution,*
> 11 Aug. 2008, p. A3.

author   title   publication

7. ORGANIZATION OR GOVERNMENT AS AUTHOR

> Organization Name. *Title*. Publisher, Date.

> Diagram Group. *The Macmillan Visual Desk Reference*. Macmillan, 1993.

For a government publication, give the name of the government first, followed by the names of any department and agency.

> United States, Department of Health and Human Services, National
> Institute of Mental Health. *Autism Spectrum Disorders*.
> Government Printing Office, 2004.

When the organization is both author and publisher, start with the title and list the organization only as the publisher.

> *Stylebook on Religion 2000: A Reference Guide and Usage Manual*.
> Catholic News Service, 2002.

Articles and Other Short Works

Articles, essays, reviews, and other shorts works are found in journals, magazines, newspapers, other periodicals, and books—all of which you may find in print, online, or in a database. For most short works, you'll need to provide information about the author, the titles of both the short work and the longer work, any page numbers, and various kinds of publication information, all explained below.

8. ARTICLE IN A JOURNAL

PRINT

> Author's Last Name, First Name. "Title of Article." *Name of Journal*,
> Volume, Issue, Date, Pages.

Documentation Map (MLA)

Article in a Print Journal

Marge Simpson, Blue-Haired Housewife: ← Title of article
Defining Domesticity on *The Simpsons*

JESSAMYN NEUHAUS ← Author

MORE THAN TWENTY SEASONS AFTER ITS DEBUT AS A SHORT ON *THE Tracy Ullman Show* in 1989, pundits, politicians, scholars, journalists, and critics continue to discuss and debate the meaning and relevance of *The Simpsons* to American society. For academics and educators, the show offers an especially dense pop culture text, inspiring articles and anthologies examining *The Simpsons* in light of American religious life, the representation of homosexuality in cartoons, and the use of pop culture in the classroom, among many other topics (Dennis; Frank; Henry "The Whole World's Gone Gay"; Hobbs; Kristiansen). Philosophers and literary theorists in particular are intrigued by the quintessentially postmodern self-aware form and content of *The Simpsons* and the questions about identity, spectatorship, and consumer culture it raises (Alberti; Bybee and Overbeck; Glynn; Henry "The Triumph of Popular Culture"; Herron; Hull; Irwin et al.; Ott; Parisi).

Simpsons observers frequently note that this TV show begs one of the fundamental questions in cultural studies: can pop culture ever provide a site of individual or collective resistance or must it always ultimately function in the interests of the capitalist dominant ideology? Is *The Simpsons* a brilliant satire of virtually every cherished American myth about public and private life, offering dissatisfied Americans the opportunity to critically reflect on contemporary issues (Turner 435)? Or is it simply another TV show making money for the Fox Network? Is *The Simpsons* an empty, cynical, even nihilistic view of the world, lulling its viewers into laughing hopelessly at the pointless futility of

Volume ←

Name of journal → *The Journal of Popular Culture*, Vol. 43, No. 4, 2010 ← Year
© 2010, Wiley Periodicals, Inc.

Issue →

515–23
for more
on citing
articles
MLA style

Neuhaus, Jessamyn. "Marge Simpson, Blue-Haired Housewife: Defining Domesticity on *The Simpsons*." *The Journal of Popular Culture*, vol. 43, no. 4, 2010, pp. 761-81.

Cooney, Brian C. "Considering *Robinson Crusoe*'s 'Liberty of Conscience' in an Age of Terror." *College English,* vol. 69, no. 3, Jan. 2007, pp. 197-215.

ONLINE

Author's Last Name, First Name. "Title of Article." *Name of Journal,* Volume, Issue, Date, Pages (if any), URL. Accessed Day Month Year.

Gleckman, Jason. "Shakespeare as Poet or Playwright? The Player's Speech in *Hamlet." Early Modern Literary Studies,* vol. 11, no. 3, Jan. 2006, purl.oclc.org/emls/11-3/glechaml.htm. Accessed 31 Mar. 2015.

9. ARTICLE IN A MAGAZINE

PRINT

Author's Last Name, First Name. "Title of Article." *Name of Magazine,* Date, Pages.

Neyfakh, Leon. "The Future of Getting Arrested." *The Atlantic,* Jan.-Feb. 2015, pp. 26+.

ONLINE

Author's Last Name, First Name. "Title of Article." *Name of Magazine,* Date on web, Pages (if any), URL. Accessed Day Month Year.

Khazan, Olga. "Forgetting and Remembering Your First Language." *The Atlantic,* 24 July 2014, www.theatlantic.com/international/ archive/2014/07/learning-forgetting-and-remembering-your-first-language/374906/. Accessed 2 Apr. 2015.

10. ARTICLE IN A NEWSPAPER

PRINT

Author's Last Name, First Name. "Title of Article." *Name of Newspaper,*
Date, Pages.

Saulny, Susan, and Jacques Steinberg. "On College Forms, a Question of
Race Can Perplex." *The New York Times*, 14 June 2011, p. A1.

To document a particular edition of a newspaper, list the edition (*late ed.*,
natl. ed., and so on) after the date. If a section of the newspaper is numbered, put that detail after the edition information.

Burns, John F., and Miguel Helft. "Under Pressure, YouTube Withdraws
Muslim Cleric's Videos." *The New York Times,* 4 Nov. 2010, late ed.,
sec. 1, p. 13.

ONLINE

Author's Last Name, First Name. "Title of Article." *Name of Newspaper,*
Date on web, URL. Accessed Day Month Year.

Banerjee, Neela. "Proposed Religion-Based Program for Federal Inmates
Is Canceled." *The New York Times,* 28 Oct. 2006, www.nytimes.
com/2006/10/28/us/28prison.html?_r=0. Accessed 4 Apr. 2015.

11. ARTICLE ACCESSED THROUGH A DATABASE

Author's Last Name, First Name. "Title of Article." *Name of Periodical,*
Volume, Issue, Date, Pages. *Name of Database,* DOI or URL.
Accessed Day Month Year.

Stalter, Sunny. "Subway Ride and Subway System in Hart Crane's 'The
Tunnel.'" *Journal of Modern Literature,* vol. 33, no. 2, Jan. 2010,
pp. 70-91. *JSTOR*, doi: 10.2979/jml.2010.33.2.70. Accessed 30 Mar.
2015.

author   title   publication

Documentation Map (MLA)

Article in an Online Magazine

URL

Name of magazine

Title of article

Author

Date

529–31
for more
on citing
websites
MLA style

Segal, Michael. "The Hit Book That Came from Mars." *Nautilus*,
8 Jan. 2015, nautil.us/issue/20/creativity/the-hit-book-that-
came-from-mars. Accessed 10 Oct. 2016.

Documentation Map (MLA)

Journal Article Accessed through a Database

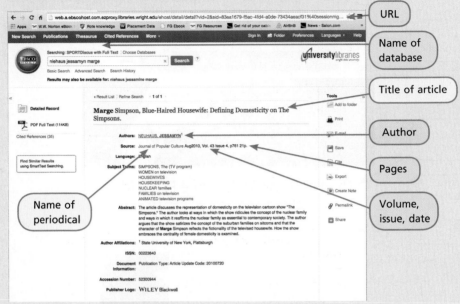

Neuhaus, Jessamyn. "Marge Simpson, Blue-Haired Housewife: Defining
    Domesticity on *The Simpsons*." *Journal of Popular Culture*, vol. 43,
    no. 4, Aug. 2010, pp. 761-81. *SPORT Discus with Full Text*, ezproxy.
    libraries.wright.edu/login?url=http://search.ebscohost.com/login.aspx?
    direct=true&db=a9h&AN=52300944&site=ehost-live. Accessed 24 Mar.
    2016.

12. ENTRY IN A REFERENCE WORK

PRINT

Author's Last Name, First Name (if any). "Title of Entry." *Title of Reference Book,* edited by Editor's First and Last Names (if any), Edition number, Publisher, Date, Pages.

"California." *The New Columbia Encyclopedia*, edited by William H. Harris and Judith S. Levey, 4th ed., Columbia UP, 1975, pp. 423-24.

"Feminism." *Longman Dictionary of American English*, Longman, 1983, p. 252.

If there's no author given, start with the title of the entry.

ONLINE

Document online reference works the same as print ones, adding the URL and access date after the date of publication.

"Baseball." *The Columbia Electronic Encyclopedia,* edited by Paul Lagassé, 6th ed., Columbia UP, 2012. www.infoplease.com/encyclopedia. Accessed 25 May 2016.

13. EDITORIAL

PRINT

"Title of Editorial." Editorial. *Name of Periodical,* Date, Page.

"Gas, Cigarettes Are Safe to Tax." Editorial. *The Lakeville Journal,* 17 Feb. 2005, p. A10.

ONLINE

"Title of Editorial." Editorial. *Name of Periodical,* Date on web, URL.
Accessed Day Month Year.

"Keep the Drinking Age at 21." Editorial. *Chicago Tribune*, 28 Aug.
2008, articles.chicagotribune.com/2008-08-26/news/0808250487_1_
binge-drinking-drinking-age-alcohol-related-crashes. Accessed
26 Apr. 2015.

14. LETTER TO THE EDITOR

Author's Last Name, First Name. "Title of Letter (if any)." Letter. *Name
of Periodical,* Date on web, URL. Accessed Day Month Year.

Pinker, Steven. "Language Arts." Letter. *The New Yorker,* 4 June 2012,
www.newyorker.com/magazine/2012/06/04/language-arts-2. Accessed
6 Apr. 2015.

15. REVIEW

PRINT

Reviewer's Last Name, First Name. "Title of Review." Review of *Title,* by
Author's First and Last Names. *Name of Periodical,* Date, Pages.

Frank, Jeffrey. "Body Count." Review of *The Exception,* by Christian
Jungersen. *The New Yorker,* 30 July 2007, pp. 86-87.

If a review has no author or title, start with what's being reviewed:

Review of *Ways to Disappear,* by Idra Novey. *The New Yorker,* 28 Mar.
2016, p. 79.

author   title   publication

ONLINE

Reviewer's Last Name, First Name. "Title of Review." Review of *Title,*
    by Author's First and Last Names. *Name of Periodical,* Date, URL.
    Accessed Day Month Year.

Donadio, Rachel. "Italy's Great, Mysterious Storyteller." Review
    of *My Brilliant Friend,* by Elena Ferrante. *The New York Review
    of Books,* 18 Dec. 2014, www.nybooks.com/articles/2014/
    12/18/italys-great-mysterious-storyteller. Accessed 28 Sept. 2015.

16. COMMENT ON AN ONLINE ARTICLE

Commenter. Comment on "Title of Article." *Name of Periodical,*
    Date posted, Time posted, URL. Accessed Day Month Year.

Nick. Comment on "The Case for Reparations." *The Atlantic,* 22 May
    2014, 3:04 p.m., www.theatlantic.com/business/archive/2014/05/
    how-to-comment-on-reparations/371422/#article-comments.
    Accessed 8 May 2015.

Books and Parts of Books

For most books, you'll need to provide information about the author, the
title, the publisher, and the year of publication. If you found the book
inside a larger volume, a database, or some other work, be sure to specify
that as well.

Documentation Map (MLA)
Print Book

523–29
for more
on citing
books
MLA style

Fontanella-Khan, Amana. *Pink Sari Revolution: A Tale of Women and Power in India.* W. W. Norton, 2013.

17. BASIC ENTRIES FOR A BOOK

PRINT

Author's Last Name, First Name. *Title*. Publisher, Year of publication.

Watson, Brad. *Miss Jane*. W. W. Norton, 2016.

EBOOK

Document an ebook as you would a print book, but add information about the ebook—or the type of ebook if you know it.

Watson, Brad. *Miss Jane*. Ebook, W. W. Norton, 2016.

Watson, Brad. *Miss Jane*. Kindle ed., W. W. Norton, 2016.

IN A DATABASE

Author's Last Name, First Name. *Title*. Publisher, Year of publication.
    Name of Database, DOI or URL. Accessed Day Month Year.

Anderson, Sherwood. *Winesburg, Ohio*. B. W. Huebsch, 1919.
    Bartleby.com, www.bartleby.com/156/. Accessed 8 Apr. 2015.

18. ANTHOLOGY

Last Name, First Name, editor. *Title*. Publisher, Year of publication.

Hall, Donald, editor. *The Oxford Book of Children's Verse in America*.
    Oxford UP, 1985.

19. WORK(S) IN AN ANTHOLOGY

Author's Last Name, First Name. "Title of Work." *Title of Anthology,*
    edited by First and Last Names, Publisher, Year of publication,
    Pages.

Achebe, Chinua. "Uncle Ben's Choice." *The Seagull Reader: Literature,*
    edited by Joseph Kelly, W. W. Norton, 2005, pp. 23-27.

TWO OR MORE WORKS FROM ONE ANTHOLOGY

Prepare an entry for each selection by author and title, followed by the anthology editors' last names and the pages of the selection. Then include an entry for the anthology itself (see no. 18).

> Author's Last Name, First Name. "Title of Work." Anthology Editors' Last Names, Pages.

> Hiestand, Emily. "Afternoon Tea." Kitchen and Jones, pp. 65-67.

> Ozick, Cynthia. "The Shock of Teapots." Kitchen and Jones, pp. 68-71.

20. MULTIVOLUME WORK

ALL VOLUMES

> Author's Last Name, First Name. Title of Work. Publisher, Year(s) of publication. Number of vols.

> Churchill, Winston. The Second World War. Houghton Mifflin, 1948-53. 6 vols.

SINGLE VOLUME

> Author's Last Name, First Name. Title of Work. Vol. number, Publisher, Year of publication. Number of vols.

> Sandburg, Carl. Abraham Lincoln: The War Years. Vol. 2, Harcourt, Brace & World, 1939. 4 vols.

21. BOOK IN A SERIES

> Author's Last Name, First Name. Title of Book. Edited by First and Last Names, Publisher, Year of publication. Series Title.

> Walker, Alice. Everyday Use. Edited by Barbara T. Christian, Rutgers UP, 1994. Women Writers: Texts and Contexts.

author   title   publication

22. GRAPHIC NARRATIVE

Author's Last Name, First Name. *Title*. Publisher, Year of publication.

Bechdel, Alison. *Fun Home: A Family Tragicomedy*. Houghton Mifflin, 2006.

If the work has both an author and an illustrator, start with the one whose work is more relevant to your research, and label the role of anyone who's not an author.

Pekar, Harvey. *Bob & Harv's Comics*. Illustrated by R. Crumb, Running
    Press, 1996.

Crumb, R., illustrator. *Bob & Harv's Comics*. By Harvey Pekar, Running
    Press, 1996.

23. SACRED TEXT

If you cite a specific edition of a religious text, you need to include it in your works cited list.

The New English Bible with the Apocrypha. Oxford UP, 1971.

The Torah: A Modern Commentary. Edited by W. Gunther Plaut, Union
    of American Hebrew Congregations, 1981.

24. EDITION OTHER THAN THE FIRST

Author's Last Name, First Name. *Title*. Name or number of edition,
    Publisher, Year of publication.

Fowler, H. W. *A Dictionary of Modern English*. 2nd ed., Oxford UP, 1965.

25. REPUBLISHED WORK

Author's Last Name, First Name. *Title*. Year of original publication.
    Current publisher, Year of republication.

Bierce, Ambrose. *Civil War Stories*. 1909. Dover, 1994.

26. FOREWORD, INTRODUCTION, PREFACE, OR AFTERWORD

Part Author's Last Name, First Name. Name of Part. *Title of Book,*
by Author's First and Last Names, Publisher, Year of publication,
Pages.

Tanner, Tony. Introduction. *Pride and Prejudice*, by Jane Austen, Penguin,
1972, pp. 7-46.

27. PUBLISHED LETTER

Letter Writer's Last Name, First Name. Letter to First and Last
Names. Day Month Year. *Title of Book,* edited by First and Last
Names, Publisher, Year of publication, Pages.

White, E. B. Letter to Carol Angell. 28 May 1970. *Letters of E. B. White,*
edited by Dorothy Lobarno Guth, Harper & Row, 1976, p. 600.

28. PAPER AT A CONFERENCE

PAPER PUBLISHED IN CONFERENCE PROCEEDINGS

Author's Last Name, First Name. "Title of Paper." *Title of Published
Conference Proceedings,* edited by First and Last Names, Publisher,
Year of publication, Pages.

Flower, Linda. "Literate Action." *Composition in the Twenty-first Century:
Crisis and Change,* edited by Lynn Z. Bloom et al., Southern Illinois
UP, 1996, pp. 249-60.

PAPER HEARD AT A CONFERENCE

Author's Last Name, First Name. "Title of Paper." *Title of Conference,*
Day Month Year, Location, City.

Hern, Katie. "Inside an Accelerated Reading and Writing Classroom."
Conference on Acceleration in Developmental Education, 15 June
2016, Sheraton Inner Harbor Hotel, Baltimore.

author   title   publication

29. DISSERTATION

> Author's Last Name, First Name. *Title.* Diss. Institution, Year, Publisher,
> Year of publication.

> Goggin, Peter N. *A New Literacy Map of Research and Scholarship in
> Computers and Writing.* Diss. Indiana U of Pennsylvania, 2000,
> University Microfilms International, 2001.

For an unpublished dissertation, put the title in quotation marks, and end
with the institution and the year.

> Kim, Loel. "Students Respond to Teacher Comments: A Comparison of
> Online Written and Voice Modalities." Diss. Carnegie Mellon U, 1998.

Websites

Many sources are available in multiple media—for example, a print periodical that is also on the web and contained in digital databases—but
some are published only on websites. This section covers the latter.

30. ENTIRE WEBSITE

> Last Name, First Name, role. *Title of Site.* Publisher, Date, URL.
> Accessed Day Month Year.

> Zalta, Edward N., principal editor. *Stanford Encyclopedia of Philosophy.*
> Metaphysics Research Lab, Center for the Study of Language, Stanford
> U, 1995-2015, plato.stanford.edu/index.html. Accessed 21 Apr. 2015.

PERSONAL WEBSITE

> Author's Last Name, First Name. *Title of Site.* Date, URL. Accessed Day
> Month Year.

> Heath, Shirley Brice. *Shirley Brice Heath.* 2015, shirleybriceheath.net.
> Accessed 6 June 2015.

Documentation Map (MLA)

Work on a Website

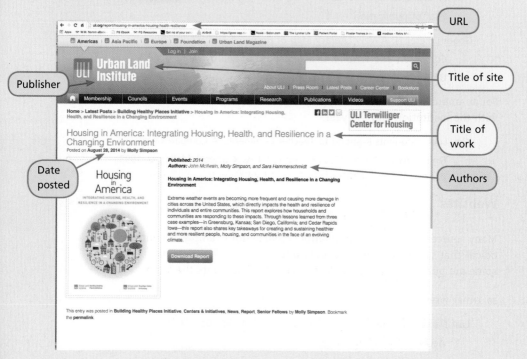

URL

Publisher

Title of site

Title of work

Date posted

Authors

McIlwain, John, et al. "Housing in America: Integrating Housing, Health, and Resilience in a Changing Environment." *Urban Land Institute*, Urban Land Institute, 28 Aug. 2014, uli.org/report/housing-in-america-housing-health-resilience. Accessed 17 Sept. 2015.

31. WORK ON A WEBSITE

> Author's Last Name, First Name (if any). "Title of Work." *Title of Site,*
>   Publisher, Date, URL. Accessed Day Month Year.

> "Global Minnesota: Immigrants Past and Present." *Immigration History*
>   *Research Center,* U of Minnesota, 2015, cla.umn.edu.ihrc. Accessed
>   25 May 2016.

32. BLOG ENTRY

> Author's Last Name, First Name. "Title of Blog Entry." *Title of*
>   *Blog,* Date, URL. Accessed Day Month Year.

> Hollmichel, Stefanie. "Bringing Up the Bodies." *So Many Books,* 10 Feb.
>   2014, somanybooksblog.com/2014/02/10/bring-up-the-bodies/.
>   Accessed 12 Feb. 2014.

Document a whole blog as you would an entire website (no. 30) and a comment on a blog as you would a comment on an online article (no. 16).

33. WIKI

> "Title of Entry." *Title of Wiki,* Publisher, Date, URL. Accessed Day Month
>   Year.

> "Pi." *Wikipedia,* Wikimedia Foundation, 28 Aug. 2013, en.wikipedia.org/
>   wiki/Pi. Accessed 25 Oct. 2013.

Personal Communication and Social Media

34. PERSONAL LETTER

> Sender's Last Name, First Name. Letter to the author. Day Month Year.

> Quindlen, Anna. Letter to the author. 11 Apr. 2013.

35. EMAIL

> Sender's Last Name, First Name. "Subject Line." Received by First and
>   Last Names, Day Month Year.

Smith, William. "Teaching Grammar—Some Thoughts." Received by
Richard Bullock, 19 Nov. 2013.

36. TEXT MESSAGE

Sender's Last Name, First Name. Text message. Received by First and Last
Names, Day Month Year.

Douglass, Joanne. Text message. Received by Kim Yi, 4 June 2015.

37. POST TO AN ONLINE FORUM

Author. "Subject line" or "Full text of short untitled post." *Name of
Forum,* Day Month Year, URL.

@somekiryu. "What's the hardest part about writing for you?" *Reddit,*
22 Apr. 2016, redd.it/4fyni0.

38. POST TO *TWITTER, FACEBOOK,* OR OTHER SOCIAL MEDIA

Author. "Full text of short untitled post" or "Title" or Descriptive label.
Name of Site, Day Month Year, Time, URL.

@POTUS (Barack Obama). "I'm proud of the @NBA for taking a stand
against gun violence. Sympathy for victims isn't enough—change
requires all of us speaking up." *Twitter,* 23 Dec. 2015, 1:21 p.m.,
twitter.com/POTUS/status/679773729749078016.

Black Lives Matter. "Rise and Grind! Did you sign this petition yet?
We now have a sign on for ORGANIZATIONS to lend their
support." *Facebook,* 23 Oct. 2015, 11:30 a.m., www.facebook.com/
BlackLivesMatter/photos/a.294807204023865.1073741829.
180212755483311/504711973033386/?type=3&theater.

@quarterlifepoetry. Illustrated poem about girl at Target. *Instagram,*
22 Jan. 2015, www.instagram.com/p/yLO6fSurRH/.

Audio, Visual, and Other Sources

39. ADVERTISEMENT

PRINT

Name of Product or Company. Advertisement or Description of ad.
    Title of Periodical, Date, Page.

Cal Alumni Association. Sports Merchandise ad. *California,* Spring 2016, p. 3.

AUDIO OR VIDEO

Name of Product or Company. Advertisement or Description of ad.
    Date. *Name of Host Site,* URL. Accessed Day Month Year.

Chrysler. Super Bowl commercial. 6 Feb. 2011. *YouTube,*
    www.youtube.com/watch?v=SKLZ254Y_jtc. Accessed 1 May 2015.

40. ART

ORIGINAL

Artist's Last Name, First Name. *Title of Art.* Year created, Site, City.

Van Gogh, Vincent. *The Potato Eaters.* 1885, Van Gogh Museum, Amsterdam.

REPRODUCTION

Artist's Last Name, First Name. *Title of Art.* Year created. *Title of Book,*
    by First and Last Names, Publisher, Year of publication, Page.

Van Gogh, Vincent. *The Potato Eaters.* 1885. *History of Art: A Survey of*
    the Major Visual Arts from the Dawn of History to the Present Day,
    by H. W. Janson, Prentice-Hall/Harry N. Abrams, 1969, p. 508.

ONLINE

Artist's Last Name, First Name. *Title of Art.* Year created. *Name of Site,*
    URL. Accessed Day Month Year.

Warhol, Andy. *Self-portrait.* 1979. *J. Paul Getty Museum,* www.getty.
    edu/art/collection/objects/106971/andy-warhol-self-portrait-
    american-1979/. Accessed 20 Jan. 2015.

41. CARTOON

PRINT

Author's Last Name, First Name. "Title of Cartoon." *Title of Periodical*, Date, Page.

Chast, Roz. "The Three Wise Men of Thanksgiving." *The New Yorker*, 1 Dec. 2003, p. 174.

ONLINE

Author's Last Name, First Name. "Title of Cartoon." *Title of Site*, Date, URL. Accessed Day Month Year.

Munroe, Randall. "Up Goer Five." *xkcd*, 12 Nov. 2012, xkcd.com/1133/. Accessed 22 Apr. 2015.

42. SUPREME COURT CASE

First Plaintiff v. First Defendant. *United States Reports* citation. Name of Court, Year of decision, URL. Accessed Day Month Year.

District of Columbia v. Heller. 554 US 570. Supreme Court of the US, 2008, www.lawcornell.edu/supct/html/07-290.ZS.html. Accessed 3 June 2016.

43. FILM

Name individuals based on the focus of your project—the director, the screenwriter, the cinematographer, or someone else.

Title of Film. Role by First and Last Names, Production Studio, Date.

Breakfast at Tiffany's. Directed by Blake Edwards, Paramount, 1961.

STREAMING

Title of Film. Role by First and Last Names, Production Studio, Date. *Streaming Service*, URL. Accessed Day Month Year.

Interstellar. Directed by Christopher Nolan, Paramount, 2014. *Amazon Prime Video*, www.amazon.com/Interstellar-Matthew-McConaughey/dp/B00TU9UFTS. Accessed 2 May 2015.

44. INTERVIEW

If the interview has a title, put it in quotation marks following the subject's name.

BROADCAST

Subject's Last Name, First Name. Interview or "Title of Interview."
    Title of Program, Network, Day Month Year.

Gates, Henry Louis, Jr. Interview. *Fresh Air,* NPR, 9 Apr. 2002.

PUBLISHED

Subject's Last Name, First Name. Interview or "Title of Interview." *Title
    of Publication,* Date, Pages.

Stone, Oliver. Interview. *Esquire,* Nov. 2004, pp. 170-71.

PERSONAL

Subject's Last Name, First Name. Personal interview. Day Month Year.

Roddick, Andy. Personal interview. 17 Aug. 2013.

45. MAP

"Title of Map." Publisher, URL. Accessed Day Month Year.

"National Highway System." US Department of Transportation Federal
    Highway Administration, www.fhwa.dot.gov/planning/images/nhs.pdf.
    Accessed 10 May 2015.

46. MUSICAL SCORE

Composer's Last Name, First Name. *Title of Composition.* Year of
    composition. Publisher, Year of publication.

Stravinsky, Igor. *Petrushka.* 1911. W. W. Norton, 1967.

47. ONLINE VIDEO

Author's Last Name, First Name. *Title. Name of Host Site,* Date, URL.
    Accessed Day Month Year.

Westbrook, Adam. *Cause/Effect: The Unexpected Origins of Terrible Things.* *Vimeo*, 9 Sept. 2014, vimeo.com/105681474. Accessed 20 Dec. 2015.

48. ORAL PRESENTATION

Presenter's Last Name, First Name. "Title of Presentation." Sponsoring Institution, Date, Location.

Cassin, Michael. "Nature in the Raw—The Art of Landscape Painting." Berkshire Institute for Lifelong Learning, 24 Mar. 2005, Clark Art Institute, Williamstown.

49. PODCAST

If you accessed a podcast online, give the URL and date of access; if you accessed it through a service such as *iTunes* or *Spotify*, indicate that instead.

Last Name, First Name, role. "Title of Episode." *Title of Program,* season, episode, Sponsor, Date, URL. Accessed Day Month Year.

Koenig, Sarah, host. "DUSTWUN." *Serial,* season 2, episode 1, WBEZ, 10 Dec. 2015, serialpodcast.org/season-two/1/dustwun. Accessed 23 Apr. 2016.

Foss, Gilad, writer and performer. "Aquaman's Brother-in-Law." *Superhero Temp Agency,* season 1, episode 1, 16 Apr. 2015. *iTunes.*

50. RADIO PROGRAM

Last Name, First Name, role. "Title of Episode." *Title of Program,* Station, Day Month Year of broadcast, URL. Accessed Day Month Year.

Glass, Ira, host. "In Defense of Ignorance." *This American Life*, WBEZ, 22 Apr. 2016, thisamericanlife.org/radio-archives/episode/585/ in-defense-of-ignorance. Accessed 2 May 2016.

51. SOUND RECORDING

ONLINE

Last Name, First Name. "Title of Work." *Title of Album,* Distributor, Date. *Name of Audio Service.*

Simone, Nina. "To Be Young, Gifted and Black." *Black Gold*, RCA Records,
1969. *Spotify*.

CD

Last Name, First Name. "Title of Work." *Title of Album,* Distributor, Date.

Brown, Greg. "Canned Goods." *The Live One,* Red House, 1995.

52. TV SHOW

ORIGINAL BROADCAST

"Title of Episode." *Title of Show,* role by First and Last Names,
season, episode, Network, Day Month Year.

"The Silencer." *Criminal Minds,* written by Erica Messer, season 8,
episode 1, NBC, 26 Sept. 2012.

DVD

"Title of Episode." Broadcast Year. *Title of DVD,* role by First and Last
Names, season, episode, Production Studio, Release Year, disc number.

"The Pants Tent." 2003. *Curb Your Enthusiasm: Season One*, performance
by Larry David, season 1, episode 1, HBO Video, 2006, disc 1.

ONLINE

"Title of Episode." *Title of Show,* season, episode, role by First and Last
Names (if any), Production Studio, Day Month Year. *Name of Host
Site,* URL. Accessed Day Month Year.

"Shadows in the Glass." *Marvel's Daredevil*, season 1, episode 8, Netflix,
10 Apr. 2015. *Netflix*, www.netflix.com/watch/80018198?trackId
=13752289&tctx=0%2C7%2Cbcfd6259-6e64-4d51-95ab-2a9f747e-
abf0-158552415. Accessed 3 Nov. 2015.

53. VIDEO GAME

Last Name, First Name, role. *Title of Game.* Distributor, Date of release.
Gaming System or Platform.

Metzen, Chris, and James Waugh, writers. *StarCraft II: Legacy of the Void*. Blizzard Entertainment, 2015. OS X.

FORMATTING A RESEARCH PAPER

Name, course, title.   MLA does not require a separate title page. In the upper left-hand corner of your first page, include your name, your professor's name, the name of the course, and the date. Center the title of your paper on the line after the date; capitalize it as you would a book title.

Page numbers.   In the upper right-hand corner of each page, one-half inch below the top of the page, include your last name and the page number. Number pages consecutively throughout your paper.

Font, spacing, margins, and indents.   Choose a font that is easy to read (such as Times New Roman) and that provides a clear contrast between regular and italic text. Double-space the entire paper, including your works cited list. Set one-inch margins at the top, bottom, and sides of your text; do not justify your text. The first line of each paragraph should be indented one-half inch from the left margin.

Long quotations.   When quoting more than three lines of poetry, more than four lines of prose, or dialogue between characters in a drama, set off the quotation from the rest of your text, indenting it one-half inch (or five spaces) from the left margin. Do not use quotation marks, and put any parenthetical documentation *after* the final punctuation.

In *Eastward to Tartary*, Kaplan captures ancient and contemporary Antioch for us:

> At the height of its glory in the Roman-Byzantine age, when it had an amphitheater, public baths, aqueducts, and sewage pipes, half a million people lived in Antioch. Today the population is only 125,000. With sour relations between Turkey and Syria, and unstable politics throughout the Middle East, Antioch is now a backwater — seedy and tumbledown, with relatively few tourists. I found it altogether charming. (123)

author   title   publication

In the first stanza of Arnold's "Dover Beach," the exclamations make clear
that the speaker is addressing someone who is also present in the scene:

> Come to the window, sweet is the night air!
>
> Only, from the long line of spray
>
> Where the sea meets the moon-blanched land,
>
> Listen! You hear the grating roar
>
> Of pebbles which the waves draw back, and fling. (6-10)

Be careful to maintain the poet's line breaks. If a line does not fit on one
line of your paper, put the extra words on the next line. Indent that line
an additional quarter inch (or two spaces).

Illustrations.   Insert illustrations close to the text that discusses them.
For tables, provide a number (*Table* 1) and a title on separate lines above
the table. Below the table, provide a caption and information about the
source. For graphs, photos, and other figures, provide a figure number
(*Fig.* 1), caption, and source information below the figure. If you give only
brief source information (such as a parenthetical note), or if the source is
cited elsewhere in your text, include it in your list of works cited. Be sure
to make clear how any illustrations relate to your point.

List of Works Cited.   Start your list on a new page, following any notes.
Center the title and double-space the entire list. Begin each entry at the
left margin, and indent subsequent lines one-half inch (or five spaces).
Alphabetize the list by authors' last names (or by editors' or translators'
names, if appropriate). Alphabetize works with no author or editor by
title, disregarding *A*, *An*, and *The*. To cite more than one work by a single
author, list them as in no. 4 on page 514.

SAMPLE RESEARCH PAPER

The following report was written by Dylan Borchers for a first-year writing
course. It's formatted according to the guidelines of the MLA (style.mla.org).

Last name and page number.

Borchers 1

Dylan Borchers

Professor Bullock

English 102, Section 4

4 May 2012

Title centered.

Against the Odds:

Harry S. Truman and the Election of 1948

Double-spaced throughout.

Just over a week before Election Day in 1948, a *New York Times* article noted "[t]he popular view that Gov. Thomas E.

No page number needed for one-page source.

Dewey's election as President is a foregone conclusion" (Egan). This assessment of the race between incumbent Democrat Harry S. Truman and Dewey, his Republican challenger, was echoed a week later when *Life* magazine published a photograph whose caption labeled Dewey "The Next President" (Photo of Truman 37). In a *Newsweek* survey of fifty prominent political writers, each one predicted Truman's defeat, and *Time* correspondents declared that Dewey would carry 39 of the 48 states (Donaldson 210). Nearly every major media outlet across the United States endorsed Dewey and lambasted Truman. As historian Robert H. Ferrell observes, even

Author named in signal phrase, page number in parentheses.

Truman's wife, Bess, thought he would be beaten (270).

The results of an election are not so easily predicted, as the famous photograph in fig. 1 shows. Not only did Truman win the election, but he won by a significant margin, with 303 electoral votes and 24,179,259 popular votes, compared to Dewey's 189 electoral votes and 21,991,291 popular votes (Donaldson 204-07). In fact, many historians and political analysts argue that Truman

Borchers   2

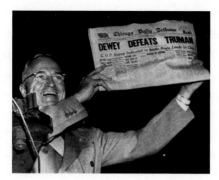

Fig. 1. President Harry S. Truman holds up an edition of the *Chicago Daily Tribune* that mistakenly announced "Dewey Defeats Truman" (Rollins).

Illustration is positioned close to the text to which it relates, with figure number, caption, and parenthetical documentation.

would have won by an even greater margin had third-party Progressive candidate Henry A. Wallace not split the Democratic vote in New York State and Dixiecrat Strom Thurmond not won four states in the South (McCullough 711). Although Truman's defeat was heavily predicted, those predictions themselves, Dewey's passiveness as a campaigner, and Truman's zeal turned the tide for a Truman victory.

     In the months preceding the election, public opinion polls predicted that Dewey would win by a large margin. Pollster Elmo Roper stopped polling in September, believing there was no reason to continue, given a seemingly inevitable Dewey landslide. Although the margin narrowed as the election drew near, the other pollsters

1″

predicted a Dewey win by at least 5 percent (Donaldson 209). Many historians believe that these predictions aided the president in the long run. First, surveys showing Dewey in the lead may have prompted some of Dewey's supporters to feel overconfident about their candidate's chances and therefore to stay home from the polls on Election Day. Second, these same surveys may have energized Democrats to mount late get-out-the-vote efforts ("1948 Truman-Dewey Election"). Other analysts believe that the overwhelming predictions of a Truman loss also kept at home some Democrats who approved of Truman's policies but saw a Truman loss as inevitable. According to political analyst Samuel Lubell, those Democrats may have saved Dewey from an even greater defeat (Hamby, *Man* 465). Whatever the impact on the voters, the polling numbers had a decided effect on Dewey.

Historians and political analysts alike cite Dewey's overly cautious campaign as one of the main reasons Truman was able to achieve victory. Dewey firmly believed in public opinion polls. With all indications pointing to an easy victory, Dewey and his staff believed that all he had to do was bide his time and make no foolish mistakes. Dewey himself said, "When you're leading, don't talk" (Smith 30). Each of Dewey's speeches was well crafted and well rehearsed. As the leader in the race, he kept his remarks faultlessly positive, with the result that he failed to deliver a solid message or even mention Truman or any of Truman's policies. Eventually, Dewey began to be perceived as aloof and stuffy. One

No signal phrase; author and page number in parentheses.

Paragraphs indented $\frac{1}{2}$ inch or 5 spaces.

Borchers   4

observer compared him to the plastic groom on top of a wedding
cake (Hamby, "Harry S. Truman"), and others noted his stiff, cold
demeanor (McCullough 671–74).

> Two works cited within the same sentence.

As his campaign continued, observers noted that Dewey
seemed uncomfortable in crowds, unable to connect with ordinary
people. And he made a number of blunders. One took place at a
train stop when the candidate, commenting on the number of
children in the crowd, said he was glad they had been let out of
school for his arrival. Unfortunately for Dewey, it was a Saturday
("1948: The Great Truman Surprise"). Such gaffes gave voters the
feeling that Dewey was out of touch with the public.

> Title used when there's no known author.

Again and again through the autumn of 1948, Dewey's
campaign speeches failed to address the issues, with the candidate
declaring that he did not want to "get down in the gutter" (Smith
515). When told by fellow Republicans that he was losing ground,
Dewey insisted that his campaign not alter its course. Even *Time*
magazine, though it endorsed and praised him, conceded that
his speeches were dull (McCullough 696). According to historian
Zachary Karabell, they were "notable only for taking place, not for
any specific message" (244). Dewey's numbers in the polls slipped
in the weeks before the election, but he still held a comfortable
lead over Truman. It would take Truman's famous whistle-stop
campaign to make the difference.

Few candidates in US history have campaigned for the
presidency with more passion and faith than Harry Truman. In

the autumn of 1948, he wrote to his sister, "It will be the greatest campaign any President ever made. Win, lose, or draw, people will know where I stand" (91). For thirty-three days, Truman traveled the nation, giving hundreds of speeches from the back of the *Ferdinand Magellan* railroad car. In the same letter, he described the pace: "We made about 140 stops and I spoke over 147 times, shook hands with at least 30,000 and am in good condition to start out again tomorrow for Wilmington, Philadelphia, Jersey City, Newark, Albany and Buffalo" (91). McCullough writes of Truman's campaign:

> No President in history had ever gone so far in quest of support from the people, or with less cause for the effort, to judge by informed opinion. . . . As a test of his skills and judgment as a professional politician, not to say his stamina and disposition at age sixty-four, it would be like no other experience in his long, often difficult career, as he himself understood perfectly. More than any other event in his public life, or in his presidency thus far, it would reveal the kind of man he was. (655)

He spoke in large cities and small towns, defending his policies and attacking Republicans. As a former farmer and relatively late bloomer, Truman was able to connect with the public. He developed an energetic style, usually speaking from notes rather than from a prepared speech, and often mingled with the crowds that met his train. These crowds grew larger as the campaign

Quotations of more than 4 lines indented $\frac{1}{2}$ inch (5 spaces) and double-spaced.

Parenthetical reference after final punctuation.

progressed. In Chicago, over half a million people lined the streets as he passed, and in St. Paul the crowd numbered over 25,000. When Dewey entered St. Paul two days later, he was greeted by only 7,000 supporters ("1948 Truman-Dewey Election"). Reporters brushed off the large crowds as mere curiosity seekers wanting to see a president (McCullough 682). Yet Truman persisted, even if he often seemed to be the only one who thought he could win. By going directly to the American people and connecting with them, Truman built the momentum needed to surpass Dewey and win the election.

The legacy and lessons of Truman's whistle-stop campaign continue to be studied by political analysts, and politicians today often mimic his campaign methods by scheduling multiple visits to key states, as Truman did. He visited California, Illinois, and Ohio 48 times, compared with 6 visits to those states by Dewey. Political scientist Thomas M. Holbrook concludes that his strategic campaigning in those states and others gave Truman the electoral votes he needed to win (61, 65).

The 1948 election also had an effect on pollsters, who, as Elmo Roper admitted, "couldn't have been more wrong." *Life* magazine's editors concluded that pollsters as well as reporters and commentators were too convinced of a Dewey victory to analyze the polls seriously, especially the opinions of undecided voters (Karabell 256). Pollsters assumed that undecided voters would vote in the same proportion as decided voters—and that turned out to be a false assumption (Karabell 257). In fact, the lopsidedness of the polls might have led voters who supported Truman to call themselves undecided out of an unwillingness to associate themselves with the losing side, further skewing the polls' results (McDonald et al. 152). Such errors led pollsters to change their methods significantly after the 1948 election.

Work by 3 or more authors is shortened using et al.

After the election, many political analysts, journalists, and historians concluded that the Truman upset was in fact a victory for the American people, who, the *New Republic* noted, "couldn't be ticketed by the polls, knew its own mind and had picked the rather unlikely but courageous figure of Truman to carry its banner" (T.R.B. 3). How "unlikely" is unclear, however; Truman biographer Alonzo Hamby notes that "polls of scholars consistently rank Truman among the top eight presidents in American history" (*Man* 641). But despite Truman's high standing, and despite the fact that the whistle-stop campaign is now part of our political landscape, politicians have increasingly imitated the style of the Dewey campaign, with its "packaged candidate who ran so as not to lose, who steered clear of controversy, and who made a good show of appearing presidential" (Karabell 266). The election of 1948 shows that voters are not necessarily swayed by polls, but it may have presaged the packaging of candidates by public relations experts, to the detriment of public debate on the issues in future presidential elections.

1″

Works Cited

Donaldson, Gary A. *Truman Defeats Dewey*. UP of Kentucky, 1999.

Egan, Leo. "Talk Is Now Turning to the Dewey Cabinet." *The New York Times*, 20 Oct. 1948, p. 8E, www.nytimes.com/timesmachine/1948/10/26/issue.html. Accessed 18 Apr. 2012.

Ferrell, Robert H. *Harry S. Truman: A Life*. U of Missouri P, 1994.

Hamby, Alonzo L., editor. "Harry S. Truman: Campaigns and Elections." *American President*, Miller Center, U of Virginia, 11 Jan. 2012, millercenter.org/president/biography/truman-campaigns-and-elections. Accessed 17 Mar. 2012.

- - -. *Man of the People: A Life of Harry S. Truman*. Oxford UP, 1995.

Holbrook, Thomas M. "Did the Whistle-Stop Campaign Matter?" *PS: Political Science and Politics*, vol. 35, no. 1, Mar. 2002, pp. 59-66.

Karabell, Zachary. *The Last Campaign: How Harry Truman Won the 1948 Election*. Alfred A. Knopf, 2000.

McCullough, David. *Truman*. Simon and Schuster, 1992.

McDonald, Daniel G., et al. "The Spiral of Silence in the 1948 Presidential Election." *Communication Research*, vol. 28, no. 2, Apr. 2001, pp. 139-55.

"1948: The Great Truman Surprise." *The Press and the Presidency*, Dept. of Political Science and International Affairs, Kennesaw State U, 29 Oct. 2003, kennesaw.edu/pols.3380/pres/1984.html. Accessed 10 Apr. 2012.

Heading centered.

Double-spaced.

Alphabetized by authors' last names.

Each entry begins at the left margin; subsequent lines are indented.

Multiple works by a single author listed alphabetically by title. For second and subsequent works, replace author's name with three hyphens.

Sources beginning with numerals are alphabetized as if the number were spelled out.

"1948 Truman-Dewey Election." *American Political History*, Eagleton
　　　　Institute of Politics, Rutgers, State U of New Jersey,
　　　　1995-2012, www.eagleton.rutgers.edu/research/
　　　　americanhistory/ap_trumandewey.php. Accessed 18 Apr. 2012.

Photo of Truman in San Francisco. *Life*, 1 Nov. 1948, p. 37. *Google
　　　　Books*, books.google.com/books?id=ekoEAAAAMBAJ&printsec=
　　　　frontcover#v=onepage&q&f=false. Accessed 20 Apr. 2012.

Rollins, Byron. "President Truman with *Chicago Daily Tribune*
　　　　Headline of 'Dewey Defeats Truman.'" Associated Press,
　　　　4 Nov. 1948. *Harry S. Truman Library & Museum*, www.
　　　　trumanlibrary.org/photographs/view.php?id=25248. Accessed
　　　　20 Apr. 2012.

Roper, Elmo. "Roper Eats Crow; Seeks Reason for Vote Upset."
　　　　Evening Independent, 6 Nov. 1948, p. 10. *Google News*, news.
　　　　google.com/newspapers?nid=PZE8UkGerEcC&dat=19481106&
　　　　printsec=frontpage&hl=en. Accessed 13 Apr. 2012.

Smith, Richard Norton. *Thomas E. Dewey and His Times*. Simon and
　　　　Schuster, 1982.

T.R.B. "Washington Wire." *The New Republic*, 15 Nov. 1948, pp. 3-4.
　　　　EBSCOhost, search.ebscohost.com/login.aspx?direct=true&db
　　　　=tsh&AN=14779640&site=ehost-live. Accessed 20 Apr. 2012.

Truman, Harry S. "Campaigning, Letter, October 5, 1948." *Harry S.
　　　　Truman*, edited by Robert H. Ferrell, CQ P, 2003, p. 91.

A range of
dates is given
for web projects
developed over a
period of time.

Every source
used is in the list
of works cited.

APA Style **53**

American Psychological Association (APA) style calls for (1) brief documentation in parentheses near each in-text citation and (2) complete documentation in a list of references at the end of your text. Throughout this chapter, you'll find models and examples that are color-coded to help you see how writers include source information in their texts and reference lists: brown for author or editor, yellow for title, gray for publication information: place of publication, publisher, date of publication, page number(s), and so on. These models and examples draw on the *Publication Manual of the American Psychological Association*, 6th edition (2009). Additional information is available at www.apastyle.org.

A DIRECTORY TO APA STYLE

In-Text Documentation   552

author   title   publication

IN-TEXT DOCUMENTATION

Brief documentation in your text makes clear to your reader precisely what you took from a source and, in the case of a quotation, precisely where (usually, on which page) in the source you found the text you are quoting.

478–90

PARAPHRASES and SUMMARIES are more common than QUOTATIONS in APA-style projects. As you cite each source, you will need to decide whether to name the author in a signal phrase—"as McCullough (2001) wrote"— or in parentheses—"(McCullough, 2001)." Note that APA requires you to use the past tense or present perfect tense for verbs in SIGNAL PHRASES:

487–90

"Moss (2003) argued," "Moss (2003) has argued."

1. AUTHOR NAMED IN A SIGNAL PHRASE

If you are quoting, you must give the page number(s). You are not required to give the page number(s) with a paraphrase or a summary, but APA encourages you to do so, especially if you are citing a long or complex work; most of the models in this chapter do include page numbers.

AUTHOR QUOTED

Put the date in parentheses right after the author's name; put the page in parentheses as close to the quotation as possible.

> McCullough (2001) described John Adams as having "the hands of a man accustomed to pruning his own trees, cutting his own hay, and splitting his own firewood" (p. 18).

Notice that in this example, the parenthetical reference with the page number comes *after* the closing quotation marks but *before* the period at the end of the sentence.

AUTHOR PARAPHRASED OR SUMMARIZED

Put the date in parentheses right after the author's name; follow the date with the page.

John Adams's hands were those of a laborer, according to McCullough (2001, p. 18).

2. AUTHOR NAMED IN PARENTHESES

If you do not mention an author in a signal phrase, put his or her name, a comma, and the year of publication in parentheses as close as possible to the quotation, paraphrase, or summary.

AUTHOR QUOTED

Give the author, date, and page in one parenthesis, or split the information between two parentheses.

> One biographer (McCullough, 2001) has said John Adams had "the hands of a man accustomed to pruning his own trees, cutting his own hay, and splitting his own firewood" (p. 18).

AUTHOR PARAPHRASED OR SUMMARIZED

Give the author, date, and page in one parenthesis toward the beginning or the end of the paraphrase or summary.

> John Adams's hands were those of a laborer (McCullough, 2001, p. 18).

3. AUTHORS WITH THE SAME LAST NAME

If your reference list includes more than one person with the same last name, include initials in all documentation to distinguish the authors from one another.

> Eclecticism is common in contemporary criticism (J. M. Smith, 1992, p. vii).

4. TWO AUTHORS

Always mention both authors. Use *and* in a signal phrase, but use an ampersand (&) in parentheses.

Carlson and Ventura (1990) wanted to introduce Julio Cortázar, Marjorie Agosín, and other Latin American writers to an audience of English-speaking adolescents (p. v).

According to the Peter Principle, "In a hierarchy, every employee tends to rise to his level of incompetence" (Peter & Hull, 1969, p. 26).

5. THREE OR MORE AUTHORS

In the first reference to a work by three to five persons, name all contributors. Use *and* in a signal phrase, but use an ampersand (&) in parentheses. In subsequent references, name the first author followed by *et al.*, Latin for "and others." Whenever you refer to a work by six or more contributors, name only the first author, followed by *et al.* (See no. 4.)

Faigley, George, Palchik, and Selfe (2004) have argued that where there used to be a concept called *literacy*, today's multitude of new kinds of texts has given us *literacies* (p. xii).

Peilen et al. (1990) supported their claims about corporate corruption with startling anecdotal evidence (p. 75).

6. ORGANIZATION OR GOVERNMENT AS AUTHOR

If an organization has a long name that is recognizable by its abbreviation, give the full name and the abbreviation the first time you cite the source. In subsequent references, use only the abbreviation. If the organization does not have a familiar abbreviation, always use its full name.

FIRST REFERENCE

(American Psychological Association [APA], 2008)

SUBSEQUENT REFERENCES

(APA, 2008)

author   title   publication

7. AUTHOR UNKNOWN

Use the complete title if it is short; if it is long, use the first few words of the title under which the work appears in the reference list.

> *Webster's New Biographical Dictionary* (1988) identifies William James as "American psychologist and philosopher" (p. 520).

> A powerful editorial asserted that healthy liver donor Mike Hurewitz died because of "frightening" faulty postoperative care ("Every Patient's Nightmare," 2007).

8. TWO OR MORE WORKS CITED TOGETHER

If you cite multiple works in the same parenthesis, place them in the order that they appear in your reference list, separated by semicolons.

> Many researchers have argued that what counts as "literacy" is not necessarily learned at school (Heath, 1983; Moss, 2003).

9. TWO OR MORE WORKS BY AN AUTHOR IN THE SAME YEAR

If your list of references includes more than one work by the same author published in the same year, order them alphabetically by title, adding lowercase letters ("a," "b," and so on) to the year.

> Kaplan (2000a) described orderly shantytowns in Turkey that did not resemble the other slums he visited.

10. SOURCE QUOTED IN ANOTHER SOURCE

When you cite a source that was quoted in another source, let the reader know that you used a secondary source by adding the words *as cited in*.

> During the meeting with the psychologist, the patient stated repeatedly that he "didn't want to be too paranoid" (as cited in Oberfield & Yasik, 2004, p. 294).

11. WORK WITHOUT PAGE NUMBERS

Instead of page numbers, some electronic works have paragraph numbers, which you should include (preceded by the abbreviation *para.*) if you are referring to a specific part of such a source. In sources with neither page nor paragraph numbers, refer readers to a particular part of the source if possible, perhaps indicating a heading and the paragraph under the heading.

> Russell's dismissals from Trinity College at Cambridge and from City
> College in New York City have been seen as examples of the controversy
> that marked his life (Irvine, 2006, para. 2).

12. AN ENTIRE WORK

You do not need to give a page number if you are directing readers' attention to an entire work.

> Kaplan (2000) considered Turkey and Central Asia explosive.

When you are citing an entire website, give the URL in the text. You do not need to include the website in your reference list. To cite part of a website, see no. 20 on page 566.

> Beyond providing diagnostic information, the website for the Alzheimer's
> Association includes a variety of resources for family and community
> support of patients suffering from Alzheimer's disease (http://www.alz.org).

13. PERSONAL COMMUNICATION

Document email, telephone conversations, interviews, personal letters, messages from nonarchived discussion sources, and other personal texts as *personal communication*, along with the person's initial(s), last name, and the date. You do not need to include such personal communications in your reference list.

> L. Strauss (personal communication, December 6, 2013) told about
> visiting Yogi Berra when they both lived in Montclair, New Jersey.

author   title   publication

NOTES

You may need to use content notes to give an explanation or information that doesn't fit into your text. To signal a content note, place a superscript numeral at the appropriate point in your text. If you have multiple notes, number them consecutively throughout your text. Put the notes themselves on a separate page with the heading *Notes*, after your reference list. Here is an example from *In Search of Solutions: A New Direction in Psychotherapy* (2003).

TEXT WITH SUPERSCRIPT

An important part of working with teams and one-way mirrors is taking the consultation break, as at Milan, BFTC, and MRI.[1]

CONTENT NOTE

[1]It is crucial to note here that while working within a team is fun, stimulating, and revitalizing, it is not necessary for successful outcomes. Solution-oriented therapy works equally well when working solo.

REFERENCE LIST

A reference list provides full bibliographic information for every source cited in your text with the exception of entire websites and personal communications. See page 578 for guidelines on preparing such a list; for a sample reference list see pages 588–89.

Print Books

For most books, you'll need to provide the author, the publication date, the title and any subtitle, and the place of publication and publisher.

IMPORTANT DETAILS FOR DOCUMENTING PRINT BOOKS

- **AUTHORS**: Use the author's last name, but replace the first and middle names with initials (D. Kinder for Donald Kinder).

- **DATES**: If more than one year is given, use the most recent one.

- **TITLES**: Capitalize only the first word and proper nouns and proper adjectives in titles and subtitles.

- **PUBLICATION PLACE**: Give city followed by state (abbreviated) or country, if outside the United States (for example, Boston, MA; London, England; Toronto, Ontario, Canada). If more than one city is given, use the first. Do not include the state or country if the publisher is a university whose name includes that information.

- **PUBLISHER**: Use a shortened form of the publisher's name (Little, Brown for Little, Brown and Company), but retain *Association*, *Books*, and *Press* (American Psychological Association, Princeton University Press).

1. ONE AUTHOR

Author's Last Name, Initials. (Year of publication). *Title*. Publication City, State or Country: Publisher.

Louis, M. (2003). *Moneyball: The art of winning an unfair game*. New York, NY: Norton.

2. TWO OR MORE WORKS BY THE SAME AUTHOR

If the works were published in different years, list them chronologically.

Lewis, B. (1995). *The Middle East: A brief history of the last 2,000 years*. New York, NY: Scribner.

Lewis, B. (2003). *The crisis of Islam: Holy war and unholy terror*. New York, NY: Modern Library.

If the works were published in the same year, list them alphabetically by title, adding "a," "b," and so on to the year (see p. 560).

author   title   publication

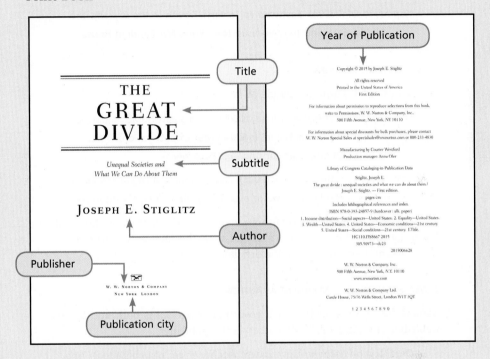

Documentation Map (APA)

Print Book

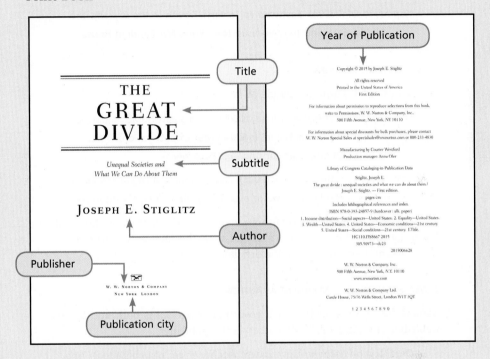

Title → THE GREAT DIVIDE

Subtitle → Unequal Societies and What We Can Do About Them

Author → JOSEPH E. STIGLITZ

Publisher → W. W. NORTON & COMPANY NEW YORK LONDON

Publication city

Year of Publication → Copyright © 2015 by Joseph E. Stiglitz

All rights reserved
Printed in the United States of America
First Edition

For information about permission to reproduce selections from this book,
write to Permissions, W. W. Norton & Company, Inc.,
500 Fifth Avenue, New York, NY 10110

For information about special discounts for bulk purchases, please contact
W. W. Norton Special Sales at specialsales@wwnorton.com or 800-233-4830

Manufacturing by Courier Westford
Production manager: Anna Oler

Library of Congress Cataloging-in-Publication Data

Stiglitz, Joseph E.
The great divide : unequal societies and what we can do about them /
Joseph E. Stiglitz. — First edition.
pages cm
Includes bibliographical references and index.
ISBN 978-0-393-24857-9 (hardcover : alk. paper)
1. Income distribution—Social aspects—United States. 2. Equality—United States.
3. Wealth—United States. 4. United States—Economic conditions—21st century.
5. United States—Social conditions—21st century. I. Title.
HC110.I5S8667 2015
305.50973—dc23
2015006628

W. W. Norton & Company, Inc.
500 Fifth Avenue, New York, N.Y. 10110
www.wwnorton.com

W. W. Norton & Company Ltd.
Castle House, 75/76 Wells Street, London W1T 3QT

1 2 3 4 5 6 7 8 9 0

557–63
for more on
citing books
APA style

Stiglitz, J. E. (2015). *The great divide: Unequal societies and what we can do about them.* New York, NY: Norton.

Kaplan, R. D. (2000a). *The coming anarchy: Shattering the dreams of the post cold war.* New York, NY: Random House.

Kaplan, R. D. (2000b). *Eastward to Tartary: Travels in the Balkans, the Middle East, and the Caucasus.* New York, NY: Random House.

3. TWO OR MORE AUTHORS

For two to seven authors, include all names.

First Author's Last Name, Initials, Next Author's Last Name, Initials, & Final Author's Last Name, Initials. (Year of publication). *Title.* Publication City, State or Country: Publisher.

Leavitt, S. D., & Dubner, S. J. (2005). *Freakonomics: A rogue economist explores the hidden side of everything.* New York, NY: Morrow.

For a work by eight or more authors, name just the first six authors, followed by three ellipsis points, and end with the final author (see no. 21 for an example from a magazine article).

4. ORGANIZATION OR GOVERNMENT AS AUTHOR

Sometimes an organization or a government agency is both author and publisher. If so, use the word *Author* as the publisher.

Organization Name or Government Agency. (Year of publication). *Title.* Publication City, State or Country: Publisher.

Catholic News Service. (2002). *Stylebook on religion 2000: A reference guide and usage manual.* Washington, DC: Author.

5. AUTHOR AND EDITOR

Author's Last Name, Initials. (Year of edited edition). *Title.* (Editor's Initials Last Name, Ed.). Publication City, State or Country: Publisher. (Original work[s] published year[s])

Dick, P. F. (2008). *Five novels of the 1960s and 70s.* (J. Lethem, Ed.). New York, NY: Library of America. (Original works published 1964-1977)

6. EDITED COLLECTION

First Editor's Last Name, Initials, Next Editor's Last Name, Initials, & Final Editor's Last Name, Initials. (Eds.). (Year of edited edition). *Title.* Publication City, State or Country: Publisher.

Raviv, A., Oppenheimer, L., & Bar-Tal, D. (Eds.). (1999). *How children understand war and peace: A call for international peace education.* San Francisco, CA: Jossey-Bass.

7. WORK IN AN EDITED COLLECTION

Author's Last Name, Initials. (Year of publication). Title of article or chapter. In Initials Last Name (Ed.), *Title* (pp. pages). Publication City, State or Country: Publisher.

Harris, I. M. (1999). Types of peace education. In A. Raviv, L. Oppenheimer, & D. Bar-Tal (Eds.), *How children understand war and peace: A call for international peace education* (pp. 46-70). San Francisco, CA: Jossey-Bass.

8. UNKNOWN AUTHOR

Title. (Year of publication). Publication City, State or Country: Publisher.

Webster's new biographical dictionary. (1988). Springfield, MA: Merriam-Webster.

If the title page of a work lists the author as *Anonymous,* treat the reference-list entry as if the author's name were Anonymous, and alphabetize it accordingly.

9. EDITION OTHER THAN THE FIRST

Author's Last Name, Initials. (Year). *Title* (name or number ed.). Publication City, State or Country: Publisher.

Burch, D. (2008). *Emergency navigation: Find your position and shape your course at sea even if your instruments fail* (2nd ed.). Camden, ME: International Marine/McGraw-Hill.

10. TRANSLATION

Author's Last Name, Initials. (Year of publication). *Title* (Translator's Initials Last Name, Trans.). Publication City, State or Country: Publisher. (Original work published Year)

Hugo, V. (2008). *Les misérables* (J. Rose, Trans.). New York, NY: Modern Library. (Original work published 1862)

11. MULTIVOLUME WORK

Author's Last Name, Initials. (Year). *Title* (Vols. numbers). Publication City, State or Country: Publisher.

Nastali, D. P., & Boardman, P. C. (2004). *The Arthurian annals: The tradition in English from 1250 to 2000* (Vols. 1-2). New York, NY: Oxford University Press USA.

ONE VOLUME OF A MULTIVOLUME WORK

Author's Last Name, Initials. (Year). *Title of whole work (Vol. number).* Publication City, State or Country: Publisher.

Spiegelman, A. (1986). *Maus* (Vol. 1). New York, NY: Random House.

12. ARTICLE IN A REFERENCE BOOK

UNSIGNED

Title of entry. (Year). In *Title of reference book* (Name or number ed., Vol. number, pp. pages). Publication City, State or Country: Publisher.

Macrophage. (2003). In *Merriam-Webster's collegiate dictionary* (11th ed., p. 745). Springfield, MA: Merriam-Webster.

author   title   publication

SIGNED

Author's Last Name, Initials. (Year). Title of entry. In *Title of reference book* (Vol. number, pp. pages). Publication City, State or Country: Publisher.

Wasserman, D. E. (2006). Human exposure to vibration. In *International encyclopedia of ergonomics and human factors* (Vol. 2, pp. 1800-1801). Boca Raton, FL: CRC.

Print Periodicals

For most articles, you'll need to provide information about the author; the date; the article title and any subtitle; the periodical title; and any volume or issue number and inclusive page numbers.

IMPORTANT DETAILS FOR DOCUMENTING PRINT PERIODICALS

- **AUTHORS:** List authors as you would for a book (see pp. 558–60).
- **DATES:** For journals, give year only. For magazines and newspapers, give year followed by a comma and then month or month and day.
- **TITLES:** Capitalize article titles as you would for a book. Capitalize the first and last words and all principal words of periodical titles. Do not capitalize *a*, *an*, *the*, or any prepositions or coordinating conjunctions unless they begin the title of the periodical.
- **VOLUME AND ISSUE:** For journals and magazines, give volume or volume and issue, depending on the journal's pagination method. For newspapers, do not give volume or issue.
- **PAGES:** Use *p.* or *pp.* for a newspaper article but not for a journal or magazine article. If an article does not fall on consecutive pages, give all the page numbers (for example, 45, 75-77 for a journal or magazine; pp. C1, C3, C5-C7 for a newspaper).

13. ARTICLE IN A JOURNAL PAGINATED BY VOLUME

Author's Last Name, Initials. (Year). Title of article. *Title of Journal, volume*, pages.

Gremer, J. R., Sala, A., & Crone, E. E. (2010). Disappearing plants: Why they hide and how they return. *Ecology, 91*, 3407-3413.

14. ARTICLE IN A JOURNAL PAGINATED BY ISSUE

Author's Last Name, Initials. (Year). Title of article. *Title of Journal, volume*(issue), pages.

Weaver, C., McNally, C., & Moerman, S. (2001). To grammar or not to grammar: That is *not* the question! *Voices from the Middle, 8*(3), 17-33.

15. ARTICLE IN A MAGAZINE

If a magazine is published weekly, include the day and the month. If there are a volume number and an issue number, include them after the magazine title.

Author's Last Name, Initials. (Year, Month Day). Title of article. *Title of Magazine, volume*(issue), page(s).

Gregory, S. (2008, June 30). Crash course: Why golf carts are more hazardous than they look. *Time, 171*(26), 53.

If a magazine is published monthly, include the month(s) only.

16. ARTICLE IN A NEWSPAPER

If page numbers are consecutive, separate them with a hyphen. If not, separate them with a comma.

Author's Last Name, Initials. (Year, Month Day). Title of article. *Title of Newspaper*, p(p). page(s).

Schneider, G. (2005, March 13). Fashion sense on wheels. *The Washington Post*, pp. F1, F6.

17. ARTICLE BY AN UNKNOWN AUTHOR

> Title of article. (Year, Month Day). *Title of Periodical, volume*(issue),
>   page(s) or p(p). page(s).

> Hot property: From carriage house to family compound. (2004,
>   December). *Berkshire Living, 1*(1), 99.

> Clues in salmonella outbreak. (2008, June 21). *New York Times*, p. A13.

18. BOOK REVIEW

> Reviewer's Last Name, Initials. (Date of publication). Title of review
>   [Review of by the book *Title of Work*, by Author's Initials Last Name].
>   *Title of Periodical, volume*(issue), page(s).

> Brandt, A. (2003, October). Animal planet [Review of the book
>   *Intelligence of apes and other rational beings*, by D. R. Rumb
>   & D. A. Washburn]. *National Geographic Adventure, 5*(10), 47.

If the review does not have a title, include the bracketed information about the work being reviewed, immediately after the date of publication.

19. LETTER TO THE EDITOR

> Author's Last Name, Initials. (Date of publication). Title of letter [Letter to
>   the editor]. *Title of Periodical, volume*(issue), page(s) or p(p). page(s).

> Hitchcock, G. (2008, August 3). Save our species [Letter to the editor].
>   *San Francisco Chronicle*, p. P-3.

Online Sources

Not every online source gives you all the data that APA would like to see in a reference entry. Ideally, you will be able to list author's or editor's name; date of first electronic publication or most recent revision; title of document; information about print publication if any; and retrieval information: DOI (digital object identifier, a string of letters and numbers that

identifies an online document) or URL. In some cases, additional information about electronic publication may be required (title of site, retrieval date,
name of sponsoring institution).

IMPORTANT DETAILS FOR DOCUMENTING ONLINE SOURCES

- **AUTHORS**: List authors as you would for a print book or periodical.

- **TITLES**: For websites and electronic documents, articles, or books, capitalize titles and subtitles as you would for a book; capitalize periodical
  titles as you would for a print periodical.

- **DATES**: After the author, give the year of the document's original
  publication on the web or of its most recent revision. If neither of
  those years is clear, use *n.d.* to mean "no date." For undated content
  or content that may change (for example, a wiki entry), include
  the month, day, and year that you retrieved the document. You
  don't need to include the retrieval date for content that's unlikely
  to change.

- **DOI OR URL**: Include the DOI instead of the URL in the reference
  whenever one is available. If no DOI is available, provide the URL of the
  home page or menu page. If you do not identify the sponsoring institution, you do not need a colon before the URL or DOI. Don't include any
  punctuation at the end of the URL or DOI. When a URL won't fit on the
  line, break the URL before most punctuation, but do not break *http://*.

20. WORK FROM A NONPERIODICAL WEBSITE

Author's Last Name, Initials. (Date of publication). Title of work. *Title of
site*. DOI or Retrieved Month Day, Year [if necessary], from URL

Cruikshank, D. (2009, June 15). Unlocking the secrets and powers of the
brain. *National Science Foundation*. Retrieved from http://www.nsf.gov
/discoveries/disc_summ.jsp?cntn_id=114979&org=NSF

When citing an entire website, include the URL in parentheses within the
text. Do not include the website in your list of references.

author   title   publication

Documentation Map (APA)

Work from a Website

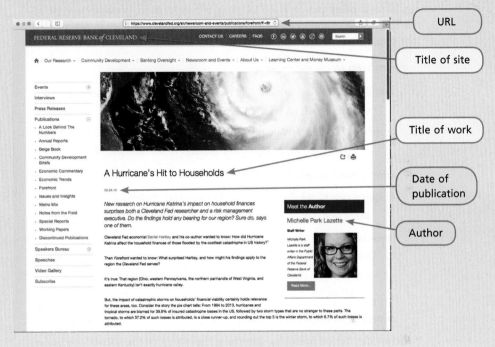

URL

Title of site

Title of work

Date of publication

Author

565–73
for more
on citing
websites
APA style

Lazette, M. P. (2015, February 25). A hurricane's hit to households. *Federal Reserve Bank of Cleveland.* Retrieved from https://www.clevelandfed .org/en/Newsroom%20and%20Events/Publications/Forefront /Katrina.aspx

21. ARTICLE IN AN ONLINE PERIODICAL

When available, include the volume number and issue number as you would for a print source. If no DOI has been assigned, provide the URL of the homepage or menu page of the journal or magazine, even for articles that you access through a database.

ARTICLE IN AN ONLINE JOURNAL

Author's Last Name, Initials. (Year). Title of article. *Title of Journal,*
volume(issue), pages. DOI or Retrieved from URL

Corbett, C. (2007). Vehicle-related crime and the gender gap. *Psychology,*
Crime & Law, 13, 245-263. doi:10.1080/10683160600822022

ARTICLE IN AN ONLINE MAGAZINE

Author's Last Name, Initials. (Year, Month Day). Title of article. *Title of*
Magazine, volume(issue). DOI or Retrieved from URL

Barreda, V. D., Palazzesi, L., Tellería, M. C., Katinas, L., Crisci, J. N.,
Bromer, K., . . . Bechis, F. (2010, September 24). Eocene Patagonia
fossils of the daisy family. *Science, 329,* 1621. doi:10.1126/science
.1193108

ARTICLE IN AN ONLINE NEWSPAPER

If the article can be found by searching the site, give the URL of the home page or menu page.

Author's Last Name, Initials. (Year, Month Day). Title of article. *Title of*
Newspaper. Retrieved from URL

Collins, G. (2012, September 12). Game time. *The New York Times.*
Retrieved from http://www.nytimes.com

22. ARTICLE AVAILABLE ONLY THROUGH A DATABASE

Some sources, such as an out-of-print journal or rare book, can be accessed only through a database. When no DOI is provided, give either the name of the database or its URL. (See p. 571 for a template and example.)

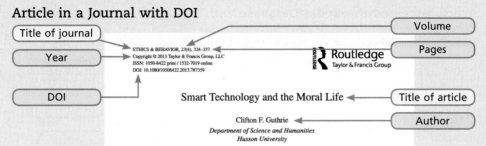

Documentation Map (APA)

Article in a Journal with DOI

Title of journal

Year

DOI

Volume

Pages

Title of article

Author

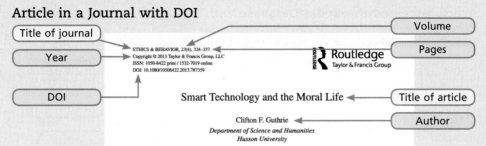

ETHICS & BEHAVIOR, 23(4), 324–337
Copyright © 2013 Taylor & Francis Group, LLC
ISSN: 1050-8422 print / 1532-7019 online
DOI: 10.1080/10508422.2013.787359

Routledge
Taylor & Francis Group

Smart Technology and the Moral Life

Clifton F. Guthrie
Department of Science and Humanities
Husson University

Smart technology is recording and nudging our intuitive and behavioral reactions in ways that are not fully shaped by our conscious ethical reasoning and so are altering our social and moral worlds. Beyond reasons to worry, there are also reasons to embrace this technology for nudging human behavior toward prosocial activity. This article inquires about four ways that smart technology is shaping the individual moral life: the persuasive effect of promptware, our newly evolving experiences of embodiment, our negotiations with privacy, and our experiences of risk and serendipity.

Keywords: persuasive technology, morality, ethics, virtue

PERSUASIVE TECHNOLOGY

For some time, cars have worked to shape our behaviors, beeping to warn us when a door is unlocked or a seat belt unfastened, or giving us fuel efficiency feedback. These straightforward but persuasive sensor systems nudge us toward a repertoire of safe driving behaviors, and we often cannot override them even if we want to. Newer cars include an increasing number of smart technologies that interact with us more intelligently. Some detect the presence of electronic keys and make it impossible for drivers to lock themselves out. Others use sensors to monitor approaching obstacles or lane boundaries and give warnings or even apply the brakes. We are seeing the emergence of street intersections that communicate directly with cars and cars that can communicate with one another (Dean, Fletcher, Porges, & Ulrich, 2012). These are so-called smart technologies because they draw data from the environment and from us, and often make decisions on our behalf. A leading researcher in automated driving noted, "The driver is still in control. But if the driver is not doing the right thing, the technology takes over" (Markoff & Sengupta, 2013).

As cars become smarter they are helping to lead us into what technologists describe as a pervasive, ambient, or calm computing environment. In 1991, Mark Weiser of the Palo Alto Research Center presciently called it "ubiquitous computing" or "ubicomp" in a much-quoted article from *Scientific American*, in which he outlined what has come to be accepted as a standard interpretation of the history of human interaction with computers. This is the age in which computers are increasingly liberated from manual input devices like laptops and cell phones to become an invisible, interactive, computational sensorium. Early examples include motion sensors, smart

Correspondence should be addressed to Clifton F. Guthrie, Department of Science and Humanities, Husson University, 1 College Circle, Bangor, ME 04401. E-mail: cfguthrie@gmail.com

563–65, 568
for more
on citing
journals
APA style

566
for more
on DOIs

Guthrie, C. F. (2013). Smart Technology and the Moral Life. *Ethics & Behavior, 23,* 324-337. doi: 10.1080/10508422.2013.787359

Documentation Map (APA)

Article Accessed through a Database with DOI

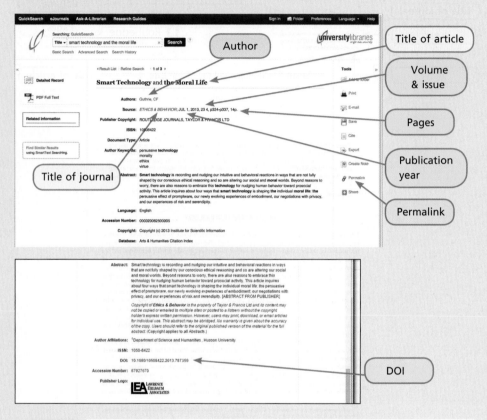

568, 571
for more
on citing an
article in a
database
APA style

Guthrie, C. F. (2013). Smart technology and the moral life. *Ethics &
Behavior 23*(4), 324-337. doi:10.1080/10508422.2013.787359

author   title   publication

Author's Last Name, Initials. (Year). Title of article. *Title of Journal,*
volume(issue), pages. DOI or Retrieved from Name of database
or URL

Simpson, M. (1972). Authoritarianism and education: A comparative
approach. *Sociometry, 35*(2), 223-234. Retrieved from http://www.jstor
.org/stable/2786619

23. ARTICLE OR CHAPTER IN A WEB DOCUMENT OR ONLINE REFERENCE WORK

For a chapter in a web document or an article in an online reference
work, give the URL of the chapter or entry if no DOI is provided.

Author's Last Name, Initials. (Year). Title of entry. In Initials Last Name
(Ed.), *Title of reference work*. DOI or Retrieved from URL

Korfmacher, C. (2006). Personal identity. In J. Fieser & B. Dowden (Eds.),
Internet encyclopedia of philosophy. Retrieved from http://www.iep
.utm.edu/person-i/

24. ELECTRONIC BOOK

Author's Last Name, Initials. (Year). *Title of book*. DOI or Retrieved from URL

TenDam, H. (n.d.). *Politics, civilization & humanity*. Retrieved from http://
onlineoriginals.com/showitem.asp?itemID=46&page=2

For an ebook based on a print version, include a description of the digital
format in brackets after the book title.

Blain, M. (2009). *The sociology of terror: Studies in power, subjection,*
and victimage ritual [Adobe Digital Editions version]. Retrieved
from http://www.powells.com/sub/AdobeDigitalEditionsPolitics
.html?sec_big_link=1

25. WIKI ENTRY

Give the entry title and the date of posting, or *n.d.* if there is no date. Then
include the retrieval date, the name of the wiki, and the URL for the entry.

> Title of entry. (Year, Month Day). Retrieved Month Day, Year, from Title
> of wiki: URL

Discourse. (n.d.). Retrieved November 8, 2013, from Psychology Wiki:
　　http://psychology.wikia.com/wiki/Discourse

26. ONLINE DISCUSSION SOURCE

If the name of the list to which the message was posted is not part of the
URL, include it after *Retrieved from*. The URL you provide should be for the
archived version of the message or post.

> Author's Last Name, Initials. (Year, Month Day). Subject line of message
> [Descriptive label]. Retrieved from URL

Baker, J. (2005, February 15). Re: Huffing and puffing [Electronic
　　mailing list message]. Retrieved from American Dialect Society
　　electronic mailing list: http://listserv.linguistlist.org/cgi-bin
　　/wa?A2=ind0502C&L=ADS-L&P=R44

Do not include email or other nonarchived discussions in your list of
references. Simply give the sender's name in your text. See no. 13 on
page 556 for guidelines on identifying such sources in your text.

27. BLOG ENTRY

> Author's Last Name, Initials. (Year, Month Day). Title of post [Blog post].
> Retrieved from URL

Collins, C. (2009, August 19). Butterfly benefits from warmer springs?
　　[Blog post]. Retrieved from http://www.intute.ac.uk/blog
　　/2009/08/19/butterfly-benefits-from-warmer-springs/

28. ONLINE VIDEO

> Last Name, Initials (Writer), & Last Name, Initials (Producer). (Year, Month
> Day posted). *Title* [Descriptive label]. Retrieved from URL

Coulter, J. (Songwriter & Performer), & Booth, M. S. (Producer). (2006, September 23). *Code Monkey* [Video file]. Retrieved from http:// www.youtube.com/watch?v=v4Wy7gRGgeA

29. PODCAST

Writer's Last Name, Initials. (Writer), & Producer's Last Name, Initials. (Producer). (Year, Month Day). Title of podcast. *Title of site or program* [Audio podcast]. Retrieved from URL

Britt, M. A. (Writer & Producer). (2009, June 7). Episode 97: Stanley Milgram study finally replicated. *The Psych Files Podcast* [Audio podcast]. Retrieved from http://www.thepsychfiles.com/

Other Kinds of Sources

30. FILM, VIDEO, OR DVD

Last Name, Initials (Producer), & Last Name, Initials (Director). (Year). *Title* [Motion picture]. Country: Studio.

Wallis, H. B. (Producer), & Curtiz, M. (Director). (1942). *Casablanca* [Motion picture]. United States: Warner.

31. MUSIC RECORDING

Composer's Last Name, Initials. (Year of copyright). Title of song. On *Title of album* [Medium]. City, State or Country: Label.

Veloso, C. (1997). Na baixado sapateiro. On *Livros* [CD]. Los Angeles, CA: Nonesuch.

32. PROCEEDINGS OF A CONFERENCE

Author's Last Name, Initials. (Year of publication). Title of paper. In *Proceedings Title* (pp. pages). Publication City, State or Country: Publisher.

Heath, S. B. (1997). Talking work: Language among teens. In *Symposium about Language and Society—Austin* (pp. 27-45). Austin: Department of Linguistics at the University of Texas.

33. TELEVISION PROGRAM

Last Name, Initials (Writer), & Last Name, Initials (Director). (Year). Title of episode [Descriptive label]. In Initials Last Name (Producer), *Series title*. City, State or Country: Network.

Dunkle, R. (Writer), & Lange, M. (Director). (2012). Hit [Television series episode]. In E. A. Bernero (Executive Producer), *Criminal minds*. New York, NY: NBC.

34. SOFTWARE OR COMPUTER PROGRAM

Title and version number [Computer software]. (Year). Publication City, State or Country: Publisher.

Elder Scrolls V: Skyrim [Computer software]. (2011). Rockwood, MD: Bethesda.

35. GOVERNMENT DOCUMENT

Government Agency. (Year of publication). *Title*. Publication City, State or Country: Publisher.

U.S Department of Health and Human Services, Centers for Disease Control and Prevention. (2009). *Fourth national report on human exposure to environmental chemicals.* Washington, DC: Government Printing Office.

ONLINE GOVERNMENT DOCUMENT

Government Agency. (Year of publication). *Title* (Publication No. [if any]). Retrieved from URL

U.S Department of Health and Human Services, National Institutes of
Health, National Institute of Mental Health. (2006). *Bipolar disorder*
(NIH Publication No. 06-3679). Retrieved from http://www.nimh.nih
.gov/health/publications/bipolar-disorder/nimh-bipolar-adults.pdf

36. DISSERTATION

Include the database name and accession number for dissertations that
you retrieve from a database.

> Author's Last Name, Initials. (Year). *Title of dissertation* (Doctoral
> dissertation). Retrieved from Name of database. (accession number)

> Knapik, M. (2008). *Adolescent online trouble-talk: Help-seeking in
> cyberspace* (Doctoral dissertation). Retrieved from ProQuest
> Dissertation and Theses database. (AAT NR38024)

For a dissertation that you access on the web, include the name of institution
after *Doctoral dissertation*. For example: (Doctoral dissertation, University of
North Carolina). End your documentation with *Retrieved from* and the URL.

37. TECHNICAL OR RESEARCH REPORT

> Author's Last Name, Initials. (Year). *Title of report* (Report number).
> Publication City, State or Country: Publisher.

> Elsayed, T., Namata, G., Getoor, L., & Oard, D. W. (2008). *Personal name
> resolution in email: A heuristic approach* (Report No. LAMP-TR-150).
> College Park: University of Maryland.

Sources Not Covered by APA

To document a source for which APA does not provide guidelines, look at
models similar to the source you have cited. Give any information readers
will need in order to find it themselves — author; date of publication; title;
publisher; information about electronic retrieval (DOI or URL); and any
other pertinent information. You might want to try your reference note
yourself, to be sure it will lead others to your source.

FORMATTING A PAPER

Title page. APA generally requires a title page. At the upper left-hand corner of the page, include "Running head:" and a shortened version of your title in capital letters. The page number (1) should go in the upper right-hand corner. Center the full title of the paper, your name, and the name of your school on separate lines about halfway down the page. You may add an "Author Note" at the bottom of the page to provide course information, acknowledgments, or contact information.

Page numbers. Use a shortened title in capital letters in the upper left-hand corner of each page; place the page number in the upper right-hand corner. Number pages consecutively throughout your paper.

Fonts, spacing, margins, and indents. Use a serif font (such as Times New Roman or Bookman) for the text, and a sans serif font (such as Calibri or Verdana) for figure labels. Double-space the entire paper, including any notes and your list of references. Leave one-inch margins at the top, bottom, and sides of your text; do not justify the text. Paragraphs should be indented one-half inch (or five to seven spaces) from the left margin. APA recommends using two spaces after end-of-sentence punctuation.

Headings. Though they are not required in APA style, headings can help readers follow your organization. The first level of heading should be bold, centered, and capitalized as you would any other title; the second level of heading should be bold and flush with the left margin; the third level should be bold and indented, with only the first letter and proper nouns capitalized and with a period at the end of the heading, with the text following on the same line.

First Level Heading

Second Level Heading

    Third level heading.

Long quotations. Indent quotations of more than forty words to one-half inch (or five to seven spaces) from the left margin. Do not use quotation marks, and place page number(s) in parentheses after the end punctuation.

> Kaplan (2000) captured ancient and contemporary Antioch for us:
>> At the height of its glory in the Roman-Byzantine age, when it had an amphitheater, public baths, aqueducts, and sewage pipes, half a million people lived in Antioch. Today the population is only 125,000. With sour relations between Turkey and Syria, and unstable politics throughout the Middle East, Antioch is now a backwater—seedy and tumbledown, with relatively few tourists. (p. 123)
>
> Antioch's decline serves as a reminder that the fortunes of cities can change drastically over time.

Illustrations. For each table, provide a number (*Table* 1) and a descriptive title on separate lines above the table; below the table, include a note with information about the source. For figures — charts, diagrams, graphs, photos, and so on — include a figure number (*Figure* 1) and information about the source in a note below the figure. Number tables and figures

Table 1
Hours of Instruction Delivered per Week

	American classrooms	Japanese classrooms	Chinese classrooms
First grade			
Language arts	10.5	8.7	10.4
Mathematics	2.7	5.8	4.0
Fifth grade			
Language arts	7.9	8.0	11.1
Mathematics	3.4	7.8	11.7

Note. Adapted from "Peeking Out from Under the Blinders: Some Factors We Shouldn't Forget in Studying Writing," by J. R. Hayes, 1991, National Center for the Study of Writing and Literacy (Occasional Paper No. 25). Retrieved from National Writing Project website: http://www.nwp.org/

separately, and be sure to refer to any illustrations in your text and clarify how they relate to the rest of your text.

Abstract.   An abstract is a concise summary of your paper that briefly introduces readers to your topic and main points. Most scholarly journals require an abstract; check with your instructor about his or her preference. Put your abstract on the second page, with the word *Abstract* centered at the top. Unless your instructor specifies a length, limit your abstract to 250 words or fewer.

List of references.   Start your list on a new page after the text but before any endnotes. Center the title and double-space the entire list. Each entry should begin at the left margin, and subsequent lines should be indented one-half inch (or five to seven spaces). Alphabetize the list by authors' last names (or by editors' names, if appropriate). Alphabetize works that have no author or editor by title, disregarding *A*, *An*, and *The*. Be sure every source listed is cited in the text; don't include sources that you consulted but didn't cite.

SAMPLE RESEARCH PAPER

Carolyn Stonehill wrote the following paper for a first-year writing course. It is formatted according to the guidelines of the *Publication Manual of the American Psychological Association,* 6th edition (2009). While APA guidelines are used widely in linguistics and the social sciences, exact requirements may vary from discipline to discipline and course to course. If you're unsure about what your instructor wants, ask for clarification.

Running head: IT'S IN OUR GENES   1

Page number.

"Running head:" and shortened title.

It's in Our Genes:

The Biological Basis of Human Mating Behavior

Carolyn Stonehill

Wright State University

Title, name, and school name.

IT'S IN OUR GENES   2

Abstract

While cultural values and messages certainly play a part in the process of mate selection, the genetic and psychological predispositions developed by our ancestors play the biggest role in determining to whom we are attracted. Women are attracted to strong, capable men with access to resources to help rear children. Men find women attractive based on visual signs of youth, health, and, by implication, fertility. While perceptions of attractiveness are influenced by cultural norms and reinforced by advertisements and popular media, the persistence of mating behaviors that have no relationship to societal realities suggests that they are part of our biological heritage.

Heading centered.

Limited to 250 words or fewer.

Two spaces after end punctuation.

It's in Our Genes:

Title centered.

The Biological Basis of Human Mating Behavior

Double-spaced throughout.

Consider the following scenario: It's a sunny afternoon on campus, and Jenny is walking to her next class. Out of the corner of her eye, she catches sight of her lab partner, Joey, parking his car. She stops to admire how tall, muscular, and stylishly dressed he is, and she does not take her eyes off him as he walks away from his shiny new BMW. As he flashes her a pearly white smile, Jenny melts, then quickly adjusts her skirt and smooths her hair.

This scenario, while generalized, is familiar: Our attraction to people—or lack of it—often depends on their physical traits. But why this attraction? Why does Jenny respond the way she does to her handsome lab partner? Why does she deem him handsome at all? Certainly Joey embodies the stereotypes of physical attractiveness prevalent in contemporary American society. Advertisements, television shows, and magazine articles all provide Jenny with signals telling her what constitutes the ideal American man. Yet she is also attracted to Joey's new sports car even though she has a new car herself. Does Jenny find this man striking because of the influence of her culture, or does her attraction lie in a more fundamental part of her constitution? Evolutionary psychologists, who apply principles of evolutionary biology to research on the human mind, would say that Jenny's responses in this situation are due largely to mating strategies developed by her prehistoric ancestors. Driven by the need to reproduce and

Paragraphs indent 5 to 7 spaces ($\frac{1}{2}$ inch).

IT'S IN OUR GENES   4

propagate the species, these ancestors of ours formed patterns
of mate selection so effective in providing for their needs and
those of their offspring that they are mimicked even in today's
society. While cultural values and messages clearly play a part
in the process of mate selection, the genetic and psychological
predispositions developed by our ancestors play the biggest role in
determining to whom we are attracted.

First-level headings boldface, centered.

● **Women's Need to Find a Capable Mate**

Pioneering evolutionary psychologist R. Trivers (as cited in
Allman, 1993) observed that having and rearing children requires
women to invest far more resources than men because of the length
of pregnancy, the dangers of childbirth, and the duration of infants'

Authors referred to by last name.

● dependence on their mothers (p. 56). According to H. Fisher (as cited
● in Frank, 2001), one of the leading advocates of this theory, finding a

Source quoted in another source; secondary source and date in first parentheses, page number in second parentheses.

capable mate was a huge preoccupation of all prehistoric reproductive
women, and for good reason: "A female couldn't carry a baby in
one arm and sticks and stones in the other arm and still feed and
protect herself on the very dangerous open grasslands, so she began
● to need a mate to help her rear her young" (p. 85). So because of this
it became advantageous for the woman to find a strong, capable
man with access to resources, and it became suitable for the man
to find a healthy, reproductively sound woman to bear and care for
his offspring. According to evolutionary psychologists, these are the
bases upon which modern mate selection is founded, and there are
many examples of this phenomenon to be found in our own society.

IT'S IN OUR GENES   5

One can see now why Jenny might be attracted by Joey's
display of resources—his BMW. In our society, men with good job
prospects, a respected social position, friends in high places, or any
combination thereof have generally been viewed as more desirable
mates than those without these things because they signal to
women that the men have resources (Buss & Schmitt, 1993, p. 226).
Compared with males, females invest more energy in bearing and
raising children, so it is most advantageous for females to choose
mates with easy access to resources, the better to provide for their
children.

Author names in parentheses when no signal phrase is used.

Men's Need to Find a Healthy Mate

For men, reproductive success depends mainly on the
reproductive fitness of their female counterpart: No amount of
available resources can save a baby miscarried in the first month
of gestation. Because of this need for a healthy mate, men have
evolved a particular attraction "radar" that focuses on signs of
a woman's health and youth, markers that are primarily visual
(Weiten, 2001, p. 399). Present-day attractiveness ratings are based
significantly on this primitive standard: "Some researchers have
suggested that cross-cultural standards of beauty reflect an evolved
preference for physical traits that are generally associated with
youth, such as smooth skin, good muscle tone, and shiny hair"
(Boyd & Silk, 2000, p. 625). This observation would explain why
women of our time are preoccupied with plastic surgery, makeup,
and—in Jenny's case—a quick hair check as a potential date

Ampersands used in parenthetical references, and used in signal phrases.

Author named in a signal phrase, publication date in parentheses after the name.

approaches. As Cunningham, Roberts, Barbee, Druen, and Wu (1995) noted, "A focus on outer beauty may have stemmed from a need for desirable inner qualities," such as health, strength, and fertility, and "culture may build on evolutionary dynamics by specifying grooming attributes that signal successful adaptation" (pp. 262-263).

The Influence of the Media on Mate Selection

There is, however, a good deal of opposition to evolutionary theory. Some critics say that the messages fed to us by the media are a larger influence on the criteria of present-day mate selection than any sort of ancestral behavior. Advertisements and popular media have long shown Americans what constitutes a physically ideal mate: In general, youthful, well-toned, symmetrical features are considered more attractive than aging, flabby, or lopsided ones. Evolutionary psychologists argue that research has not determined what is cause and what is effect. Cosmides and Tooby (1997) offered the following analogy to show the danger of assigning culture too powerful a causal role:

Quotations of 40+ words indented 5 to 7 spaces.

> For example, people think that if they can show that there is information in the culture that mirrors how people behave, then *that* is the cause of their behavior. So if they see that men on TV have trouble crying, they assume that their example is *causing* boys to be afraid to cry. But which is cause and which effect? Does the fact that men don't cry much on TV *teach* boys to not cry, or does it merely *reflect* the way boys normally develop? In the absence of research on the particular topic,

IT'S IN OUR GENES   7

there is no way of knowing. ("Nature and Nurture: An

Adaptationist Perspective," para. 16)

We can hypothesize, then, that rather than media messages
determining our mating habits, our mating habits determine the
media messages. Advertisers rely on classical conditioning to
interest consumers in their products. For instance, by showing an
image of a beautiful woman while advertising a beauty product,
advertisers hope that consumers will associate attractiveness
with the use of that particular product (Weiten, 2001). In order
for this method to be effective, however, the images depicted in
conjunction with the beauty product must be ones the general
public already finds attractive, and an image of a youthful, clear-
skinned woman would, according to evolutionary psychologists, be
attractive for reasons of reproductive fitness. In short, what some
call media influence is not an influence at all but merely a mirror in
which we see evidence of our ancestral predispositions.

If Not Media, Then What?

Tattersall (2001), a paleoanthropologist at the American
Museum of Natural History, offered another counterargument to
the evolutionary theory of mate selection. First, he argued that the
behavior of organisms is influenced not only by genetics, but also
by economics and ecology working together (p. 663). Second, he
argued that no comparisons can be made between modern human
behavior and that of our evolutionary predecessors because the
appearance of *Homo sapiens* presented a sudden, qualitative change

Major heading
and paragraph
number cited
for quote from
unpaginated
work from a
website.

from the Neanderthals—not a gradual evolution of behavioral traits:

> As a cognitive and behavioral entity, our species is truly unprecedented. Our consciousness is an emergent quality, not the result of eons of fine-tuning of a single instrument. And, if so, it is to this recently acquired quality of uniqueness, not to the hypothetical "ancestral environments," that we must look in the effort to understand our often unfathomable behaviors. (p. 665)

End punctuation before parentheses in block quotations.

The key to Tattersall's argument is this "emergent quality" of symbolic thought; according to his theories, the ability to think symbolically is what separates modern humans from their ancestors and shows the impossibility of sexual selection behaviors having been passed down over millions of years. Our sexual preferences, Tattersall said, are a result of our own recent and species-specific development and have nothing whatsoever to do with our ancestors.

Opponents of the evolutionary theory, though, fail to explain how "unfathomable" mating behaviors can exist in our present society for no apparent or logical reason. Though medicine has advanced to the point where fertility can be medically enhanced, Singh (1993) observed that curvy women are still viewed as especially attractive because they are perceived to possess greater fertility—a perception that is borne out by several studies of female fertility, hormone levels, and waist-to-hip ratio (p. 304). Though

IT'S IN OUR GENES   9

more and more women are attending college and achieving high-
paying positions, women are still "more likely than men to consider
economic prospects a high priority in a mate" (Sapolsky, 2001-2002,
p. 18). While cultural norms and economic conditions influence our
taste in mates, as Singh (1993) showed in observing that "the degree
of affluence of a society or of an ethnic group within a society may,
to a large extent, determine the prevalence and admiration of
fatness [of women]" (pp. 304-305), we still react to potential mates
in ways determined in Paleolithic times. The key to understanding
our mating behavior does not lie only in an emergent modern
quality, nor does it lie solely in the messages relayed to us by
society; rather, it involves as well the complex mating strategies
developed by our ancestors.

References

Heading centered.

Allman, W. F. (1993, July 19). The mating game. *U.S. News & World Report, 115*(3), 56-63.

Alphabetized by authors' last names.

Boyd, R., & Silk, J. B. (2000). *How humans evolved* (2nd ed.). New York, NY: Norton.

All lines after the first line of each entry indented.

Buss, D. M., & Schmitt, D. P. (1993). Sexual strategies theory: An evolutionary perspective on human mating. *Psychological Review, 100*(2), 204-232.

Cosmides, L., & Tooby, J. (1997). Evolutionary psychology: A primer. Center for Evolutionary Psychology. Retrieved April 30, 2013, from http://www.psych.ucsb.edu/research/cep/primer.html

Cunningham, M. R., Roberts, A. R., Barbee, A. P., Druen, P. B., & Wu, C.-H. (1995). "Their ideas of beauty are, on the whole, the same as ours": Consistency and variability in the cross-cultural perception of female physical attractiveness. *Journal of Personality and Social Psychology, 68*, 261-279.

Frank, C. (2001, February). Why do we fall in—and out of—love? Dr. Helen Fisher unravels the mystery. *Biography*, 85-87, 112.

Sapolsky, R. M. (2001-2002, December-January). What do females want? *Natural History*, 18-21.

Singh, D. (1993). Adaptive significance of female physical attractiveness: Role of waist-to-hip ratio. *Journal of Personality and Social Behavior, 65*, 293-307.

IT'S IN OUR GENES   11

Tattersall, I. (2001). Evolution, genes, and behavior. *Zygon: Journal of Religion & Science, 36,* 657-666. doi:10.1111/0591=2835.00389

Weiten, W. (2001). *Psychology: Themes & variations* (5th ed.). San Bernardino, CA: Wadsworth.

All sources cited in the text are listed.

Media / Design

Consciously or not, we design all the texts we write, choosing typefaces, setting up text as lists or charts, deciding whether to add headings — and then whether to center them or align them on the left. Sometimes our genre calls for certain design elements — essays begin with titles, letters begin with salutations ("Dear Auntie Em"). Other times we design texts to meet the demands of particular audiences, formatting documentation in MLA or APA or some other style, setting type larger for young children, and so on. And our designs always depend upon our medium. A memoir might take the form of an essay in a book, be turned into a bulleted list for a slide presentation, or include links to images or other pages if presented on a website. The chapters in this part offer advice for CHOOSING MEDIA; working with DESIGN, IMAGES, and SOUND; WRITING ONLINE; and GIVING PRESENTATIONS.

Media / Design

Choosing Media 54

USA Today reports on contract negotiations between automakers and auto-workers with an article that includes a large photo and a colorful graph; the article on the same story on *nytimes.com* includes a video of striking workers. In your economics class, you give a presentation about the issue that includes *Prezi* slides.

These examples show how information about the same events can be delivered using three different media: print (*USA Today*), electronic (*nytimes.com*), and spoken (the main medium for your class presentation). They also show how different media offer writers different modes of expressing meaning, ranging from words to images to sounds and hyper-links. A print text can include written words and still visuals; online, the same text can also incorporate links to moving images and sound as well as to other written materials. A presentation with slides can include both spoken and written words, can incorporate video and audio elements — and can also include print handouts.

In college writing, the choice of medium often isn't up to you: your instructor may require a printed essay or a classroom talk, a website, or some combination of media. Sometimes, though, you'll be the one deciding. Because your medium will play a big part in the way your audience receives and reacts to your message, you'll need to think hard about what media best suits your audience, purpose, and message. This chapter will help you choose media when the choice is yours.

academic literacies

rhetorical situations

genres

processes

strategies

research MLA / APA

media / design

readings

handbook

Print

When you have a choice of medium, print has certain advantages over spoken and electronic text in that it's more permanent and doesn't depend on audience access to technology. Depending on your own access to technology, you can usually insert photos or other visuals and can present data and other information as graphs or charts. Obviously, though, print documents are more work than electronic ones to update or change, and they don't allow for sound, moving images, or hyperlinks to other materials.

Electronic

Online writing is everywhere: on course learning platforms and class websites; in virtual discussion groups and wikis; in emails, text messages, tweets, and other social media. And when you're taking an online course, you are, by definition, always using an electronic medium. Remember that this medium has advantages as well as limitations and potential pitfalls. You can add audio, video, and hyperlinks — but your audience may not have the same access to technology that you do. These are just some of the things you'll need to keep in mind when deciding, say, whether to include or to link to videos or a site that has restricted access.

Spoken

If you deliver your text orally, as a speech or presentation, you have the opportunity to use your tone of voice, gestures, and physical bearing to establish credibility. But you must write your text so that it's easy to understand when it is heard rather than read. The spoken medium can be used alone with a live, face-to-face audience, but it's often combined with print, in the form of handouts, or with electronics, in the form of presentation software like *PowerPoint* or *Prezi*, or designed for remote audiences in formats like webcasts, webinars, podcasts, or video-calling services such as *Skype*.

Multimedia

It's increasingly likely that you'll be assigned to create a multimedia text, one that includes some combination of print, oral, and electronic elements. It's also possible that you'll have occasion to write a multimodal text, one that uses more than one mode of expression: words, images, audio, video, hyperlinks, and so on. The words *multimedia* and *multimodal* are often used interchangeably, but *multimodal* is the term that's used most often in composition classes, whereas *multimedia* is the one used in other disciplines and in industry. In composition classes, the word generally refers to writing that includes more than just words.

For example, let's say that in a U.S. history class you're assigned to do a project about the effects of the Vietnam War on American society. You might write an essay using words alone to discuss such effects as increased hostility toward the military and government, generational conflict within families and society at large, and increased use of recreational drugs. But you could also weave such a text together with many other materials to create a multimodal composition.

If you're using print, for example, you could include photographs from the Vietnam era, such as of antiwar protests or military funerals. Another possibility might be a time line that puts developments in the war in the context of events going on simultaneously elsewhere in American life, such as in fashion and entertainment or in the feminist and civil rights movements. If you're posting your project online, you might also incorporate video clips of TV news coverage of the war and clips from films focusing on it or its social effects, such as *Apocalypse Now* or *Easy Rider*. Audio elements could include recorded interviews with veterans who fought in the war, people who protested against it, or government officials who were involved in planning or overseeing it. Many of these elements could be inserted into your document as hyperlinks.

If your assignment specifies that you give an oral presentation, you could play some of the music of the Vietnam era, show videos of government officials defending the war and demonstrators protesting it, maybe hang some psychedelic posters from the era.

Considering the Rhetorical Situation

55–56 **PURPOSE**   What's your purpose, and what media will best suit that purpose? A text or email may be appropriate for inviting a friend to lunch, but neither would be ideal for demonstrating to a professor that you understand a complex historical event; for that, you'd likely write a report, either in print or online — and you might include photos or maps or other such texts to provide visual context.

57–60 **AUDIENCE**   What media are your audience likely to expect — and be able to access? A blog may be a good way to reach people who share your interest in basketball or cupcakes, but to reach your grandparents, you may want to put a handwritten note in the mail. Some employers require applicants to submit résumés and applications online, while others prefer to receive them in print form.

61–63 **GENRE**   Does your genre require a particular medium? If you're giving an oral presentation, you'll often be expected to include slides. Academic essays are usually formatted to be printed out, even if they are submitted electronically. An online essay based on field research might include audio files of those you've interviewed, but if your essay were in print, you'd need to quote (or paraphrase or summarize) what they said.

64–67 **STANCE**   If you have a choice of media, think about whether a particular medium will help you convey your stance. A print document in MLA format, for instance, will make you seem scholarly and serious. Tweeting or blogging, however, might work better for a more informal stance. Presenting data in charts will sometimes help you establish your credibility as a knowledgeable researcher.

Once you decide on the media and modes of expression you're using, you'll need to design your text to take advantage of their possibilities and to deal with their limitations. The next chapters will help you do that.

Designing Text

You're trying to figure out why a magazine ad you're looking at is so funny, and you realize that the font used for the text is deliberately intended to make you laugh. In giving an assignment for a research paper, your psychology professor specifies that you are to follow APA format. Your classmates complain that the *PowerPoint* slides you use for a presentation are hard to read, and one of them suggests that it's because there's not enough contrast between the colors of the words and the background. Whether you're putting together your résumé, creating a website for your intramural soccer league, or writing a research essay for a class, you need to think about how you design what you write.

Sometimes you can rely on established conventions: in academic writing using MLA and APA style, for example, there are specific guidelines for margins, headings, and the use of single-, double-, or triple-spaced lines of text. But often you'll have to make design decisions on your own — and not just about words and spacing. If what you're writing includes photos, charts, tables, graphs, or other visuals, you'll need to figure out how to integrate these with your written text in the most attractive and effective way; online, you may also need to decide where and how to include video clips and hyperlinks. You might even use scissors, glue, and staples to attach objects to a poster or create pop-ups in a brochure.

No matter what your text includes, its design will influence how your audience responds to it and therefore how well it achieves your purpose. This chapter offers general advice on designing print and online texts to suit your purpose, audience, genre, and stance.

Considering the Rhetorical Situation

As with all writing tasks, your rhetorical situation should affect the way you design a text. Here are some points to consider:

55–56 **PURPOSE** How can you design your text to help achieve your purpose? If you're reporting information, for instance, you may want to present statistical data in a chart or table rather than in the main text to help readers grasp it more quickly. If you're trying to get readers to care about an issue, a photo or pull quote—a brief selection of text "pulled out" and reprinted in a larger font—might help you do so.

57–60 **AUDIENCE** How can you make your design appeal to your intended audience? By using a certain font style or size to make your text look hip, serious, or easy to read? What kind of headings — big and bold, simple and restrained? — would your readers expect or find helpful? What colors would appeal to them?

61–63 **GENRE** Are you writing in a genre that has design conventions, such as an annotated bibliography, a lab report, or a résumé? Do you need to follow a format such as those prescribed in MLA or APA style?

64–67 **STANCE** How can your design reflect your attitude toward your audience and subject? Do you need a businesslike font or a playful one? Would tables and graphs help you establish your credibility? How can illustrations help you convey a certain tone?

Some Basic Principles of Design

Be consistent. To keep readers oriented while reading documents or browsing multiple webpages, any design elements should be used consistently. In a print academic essay, that task may be as simple as using the same font throughout for your main text and using boldface or italics for headings. If you're writing for the web, navigation buttons and other major elements should be in the same place on every page. In a presentation, each slide should use the same background and the same font unless there's a good reason to introduce differences.

Keep it simple.   One of your main design goals should be to help readers see quickly — even intuitively — what's in your text and how to find specific information. Adding headings to help readers see the parts, using consistent colors and fonts to help them recognize key elements, setting off steps in lists, using white space to set off blocks of text or to call attention to certain elements, and (especially) resisting the temptation to fill pages with fancy graphics or unnecessary animations: these are all ways of making your text simple to read.

Look, for example, at a furniture store's simple, easy-to-understand webpage design on page 600. This webpage contains considerable information: a row of links across the top, directing readers to various products; a search option; a column down the right side that provides details about the chair shown in the wide left-hand column; thumbnail photos below the chair, showing its various options; and suggestions across the bottom for furniture to go with it. Despite the wealth of content, the site's design is both easy to figure out and, with the generous amount of white space, easy on the eyes.

Aim for balance.   On the webpage on page 600, the photo takes up about a quarter of the screen and is balanced by a narrower column of text, and the "Matching Products" and "More POÄNG series" sections across the page bottom balance the company logo and links bar across the top. For a page without images, balance can be created through the use of margins, headings, and spacing. In the journal page shown on page 516, notice how using white space around the article title and the author's name, as well as setting both in larger type and the author's name in all capital letters, helps to balance them vertically against the large block of text below.

The large initial letter of the text also helps to balance the mass of
smaller type that follows. MLA and APA styles have specific design guidelines for academic research papers that cover these elements. A magazine

academic literacies

rhetorical situations

genres

processes

strategies

research MLA / APA

media / design

readings

handbook

page might create a sense of balance by using pull quotes and illustrations to break up dense vertical columns of text.

Use color and contrast carefully. Academic readers usually expect black text on a white background, with perhaps one other color for headings. Presentation slides and webpages are most readable with a plain, light-colored background and dark text that provides contrast. Remember that not everyone can see all colors and that an online text that includes several colors might be printed out and read in black and white; make sure your audience will be able to distinguish any color variations well enough to grasp your meaning. Colored lines on a graph, for example, should be distinguishable even if readers cannot see the colors. Red-green contrasts are especially hard to see and should be avoided.

Use available templates. Good design takes time, and most of us do not have training as designers. If you're pressed for time or don't feel up to the challenge of designing your own text, take advantage of the many templates available. In *Microsoft Word*, for example, you can customize "styles" to specify the font, including its size and color; single- or double-spacing; paragraph indentations; and several other features that will then automatically apply to your document. Websites that host personal webpages and blogs offer dozens of templates that you can use or modify to suit your needs. And presentation software offers many templates that can simplify creating slides.

Some Elements of Design

Fonts. You can usually choose from among many fonts, and the one you choose will affect how well the audience can read your text and how they will perceive your **TONE**. Times Roman will make a text look businesslike or academic; Comic Sans will make it look playful. For most academic writing,

65

you'll want to use a font size between 10 and 12 points and a serif font (such as Times Roman or Bookman) rather than a sans serif font (such as Arial, Verdana, or Calibri) because serif fonts are generally easier to read. Reserve sans serif for headings and parts of the text that you want to highlight. Decorative fonts (such as *Magneto*, *Amaze*, Chiller, and Jokerman) should be used sparingly and only when they're appropriate for your audience, purpose, and the rest of your RHETORICAL SITUATION. If you use more than one font in a text, use each one consistently: one for HEADINGS, one for captions, one for the main body of your text. And don't go overboard—you won't often have reason to use more than two or, at most, three fonts in any one text.

Every font has regular, **bold**, and *italic* forms. In general, choose regular for the main text and lower-level headings, bold for major headings, and italic within the main text to indicate titles of books and other long works and, occasionally, to emphasize words or brief phrases. Avoid italicizing or boldfacing entire sentences or paragraphs, especially in academic writing. If you are following MLA, APA, or some other style format, be sure your use of fonts conforms to its requirements.

Finally, consider the line spacing of your text. Generally, academic writing is double-spaced, whereas JOB LETTERS and RÉSUMÉS are usually single-spaced. Some kinds of REPORTS may call for single-spacing; check with your instructor if you're not sure. You'll often need to add extra space to set off parts of a text—items in a list, for instance, or headings.

Layout. Layout is the way text is arranged on a page. An academic essay, for example, will usually have a title centered at the top, one-inch margins all around, and double-spacing. A text can be presented in paragraphs—or in the form of LISTS, TABLES, CHARTS, GRAPHS, and so on. Sometimes you'll need to include other elements as well: headings, images and other graphics, captions, lists of works cited.

Paragraphs. Dividing text into paragraphs focuses information for readers and helps them process the information by dividing it into manageable chunks. If you're writing a story for a print newspaper with narrow columns, for example, you'll divide your text into shorter paragraphs

53 ▪
604–5 ▢

MLA 500–548 ●
APA 549–90

253–64 ▲
129–55

603 ▢
609–11

academic literacies · rhetorical situations · genres · processes · strategies · research MLA/APA · media/design · readings · handbook than you would if you were writing an academic essay. In general, indent paragraphs five to seven spaces (one-half inch) when your text is double-spaced; either indent or skip a line between paragraphs that are single-spaced.

Lists. Put information into list form that you want to set off and make easily accessible. Number the items in a list when the sequence matters (in instructions, for example); use bullets when the order is not important. Set off lists with an extra line of space above and below, and add extra space between the items on a list if necessary for legibility. Here's an example:

> Darwin's theory of how species change through time derives from three postulates, each of which builds on the previous one:
>
> 1. The ability of a population to expand is infinite, but the ability of any environment to support populations is always finite.
> 2. Organisms within populations vary, and this variation affects the ability of individuals to survive and reproduce.
> 3. The variations are transmitted from parents to offspring.
>
> —Robert Boyd and Joan B. Silk, *How Humans Evolved*

Do not set off text as a list unless there's a good reason to do so, however. Some lists are more appropriately presented in paragraph form, especially when they give information that is not meant to be referred to more than once. In the following example, there is no reason to highlight the information by setting it off in a list—and bad news is softened by putting it in paragraph form:

> I regret to inform you that the Scholarship Review Committee did not approve your application for a Board of Rectors scholarship for the following reasons: your grade-point average did not meet the minimum requirements; your major is not among those eligible for consideration; and the required letter of recommendation was not received before the deadline.

Presented as a list, that information would be needlessly emphatic.

Headings.   Headings make the structure of a text easier to follow and help readers find specific information. Some genres require standard headings—announcing an ABSTRACT, for example, or a list of WORKS CITED. Other times you will want to use headings to provide an overview of a section of text. You may not need any headings in brief texts, but when you do, you'll probably want to use one level at most, just to announce major topics. Longer texts, information-rich genres such as brochures or detailed **REPORTS**, and websites may require several levels of headings. If you decide to include headings, you will need to decide how to phrase them, what fonts to use, and where to position them.

183–87 ▲
539 ●
129–56 ▲

Phrase headings concisely.   Make your headings succinct and parallel in structure. You might make all the headings nouns (**Mushrooms**), noun phrases (**Kinds of Mushrooms**), gerund phrases (**Recognizing Kinds of Mushrooms**), or questions (**How Do I Identify Mushrooms?**). Whatever form you decide on, use it consistently for each heading. Sometimes your phrasing will depend on your purpose. If you're simply helping readers find information, use brief phrases:

HEAD   **Forms of Social Groups among Primates**
SUBHEAD   *Solitary Social Groups*
SUBHEAD   *Monogamous Social Groups*

If you want to address your readers directly with the information in your text, consider writing your headings as questions:

How can you identify morels?
Where can you find morels?
How can you cook morels?

Make headings visible.   Headings need to be visible, so if you aren't following an academic style like MLA or APA, consider making them larger than the regular text, putting them in **bold** or *italics*, or using <u>underlining</u> — or a different font. For example, you could make your main text a serif font like Times Roman and your headings in a sans serif font like Arial. On the web, consider making headings a different color from the body text.

academic literacies   rhetorical situations   genres   processes   strategies   research MLA/APA   media/design   readings   handbook

When you have several levels of headings, use capitalization, bold, and italics to distinguish among the various levels:

First-Level Head
Second-Level Head
Third-level head

APA format requires that each level of heading appear in a specific style: centered bold uppercase and lowercase for the first level, flush-left bold uppercase and lowercase for the second level, and so on.

● 576

Position headings appropriately. If you're following APA format, center first-level headings. If you are not following a prescribed format, you get to decide where to position your headings: centered, flush with the left margin, or even alongside the text in a wide left-hand margin. Position each level of head consistently throughout your text. Generally, online headings are positioned flush left.

White space. Use white space to separate the various parts of a text. In general, use one-inch margins for the text of an essay or report. Unless you're following MLA or APA format, include space above headings, above and below lists, and around photos, graphs, and other visuals. See the two SAMPLE RESEARCH PAPERS in this book for examples of the formats required by MLA and APA.

● MLA 539–48

APA 578–89

Evaluating a Design

Does the design suit your PURPOSE? Does the overall look of the design help convey the text's message, support its argument, or present information?

■ 55–56

How well does the design meet the needs of your AUDIENCE? Will the overall appearance of the text appeal to the intended readers? Is the font large enough for them to read? Are there headings to help them find their way through the text? Does the design help readers find the information they need?

■ 55–56

61–63
How well does the text meet any GENRE requirements?   Can you tell by looking at the text that it is an academic essay, a lab report, a résumé, a blog? Do its fonts, margins, headings, and page layout meet the require-

MLA 538–39
APA 576–79
ments of **MLA**, **APA**, or whatever style is being followed?

64–67
How well does the design reflect your STANCE?   Do the page layout and fonts convey the appropriate tone — serious, playful, adventuresome, conservative, or whatever other tone you intended?

Using Visuals, Incorporating Sound 56

For an art history class, you write an essay comparing two paintings by Willem de Kooning. For an engineering class project, you design a model of a bridge and give an in-class presentation explaining the structures and forces involved, which you illustrate with slides. For a psychology assignment, you interview several people who've suffered foreclosures on their homes in recent years about how the experience affected them and how they've tried to cope with the resulting stress — and then create an online text weaving together a slideshow of photos of the people outside their former homes, a graph of foreclosure rates, video and audio clips from the interviews, and your own insights.

All of these writing tasks require you to incorporate and sometimes to create visuals and sound. Many kinds of visuals can be included in print documents: photos, diagrams, graphs, charts, and more. And with writing that's delivered online or as a spoken presentation, your choices expand to include audio and video, voice-over narration, and links to other materials.

Visuals and sound aren't always appropriate, however, or even possible — so think carefully before you set out to include them. But they can help you make a point in ways that words alone cannot. Election polling results are easier to see in a bar graph than the same information would be in a paragraph; an audio clip can make a written analysis of an opera easier to understand. This chapter provides some tips for using visuals and incorporating sound in your writing.

Considering the Rhetorical Situation

Use visuals that are appropriate for your audience, purpose, and the rest of your **RHETORICAL SITUATION**. If you're trying to persuade voters in your

■ 53

town to back a proposal on an issue they don't know or care much about, for example, you might use dramatic pictures just to get their attention. But when it's important to come across as thoughtful and objective, maybe you need a more subdued look — or to make your points with written words alone. A newspaper article on housing prices might include a bar graph or line graph and also some photos. A report on the same topic for an economics class would probably have graphs with no photos; a community website might have graphs, links to related sites, and a video interview with a home owner.

In your academic writing, especially, be careful that any visuals you use support your main point — and don't just serve to decorate the text. (Therefore, avoid clip art, which is primarily intended as decoration.) Images should support what you say elsewhere with written words and add information that words alone can't provide as clearly or easily.

Using Visuals

Photos, videos, tables, pie charts, bar graphs: these are many kinds of visuals you could use.

An essay discussing the work of Willem de Kooning might contrast one of his more representational works (such as the one on the left) with one that's more abstract (right).

Photographs.   Photos can support an **ARGUMENT**, illustrate **NARRATIVES** and **PROCESSES**, present other points of view, and help readers "place" your information in time and space. You may use photos you take yourself, or you can download photos and other images from the internet — within limits. Most downloadable photos are copyrighted, meaning that you can use them without obtaining permission from the copyright owner only if you are doing so for academic purposes, to fulfill an assignment. If you are going to publish your text, either in print or on the web, you must have permission. Consider, too, the file size of digital images; large files can clog readers' email in-boxes, take a long time to display on their screens, or be hard for you to upload in the first place, so you may have to compress an image or reduce its resolution (which can diminish its sharpness).

355–73
419–27
414–18

Videos.   If you're writing online, you can include video clips for readers to play. If you're using a video already available online, such as on *YouTube*, you can show the opening image with an arrow for readers to click on to start the video, or you can simply copy the video's URL and paste it into your text as a **LINK**. In either case, you need to introduce the video in your text with a **SIGNAL PHRASE**. As with any other source, you need to provide an in-text citation and full documentation.

613–14
487–90

   If you want to include a video you made yourself, you can edit it using such programs as *iMovie* or *Windows Movie Maker*. Once you're ready to insert it into your document, the easiest way is to first upload it to *You-Tube*, choosing the Private setting so only those you authorize may view it, and then create a link in your document.

Graphs, charts, and tables.   Statistical and other numerical information is often best presented in graphs, charts, and tables. If you can't find the right one for your purpose, you can create your own, as long as it's based on sound data from reliable sources. To do so, you can use various spread-sheet programs or online chart and graph generators.

   In any case, remember to follow basic design principles: be **CONSISTENT**, label all parts clearly, and **KEEP THE DESIGN SIMPLE**, so readers can focus on the information and not be a distracted by a needlessly complex design. In particular, use color and contrast wisely to emphasize what's

598–99

RACE TO 25 MILLION
Global unique visitors in millions

Line graphs are a good way of showing changes in data over time. Each line here represents a different social networking site. Plotting the lines together allows readers to compare the data at different points in time. Be sure to label the *x* and *y* axes and limit the number of lines to four at the most.

REVENUE
In billion euros

Bar graphs are useful for comparing quantitative data, measurements of how much or how many. The bars can be horizontal or vertical. This graph shows IKEA's earnings between 2000 and 2011. Some software offers 3-D and other special effects, but simple graphs are often easier to read.

Revenue for the four English leagues 2010/11

Pie charts can be used to show how a whole is divided into parts or how parts of a whole relate to one another. The segments in a pie should always add up to 100 percent, and each segment should be clearly labeled.

ECONOMY WATCH
A snapshot of key figures for the world's largest economies.

Tables are useful for displaying numerical information concisely, especially when several items are being compared. Presenting information in columns and rows permits readers to find data and identify relationships among them.

Diagrams and flowcharts are ways of showing relationships and processes. This diagram shows how carbon moves between the Earth and its atmosphere. Flowcharts can be made using widely available templates; diagrams, on the other hand, can range from simple drawings to works of art. Some simple flowcharts may be found in the Genre chapters (for example, p. 252).

academic literacies　rhetorical situations　genres　processes　strategies　research MLA / APA　media / design　readings　handbook

most significant. Choose **COLORS** that are easy to distinguish from one another — and that remain so if the graph or chart is printed out in black and white. (Using gradations of color from light to dark will show in black and white.) Some common kinds of graphs, charts, and tables are shown on the facing page.

◻ 601

SOME TIPS FOR USING VISUALS

- Position images as close as possible to the discussion to which they relate. In *Microsoft Word*, simply position your cursor where you want to insert an image; click Picture on the Insert tab; choose the appropriate image from your files; and click Insert. You may then need to adjust the way the text flows or wraps around the image: in the Page Layout tab, choose the appropriate option in Wrap Text.

- In academic writing, number all images, using separate sequences of numbers for figures (photos, graphs, diagrams, video clips, and drawings) and tables: Fig. 1, Fig. 2; Table 1, Table 2.

- Explain in your written text whatever information you present in an image — don't expect it to speak for itself. Refer to the image before it appears, identifying it and summarizing its point. For example: "As Table 1 shows, Italy's economic growth rate has been declining for thirty years."

- Provide a title or caption for each image to identify it and explain its significance for your text. For example: "Table 1: Italy's Economic Growth Rate, 1985–2015."

- Label the parts of visuals clearly to ensure that your audience will understand what they show. For example, label each section of a pie chart to show what it represents.

- Cite the source of any images you don't create yourself. You need not document visuals you create, based on data from your own experimental or field research, but if you use data from a source to create a graph or chart, **CITE THE SOURCE** of the data.

● 491–94

- In general, you may use visuals created by someone else in your academic writing as long as you include full **DOCUMENTATION**. If you post your writing online, however, you must first obtain permission from the copyright owner.

● 496–99

Incorporating Sound

Audio clips, podcasts, and other sound files can serve various useful purposes in online writing. Music, for example, can create a mood for your text, giving your audience hints about how to interpret the meaning of your words and images or what emotional response you're evoking. Other types of sound effects — such as background conversations, passing traffic, birdsongs, crowd noise at sports events — can provide a sense of immediacy, of being part of the scene or event you're describing. Spoken words can serve as the primary way you present an online text or as an enhancement of or even a counterpoint to a written text. (And if your audience includes visually impaired people, an audio track can allow or help them to follow the text.)

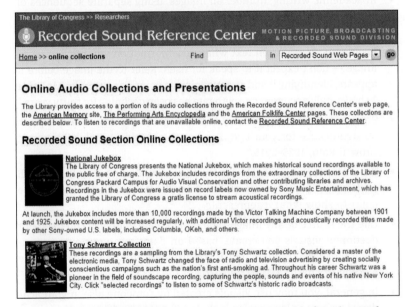

The Library of Congress is a good source for online recordings of music, speeches, and radio broadcasts.

academic literacies   rhetorical situations   genres   processes   strategies   research MLA / APA   media / design   readings   handbook

You can download or link to various spoken texts online, or you can record voice and music as podcasts using programs such as *GarageBand* and *Audacity*. Remember to provide an **IN-TEXT CITATION** and full **DOCUMENTA-TION** of any sound material you obtain from another source.

● 496–99

Adding Links

If you're writing an online text in which you want to include images, video, or sound material available on the web, it's often easier and more effective to create links to them within the text than to embed them by copying and pasting. Such links allow readers to see the materials' original context and to explore it if they wish.

The example below shows a blog post from the Archives of American Art with links to additional detail and documentation.

John Singer Sargent

This lively caricature from the Francis Davis Millet and Millet family papers features an artist fervently painting his subject, just in the background. Most likely it is John Singer Sargent at work on his painting *Carnation, Lily, Lily, Rose*. His posture and the expression on his face suggest an exuberance that matches the action of the paint dripping and splashing as it prepares to meet the canvas with energetic strokes.

Caricature of an artist painting vigorously, ca. 1885-1886. Francis Davis Millet and Millet family papers, Archives of American Art, Smithsonian Institution.

SOME TIPS FOR CREATING LINKS

487–90 ●

- Indicate links with underlining and color (most often blue), and introduce them with a **SIGNAL PHRASE**.
- Don't include your own punctuation in a link. In the example on page 613, the period is not part of the link.
- Try to avoid having a link open in a new browser window. Readers expect links to open in the same window.

Editing Carefully — and Ethically

You may want to edit a photograph, cropping to show only part of it or using *Photoshop* or similar programs to enhance the colors or otherwise alter it. Similarly, you may want to edit a video, podcast, or other audio file to shorten it or remove irrelevant parts. If you are considering making a change of this kind, however, be sure not to do so in a way that misrepresents the content. If you alter a photo, be sure the image still represents the subject accurately; if you alter a recording of a speech or interview, be sure the edited version maintains the speaker's intent. Whenever you alter an image, a video, or a sound recording, tell your readers how you have changed it.

The same goes of editing charts and graphs. Changing the scale on a bar graph, for example, can change the effect of the comparison, making the quantities being compared seem very similar or very different, as shown in the two bar graphs of identical data in Figures 1 and 2.

Because of the different fund-raising goals implied by the graphs ($800 or $5,000) and the different increments of the dollars raised ($200 or $1,000), the graphs send very different messages, though the dollars raised by each fund-raiser remain the same. Just as you shouldn't edit a quotation or a photograph in a way that might misrepresent its meaning, you should not present statistical data in a way that could mislead readers.

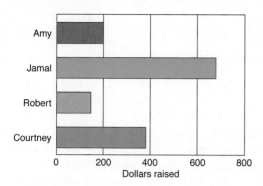

Fig. 1. Fund-raising results for the class gift.

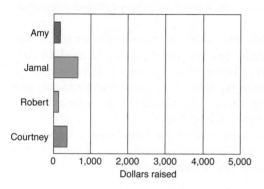

Fig. 2. Fund-raising results for the class gift.

57 Writing Online

Email. *Facebook.* Texts. Tweets. It may seem as if almost all writing is done online now. In college courses, you may still be required to turn in some writing assignments on paper, but more and more writing is not only done online but submitted that way too. And many classes are being taught online, with little or no face-to-face communication between instructors and students.

Online, your instructor and classmates usually cannot see or hear you — and that matters more than you might think. A puzzled look or a smile of recognition can start an important conversation in a face-to-face class, but in an online environment, your audience usually has only your written words to respond to. Therefore, you need to express your thoughts and feelings as clearly as you can *in writing.*

So it's useful to think about how the electronic medium affects the way we write — and how we can express ourselves most effectively when we write online. This chapter provides some advice.

Online Genres

For most of us, email, texting, and social networking sites like *Facebook* are already parts of everyday life. But using them for academic purposes may require some careful attention. Following are some guidelines.

Email. When emailing faculty members and school administrators, you are writing in an academic context, so your messages should reflect it: use an appropriate salutation ("Dear Professor Hagzanian"); write clearly and concisely in complete sentences; use standard capitalization and punctuation; proofread; and sign your full name. If you're writing about a specific

academic literacies
rhetorical situations
genres
processes
strategies
research MLA / APA
media / design
readings
handbook

course or group work, identify the course or group explicitly. Also, craft a specific subject line; instead of writing "Question about paper," be specific: "Profile organization question." If you change topics, change your subject line as well rather than simply replying to an old email. And be careful before you hit Send — you want to be good and sure that your email neither says something you'll regret later (don't send an email when you're angry!) nor includes anything you don't want the whole world reading (don't put confidential or sensitive information in email).

Texts. Texting is inherently informal and often serves as an alternative to a phone call. Since texting often takes place as a conversation in real time (and phone keyboards can be hard to use), those who write texts often use acronyms, shorthand, and emoticons — ROTFL (rolling on the floor laughing), OST (on second thought), 2nite (tonight), 10Q (thank you), :) (happy) — to get their meaning across quickly and efficiently. If you use these abbreviations, though, be sure your readers will understand them!

Social media. You may take a course that involves using *Facebook* or another social media site as a way for class members to communicate or as part of a **LEARNING MANAGEMENT SYSTEM**. If so, you need to consider your rhetorical situation to make sure your course postings represent you as a respectful (and respectable) member of the class. Also, remember that many employers routinely check job applicants' social media pages, so don't post writing or photos that you wouldn't want a potential employer to see.

⬚ 622–24

Websites. Websites are groups of webpages organized around a homepage and connected to one another (and to other websites) through hyperlinks, which take users automatically from one page to another. While it's possible to create your own websites from scratch, free website builders such as *Weebly*, *Google Sites*, or *Wix* make it easy to create a site by providing templates for homepages, page designs, and navigation systems.

One key element in a website is the use of links to bring material from other sources into your text. You can link to the definition of a key term, for instance, rather than defining it yourself, or you can summarize a

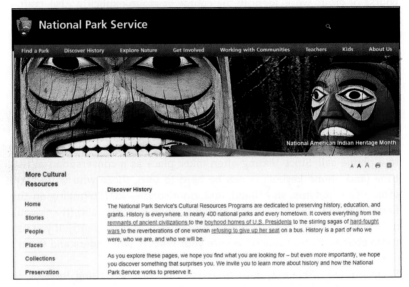

The homepage of Discover History, the National Park Service cultural resource program, provides a navigation menu on the left that leads to various sections of the site. Links embedded within the introductory text connect to Park Service pages outside the program.

source and link to the full text rather than quoting or paraphrasing it. Providing links lets readers decide whether they need or want to see more detailed information — or not.

Blogs.   Blogs are websites that generally focus on a single topic — politics, celebrities, gaming, baseball, you name it. They're maintained and updated regularly by individuals or groups who post opinions, reflections, information, and more — with writing, photos, video and audio files, and links to other sites. Blogs are an easy way to share your writing with others — and to invite response. Free blog hosting sites such as *WordPress*, *Tumblr*, or *Blogger* offer templates that let you create a blog and post to it easily, and some learning management systems include blogging capability as well.

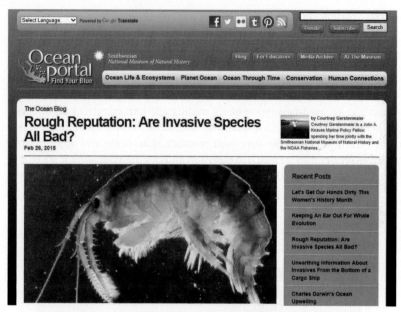

This blog, hosted by the Smithsonian Institution, focuses on marine biology and includes video, audio, slideshows, and written narratives. Readers can interact with and respond to the text by clicking on icons for Facebook, Twitter, and other social networking sites.

If your blog is public, anyone can read it, including potential employers, so just as with *Facebook* and other social media, you'll want to be careful about how you present yourself and avoid posting anything that others could see as offensive. (Think twice before posting when you're angry or upset.) You may want to activate privacy settings that let you restrict access to some of the content or that make your blog unsearchable by *Google* and other search tools. Also, assume that what you post in a blog is permanent: your friends, family, employer — anyone — may read a posting years in the future, even if the blog is no longer active.

Wikis.   Wikis are websites that allow a group to work collaboratively, with all users free to add, edit, and delete content. *Wikipedia*, the online encyclopedia, is one of the most famous wikis: its content is posted and edited by people all over the world. You may be asked to contribute to a class wiki, such as the one below from a writing course at Bloomsburg University of Pennsylvania. Students post their work to the wiki, and everyone in the class has access to everyone else's writing and can comment on or revise it. When contributing to a wiki, you should be careful to write precisely, edit carefully, and make sure your research is accurate and appropriately cited — others may be quick to question and rewrite your work if it's sloppy or inaccurate. Free wiki apps include *MediaWiki*, *Tiki Wiki*, and *DokuWiki*.

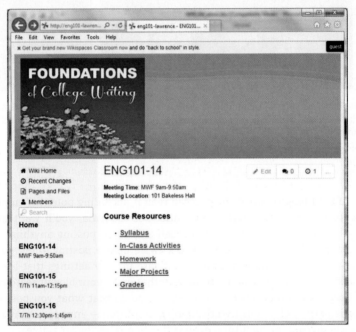

A writing-course wiki from Bloomsburg University of Pennsylvania.

academic literacies

rhetorical situations

genres

processes

strategies

research MLA / APA

media / design

readings

handbook

Managing Online Course Work

Because so much of your college work will be done online — at the very least, you'll do most of your writing on a computer and submit some assignments via email — it's important to set up some procedures for yourself. In a single writing course, for example, you may write three or four drafts of four essays — that's twelve to sixteen documents. To keep track of your files, you'll need to create folders, establish consistent file names, and back up your work.

Creating folders.　Create a folder for each course, and name it with the course title or number and the academic term: ENG 101 Fall 2016. Within each course folder, create a folder for each major assignment. Save your work in the appropriate folder, so you can always find it.

Saving files.　Your word processor likely saves documents to a specific format identified by a three- or four-letter ending automatically added to the file name: .doc, .docx, .txt, and so on. However, this default format may not be compatible with other programs. If you're not sure what format you'll need, use the Save As command to save each document in Rich Text Format, or .rtf, which most word processors can read.

Naming files.　If you are expected to submit files electronically, your instructor may ask you to name them in a certain way. If not, devise a system that will let you easily find the files, including multiple drafts of your writing. For example, you might name your files using *Your last name + Assignment + Draft number + Date:* Jones Evaluation Draft 2 10-5-2013.docx. You'll then be able to find a particular file by looking for the assignment, the draft number, or the date. Saving all your drafts as separate files will make it easy to include them in a portfolio; also, if you lose a draft, you'll be able to use the previous one to reconstruct it.

Backing up your work.　Hard drives fail, laptops and tablets get dropped, flash drives are left in public computers. Because files stored in computers can be damaged or lost, you should save your work in several places: on your computer, on a flash drive or portable hard drive, in space supplied by your school, or online. You can also ensure that an extra copy of your work exists by emailing a copy to yourself.

Finding Basic Course Information

You'll need to learn some essential information about any online courses you take:

- *The phone number for the campus help desk* or technology center. Check the hours of operation, and keep the number handy.

- *The syllabus,* list of assignments, and calendar with deadlines.

622–24
- *Where to find tutorials* for your school's **LEARNING MANAGEMENT SYSTEM** and other programs you may need help with.

- *How and when you can contact your instructor* — in person during office hours? by phone or email? — and how soon you can expect a response.

- *What file format you should use* to submit assignments — .doc, .docx, .rtf, .pdf, something else? — and how to submit them.

- *How to use the spellcheck function* on your word processor or learning management system.

- *How to participate in online discussions* — will you use a discussion board? a chat function in a learning management system? a blog? a social network? something else?

Using Learning Management Systems

Whether you're in a face-to-face, hybrid, or online class, you may be asked to do some or all of your classwork online using a learning management system (LMS) such as *Blackboard* or *Desire2Learn*. An LMS is a web-based educational tool that brings together all the course information your

A course homepage from Wright State's Pilot LMS.

instructor wants you to have, along with features that allow you to participate in the class in various ways. Your school's LMS likely includes the following features that you'll be expected to use:

A course homepage   contains posts from your instructor; a calendar with due dates for assignments; and links to the course syllabus, other course content, and additional features available on the site.

A discussion board   allows you to communicate with classmates even if everyone isn't logged in to the board at the same time. These conversations may be organized in "threads" so that posts on a particular topic appear together and may be read in order. When you contribute to a threaded discussion, treat it as an ongoing conversation: you need not introduce the topic but can simply add your comments.

A chat tool allows you to engage in written conversations in real time, with all participants logged in simultaneously. In a classroom, doing this may be like texting with many others at once, so the rules for class discussion apply: be patient while waiting for a response; focus on the topic being discussed; avoid sarcasm or personal attacks.

A dropbox is a place where you submit assignments online. If your course dropbox has folders for each assignment, be sure to upload your assignment into the correct folder. Keep in mind that systems go down, so don't wait until the last minute to submit a file. It's a good idea to double-check that the file you've submitted has been uploaded; often you can simply exit the dropbox and then return to it to see that your file is where it should be.

Online portfolios. Many LMSs allow you to create an online portfolio where you may post your coursework as well as photos, personal information, and links to other websites.

Additional features. An LMS may also include email; a space to keep a journal; a whiteboard for posting images, graphics, and presentations; a gradebook; a social network (sometimes called a Ning) for class members only; and other features that can help you keep track of your work in a class.

Giving Presentations

In a marketing class, you give a formal presentation that includes slides and handouts as part of a research project on developing brand loyalty to clothing labels among college students. As a candidate for student government, you deliver several speeches to various campus groups that are simultaneously broadcast over the web. At a good friend's wedding, after you make a toast to the married couple, another friend who couldn't attend in person toasts them remotely using *Skype*; a third guest records both toasts on his cell phone and uploads them to *Facebook*. Whether or not you include electronic and print media, whenever you are called on to give a spoken presentation, you need to make your points clear and memorable. This chapter offers guidelines to help you prepare and deliver effective presentations. We'll start with two good examples.

ABRAHAM LINCOLN
Gettysburg Address

Given by the sixteenth president of the United States, at the dedication of the Gettysburg battlefield as a memorial to those who died in the Civil War, this is one of the most famous speeches ever delivered in the United States.

> Four score and seven years ago our fathers brought forth on this continent, a new nation, conceived in Liberty, and dedicated to the proposition that all men are created equal.
> Now we are engaged in a great civil war, testing whether that nation, or any nation so conceived and so dedicated, can long endure.

We are met on a great battle-field of that war. We have come to dedicate a portion of that field, as a final resting place for those who here gave their lives that that nation might live. It is altogether fitting and proper that we should do this.

But, in a larger sense, we can not dedicate — we can not consecrate — we can not hallow — this ground. The brave men, living and dead, who struggled here, have consecrated it, far above our poor power to add or detract. The world will little note, nor long remember what we say here, but it can never forget what they did here. It is for us the living, rather, to be dedicated here to the unfinished work which they who fought here have thus far so nobly advanced. It is rather for us to be here dedicated to the great task remaining before us — that from these honored dead we take increased devotion to that cause for which they gave the last full measure of devotion — that we here highly resolve that these dead shall not have died in vain — that this nation, under God, shall have a new birth of freedom — and that government of the people, by the people, for the people, shall not perish from the earth.

You won't likely be called on to deliver such an address, but the techniques Lincoln used — brevity, rhythm, recurring themes — are ones you can use in your own spoken texts. The next example represents the type of spoken text we are sometimes called on to deliver at important occasions in the lives of our families.

JUDY DAVIS

Ours Was a Dad . . .

This short eulogy was given at the funeral of the writer's father, Walter Boock. Judy Davis lives in Davis, California, where she was for many years the principal of North Davis Elementary School.

Elsa, Peggy, David, and I were lucky to have such a dad. Ours was a dad who created the childhood for us that he did not have for himself.

The dad who sent us airborne on the soles of his feet, squealing with delight. The dad who built a platform in the peach tree so we could eat ourselves comfortably into peachy oblivion. The dad who assigned us chores and then did them with us. The dad who felt our pain when we skinned our knees.

Ours was the dad who took us camping, all over the U.S. and Canada, but most of all in our beloved Yosemite. The one who awed us with his ability to swing around a full pail of water without spilling a drop and let us hold sticks in the fire and draw designs in the night air with hot orange coals.

Our dad wanted us to feel safe and secure. On Elsa's eighth birthday, we acquired a small camping trailer. One very blustery night in Minnesota, Mom and Dad asleep in the main bed, David suspended in the hammock over them, Peggy and Elsa snuggled in the little dinette bed, and me on an air mattress on the floor, I remember the most incredible sense of well-being: our family all together, so snug, in that little trailer as the storm rocked us back and forth. It was only in the morning that I learned about the tornado warnings. Mom and Dad weren't sleeping: they were praying that when morning came we wouldn't find ourselves in the next state.

Ours was the dad who helped us with homework at the round oak table. He listened to our oral reports, taught us to add by looking for combinations of 10, quizzed us on spelling words, and when our written reports sounded a little too much like the *World Book* encyclopedia, he told us so.

Ours was a dad who believed our round oak table that seated twelve when fully extended should be full at Thanksgiving. Dad called the chaplain at the airbase, asked about homesick boys, and invited them to join our family. Or he'd call International House in Berkeley to see if someone from another country would like to experience an American Thanksgiving. We're still friends with the Swedish couple who came for turkey forty-five years ago. Many people became a part of our extended family around that table. And if twelve around the table was good, then certainly fourteen would be better. Just last fall, Dad commissioned our neighbor Randy to make yet another leaf for the table. There were fourteen around the table for Dad's last Thanksgiving.

Ours was a dad who had a lifelong desire to serve. He delivered Meals on Wheels until he was eighty-three. He delighted in picking up the day-old doughnuts from Mr. Rollen's shop to give those on his route an extra treat. We teased him that he should be receiving those meals himself! Even after walking became difficult for him, he continued to drive and took along an able friend to carry the meals to the door.

Our family, like most, had its ups and downs. But ours was a dad who forgave us our human failings as we forgave him his. He died in peace, surrounded by love. Elsa, Peggy, David, and I were so lucky to have such a dad.

This eulogy, in honor of the writer's father, provides concrete and memorable details that give the audience a clear image of the kind of man he was. The repetition of the phrase "ours was a dad" provides a rhythm and unity that moves the text forward, and the use of short, conventional sentences makes the text easy to understand — and deliver.

Key Features / Spoken Presentations

A clear structure.   Spoken texts need to be clearly organized so that your audience can follow what you're saying. The **BEGINNING** needs to engage their interest, make clear what you will be talking about, and perhaps forecast the central parts of your talk. The main part of the text should focus on a few main points — only as many as your listeners can be expected to absorb and retain. (Remember, they can't go back to reread!) The **ENDING** is especially important: it should leave your audience with something, to remember, think about, or do. Davis ends as she begins, saying that she and her sisters and brother "were so lucky to have such a dad." Lincoln ends with a dramatic resolution: "that government of the people, by the people, for the people, shall not perish from the earth."

Signpost language to keep your audience on track.   You may need to provide cues to help your listeners follow your text, especially **TRANSITIONS** that lead them from one point to the next. Sometimes you'll also want to stop and **SUMMARIZE** a complex point to help your audience keep track of your ideas and follow your development of them.

331–38

338–42

349

486–87

A tone to suit the occasion.   Lincoln spoke at a serious, formal event, the dedication of a national cemetery, and his address is formal and even solemn. Davis's eulogy is more informal in TONE, as befits a speech given for friends and loved ones. In a presentation to a panel of professors, you probably would want to take an academic tone, avoiding too much slang and speaking in complete sentences. If you had occasion to speak on the very same topic to a neighborhood group, however, you would likely want to speak more casually.

65

Repetition and parallel structure.   Even if you're never called on to deliver a Gettysburg Address, you will find that repetition and parallel structure can lend power to a presentation, making it easier to follow — and more likely to be remembered. "We can not dedicate — we can not consecrate — we can not hallow": the repetition of "we can not" and the parallel forms of the three verbs are one reason these words stay with us more than 150 years after they were written and delivered. These are structures any writer can use. See how the repetition of "ours was a dad" in Davis's eulogy creates a rhythm that engages listeners and at the same time unifies the text.

Slides and other media.   Depending on the way you deliver your presentation, you will often want or need to use other media — *PowerPoint, Prezi,* or other presentation slides, video and audio clips, handouts, flip charts, whiteboards, and so on — to present certain information and to highlight key points.

Considering the Rhetorical Situation

As with any writing, you need to consider your rhetorical situation when preparing a presentation:

PURPOSE   Consider what your primary purpose is. To inform? persuade? entertain? evoke another kind of emotional response?

55–56

57–60 **AUDIENCE**   Think about whom you'll be addressing and how well you know them. Will they be interested, or will you need to get them interested? Are they likely to be friendly? How can you get and maintain their attention, and how can you establish common ground with them? How much will they know about your subject — will you need to provide background or define any terms?

61–63 **GENRE**   The genre of your text will affect the way you structure and present it. If you're making an argument, for instance, you'll need to consider counterarguments — and, depending on the way you're giving the presentation, perhaps to allow for questions and comments from members of the audience who hold other opinions. If you're giving a report, you may have reasons to prepare handouts with detailed information you don't have time to cover in your spoken text, or links to online documents or websites.

64–67 **STANCE**   Consider the attitude you want to express. Is it serious? thoughtful? passionate? well informed? humorous? something else? Choose your words and any other elements of your presentation accordingly. Whatever your attitude, your presentation will be received better by your listeners if they perceive you as comfortable and sincere.

A Brief Guide to Writing Presentations

Whether you're giving a poster presentation at a conference or an oral report in class, what you say will differ in important ways from what you might write for others to read. Here are some tips for composing an effective presentation.

Budget your time.   A five-minute presentation calls for about two and a half double-spaced pages of writing, and ten minutes means only four or five pages. Your introduction and conclusion should each take about one-tenth of the total time available; time for questions (if the format allows for them) should take about one-fifth; and the body of the talk, the rest. In a ten-minute presentation, then, allot one minute for your introduction, one minute for your conclusion, and two minutes for questions, leaving six minutes for the body of your talk.

Organize and draft your presentation.   Readers can go back and reread if they don't understand or remember something the first time through a text. Listeners can't. Therefore, it's important that you structure your presentation so that your audience can follow your text — and remember what you say.

- *Craft an introduction* that engages your audience's interest and tells them what to expect. Depending on your rhetorical situation, you may want to **BEGIN** with humor, with an anecdote, or with something that reminds them of the occasion for your talk or helps them see the reason for it. In any case, you always need to summarize your main points, provide any needed background information, and outline how you'll proceed.

331–38

- *In the body of your presentation,* present your main points in more detail and support them with **REASONS** and **EVIDENCE**. As you draft, you may well find that you have more material than you can present in the time available, so you'll need to choose the most important points to focus on and leave out the rest.

359–67

- *Let your readers know you're concluding* (but try to avoid saying "in conclusion"), and then use your remaining time to restate your main points and to explain why they're important. End by saying "thank you" and offering to answer questions or take comments if the format allows for them.

Consider whether to use visuals.   You may want or need to include some visuals to help listeners follow what you're saying. Especially when you're presenting complex information, it helps to let them see it as well as hear it. Remember, though, that visuals should be a means of conveying information, not mere decoration.

DECIDING ON THE APPROPRIATE VISUALS

- *Slides* are useful for listing main points and for projecting illustrations, tables, and graphs.

- *Videos, animations, and sounds* can add additional information to your presentations.

- *Flip charts, whiteboards, or chalkboards* allow you to create visuals as you speak or to keep track of comments from your audience.

- *Posters* sometimes serve as the main part of a presentation, providing a summary of your points. You then offer only a brief introduction and answer any questions.

- *Handouts* can provide additional information, lists of works cited, or copies of any slides you show.

What visual tools (if any) you decide to use is partly determined by how your presentation will be delivered. Will you be speaking to a crowd or a class, delivering your presentation through a podcast, or creating an interactive presentation for a web conference? Make sure that any necessary equipment and programs are available — and that they work. If at all possible, check out any equipment in the place where you'll deliver your presentation before you go live. If you bring your own equipment for a live presentation, make sure you can connect to the internet if you need to and that electrical outlets are in reach of your power cords. Also, make sure that your visuals can be seen. You may have to rearrange the furniture or the screen to make sure everyone can see.

And finally, have a backup plan. Computers fail; projector bulbs burn out; marking pens run dry. Whatever your plan is, have an alternative in case any problems occur.

academic literacies   rhetorical situations   genres   processes   strategies   research MLA / APA   media / design   readings   handbook

Presentation software.   *PowerPoint, Keynote,* and other presentation software can include images, video, and sound in addition to displaying written text. They are most useful for linear presentations that move audiences along one slide at a time. Cloud-based programs like *Prezi* also allow you to arrange words or slides in various designs, group related content together, and zoom in and out. Here are some tips for writing and designing slides:

- *Use* **LISTS** *or images, not paragraphs.* Use slides to emphasize your main points, not to reproduce your talk onscreen: keep your audience's attention focused on what you're saying. A list of brief points, presented one by one, reinforces your words. An image can provide additional information that your audience can take in quickly.

□ 603

- *Make your text easy for your audience to read.* **FONTS** should be at least 18 points, and larger than that for headings. Projected slides are easier to read in sans serif fonts like Arial, Helvetica, and Tahoma than in serif fonts like Times New Roman. And avoid using all capital letters, which can be hard to read.

□ 601–2

- *Choose colors carefully.* Your text and any illustrations must contrast with the background. Dark content on a light background is easier to read than the reverse. And remember that not everyone sees all colors; be sure your audience doesn't need to be able to see particular colors or contrasts in order to get your meaning. Red-green and blue-yellow contrasts are especially hard for some people to see and should be avoided.

- *Use bells and whistles sparingly, if at all.* Presentation software offers lots of decorative backgrounds, letters that fade in and out or dance across the screen, and sound effects. These features can be more distracting than helpful; use them only if they help to make your point.

- *Mark your text.* In your notes or prepared text, mark each place where you need to click a mouse to call up the next slide.

This Prezi *presentation rotates, includes audio and video, and zooms in and out to let viewers take a closer look.*

Truman

- Conducted whistle-stop campaign
- Made hundreds of speeches
- Spoke energetically
- Connected personally with voters
- Focused on key states

Truman's Whistle-Stop Campaign

Two PowerPoint slides on the U.S. presidential election of 1948. The slide on the left outlines the main points; the one on the right shows a map of Truman's whistle-stop campaign, providing a graphic illustration of the miles he traveled as he campaigned to be president.

Handouts. When you want to give your audience information they can refer to later — reproductions of your visuals, bibliographic information about your sources, printouts of your slides — do so in the form of handouts. Refer to the handouts in your presentation, but unless they include material your audience needs to consult before or as you talk, wait until you are finished to distribute them so as not to distract listeners. Clearly label everything you give out, including your name and the date and title of the presentation.

Delivering a Presentation

The success of a presentation often hinges on how you deliver it. As you work on your spoken texts, bear in mind the following points:

Practice. Practice, practice, and then practice some more. The better you know your talk, the more confident you will be, and your audience will respond positively to that confidence. If you're reading a prepared text, try to write it as if you were talking. Then practice by recording it as you read it; listen for spots that sound as if you're reading, and work on your delivery to sound more relaxed. As you practice, pay attention to keeping within your time limit. If possible, rehearse your talk with a small group of friends to test their response and to get used to speaking in front of an audience.

Speak clearly. When you're giving a spoken presentation, your first goal is to be understood by your audience. If listeners miss important words or phrases because you don't pronounce them distinctly, your talk will not succeed. Make sure, too, that your pace matches your audience's needs. Often you'll need to make yourself speak more slowly than usual to explain complex material (or to compensate for nerves); sometimes you may need to speed up to keep your audience's attention. In general, though, strive for a consistent pace throughout, one that ensures you don't have to rush at the end.

Pause for emphasis.   In writing, you have white space and punctuation to show readers where an idea or discussion ends. When speaking, you need to pause to signal the end of a thought, to give listeners a moment to consider something you've said, or to get them ready for a surprising or amusing statement.

Stand up (or sit up) straight and look at your audience.   If you're in the same physical space as your audience, try to maintain some eye contact with them. If that's uncomfortable, fake it: pick a spot on the wall just above the head of a person in the back of the room, and focus on it. You'll appear as if you're looking at your audience even if you're not looking them in the eye. And if you stand or sit up straight, you'll project the sense that you have confidence in what you're saying. If you appear to believe in your words, others will, too. If you're speaking via an online forum like *Skype*, look at the computer's camera — not at the screen. Also, make sure the camera is positioned at your eye level, so you aren't looking down at it (and showing your viewers the ceiling behind you!).

Use gestures for emphasis.   If you're not used to speaking in front of a group, you may let your nervousness show by holding yourself stiffly, elbows tucked in. To overcome some of that nervousness, take some deep breaths, try to relax, and move your arms and the rest of your body as you would if you were talking to a friend. Use your hands for emphasis: most public speakers use one hand to emphasize specific points and both hands to make larger gestures. Watch politicians on C-SPAN to see how people who speak on a regular basis use gestures as part of their overall delivery.

part 8

Analog

"Read, read, read. Read everything — trash, classics, good and bad, and see how they do it." So said the American writer William Faulkner, and on the following pages you will find an anthology of readings that shows how your fellow University of Alabama students get it done. Read on, and pay attention to how these writers use the KEY FEATURES and STRATEGIES that you yourself are learning to use. The anthology includes readings in eight GENRES and a chapter of readings that mix genres; you'll find a menu of readings in the back of the book.

Analog

Introduction

LUKE NIILER

Director, University of Alabama First-Year Writing Program

You are reading *Analog*, a collection of student essays from the University of Alabama's First-Year Writing Program. *Analog* is intended to supplement readings in 100-level writing classes; augment the creative writing culture of UA's English Department with expository/academic prose; and help students more closely identify as writers. I should note at the outset that this work would not have been possible without the hard work and dedication of Chase Burke, Sarah Cantrell, Candace Chambers, Julia Coursey, Sarah Scarr, and Marni Presnall, who assisted with the many aspects of this project.

This project came about as I explored how writing teachers could help student writers identify as, well, writers. And by "writers" I mean people doing authentic and meaningful work to express, interrogate, and argue about topics that matter to them—not just submitting essays for grades. I reflected on my teaching career and realized my students were most likely to work this way when they worked with model texts. I did some digging and learned that teachers' use of writing models helps students see, practice, and develop critical writing skills, from "higher order" matters (such as development, voice, and argument) to "lower order" concerns (grammar, punctuation, and mechanics). The idea of models is not new; in fact, it goes back to ancient Greece and Rome. Students of public oratory studied *topoi*, or "commonplaces," key passages that enabled them to craft strong speeches. By imitating models, students learned the key moves that good public speakers make. The same is true of writing classes.

Writing students, in turn, do their most authentic, meaningful, and "writerly" work *when the texts they work with are written by fellow students.* This is true, certainly, in the revision process, in which students practice various forms of peer review and workshop strategies—strategies that have been in play in writing classrooms since the process movement in the 1970s, and championed by the likes of Donald Murray, Peter Elbow, and Wendy Bishop They exchange, read, and discuss each other's drafts. They use rubrics to evaluate and assess. They get a sense of one another's topics and rhetorical strategies, and they seek to imitate, interrogate, or extend their peers' work in their own. All of these forms of engagement help students cultivate a sense of a writerly self-efficacy. They feel more like writers because they are doing the things writers do.

Analog, accordingly, features instructor-nominated and student/faculty-reviewed essays from the University of Alabama's First-Year Writing Program. As you'll see from the table of contents, *Analog* has been designed to supplement classroom instruction from the *Norton Field Guide to Writing*—but the kinds of essays featured here could be considered staples in any First-Year Writing classroom. And you can count on *Analog* to change and evolve, even as the University of Alabama's First-Year Writing Program changes and evolves over time.

A note about the title, *Analog.* While I certainly enjoy the myriad benefits of digital media, there's just something about print. Print has an aspirational quality; I want you to want to not only see but also touch your work—to experience it as a tangible object fraught with significance. Perhaps this publication will encourage many of you to set aside some space in your lives for books.

I encourage you to read *Analog,* and see it as an example of what is possible in the First-Year Writing classroom. Perhaps you'll use some essays as models of subjects, themes, or approaches. Or you'll see insights, points of departure. Maybe you'll understand these essays in terms of craft, ways of forming and shaping language. Maybe you'll read these essays and see only the flaws. And make no mistake, there are

academic literacies · rhetorical situations · genres · processes · strategies · research MLA / APA · media / design · readings · handbook

flaws; this collection has been lightly edited on purpose, to preserve as much of the authors' unique and often noteworthy voices as possible. In this spirit, then, I hope that any missteps can become fruitful, productive points of inquiry for you. Remember, too, that these essays were shaped and formed in writing classrooms by writing students for writing teachers. By working with these essays, you complete the creative circle.

A note on production:

This collection includes essays from the 2015–2016, 2016–2017, and 2017–2018 academic years. Teachers submitted these essays on behalf of their students to *Analog* at analog@ua.edu. The editorial staff secured author permissions, reviewed the drafts, and edited for clarity.

59 Literacy Narratives

academic literacies · rhetorical situations · genres · processes · strategies · research MLA / APA · media / design · readings · handbook

LAKEIDRA SMITH

Decoding My Future

BY AGE TEN, I already knew what I wanted to do for the rest of my life. Sure, it seems like an early age to make important, life-long career choices, but honestly – it was a subconscious decision at best and an abstract idea at worst. During my brief life, my career plans have changed dozens of times. First, I aspired to be a teacher, until I admitted to myself that I didn't like children. Then, my dreams shifted to becoming a fashion designer, until I discovered their average salary. After numerous other fallen dreams – ranging from dancer to actress – I came to the realization that my dream career had been sitting in front of me all along.

For as long as I can remember, I have loved technology. Computers, cellphones, the internet, it all fascinated me. Watching technology evolve during my childhood was beyond exciting. Desktops became laptops which soon morphed into tablets, cellphones turned from a fad into a necessity, and dial-up became high-speed internet with wireless capabilities. Even though I was only four, I still vividly remember the first time I used a computer. My parents had just recently painted my sister Kalisha's bedroom a blinding shade of neon yellow. In my opinion, the color choice was a bit tacky, but it wasn't my room, therefore I had no say in the matter. My sister sat me in her lap as she sat in front of her desktop computer. Her desk was a cluttered mess of sticky notes, pencil shavings, and notebook paper, but that didn't faze me in the least. The simple fact that she let me guide the mouse of the computer was incredible to me, despite the fact that she wouldn't allow me to click anything and whenever I moved my index finger even a centimeter, she hit me with a stark stare. Despite all of that, I savored every moment. In a world yet to be flooded with Wi-Fi and smartphones, I was astounded by what this remarkable contraption – this marvel – in front of me was capable of.

As I grew older, I began to dive deeper into the vast world of electronic devices. I learned to navigate the internet with such ease that

I accidentally ordered a printer – a costly one. When it landed on our doorstep, I suppose it was quite obvious who the culprit was. At least my family put the printer to good use. Soon, playing video games on the computer became one of my favorite pastimes. I constantly wondered what was driving the movements of my adored, tiny animated characters. Intense curiosity began to ensue in my mind. Was it something hidden behind the screen? Maybe the magic was buried deep within the massive box that accompanied the desktop computer. I absolutely had to find out. I had to discover what was within this machine that made it work so smoothly.

However, I never truly considered technology as a career choice. Perhaps it was because I didn't know anyone with a career in the STEM field – especially a woman. When my friends would talk about their dream careers, they were abstract and exceptionally unattainable dreams. My childhood best friend proclaimed she wanted to be an archaeologist, simply, because we thought we found a fossil on the playground. Maybe that's where I got the idea to become a fashion designer. Nothing was unattainable – at least it didn't feel like it at that age. I would sketch designs daily, and even though it was enjoyable, it wasn't as fulfilling as I wanted it to be.

As the years flew by, I continued to nurture my first love. After my mom bought me my first laptop as a Christmas gift when I was nine, I learned how to fix software problems by tinkering with the things that I'd broken. This led me to the realization that I enjoy solving software problems. It was a thrilling experience. Downloading and installing programs got me into trouble with viruses more than a few times, but my curiosity and problem solving skills combined to fight dangerous spyware, trojans, and malware. However, I still did not contemplate making it into my career.

With the aid of better equipment and a keener skill set, I was charging people for my services by the age of fifteen. From virus removal to graphic design, I was the go-to for technical problems and tasks. While family and friends were my only clients, my business was steadily growing by word-of-mouth. Driven by a higher level of motivation to succeed and the realities of high school graduation, I felt pressure to decide on a career path, and that pushed me to pursue my passion further.

academic literacies · rhetorical situations · genres · processes · strategies · research MLA / APA · media / design · readings · handbook

Tinkering with small programs and crafting the programs for basic website designs became my hobby. While continuing to hone my skills, I was becoming proficient in many modern coding languages, like Python and Ruby. Although, I am still not completely literate in the field of technology and coding – C, a programming language created in the dinosaur age, is still my biggest enemy – I am well on my way. For some strange reason, going in circles for hours on end to come to a conclusion that was stamped directly on my forehead in scarlet red ink is my idea of a good time. To find a solution to a problem and make something work after hours of trial, error, and headaches was exhilarating.

Until this day, my love for computers, technology, and software has not dissipated and neither has my curiosity. Currently, I am pursuing my bachelor's degree in Computer Science with a concentration in Software Engineering. However, I never quite imagined that this is what my future was destined to be, but perhaps that was a wonderful thing in the end.

RACHEL FROST

The Only True Sport

I HAD TUNNEL VISION. I felt like the entire world had been picked up and dropped on my chest, but there I was, standing at the starting line. I knew there were people around me, not just people, but my teammates. Though I was a mere freshman and had only known them for a few weeks, these teammates were already my closest companions. I knew they were there, but all I could hear was my heart hammering. My coach was in my head, telling me over and over, "Running is 90% mental, and only 10% physical." All I could feel was the tenseness in my shoulders and the thick soreness in my calves from the excruciating practices all week. The taste of Gatorade was still in my mouth from trying to hydrate all morning, and the beads of sweat from my forehead dripped into my eyes. I could only focus on miniscule, seemingly insignificant details instead of what I should have actually been focusing on. I had a laborious task ahead. Before I could prepare myself, the command "Runners, take your mark," boomed through a megaphone and the click of the starter gun rang in my ears. I was off.

Right foot, left foot, breathe in, breathe out was my mantra. This was my first high school cross country meet, which shouldn't have been so scary due to my previous experiences with running in middle school, but something about it made it terrifying. Was it the height of the sophisticated seniors who seemed to be decades older me? Was it the pressure of wearing the Hoover High School "H" on my chest? All I could think to myself was, "What have I gotten myself into- again?" There was no turning back after the gun went off, and the sun seemed to singe my shoulders. I ran across a vast field filled with hundreds of athletes- long legged, spindly and tall girls who seemed to mock my short stature.

I am a runner. I had run all throughout middle school, so running wasn't slightly new to me. After trying out sport after sport, from swimming, to softball to dance team, I finally found something I loved: cross country. I liked how it was an individual sport, but at the same time, a team sport. Fast forward two years, and my measly two mile run at meets had turned into a 5K with not just two grades of girls, but four. The pressure I felt had increased incredibly, which was why the feeling of each time my foot hit the gravel seemed to be the most important step of my life. I wanted so badly to make my new team proud–so I ran. Quickly I felt the difference of middle school cross country and high school cross country–just one year had upped the competition more than I thought possible. Despite my shoe coming untied halfway through the second mile and girls' elbows digging into my ribcage as I passed them, I ran to make my new teammates and coaches proud.

Mile two was where I started to feel the immense pain. Cramps felt like someone was twisting a knife in my side, and I was used to finishing the race at that point like I did in middle school. A little after mile two I turned the corner to see my coach- his weathered face and lanky build from years and years of running greeted me with a loud "I know you can do better than that!" and he was right. All I could think about was the months of practice, the blood and more sweat than I ever thought was possible that I had put into this sport, all leading up to this moment. My legs had gone through hell and back and were programmed to be doing what they were doing. The middle of the race is the hardest part- it seems like the final mile is a light at the end of a long, distant tunnel filled with more cramps and blows to the ribs.

Right foot, left foot, breathe in, breathe out ran through my head over 5 and over. My shiny new black spikes crushed the changing course under my feet. From grass to gravel, from flat to uphill, and even through a creek they were somehow still on despite one being untied. I flew over a hill and saw one of my coaches, Coach Maddox, cheering from the bottom. Coach Maddox had been my inspiration throughout summer training and our first few practices. She was bound to a wheelchair because of a car wreck she had been in during here time at college as a track and cross country star, and was paralyzed. Her love for running pushed her to become a coach, and whenever I wanted to give up, I decided I would run the rest of that race or workout for her. I saw her at the bottom of what felt like Mount Everest and a smile broke out across my face. She yelled to me, encouraging me that I only had three laps around the track left–about three quarters of a mile to go. Never had I felt like I could run harder than that moment. A huge burst of energy came from depths that I didn't even know I had. I was almost done with my first meet and despite my exhaustion, being a little underprepared, and shoe malfunctions, I wanted to finish and finish for her. At the end of the race my most important job was to pass as many people as I possibly could, so pass I did.

I rounded a corner and before my eyes stood the finish chute. A runners' finish is one of the key parts to a race. I kept a steady pace the whole race but for the last 200 meters, my job was to sprint and advance past as many people as I could so I could earn more points for my team. My feet dug into the ground, kicking up chunks of dirt and grass sending them flying everywhere. Accustomed to running long distance, my body was now sprinting and the race clock loomed large, right before my eyes. I soared under the clock, hearing my parents and teammates cheering my name; I had finally finished. I felt a sense of accomplishment stronger than I had felt in any of my years of high school. My legs were shaky, my jersey was sweaty, and my arms were weak. But when I saw Coach Maddox sitting at our team tent, I smiled to myself, knowing I had finished my race for her. When I got to our tent she greeted me with immense congratulations on finishing my first meet.

Last year, Coach Maddox passed away due to health complications. Her quality of life was not the best, so when she passed, the team grieved but also celebrated because we knew she was finally able to run again. Now when I run, whether it be a short jog or a half marathon, I run with Coach Maddox in my mind even more than I did beforehand. My first high school cross country meet is something that will stay with me forever, and the seemingly insignificant details at the beginning of the race proved to be hugely significant.

DUSTIN CHILDERS

Rifles and Wrenches

AIRFRAME MECHANICS HOLD A SACRED, silent, and small place in an aviation team of hundreds who support the logistic and transportation battle the United States Marine Corps fights every hour of every day. This is the same pitch I heard from my recruiter right after high school in 2010. I thought to myself, "You mean to tell me I can be a Marine and turn wrenches on multimillion-dollar aircraft? Where do I sign?" I went to a vocational school specializing in automotive services for half the day in high school. It did not take much effort to convince me to join a noble cause like that. Needless to say, I was ecstatic to finally get out of my hometown and be a part of something bigger than me.

In order to earn the title of Marine, I first had to complete Boot Camp and Marine Combat Training. Then I attended 'A' and 'C' schools to become a MV-22 Osprey Airframes Mechanic. After graduating all these camps and schools, and claiming my title of Marine and aircraft maintainer, the final step was to enter what we called the "Fleet." In civilian terms, the Fleet is better understood as the labor force. I was feeling rather accomplished at this point. But I would later learn that I probably should have paid a little more attention in the classroom. Mercifully relieved of my studies, I was finally in my unit, or squadron, where I would take what I used in school and apply it to a real operational aircraft instead of the ancient mock models we practiced on.

Squadrons are full of strangers that, over time, become something more. They become a band of brothers and sisters. We clocked more hours at work than we did at home and when we were deployed, work was home. Strangely, some of the guys would rather be on a deployment. I, however, thought these expeditions were exhausting. I would prefer to be on a beach with a beer in my hand and in a country whose primary language is English. Individual preferences aside, we developed into a fraternity with semi-automatic rifles and Snap-on wrenches instead of pastel polos and leather loafers. Unlike a fraternity, there was no pledging process or initiation ceremony. My classmates and I were simply tossed to wolves that like to play with their food.

We then discovered the firehose classes in school gave us very little understanding of the aircraft, and we had no clue how to apply the scarce knowledge we did retain. With the squadron being involuntarily forced to accept new members of the family, existing members were reluctant to accept and teach us the vital lessons we needed to know. Over time, the invisible walls between mentor and mentee began to wither away. I started learning more and taking on responsibilities that, originally, would have been out of my comfort zone. I was out on the aircraft every day with busted bloody knuckles and impermeable black grease worn as war paint, despite the unpredictable and sometimes harsh weather conditions. My performance was improving beyond those of my peers and my mentors were beginning to notice. I was learning to become a wolf.

Once I became a wolf, I needed to join the pack. In order to become 5 a trusted and productive member of my squadron, I was required to obtain qualifications on equipment that was needed to test and service the aircraft. Along with that, my knowledge of the aircraft and how its components work would play an essential role in advancing in the Airframes field. However, the tricks of the trade are not written down in any book or manual. This is where Sergeants Racine, Reeves, and Henry worked as a team, and taught me their personal tips and tricks that helped them in the past. One specific stern piece of advice Racine kept telling me was, "Do each maintenance evolution step-by-step so I do not have to tell you to go back and do it twice." Their guidance steered me clear of obstacles that they had to overcome the hard way and also pushed me to excel beyond what I thought was possible.

Ultimately, they molded me to fit the bill of Collateral Duty Inspector, a decorative title for someone who is a Quality Assurance Representative outside of the Quality Assurance department. Only the Marines who are trusted and possess sound judgment claim this distinction. This means I was responsible for verifying the quality and accuracy of the work performed by those under me. I was the first of my peer group to receive this title, but I made sure I was not the last. Just as my mentors provided me with guidance, I went on to help my former peers fill a Collateral Duty Inspector bill as well. I now consider my sergeants to be my lifelong brothers for their support not only at work, but outside of work as well.

Learning this trade and having the opportunity to meet such wonderful people along the way has shaped me into who I am today. I now hold myself to a higher standard in everything I do and people tend to notice. I also feel as though I am a better person, in a general sense, because of my reinvented respect for others. Though I lacked knowledge in the beginning, the support of my adopted family helped me to fulfill the requirements necessary to move forward in my short career.

However, my five-year career technically never stopped. Following this adventure, I went on to earning my FAA Airframes Certification, which allows me to work on any civilian aircraft at my heart's desire. From wooden planes to big commercial airliners, I am your man. Even now, my journey has yet to find its end. I am now attending my freshman year at the University of Alabama to become an Aerospace Engineer in hopes of one day being able to design the aircraft instead of fixing it. My ultimate goal is to continue contributing to the MV-22 Osprey community on the opposite side of the assembly line. I want to make life easier for these brave men and women by simplifying these complicated modern marvels, one design at a time.

60 Textual Analyses

academic
literacies

rhetorical
situations

genres

processes

strategies

research
MLA / APA

media /
design

readings

handbook

RUDI JOHNSTON

Metaphor, Flashback, and Point of View in Leslie Jamison's The Empathy Exams

EMPATHY IS A WORD everyone throws around but no one really catches. We've all heard the phrase, "you can't understand another person's experience until you've walked a mile in their shoes," and we've replaced empathy with this idea. We've decided that we can empathize with someone if we've shared a similar experience. In her book, The Empathy Exams, Leslie Jamison explores the idea of empathy and what it truly means. Jamison has multiple stories of personal experiences that have shaped her understanding of empathy. In two of the small essays, "The Empathy Exams" and "La Frontera," she uses metaphor, flashback, and point of view to illustrate what she believes empathy to be.

"The Empathy Exams" is an account of Jamison's time spent working as a medical actor, performing as a patient for medical students' exams. Throughout this essay, Jamison goes back and forth between her present working this job and her past experiences with an abortion and a heart surgery. She utilizes flashback to reminisce about when she first kissed her past boyfriend and times spent focused on him, as well as all of the time she spent in a doctor's office. Jamison describes her situation juggling the two procedures—abortion and heart surgery—as a time when she realized just how frail she was. She was scared, as her frail body was put in the hands of men and "dependent on the care of a man [she] was just beginning to love" (7). Jamison put her heart in the hands of the doctors and the hands of a man from whom she wanted more. She wanted him to help her in this difficult time. However, she felt disconnected from him; her thoughts were sprinting around her head. "Couldn't he just trust that I felt something, and that I'd wanted something from him?" she writes. "I needed his empathy not just to comprehend the emotions I was describing, but to help me discover which emotions were actually there" (10). Jamison was longing for someone to empathize with her. She wanted someone to know her perspective without having had to step into her shoes. She didn't expect Dave to understand, she just expected him to try to.

Jamison explores the meaning of empathy further and further when she steps into the office of her cardiologist. Jamison recalls how her doctor would ask simple questions every time they met and then "when she left the room to let me dress, I could hear her voice speaking into a tape recorder in the hallway" (17). Jamison never felt a strong connection with her doctor, as Dr. M. was rude and inconsiderate towards Jamison's feelings. So she learned about fake empathy. Dr. M. would quickly record what she'd learned from her standard questions just so that she could listen to the recording five minutes before their next meeting and seem to actually care. Jamison recognized this and learned more about how empathy is a form of caring. Jamison's first-person point of view throughout the essays helps to establish her interpretation of empathy. When she is feeling down, she recounts that "[she] wanted him to hurt whenever [she] hurt, to feel as much as [she] felt. But it's exhausting to keep tabs on how much someone is feeling for you. It can make you forget that they feel too" (19). Empathy is oftentimes a two way road with one side blocked off. She wanted her boyfriend to empathize with her without thinking about how it could be hard for him to. His girlfriend was pregnant. His girlfriend was having heart surgery. Through her personal experience, Jamison learns more about what empathy is and how to be empathetic.

In "La Frontera," Jamison recounts her time traveling through different cities in Mexico near the United States border. She visits cities that have been overtaken with violence, and cities that are practically suburban. Jamison tries to connect with each city individually, as she's trying to really understand what's happening beneath the surface. She consistently uses metaphors to explain what she's beginning to understand empathy to be. She travels to Tijuana, a place that used to be completely overcome with violence but was beginning to become a little bit safer. She notes that there are many cheap tourist stands lining the streets, but not many tourists for them to cater to. She assumes that the past violence scared away most of the tourists, those who focus on the surface. Jamison explores the truths about tourism, that we believe that "bringing our bodies somewhere draws that place closer to us, or we to it" (59). She realizes that this is not true, but it is what most people think: it's a "quick fix of empathy" (59). Jamison notes that it's almost something to just make us feel better, like drugs or alcohol or a one-night stand. She notes that "sometimes the city fucks on the first date, and sometimes it doesn't. But always, *always*, we wake up in the morning and find we didn't know it at all" (59). We pretend to be empathetic on the surface, but we're really only escaping ourselves.

Jamison's description in "La Frontera" alludes to the fact that many 5 people try to be empathetic to feel better about themselves, to feel like they're being a good person. In reality, true empathy is about others. Jamison meets a man named Marco on her journey and talks with him about his home. Marco recounts how the morning before he left for the *encuentro*, he woke up and hit the snooze button just to be woken back up minutes later by a grenade explosion followed by machine-gun fire. Marco finds it normal, "'Like a conversation,' he says, 'one voice and then the response'" (62). That's part of his daily life. Later, Jamison expands on this thought, realizing that the conversation is the constant violence. She visits many different cities and experiences different types of hurt. She leaves and knows there's no way she could do anything about it; she can't even begin to understand how these people live. "So the conversation continues" (68). The violence continues. Grenade explosions are answered by gunfire. Drug lords continue to send their messages on dead bodies. Poets continue to try to explain. The conversation gets them nowhere because everyone is trying to talk the loudest; and with a jumbled mess of words, how could any outsider understand what these people are going through?

Jamison uses different techniques throughout her book to explain what she believes empathy to be. In the essay "The Empathy Exams" she uses mainly flashback and point of view, and in "La Frontera" she uses mainly metaphor. "The Empathy Exams" is a more personal account, as

Jamison shares her past struggles and heartache. She was vulnerable and needed someone to understand her emotions for her: "couldn't he just trust that [she] felt something, and that [she'd] wanted something from him? [She] needed his empathy not just to comprehend the emotions [she] was describing, but to help [her] discover which emotions were actually there" (10). Those flashbacks are effective in demonstrating how Jamison was seeking empathy and exactly what she was wanting. She was waiting for someone to understand her while realizing that he couldn't know exactly how she felt. The metaphors used in "La Frontera" are more of an attempt to characterize how the general public views empathy and how these views are flawed. Her metaphor of the tourist cities as one night stands is effective in showing how our 'quick fixes' of empathy don't mean anything. She says that "always, *always*, we wake up in the morning and find we didn't know [the city] at all" (59). The general view of empathy is feeling for someone in a hard situation. Jamison's view of empathy is something much deeper. We have to understand someone's pain without understanding their circumstance, and that in itself is understanding.

Both "The Empathy Exams" and "La Frontera" are used to interpret empathy. Jamison uses different strategies to bring forth the same concept: there are things that cannot be understood by an outsider, but that outsider should still try to understand. Through her flashbacks of her own times struggling with desiring empathy and her metaphors for cities and violence within them, she successfully defines empathy as something everyone wants but barely anyone is able to give. It is something that requires selflessness and acceptance that understanding is not possible in every situation. Leslie Jamison throws the word empathy around, and actually catches it.

Works Cited

Jamison, Leslie. *The Empathy Exams*. Graywolf Press, 2014.

SIMON WILDING

Hansel and Gretel: *Behind the Story*

HANSEL AND GRETEL is one of the most famous tales told by Jacob and Wilhelm Grimm. It was first published in the 1812 collection of German tales for children "Kinder- und Haus-Märchen." The story is about a woodcutter, his wife, and their two children, Hansel and Gretel, who live in harsh conditions as a famine sweeps over the country. As the father struggles to provide food for his family, his wife develops an evil plan to better the situation for her and her husband. The children will be led out to the forest and left there to starve. After the siblings are left behind and wander around the wilderness for days, they discover a house made out of bread and sugar, which in turn lures them into the arms of a witch. Hansel and Gretel escape their imprisonment by killing the evil woman and returning home to their father with arms full of jewels found in the witch's house. Although it is commonly referred to as a fairy tale, the original 1812 version is a realistic portrayal of German society and culture at that time.

The Grimm brothers' depiction of the children's parents truthfully portrays German society in the 19th century. In the second edition of *Hansel and Gretel*, published in 1819, Wilhelm Grimm changes the biological mother to a stepmother, which reflected a common practice in early 19th century Germany: fathers remarrying because many mothers died during childbirth. (However, the change could also have had a more personal reason for the authors, as Jack Zipes refers to in his book *Happily Ever After*: "Is it possible that because he [Wilhelm] and Jacob revered their own mother, they did not want to depict a biological mother abandoning her own children?" (49)). During the 19th century, major famines hit the country and left numerous families with little to no food behind. This led to a rise in child abandonment across the nation and forced many parents to desert their little ones in order to provide food for themselves. The new change brings up similarities between the stepmother and the witch, with both depicted as evil and cold-hearted. One of the ways Wilhelm Grimm accomplishes this connection is when he lets both women use the phrase "lazybones" to wake the children (*The Golden Age*, 127). This image of the evil stepmother continues on and is still around today, as seen in modern day literature and media. Moreover, an evil element is often considered an essential part of a fairy tale; take, for instance, the bad wolf in *Little Red Riding Hood* or the Evil Queen from *Snow White*. In this story, the wickedness we see comes in the form of the cold-hearted mother/stepmother who encourages the abandonment of her children to the witch. While there were no actual witches eating children in Germany, these evil women represent the poor guardianship some of Germany's youth had to endure.

In addition to the mother and witch symbolizing evil, the forest is arguably a symbol for Germany and its dark outlook in the 19th century. For the most part, the story of Hansel and Gretel takes place in the forest, a widely used scene in the fairytale genre, which is suitable, given that forests once comprised the majority of Germany's landscape. Forests in literature have always been a somewhat dark and gloomy place that humans avoid at any cost. As seen in other tales like *Little Red Riding Hood* or *Baba Yaga*, the wilderness is home to many terrifying creatures. Whereas castles, towns or homes generally stand for security and certainty, these values are lost in the forest. When Hansel and Gretel are left behind in the woods and experience this loss of values, they undergo a character transformation, which is a common theme in Grimm's tales, by killing the witch and overcoming their present struggles. Grimm's description of Hansel and Gretel's hopelessness when lost in the forest ("They walked another day, but they could not find their way out of the woods") symbolizes the desperation Germany faced during that time (Zipes, *The Golden Age*, 125). Just like the two siblings, the nation seemed to be unable to find a solution for their struggles. There are clear similarities between Germany and the forest Hansel and Gretel are trapped in, as both cannot provide for the well-being of their inhabitants. Once the siblings overpower the witch, "They filled their pockets [with jewels], then ran away and found their way back home" (Zipes, *The Golden*

academic literacies   rhetorical situations   genres   processes   strategies   research MLA / APA   media / design   readings   handbook

Age, 126). In order to receive the typical fairytale ending, Hansel and Gretel found the resources they needed to live a happy life ever after. Similarly, the upswing in German economy led to an accumulation of wealth and restored the nation's prosperity. Hansel and Gretel found their way out of despair by overcoming the suffering of the forest, while Germany found the solution to its problems in itself.

Furthermore, *Hansel and Gretel* represents the struggle of historic Germany is the need for nourishment, which was particularly caused by major famines during that time period. Just like Hansel and Gretel's family, a major part of the German population suffered under those conditions and had trouble providing food on the table. This struggle is reflected in the harsh decision of abandoning their children many parents had to make. The tale depicts this conflict in the nightly discussions Hansel and Gretel's parents had. Grimm tries to transmit the importance of bread to people at that time by continuously mentioning it in the tale. The mother of the two siblings emphasizes the importance of rations and self-control, stating, "Here's a piece of bread for each of you. But be smart and don't eat it until noon" (Zipes, *The Golden Age*, 123). This further intensifies the desperate decision Hansel makes to use breadcrumbs as waymarkers, as that loaf of bread doesn't just represent a day's provision, but is symbolic of an entire nation's need for food he is giving away. While commonly assumed the witch's house is made of gingerbread, it was actually regular bread that was used in the original version. The relief the siblings experienced when stumbling upon the house of bread is illustrative of the simple desire of most every person at that time: basic nourishment. People didn't long for fancy meals or exotic drinks, but rather looked for the fundamental satisfaction, which brings the focus back to one of the core symbols of this tale, bread. This mentality is still evident in today's German culture compared to other nations like America. While the United States is known for its lavish high-life, endless aisles at grocery stores and its wasteful nature, Germany has kept its modest attitude. Even though there are exceptions to every generalization, it could be argued that tales like Hansel and Gretel somewhat shaped and reflect the country's outlook today.

To conclude, the story of the two abandoned siblings Hansel and 5
Gretel accurately depicts some conditions in Germany in the 19th
century. Grimm emphasizes on the shift in traditional family life by
relating Hansel and Gretel's desertion to the actual rise in child abandonment in Germany. Moreover, the symbolism of the dark and gloomy
forest in place of the suffering country shows the deep sense of reality
Grimm wanted to include in his fairytale. In the same way, the nation's
desire for nourishment is illustrated throughout this story through the
illusion of bread and the gluttony the siblings have as they stumble over
the witch's house. Through these examples, Germany's present values
and culture can be related back to the struggles Hansel and Gretel had
to endure in their adventure in the forest.

Works Cited

Zipes, Jack. "Hansel and Gretel." *The Golden Age of Folk and Fairy Tales:
from the Brothers Grimm to Andrew Lang*, Hackett Publishing Company, Inc., Indianapolis, 2013.

Zipes, Jack. "The Rationalization of Abandonment and Abuse in Fairy
Tales: The Case of Hansel and Gretel ." *Happily Ever after: Fairy
Tales, Children, and the Culture Industry*, Routledge, New York, 1997.

Annotated Bibliography **61**

ADRIENNE POWERS
Annotated Bibliography: Seoul Meets Body 662

See also:

MICHAEL BENTON,
MARK DOLAN, AND
REBECCA ZISCH,
Teen Film$ 188

JESSICA ANN
OLSON, *Global
Warming* 190

ADRIENNE POWERS

Annotated Bibliography: Seoul Meets Body

Bblogger, Jerlene. "Collagen Skincare and Supplements: Do They
  Work?" *Musical Houses*, 13 Jan. 2013, *www.musicalhouses.blogspot.
  nl/2013/01/collagen-skincare-and-supplements-do.html.*

JERLENE **B**BLOGGER'S **ARTICLE** "Collagen Skincare and Supplements: Do
They Work?" covers the effectiveness of collagen in different mediums.
The article opens with an explanation of why topically applied collagen
is a useless anti-aging ingredient. Bblogger notes that skin cannot absorb
molecules larger than 500 Daltons and collagen molecules are much too
large at around 5,000 Daltons. Although companies advertise skincare
products with smaller, more absorbable collagen, it is still significantly
too large to penetrate skin.

The author states that collagen does have the ability to moisturize skin and make wrinkles and skin texture appear smoother. "As you
might guess, this is a temporary effect - it's gone as soon as you wash
your face, and wash the film off," says Bblogger. "It definitely does not
have any long-term effect."

The article also explains why collagen dietary supplements are ineffective at improving skin because collagen, like all proteins, is broken
down to amino acids during digestion.

Bblogger offers a thorough explanation of collagen effectiveness in
topical products and dietary supplements. The article is also filled with
helpful diagrams and illustrations to better understand its message: collagen is overhyped in both the beauty and health industries. Although
I appreciate the author's humor and dedication to this topic, her credibility decreased when I was unable to find her name located anywhere
on her website, *Musical Houses*. Eventually, I located her on Facebook as
"Jerlene Bblogger." Regardless of this, the information Bblogger presented
is especially informative on Daltons and how they relate to lack of collagen absorbability.

academic literacies   rhetorical situations   genres   processes   strategies   research MLA / APA   media / design   readings   handbook

Fabi, Sabrina, et al. "The Effects of Filtrate Secretion of the *Cryptomphalus aspersa* on Photoaged Skin." *Journal of Drugs in Dermatology*, vol. 12, no. 4, Spring 2013, pp. 453-57, worldsbestskincare.net/docs/jdd.pdf.

"The Effects of Filtrate Secretion of the *Cryptomphalus aspersa* on Photo- [5] aged Skin" by Sabrina Fabi et al. covers a study regarding the effectiveness of snail slime applied topically to photodamaged skin. The double-blind, randomized study lasted 14 weeks and focused on 25 participants with photodamaged skin.

Although the study was small, the findings were significant. After eight weeks, participants saw visible improvement in fine lines, deep wrinkles, and overall skin texture (Fabi et al. 455). Accurate data was recorded by 3-D imaging the participants during the entirety of the study.

This article was a tough read due to its scientific terminology, but it is extremely thorough. Each step of the study is described in detail and accompanied with related photographs and diagrams. It was originally published by the *Journal of Drugs in Dermatology* and produced by a team of five doctors which lends to its credibility. I have also seen this article referenced in many other articles, including major news sources.

This source is useful because the information is presented without bias, seems highly credible, and is relevant to my research topic.

Lee, Hyun-Sun, et al. "Fermenting Red Ginseng Enhances Its Safety and Efficacy as a Novel Skin Care Anti-Aging Ingredient: In Vitro and Animal Study." *Journal of Medicinal Food*, vol. 15, no. 11, Winter 2012, pp. 1015-23, www.ncbi.nlm.nih.gov/pmc/articles/PMC3491619/.

This study by Hyun-Sun Lee et al. focuses on the differences between red ginseng and fermented red ginseng as an anti-aging ingredient in cosmetics. Lee starts by introducing red ginseng, a traditional medicinal ingredient used for thousands of years in Asia. This herb has been studied extensively and, "Many previous studies have reported that P. ginseng has anti-wrinkle effects, protects against ultraviolet radiation-induced skin aging, and has anti-melanogenesis effects" (Lee et al.).

The study tested the safety of red ginseng on guinea pigs. A topical concentration of either red ginseng or fermented red ginseng was

applied to the test subjects. The guinea pigs tested with fermented red
ginseng had significantly less skin sensitization than those with red
ginseng. Researchers implied that this "reduced toxicological potency"
makes fermented red ginseng safer to use on skin, with less possibility of allergic reactions or sensitivities (Lee et al.). The fermented red
ginseng was also found to contain higher amounts of certain anti-aging
components including antioxidants, polyphenols, and uronic acid. Lee
et al. suggests that these findings make fermented red ginseng a more
potent anti-aging ingredient than red ginseng.

This article was difficult to read and understand due to its scientific terminology. Words like "tyrosinase" and "dinitrochlorobenzene"
popped up all too often and forced me to research further into this
topic. Although hard to ingest, the message of this study is clear: the
fermentation of red ginseng amplifies the anti-aging components found
in red ginseng. The findings were also significant in the skin toxicity
test on guinea pigs. This test hasn't been conducted on humans (to
my knowledge), so it is hard to say if the reduced sensitization from
fermented red ginseng has the same effect on humans.

This article is relevant to my research topic as it was funded by the
Korea Institute for Advancement of Technology. Although it doesn't focus
on the effects of fermented skincare ingredients in general, it shows
how the fermentation of red ginseng increases potency of certain elements like antioxidants and implies promising results in reducing skin
allergens and reactions. Locating scientific studies related to fermented
skincare has been difficult and I'm very excited to add this one to my
arsenal.

Romanowski, Perry. "Is Collagen a Good Anti-Aging Ingredient?"
The Beauty Brains, March 2015, thebeautybrains.com/2015/03/is-
collagen-a-good-anti-aging-ingredient/.

Perry Romanowski's article "Is Collagen a Good Anti-Aging Ingredient?"
focuses on the effectiveness of collagen in a variety of mediums including topical products, injections, and dietary supplements. The author
examines these different applications and finds a wide range of results
from completely ineffective to immediately noticeable improvements.

academic literacies · rhetorical situations · genres · processes · strategies · research MLA / APA · media / design · readings · handbook

Due to the large size of collagen molecules, topically applied collagen is unable to penetrate the skin. Romanowski says that, "Even if native collagen could penetrate to the dermis, it is inconceivable that the molecules could form fibers or integrate with existing collagen fibers because the precursors for fiber assembly are soluble precollagen."

The article also discusses collagen injections which give fast results, [15] but are expensive and must be repeated every three to six months optimally. Romanowski gave the effectiveness of collagen dietary supplements a mixed review, although he does cite promising studies which suggest that they may have a positive effect on skin.

I really appreciate the skepticism of the author and how he tackled the topic of collagen. Romanowski opens the article with, "When it comes to anti-aging products, it's easy to be tricked into spending a lot of money on products that aren't worth it. That's because there's so much pseudoscientific misinformation out there about anti-aging cosmetic ingredients." I feel that the author wrote this article with an unbiased perspective which is an extremely rare and useful find among beauty articles. Romanowski uses outside sources and studies to defend his opinions on collagen topical products, injections, and dietary supplements. He also gains credibility as a cosmetology chemist of nearly twenty years. These observations make Romanowski's article an extremely valuable source.

Thomas, Steve. "Medicinal Use of Terrestrial Mollusks (Slugs and Snails) With Particular Reference to Their Role in the Treatment of Wounds and Other Skin Lesions." *World Wide Wounds,* July 2013, www.worldwidewounds.com/2013/July/Thomas/slug-steve-thomas.html.

"Medicinal Use of Terrestrial Mollusks (Slugs and Snails) With Particular Reference to Their Role in the Treatment of Wounds and Other Skin Lesions" by Thomas Steve discusses the historical uses of snail slime for treating ailments including warts, burns, rashes, wounds, and toothaches. The author mentions that, "Hippocrates reportedly recommended the use of crushed snails to relieve inflamed skin..." (Thomas).

The article also mentions how the snail slime craze started. The first marketed product containing snail slime originated in Chile after snail farmers noticed how much quicker their wounds healed after handling their snails (Thomas). From there, the snail slime trend took off in Korean beauty products.

Thomas also covers the composition of snail slime, including naturally found substances that are artificially derived in other skincare products (including copper peptides and hyaluronic acid).

20 Although this article shares valuable information on the history and uses of snail slime, it falls short in a couple areas. The article hasn't been updated since 2013 and the look of its website is less than professional. I was also unable to find background information on the author and why he is qualified to write about this topic. Even with these observations, the article still contains information that is valuable to my research question. It is well written and followed with a long list of references cited in the reading.

Vukovic, Kristen. "Fermentation Phenomenon." *American Spa,* 20 Dec. 2016, americanspa.com/skincare/fermentation-phenomenon.

"Fermentation Phenomenon" by Kristen Vukovic describes the fermentation processes used for cosmetics and how it is similar to making fermented foods like kimchi. The article also explains that fermented ingredients in beauty products are more effective than non-fermented ingredients due to their smaller molecular particles, which absorb more readily into the skin (Vukovic 2). The article proposes that fermented ingredients benefit the skin by, "...calming and brightening the skin, as well as providing enhanced antioxidants and anti-inflammatory properties—plus, the skin readily absorbs them" (Vukovic 2).

"Fermentation Phenomenon" is a short read, but it shares information that is relevant to my research question. It seems biased due to plugs for skincare products containing fermented ingredients throughout its entirety. The article also doesn't mention any kind of science behind the effectiveness of fermented skincare ingredients, but makes bold claims about their abilities of brightening and calming skin. Vukovic

academic literacies | rhetorical situations | genres | processes | strategies | research MLA / APA | media / design | readings | handbook

does provide decent background information though, which is specifically focused on Korean skincare products and relevant to my research.

The research materials I have gathered both supports and denies the effectiveness of certain unique ingredients in Korean skincare products including snail mucin, collagen, and fermented ingredients. From these materials, it seems that snail slime is proven effective in improving fine lines. It may also have other benefits including increased wound healing. After reviewing the article "Collagen Skincare and Supplements: Do They Work?" I feel that the effects of topically applied collagen are overhyped by beauty companies. My takeaway is that collagen may have the short-term benefit of making skin look smoother, but the effect only lasts while the product is on the skin. This is due to the large molecule size of collagen, making it not absorbable in skin. Finding solid information on the effectiveness of fermented ingredients in skincare has been a challenge. The article "Fermentation Phenomenon" mentions amazing benefits of using fermented skincare products but doesn't have any scientific basis for its claims.

I feel that there are big gaps in my research so far. I would like to find sources that explain the effects of different compounds found naturally in snail slime (such as hyaluronic acid) to better understand how it effects the skin. My biggest gap falls onto fermented ingredients. I have looked at many different articles proclaiming their effectiveness, but it's usually to advertise brands or new products. The idea that fermented ingredients have a smaller molecule size that absorb more readily into the skin sounds great on paper, but I have yet to find any scientific findings to support this.

I have decided to keep my topic focused on Korean beauty products 25 rather than Asian beauty products. It makes sense because snail slime and fermented ingredients are both common additions to Korean beauty products. As mentioned, I am having difficulty finding research related to fermented ingredients. I do not want to modify this part of my research topic and believe that if I keep searching I'll be able to find a definitive answer.

62 Arguments

academic
literacies

rhetorical
situations

genres

processes

strategies

research
MLA / APA

media /
design

readings

handbook

ADRIENNE POWERS

Seoul Meets Body

T HE KOREAN STANDARD OF BEAUTY has become a global obsession. The pursuit of Chok Chok, or skin that appears youthful, radiant, and glowing is no longer limited to Korea. The practice of using a ten-step skincare regime has gained traction worldwide and fueled a beauty industry that is expected to reach more than thirteen billion dollars by 2020 (Park). According to Jane Jang, senior beauty analyst at Mintel, "The Korean beauty market remains buoyant thanks to fast-paced innovations and highly engaged customers who don't hesitate to adopt novel products delivering new beauty experiences" ("A Bright Future"). In this highly competitive market, research and product design must be pushed to the limit to contend with thousands of Korean beauty companies vying for shelf space. The huge demand for these coveted products has been fed by a growing presence of online stores specializing in Korean beauty, fondly referred to as K-beauty by devoted fans. Even U.S. stores like Target, Sephora, and Urban Outfitters are stocking their shelves with Korean beauty items. The addition of unique ingredients including snail mucin (slime collected from snails), fermented red ginseng, and collagen helps products stand out from this massive crowd of competitors. Korean companies also make bold statements on product efficacy and anti-aging properties to entice hopeful customers. Although Korean beauty companies' claims about snail mucin and fermented ginseng are supported by scientific studies, consumers should avoid products containing collagen because it does not perform as advertised.

The introduction of snail mucin in Korean skincare products took the world by storm, quickly becoming the star ingredient in many now cult-favorite creams, gels, serums, and masks. Snail mucin is collected from snails that have been stimulated (often with an electrical current) to increase their slime production. The mucin is fit for use in beauty products after undergoing a series of filtration processes. Although the first Korean product hit the shelves in 2010, snails have a long history as a medicinal treatment for rashes, warts, wounds, and toothaches dating back to the time of Hippocrates (Thomas). Today, Korean beauty companies tout snail mucin as a super effective anti-aging ingredient that aids in repairing wrinkles and improving overall skin texture.

Snail mucin naturally contains certain ingredients often found in other skincare products such as hyaluronic acid and copper peptides which are associated with anti-aging effects. A study published in the *Journal of Drugs in Dermatology* tested the efficacy of topically applied snail mucin emulsion on photoaged skin. Although the study was small with only twenty-five participants, the findings were significant. After eight weeks, participants saw visible improvement in fine lines, deep wrinkles, and overall skin texture (Fabi et al. 455). Participants continued to see improvements even after discontinuing application of the snail mucin emulsion for two weeks.

Another effective anti-aging ingredient used in Korean beauty products is fermented red ginseng. Like snail mucin, red ginseng has a rich history dating back thousands of years in Asia. The herb has been researched extensively in its unfermented state and, "Many previous studies have reported that P. Ginseng [red ginseng] has anti-wrinkle effects, protects against ultraviolet radiation-induced skin gaining, and has anti-melanogenesis effects" (Lee et al.). Although fermentation of skincare ingredients is new to the K-beauty scene, the process is similar to making fermented foods such as yogurt, sauerkraut, and Korea's beloved national dish: kimchi. According to Kristin Vukovic, a lifestyle and beauty author, "Fermented extracts within skincare products have many benefits, including calming and brightening the skin, as well as providing enhanced antioxidant and anti-inflammatory properties— plus, the skin readily absorbs them."

A two-part study funded by the **Korea Institute for Advancement** 5 **of Technology** focused on the differences between red ginseng and fermented red ginseng as an anti-aging ingredient in cosmetics. The study tested the safety of red ginseng on guinea pigs. A topical concentration of either red ginseng or fermented red ginseng was applied to the test subjects. The guinea pigs tested with fermented red ginseng had significantly less skin sensitization than those with red ginseng. Researchers

academic literacies   rhetorical situations   genres   processes   strategies   research MLA / APA   media / design   readings   handbook

implied that this "reduced toxicological potency" makes fermented red ginseng safer to use on skin, with less allergic reactions or sensitivities (Lee et al.). The fermented red ginseng was also found to contain higher amounts of certain anti-aging components including antioxidants, polyphenols, and uronic acid. The authors suggest that these findings make fermented red ginseng a more potent anti-aging ingredient than red ginseng. This traditional herb is the featured star of many K-beauty products including toners, sheet masks, and emulsions in both a fermented and non-fermented state. Fermented ginseng is a valuable ally in the battle against aging, although it is sometimes combined with other ingredients that do not have its impressive track record.

Another "miracle" ingredient in the Korean beauty industry is collagen. *Peach and Lily*, one of the largest online Korean beauty suppliers, claims that applying collagen can help prevent the formation of wrinkles, dark spots, and sagging and "will help infuse collagen into the skin" (Yoon). This unfortunately is far from the truth. According to cosmetology chemist Perry Romanowski, there is no way for skin to absorb collagen from a foreign source and magically assimilate it into the skin's existing collagen. Topically applied collagen is also ineffective due to its large molecular size, which inhibits skin absorbability. Molecules larger than 500 Daltons are unable to penetrate skin and collagen molecules are significantly too large at around 5,000 Daltons (Bblogger). K-beauty companies often advertise smaller, more absorbable collagen molecules (known as hydrolyzed collagen), but the particles are still too big to be absorbed by skin. Beauty expert Jerlene Bblogger states that collagen does have the ability to moisturize skin and make wrinkles appear smoother but, "As you might guess, this is a temporary effect—it's gone as soon as you wash your face, and wash the film off. It definitely does not have any long-term effect." Injections are the only effective use of collagen. Results are instant, but the process is expensive and must be done somewhat regularly to maintain the desired effect.

Korea has many innovative and cutting-edge beauty products which are now easily accessible worldwide. It is even believed that the K-beauty industry is twelve to fourteen years more advanced than United States' beauty technology (Park). Even with this high level of expertise, not all

Korean beauty products are effective or advertised honestly. "When it comes to anti-aging products, it's easy to be tricked into spending a lot of money on products that aren't worth it," says Romanowski. "That's because there's so much pseudoscientific misinformation out there about anti-aging cosmetic ingredients." Research has shown that both snail mucin and fermented red ginseng are beneficial skincare ingredients. Snail mucin is effective at combating signs of aging by reducing wrinkles and improving overall skin texture. Fermented red ginseng is a more potent version of non-fermented ginseng, with a higher prevalence of anti-aging components such as antioxidants. It is also likely associated with decreased skin allergies and sensitivities. While found in a multitude of Korean beauty products, collagen is ineffective even in a hydrolyzed form when applied topically. Beauty savvy consumers pursuing improved skin or even the elusive look of *Chok Chok* should continue slathering on snail mucin and fermented ginseng, but should avoid products containing collagen—an overhyped and poorly advertised ingredient in Korean beauty.

Works Cited

"A Bright Future: South Korea Ranks Among the Top 10 Beauty Markets Globally." *Mintel*, 4 Apr. 2017, http://www.mintel.com/press-centre/beauty-and-personal-care/a-bright-future-south-korea-ranks-among-the-top-10-beauty-markets-globally

Bblogger, Jerlene. "Collagen Skincare and Supplements: Do They Work?" *Musical Houses*, 13 Jan. 2013, www.musicalhouses.blogspot.nl/2013/01/collagen-skincare-and-supplements-do.html.

Fabi, Sabrina, et al. "The Effects of Filtrate Secretion of the *Cryptomphalus aspersa* on Photoaged Skin." *Journal of Drugs in Dermatology*, vol. 12, no. 4, Spring 2013, pp. 453-57, worldsbestskincare.net/docs/jdd.pdf.

Lee, Hyun-Sun, et al. "Fermenting Red Ginseng Enhances Its Safety and Efficacy as a Novel Skin Care Anti-Aging Ingredient: In Vitro and Animal Study." *Journal of Medicinal Food*, vol. 15, no. 11, Winter 2012, pp. 1015-23, www.ncbi.nlm.nih.gov/pmc/articles/PMC3491619/.

Park, Anna. "Why K-Beauty is Leading the Beauty Industry Worldwide." *W2Beauty*, May 2017, w2beauty.com/2017/05/k-beauty-leading-beauty-industry/.

Romanowski, Perry. "Is Collagen a Good Anti-Aging Ingredient?" *The Beauty Brains*, Mar. 2015, thebeautybrains.com/2015/03/is-collagen-a-good-anti-aging-ingredient/.

Thomas, Steve. "Medicinal Use of Terrestrial Mollusks (Slugs and Snails) With Particular Reference to Their Role in the Treatment of Wounds and Other Skin Lesions." *World Wide Wounds*, July 2013, www.worldwidewounds.com/2013/July/Thomas/slug-steve-thomas.html.

Vukovic, Kristen. "Fermentation Phenomenon." *American Spa*, 20 Dec. 2016, americanspa.com/skincare/fermentation-phenomenon.

Yoon, Alicia. "Collagen is King." *Peach and Lily*, July 2015, www.peachandlily.com/blogs/news/51230149-collagen-is-king

CHANDLER NICHOLS

The Magic of Self-Healing: A Lost Art

THROUGHOUT TIME, magic has been a sought-after yet feared phenomenon. Historically, scientific and mathematical concepts developed, extinguishing magic and labeling it a fictitious power, a way of interpreting anything with unfamiliar causes or functions. Science, in turn, was said to explain everything. Yet, what if magic were needed to explain science? The powers of the subconscious mind are yet to be understood. Theories—logical, medicinal, psychological, and historical alike—attempt to discover how subliminal thoughts are able to manifest physical change.

Imagine a man, muscular and healthy, who devoted his life to health and fitness, yet suddenly deteriorated from an unexplainable, severe case of congestive heart failure. Such a nightmare happened to R. Larry Nichols in the summer of 2012. Within several months' time, Nichols went from performing his daily exercise routines to not being able to stand on swollen feet. He had never smoked and was never obese or even overweight. An otherwise brief visit to the doctor was prolonged when he was told his heart was failing, thus causing the edema, or swelling, in his legs and abdomen. He was admitted for open-heart surgery. His surgeon performed miraculous work, although he did not expect Nichols to survive the operation. His doctors said his condition was unexplainable, with the only possible causes being viral or genetic. Nonetheless, Nichols survived and returned to an almost normal lifestyle. Unfortunately, his condition attacked once again in the summer of 2015, this time with a vengeance. Nichols' health declined so rapidly that in a few months, he could not eat nor walk due to swelling. He was admitted to the local hospital where his first cardiologist worked. The use of high-powered diuretics did not help, and Nichols' condition continued to deteriorate. He could not eat. The cardiologist suggested having an LVAD (Left Ventricle Assist Device) implanted, even though such a device is hindering and often a last resort, and, at the time, Nichols was too weak for surgery. Worse, his congestive heart failure began shutting down his organs, causing liver cirrhosis. Things were looking dire.

The doctors told Nichols and his family that the best course of action would be to deactivate his defibrillator and let him return home and live out his last days in peace. Nichols, headstrong and determined to live, refused. His cardiologist transferred him to a faith-based hospital in Nashville, Tennessee, where cardiac specialists performed vigorous tests to determine the root cause of his condition. Meanwhile, he fought mentally and physically to survive, while friends and family sent love, prayers, and positive thoughts his way. Suddenly and miraculously, Nichols' ammonia levels decreased and his body stopped retaining fluid. He began to eat. He began to walk. Soon, he was sent home, and he is currently recovering.

Nichols' condition is extremely rare, but what is even more peculiar is what healed him. The medicines he was given were mild; no further extensive surgery was performed after his heart surgery. Even the doctors doubted his survival, yet he defied their predictions. There are more "magical" than scientific factors at work here, as it seems most of his healing was the result of willpower, faith, and persistent optimism. Hence the question arises: What is the true power of the mind?

First, it is important to understand the concept of thought. Thought, a power of the mind, can be separated into two states: mind, which is subjective, and brain, which is objective (Schimmel 488). This categorization, known as the double aspect theory, describes how mental activity has both physical and metaphysical properties, and though the two can collaborate as one, they are ultimately individualized. Furthermore, the mind consists of intellectual and active powers, the former consisting of understanding and the latter involving will (Jaffro 197). Jaffro elaborates on this, noting, "[Intellectual powers] are powers to conceive, perceive, remember, believe, judge, reason, etc. [Active powers] are powers to produce changes in the world, to move our body, to direct our thought" (197). And, again, just as the mind and brain are separate yet interdependent, so are the powers of will and understanding. Will, the origin of action, must therefore have a source of understanding that the action will occur.

An idea or thought is created from experience into consciousness; then, the subconscious mind utilizes will to bring forth an action inspired by the idea.

The idea of willpower spread rapidly in the nineteenth century when Spiritualism appeared. Spiritualists and likeminded psychiatrists promoted the idea that the mind was not limited to the body or bound by the physical self (Alvarado 98). Rather, the subconscious mind was capable of powers such as mediumship, hypnosis, telepathy, creativity, and even self-healing. Divine healing, an idea brought forth during the Faith Movement, suggested that faith in God and constant prayer would cure illnesses (Pretorius 2). The "force of faith" is a category within the "power of the mind" (Pretorius 5). Denying symptoms and meditating on the promise of renewed health was a step-by-step process that the Faith Movement promoted (Pretorius 4). This seemingly spell-like ritual works thus: people are convinced they can be healed, and so they are healed. Faith is a key ingredient in self-healing, and along with optimism the subconscious mind begins to manifest the will to heal.

The belief of willpower and self-healing dissipated after the nineteenth century, and was dismissed as a false, as it was not provable by science. However, long before, the ancient Greeks utilized placebos as a sincere form of healing. Better known today is Hippocratic, or naturalized, medicine, which administers physical cures such as medicines or surgeries to patients to heal them. Asklepian healing, which was a religious healing, did not combat this idea, but was rather utilized in collaboration with it to optimize recovery (Collins 33). This form of healing took place in temples that were built on sacred grounds, providing an atmosphere of mystery and enthusiasm for the healing that awaited inside. Visitors would arrive with the expectation of being cured. They would enter a chamber and sleep, and then their dreams would be interpreted to determine what cure they would need (Collins 35). There are two important factors here: one, the patients arrived optimistically, and two, the subconscious mind (through dreaming) was utilized. The conscious mind recognized an illness in the patient, who then turned to the Asklepian temple for help. By entering the temple with optimism and the enthusiasm to be cured, the conscious experience would translate into the subconscious mind, which would activate powers of self-healing.

Placebos are now seen to have real effects, based on the brain and nervous system. The word placebo translates from Latin, "I shall please." Placebos and will are a way for thoughts to be interpreted and converted into action. In the 1980s a study by Dr. Daniel Ellis Moerman tested placebos explicitly. Two groups with stomach ulcers were given pills; one group was given actual medicine, and the other a placebo. Dr. Moerman found that the placebo produced a result in at best 90% of cases, which was more than that of the pharmaceutical. Furthermore, the ulcers tended to reappear in the patients that were given the drug, but did not return with the patients who took the placebo (Sachs 344). In fact, medical research has shown that placebos, when actual medicine is absent, work 33% of the time (Collins 38). Martin Ingvar used PET brain scans to monitor reactions of the brain in an experiment. One group of test subjects was given a painkiller medicine, while the other group was injected with saline solution and told it was painkiller. All test subjects then touched a hot rod. The brain scans were very similar in both groups, showing that both groups felt (or imagined) the same level of pain, even though one group was not even given the drug (Sachs 344).

Desires fuel willpower, yet will is also the "ability to resist temptations, to suppress feelings of desire, to practice self-denial, [and] to overcome habits" (Kugelmann 484). Self-control is constituted of control of the physical body and its reactions, and is especially evident during times of adversity or illness (Kugelmann 485). Will also allows an individual to endure and persevere, especially through adversity. Furthermore, it is a tool that can be used to influence others. Therefore, the attitude a healthcare professional has with his or her patient is a major factor in determining the outcome of the patient's recovery.

Willpower, I believe, is the source of the placebo effect; and faith, 10 steadfastness, positivity, a compassionate environment, denial of symptoms or negativity, and expectation are the ingredients necessary to activate it. Similarly, Sachs argues that energy can be focused into one part of the body to cure illnesses (343). Activating a placebo effect can therefore be written into a formula of sorts: 1. An experience is observed by the conscious and analyzed by the subconscious mind; 2. The subconscious mind, in conjunction with the conscious brain, finds a purpose in the experience and develops reasons to overcome or submit to it; 3. If the adversity is to be overcome, optimistic emotions, the belief that one will prevail, faith, and perseverance will form subconsciously; and in reaction to a positive environment and denial of negativity, the conscious brain will also add purpose; 4. With a purpose to live or overcome adversity defined, willpower will activate the nervous system to invoke self-healing. Comparably, Pretorius mentions:

> The process of obtaining healing is as follows: have faith in the Scriptures, which declare that healing comes through the atonement of Christ; deny any symptoms of sickness, but instead confess the Word that declares healing; and persist with the confession, over and over, until healing manifests itself (5).

This manifestation of healing is seen in the case of Mr. Nichols. He managed to utilize self-healing by following the placebo formula. Though this formula exists, and there are certain ingredients needed to activate it, he had not studied the subject. This demonstrates that having a conscious understanding of the placebo process is unnecessary for the process to work, thus showing that will and placebos act subconsciously, even though the conscious mind is necessary to understand the situation (as explained by the double aspect theory).

When faced with grave illness, Nichols refused to succumb to the inevitability of casualty. Instead of letting negativity flood his mind, he developed positive emotions, and even directed anger towards his condition, rather than himself, because he knew he was not the cause of his heart failure. "In the Asklepian tradition, it was the supplicant's willingness to engage in the healing process with enthusiasm (to be divinely inspired) that created a deep sense of openness and provided a means of activating their endogenous resources for healing" (Collins 41). He convinced himself that he would live and return to a normal life. He fought because he told himself he had more to do and see in life, and it was not yet his time to go. His friends and family also supported him through love and faith, which in turn may have inspired his own faith. "The possession of healing comes through the exercise of faith... 'Name it and claim it' and 'Believe it and receive it'. Faith is defined as speaking or confessing with authority in the full expectation that what is spoken will happen" (Pretorius 4).

It is interesting to observe the differences between the two hospitals where Mr. Nichols was cared for during the 2015 incident. In the first hospital, he and his family were told his condition would be impossible to improve, so the best course of action would be to turn off his defibrillator and go home to pass in peace rather than prolong suffering. During this time, Mr. Nichols developed liver cirrhosis and accumulated life-threatening ammonia levels. His health declined rapidly. Yet, after he asserted his will to live, he was transported to a faith-based hospital in Nashville. The atmosphere was a stark contrast to the previous hospital, as the healthcare professionals there were as optimistic as he was. Though no new medications were prescribed, Mr. Nichols healed in the short time he spent there. The positive relationship established with the doctors, as well as the spiritual atmosphere, provided more of the variables presented in the placebo formula. He thought positively, was now surrounded by others who shared his compassion and perseverance for recovery, and was convinced he would live. All of the ingredients to activate self-healing were present, allowing his willpower to bring about the action and repair his heart, liver, and the rest of his body. The process is continuing as he regains healthy weight and returns to living normally. He still has the determination and other factors in his subconscious mind to allow his body to continue to heal, and as long as this is so he will keep improving.

The case of Mr. Nichols shows the importance of healthcare professionals' attitudes towards their patients. If a patient shows the will to live, it is the duty of the healthcare professional to support that will in every way he or she can. This does not mean lying to the patient, but presenting the patient with the facts while also supporting any decisions to fight an illness. For example, cardiologist Dr. Bernard Lown told one of his patients who had a serious heart condition that the heartbeat was "a wholesome very good third-sound gallop." Though this is not good in medical terms, the patient interpreted it to mean that his heart was "as strong as a horse." Because of his imagining that his heart was strong, he expected to recover, and he did indeed heal. "It is humbling to imagine that a man who was expected to die of a heart condition recovered, because his imagination connected with the idea that he had a heart as strong as a horse" (Collins 39).

Multiple disciplines, from history to psychology to logic, have attempted to explain the mysterious placebo. From this information, ingredients needed to activate the placebo effect can be identified and thus be arranged into a formula: optimism, faith, denial of symptoms, compassionate atmosphere, determination to heal, and expectation to heal. Essentially, all of these ingredients can be simplified to positive thinking. By devoting oneself to the thought of healing, the body can heal itself through a conscious-subconscious relationship, known as the double aspect theory. Mr. Nichols overcame dire circumstances by healing himself. An experience alerted his consciousness of adversity; his conscious thoughts provoked subconscious analysis; the subconscious found a purpose through the object of experience; willpower, along with other ingredients, activated self-healing. Mr. Nichols defied his doctors' predictions; he defied science. Currently, placebos are not understood in their entirety, and are thus considered "magic." Yet, I believe that placebos will become scientific in the near future. The power of the mind, including will and self-healing, is increasing in popularity as an area of study. Just as thoughts can be manifested into action, what was once considered a figment of imagination is now becoming reality.

Works Cited

Alvarado, Carlos S. "Mediumship, Psychical Research, Dissociation, And The Powers Of The Subconscious Mind." *Journal Of Parapsychology* vol. 78, no. 4, 2014, pp. 98-114. PsycINFO, http://eds.b.ebscohost. com/ehost/detail/detail?vid=6&sid=771f8315-de2c-480a-b464011dc 4fcdedc%40sessionmgr104&bdata=JnNpdGU9ZWhvc3QtbGl2ZQ%3d %3d#AN=2014-31800-006&db=psyh

Collins, Mick. "Asklepian Dreaming And The Spirit Of Transformational Healing: Linking The Placebo Response To Therapeutic

academic literacies · rhetorical situations · genres · processes · strategies · research MLA / APA · media / design · readings · handbook

Uses Of Self." *Journal Of Religion And Health* vol. 52, no. 1, 2013, pp. 32-45. *PsycINFO*, http://eds.b.ebscohost.com/ehost/detail/detail?vid=8&sid=771f8315-de2c-480a-b464011dc4fcdedc%40sessionmgr104&bdata=JnNpdGU9ZWhvc3QtbGl2ZQ%3d%3d#AN=2013-03581-004&db=psyh

Jaffro, Laurent. "Reid On Powers Of The Mind And The Person Behind The Curtain." *Canadian Journal Of Philosophy* vol. 41, no. S1, 2014, pp. 197-213. *Academic Search Premier*, http://eds.b.ebscohost.com/ehost/detail/detail?vid=3&sid=f5c8938b-47e9-4fb5-a52d1b63fe100c7c%40sessionmgr120&bdata=JnNpdGU9ZWhvc3QtbGl2ZQ%3d%3d#AN=98942454&db=aph

Kugelmann, Robert. "Willpower." *Theory & Psychology*, vol. 23, no. 4, 2013, pp. 479-498. *PsycINFO*, http://eds.a.ebscohost.com/ehost/detail/detail?vid=4&sid=7fd3c761-d511-4d8f-b01c1d7fb2921dc0%40sessionmgr4007&bdata=JnNpdGU9ZWhvc3QtbGl2ZQ%3d%3d#AN=2013-30895-004&db=psyh

Pretorius, Stephan P. "Is 'Divine Healing' In The 'Faith Movement' Founded On The Principles Of Healing In The Bible Or Based On The Power Of The Mind?." *Hervormde Teologiese Studies*, vol. 65, no. 1, 2009, pp. 399-405. *Academic Search Premier*, http://eds.b.ebscohost.com/ehost/detail/detail?vid=3&sid=2edcdcf8-2fbf-4121-8ee28a9d94820130%40sessionmgr104&bdata=JnNpdGU9ZWhvc3QtbGl2ZQ%3d%3d#AN=48238679&db=aph

Sachs, Lisbeth. "Effects Of Magic Come In From The Cold: Pictorial Evidence Of Placebo Effect." *Scandinavian Journal Of Public Health*, vol. 34, no. 4, 2006, pp. 342-345, *CINAHL Plus with Full Text*, http://eds.b.ebscohost.com/ehost/detail/detail?vid=3&sid=27e1b38b-e403-488a-bafd-fef63b05c76f%40pdc-v-sessmgr01&bdata=JnNpdGU9ZWhvc3QtbGl2ZQ%3d%3d#AN=106339053&db=rzh

Schimmel, Paul. "Mind Over Matter? II: Implications For Psychiatry." *Australian & New Zealand Journal Of Psychiatry*, vol. 35, no. 4, 2001, pp. 488-494. *Academic Search Premier*, http://eds.b.ebscohost.com/ehost/detail/detail?vid=5&sid=39a0d727-dac5-474b-ab1d-4a4aa595ace6%40sessionmgr102&bdata=JnNpdGU9ZWhvc3QtbGl2ZQ%3d%3d#AN=5024704&db=aph

JANNA HOOD

A Wash with UA's Machine

FROM SGA TO HOMECOMING QUEEN, and throughout the campus of the University of Alabama, there are students upset about a racist Machine destroying the democracy and integration on campus. For many years, the University has been known for its deep southern roots in segregation. Being an institution at which the first African American students had to be escorted in through the doors, amidst the speech of Governor George Wallace attempting to prevent integration, segregation has left its scar across campus. Not only is the problem with racial prejudice, but also political prejudice on campus. The Machine is a very private and secretive, campus-wide, political organization, which usually chooses the campus's winning candidates by using its power to gain control over voters. The fact is that the Machine is made up of all-white, Greek-system members, and the racism on campus will not stop until the members of the organization are found and prevented from allowing their political agenda to plague campus any longer.

The Machine began as a fraternity called Theta Nu Epsilon, whose Greek initials spell out ONE since the Greek letter Theta is shaped like the English letter O. Theta Nu Epsilon's goal was to teach its members how to gain and use power to be the pinnacle political leaders (Weiss). Today, its members allegedly make up the majority of the Student Senate, which votes on topics relating to campus student organizations. If the Machine chooses a student running for a campus office, or social position, and the many members support this student, he or she will most likely win the seat and use the position's power to implement the Machine's objectives. The power does not stop there, however, because organizations now try to please the Machine by supporting whomever it supports in order for their candidates to be supported in the next election. The Machine runs on power and scare tactics, such as social

academic literacies · rhetorical situations · genres · processes · strategies · research MLA / APA · media / design · readings · handbook

excommunication and incidents of violence in past years, in order to maintain their control over campus democracy (Smith).

One example of such wielding of political power was the 2015 vote for Homecoming Queen at Alabama. One of the African American, Alpha Gamma Delta sorority members, Halle Lindsay, was running for Queen when the Machine chose to support a Caucasian member of the Court instead, Katelyn Katsafanas. This led all of the Greek system members to vote in favor of the Machine candidate, including Lindsay's own sorority sisters. One quote from a social media thread between the sorority's members read, "We are supporting [Katsafanas], we have to support what the Machine says to support" (Mosely). Despite Lindsay having many admirable qualities that set her apart from the other contestants, the Machine chose not to support her. While many see this as a racial controversy, others see it as a blatant lack of the freedom to vote for whomever the voter thinks is the most deserving candidate. In an interview with Lindsay herself, she states, "The greatest disappointment I feel is seeing my sorority sisters oppressed and unable to individually express themselves because of the politics involved. The goal for any election is to do your research and vote to support whom you believe is most qualified" (Enoch). The Alpha Gamma Delta members felt the need to choose between their own sister and a social presence on campus, which resulted in a win for Katsafanas and the Machine.

While much of the University's students and faculty are taking steps to become more of a diverse and integrated campus, the Greek system remains quite segregated. One CNN interview with a journalist from the *Crimson White* spoke about two African American women being blocked from pledging a sorority despite their 4.0 GPAs and outstanding credentials from public service work (Baldwin). Another example of this same thing happening was with Melody Twilley, when she decided to rush at Alabama but failed to be admitted two years in a row. She was a daughter of an upper-middle-class family in the black belt of Alabama, and was picked out of her high school to go to a prestigious academic boarding school in Mobile, the Alabama School of Math and Sciences. Being completely eligible to join a sorority, she wanted to rush with all of her friends and join a family of women who would become lifelong friends and make her college experience great. However, by day three of the rush week, she was informed that she had been dropped. Despite being "bright, attractive, and a member of the upper class," she was dropped on what appeared to be an only racial basis (Zengerle).

In recent years, more African American women are being allowed to join typically all-white sororities, but there is still work to be done to integrate a system that should have been integrated when the rest of the school was working through desegregation. However, instead of the University Board demanding all sororities allow African American students, students of color chose to form their own Greek system on campus. Alpha Kappa Alpha's Theta Sigma chapter is the only house on Sorority Row devoted especially to African American women who want to have the same experience their fellow Caucasian women do (Theta Sigma Chapter). Now, there are about nine sororities and fraternities on campus devoted solely to African American students; however, even they allow some Caucasian students to join with less hassle than a person of color joining a traditionally white Greek organization. On a campus as ethnically diverse as the University of Alabama is, the fact that the Greek system is still as segregated as it is raises the question of why that is so.

While many advocates for racial integration are battling for a less segregated Greek system, it is unfortunate that one organization, the Machine, is attempting to halt their progress. The Machine's members consist of chapter presidents and officers from twenty-eight of Alabama's sororities and fraternities, and they use this influential power to sway political votes for the members they support. Members of the Machine have also infiltrated the Student Senate, which votes on topics brought to it by the student body. This makes passing any policy that could potentially punish members of the Machine for telling people how to vote nearly impossible, despite how many students request solutions to the issue.

One possible solution to the dictatorship that is the Machine is a campus hotline for any suspicion of voting fraud, and a punishment for any members found to be associated with the Machine. Hotlines have been used for many issues where callers wish to anonymously help someone, or confidentially receive help for themselves. One example is the Domestic Violence Hotline put in place by President Bill Clinton, following the passage of Violence Against Women Act of 1994, to provide twenty-four-hour access to trained counselors ("Off Our Backs"). The University of Alabama itself implemented a Hazing Hotline in 2001, which has proven to be helpful in making campus a safer environment. Just last semester, September of 2015, five fraternity brothers were arrested for hazing due to an anonymous call to the hotline (*Crimson White* Staff). Although the risk of being caught did not prevent the act, the hotline provided a way for action to be made to stop the hazing, catch the hazers, and punish them for their actions. If there were a way for witnesses of Machine work to anonymously call, text, or email their allegations to a task force committee, there would be a greater chance of finding members of the Machine and preventing them from influencing elections.

Along with the hotline, there should be a form of punishment for those found to be involved with the Machine's political regime. Revoking their right to vote in campus elections would not be ethical. But they could be placed on probation by, or removed from, the Student Senate. They could be prohibited from running for Student Government Association positions for an allotted number of elections. While these measures will not stop the Machine from functioning altogether, they could help take power away from the Machine, and give it to the voters.

Many colleges have been criticized for being steeped in traditions that have, over the years, become increasingly outdated. Whether working to change racist mascots, buildings named after historical people with less than moral backgrounds, or even student-led organizations whose sole purpose since their founding was to gain and keep power, there are many ways universities can change for the better. The problem might be solved by implementing a hotline to mitigate the Machine's corruption of campus democracy. The people's vote should be that of individual opinion and not based on an organization that chooses candidacy based on ethnicity or popularity. Slowing the progress of the Machine will not immediately integrate the University of Alabama's Greek systems, but by creating more equal opportunities for every race and ethnicity in Greek life, Student Government Association, and everyday campus life, the university will be more accepting of the diverse student body already present on campus. While there will always be amoral people and organizations, if the majority of the people come together for one common goal of fairness and equality, the few left behind will only remain in the past with the traditions they fought so desperately to preserve.

Works Cited

"Allegations of Racism at University of Alabama Sororities; Kidman Collides with Pap; Brain-Eating Amoeba Makes Louisiana Water." *CNN Newsroom*, 13 Sept. 2013, https://www.cnn.com/2013/09/18/us/alabama-sororities/index.html

Enoch, Ed. "Controversy amid University of Alabama Homecoming Queen Crowning." *TuscaloosaNews.com*. N.p., 10 Oct. 2015, http://www.tuscaloosanews.com/article/DA/20151010/News/605156964/TL/

"Five University Students Arrested Due to an Investigation of Hazing Allegations." - *The Crimson White*. The University of Alabama, 1 Oct. 2015, http://www.cw.ua.edu/article/2015/09/five-university-of-alabama-students-arrested-due-to-an-investigation-of-hazing-allegations

Mosely, Erin. "Believe It or Not: A Sorority Horror Story." - *The Crimson White*. University of Alabama, 10 Aug. 2015, http://www.cw.ua.edu/article/2015/10/believe-it-or-not-a-sorority-horror-story

"New Domestic Violence Hotline". "New Domestic Violence Hotline". *Off Our Backs* vol. 26, no. 5, 1996, p. 3. https://www.jstor.org/stable/20835468?Search=yes&resultItemClick=true&searchText=new&searchText=domestic&searchText=violence&searchText=hotline&searchUri=%2Faction%2FdoBasicSearch%3Ffilter%3D%26amp%3BQuery%3Dnew%2Bdomestic%2Bviolence%2Bhotline&refreqid=search%3A70a3ec7af0b1e55d6adc7d1852d70865&seq=1#page_scan_tab_contents

Smith, Alex. "Why I'm Leaving the Machine." - *The Crimson White*. University of Alabama, 26 Oct. 2015, http://www.cw.ua.edu/article/2015/10/why-im-leaving-the-machine

"Theta Sigma Chapter." *The National Pan-Hellenic Council.* Alpha Kappa Alpha, n.d. nphchq.org. 04 Apr. 2016.

Weiss, Philip. "The Most Powerful Fraternity in America." *Welcome to the Machine.* Esquire, April 1992, http://www.welcometothemachine. info/pdf/esquire.pdf

Zengerle, Jason. "This Student Took on University of Alabama's Segregated Sororities. It Didn't Turn Out As She'd Hoped." *New Republic.* N.p., 3 Feb. 2012. https://newrepublic.com/article/119156/ segregation-lives-university-alabamas-sorority-row

KRISTEN GOCHETT

Being Black in America: How Race Plays a Role in Police Brutality

THE RECENT INCREASE IN DEATHS of unarmed African Americans at the hands of law enforcement officers has sparked the Black Lives Matter movement. Black Lives Matter attempts to emphasize the importance of black lives in a racially discriminatory criminal justice system. Black Lives Matter is not implying that all lives do not matter; the movement highlights the injustice that African Americans face in present day America (decades after the Civil Rights Movement). Trayvon Martin, a seventeen-year-old African American youth from Sanford, Florida, was shot and killed by George Zimmerman, a community watchman, while walking down the street with Skittles and an Arizona iced tea because he was deemed "suspicious." Tamir Rice, a twelve-year-old youth from Cleveland, Ohio was fatally shot by police after playing on a swing set at the park with a plastic pistol. Michael Brown, an eighteen-year-old African American man from Ferguson, Missouri was shot in the back six times and killed after an altercation between him and officer Darren Wilson. Eric Garner, a forty-three-year-old African American man from Staten Island, New York, was placed in a fatal chokehold that led to his death after reports that he uttered "I Can't Breathe" eleven times. Walter Scott, thirty-three years old and from North Charleston, South Carolina, was shot in the back and killed after fleeing from police after a traffic stop from a non-functioning tail light. Finally, Sandra Bland, a twenty-eight-year-old from Walter County, Texas was taken into custody after a minor traffic violation and was later found hanging from the ceiling in her jail cell. All black, all unarmed. After the verdict of no indictment from their deaths and numerous others, the African American community has taken action to demand justice in a criminal justice system that fails to protect its people of color.

academic literacies · rhetorical situations · genres · processes · strategies · research MLA / APA · media / design · readings · handbook

In recent discussions of police brutality, a controversial issue has been whether race contributes to the use of deadly force by law enforcement officers on African Americans. On the one hand, some politicians argue that law enforcement officers use necessary force to subdue those who are in violation of the law regardless of their race. From this perspective, Heather MacDonald, an American political commentator and journalist, suggests police officers target African Americans only if they commit crimes. On the other hand, African American political scientists and professors from colleges around the nation charge that race is the primary factor in law enforcement's use of excessive force. In the words of Sundiata Cha-Jua, African American Studies and History professor at the University of Illinois, "police brutality is the current form of state-sanctioned violence against people of color" (par. 1). According to this view, recent reports of police brutality are a continuation of the 500 years of violence African Americans have endured in the United States. In order to address the police's abuse and improve the public's opinion of policing, common ground must be reached between those who are for and against the use of deadly force, and there must be reform in the policing profession.

The Black Lives Matter movement arose as a response to the continued murders and brutal arrests of African Americans through the excessive force of police officers. The movement started from a social media post expressing outrage in response to Michael Brown's death. After a vivid rant of injustice, a user used the hashtag followed by the three now-famous words "Black Lives Matter." These three words became a rallying cry from the African American community to demand recognition as human beings in a society of racial disparity. The deaths of Martin, Rice, Brown, Garner, Scott, and Bland highlight the need for justice in the criminal justice system. In the film *Black Twitter After Ferguson,* Black Twitter activist Johnetta Elzie asserts that "It doesn't matter what black people do. We are walking targets just because." The film explains the atmosphere of the African American community on Twitter after the death of Michael Brown. The death of Brown resulted in mass demonstrations in Ferguson, Missouri, with protestors demanding justice as human beings in a nation that claims to treat every man equally regardless of physical characteristics or socioeconomic status. Although riots proved not to be the most efficient way to demand the justice Black Americans wanted, the riots created a media frenzy that brought nationwide awareness to the Black Lives Matter movement, which eventually led to the question: how many more unarmed African Americans must lose their lives in this ongoing battle for equality?

While Elzie explains the toll the death of Brown had on the African American community, John A. Powell's recent article in *The Washington Informer* provides overwhelming statistics of racial injustice in federal, state, and local government. After several verdicts of no indictment from a continuation of murders of unarmed blacks, the African American community faced the harsh reality of no punishment for the officers who took the lives of innocent citizens. Police continue to murder Black Americans without consequences for the actions committed. In his article "Let's Have a Real Conversation About Race," professor of law and African American studies at the University of California, Berkeley, John A. Powell asserts that "our young black males are at a twenty-one times greater risk of being shot dead by police than their white counterparts" (par. 2). Similarly, Jennifer Eberhardt, social psychologist and professor at Stanford University explains that "black defendants who have what are considered stereotypically "black features" serve up to eight months longer and receive more death sentences than their white counterparts" (par. 6). ProPublica, a non-profit newsroom that produces investigative journalism in public interest, also gathered statistics for means of determining what factors influenced police brutality. According to the gathered statistics, "1,217 deadly police shootings from 2010 to 2012 captured in the federal data show that blacks, age 15 to 19, were killed at a rate of 31.17 per million, while just 1.47 per million white males in that age range died at the hands of police." The statistics in these studies are evidence that race does play a role in the unequal treatment of citizens in the American criminal justice system.

Given the documented statistics of racial injustice in the criminal justice system, it can be inferred that police are intimidated by African Americans resulting in the use of excessive force. Recent findings from national statistics prove that racial bias is the deciding factor when a   5

academic literacies   rhetorical situations   genres   processes   strategies   research MLA / APA   media / design   readings   handbook

law enforcement officer decides if use of deadly force is necessary. In his article, "Why Police So Often See Unarmed Black Men as Threats," journalist German Lopez suggests that "everyone carries a subconscious prejudice … this implicit bias contributes to the many racial disparities in law enforcement" (par. 2). University of Colorado Boulder psychology professor Josh Correll ran tests to prove racial bias in police shootings with a shooter video game. Correll argues that "officers generally did a good job of avoiding shooting all races…when shooting was warranted, officers pulled the trigger more quickly against black suspects than white ones" (par 9). The evidence in these studies is further explained in a national study from the Federal Bureau of Statistics in 2007. The findings showed that black and white low class citizens were equally likely to be stopped by police, but blacks were more likely to have had excessive force used against them. These statistics support the claim that race is a motive in deciding when and when not to fire a gun or act excessively causing harm to the citizen.

While the statistics from various studies involving race and excessive force conclude that race does in fact play a role in police brutality, the definition of deadly force marks the primary division between those who approve and oppose it. Police define use of deadly force as shooting to kill. There are arguments that use of deadly force is very much necessary to ensure the safety of law enforcement officers. From this perspective, Oak Ridge, Tennessee Police Department Sergeant Randy Tedford proposes, "Cops don't shoot to kill. If we have to shoot, we are shooting to survive" (par. 10). According to Tedford, police utilize deadly force when absolutely necessary. Tedford also explains that police have a dual job each day. They are forced to protect the citizens of our country and maintain healthy relationships with their families. He also asserts that they sometimes fear if they do not use deadly force when they feel threatened, they may not make it home to see their families at the end of their shift. He explains that guns are the last resort in attempting to detain all citizens, not just African Americans. According to the federal use-of-force continuation, police are supposed to determine their level of force in any situation based on the actions of the individual they are in contact with. Although this may be true for some officers, not all abide by this standard. If police only shoot to survive, how can the deaths of unarmed African Americans who pose no threat to law enforcement officers be justified?

While there are various citizens around the nation who approve of the use of excessive force by police officers, there are also those who oppose it. *Debate.org*, a public opinion web site, ran a poll to ask the general public if police should be allowed to use deadly force. Although sixty-two percent who answered the survey chose yes and thirty-eight percent chose no, it is clear that there is division among citizens regarding deadly force. An anonymous user answered the question proposing that "Police should be forced to retreat from a situation just as any other civilian...they make a bad situation worse when they arrive and usually are the reason the person completes the act they're threatening." The proposed opinion suggests that there are better solutions to handling a situation in which force is necessary. The anonymous user goes on to suggest, "I would even offer only carrying less lethal weapons and reserving deadly weapons for specialized trained officers." The user argues that it is justifiable for police to use force to detain individuals; however, deadly force only makes a bad situation worse.

Given the opinions of those who are for and against the use of deadly force, or any force at all, it is understandable that this is a heavily debated topic among politicians, law enforcement, and the public. In the article "Law Enforcement and Violence: The Divide Between Black and White Americans," many researchers from the University of Chicago contributed to statistics from both Black and White Americans and their opinions of policing. According to the statistics, "Blacks and whites agree that changes in policies and procedures could be effective in reducing tensions between minorities and police and in limiting violence against civilians." Everyone has their opinions, whether for or against force. However, finding an adequate solution to the problem is not as simple. In her article in *The Huffington Post*, politics reporter Julia Craven avers, "we want a world where police don't kill people (par. 1). According to her view, black activists around the nation are proposing solutions to bring a better name to policing and to mend the broken relationship between law enforcement and African Americans. Of the proposed solutions, community policing and body cameras appear to be the most promising ways to reform policing and boost the public's image of the profession.

Community policing is a way that the police can interact with the ones they serve in their respective communities. In *Police*, a publication for law enforcement officers, the article "Community Policing Can Be Effective If Properly Practiced" explains that community policing "emphasizes the individual initiatives and skills of officers as well as interacting with local citizens to build relationships" (par 1). This is an attempt for the public to regain their trust in policing, and it also reforms policing. In community policing, the officers form a relationship with the citizens they are meant to protect. Another solution for boosting the public's morale is the use of body cameras. Body cameras record an officer's routine procedures and arrests that can be used in case of claims of police misconduct. According to his article "Mixed Messages: Body Camera Rules," former attorney-general Eric Holder acknowledges that "body cameras tend to reduce the number of complaints and are a very useful tool in trying to determine what was the nature of action between someone in the community" (par. 1). Body cameras record officer-citizen interaction and provide visual evidence in a case of injustice. These solutions black activists proposed could possibly be the solution to the ongoing tension between police and African Americans.

In the final analysis, the best solution for decreasing police brutal- 10 ity against the African American community and changing the public's opinion of policing is for common ground to be reached in deciding the differentiating factor of what is considered deadly force and what is not to reform policing. The police are meant to protect our well-being. However, there is evidence that police do not always abide by moral standards. The deaths of Martin, Rice, Brown, Scott, and Bland serve as reminders of the injustices that the African American community have faced. They sparked a movement that demanded justice for better treatment of African Americans. Although their deaths prompted a divide within the nation, it also allowed citizens to reach mutual agreements as to what needs to be done to ensure these types of fatalities will never happen again. In the end, we, as well as law enforcement officers, must fulfill our duties as United States citizens to ensure safety for all and more unified nation.

Works Cited

McDonald, Brent. "Black Twitter After Ferguson." *NYTimes. com Video Collection*, 2015, https://www.nytimes.com/video/us/100000003841604/blacktwitter-after-ferguson.html

Cha-Jua, Sundiata Keita. "Racism Is a Factor in Police Violence." *Police Brutality*, edited by Helen Cothran, Greenhaven Press, 2001. Opposing Viewpoints. *Opposing Viewpoints in Context*, http://link.galegroup.com/apps/doc/EJ3010156237/OVIC?u=tusc49521&xid=8d13384e. Accessed 20 Mar. 2018. Originally published as "Contemporary Police Brutality and Misconduct: A Continuation of the Legacy of Racial Violence," 2001.

"Community Policing Can Be Effective If Properly Practiced." *Community Policing*, edited by Roman Espejo, Greenhaven Press, 2014. Opposing Viewpoints. *Opposing Viewpoints in Context*, http://link.galegroup.com/apps/doc/EJ3010903212/OVIC?u=tusc49521&xid=8412f40b. Accessed 20 Mar. 2018. Originally published as "Does Community Policing Work?" *Police*, Dec. 2005.

Craven, Julia. "Here's What Black Lives Matter Activists Want Politicians to Do About Police Violence." *HuffingtonPost.com*. 24 Aug. 2015. https://www.huffingtonpost.com/entry/black-lives-matter-policy-demands_us_55d7392ae4b0a40aa3aa9443

Mac Donald, Heather. "Racial Profiling Does Not Exist." *Racial Profiling*, edited by David Erik Nelson, Greenhaven Press, 2009. Opposing Viewpoints. *Opposing Viewpoints in Context*, http://link.galegroup.com/apps/doc/EJ3010572207/OVIC?u=tusc49521&xid=9a4986c4. Accessed 20 Mar. 2018. Originally published as "Reporting While Wrong: The New York Times Peddles More 'Driving While Black' Malarkey," *National Review*, vol. 57, no. 17, 26 Sept. 2005.

"Law Enforcement and Violence: The Divide Between Black and White Americans." *NORC.org*, July 2015, http://www.apnorc.org/projects/ Pages/law-enforcement-and-violence-the-divide-between-black-and-white-americans.aspx

Lopez, German. "Why Police So Often See Unarmed Black Men as Threats." *Vox Policy & Politics*, 29 Dec. 2015, https://www.vox. com/2014/8/28/6051971/police-implicit-bias-michael-brown-ferguson-missouri

Powell, John A. "Let's Have a Real Conversation about Race in the United States." *Dallas Examiner*, http://dallasexaminer.com/ news/2014/dec/28/lets-have-real-conversation-about-race-united-stat/

Shackford, Scott. "Mixed messages: body camera rules." *Reason*, Mar. 2016, p. 12+. *Opposing Viewpoints in Context*, http://link.galegroup. com/apps/doc/A443399242/OVIC?u=tusc49521&xid=4d6d9161. Accessed 20 Mar. 2018.

Tedford, Randy. "The Use of Deadly Force Is Sometimes Necessary." *Police Brutality*, edited by Louise I. Gerdes, Greenhaven Press, 2004. Current Controversies. *Opposing Viewpoints in Context*, http://link.galegroup.com/apps/doc/EJ3010057234/ OVIC?u=tusc49521&xid=4ece73aa. Accessed 20 Mar. 2018.

GAVIN REID

The True Enshrinement of American Ideals: The Electoral College

IMAGINE THAT YOU HAVE just cast your vote for president, and you are sitting in your living room impatiently waiting for the results of the election to come in so that you can know who will be the next president of the United States of America. All of the results come in and you are excited to see that the candidate you voted for won the majority of votes across the country...but then you realize they somehow lost in the Electoral College. This was a reality for citizens who voted in the presidential election of 1824, 1876, 1888, 2000, and now the presidential election of 2016. This fact can stir a lot of emotions and understandably so. It can seem incomprehensible that a candidate can win most of the votes and yet still lose the election. However, we must analyze the Electoral College and its purpose before we jump to any conclusions about the fate of the Electoral College. Many news articles have recently declared that the Electoral College should be done away with. However, the Electoral College must remain, because it was instated by the nation's founding fathers for very good reason, solidly embodies the ideals of the United States of America, and its benefits strongly outweigh any possible shortcomings.

The Electoral College was instated by our nation's founding fathers to prevent one region from controlling the course of the country. A prominent fear of small states at the time was that the new government would allow the larger states to force their will upon them. At the time of our country's formation a majority of the population was concentrated within a few states and these few states would be able to dominate the government if the government were a pure democracy. Because of this population disparity, many small states feared that the larger ones would force them to conform to any laws and legislation that the larger states desired. The founding fathers recognized that a pure democracy could lead to this tyranny of the majority, so they put multiple measures into place to avoid this tyranny. One of those measures is the Electoral College, which allows each state a more equal voice while also reflecting the opinion of the population.

The Electoral College consists of multiple groups of electors from each state. The number of electors for each state is equal to the sum of the number of the state's representatives in the House of Representatives and the two Senators granted to each state. There are 538 total electors. Each state legislature nominates the electors for the state, and the people choose which group of electors they want by voting for their presidential candidate ("U.S. Electoral College: What is the Electoral College?"). This strategy gives each state a more equal voice, grants each state two electors regardless of population, and grants additional electors based on each state's population. Without the Electoral College, urban areas could potentially dominate politics. If the president were simply decided by the popular vote, then vast regions of America wouldn't be properly represented and would be ignored. The founding fathers also appreciated the quality of votes as opposed to the quantity. Michael Uhlmann, a political science professor in the Department of Politics and Policy at Claremont Graduate University, states that the Electoral College "teaches us that the character of a majority is more important than its size alone." While a majority vote of the population could come solely from urban areas, Richard Posner, a past judge on the United Sates Seventh Court of Appeals, a professor at the University of Chicago, and a Harvard Law School graduate, states that "The Electoral College requires a presidential candidate to have trans-regional appeal." The president can't win the election by earning the support of simply one geographic area or demographic of the population. The Electoral College forces the future president to appeal to people of various demographics, regions, and subcultures.

The Electoral College, despite popular belief, solidly embodies the ideals of our government. Many Americans believe that since the Electoral College does not always reflect the will of the majority: that it is, in effect, undemocratic. The short response to that comment is, "Yes, it is absolutely undemocratic." The longer response requires a more thorough understanding of the founding of our nation. Anyone who tells you that the United States of America is simply a democracy is completely misinformed. The framers of the Constitution formed a government that consists of aspects of a democracy, a republic, and a federalist system. While a democracy focuses solely on the will and desires of the majority of a population, a republic allows the people to elect representatives who will represent the population in legal matters by doing what they believe is best for the nation. A federalist system, in turn, separates the powers of a government into multiple tiers to ensure that more local areas are governed in a way that more accurately represents the local population. While the Electoral College may seem to contradict the ideals of a democracy, it accomplishes the goals set forth by a republic and federalist system. Representatives chosen by the public ultimately are the ones responsible for electing the president and the state legislatures assume responsibility for nominating the members of the Electoral College. The founding fathers were wary of majority rule in a democracy and wanted to ensure that their country was protected from itself. A memorable quote from Thomas Jefferson is that "Democracy is nothing more than mob rule, where 51% of the people may take away the rights of the other 49%." The American people must be aware and cautious of this mob rule and strive to protect and secure the rights of the 49%. America is the great country that it is today because the founding fathers promised American citizens certain unalienable rights, and we must be cautious of any political reform that could possible jeopardize these rights.

Opponents of the Electoral College would argue that it should be 5 removed due to its negative effects on our country. A prominent argument is that presidential campaigning focuses on certain key swing states and "has just taken a lot of states off of the presidential map" (Dotinga). Bypassing or abolishing the Electoral College would supposedly "allow long-ignored states to get attention again in presidential campaigns" (Dotinga). While the concentration of campaigns in certain states is upsetting, it is unreasonable to assume that candidates would then give equal attention to every region of the country if the

academic literacies   rhetorical situations   genres   processes   strategies   research MLA / APA   media / design   readings   handbook

Electoral College were abolished. If the Electoral College were done away with, then campaigning would shift its focus to regions with multiple high population urban areas such as the northeast and the west coast. Although candidates may have to adjust their campaign strategies, large sections of America, especially rural areas, would remain ignored. Another argument is that abolishing the Electoral College would make every vote more important and would open our political system more accommodating of third parties. Instead of ignoring the votes that do not align with the majority of voters in each state and the opinions of voters supporting third parties, every individual's vote would have an equal effect on the outcome of the election and allow third parties to become more significant. Uhlmann states that, "What the people would get by choosing direct election is the disintegration of the state-based two-party system." He notes that removing the Electoral College would allow "the rise of numerous factional parties based on region, class, ideology, or cult of personality." Although this may be true, we must again look back at the initial purpose of the Electoral College and not let the appeal of the statement "every vote counts" overshadow the purpose and intentions of the Electoral College. Just because a system has flaws does not mean that reform would make it a more just and reasonable system. As long as government is organized by mankind and humans continue to be imperfect creatures, we must accept that our political system will be flawed to a degree and decide whether or not reform would truly be beneficial. It is too easy to simply make a decision that sounds pleasing to the ear and makes us feel good. We must closely analyze each consequence of our choices before we decide on a course of action.

The United States of America must keep the Electoral College as a part of its government structure. Although the complaints against it are understandable, we must analyze and study the profound reasons that it was initially created; to ensure a proper representation of each state, region, and people of the United States in the presidential election. The Electoral College prevents regional tyranny in our government, maintains our current government structure, and embodies the ideals embedded in our government system. As appealing as a direct election may sound, we must remember what the founding fathers had in mind for our country and how the institutions they put in place were created for the protection of our freedom and way of life.

Works Cited

Dotinga, Randy. "The Electoral College Weakens Federalism." *The Presidential Election Process*, edited by Tom Lansford, Greenhaven Press, 2008, *Opposing Viewpoints in Context*, ic.galegroup.com/ic/ovic/?p=OVIC%3AGIC&u=tusc49521. Originally published as "A Backdoor Plan to Thwart the Electoral College," *Christian Science Monitor*, vol. 98, no. 141, 16 June 2006, pp. 1-10.

Uhlmann, Michael M. "The Electoral College Strengthens Federalism." *The Presidential Election Process*, edited by Tom Lansford, Greenhaven Press, 2008, *Opposing Viewpoints in Context*, ic.galegroup.com/ic/ovic/?p=OVIC%3AGIC&u=tusc49521. Originally published as "The Old (Electoral) College Cheer: Why We Have It; Why We Need It," *National Review*, vol. 56, no. 21, 8 Nov. 2004, p. 28.

Posner, Richard. "In Defense of the Electoral College." *Slate*, 11 Nov. 2016, www.slate.com/articles/news_and_politics/view_from_chicago/2012/11/defending_the_electoral_college.html

"U.S. Electoral College: What is the Electoral College?" *National Archives and Records Administration*, n.d., www.archives.gov/federal-register/electoral-college/about.html.

Evaluation **63**

HUNTER STANLEY

Hey...

DEPRESSION IS A TOPIC that's difficult to discuss, address, and explain. Many face it. The crippling reality of depression is there is no good 'fix,' no perfect method of consoling those whose lives are affected by it. It is difficult to relate to unless you have walked in those shoes. Nonetheless, hip hop artist George Watsky aims to lighten the burden of those who have, or have had, depression with a song that addresses this ailment. With soft, simple, and soothing melodies, a smooth lyrical rhythm, and truly inspiring words, "Hey As***le" addresses this all-too-common mental illness.

The song begins with singer-songwriter Kate Nash's vocals floating beautifully over a simple, melodic track. An acoustic guitar accompanies the arrangement. Even though the lyrics include profanity, the mood of the piece comes across as sweet and melancholy. Throughout the song, the gentle melody can be heard playing in the background.

Following on the coattails of the chorus is the rapping of our songwriter, George Watsky, who states, "This kind of shot comes once / Another opportunity of a lifetime just slipped away / And that's the fifth this month." Here, Watsky begins to explain the shackling effect depression has on individuals. Even so, he appeals to our sense of rhythm and rhyme. Later, he transitions into a faster and more exhaustive rap. Adamantly, Watsky raps, "I'm climbing up a ladder that has got no end / Hung up on a rung I'll never make it to the top." Watsky allows the natural oration of these words to create a syncopation that pushes the emotion of this piece. Again, he rhymes most lines using the "ABCBBBDB" structure. This lets the listener feel the pulse of the song and the intensity of his emotion drift into the tapping of their foot or the nodding of their head. Not only does he engage the audience's brain with his imaginative use of words and their bodies with his movement-inducing cadences, but he invokes their heart and soul with his inspiring lyrics.

At the conclusion of almost every stanza, Watsky adds phrases of encouragement to establish hope and perseverance in his listeners. He intentionally finishes every segment of the song with positivity, reflecting the theme that there is always light at the end of the tunnel. At the finale of the first fast-paced segment he raps, "Don't you ever forget/ Why you get up and you put one foot in front of the next." Here, he is trying to clarify the overbearing thundercloud of doubt and lack of self-worth while simultaneously hoping to provide an umbrella for those caught underneath it. This illness is an uphill battle. Watsky expresses this best when he raps, "Spent a half an hour sitting at the bottom of my shower / Letting the water run over my body and dammit I wanted to get up / But I didn't have the power." Depression can be debilitating, and this quote does a sufficient job of explaining the absence of desire while within its grip. However, he implores the hearer to continue to fight. In a final effort to inspire and uplift, his last lyrics are "I'll keep on coming and coming until I'm coming with the stamina of a salmon / Who's heading upstream." This song ensures that hope is not lost. Even though the battle is uphill, underwater, out of breath, or darn near close to death, there is success.

This optimistic opinion is not universal. Some may find the lyrics [5] and overall tone inherently sad instead of finding the morsels of hope scattered within the artistry of this song. After all, the title of this song is indeed an expletive. Many of the song's lyrics elaborate on the crippling effects of depression. There is mention of a lack of energy, low self esteem, incapability, and denial. Others may say the tune itself is gloomy, mistaking the sweet overtones for a miserable melody. The rap could be construed as the pinnacle of the heated argument between battling wills inside the mind of someone living under the conditions of the disease. Although some may choose to view this song as morose, one could also arrive at the conclusion that it contains the tools of living with and eventually conquering depression. The message of hope lying within every stanza is a continual reminder to its listeners that they are stronger than their adversary.

"Hey A****le" addressed the pains of depression with its use of a soft melodic motif, a consistent and unfailing beat, and inspiring lyrics.

Many people struggle with this ailment, and George Watsky intended to give his two cents to the world about it. Through the melody and chorus we feel the bittersweet melancholy quality of the illness. Within the rhythms and raps we feel the pressure and dulling feeling many scuffle with. Contained in the meaningful lyrics we feel hope and inspiration addressed to those caught in the grips of this ugly pain. This song does a noble job of bringing awareness and compassion to those afflicted by depression.

Works Cited

Watsky. "Hey Asshole." *Cardboard Castles*, Steel Wool Records, 2013.

Memoirs **64**

See also:

RICK BRAGG
*All Over but
the Shoutin'*　216

CALLAHAN SMITH

The Inside

I LOOKED AT MY INSTRUCTOR, Noah, admiring his white lab coat. His name was inscribed on it in a fancy cursive font. He seemed so official, like a real doctor, even though he was just a medical student. I could only wonder if I would be wearing one someday. I had dreamed of becoming a doctor for as long as I could remember. But I feared that could all change today.

It was the fifth day of my course at Brown University, the day I had been anticipating all week. Today was the day I was going to see the inside of the human cadaver lab.

I zoned back into the Noah's speech. He informed us that, "At least one med student every year passes out during their first time in the lab. So, don't worry if you feel like you're going to. Just try to tell me before you actually do." I wasn't sure whether his goal had been to scare us or make us feel better, but those three sentences had crushed the very little confidence I did have. I hoped that wouldn't happen to me, that seeing cadavers wouldn't terrify me so much that I would no longer want to be a doctor. But, it was definitely possible.

I had scrubbed in. My blue latex gloves were on. Everything was ready, but I wasn't sure if I was. I was only sixteen, and I was about to see dead bodies. Today would be my first experience with death, and I would be looking it straight in the face.

As soon as Noah opened the door, our hallway became invaded by 5 the atrocious odor that had escaped from the lab. It was the chemicals used to preserve the bodies. It was nauseating. My nose was burning and my head was throbbing. It only got worse with each breath.

The lab was chilly and bright. It was empty for the most part, except for three silver tables. Lying on top of each one was a big, black bag.

Those were the cadavers.

My stomach dropped. I reluctantly joined the rest of my class in the huddle they formed in front of Noah. Lying there between Noah and the rest of my class was one of the cadavers. *I can do this...* I repeated it in my head, desperately trying to convince myself it was true.

Noah reached for the bag. My legs began to tremble and my knees felt like they would give out any second. He grabbed the zipper. I was fighting my urge to bolt for the door. I could feel my heart beating faster and faster, pounding throughout my entire body. Noah slowly unzipped the bag, revealing more and more of the man's body- first his curly gray hair, then his big pointy nose. His lips showed no expression, not a smile or a frown. His wrinkled skin was pale with a slight tint of yellow and gray. His skin looked abnormally stiff. His naked body stretched across the entire table. He was completely exposed.

When I looked at his face, all I could think about was this man's life. He had a family, people who cared about him. He had dreams and passions. I wondered what kind of job he had and what state he lived in. He got out of bed every morning for decades, until one day he didn't. The thought sent chills down my spine.

He opened the next bag, revealing another man, one that had already been dissected. His face had been covered with a sheet. For some reason, this cadaver didn't freak me as much. You would think that seeing someone's insides, all of their organs right there in front of you, would be a lot more terrifying, but it wasn't. But when I looked at the man who hadn't been cut open yet, all I could think about was that I was looking at death.

Noah told us that it was now time for us to actually study the cadavers, which meant that we were actually hold their organs. Looking at cadavers was hard enough, but having my hands inside another person's body would be an entirely new challenge.

His incision began right below his neck and ended right below his belly button. His skin was stretched, his chest was cracked, and his ribs were separated, all of which contributed to the hole in the middle of his body. It was packed with at least twenty organs. They were overlapping, intertwined, and all piled up on top of one another. I was fascinated by how many organs could fit into such a small place. They were like puzzle pieces, each had an assigned spot where it needed to be for it all to work.

I reached my hands inside of this man's frigid body and moved them around to touch each organ. The preservative in his body began to seep through my gloves. I made my way to his heart. I grabbed it and took it out from his chest. It was much larger than I had expected; it was strong and stiff. Small pieces of yellow fat lined his heart. His aorta was big enough to stick my finger through. This was the first human organ I had ever held.

Noah wheeled out two more tables. Among the variety of organs 15 were multiple hearts, lungs, livers. I compared the two sets of lungs. One was a healthy pair of lungs and the other belonged to a smoker. The smoker's lungs were completely black. They were shriveled up and felt like a crumbled-up trash bag. The smoker's lungs looked like completely different organs.

I picked up one of the brains. I held it in my hands, admiring how powerful this one organ is. It once served as an entire control center for one person. It once stored every memory that person had from their entire life.

I had studied all of the organs, and the only thing left on the table terrified me. It was a human head. It had been cut off from the rest of its body and sawed in half. I held one half in each hand with my fingertips resting on his ginger hair. I placed the two halves together. I felt terrible for him. He donated his body to science and this is what he got.

I walked out of the cadaver lab feeling guilty more than anything. Guilt for what I had just done. At times, I had been so focused on the organs that I completely forgot about the people they had belonged to. I had dehumanized these people. This is advice often given to medical students and doctors to help them focus more on the medicine, but it made me feel sick. Yet, the more I thought about these people, the more confused I became. My hands had been inside of their bodies, yet I knew absolutely nothing about them. No name, no age, no cause of death. Nothing.

It had been easier not to think about these people, but it did not feel right. This would be something that I would continue to struggle with, finding a balance between focusing just on the medicine and having compassion for the person.

It hadn't been easy, but I had survived my first cadaver lab. For now, 20 I could continue to dream of becoming a doctor.

academic literacies   rhetorical situations   genres   processes   strategies   research MLA / APA   media / design   readings   handbook

COURTNEY POMEROY

Driving Forward

MY DOOR OPENS SLOWLY. Courtney gets inside and puts her hands on my steering wheel. I can feel them shaking. She takes them off. She shakes her blonde hair and places her hands back on my wheel. Off again, on again. I can feel her nervousness. Come on girl, I think to myself. You can do this. She places her right foot on my brake and shifts the gear to drive.

We stroll down the cul-de-sac. The sun shines on my white exterior. We pass the house where Courtney babysits. At least, I think she does. I see her over there playing with kids sometimes. I see a patch of ice approaching and brace myself. *Deep breath*, I think. *I can do this.* I glide over the ice and take a left past the mailbox. I know where I'm headed at this point. A right again, another right, a few blocks, another right. I can feel Courtney start to ease off the gas. We reach Matt's home.

His old red truck is sitting in the driveway. I always scoff at the sight of that thing...the truck is a little downtrodden for my liking. I should've known Courtney and Matt weren't meant to be from the start. I mean, she drives me, a shiny white Volvo. He drives a Ford.

Courtney picks up the phone again and I hear Matt's voice over my Bluetooth. "Hey," he says bluntly.

"Hi," Courtney hesitates. "I'm here."   5

"Why don't you come inside?"

"Will you just come out to my car?"

There's a long pause over my speaker. "Sure," he sighs.

I see Matt walk towards me. He's wearing sweats with his hood on. He drags his feet along the blacktop, knowing somehow that he is heading toward his impending doom. He gets into my passenger side and slinks into the seat. No one says anything for awhile.

Jesus, Courtney, speak! This is getting a little awkward.   10

Courtney looks over in his direction with a pained smile. "So, um, I've just been thinking a lot lately. And college is coming soon..."

Wait, college? The calendar on my dashboard says it's only February...

"And I was just thinking about how you and I want different things, you know? Like, I don't want to go in to college with a boyfriend. So, I think maybe we should just go our separate ways."

Boy, that speech was painful. Courtney glances over at my cup holders as she struggles to make eye contact.

I feel a drop of liquid pelt my tan leather seat. Oh dear, is he crying? 15 I wait for him to say something. Courtney waits too. I wish I could make the clock on my screen move faster.

"I still care about you," Courtney offers up a plea for a response from him. He shakes his head, grabs my handle, and gets out. Courtney watches, surprised, probably because of his lack of words.

Listen here, her 'college' excuse was absolute BS. Let me tell you what really happened.

***

It's April, ten months prior to the break up. Courtney comes out her front door in a long pink dress that laces up and reveals her tan back. Her hair is curled and pinned up, and she's holding a flower in her hand.

"Courtney?" Her mom pops out the front door. Courtney turns around and her dress billows in the spring air. "He's not picking you up?" Her mom questions. *Good question.* I think he should be the one to drive, but I'm a little more old-fashioned. Courtney shakes her head no.

"Okay, be home by midnight." 20

We pull up to Matt's house. I can feel Courtney's hands shake a little with nerves. Good nerves, though. Matt opens the door and greets her. "Hey," he looks her up and down and adjusts his tie. "You look good."

Good? That's all? I shrug my bumpers. "Thank you," Courtney blushes. "Ready?" She puts me into drive.

We stroll past the dirt roads, and the flowery trees, and the red rocks, and the mountains of Colorado. The two lovebirds don't have much to say for the half hour drive.

"Are you excited?" Courtney breaks the silence.

"Sure." Matt says. "My friends are crazy fun." Courtney nods. "Are 25 you?" He asks in return.

"Yes!" Courtney smiles. "I wish we had gone to my school's prom too, though."

Matt grunts. "You know I didn't really want to go to a Catholic school prom... my school's prom will be a lot better."

I roll my headlights at his response. That was a little unnecessary, don't you think? I pull up to a golf course where dressed up couples are all taking photos. Matt jumps out of me and I watch as he runs over to his friends and fist-bumps them. He doesn't bother opening me from Courtney's side. Courtney blinks with surprise, gets out on her own, and strolls over to Matt and his friends.

***

"Oh my gosh, that movie was so scary!" Courtney exclaims as her and Matt sit down in my seats.

He looks at her and smiles. "I think I was more scared than you 30 were!" They laugh and spill some of the leftover popcorn. Matt wipes the spare kernels off of his old sweatpants and onto my floor. *Ew, get this greasy stuff off of me!*

Courtney drives me back to Matt's house. He turns to open my door, but stops. "Hey, so I had fun with you at prom the other night and I really like spending time with you." Matt looks over at Courtney. She starts to fiddle with the laces of my steering wheel—a nervous habit of hers. "Would you want to, uh, make this official?"

Courtney pauses. "Sure." *Sure?* That seemed a little too casual. But what do I know? We drive away and she looks back at him through my rearview mirror, grinning from ear to ear.

***

My tires hit the dirt road and the crisp Colorado wind whistles around my exterior. The stars begin to shine brightly and we seem to get closer and closer to them as we make our way up to our destination: Daniel's Park.

Daniel's Park, from what I can tell, is the hangout spot for most teenagers. It's a place for kids who need to hide out from their parents, kids who want to wander around and get lost in the different trails, kids who just want to come up for fresh air. There's a perfect view of the Rocky Mountains during the day and Denver's city lights at night, all easily seen through a car windshield.

Courtney and Matt don't say much to each other. It's kind of their relationship's trademark. Courtney has given up on asking questions that often end in a one word response. She seems to be running low on gas when it comes to spending time with him. They watch the sun set and peer through the sunroof at the stars. He puts his arm around her and kisses her, and for some reason, the stars weren't shining quite as brightly when she glanced back up at them.

***

"Hey! How was your day?" Courtney chirps into the Bluetooth.

"Fine." Matt snarls.

"Is something wrong?"

"Whatever. I'm fine I guess."

"Well," Courtney hesitates. "Do you still want me to pick you up?"

"Not really." I panic at this response. I brace my tires for whatever is going to happen next.

Sure enough, Courtney slams my brake. "What?" She jerks me into a U-turn. Her face turns as bright red as my brake lights.

"I'm just not in the mood." *Alright, Matt. Lose the attitude.*

"Hm." Courtney interjects. Matt proceeds to ask her if there is a problem. She hesitates. Confrontation is hard for her. "You know what, Matt, I'm sorry if you've had a bad day, but I don't think that's my fault?" She raises her pitch at the end as if she's asking a question.

"It isn't."

"Okay, so how come you're acting this way? You always do this. How many times have I told you that you can't take every little thing that happens to you out on me?" My speed increases as Courtney's heart rate does.

Matt mumbles a few words. Courtney ends the conversation and accelerates back home. Her phone dings and vibrates but her eyes remain fixed on the road with her brows furrowed.

***

"I love you." Matt slurs his words from the passenger side.

"What did you just say?"

"I said," He pauses to burp, "I love you." 50

"Matt," Courtney stops him. "You're drunk."

It's 2 o'clock in the morning. Well past Courtney and I's bedtime. She had thrown on a jacket and ran out of her front door into the moonlight to pick up Matt from a party.

He leans over and tries to kiss her cheek, but she rejects it. The magnitude of that four-letter word sinks into her and she turns the radio off. We finish the ride in silence. I watch as Courtney walks over to Matt's side and helps him into his home. She comes back shortly with one hand wrapped around her keys and the other wiping a tear from her face. Her head falls to my wheel and her hands grip my seat. I hear sniffling and soft sobs. "I'm so confused," she whispers under her breath. No matter where my GPS could navigate her, I know she'd still be lost.

***

So, there you have it. Courtney wasn't worried about college. I've heard her tell her friends that ride shotgun with us that Matt has ignored her out in public. That his gift to her for Valentine's day was his own wrestling team's t-shirt. That he's been mad at her for not always clearing her schedule for him. She wasn't worried about college. She was worried about her own sanity. Her emotions. Her heart.

Courtney watches Matt as he sulks back into his house, taking nine 55 months of frustration and pain with him. I examine Courtney's eyes in the rearview mirror. Not a tear. Just relief.

She puts me back into drive and we zoom out of his neighborhood, leaving behind a trail of dust and unhappy memories. Courtney turns on the radio as we twist and turn around corners.

Courtney and I had driven around nine thousand miles together over the course of this relationship. And she wasn't going to stop driving now. So, we drive forward.

65 Profiles

See also:

academic literacies

rhetorical situations

genres

processes

strategies

research MLA / APA

media / design

readings

handbook

MADELINE TURNER

Hillary Clinton: Trailblazer, Role Model, and Grandmother

I n the early morning of November 9, 2016, presidential hopeful Hillary Clinton conceded the 2016 election to the new President-elect Donald Trump, thus ending a historical race between the two. While Clinton did not make history in becoming the first female president of the UnitedStates, her campaign and journey to election day inspired millions of women nationwide to become proactive in American politics. The lack of women involved in politics and businesses is a problem in America. However, since Clinton's defeat to Trump, a businessman who had no political experience and ran a questionable campaign, more and more women have stepped up and disclosed their interest in running for political office both on the national and local level. Women in America have the unique opportunity to learn and grow from the loss of the 2016 presidential election. Clinton has encouraged women in many different ways: to take a chance and be more involved in politics, to have confidence in themselves, to stand up to bullies, and to know that winning does not always justify success. Clinton boldly addressed the saddened and angry crowd during her concession speech. She stated, "And to all the women, and especially the young women, who put their faith in this campaign and in me, I want you to know that nothing has made me prouder than to be your champion." She is and will continue to be a champion for all women from 1 to 99, and her many achievements in politics should encourage women to get involved.

Hillary Clinton was certainly not the only trailblazer for women in politics; however, her efforts to fight for equality in America will put her name down in history books. The first woman who held an elected office position in United States politics was in 1887. Her name was Susanna Salter and she was elected to serve as the mayor for her small town of Arkansas. Nearly 100 years later, Hillary Clinton stepped into the political spotlight in 1978 as First Lady of Arkansas, and in 1992 she became First Lady of the United States. After her days as First Lady came to an end in 1998, Clinton shocked the nation by announcing her candidacy to serve as a senator for New York. Women had been members of the United States Senate so having a woman run did not come as a surprise; instead, having a former First Lady of the United States run was quite surprising. However, there was no question about whether or not Clinton was qualified to be a senator. As First Lady, Clinton was fairly active politically in policies dealing with women's rights and healthcare. Before First Lady Clinton, the first lady's job was often to coordinate parties, look pretty, and always support their husband. The fact that a first lady was interested in politics and working with her husband was something this country had never seen before. After serving as a senator for the state of New York for two terms, Clinton announced that she would be seeking the Democratic Presidential Nominee in 2008. This is where Clinton, First Lady, lawyer, and senator, took her first loss. The party nominated Barack Obama as their presidential nominee, who would later become the first African American President of the United States. Clinton did not shy away from the public's eye after this devastating loss. Obama appointed her to be his Secretary of State. She served on the Obama administration's cabinet for both terms. In 2015, Clinton once again announced that she would be seeking to be the Democratic Presidential Nominee. Little did Clinton know she was about to enter one of the most historical election seasons this country had ever seen.

After months of hard work campaigning, advertising, hosting fundraising parties, and debating alongside Donald Trump, the campaign season came to an end. It was now election night, a night Secretary Clinton hoped would end in her becoming the first female president of the United States. However, in a sudden and surprising turn of events, many of the swing states that political scientists thought for sure would vote as Democrats voted Republican instead. The result was another loss for Hillary Clinton, and some even considered it a loss for women nationwide. An extremely qualified woman candidate was defeated by an openly sexist businessman with no political experience. However, in the months that have followed Clinton's defeat, there has been a surge of women wanting to get involved in politics, both locally and nationally.

The surge of women wanting to become involved has been most noticed on a local level. A fundraising group in Maryland that raises money for potential democratic, woman candidates, found that nearly 175 more women signed up to attend the event after Clinton lost (Wiggins 1). The increase in women getting involved may seem like a very minuscule change, but it makes a difference. One must take into account the fact that this is on a local level and that this is a group aimed towards a very specific cause. Research from Jennifer Lawless from American University shows "women are less likely than men to show interest in running for elected office [. . . this] is a tendency among women to doubt their qualifications. Watching Clinton lose to Trump, despite her extensive political experience, could reinforce those doubts" (Foran 1). Losing to any candidate would set women in politics back, but losing to a candidate like Donald Trump discouraged women even more. Trump was very vocal about his negative views on women and ran his campaign for the white men in America who "wanted their country 'back'" (CNN 1). The country elected an underqualified man who has referred to women as "pigs" as their president, as opposed to Hillary Clinton, who was extremely qualified and made sure she did not say anything blatantly negative about her opponents. After Clinton's loss, if women were not getting involved in politics, then they were showing their support in different ways, such as protesting. In the days that followed Secretary Clinton's loss, many organizations protested Trump's win. One group in particular was composed mostly of women. The "Not Our President" protest movement held peaceful rallies in many large cities across the country, as well as protesting via social media. Anyone who kept up with the news during the 2016 election cycle would know that Secretary Clinton was far more qualified for holding the most coveted elected position in the United States than her opponent. Even though there has been a small influx in Maryland, the question still remains: how, after such a devastating loss, can women be encouraged to get involved in politics? The answer is simple; women must learn from Secretary Clinton's loss and use it to their advantage to empower one another.

Now, nearly six months after the final votes were counted and Clinton conceded to President Trump, it is time for women to fight back and honor Secretary Clinton by empowering one another. The United States was founded by men, causing much of US history to be about the powerful men who founded this great nation, but what about the women? In order for women to become more involved in politics, there needs to be a change in the way educators portray women in history. Instead of focusing on just the male politicians who have made a difference, more effort needs to be put into the female politicians who have made a significant difference on US history. For example, public elementary schools across the state of Alabama teach Alabama history in the fourth grade, and while Supreme Court Justice Hugo Black is in the curriculum, former Secretary of State Condoleezza Rice is omitted from the curriculum (ALSDE.com). This could cause young girls in Alabama to think that only men write history and that only men can be powerful and hold a political office. If public school curricula were to be modified nationwide to include more history on the impacts women have had on the US, then in years to come those students would be more likely to run for office knowing that another woman has run and has been elected. Fear is a large factor in preventing women to run for an elected position.

It is normal for women to have a healthy and nervous fear before entering into any workplace dominated by men. It is not normal, however, for women to be so intimidated by men that they do not try to enter into the workplace at all. The latter of these two feelings is what most women who have considered running for office and then backed out have felt. One of the fears includes being judged. According to an article published by *The Atlantic*, "both men and women judge [powerful women] more harshly than they judge powerful men" (Beinart 2). The fear of being in the public eye and then being scrutinized more so than their male counterpart is enough to discourage women to run for elections. In order for this problem to be solved, there needs to be laws limiting the power journalists have on public opinion, without breaching any of the rights given in the First Amendment. Claire Landsbaum gives another reason women are fearful to enter politics. Landsbaum writes, "[women have] concerns that a career in politics will prevent them from having children" (1). The solution for this is simple: implement a maternity leave into the job contracts of both members of the House of Representatives and the Senate. This maternity leave would be available for both male and female congress members. Women should no longer have to pick between having a career and having a family. Secretary

Clinton's loss should not be considered a failure. Her positive strides for women in politics should be appreciated by women all across the nation.

Secretary Clinton has stayed away from the public light since her concession speech. She has been able to spend time with her husband, Bill, her daughter, Chelsea, and her granddaughter, Charlotte. According to the article "The Iconic Hillary Clinton," "Clinton's transgressions may be largely forgiven by her supporters and largely forgotten by the public" (Frazier 2). Secretary Clinton will not be remembered as a loser, or a liar with a closet full of skeletal emails; instead, she will be remembered and cherished as a feminist icon.

Works Cited

Alabama State Department of Education. *Curriculum Guide to the Alabama Course of Study: Social Studies, Grades K-12.* 17 February 2012, www.alsde.edu/sec/ses/Curriculum%20Guides/cgsocialstudies.pdf.

Beinart, Peter. "Fear of a Female President." *The Atlantic,* October 2016, www.theatlantic.com/magazine/archive/2016/10/fear-of-a-female-president.

"Cracked but not shattered: 20 women on Clinton's run." *CNN Wire,* 10 Nov. 2016. *Opposing Viewpoints in Context,* link.galegroup.com/apps/doc/A469605313/OVIC?u=tusc49521&xid=a99865d2.

Foran, Clare. "Will Hillary Clinton's Defeat Set Back Women in Politics?" *The Atlantic,* 27 Nov. 2016, www.theatlantic.com/politics/archive/2016/11/hillary-clinton-donald-trump-women/508340/.

Frazier, Caitlin. "The Iconic Hillary Clinton." *The Atlantic,* 13 Nov. 2016, www.theatlantic.com/politics/archive/2016/11/hillary-clinton-icon/507503/.

Landsbaum, Claire. "How to Get More Women Involved in Politics." *The Cut,* 16 Nov. 2016, www.thecut.com/2016/11/how-to-get-more-women-involved-in politics.html

Wiggins, Ovetta. "Clinton's loss sparks surge of interest in electing women." *Washington Post,* 10 Dec. 2016. *Opposing Viewpoints in Context,* link.galegroup.com/apps/doc/A473470128/OVIC?u=tusc49521&xid=d93e23ec.

ERIN BILDER
Bonded Together By Tailgating

"**T**AILGATING IS A TRADITION** as old as the SEC itself. Each campus has its own tailgating style, and at Alabama, students and alumnae alike spare no expense when it comes to everything from the tent to the music to the perfect menu of game day snacks and beverages" (Baggett). Students, residents, and visitors share a feeling of euphoria on Saturdays during the fall. I watch the Quad go from beautifully bare to filling with tents as I walk to class all week and count down the days until game day. My roommates and I, much like many others, awaken on game day mornings after a long week of classes or tedious work. We blast "Sweet Home Alabama" over our speakers and prepare to start our day, which will be filled with family, friends, fun, and of course, lots of food and drinks.

tailgating is a full day affair that is taken very seriously at the University of Alabama. "'We get here at 6 a.m. and set everything up," says Sherman Hargrove, a fan from Ardmore, Alabama. "It takes 30 minutes. We have Bloody Marys and we cook breakfast. Sometimes we go into the game and sometimes we stay here and watch the game on TV'" (Klass). The most die-hard fans need about eight hours to get their full experience of tailgating, a ritual they will repeat every other week, sometimes even at away games.

Tailgating is filled with all different types of people that unite for one main cause, rolling with the Crimson Tide. As I walk through the quad with my friends and game-day date, I notice all the different variations of people unexpectedly bonding together to cheer on their favorite team. There are college girls dressed to the nines in crimson, black, or white dresses, accompanied by a stylish pair of heels or cowgirl boots, supporting their respective sorority with decorated buttons that exclaim how much their group "loves the Tide." Their hands usually sport red solo cups filled with various colors of mixed, fruity drinks. There are fraternity boys wearing button-downs and khakis, sporting the sticker matching their game-day date's button. There are "new-boys" pledging

academic literacies | rhetorical situations | genres | processes | strategies | research MLA / APA | media / design | readings | handbook

fraternities as well. They have been required to wear a blazer and dress slacks even in the hottest of weather, and expected to supply their older brothers' needs. There are older, die-hard Alabama fans sporting their houndstooth print garments to remember the legendary coach of their era, Paul W. Bear Bryant. They often offer younger, college-aged fans food and drinks as they walk around the Quad. There are families with young children, already expecting their children to attend the University of Alabama when they grow up. Their daughters are dressed up in Alabama cheerleader uniforms, sporting pigtails and fake tattooed A's on their faces, and their sons wear their favorite Alabama t-shirts and hats. All these different types of people unite on the Quad, proudly exclaiming "Roll Tide!" to each other before cheering on their favorite team together in Bryant-Denny Stadium with their white and crimson shakers.

As I walk through the Quad and look around on scorching Saturday afternoons, it is filled beyond capacity. The only walking room is in the lanes restricted to emergency vehicles. The remaining area is filled with crimson and white tents all containing similar commodities. There are tables lined with delicious-smelling catered food, coolers filled with water and various alcoholic drinks, people proudly decked out in their best gameday outfits, and speakers playing sing-along songs that fans bond over every week, like "Sweet Home Alabama" and Dixieland Delight." Sometimes I see televisions and a mass of chairs, since some people come to the Quad just for the tailgating and often watch the games with new friends on television. It is just as much of an excitement as the game itself.

Other than my own home, I never feel as welcomed as I do on the Quad as I walk around getting ready for the game with fellow friends. During the last home game I attended with my three roommates, an older, friendly couple asked to take a picture of us because of "how cute our outfits were," and we were invited into many different tents filled with food and drinks. I had never met any of these people before, but we shared a special bond in the team we root for. Our love of the Tide seems to make us friends for the day and sometimes even friends at the upcoming home games. In other situations, actions like this would not be considered normal and a majority of people would not invite random others to eat their food or drink their drinks. The pride that older fans feel for the team is what radiates into my generation to keep it going.

Tailgating at the University of Alabama is a tradition that outlives most of the students that go to the university, including myself. To me, it seems like a way to unite the different generations for a few hours and proposes a way to keep the tradition going into the future since we college students of the present get tailgating ideas from generations past. I have bonded with fans of all different ages while discussing the Tide's chances of making it to the championship for the seventeenth time. I have bonded while debating how much the Tide will dominate their opponent this week compared to last. I watch people chat with neighboring tents and exchange things back and forth, creating lifelong friendships that are renewed every football season. It's an unlikely alliance between people that may never have associated with each other if the circumstances were different. An older fan, Kevin Crawford said of his tailgating location on the Quad, "'I've been in this same spot for 10 years." "The people all around, we've all pretty much been here the same time. We go about four months without seeing each other and football season starts, and boom, we're back and it's wonderful'" (Klass). Tailgating is its own form of socializing and connecting with new people of all different backgrounds when in Tuscaloosa.

The University of Alabama uses its almost too-good-to-be-true football team to bring in students from all different regions of the United States and bring in profits that would have been impossible without the team. This thought is exemplified in a *New York Times* article that notes, "Many newcomers are like Molly Brautigan, 18, who says Saban and his football team brought her south from Montclair, N.J. She wanted to spend Saturday mornings like this one — trying on and discarding outfits — for a brunch date at the Pi Kappa Alpha fraternity house" (Drape). UA has recruited an immense amount of people from all over the United States. In fact, this is the first year that out-of-state students have outnumbered in-state students, again (and perhaps coincidentally) after a National Championship win. Not only do those out-of-state students pay much more in tuition than in-state students, Bryant-Denny stadium is always packed. The University, in turn, benefits financially.

academic literacies   rhetorical situations   genres   processes   strategies   research MLA / APA   media / design   readings   handbook

The Alabama football team made the University of Alabama what is today. Football and tailgating are American traditions everywhere, but there is no similar experience that can match up to Saturdays in Tuscaloosa.

Works Cited

Baggett, Will. "Own the Quad: Tailgate Tips and Traditions." *The Crimson White*, 12 Sept. 2016, www.cw.ua.edu/article/2016/09/alabama-tailgate-tips-and-traditions.

Drape, Joe. "Alabama Is Rolling in Cash, With Tide Lifting All Boats." *The New York Times*, 6 Nov. 2015, www.nytimes.com/2015/11/07/alabama-crimson-tide-football-marketing.

Klass, Kym. "Alabama Football: A Tradition, Dynasty." *The Montgomery Advertiser*, 10 Sept. 2016, Montgomeryadvertiser.com/story/news//2016/09/10/Alabama-football-a-tradition-dynasty/90199766.

Klass, Kym. "Top-notch Tailgating at Alabama: '7 Great Weekends'" *The Montgomery Advertiser*, 29 Sept. 2016, montgomeryadvertiser.com/story/life/livinglarge/top-notch-tailgating-alabama-7-great-weekends/90261582.

MATTHEW BRIES

Warren G. Harding, Newspaperman

JUNE 12, 1920: It was the fourth day of the Republican National Convention. After nine ballots, no one had yet been nominated to run for president. The votes were deadlocked between three of the major candidates, General Leonard Wood, Illinois Governor Frank Lowden, and California Senator Hiram Johnson. After realizing that no agreement could be reached between these candidates, delegates of the Republican Party discussed possible alternatives, including Warren G. Harding, in an infamous "smoke-filled room." As the roll for the tenth ballot progressed, the candidate Governor Sproul of Pennsylvania entered the floor, made his way to his state's delegation, and released his votes to Harding. These were the last votes that Harding needed to win the nomination. Cheers erupted, and a procession holding large images of Harding marched triumphantly around the hall ("Harding and Coolidge Named By Republicans"). By the time all the delegates' votes were counted, Harding had obtained 692 votes over Leonard Wood's 156. Though it took special circumstances to win him the nomination, it would be a different task altogether to win the election. The qualities that led him to win the nomination—in particular, his experience as a newspaperman and skill at public speaking—combined with a well-run, modern campaign, led Harding to win the White House.

Born on his grandfather's farm in Morrow County, Ohio, Warren Harding was the oldest of eight children. When Harding was just nineteen, he moved to Marion, Ohio and took a job with The Mirror, a small weekly newspaper. Though he had tried several other careers previously, after working there for a few months he realized that being a newspaperman was his calling. This led him and two of his best friends to purchase a bankrupt local newspaper, The Marion Star, in his new hometown for $300 (Cunningham). He would devote most of his time to the success of this paper and just a year later he became its sole owner.

academic literacies   rhetorical situations   genres   processes   strategies   research MLA / APA   media / design   readings   handbook

It was here at his paper that his political life began and where his skills and personality that eventually led him to the presidency would shine through. One example that highlights the content of his character is the creed that he created for his newly purchased newspaper which included points such as:

Remember there are two sides to every question. Get them both.
Be decent, be fair, be generous.
Boost, don't knock.
There's good in everybody.
Bring out the good and never needlessly hurt the feelings of anybody . . .
("Harding a Farm Boy Who Rose By Work")

Harding himself fully embodied this creed in his daily life and as a result was generally well liked and non-confrontational. It was because of these tendencies not to offend people and to remain balanced that he would later win the Republican nomination, even though he was not initially a major candidate. His position with the paper would also help him form powerful connections and get him involved with the Republican party.

A newspaperman at heart, he was almost always hesitant about running for office, much preferring to continue his work with his newspaper. When he learned of the desire to nominate him for the U.S. Senate, "he was so reluctant to become a candidate that he left the State for two months on a hunting trip to Texas," ("Harding a Farm Boy Who Rose By Work"). However, his speaking skills and ability to talk on his feet led fellow politicians to encourage him to run for office on many occasions, with varying success. In the early 1890s, Harding began giving speeches for the Republican party and many members were impressed. One even told him after his second speech, "Young man, you have the gift of gab. Keep it up and some day you'll be President of the United States." ("Harding a Farm Boy Who Rose By Work"). Little did he know that this would actually come to fruition. In 1898, he ran for his first office as an Ohio State Senator. He would eventually achieve the offices of Lieutenant Governor of Ohio, State Senator, and U.S. Senator, as well as speak at the 1908 and 1916 Republican National Conventions. After pressure from colleagues and friends, he began a run for the White House in the 1920 election. Not having taken primary campaigning very seriously, spending much less than the other candidates, and doing only modest campaigning, he handily won the Republican nomination anyways. In fact, he spent less than the other major candidates, which helped him avoid accusations of attempting to buy the nomination.

His presidential campaign was taken much more seriously and featured several components that made it especially successful. The first was using a form of campaigning not commonly used since the time of William McKinley, 24 years earlier, a "front porch" style campaign. Harding's campaign even remodeled his house to more resemble McKinley's, going so far as to put McKinley's flag pole in Harding's front lawn (Morello 50). In a front porch style campaign, rather than going around and campaigning throughout the country, he stayed at his home in Marion and gave speeches to visiting delegations. In total, 600,000 people made the trip to his home between July and September of that year (Morello 63). This allowed him and his campaign managers to carefully control who he was speaking to, what he was saying and how the press could cover the event. Harding, having had several extra-marital affairs, was at great risk of saying something that could potentially ruin his campaign. However, in large part to the style of his campaign, he managed to keep it quiet during the election. As a newspaperman, Harding knew what the members of the press would want and built a small building near his house so that they could work and gave almost daily press conferences to them. The Republican party also hired ad-man Albert Lasker to help publicize him. Together they used Lasker's "reason why" advertising techniques to show the American people that Harding was a hardworking person that they could relate to through speeches, film, radio, the phonograph, and even celebrity endorsements. The long list of celebrity endorsements included "The World's Greatest Entertainer," Al Jolson, and silent movie star Douglas Fairbanks (Morello 54). His campaign also focused on producing targeted advertisements for specific interest groups such as farmers, African-Americans, and women, who had just earned the right to vote in all states. Because of his extensive use of modern communication methods, he was able to insert himself into the lives of millions of Americans, without even leaving his front porch.

With Lasker's management and the front porch campaign, all Harding had left to do was supply a solid and inspiring platform. The root of this was his idea of a "Return to Normalcy" which had great success in relating with the feelings of many, if not most Americans. Having just exited the first World War two years prior, people in the US were facing a post war recession and feeling the consequences of the war. People wished to go back to the times before the war, and Harding played on these concerns with his theme. He called for doing this in a subtle, gentle manner, for tax cuts and for more efficient government. In a speech he declared: "America's present need is not heroics, but healing; not nostrums, but normalcy; not revolution, but restoration; not agitation, but adjustment" (Freidel and Sidey). The war had been a drastic change for Americans, and this statement resonated with them. The universality of his platform allowed him to garner the vote of the people.

James Cox, who was running himself ragged campaigning all across the country, was no match for Harding in the election. Though he put in a tremendous effort, he was not as well advertised as Harding and did not resonate with the post-war feelings of Americans. In all it was his modern campaign, Harding's speaking skills, and his experience as a newspaper man that led him to enter and win the election. In the end, Harding captured a commanding 60.2% of the popular vote, and won in 37 of the 48 states, one of the largest margins in American history.

Works Cited

Cunningham, Lillian. "Warren G. Harding." *Presidential Podcast*, 17 July 2013, https://www.washingtonpost.com/graphics/business/presidential-podcast/.

Freidel, Frank, and Hugh Sidey. "Warren G. Harding." *The White House*, The White House, 30 Dec. 2014, https://www.whitehouse.gov/1600/presidents/warrenharding.

"Harding a Farm Boy Who Rose By Work." *New York Times* 3 Aug. 1923: pg. 3 *ProQuest Historical Newspapers*. 12 Oct. 2016, http://search.proquest.com/news/docview/103201702

"Harding and Coolidge Named By Republicans." St. Louis Post-Dispatch 13 Jun. 1920: pg. B1 *ProQuest Historical Newspapers*, http://search.proquest.com/docview/578812530/

Morello, John. *Selling the President, 1920*. Praeger, 2001.

academic literacies

rhetorical situations

genres

processes

strategies

research MLA / APA

media / design

readings

handbook

Reflections **66**

See also:

**JONATHAN
SAFRAN FOER**
My Life as a Dog   245

ALEX MAZZAFERRO
Gasping for Air

IN MOVIES, ASTHMA DOESN'T SEEM TOO BAD. In the movie It, based on
the novel by Stephen King, the loveable, nerdy kid runs a few paces,
pretends to wheeze, whips out his handy-dandy inhaler, takes one puff,
immediately exhales, and he's good to go. Not too bad, right? Well, after
running a few minutes, my esophagus starts to close, my chest gets tight,
and I start wheezing. I usually have to sit down because I can't breathe
at all. I reach for my rescue inhaler, pull off the cap, and shake it for a
few seconds. I exhale as hard as I can, so I can empty my lungs. I have
to follow this routine because I need to prepare myself for the following
gigantic gasp for air. I suck in as deeply as humanly possible with my
extremely inadequate lungs, while I squeeze my inhaler and a cloud of
white, dusty air enters deep into my diaphragm. I hold my breath for
twenty agonizing seconds, and at the last second I cough out the stale
air. At this point, my vision may go dark or I might get light-headed, but
I'm not done yet. I have to wait sixty seconds then repeat the process to
take another dose. On top of everything, my inhaler doesn't provide a
clean, seamless transition from choking to easy breathing. That would
be far too convenient; I usually spend the next minute or two coughing
my brains out so that my body can clear its passages.

The media is at fault for not showing the varying severity of many
cases of asthma. As a result, people always assumed that I was faking
my symptoms so that I would get out of sprints for football practice, or
so I wouldn't have to run the mile in gym class. Coaches would shake
their heads in disapproval, and my peers would stare as I slowed down
to a stop and took a puff in the middle of a workout. One time, while I
was holding in a breath after using my inhaler, my gym teacher came up
to me and said, "You know that there are Olympic athletes with asthma,
right? It's not a good excuse to quit. Get out there and quit messing
around." If only he knew that there are varying degrees of the disease.
The Olympic athletes that my teacher was talking about were probably

never hospitalized after an asthma attack in the middle of the night like I have been.

My coaches and peers probably didn't know that I truly could not breathe during a sprint. They probably thought that a small wheeze was the only symptom I had. In reality, I couldn't participate because it felt like someone was sitting on my chest and strangling me more and more with each breath. The only way to experience a similar feeling would be to run while only breathing through a straw. If my coaches could try it, I bet they wouldn't get very far before spitting the straw out. Probably, they'd get as far as I would get before needing to use my inhaler.

During practice, I wanted so badly to fit in and be able to run like everyone else without drawing a ton of attention every time I experienced an attack. However, keeping a low profile was difficult when my lungs made a noise that drew every eye within a fifty-foot radius. Nearly every day, I'd have to decide which would be more embarrassing: walking off the field alone to use my inhaler as my peers and superiors watched, or continuing to wheeze and choke.

Before I joined football or baseball, I used to see my inhaler as a   5 safety net. If I ever got into a life-threatening situation, I could always count on the cold cloud of Albuterol to rescue me. As time went on, I started joining organized sports, and my inhaler went from being my safety net to a spotlight that highlighted my worst quality. I was so embarrassed because I didn't want to be different. I projected all of my frustrations that stemmed from my asthma onto it. I didn't realize that my inhaler wasn't the thing that set me apart from everyone else, but it was easier to blame my problems on a physical object. I tried hiding it, or not using it when I needed it because it made me feel inferior. People didn't understand my condition, so I looked to my inhaler instead of the people who were really at fault for my embarrassment.

As for many lucky people, my symptoms started to vanish with age. My awful wheeze has been tamed, I don't get winded after a walk up a flight of stairs, and my lungs have strengthened. I'm free to live a healthy, active life. Nowadays, I can go for a run, and I feel safe leaving my inhaler at home. Unless I get sick, I don't ever struggle to breathe. I almost forgot how bad I had asthma until I grabbed my inhaler to describe it. Even though movies have incorrectly portrayed the use of inhalers, they've nailed the aesthetics. The actual medicine in my inhaler is in a metal cylinder with a small plastic nozzle at the bottom. The cylinder is the thickness of a piece of sidewalk chalk and about two inches long. It slides into a blue, plastic case which creates the mist I inhale. My inhaler fits in my hand comfortably. It has a modern, almost futuristic style, and it's very pleasing to look at. Whenever I look in my medicine cabinet, my inhaler usually catches my eye. For a fleeting second, I feel a barrage of emotions. I remember all of the situations in which using my inhaler made me feel so different from everyone else. I remember all of the trips to the nurse's office after running around at recess, or all of the stares I would get while taking a break in the middle of sprints. But now when I look at it, I feel stronger since I've outgrown my asthma and I'm no longer dependent on it.

I've had many years to think about the people who have passed judgment on me. I've decided to forgive them because it's not their fault for being misinformed. Society is more to blame than any individual. If movies and television could accurately depict the struggles of asthmatic children, they may not be treated as harshly. I hope that things change in the near future, and coaches across the country become more informed.

For the longest time, my inhaler was the symbol of my inadequacy. Now my inhaler is a dusty trophy that I have for beating my asthma. I don't have to keep it in my pocket or backpack at all times, and it serves as a reminder that I will no longer ever be held back due to a physical condition. Instead of being embarrassed about it, I can brag about how terrible my asthma used to be and how far I've come. I respect my inhaler now, and realize that it wasn't at fault for all of my asthma related issues; misinformed people as a product of our society were.

academic literacies   rhetorical situations   genres   processes   strategies   research MLA / APA   media / design   readings   handbook

JACOB DRISKILL

A Missionary's Guilt

I PUT MY EARBUDS IN AND CLOSED MY EYES. I only had 27% battery left and I was a week away from an outlet I could use to charge it, but I didn't care. I needed something to distract myself from the world outside the bus. If I turned the music up loud enough, I might even be able to get some sleep. That was just wishful thinking, though. There was no way I would be able to sleep in this heat. Sweat had soaked through my clothes, which had began sticking to the seats.

I jerked my head up as the bus came screeching to a stop. Brake-lights ahead. I was not surprised. Traffic in Port-au-Prince was a cycle of traffic jams interrupted by frantic 80 mile per hour sprints.

I looked out the window to my left to a warzone. Rubble and trash lined the streets, buildings looked like they had been hit by bombs, and of course, the UN soldiers with their white helmets and assault rifles.

***

I forgot whose idea it was originally. A youth mission trip to our sister church in Haiti. Even though I really didn't want to go, I never refused, preferring to instead imagine the future as a dream.

In the coming months, I went through the motions, always denying. 5 "The trip isn't for another 7 months, I don't have anything to worry," I told myself.

"I still have a whole month until I leave."

"I leave tomorrow." Reality hit me. It was real now and I couldn't procrastinate any longer.

***

I stepped off the plane into the sea of dusty tarmac. The sun beat down on our little convoy, heavy and suffocating like a wet blanket. There were ten of us, the youth group at my church, although there were more parents than there were kids. The rest of the kids had backed out in the last few months, all of them possessing a foresight I wish I hadn't lacked.

A gust of refreshing air hit me in the face as we walked in the airport. The building's temperature felt like it sat in the low 80's, a far cry from the sweltering heat of outside, but definitely not freezing. This place was practically brand-new. According to Brother Harry, the government had used a good portion of the aid on rebuilding it after the earthquake. The airport had air-conditioning and internet, two commodities that were far from common elsewhere in the country. I couldn't help but notice the flickering lights, the dirty tile floors, the musty smell, and of course the sputtering air conditioner.

"It doesn't get better than this!" Brother Harry turned around and bellowed, a big grin on his face. I matched his smile as dread struck my stomach.

Brother Harry had been preaching at New Life Christian Center since before I was born, and I grew up listening to him behind the pulpit. He was used to this airport by now, he had gone on countless mission trips here. He was about as native as a pasty southern boy could get, and he took great pride in how the Haitians pronounced his name: "Pastor 'Arreh."

***

It was 2:00 p.m. on a weekday, but it seemed most of the city was on the streets. Peddlers were on the corners selling their wares, which usually consisted of sunhats or flip-flops. Families slept under houses made of tarps. Cellphones were everywhere, which I found odd. Most of these people were homeless, but they all had phones. There were plywood shacks every 100 yards dedicated to charging them, always with a herd of people huddled around.

The bus was quiet. It seemed that everyone was as speechless as I was. They all had the same expression on their face, leaning up against the bus window, their dead eyes taking in the world outside.

Up ahead was a Volkswagen dealership. The glint of the sun bouncing off of the brand-new SUVs blinded me. "What are you doing here?" I wanted to ask. "You don't belong here."

Although, I suppose, neither do I.

***

We proceeded through immigration and got our luggage. We were met by a crowd of people in the lobby, and among them was Pastor Baptiste. He was a smallish man, but I could tell that he was a person that people respected. Immediately, I stood up straight and put on best smile, eager to show him the respect he seemed to deserve. Brother Harry, on the other hand, greeted him with a hug. The two had been close friends for the last 19 years, since they opened a church (and later a school) together in Pastor Baptiste's hometown of Brossier.

The two talked to each other in Haitian Creole. Even in another language, Brother Harry's redneck twang was hard to miss. Pastor Baptiste then made his introductions to the rest of us and led us out the door. On the other side, hundreds of Haitians swarmed us, looking for handouts. Baptiste forced a path through them and we eventually made our way to an old school bus, rusted and dirty. We threw our luggage in the back and climbed aboard.

***

The bus crept forwards. A horn blasted us from behind. I was used to the sound of horns by now. People used their horns more than their brakes around here.

A crew of Haitians made their way to the bus. They approached and started the usual cries for money. We had had beggars approach the bus many times since we left the airport, but this crew seemed especially persistent.

A teen not much older than I seemed to be the head of the little 20 crew. He started smacking the window in front of me, and when that didn't get anyone's attention, he jumped up and grabbed a handful of the hair from the lady sitting in front of me. Her shrieks seemed to ignite the gang, and more started smacking windows and rocking the bus as their cries for money got even louder.

Panic gripped me. I lunged backwards, away from the windows. Pastor Baptiste jumped up and swung at the teen's hand, knocking it out of the bus.

Pastor Baptiste stared down the teen and shouted something in Creole. With that one word the rest of the crew backed off. The bus shuddered forward. The pastor never broke eye contact even as we drove off, giving the teen a look that would drive off the devil.

***

The bus screeched around a bend at 50 miles an hour, two wheels kicking in the air. There were more trees on this road, and the world around us was more green than it was grey. We were finally leaving the city. I said a quick prayer, thanking the Lord for safe passage thus far. I closed my eyes and finally tried to sleep.

I began to get a feeling that I hadn't felt before. I felt shame. Driving through the city, I was thinking about myself. "How am I gonna get through this?" I asked myself. I may I have felt sorrow while I was there, but it was me feeling bad about the situation I was in, not sorrow for the people living here. I may have wanted to change things, but I was more concerned with changing *my* circumstances rather than those around me.

I turned up the volume on my phone to drown out my guilt.   25

academic literacies   rhetorical situations   genres   processes   strategies   research MLA / APA   media / design   readings   handbook

Texts That Mix Genres **67**

See also:

ANNA QUINDLEN
*Write for Your
Life*   265

RACHEL HUIE

Becoming Margaret

WHEN SOMEONE FINALLY SENT ME A PHOTOGRAPH — CRACKLED, pale, incomplete — of Margaret Elizabeth O'Brien Davis, I was disappointed, to say the least. She didn't look like me. Or perhaps I should say, I didn't look like her, given that her death had preceded my birth by one hundred years (thinking on the spot has never been my strong suit). With the hindsight of a year and a half, I can admit that our differences in physiognomy were only partly to blame for that initial, fleeting disappointment. The other culprit was that Mrs. Davis didn't fit the mental image I had kept, smoke and mirror-like, of the stereotypical Victorian woman. She had no meticulous bouffant or elegant dress, but there was a determination in the eyes, a practiced tilt of the eyebrows that could be read either as arrogance or ambition.

That I could work with.

*

Before she married the doctor, when she was still only Margaret O'Brien the aspiring authoress, her father established the first theater in Birmingham. He was an Irish émigré who found the lack of culture in the newborn city depressing, so he painted the props, contracted a troupe, and rallied the town. On opening night, when the gas lanterns fell apart, he took the lamps from nearby trains to illuminate the stage ("Captain").

He would become mayor in 1909. Margaret did not live to see it.

*

The day I dressed up to portray Margaret Davis at the cemetery's annual fall pilgrimage — that one afternoon in mid-October when the carriage-ways and shattered crypts became a living village — it rained. For the first time in three months, it rained. My meticulous bouffant fell flat beneath the magnolia tree whose roots tore through the O'Malley family plot. I had sought shelter there alongside the undertaker (an actor, monologue

5

shifting from anger at the low turnout to hopefulness for his dehydrated garden), the town madam (an actress, classically trained, whose performance was considered the highlight of the tour), and a den mother. Of us, she was the only real one.

*

When Margaret O'Brien was eighteen, she published a historical novel of some renown in which the protagonist, Judith Iscariot, committed suicide after aiding the Roman emperor's persecution of Christians. One year later, the gynecologist who would become her husband shot a rival doctor in a duel ("Dr.").

*

Once the rain stopped, we left our cover and returned to the grave sites. My heels sunk into the mossy hillside of the O'Brien plot. I resorted to pacing the brick stacks outlining each individual grave, unaware that I had just put myself on display. A family of fourteen immediately clustered around, said something about how I looked like a "real live ghost" in the post-storm fog, pushed me into a selfie and left with only an apathetic grunt when I tried to tell them "I'm Margaret Davis."

It occurred to me then, standing forgotten in my crumpled costume after the whirlwind moved on to the *Titanic* survivor, that the curtain between me and the reenactors I saw at home tours and on battlefields had been lifted. They were people, too, I realized, whose life stories, assets, and flaws went unseen by the guests they interacted with, dreamlike, as they spun their stories. There is a certain camaraderie amongst the people who hide themselves behind a character in the name of entertainment. I felt it there. When the undertaker photobombed a picture of me to the startled delight of its photographer. How at any given moment a visitor en route to the bathroom would stumble wide-eyed across a group of Victorian women hiding in the chapel with cell phones and convenience store cookies. The way the railroad baron, strolling past with a guest on each arm, more in character than most, bowed and offered me a "good afternoon" two octaves beneath his usual tone. The whole thing was a masquerade.

I loved every minute of it.

*

Margaret Davis died young. Nine years older than I was when I portrayed her, nine months into her marriage, she contracted an illness from which her physician husband couldn't save her ("Death"). Legend has it that, after her death, her father donated three hundred books to the library at Avondale ("Avondale"). Her sister, the suffragette, named her firstborn in her honor. Her husband never remarried — local lore says he devoted himself to his work. I wonder, though, if that particular suggestion might have been wrong: if he ever felt something like guilt, his devotion a mask for grief.

10

*

The day ended, as they have a habit of doing, and I walked down the hill alone. The undertaker had been gone an hour, the *Titanic* survivor emerged from the chapel in blue jeans and tennis shoes, and an irate visitor intercepted me to demand a refund because she had gotten separated from her tour group. Fourteen hours later, I was back at school, daydreaming through 8 a.m. Latin. I was still too transfixed on the dead characters I had left behind to care about a dead language. *I am trying to understand what has happened to me,* I scribbled in the margins of my Vergil translation, partly to stop myself from forgetting the past and partly in order to figure out the future. I was in one of my melodramatic moods. I blamed it on the method acting.

*

If you search online for Margaret O'Brien Davis, most of the results will revolve around an actress, an infant prodigy who lived to an advanced age, though in the pictures she is immortalized only as a child. For a long time, these were the only results. It seemed there was little interest in a forgotten author with simplistic hair who died young in a death-obsessed age. For months, I agreed. During pilgrimage rehearsals, I shied away from performing Margaret on our main stage, cited lack of "interesting" information and a self-imposed exile from the performing arts. Nevertheless, there was something that drew me — and so many of our visitors — to her that I am just beginning to understand. This is what haunted me: the four-year-old who dragged his mother away from a tour so he could timidly pet the ruffles in my hem — the dry cleaner who insisted my costume must have been made "back when they made things right" — the preteen who sulked in her pictures with me but later told the director my dress looked straight out of her favorite historical drama.

When you put on the costume, it becomes inevitable that you also assume the character's traits over your own, exchanging them just as you would a jacket or a pin in order to suspend your audience's disbelief. To them, you are a fleeting image; they never know your reality. The opposite happened internally: performing Margaret's character gave me a greater self-awareness that, coupled with my rekindled love of the performing arts, began pushing me from my reluctantly-proposed government career to one in entertainment/media advocacy. After years of being slightly uncomfortable with myself, I finally had the confidence to take off my mask of timidity and learn to love addressing an audience. In short, courtesy of the theater-owner's daughter, I had caught the acting bug.

Works Cited

"Avondale Library history." *Birmingham Public Library*, bplonline.cdmhost. com/digital/collection/p4017coll2/id/54. Accessed 15 Mar. 2018.

"Captain O'Brien Gives Birth to Theatre in Birmingham." *History Engine: Tools for Collaborative Education and Research*, www.historyengine. richmond.edu/episodes/view/5232. Accessed 15 Mar. 2018.

"Death List of a Day: Mrs. Margaret O'Brien Davis." *New York Times*, 2 Apr.1898, p. 9, www.nytimes.com/1898/04/02/archives/death-list-of-a-day-mrs-margaret-obrien   davis.html. Accessed 15 Mar. 2018.

"Dr. William Locke Chew." *Find A Grave*, 14 Sept. 2012, www.findagrave. com/memorial/97071569/william-locke-chew. Accessed 8 Mar. 2018.

T.J. RUTLAND

A Search for the Upside of Downs

ALONG WITH HER HUSBAND AND THEIR TWO YEAR OLD SON, Monique was thrilled when she learned she'd be welcoming a new addition to her family. She was pleased that her two-year-old son would have a sibling to grow up with. But during her first trimester, Monique received a telephone call from her obstetrician's office that set many other things in motion. That single moment forever changed the way she and her family defined their meanings of life, love, and family.

"I've got some bad news." Monique said. Monique, a 42 year-old petite woman, was on the phone with her mother, Sandra, at the time. This was nearly three years ago. Monique was seated in the driver's seat of the car while her husband was sitting beside her in the front passenger seat. Monique remembers this moment very vividly. "We were just sitting there, totally devastated . . . I was crying and my husband had his head down just looking at the floor of the car." Monique tells me that she never would have expected to be in that situation. "We didn't expect this to happen . . .we were expecting something completely different." That day was an ordinary Thursday in March. It was ordinary for Monique and her family right up until the moment they were leveled with the news that the child Monique was carrying, her son, had tested positive for the genetic chromosomal condition, Down Syndrome.

According to the National Down Syndrome Society, Down Syndrome occurs when an individual has a partial or full copy of chromosome 21. Down Syndrome is medically referred to as Trisomy 21. The additional chromosome material alters the course of development, which can contribute to cognitive and physical developmental delays. Down Syndrome is the most common chromosomal condition. Statistics show that one in every 700 babies in the U.S. are born with Down Syndrome. Maternal age has been linked as one of the factors that could contribute to Down Syndrome. The National Down Syndrome society states that statistically, once the age of the mother reaches 25, the probability for Down

academic literacies   rhetorical situations   genres   processes   strategies   research MLA / APA   media / design   readings   handbook

Syndrome jumps. At the maternal age of 40, the odds are estimated at a probability of 1 in 100. At 49, the odds are close to 1 in 10. "My doctor explained that we'd need to have certain tests performed because of our age . . . I was 42 at the time, but everything was fine with our first son, so we expected everything to be fine this time too." Monique explains.

Earlier in this pregnancy, Monique took a prenatal blood test that screened the child for certain genetic conditions. "The doctor's office called me and explained they wanted me to come in with my husband to see the doctor . . . we were awaiting a phone call for the lab results and it seemed very strange to call us and ask us to come visit with my doctor." During the visit, they were walked back to a patient room and asked to wait for the physician. "The doctor came into the room and explained the results of the blood test to us . . .everything changed from that moment on." Monique and her husband were given the options that they could continue with the pregnancy, or the pregnancy could be terminated.

Studies have reported that nearly 9 out of every 10 pregnancies that 5 have received a prenatal diagnosis for Down Syndrome are terminated. Right now, the ACLU (American Civil Liberties Union) of Ohio is suing to halt and block a state law that bans abortions "because an unborn child has or may have Down syndrome." (par. 1) Monique and her husband stared this decision directly in the face. They were of two minds. Monique wanted to allow the pregnancy to continue while her husband, out of fear of the uncertainty, felt it would be best to terminate the pregnancy. "We couldn't bring ourselves to talk about it," she says. "Once we both realized we saw this choice differently, I think it became too big for us." Monique says that she and her husband would almost treat each other like two new roommates living together, each one not sure of where the boundaries were – and not wanting to offend the other. "It was so horrible," she says. "I felt very alone and fearful and I wanted to be close to him, but I wasn't sure that he would understand how I felt."

Monique began to feel the weight and gravity of the pregnancy decision looming before them. The decision they needed to make began to take a toll on their marriage. "My husband had it in his mind that we could just try again," Monique says. She explains that it was not her husband's intentions to be cold, unloving, or indifferent to their child.

On the contrary, Monique says her husband felt they could protect their son from pain, challenges, and a difficult life. "My husband said we were being selfish to choose this life for him – because our son would have to live with our choice and we wouldn't." Monique was not sure if her marriage would survive – and this feeling made her feel even more alone without anywhere to turn for comfort, reassurance, or encouragement.

One fear many parents face when they learn their child has Down Syndrome is the fear that their baby will be different. *Parents Magazine* hosts many articles written by parents of children with Down Syndrome, and these articles help dispel this fear (parents.com/home/health/down-syndrome). Studies show although children with Down Syndrome may develop at a different pace than a child without the diagnosis, the children with Down Syndrome still achieve the developmental milestones used to grade and assess most children's development. Monique heavily researched information that pertained to the lives of children with Down Syndrome. "I wanted to find out what we could expect . . .I was very pleased to learn everything was not all the gloom and doom you hear about . . . most of the information was very helpful to me and left me feeling hopeful."

Monique and her husband never sat down to have a hard-lined discussion about their situation. For the most part, the two of them had made up their minds – and were waiting to find out which of them would give in first. In the end, their collective indecisiveness to not firmly make a decision concerning the pregnancy made the decision for them. The pregnancy continued to progress, and now Monique was past the point in her pregnancy where a termination of the pregnancy could occur. Monique explains that this was the time when everything became so real and overwhelming. "It was no longer, 'We received the Down Syndrome news,'" she said. "The focus shifted to 'Our son will have Down Syndrome.'" Monique turned to her faith to prepare herself for the remainder of the pregnancy and to pray for the commitment from her husband. They both received spiritual counseling where their pastor counseled them and prayed for their family and their soon- to- be- born son.

As the pregnancy grew closer to term, Monique's mother, Sandra, became an ever-present figure in the life of her daughter. Monique's

academic literacies   rhetorical situations   genres   processes   strategies   research MLA / APA   media / design   readings   handbook

mother, and her mother's sisters, all prayed for the emotional, spiritual, and physical health of Monique and the baby. "I was so glad to have my mom there for us . . .she was such a great help and someone I could talk to" Monique states. Sandra explains that she encouraged her daughter to believe that all things are possible with God. "God cannot be limited to only what we can imagine . . . he is a much greater God than we could ever dream of," Sandra says.

On the first Tuesday in September of that year, Monique and her husband welcomed a wonderful and beautiful baby boy into the world. He resembled his older brother in appearance very much. Monique and her family learned and discovered that their son did not carry many of the classic facial and physical traits often attributed to Down Syndrome. There were those traits that were present (i.e. smaller hands, fingers, and ears), but to them, their son was beautiful. He had fine wavy hair like his mother – and tons of it. Monique never expected that the day of her son's birth would be so normal. "It finally sunk in as I held him, that he is just a baby . . . he was my baby and I loved him so much." Monique says. Monique began to affectionately call her son "Sugar Pops."

Monique and her family have emerged from this experience with a more defined purpose and a much greater devotion to each other. Monique says that by choosing to love her son unconditionally and not succumbing to fear of the unknown, she was able to see a perspective that God was offering her the opportunity to become the mother she was meant to be and called to be. By turning to her faith to recognize God's promises, Monique explains that she then had the room in her life to receive the blessing of her son. "God used my faith to move away the clutter of disbelief and doubt in my life." Monique says. "There were so many days were I would be so sad before my son was born . . .but when I had the great opportunity to meet him, I discovered just what a wonderful blessing he is and I felt encouraged and hopeful again for his future to be very bright and fulfilling." When asked what she would tell her younger self now as encouragement with accepting the pregnancy news, Monique replies "God does not make mistakes. This child puts so much light and joy into my heart, that I feel so honored to be his mother."

Works Cited

"Down Syndrome." *Parents*, March 2018, https://www.parents.com/
    health/down-syndrome/

National Down Syndrome Society. "Down Syndrome Facts." ndss.org,
    Jan. 2018. https://www.ndss.org/about-down-syndrome/down-
    syndrome-facts/

Held, Amy. "ACLU Sues To Halt 'Unconstitutional' Down Syndrome
    Abortion Law In Ohio." *National Public Radio*. Core Publisher NPR
    Digital Services, 15 Feb. 2018. https://www.npr.org/sections/
    thetwo-way/2018/02/15/586014513/aclu-sues-to-halt-
    unconstitutional-down-syndrome-abortion-law-in-ohio

Monique. Personal Interview, 20 February 2018.

Monique. Personal Interview, 21 February 2018.

Sandra. Personal Interview, 20 February 2018.

academic
literacies

rhetorical
situations

genres

processes

strategies

research
MLA / APA

media /
design

readings

handbook

part 9

Handbook

"Pfft, English, who needs that? I'm never going to England." So says the illustrious Homer Simpson on an early episode called "The Way We Was." Maybe Homer can ignore the conventions of English grammar and usage, but that's not the case for the rest of us. If we want the world to take seriously what we think and say, we need to pay attention to our grammar and language. We need to edit our SENTENCES so they're clear, choose our LANGUAGE carefully, and use PUNCTUATION purposefully. This handbook provides guidelines to help you edit what you write.

Handbook

Sentences S

academic literacies
rhetorical situations
genres
processes
strategies
research MLA / APA
media / design
readings
handbook

S-1 Elements of a Sentence

In casual situations, we often use a kind of shorthand, because we know our audience will fill in the gaps. When we say "Coffee?" to a dinner guest, he knows we mean, "Would you like some coffee?" When we text "7 @ Starbucks?" to a friend, she'll understand that we're asking, "Should we meet at 7:00 at Starbucks?" In more formal writing or speaking situations, though, our audience may not share the same context; to be sure we're understood, we usually need to present our ideas in complete sentences. This chapter reviews the parts of a sentence.

S-1a Subjects and Predicates

A sentence contains a subject and a predicate. The subject, which usually includes a **NOUN** or **PRONOUN**, names the topic of the sentence; the predicate, which always includes a **VERB**, says what the subject is or does.

Glossary
HB-29–34
HB-12–24

> S   P
> ▶ Birds fly.

> S   ┌──────────P──────────┐
> ▶ Birds are feathered vertebrates.

Sometimes the subject and the predicate contain only one word. Usually, however, both contain more than one word.

> ┌──────S──────┐┌────────P────────┐
> ▶ Birds of many kinds fly south in the fall.

> ┌────────S────────┐┌──────P──────┐
> ▶ Flying in a V formation is characteristic of geese.

> ┌──────S──────┐┌────P────┐
> ▶ One of the flock leads the others.

A sentence may contain more than one subject or verb.

> S   S   V
> ▶ Birds and butterflies fly south in the fall.

> S   V   V
> ▶ Birds fly south in the fall and return north in the spring.

academic literacies · rhetorical situations · genres · processes · strategies · research MLA / APA · media / design · readings · handbook

At times, the subject comes after the verb.

▶ Here comes the sun.

V ┌─S─┐

▶ In the attic were old photographs and toys.

V ┌────────S────────┐

Expressing subjects explicitly

English requires an explicit subject in every **CLAUSE**, even if all of the clauses in a sentence are about the same subject.

HB-6

it

▶ Although the dinner cost too much, ⌃ impressed my guests.

The only exception is commands, in which the subject is understood to be *you*.

▶ Eat smaller portions at each meal.

In informal conversation, speakers sometimes emphasize a noun subject by repeating it as a pronoun: *My friend Jing she changed her name to Jane.* In academic writing, though, don't repeat a subject this way.

▶ The visiting students ~~they~~ were detained at the airport.

Sentences beginning with *there* or *it*. In some cases where the subject comes after the verb, an **EXPLETIVE**—*there* or *it*—is required before the verb.

Glossary

There is

▶ ⌃ Is no place like home.

It is

▶ ⌃ Is both instructive and rewarding to work with young children.

You can often rephrase the sentence to avoid using the expletive.

Working with young children

▶ ~~It~~ is both instructive and rewarding ⌃ . ~~to work with young children.~~

S-1b Clauses

A clause is a group of words containing a subject and a predicate. An independent clause can function alone as a sentence: *Birds fly.* A subordinate clause begins with a **SUBORDINATING WORD** such as *because, as,* or *which* and cannot stand alone as a sentence: *because birds fly.* (See p. HB-8 for a list of common subordinating words.)

HB-8

┌─INDEPENDENT CLAUSE─┐ ┌────────SUBORDINATE CLAUSE────────┐
▶ My yard is now quiet because most of the birds flew south.

S-1c Phrases

A phrase is a word group that makes sense but lacks a subject, a verb, or both and thus cannot stand alone as a sentence. Some common ones are prepositional, appositive, participial, gerund, and infinitive phrases.

HB-56–58

A prepositional phrase starts with a **PREPOSITION** such as *at, from, of,* or *in* and usually ends with a noun or pronoun: *at school, from home, in bed.* It usually functions as an adjective or adverb.

▶ The day *after the World Series* everyone *in San Francisco* celebrated.

An appositive phrase follows and gives additional information about a noun or pronoun. It functions as a noun.

▶ We all know that computers and their spawn, *the smartphone and cellphone,* have created a very different world from several decades ago.
—Alina Tugend,
"Multitasking Can Make You Lose . . . Um . . . Focus"

Glossary

A participial phrase contains the **PRESENT PARTICIPLE** or **PAST PARTICIPLE** of a verb plus any **OBJECTS**, **MODIFIERS**, and **COMPLEMENTS**. It functions as an adjective.

▶ *Brimming with optimism,* I headed over to the neighborhood watering hole and waited. —Hal Niedzviecki, "Facebook in a Crowd"

* academic literacies
■ rhetorical situations
▲ genres
○ processes
◆ strategies
● research MLA / APA
□ media / design
▮▮ readings
⟋ handbook

▶ A study from Princeton *issued at the same times as the Duke study* showed that women in the sciences reported less satisfaction in their jobs and less of a sense of belonging than their male counterparts.
—Anna Quindlen, "Still Needing the F Word"

A gerund phrase includes the *-ing* form of a verb plus any objects, modifiers, and complements. It functions as a noun.

▶ *Asking for candy on Halloween* was called trick-or-treating, but *asking for candy on November first* was called begging.
—David Sedaris, "Us and Them"

An infinitive phrase includes an infinitive (*to* plus the base form of a verb: *to read, to write*) and any objects, modifiers, and complements. It functions as a noun, an adjective, or an adverb.

▶ The plan *to commit more troops* requires top-level approval.

▶ The point of ribbon decals is *to signal that we support our troops.*

S-2 Sentence Fragments

Sentence fragments often show up in advertising: "Got milk?" "Good to the last drop." "Not bad for something that tastes good too." We use them in informal speech and text messages as well. In other kinds of writing, though, some readers consider fragments too informal, and in many academic writing situations, it's better to avoid them altogether. This chapter helps you identify and edit out fragments.

S-2a Identifying Fragments

A sentence fragment is a group of words that is capitalized and punctuated as a sentence but is not a sentence. A sentence needs at least one **INDEPENDENT CLAUSE**, which contains a **SUBJECT** and a **VERB** and does not start with a **SUBORDINATING WORD**.

HB-6

HB-4–5

HB-12–24

HB-8

NO SUBJECT	The catcher batted fifth. Fouled out, ending the inning.
	Who fouled out?
NO VERB	The first two batters walked. Manny Ramirez again.
	What did Ramirez do again?
SUBORDINATING WORD	Although the Yankees loaded the bases.
	There is a subject (Yankees) and a verb (loaded), but although is a subordinating word. What happened after the Yankees loaded the bases?

SOME SUBORDINATING WORDS

after	because	so that	until	while
although	before	that	when	who
as	if	though	where	which
as if	since	unless	whether	why

S-2b Editing Fragments

Since some readers regard fragments as errors, it's generally better to write complete sentences. Here are four ways to make fragments into sentences.

Add a subject

▶ The catcher batted fifth. ~~Fouled out,~~ *He fouled out,* ending the inning.

Add a verb

▶ The first two batters walked. Manny Ramirez again. *walked*

Sometimes, a fragment contains a verb form, such as a present participle or past participle, that cannot function as the main verb of a sentence. In these cases, you can either substitute an appropriate verb form or add a **HELPING VERB**.

HB-17–19

▶ As the game went on, the fans started to lose interest. The pitcher's arm ~~weakening,~~ *weakened,* and the fielders ~~making~~ *made* a number of errors.

▶ The media influence the election process. Political commercials *are*
appearing on television more frequently than in years past.

Remove the subordinating word

▶ I'm thinking about moving to a large city. ~~Because~~ I dislike the lack of
privacy in my country town of three thousand residents.

Attach the fragment to a nearby sentence

▶ Some candidates spread nasty stories. ~~About~~ *about* their opponents.

▶ These negative stories can deal with many topics. ~~Such~~ *, such* as marital
infidelity, sources of campaign funds, and drug use.

▶ Put off by negative campaigning. ~~Some~~ *, some* people decide not to vote at all.

S-2c Intentional Fragments

Writers sometimes use fragments intentionally.

FOR EMPHASIS	Throughout my elementary and middle school years, I was a strong student, always on the honor roll. I never had a GPA below 3.0. I was smart, and I knew it. *That is, until I got the results of the proficiency test.* —Shannon Nichols, "'Proficiency'"
TO BE INFORMAL	The SAT writing test predicts how successful a student will be in college. *Since when?*
TO LIST SEVERAL EXAMPLES	The small details stand out. *The bathrooms with green stalls and mirrors with painted Ducks slugging conference foes. The extra-large furniture tested to withstand 500 pounds. The elevators decorated with famous plays in Oregon football history, the actual plays, drawn up in Xs and Os by a coach. The room for*

*professional scouts to watch footage of Oregon players. The
ticker running sports scores.*
—Greg Bishop, "We Are the University of Nike."

Though fragments are common in informal contexts, they are often considered errors in academic writing.

S-3 Comma Splices, Fused Sentences

You'll sometimes see a comma splice in ads or literary works: "He dropped the bucket, the paint spilled on his feet." Or the comma may be omitted, forming a fused sentence: "He dropped the bucket the paint spilled on his feet." A comma splice or a fused sentence is generally regarded as an error in academic writing. This chapter shows how to recognize comma splices and fused sentences and edit them out of your writing.

S-3a Identifying Comma Splices and Fused Sentences

HB-6

A comma splice occurs when two or more **INDEPENDENT CLAUSES** follow one another with only a comma between them.

> **COMMA SPLICE**   T. S. Eliot is best known for his poetry, he also wrote several plays.

A fused sentence occurs when two or more independent clauses follow one another with no punctuation in between.

> **FUSED SENTENCE**   The school board debated the issue for three days they were unable to reach an agreement.

S-3b Editing Comma Splices and Fused Sentences

There are several ways to edit out comma splices and fused sentences.

Make the clauses two sentences

▶ T. S. Eliot is best known for his poetry, ~~he~~ also wrote several plays. *. He*

Use a comma and a **COORDINATING CONJUNCTION**

HB-38

▶ The school board debated the issue for three days *, but* they were unable to reach an agreement.

Use a semicolon

If the relationship between the two clauses is clear without a coordinating conjunction, you can simply join them with a semicolon.

▶ Psychologists study individuals' behavior*;* sociologists focus on group-level dynamics.

When clauses are linked by a **TRANSITION** such as *therefore* or *as a result*, the transition needs to be preceded by a semicolon and followed by a comma.

✳ 13

▶ The hill towns experienced heavy spring and summer rain*;* therefore, the fall foliage fell far short of expectations.

Recast one clause as a subordinate clause

Add a **SUBORDINATING WORD** to clarify the relationship between the two clauses.

HB-8

▶ ~~Initial~~ critical responses to *The Waste Land* were mixed, the poem has been extensively anthologized, read, and written about. *Although initial*

S-3c Intentional Comma Splices

Writers sometimes use only a comma between clauses that are very brief or closely parallel in structure, as in proverbs like *Marry in haste, repent at leisure.* In academic writing, though, such sentences may be seen as mistakes.

S-4 Verbs

Verbs are the engines of sentences, giving energy, action, and life to writing. "I Googled it" is much more vivid than "I found it on the Internet"—and the difference is the verb. Sometimes, however, our use of verbs can obscure our meaning, as when a politician avoids taking responsibility by saying, "Mistakes were made." Our choice of verbs shapes our writing in important ways, and this chapter reviews ways of using verbs appropriately and effectively.

S-4a Verb Tenses

To express time, English verbs have three simple tenses—present, past, and future. In addition, each of these verb tenses has perfect and progressive forms that indicate more complex time frames. The present perfect, for example, can be used to indicate an action that began in the past but is continuing into the present. The lists that follow show each of these tenses for the regular verb *talk* and the irregular verb *write*.

Simple tenses

PRESENT	PAST	FUTURE
I talk	I talked	I will talk
I write	I wrote	I will write

Use the simple present to indicate actions that take place in the present or that occur habitually. Use the simple past to indicate actions that were completed in the past. Use the simple future to indicate actions that will take place in the future.

▶ Most wealthy industrialized countries *operate* national health-insurance systems.

▶ In 2010, Congress *approved* the Affordable Care Act.

▶ Prohibiting English *will do* for the language what Prohibition *did* for liquor.   —Dennis Baron, "Don't Make English Official—Ban It Instead"

Use the present tense to express a scientific fact or a general truth even when the rest of the sentence is in the past tense.

>   *lose*
> ▶ Agatston showed that South Beach dieters ~~lost~~ about ten pounds in
> the first two weeks.

In general, use the present tense to write about literature.

> ▶ In the first book of the series, Rowling *introduces* us to eleven-year-old
> Harry Potter; in the seventh and final volume, Harry *enters* full adulthood.

In **APA STYLE**, use the past tense or the present perfect to report results of an experiment and the present tense to give your own insights into or conclusions about the results.

● APA 549–89

> ▶ The bulk of the data collected in this study *validated* the research of Neal
> Miller; the subjects *appeared* to undergo operant conditioning of their
> smooth muscles in order to relax their frontalis muscles and increase their skin
> temperatures. Subjects 3 and 6 each *failed* to do this in one session; subject
> 7 *failed* to do this several times. This finding *is* difficult to explain precisely.
>   —Sarah Thomas, "The Effect of Biofeedback Training
>   on Muscle Tension and Skin Temperature"

Perfect tenses

PRESENT PERFECT	PAST PERFECT	FUTURE PERFECT
I have talked	I had talked	I will have talked
I have written	I had written	I will have written

Use the present perfect to indicate actions that took place at unspecified times in the past or that began in the past and continue into the present (or have relevance in the present).

> ▶ Many teachers and parents *have resisted* the increasing pressure for more
> standardized testing of students.

Use the past perfect for an action that was completed before another past action began.

>   *had*
> ▶ By the time I was born, the Gulf War already ended.
>
> *The war ended before the writer was born.*

Use the future perfect to indicate actions that will be completed at a specific time in the future.

▶ By this time next year, you *will have graduated*.

Progressive tenses

PRESENT PROGRESSIVE	PAST PROGRESSIVE	FUTURE PROGRESSIVE
I am talking	I was talking	I will be talking
I am writing	I was writing	I will be writing

PRESENT PERFECT PROGRESSIVE	PAST PERFECT PROGRESSIVE	FUTURE PERFECT PROGRESSIVE
I have been talking	I had been talking	I will have been talking
I have been writing	I had been writing	I will have been writing

Use progressive tenses to indicate continuing action.

▶ The Heat *are having* a great year, but the Spurs *are leading* the league.

▶ We *were watching* TV when the doorbell rang.

▶ During the World Cup, soccer fans around the world *will be watching* on TV or online.

▶ Willie joined the Grace Church Boy Choir when he was ten, and he *has been singing* ever since.

S-4b Verb Forms

There are four forms of a verb: the base form, the past, the past participle, and the present participle. Samples of each appear in the lists below. All of the various tenses are generated with these four forms.

The past tense and past participle of all regular verbs are formed by adding -ed or -d to the base form (*talked*, *lived*). Irregular verbs are not as predictable; see the list of some common ones below. The present participle consists of the base form plus -ing (*talking*, *living*).

BASE FORM   On Thursdays, we *visit* a museum.

PAST TENSE   Last week, we *visited* the Museum of Modern Art.

PAST PARTICIPLE	I have also *visited* the Metropolitan Museum, but I've not yet *been* to the Cloisters.
PRESENT PARTICIPLE	We will be *visiting* the Cooper-Hewitt Museum tomorrow to see the cutlery exhibit.

Some common irregular verbs

BASE FORM	PAST TENSE	PAST PARTICIPLE	PRESENT PARTICIPLE
be	was/were	been	being
bring	brought	brought	bringing
choose	chose	chosen	choosing
come	came	came	coming
do	did	done	doing
eat	ate	eaten	eating
find	found	found	finding
fly	flew	flown	flying
give	gave	given	giving
go	went	gone	going
hang (suspend)	hung	hung	hanging
have	had	had	having
know	knew	known	knowing
make	made	made	making
prove	proved	proved, proven	proving
rise	rose	risen	rising
set	set	set	setting
sit	sat	sat	sitting
teach	taught	taught	teaching
write	wrote	written	writing

It's easy to get confused about when to use the past tense and when to use a past participle. One simple guideline is to use the past tense if there is no helping verb and to use a past participle if there is one.

▶ For vacation last summer, my family ~~gone~~ *went* to the Outer Banks.

▶ After a week at the beach, we had ~~ate~~ *eaten* a lot of seafood.

Gerunds and infinitives

A gerund is a verb form ending in *-ing* that functions as a noun: *hopping*, *skipping*, *jumping*.

▶ Although many people like *driving*, some prefer *walking*.

An infinitive is a verb form made up of *to* plus the base form of a verb: *to hop*, *to skip*, *to jump*.

▶ Although many people like *to drive*, some prefer *to walk*.

In general, use infinitives to express intentions or desires, and use gerunds to express plain facts.

▶ I planned *to learn* Spanish, Japanese, and Arabic.

▶ I also wanted ~~studying~~ *to study* Russian.

▶ Unfortunately, I ended up *studying* only Spanish and Arabic—and *speaking* only Spanish.

▶ Just in time for Thanksgiving, the painters finished ~~to put~~ *putting* up the wallpaper.

Some verbs—*begin, continue, like, prefer*, and a few others—can be followed by either a gerund or an infinitive with little if any difference in meaning. But with several verbs—*forget, remember, stop*, and a few others—the choice of an infinitive or a gerund changes the meaning.

▶ I stopped *to eat* lunch.

In other words, I took a break so that I could eat lunch.

▶ I stopped *eating* lunch.

In other words, I no longer ate lunch.

Always use a gerund after a **PREPOSITION**.

HB-56–58

▶ The water is too cold for ~~to swim.~~ *swimming.*

S-4c Helping Verbs

Do, *have*, *be*, and **MODALS** such as *can* and *may* all function as helping verbs that are used with main verbs to form certain **TENSES** and **MOODS**. *Do*, *have*, and *be* change form to indicate different tenses; modals do not.

HB-18–19
HB-12–14
HB-20–21

FORMS OF *DO*	do, does, did
FORMS OF *HAVE*	have, has, had
FORMS OF *BE*	be, am, is, are, was, were, been
MODALS	can, could, may, might, must, should, will, would, ought to

Do, *does*, and *did* require the base form of the main verb.

▶ That professor *did take* class participation into account when calculating grades.

▶ Sometimes even the smartest students *do* not *like* to answer questions out loud in class.

Have, *has*, and *had* require the past participle of the main verb.

▶ I *have applied* for insurance through one of the new exchanges.

▶ When all of the visitors *had gone*, the security guards locked the building for the night.

Forms of *be* are used with a present participle to express a continuing action or with a past participle to express the **PASSIVE VOICE**.

HB-19

CONTINUING ACTION

▶ The university *is considering* a change in its policy on cell phone use.

▶ I *was studying* my notes from last week as I walked to class.

PASSIVE VOICE

▶ Six classes per semester *is considered* a heavy course load.

▶ Ancient Greek *was studied* by many university students in the early twentieth century, but it is not a popular major today.

Modals

Can, could, may, might, must, shall, should, will, *and* would: these are modals, a kind of helping verb used with the base form of a verb to express whether an action is likely, possible, permitted, or various other conditions.

Likelihood *will, could, may, might*

▶ The Spurs *will* win tomorrow. [*very certain*]

▶ The Lakers *could* defeat the Heat. [*somewhat certain*]

▶ The Rockets *may* win their game tonight. [*less certain*]

▶ The Knicks *might* make the playoffs someday. [*much less certain*]

Assumption *must*

▶ The dog just started barking; he *must* hear our guests arriving.

Expectation *should*

▶ Two large onions *should* be enough for this recipe.

Ability *can, could*

▶ Mick Jagger *can* still put on quite a performance, but years ago he *could* sing and throw himself around the stage more dramatically. How much longer *will* he *be able to* keep rocking?

Necessity or obligation *must, should*

▶ Travelers *must* have a passport for foreign travel.

▶ We *should* leave early tomorrow because of the holiday traffic.

Permission and requests *may, can, could, would, will*

▶ People traveling with small children *may* board the plane first.

▶ The hotel's check-in time is 4:00 PM, but travelers *can* often check in earlier.

▶ *Would* someone help me put my suitcase in the overhead rack?

▶ *Will* you please turn off your cell phone?

Advice *should*

▶ You *should* never text while driving.

Intention *will, shall*

▶ Marianna *will* bring an apple pie for Thanksgiving dinner.

▶ We *shall* overcome.

S-4d Active and Passive Voice

Verbs can sometimes be active or passive. In the active voice, the subject performs the action of the verb (*Becky solved the problem*). In the passive voice, the subject receives the action (*the problem was solved by Becky*).

ACTIVE   One year ago, almost to the day, I *asked* my hairdresser to cut off 16 inches of my hair.
—Suleika Jaouad, "Finding My Cancer Style"

PASSIVE   As a teenager I *was instructed* on how to behave as a proper señorita.
—Judith Ortiz Cofer, "The Myth of the Latin Woman"

Active verbs tend to be more direct and easier to understand, but the passive voice can be useful when you specifically want to emphasize the recipient of the action.

▶ In a sense, little girls *are urged* to please adults with a kind of coquettishness, while boys *are enjoined* to behave like monkeys toward each other.   —Paul Theroux, "Being a Man"

The passive voice is also appropriate in scientific writing when you want to emphasize the research itself, not the researchers.

▶ The treatment order was random for each subject, and it *was reversed* for his or her second treatment.
—Sarah Thomas, "The Effect of Biofeedback Training on Muscle Tension and Skin Temperature"

S-4e Mood

English verbs have three moods: indicative, imperative, and subjunctive. The indicative is used to state facts, opinions, or questions.

▶ Habitat for Humanity *has built* twelve houses in the region this year.

▶ What other volunteer opportunities *does* Habitat *offer*?

The imperative is used to give commands or directions.

▶ *Sit* up straight, and *do* your work.

The subjunctive is used to indicate unlikely or hypothetical conditions or to express wishes, requests, or requirements.

▶ We would be happier if we *had* less pressure at work.

▶ My mother wishes my brother *were* more responsible with his money.

▶ Most colleges require that each applicant *write* an essay.

The subjunctive has two types—one that is the same form as the past tense and one that is the same as the base form.

Conditional sentences

The subjunctive is used most often in conditional sentences, ones that include a clause beginning with *if* or another word that states a condition. Use the indicative in the *if* clause to show that you are confident the condition is posssible; use the subjunctive to show that it's doubtful or impossible.

If it's a fact or a possibility. When there's no doubt that the condition in the *if* clause is true or possible, use the indicative in both clauses.

▶ If an earthquake *strikes* that region, forecasters *expect* a tsunami.

▶ A century ago, if a hurricane *struck*, residents *had* very little warning.

▶ If you *follow* that diet for two weeks, you *will lose* about ten pounds.

If it's unlikely, impossible, or hypothetical. When the condition in the *if* clause is not likely or possible, use the subjunctive (same as the past form) in the *if* clause and *would* (or *could* or *might*) + the base form of a verb in the other clause. For *be*, use *were* in the *if* clause, not *was*.

▶ If I *won* the lottery, I *could pay off* my student loans.

▶ If Martin Luther King Jr. *were* alive, he *would acknowledge* progress in race relations, but he *would* also *ask* significant questions.

Because the subjunctive can sound rather formal, it's often not used in informal contexts. In formal and most academic writing, however, it's best to do so.

INFORMAL   I *wish* I *was* in Paris.

ACADEMIC   In *The Three Sisters*, Masha *wishes* she *were living* in Moscow.

When the *if* clause is about an event in the past that never happened, use the past perfect in the *if* clause and *would have* (or *could have* or *might have*) + a past participle in the other clause.

▶ If the police officer *had separated* the witnesses, their evidence *would have been* admissible in court.

Requests, recommendations, and demands

In *that* clauses following verbs such as *ask*, *insist*, or *suggest*, use the subjunctive to express a request, a recommendation, or a demand. Use the base form of the verb in the *that* clause.

▶ I recommended that Hannah *study* French as an undergraduate.

▶ The CEO will insist that you *be* at your desk before nine each morning.

S-4f Phrasal Verbs

Act up. Back down. Carry on. These are all phrasal verbs, composed of more than one word—usually a verb and a preposition. You know what *act* means. You know what *up* means. If English is not your primary language, however, you may need to check a dictionary to find out that *act up* means to "misbehave" (or say that using another phrasal verb, you may need to *look it up*). With phrasal verbs, knowing the meaning of each part does not always help you to know what the phrasal verb itself means.

Glossary

Phrasal verbs can be divided into two categories, separable and insepa-rable. With separable verbs, the parts can be separated by an **OBJECT**; with inseparable ones, the parts can never be separated.

> **SEPARABLE**   I used to *look up* words in a dictionary; now I *look* them *up* on my phone.

> **INSEPARABLE**   Jim and his family are *caring for* his elderly mother.

With separable phrasal verbs, you have a choice: you can put the object between the parts, or after the complete phrasal verb.

▶ With a hurricane forming nearby, NASA *called off* tomorrow's lunar launch.

▶ Darn! They *called* the launch *off*?

When the object is a long phrase, however, it almost always follows the complete verb.

▶ NASA engineers called the launch of the lunar mission scheduled for tomorrow ~~off~~. *off*

Personal pronouns — *me, you, him, her, it, us, them* — are almost always placed between the parts.

▶ The launch was scheduled for yesterday, but NASA called off ~~it~~ *it* because of the weather.

Some phrasal verbs never take an object — for example, *come over* (meaning to "visit") and *catch on* (meaning to "become popular").

▶ Why don't you *come over* and see us sometime?

▶ Even the developers of *Pinterest* were astonished by how quickly it *caught on.*

With some phrasal verbs, the meaning changes depending on whether or not there is an object. To *look something up*, for instance, means to "find information"; without an object, to *look up* means to "get better."

▶ When in doubt, *look up* phrasal verbs in a dictionary.

▶ The sun's out and the roses are in bloom; things are *looking up!*

Go to **wwnorton.com/write/fieldguidelinks** for a glossary of phrasal verbs.

Some common phrasal verbs

SEPARABLE

back up   means to "support": *Dodson's hypothesis is well stated, but the data do not back it up.*

break down   means to "divide into smaller parts": *Their analysis might be clearer if it broke the data down state by state.*

carry out   means to "fulfill" or "complete": *We plan to carry out a survey on what the students in our dorm are reading.*

find out   means to "learn" or "get information": *Some parents decide not to find out the gender before their baby is born because they want to be surprised; others just want to annoy relatives.*

point out   means to "call attention to": *The lizards blend in with the leaves so well that they were hard to see until the guide pointed them out.*

INSEPARABLE

call for   means to "require" or "deserve": *Our current economic situation calls for bold and innovative thinking.*

get over   means to "recover": *Grandma always insisted that the best way to get over a cold was to eat chicken soup.*

look into   means to "investigate": *GAO investigators are looking into allegations of fraud by some college recruiters.*

settle on   means to "decide on" or "choose": *We considered Elizabeth, Margaret, Jane, and many other names for our baby, but finally we settled on Susanna.*

touch on   means to "mention briefly": *The Wall Street Journal article focused on productivity and barely touched on issues of worker safety.*

CANNOT TAKE AN OBJECT

come about   means to "happen" or "occur": *How did the dispute come about in the first place?*

get by   means to "survive" or "manage," usually with few resources: *Many retired workers can't get by on just their pensions; they have to find part-time work as well.*

give in   means to "yield" or "agree": *After much discussion, members of the union voted not to give in to management's demands for a reduction in benefits.*

show up   means to "arrive": *Did everyone show up for the rehearsal?*

take off   means to "leave the ground": *The JetBlue flight took off an hour late because of thunderstorms in the Midwest.* It also means to "make great progress": *Sales of Anna Karenina took off in 2004, after it was recommended by Oprah Winfrey.*

S-5 Subject-Verb Agreement

Subjects and verbs should agree: if the subject is in the third-person singular, the verb should be in the third-person singular—"Dinner is on the table." Yet sometimes context affects subject-verb agreement, as when we say that "macaroni and cheese *make* a great combination" but that "macaroni and cheese *is* our family's favorite comfort food." This chapter focuses on subject-verb agreement.

S-5a Agreement in Number and Person

Subjects and verbs should agree with each other in number (singular or plural) and person (first, second, or third). To make a present-tense verb agree with a third-person singular subject, add -s or -es to the base form.

▶ A 1922 *ad* for Resinol soap *urges* women to "make that dream come true" by using Resinol.   —Doug Lantry, "'Stay Sweet as You Are'"

academic literacies | rhetorical situations | genres | processes | strategies | research MLA / APA | media / design | readings | handbook

To make a present-tense verb agree with any other subject, simply use the base form without any ending.

▶ *I listen* to NPR every morning while *I brush* my teeth.

▶ *Drunk drivers cause* thousands of preventable deaths each year.

Be and *have* have **IRREGULAR** forms and so do not follow the -s/-es rule. HB-15

▶ The test of all knowledge *is* experiment.
                 —Richard Feynman, "Atoms in Motion"

▶ The scientist *has* a lot of experience with ignorance and doubt and uncertainty, and this experience *is* of great importance.
                 —Richard Feynman, "The Value of Science"

S-5b Subjects and Verbs Separated

A verb should agree with its subject, not with another word that falls in between.

▶ In the backyard, the *leaves* of the apple tree *rattle* across the lawn.
                 —Gary Soto, "The Guardian Angel"

▶ The *price* of soybeans ~~fluctuate~~ *fluctuates* according to demand.

S-5c Compound Subjects

Two or more subjects joined by *and* are generally plural.

▶ Swiss cheese and shrimp *are* both high in vitamin B12.

However, if the parts of the subject form a single unit, they take a singular verb.

▶ Forty acres and a mule $\overset{is}{\cancel{are}}$ what General William T. Sherman promised each freed slave.

If the subjects are joined by *or* or *nor*, the verb should agree with the closer subject.

▶ Either you or she $\overset{is}{\cancel{are}}$ mistaken.

▶ Neither the teacher nor his students $\overset{were}{\cancel{was}}$ able to solve the equation.

S-5d Subjects That Follow the Verb

English verbs usually follow their subjects. Be sure the verb agrees with the subject even when the subject follows the verb, such as when the sentence begins with *there is* or *there are*.

▶ There $\overset{are}{\cancel{is}}$ too many unresolved problems for the project to begin.

▶ In the middle of the room $\overset{were}{\cancel{was}}$ a desk and a floor lamp.

S-5e Collective Nouns

Collective nouns such as *group, team, audience,* or *family* can take singular or plural verbs, depending on whether the noun refers to the group as a single unit or to the individual members of the group.

▶ The choir $\overset{sings}{\cancel{sing}}$ Handel's *Messiah* every Christmas.

▶ Gregor's family *keep* reassuring themselves that things will be just fine again.   —Scott Russell Sanders, "Under the Influence"

The word themselves *shows that* family *refers to its individual members.*

S-5f *Everyone* and Other Indefinite Pronouns

Glossary

Most **INDEFINITE PRONOUNS**, such as *anyone, anything, each, either, everyone, everything, neither, nobody, no one, one, somebody, someone,* and *something,* take a singular verb, even if they seem plural or refer to plural nouns.

▶ Everyone in our dorm *has* already *signed* the petition.

▶ Each of the candidates ~~agree~~ with the president.
   agrees

Both, few, many, others, and *several* are always plural.

▶ Although there are many great actors working today, few *are* as versatile as Meryl Streep.

All, any, enough, more, most, none, and *some* are singular when they refer to a singular noun, but they are plural when they refer to a plural noun.

▶ Don't assume that all of the members of a family ~~votes~~ the same way.
   vote

▶ Most of the music we heard last night ~~come~~ from the baroque period.
   comes

S-5g *Who, That, Which*

Glossary

The **RELATIVE PRONOUNS** *who, that,* and *which* take a singular verb when they refer to a singular noun and a plural verb when they refer to a plural noun.

▶ In these songs, Lady Gaga draws on a tradition of camp that *extends* from drag queen cabaret to Broadway and disco.
                                               —Jody Rosen, review of *Born This Way*

▶ Scott Karp, who *writes* a blog about online media, recently confessed that he has stopped reading books altogether.
                              —Nicholas Carr, "Is Google Making Us Stoopid?"

One of the is always followed by a plural noun, and when the noun is followed by *who* or *that,* the verb should be plural.

▶ Jaime is one of the speakers who ~~asks~~ ^{ask} provocative questions.

> *Several speakers ask provocative questions. Jaime is one. Who refers to speakers, so the verb is plural.*

If the phrase begins with *the only one*, however, the verb should be singular.

▶ Jaime is the only one of the speakers who ~~ask~~ ^{asks} provocative questions.

> *Only one speaker asks provocative questions: Jaime. Who thus refers to one, so the verb is singular.*

S-5h Words Such as *News* and *Physics*

Words like *news*, *athletics*, and *physics* seem plural but are usually singular in meaning and take singular verb forms.

▶ The *news* of widespread layoffs *alarms* everyone in the company.

Some of these words, such as *economics*, *mathematics*, *politics*, and *statistics*, have plural meanings in some uses and take plural verbs.

▶ For my roommate, mathematics *is* an endlessly stimulating field.

▶ The complex mathematics involved in this proof *are* beyond the scope of this lecture.

S-5i Titles and Words Used as Words

Titles and words that are discussed as words are singular.

▶ *The Royal Tenenbaums* ~~depict~~ ^{depicts} three talented siblings who are loosely based on characters created by J. D. Salinger.

▶ *Man-caused disasters* ~~are~~ ^{is} a term favored by some political analysts as a substitute for the term *terrorist attacks*.

S-6 Pronouns

We use pronouns to take the place of nouns so that we don't have to write or say the same word or name over and over. Imagine how repetitive our writing would be without pronouns: *Little Miss Muffet sat on a tuffet eating Little Miss Muffet's curds and whey.* Luckily, we have pronouns, and this chapter demonstrates how to use them clearly.

S-6a Pronoun-Antecedent Agreement

Antecedents are the words that pronouns refer to. A pronoun must agree with its antecedent in gender and number.

IN GENDER	*Grandma* took *her* pie out of the oven.
IN NUMBER	*My grandparents* spent weekends at *their* cabin on White Bear Lake.

Generic nouns

Generic nouns refer to a type of person or thing (*a farmer, a soccer mom*). You'll often see or hear plural pronouns used to refer to singular generic nouns; in academic writing, however, be sure that your pronoun agrees with its antecedent.

▶ Every lab technician should always wear goggles to protect ~~their~~ *his or her* eyes while working with chemicals.

▶ ~~Every lab technician~~ *Lab technicians* should always wear goggles to protect their eyes while working with chemicals.

Indefinite pronouns like everyone *and* each

INDEFINITE PRONOUNS such as *anyone, each, either, everyone, neither, no one,* and *someone* are singular even if they seem to be plural or refer to plural nouns.

Glossary

▶ Everyone in the class did ~~their~~ *his or her* best.

If you find *his or her* awkward, you can rewrite the sentence to make the antecedents plural.

> *All of the students*
> ▶ ~~Everyone~~ in the class did their best.

In conversation and informal writing, *they* and other plural pronouns are often used to refer to indefinite pronouns or generic nouns that are grammatically singular: *Someone left their phone at the coffee shop.* In most academic writing, though, either stick to singular pronouns (such as *his or her*) or make the antecedent plural.

Collective nouns like audience and team

Collective nouns such as *audience, committee,* or *team* take a singular pronoun when they refer to the group as a whole and a plural pronoun when they refer to members of the group as individuals.

> *its*
> ▶ The winning team drew ~~their~~ inspiration from the manager.

> *their*
> ▶ The winning team threw ~~its~~ gloves in the air.

He, his, *and other masculine pronouns*

HB-67–68

To avoid **SEXIST LANGUAGE**, use *he, him, his,* or *himself* only when you know that the antecedent is male.

> *or her.*
> ▶ Before meeting a new doctor, many people worry about not liking him.

S-6b Pronoun Reference

A pronoun usually needs a clear antecedent, a specific word to which it refers.

> ▶ My grandmother spent a lot of time reading to me. She mostly read the standards, like *The Little Engine That Could.*
> —Richard Bullock, "How I Learned about the Power of Writing"

Ambiguous reference

If there is more than one word that a pronoun could refer to, rewrite the sentence to clarify which one is the antecedent.

> ► After I plugged the printer into the computer, ~~it~~ sputtered and died.
> *the printer*
>
> *What sputtered and died—the computer or the printer? The edit makes the reference clear.*

Implied reference

If a pronoun does not refer clearly to a specific word, rewrite the sentence to omit the pronoun or insert an antecedent.

Unclear reference of *this, that,* and *which*. These three pronouns must refer to specific antecedents.

> ► Ultimately, the Justice Department did not insist on the breakup of Microsoft, ~~which~~ set the tone for a liberal merger policy.
> *an oversight that*

Indefinite use of *they, it,* and *you*. Except in expressions like *it is raining* or *it seems that*, *they* and *it* should be used only to refer to people or things that have been specifically mentioned. *You* should be used only to address your reader.

> ► ~~In many~~ European countries, ~~they~~ don't allow civilians to carry handguns.
> *Many*
>
> ► ~~On the~~ Weather Channel, ~~it~~ said that storms would hit Key West today.
> *The*
>
> ► Many doctors argue that age should not be an impediment to physical exercise ~~if you~~ have always been active.
> *for people who*

Both in conversation and in writing, antecedents are often left unstated if the audience will easily grasp the meaning. For academic writing, however, it's better not to use implied or indefinite antecedents.

S-6c Pronoun Case

The pronouns below change case according to how they function in a sentence. There are three cases: subject, object, and possessive. Pronouns functioning as subjects or subject **COMPLEMENTS** are in the subject case; those functioning as **OBJECTS** are in the object case; those functioning as possessives are in the possessive case.

Glossary

SUBJECT	*We* lived in a rented house three blocks from the school.
OBJECT	I went to my room and shut the door behind *me.*
POSSESSIVE	All *my* life chocolate has made me ill.

—David Sedaris, "Us and Them"

SUBJECT	OBJECT	POSSESSIVE
I	me	my / mine
we	us	our / ours
you	you	your / yours
he / she / it	him / her / it	his / her / hers / its
they	them	their / theirs
who / whoever	whom / whomever	whose

In subject complements

Glossary

Use the subject case for pronouns that follow **LINKING VERBS** such as *be, seem, become,* and *feel.*

▶ In fact, Li was not the one who broke the code; it was ~~me~~. *I.*

If It was I *sounds awkward, revise the sentence further:* I broke it.

In compound structures

When a pronoun is part of a compound subject, it should be in the subject case. When it's part of a compound object, it should be in the object case.

▶ On our vacations, my grandfather and ~~me~~ *I* went fishing together.

▶ There were never any secrets between ~~he~~ *him* and ~~I~~ *me.*

After than *or* as

Often comparisons with *than* or *as* leave some words out. When such comparisons include pronouns, your intended meaning determines the case of the pronoun.

▶ You trust John more than *me*.

This sentence means You trust John more than you trust me.

▶ You trust John more than *I*.

This sentence means You trust John more than I trust him.

Before or after infinitives

Pronouns that come before or after an **INFINITIVE** are usually in the object case.

Glossary

             me   *her*
▶ The professor asked Scott and ~~I~~ to tell our classmates and ~~she~~ about our project.

Before gerunds

Pronouns that come before a **GERUND** are usually in the possessive case.

HB-16

             his
▶ Savion's fans loved ~~him~~ tap dancing to classical music.

With who *or* whom

Use *who* (and *whoever*) where you would use *he* or *she*, and use *whom* (and *whomever*) where you would use *him* or *her*. These words appear most often in questions and in **SUBORDINATE CLAUSES**.

Glossary

In questions. It can be confusing when one of these words begins a question. To figure out which case to use, try answering the question using *she* or *her*. If *she* works, use *who*; if *her* works, use *whom*.

    Whom
▶ ~~Who~~ do the critics admire most?

They admire her, so change who to whom.

▶ *Who*
~~Whom~~ will begin the discussion on this thorny topic?
^

She *will begin the discussion, so change* whom *to* who.

In subordinate clauses. To figure out whether to use *who* or *whom* in a subordinate clause, you need to determine how it functions in the clause. If it functions as a subject, use *who*; if it functions as an object, use *whom*.

▶ *whomever*
You may invite ~~whoever~~ you like.
^

Whomever *is the object of* you like.

▶ *whoever*
I will invite ~~whomever~~ is free that night.
^

Whoever *is the subject of* is free that night. *The clause* whoever is free that night *is the object of the whole sentence.*

When we *or* us *precedes a noun*

If you don't know whether to use *we* or *us* before a noun, choose the pronoun that you would use if the noun were omitted.

▶ *We* students object to the recent tuition increases.

Without students, *you would say* We object, *not* Us object.

▶ The state is solving its budget shortfall by unfairly charging *us* students.

Without students, *you would say* unfairly charging us, *not* unfairly charging we.

S-7 Parallelism

Been there, done that. Eat, drink, and be merry. For better or for worse. Out of sight, out of mind. All of these common sayings are parallel in structure, putting related words in the same grammatical form. Parallel structure emphasizes the connection between the elements and can make your writing rhythmic and easy to read. This chapter offers guidelines for maintaining parallelism in your writing.

S-7a In a Series or List

Use the same grammatical form for all items in a series or list—all nouns, all gerunds, all prepositional phrases, and so on.

▶ The seven deadly sins—*avarice, sloth, envy, lust, gluttony, pride,* and *wrath*—were all committed Sunday during the twice-annual bake sale at St. Mary's of the Immaculate Conception Church.   —*The Onion*

▶ After fifty years of running, biking, swimming, weight lifting, and~ *playing* tennis to stay in shape, Aunt Dorothy was unhappy to learn she needed knee surgery.

S-7b With Paired Ideas

One way to emphasize the connection between two ideas is to put them in identical grammatical forms. When you connect ideas with *and, but,* or another **COORDINATING CONJUNCTION** or with *either . . . or* or another **CORRELATIVE CONJUNCTION**, use the same grammatical structure for each idea.

HB-38

HB-38

▶ Many rural residents are voting on conservation issues and ~~agree~~ *agreeing* to pay higher taxes to keep community land undeveloped.

▶ General Electric paid millions of dollars to dredge the river and ~~for removing~~ *to remove* carcinogens from backyards.

▶ Sweet potatoes are highly nutritious, providing both dietary fiber and ~~as a good source of~~ vitamins A and C.

▶ Information on local cleanup efforts can be obtained not only from the town government but also ~~by going to~~ *at* the public library.

S-7c On Presentation Slides

PowerPoint and other presentation tools present most information in lists. Entries on these lists should be in parallel grammatical form.

During the 1946 presidential race, Truman

- Conducted a whistle-stop campaign
- Made hundreds of speeches
- Spoke energetically
- Connected personally with voters

S-7d On a Résumé

Entries on a résumé should be grammatically and typographically parallel. Each entry in the example below has the date on the left; the job title in bold followed by the company on the first line; the city and state on the second line; and the duties performed on the remaining lines, each starting with a verb.

2012–present	**INTERN**, Benedetto, Gartland, and Company New York, NY Assist in analyzing data for key accounts. Design *PowerPoint* slides and presentations.
2011, summer	**SALES REPRESENTATIVE**, Vector Marketing Corporation New York, NY Sold high-quality cutlery, developing client base.
2010, summer	**TUTOR**, Grace Church Opportunity Project New York, NY Tutored children in math and reading.

S-7e In Headings

When you add headings to a piece of writing, put them in parallel form—all nouns, all prepositional phrases, and so on. Consider, for example, the following three headings in the chapter on developing a research plan.

Acknowledging Sources
Avoiding Plagiarism
Understanding Documentation Styles

academic literacies · rhetorical situations · genres · processes · strategies · research MLA / APA · media / design · readings · handbook

S-7f With All the Necessary Words

Be sure to include all the words necessary to make your meaning clear and your grammar parallel.

▶ Voting gained urgency in cities, suburbs, and on farms.
  (insert: in)

▶ She loved her son more than her husband.
  (insert: she loved)

  The original sentence was ambiguous; it could also mean that she loved her son more than her husband did.

▶ A cat's skeleton is more flexible than a dog.
  (insert: that of)

  The original sentence compared one animal's skeleton to a whole animal rather than to another animal's skeleton.

S-8 Coordination, Subordination

When we combine two or more ideas in one sentence, we can use coordination to give equal weight to each idea or subordination to give more emphasis to one of the ideas. Assume, for example, that you're writing about your Aunt Irene. Aunt Irene made great strawberry jam. She did not win a blue ribbon at the Iowa State Fair.

COORDINATION   Aunt Irene made great strawberry jam, but she did not win a blue ribbon at the Iowa State Fair.

SUBORDINATION   Though Aunt Irene made great strawberry jam, she did not win a blue ribbon at the Iowa State Fair.

S-8a Linking Equal Ideas

To link ideas that you consider equal in importance, use a coordinating conjunction, a pair of correlative conjunctions, or a semicolon.

COORDINATING CONJUNCTIONS

and	or	so	yet
but	nor	for	

▶ The line in front of Preservation Hall was very long, *but* a good tenor sax player was wandering up and down the street, *so* I took my place at the end of the line.   —Fred Setterberg, "The Usual Story"

▶ New models of coursework may need to be developed, *and* instructors may need to be hired.
    —Megan Hopkins, "Training the Next Teachers for America"

Be careful not to overuse *and*. Try to use the coordinating conjunction that best expresses your meaning.

▶ Mosquitoes survived the high-tech zapping devices, ~~and~~ *but* bites were a

small price for otherwise pleasant evenings in the country.

CORRELATIVE CONJUNCTIONS

either . . . or	not only . . . but also	whether . . . or
neither . . . nor	just as . . . so	

▶ *Just as* the summer saw endless rain, *so* the winter brought many snowstorms.

While a semicolon alone can signal equal importance, you might use a **TRANSITION** such as *therefore* or *in fact* to make the relationship between the ideas especially clear.

13 ※

▶ Snowplows could not get through; trains stopped running.

▶ The 1996 film *Space Jam* stars Bugs Bunny and Michael Jordan, an unlikely pairing; *however,* the two are well matched in heroic status and mythic strengths.

S-8b Emphasizing One Idea over Others

HB-6–7 ◩

To emphasize one idea over others, put the most important one in an **INDEPENDENT CLAUSE** and the less important ones in **SUBORDINATE CLAUSES** or **PHRASES**.

▸ ⌈————PHRASE————⌉
▸ Wanting to walk to work, LeShawn rented a somewhat expensive apartment downtown.

▸ ⌈————SUBORDINATE CLAUSE————⌉
▸ His monthly expenses were actually lower because he saved so much money in transportation costs.

S-9 Shifts

You're watching the news when your brother grabs the remote and changes the channel to a cartoon. The road you're driving on suddenly changes from asphalt to gravel. These shifts are jarring and sometimes disorienting. Similarly, shifts in writing—from one tense to another, for example—can confuse your readers. This chapter explains how to keep your writing consistent in verb tense, point of view, and number.

S-9a Shifts in Tense

Only when you want to emphasize that actions take place at different times should you shift verb **TENSE**.

HB-12–14

▸ My plane *will arrive* in Albuquerque two hours after it *leaves* Portland.

Otherwise, keep tenses consistent.

▸ As the concert ended, several people ~~are~~ *were* already on their way up the aisle, causing a distraction.

In writing about literary works, use the present tense. Be careful not to shift to the past tense.

▸ The two fugitives start down the river together, Huck fleeing his abusive father and Jim running away from his owner. As they ~~traveled,~~ *travel,* they ~~met~~ *meet* with many colorful characters, including the Duke and King, two actors and con artists who involve Huck and Jim in their schemes.

S-9b Shifts in Point of View

Do not shift between first person (*I, we*), second person (*you*), and third person (*he, she, it, they, one*).

▶ When ~~one has~~ a cold, you should stay home to avoid infecting others.
  you have

S-9c Shifts in Number

Unnecessary shifts between singular and plural subjects can confuse readers.

▶ Because of late frosts, oranges have risen dramatically in price. But since ~~the orange is~~ such a staple, they continue to sell.
  oranges are

academic literacies · rhetorical situations · genres · processes · strategies · research MLA / APA · media / design · readings · handbook

Language   L

L-1 Appropriate Words

Cool. Sweet. Excellent. These three words can mean the same thing, but each has a different level of formality. We usually use informal language when we're talking with friends, and we use slang and abbreviations when we send text messages, but we choose words that are more formal for most of our academic and professional writing. Just as we wouldn't wear an old T-shirt to most job interviews, we wouldn't write in a college essay that *Beloved* is "an awesome book." This chapter offers you help in choosing words that are appropriate for different audiences and purposes.

L-1a Formal and Informal Words

55–56
57–60

Whether you use formal or informal language depends on your **PURPOSE** and **AUDIENCE**.

> **FORMAL**   Four score and seven years ago our fathers brought forth on this continent, a new nation, conceived in Liberty, and dedicated to the proposition that all men are created equal.
> —Abraham Lincoln, Gettysburg Address

> **INFORMAL**   Our family, like most, had its ups and downs.
> —Judy Davis, "Ours Was a Dad"

The first, more formal sentence was delivered in 1863 to twenty thousand people, including many officials and prominent citizens. The second, less formal sentence was spoken in 2004 to a small gathering of family and friends at a funeral.

Colloquial language (*What's up? No clue*) and slang (*A-list, S'up?*) are not appropriate for formal speech and most academic and professional writing.

> ▶   ~~A lot of~~ high school ~~kids~~ have so little time for lunch that they end up ~~gobbling down their food~~ as they race to class.
> *Many* *students* *eating*

L-1b Pretentious Language

Long or complicated words might seem to lend authority to your writing, but often they make it sound pretentious and stuffy. Use such words sparingly and only when they best capture your meaning and suit your RHETORICAL SITUATION.

▶ ~~Subsequent to~~ _{After} adopting the new system, managers ~~averred~~ _{claimed} that their staff worked ~~synergistically~~ _{together} ~~in a way that exceeded parameters.~~ _{better than expected.}

L-1c Jargon

Jargon is a specialized vocabulary of a profession, trade, or field and should be used only when you know your audience will understand what you are saying. A computer enthusiast might easily understand the following paragraph, but most readers would not be familiar with terms like *HDMI*, *DVI*, and *1080p*.

▶ HDMI is the easiest and most convenient way to go about high-def. Why? Because you get [video] and sound in a single, USB-like cable, instead of a nest of component cables or the soundless garden hose of DVI. Also, unless you're trying to run 1080p over 100 feet or somesuch, stay away from premium brands. Any on-spec cheapie HDMI cable will be perfect for standard living room setups.
> —Rob Beschizza, "Which Is Better, HDMI or Component?"

When you are writing for an audience of nonspecialists, resist the temptation to use overly technical language.

▶ The ~~mini-sternotomy~~ _{small incision} at the lower end of the ~~sternum resulted in~~ _{breastbone preserved} ~~satisfactory cosmesis.~~ _{her appearance.}

L-1d Clichés

Steer clear of clichés, expressions so familiar that they have become trite (*white as snow, the grass is always greener*).

> *unconventionally.*
> The company needs a recruiter who thinks ~~outside the box.~~
>   ^

> *soundly.*
> After canoeing all day, we all slept ~~like logs.~~
>   ^

> *collaborates well,*
> Nita ~~is a team player,~~ so we hope she will be assigned to the project.
>   ^

L-2 Precise Words

Serena Overpowers Sloane. Mariano Finishes Off the Sox. In each case, the writer could have simply used the word *beats*. But at least to sports fans, these newspaper headlines are a bit more precise and informative as a result of the words chosen. This chapter offers guidelines for editing your own writing to make it as precise as it needs to be.

L-2a *Be* and *Do*

Try not to rely too much on *be* or *do*. Check your writing to see where you can replace forms of these words with more precise verbs.

> *focuses on*
> David Sedaris's essay "Us and Them" ~~is about~~ his love/hate relationship
>   ^
> with his family.

> *solving*
> Some doctors no longer believe that ~~doing~~ crossword puzzles can
>   ^
> delay the onset of senility or Alzheimer's disease.

Sometimes using a form of *be* or *do* is the right choice, such as when you are describing something or someone.

> Most critics agree that *Citizen Kane, Casablanca,* and *The Shawshank Redemption are* some of the finest movies ever made.

L-2b Abstract and Concrete Words

Abstract words refer to general qualities or ideas (*truth, beauty*), whereas concrete words refer to specific things that can be perceived with our senses (*books, lipstick*). You'll often need to use words that are general or abstract, but remember that specific, concrete words can make your writing more precise and more vivid—and can make an abstract concept easier to understand.

> ▶ In Joan Didion's work, there has always been a fascination with what she once called "the unspeakable peril of the everyday"—the coyotes by the interstate, the snakes in the playpen, the fires and Santa Ana winds of California.
> —Michiko Kakutani, "The End of Life as She Knew It"

The concrete words coyotes, snakes, fires, *and* winds *help explain the abstract* peril of the everyday.

L-2c Figurative Language

Figures of speech such as **SIMILES** and **METAPHORS** are words used imaginatively rather than literally. They can help readers understand an abstract point by comparing it to something they are familiar with or can easily imagine.

Glossary

SIMILE   His body is in almost constant motion—rolling those cigarettes, rubbing an elbow, reaching for a glass—but the rhythm is tranquil and fluid, *like a cat licking its paw.*
—Sean Smith, "Johnny Depp: Unlikely Superstar"

METAPHOR   And so, before the professor had even finished his little story, *I had become a furnace of rage.*
—Shelby Steele, "On Being Black and Middle Class"

L-3 Idioms

A piece of cake. Walking on air. Cute as a button. These are just three of the thousands of English idioms and idiomatic expressions that are used every day. Most idioms are phrases (and sometimes whole sentences) whose meaning cannot be understood by knowing the meanings of the individual words. We use idioms because they give a lot of information in few words and add color and texture to what we say or write. If you're learning English, a well-chosen idiom also demonstrates your fluency in the language. Some idioms appear more often in conversation than in formal writing, but many will be useful to you in your academic work.

L-3a Recognizing Idioms

When you read or hear a phrase that seems totally unrelated to the topic, you have probably encountered an idiom.

▶ Influencing Hollywood is a little *like herding cats.*
—Jane Alexander, *Command Performance*

Cats are notoriously independent and indifferent to following directions; thus a difficult, maybe impossible task is said to be "like herding cats."

▶ As the economy contracts, we Americans are likely to find that we have been living too *high on the hog.* —*Los Angeles Times*

Ham, ribs, bacon, and other meats that are considered the most tasty and desirable are from the upper parts of the hog. People who live extravagantly or luxuriously are sometimes said to be living "high on the hog."

▶ This is about really getting *a leg up* for when you graduate. A lot of these places hire people that they intern.
—Morgan to Chelsea, *Days of Our Lives*

When a rider is mounting a horse, another person often supports the rider's left leg while the right one swings over the horse's back. Having "a leg up" means you've been given extra help or certain advantages.

▶ I love to see a young girl go out and *grab the world by the lapels.*
—Maya Angelou

Grabbing the front of a jacket, or "grabbing someone by the lapels," is a firm and aggressive move that aims to take charge of a situation.

L-3b Understanding Idioms

Idioms may seem peculiar or even nonsensical if you think about their literal meanings, but knowing where they originated can help you figure out what they mean. Many idioms, for example, originate in sports, music, and animal contexts, where their meanings are literal. Used in other contexts, their meanings are similar, if not exactly literal.

▶ When the senator introduced the bill, she thought passage would be a *slam dunk* since public opinion was strongly favorable.

In basketball, a player scores a "slam dunk" by shoving the ball through the basket in a dramatic way. As an idiom, a "slam dunk" refers to a victory gained easily or emphatically.

▶ George Saunders's commencement speech really *struck a chord* with the Syracuse graduates.

A chord is a group of musical notes that harmonize; to "strike a chord" with an audience means to make a connection by bringing up something interesting or relevant to them.

▶ Some members of Congress think that limiting food stamps will get more Americans back to work; I think they're *barking up the wrong tree.*

This idiom refers to a dog in pursuit of an animal that has disappeared into a group of trees; the dog is barking at one tree, but its prey has climbed up another. To "bark up the wrong tree" means to pursue the wrong course of action.

You can sometimes figure out the meaning of an idiom based on its context; but if you're not sure what it means or how to use it properly, look it up online—go to **wwnorton.com/write/fieldguidelinks** for links to some good sources. The *Cambridge Dictionary of American Idioms* is a good print source.

L-3c Common Idiomatic Expressions in Academic and Professional Writing

Idiomatic expressions are words that go together like peanut butter and jelly—you often find them together. You've probably encountered expressions such as *with respect to, insofar as,* or *as a matter of fact* in academic

_____ 13 ✳

or professional writing. Many of these function as **TRANSITIONS**, helping readers follow your reasoning and understand how your ideas relate to one another. You're expected to signal the connections among your ideas clearly in the writing you do in college, and the following idiomatic expressions can help you do so.

To shift to a narrower focus

with respect to, with regard to   indicate the precise topic you are addressing: _The global economic situation is much more complicated with respect to certain nations' high levels of debt._

insofar as   sets a limit or scope for a statement: _Despite her short stature, Bates is the team leader insofar as direction and determination are concerned._

in particular   points to something especially true within a generalization: _Cosmetic surgery procedures for men have increased tremendously in the last decade; liposuction and eyelid surgery, in particular, showed dramatic increases._

To give examples

a case in point   frames an example that illustrates a point: _Recent business activity shows a clear trend toward consolidation. The merger of two airlines last year is a case in point._

for instance   indicates an example that illustrates an idea: _Green vegetables are highly nutritious; one serving of kale, for instance, provides the full daily recommended value of vitamins A and C._

To add information

in addition introduces a new but related point: _Locally grown tomatoes are available nearly everywhere; in addition, they are rich in vitamin C and beta-carotene._

along the same lines   connects two similar ideas: _Many U.S. cities are now developing parking meter plans along the same lines as the system in Chicago._

by the same token   signals a point that follows the logic of the previous point: _Insider trading has damaged the reputation of the financial industry in_

general; by the same token, high-profile embezzlers like Bernie Madoff have eroded the public's confidence in many investment advisers.

as a matter of fact, in fact signal a statement that explains a previous point: *Wind power is an increasingly common energy source; as a matter of fact, wind energy generation quadrupled between 2000 and 2006.*

To emphasize something

of course emphasizes a point that is (or should be) obvious: *Fresh foods are preferable to processed foods, of course, but fresh food is not always available.*

in any case, in any event introduce something that is true regardless of other conditions: *The city has introduced new precautions to ensure the election goes smoothly; the results will be closely scrutinized in any event.*

To signal alternatives or conflicting ideas

on the one hand . . . on the other hand introduces contrasting ideas or conditions: *On the one hand, some critics have loudly rejected reality television; on the other hand, unscripted shows are often received well by the public.*

up to a point signals acceptance of part but not all of an argument or idea: *The senator's statement is correct up to a point, but her conclusions are misguided.*

have it both ways to benefit from two conflicting positions: *Tech companies want to have it both ways, asking the government to be more transparent about its use of user data while not disclosing that they are using these data for their own commercial purposes.*

of two minds signals ambivalence, validates conflicting ideas: *On the question of whether organic food is worth the extra cost, I am of two minds: I like knowing that the food is grown without chemicals, but some studies suggest that the health benefits are questionable.*

in contrast signals a change in direction or a different idea on the same subject: *Large birds such as crows can live for more than ten years; in contrast, tiny hummingbirds generally live less than three years.*

on the contrary   signals an opposite idea or opposing position: *Some bankers claim that the proposed mortgage regulations would harm the economy; on the contrary, the new rules would be the most effective means of reinvigorating it.*

in fact, as a matter of fact   signal a statement that challenges or refutes a previous statement: *Nicholas Carr suggests that Google is making us stupid; in fact, some argue that by giving us access to more information, it's making us better informed.*

To summarize or restate something

in brief, in short   introduces a short summary of points already established: *In brief, the accident was caused by a combination of carelessness and high winds.*

in other words   signals a restatement or explanation of the preceding idea: *Our opposition to the proposal is firm and unequivocal; in other words, we emphatically decline.*

in conclusion, in sum   signal the final statement or section of a text: *In conclusion, the evidence points to a clear and simple solution to the problem.*

Sports idioms in business writing. You'll encounter and use many idioms in business writing, especially ones that come from sports—probably because the competitiveness of the business world makes it easily comparable to sports. Following are some idioms that often come up in business contexts.

a team player   someone who acts in the interest of a whole team or group rather than for individual gain: *The best managers are team players, making sure that the credit for a success is shared among everyone who contributed to the effort.*

to cover all the bases   an expression that comes from baseball, where the fielders must protect all four bases against the other team's runners; as an idiom, it means to be thorough—to deal with all aspects of a situation and consider all possibilities: *Her report was well executed; it covered all the bases and anticipated all possible counterproposals.*

across the board a large board at a racetrack displays the names of all the horses in a race; to place an equal bet on every horse is to bet "across the board," so the idiom refers to something affecting all items in a group equally: *Proponents of the new health-care policy insist that it will reduce costs across the board, from doctor visits to medical procedures to prescription medicines.*

Considering context. Many idiomatic expressions are quite informal. These can be used effectively in casual conversation or social media, but they are rarely if ever appropriate in academic or professional writing. As with all writing, you need to consider your **AUDIENCE** and **PURPOSE** when you use idiomatic expressions.

57–60

55–56

In a conversation with a friend or family member, you might say *let's cut to the chase;* with a business colleague, however, it may be more appropriate to suggest that you *get right to the point,* or *focus on what's most important.*

In an email to a friend, you might say something sounds *like a piece of cake;* with your boss, it would be more appropriate to say it sounds *doable* or *easy to do.*

On Facebook, you might describe an improv show as *over the top;* in a review for a class, it would be more appropriate to say it was *excessive* or *outrageous.*

L-4 Words Often Confused

When you're tired, do you *lay* down or *lie* down? After dinner, do you eat *desert* or *dessert?* This chapter's dual purpose is to alert you to everyday words that can trip you up and to help you understand the differences between certain words that people tend to confuse.

accept, except *Accept* means "to receive willingly": *accept an award. Except* as a preposition means "excluding": *all languages except English.*

adapt, adopt *Adapt* means "to adjust": *adapt the recipe to be dairy free. Adopt* means "to take as one's own": *adopt a pet from a shelter.*

advice, advise   *Advice* means "recommendation": *a lawyer's advice. Advise* means "to give advice": *We advise you to learn your rights.*

affect, effect   *Affect* is usually a verb that means "to produce a change in": *Stress can affect health. Effect* is a noun that means "result": *The effects of smoking are well known.* As a verb, it means "to cause": *A mediator works to effect a compromise.*

all right, alright   *All right* is the preferred spelling.

allusion, illusion   *Allusion* means "indirect reference": *an allusion to Beowulf. Illusion* means "false appearance": *an optical illusion.*

a lot   Always two words, *a lot* means "a large number or amount" or "to a great extent": *a lot of voters; he misses her a lot.* The phrase is too informal for most academic writing.

among, between   Use *among* for three or more items: *among the fifty states.* Use *between* for two items: *between you and me.*

amount, number   Use *amount* for things you can measure but not count: *a large amount of water.* Use *number* for things you can count: *a number of books.*

as, as if, like   *Like* introduces a noun or noun phrase: *It feels like silk.* To begin a subordinate clause, use *as* or *as if: Do as I say, not as I do; It seemed as if he had not prepared at all for the briefing.*

bad, badly   Use *bad* as an adjective following a linking verb: *I feel bad.* Use *badly* as an adverb following an action verb: *I play piano badly.*

capital, capitol   A *capital* is a city where the government of a state, province, or country is located: *Kingston was the first state capital of New York.* A *capitol* is a government building: *the dome of the capitol.*

cite, sight, site   *Cite* means "to give information from a source by quoting, paraphrasing, or summarizing": *Cite your sources. Sight* is the act of seeing or something that is seen: *an appalling sight.* A *site* is a place: *the site of a famous battle.*

compose, comprise   The parts *compose* the whole: *Fifty states compose the Union.* The whole *comprises* the parts: *The Union comprises fifty states.*

could of   In writing, use *could have (could've).*

academic literacies   rhetorical situations   genres   processes   strategies   research MLA / APA   media / design   readings   handbook

council, counsel *Council* refers to a body of people: *the council's vote*. *Counsel* means "advice" or "to advise": *her wise counsel; she counseled victims of domestic abuse*.

criteria, criterion *Criteria* is the plural of *criterion* and takes a plural verb: *Certain criteria have been established*.

data *Data*, the plural of *datum*, technically should take a plural verb (*The data arrive from many sources*), but some writers treat it as singular (*The data is persuasive*).

desert, dessert *Desert* as a noun means "arid region": *Mojave Desert*. As a verb it means "to abandon": *He deserted his post*. *Dessert* is a sweet served toward the end of a meal.

disinterested, uninterested *Disinterested* means "fair" or "unbiased": *a disinterested jury*. *Uninterested* means "bored" or "indifferent": *uninterested in election results*.

emigrate (from), immigrate (to) *Emigrate* means "to leave one's country": *emigrate from Slovakia*. *Immigrate* means "to move to another country": *immigrate to Canada*.

etc. The abbreviation *etc.* is short for the Latin *et cetera*, "and other things." *Etc.* is fine in notes and bibliographies, but avoid using it in your writing in general. Substitute *and so on* if necessary.

everyday, every day *Everyday* is an adjective meaning "ordinary": *After the holidays, we go back to our everyday routine*. *Every day* means "on a daily basis": *Eat three or more servings of fruit every day*.

fewer, less Use *fewer* when you refer to things that can be counted: *fewer calories*. Use *less* when you refer to an amount of something that cannot be counted: *less fat*.

good, well *Good* is an adjective: *She looks good in that color; a good book*. *Well* can be an adjective indicating physical health after a linking verb (*She looks well despite her recent surgery*) or an adverb following an action verb (*He speaks Spanish well*).

hopefully In academic writing, avoid *hopefully* to mean "it is hoped that"; use it only to mean "with hope": *to make a wish hopefully*.

imply, infer Imply means "to suggest": *What do you mean to imply? Infer* means "to conclude": *We infer that you did not enjoy the trip.*

its, it's Its is a possessive pronoun: *The movie is rated R because of its language.* It's is a contraction of "it is" or "it has": *It's an action film.*

lay, lie Lay, meaning "to put" or "to place," always takes a direct object: *She lays the blanket down.* Lie, meaning "to recline" or "to be positioned," never takes a direct object: *She lies on the blanket.*

lead, led The verb lead (rhymes with *bead*) means "to guide": *I will lead the way.* Led is the past tense and past participle of lead: *Yesterday I led the way.* The noun lead (rhymes with *head*) is a type of metal: *Use copper pipes instead of lead pipes.*

literally Use literally only when you want to stress that you don't mean figuratively: *While sitting in the grass, he realized that he literally had ants in his pants.*

loose, lose Loose means "not fastened securely" or "not fitting tightly": *a pair of loose pants.* Lose means "to misplace" or "to not win": *lose an earring; lose the race.*

man, mankind Use *people, humans, humanity* or *humankind* instead.

many, much Use *many* when you refer to things that can be counted: *many books.* Use *much* to refer to something that cannot be counted: *much knowledge.*

may of, might of, must of In writing, use *may have, might have,* or *must have.*

media Media, a plural noun, takes a plural verb: *Many political scientists believe that the media have a huge effect on voting behavior.* The singular form is medium: *TV is a popular medium for advertising.*

percent, percentage Use *percent* after a number: *80 percent.* Use *percentage* after an adjective or article: *an impressive percentage; the percentage was impressive.*

principal, principle As a noun, *principal* means "a chief official" or "a sum of money": *in the principal's office; raising the principal for a down payment.* As an adjective, it means "most important": *the principal cause of death. Principle* means "a rule by which one lives" or "a basic truth or doctrine": *Lying is against her principles; the principles of life, liberty, and the pursuit of happiness.*

raise, rise   Meaning "to grow" or "to cause to move upward," *raise* always takes a direct object: *He raised his hand.* Meaning "to get up," *rise* never takes a direct object: *The sun rises at dawn.*

the reason . . . is because   Use *because* or *the reason . . . is (that)*, but not both: *The reason for the price increase was a poor growing season* or *prices increased because of a poor growing season.*

reason why   Instead of this redundant phrase, use *the reason* or *the reason that*: *Psychologists debate the reasons that some people develop depression and others do not.*

respectfully, respectively   *Respectfully* means "in a way that shows respect": *Speak to your elders respectfully. Respectively* means "in the order given": *George H. W. Bush and George W. Bush were the forty-first president and the forty-third president, respectively.*

sensual, sensuous   *Sensual* suggests sexuality: *a sensual caress. Sensuous* involves pleasing the senses through art, music, and nature: *the violin's sensuous solo.*

set, sit   *Set*, meaning "to put" or "to place," takes a direct object: *Please set the vase on the table. Sit*, meaning "to take a seat," does not take a direct object: *She sits on the bench.*

should of   In writing, use *should have* (*should've*).

stationary, stationery   *Stationary* means "staying put": *a stationary lab table. Stationery* means "writing paper": *the college's official stationery.*

than, then   *Than* is a conjunction used for comparing: *She is taller than her mother. Then* is an adverb used to indicate a sequence: *Finish your work, and then reward yourself.*

that, which   Use *that* to add information that is essential for identifying something: *The wild horses that live on this island are endangered.* Use *which* to give additional but nonessential information: *Abaco Barb horses, which live on an island in the Bahamas, are endangered.*

their, there, they're   *Their* signifies possession: *their canoe. There* tells where: *Put it there. They're* is a contraction of "they are": *They're busy.*

to, too, two   *To* is either a preposition that tells direction (*Give it to me*) or part of an infinitive (*To err is human*). *Too* means "also" or "excessively": *The younger children wanted to help, too; It's too cold to sit outside. Two* is a number: *tea for two.*

unique   Because *unique* suggests that something is the only one of its kind, avoid adding comparatives or superlatives (*more, most, less, least*), intensifiers (such as *very*), or qualifiers (such as *somewhat*).

weather, whether   *Weather* refers to atmospheric conditions: *dreary weather. Whether* refers to a choice between options: *whether to stay home or go out.*

who's, whose   *Who's* is a contraction for "who is" or "who has": *Who's the best candidate for the job? Who's already eaten? Whose* refers to ownership: *Whose keys are these? Tom, whose keys were on the table, had left.*

would of   In writing, use *would have* (*would've*).

your, you're   *Your* signifies possession: *your diploma. You're* is a contraction for "you are": *You're welcome.*

L-5 Prepositions

A great session with your favorite video game. You've finally reached the cave of the dying wise man who will tell you the location of the key that you need. He points a long, bony finger toward a table and struggles to rasp out one word, "jar." You're down to your last life. You only have one chance. Is the key *in* the jar? *under* it? *behind* it? Oh, that one little preposition makes all the difference!

Real life is seldom this dramatic, but correct prepositions do make a difference. Prepositions are words like *at, from, in,* and *with* that describe relationships, often in time and space: *at work, in an hour, with your mom.* English has a large number of prepositions compared to other languages, and sometimes it's difficult to choose the right one.

academic literacies · rhetorical situations · genres · processes · strategies · research MLA / APA · media / design · readings · handbook

Prepositions are always followed by noun or pronoun **OBJECTS**. (You can't just "write about"; you have to write about something.) Together a preposition and its object form a prepositional phrase. In the following examples, the prepositions are underlined and the prepositional phrases are italicized.

▶ This is a book _about writing._

▶ We're _in the midst of a literacy revolution._ —Andrea Lunsford

▶ Research is formalized curiosity. It is poking and prying _with a purpose._
—Zora Neale Hurston

▶ _In the years between 1969 and 1978,_ I lived, worked, and played _with the children and their families in Roadville and Trackton._
—Shirley Brice Heath

The table and lists that follow summarize the basic differences in the ways to use three common prepositions—_at, on,_ and _in._

AT a specific point	•	at home at the gym at noon
ON a line	——	on the avenue on the table on a specific day
IN a shape or enclosure	⬭	in a container in the park in two hours

Prepositions of place

AT _a specific address or business: at_ 33 Parkwood Street, _at_ McDonald's
a public building or unnamed business: at the library, _at_ the gym
a general place: at home, _at_ work

ON _a surface: on_ the floor, _on_ the grass, _on_ the wall
a street: on Ninth Street, _on_ Western Avenue
an electronic medium: on the radio, _on_ the web
public transportation: on the bus, _on_ an airplane

IN *a container, room, or area: in* the jar, *in* my office, *in* the woods
a geographic location: in San Diego, *in* the Midwest
a printed work: in the newspaper, *in* Chapter 3

Prepositions of time

AT *a specific time: at* 4:30 PM, *at* sunset, *at* lunchtime

ON *a day of the week: on* Friday
an exact date: on September 12
a holiday: on Thanksgiving, *on* Veteran's Day

IN *a defined time period: in* an hour, *in* three years
a month, season, or year: in June, *in* the fall, *in* 2011
a part of the day: in the morning, *in* the evening

L-6 Unnecessary Words

At this point in time. Really unique. In a manner of speaking. Each of these phrases includes words that are unnecessary or says something that could be expressed more concisely. This chapter shows you how to edit your own writing to make every word count.

L-6a *Really, Very,* and Other Empty Words

Intensifiers such as *really* and *very* are used to strengthen what we say. Qualifiers such as *apparently, possibly, seem,* or *tend to* are a way to soften what we say. It's fine to use words like these when they are necessary. Sometimes, however, they are not. You shouldn't say that something is "very unique," because things either are unique or they're not; there's no need to add the intensifier. And why say that someone is "really smart" when you could say that he or she is "brilliant"?

▶ Accepted by five colleges, Jackson ~~seems to be facing an apparently very~~ ^*is facing a*^ difficult decision.

academic literacies — rhetorical situations — genres — processes — strategies — research MLA / APA — media / design — readings — handbook

L-6b *There Is, It Is*

Glossary

EXPLETIVE constructions like *there is* and *it is* can be useful ways to introduce and emphasize an idea, but often they only add unnecessary words. Eliminating them not only makes the sentence more concise but also makes its verb stronger.

▶ ~~It is necessary for~~ Americans today ^must^ to learn to speak more than one language.

▶ ~~There are four~~ ^Four^ large moons and more than thirty small ones ~~that~~ orbit Jupiter.

In certain contexts, expletives can be the best choices. Imagine the ending of *The Wizard of Oz* if Dorothy had said "No place is like home" instead of the more emphatic (and sentimental) "There's no place like home."

L-6c Wordy Phrases

Many common phrases use several words when a single word will do. Editing out such wordy phrases will make your writing more concise and easier to read.

WORDY	CONCISE
as far as . . . is concerned	concerning
at the time that	when
at this point in time	now
in spite of the fact that	although, though
in the event that	if
in view of the fact that	because, since

▶ ~~Due to the fact that~~ ^Because^ Professor Lee retired, the animal sciences department now lacks a neurology specialist.

L-6d Redundancies

Eliminate words and phrases that are unnecessary for your meaning.

▶ Painting the house purple ~~in color~~ will make it stand out from the many white houses in town.

▶ Dashing ~~quickly~~ into the street to retrieve the ball, the young girl was almost hit by a car.

▶ Campers should know how much wood is ~~sufficient~~ enough for a fire to burn all night.

L-7 Adjectives and Adverbs

Adjectives and adverbs are words that describe other words, adding important information and detail. When Dave Barry writes that the Beatles "were the *coolest* thing you had ever seen" and that "they were *smart*; they were *funny*; they didn't take themselves *seriously*," the adjectives and adverbs (italicized here) make clear why he "wanted *desperately* to be a Beatle." This chapter will help you use adjectives and adverbs in your own writing.

L-7a Choosing between Adjectives and Adverbs

Glossary
HB-29–34

Adjectives are words used to modify **NOUNS** and **PRONOUNS**. They usually answer one of these questions: Which? What kind? How many?

▶ *Two* rows of *ancient oak* trees lined the *narrow* driveway.

▶ *Many* years of testing will be needed to determine whether the *newest* theories are *correct*.

▶ If you are craving something *sweet*, have a piece of fruit.

HB-12–24

Adverbs are words used to modify **VERBS**, adjectives, and other adverbs. They usually answer one of these questions: How? When? Where? Why? Under what conditions? To what degree? Although many adverbs end in -ly (*tentatively*, *immediately*), many do not (*now*, *so*, *soon*, *then*, *very*).

▶ Emergency personnel must respond *quickly* when an ambulance arrives.

▶ Environmentalists are *increasingly* worried about Americans' consumption of fossil fuels.

▶ If the senator had known that the news cameras were on, she would not have responded *so angrily*.

Well *and* good

Use *well* as an adjective to describe physical health; use *good* to describe emotional health or appearance.

▶ Some herbs can keep you feeling ~~good~~ *well* when everyone else has the flu.

▶ Staying healthy can make you feel *good* about yourself.

Good should not be used as an adverb; use *well*.

▶ Because both Williams sisters play tennis so ~~good,~~ *well,* they've frequently competed against each other in major tournaments.

Bad *and* badly

Use the adjective *bad* after a **LINKING VERB** to describe an emotional state or feeling. In such cases, the adjective describes the subject.

Glossary

▶ Arguing with your parents can make you feel *bad*.

Use the adverb *badly* to describe an **ACTION VERB**.

Glossary

▶ Arguing with your parents late at night can make you sleep *badly*.

L-7b Using Comparatives and Superlatives

Most adjectives and adverbs have three forms: the positive, the comparative, and the superlative. The comparative is used to compare two things, and the superlative is used to compare three or more things.

COMPARATIVE Who's the *better* quarterback, Eli Manning or his brother?

SUPERLATIVE Many Colts fans still consider Peyton Manning to be the *best* quarterback ever.

The comparative and superlative of most adjectives are formed by adding the endings -*er* and -*est*: *slow, slower, slowest*. Longer adjectives and most adverbs use *more* and *most* (or *less* and *least*): *clearly, more clearly, most clearly*. If you add -*er* or -*est* to an adjective or adverb, do not also use *more* or *most* (or *less* and *least*).

▶ The ~~most~~ lowest point in the United States is in Death Valley.

A few adjectives and adverbs have irregular comparatives and superlatives.

	COMPARATIVE	SUPERLATIVE
good, well	better	best
bad, badly	worse	worst
far (distance)	farther	farthest
far (time or amount)	further	furthest
little (amount)	less	least
many, much, some	more	most

L-7c Placing Modifiers Carefully

Glossary

Place adjectives, adverbs, and other **MODIFIERS** so that readers clearly understand which words they modify.

▶ The doctor explained advances in cancer treatment to the families of patients. *at the seminar.*
  (insert: *at the seminar*)

The doctor, not the patients, is at the seminar.

▶ ~~The~~ surgeons assured the patient that they intended to make only two small incisions. ~~before the anesthesiologist arrived.~~
  (insert: *Before the anesthesiologist arrived, the*)

The original sentence suggests that the incisions will be made without anesthesia, surely not the case.

To avoid ambiguity, position limiting modifiers such as *almost, even, just, merely,* and *only* next to the word or phrase they modify—and be careful that your meaning is clear. See how the placement of *only* can result in two completely different meanings.

▶ A triple-threat athlete, Martha ~~only~~ played soccer ^only^ in college.

▶ A triple-threat athlete, Martha ~~only~~ played ^only^ soccer in college.

Be careful that your placement of *not* doesn't result in a meaning you don't intend.

▶ When I attended college, every student was ^not^ ~~not~~ using a laptop.

Dangling modifiers

Modifiers are said to be dangling when they do not clearly modify any particular word in the sentence. You can usually fix a dangling modifier by adding a **SUBJECT** that the modifier clearly refers to, either in the rest of the sentence or in the modifier itself.

Glossary

▶ Speaking simply and respectfully, many people ^the doctor comforted^ ~~felt comforted by the~~ ~~doctor's~~ ^with his^ presentation.

The doctor was speaking, not the other people.

▶ While running to catch the bus, ^I was^ the shoulder strap on my bag broke.

Split infinitives

When you place a modifier between *to* and the base form of the verb in an **INFINITIVE**, you create a split infinitive: *to deliberately avoid.* When a split infinitive is awkward or makes a sentence difficult to follow, put the modifier elsewhere in the sentence.

Glossary

▶ Professional soccer players are expected to ~~rigorously~~ train ^rigorously^ every day.

Sometimes, however, a split infinitive is easier to follow.

▶ One famous split infinitive appears in the opening sequence of
   Star Trek: "to boldly go where no man has gone before."

L-8 Articles

A, *an*, and *the* are articles, words used before a noun to indicate whether
something is general or specific. Use *a* or *an* with nouns whose specific
identity is not known to your audience: *I'm reading a great book.* Use *the*
with nouns whose specific identity is known to your audience, whether
the noun describes something specific: *the new book by Dave Eggers*—or is
something you've mentioned: *Beverly is almost finished writing her book. The
book will be published next year.* Sometimes no article is needed: *Books are
now available in print and online.*

L-8a When to Use *A* or *An*

Use *a* or *an* before singular count nouns referring to something that's
not specific or that you're mentioning to your audience for the first time.
Count nouns name things that can be counted: *one book, two books.* Use
a before consonant sounds: *a tangerine, a university;* use *an* before vowel
sounds: *an orange, an hour.*

▶ *An apartment* near campus might be rather expensive.

   Any apartment near campus would be expensive, not just a specific one.

▶ I put *a carrot*, some tomatoes, and a little parsley in the salad.

   This carrot is being mentioned for the first time.

Do not use *a* or *an* before a noncount noun. Noncount nouns name abstract
items (*respect, curiosity*) and liquids and masses that cannot be measured
with numbers (*milk, sand, rice*).

▶ Our team could use *some encouragement* from the coach.

▶ The last thing Portland needs this week is *more rain.*

L-8b When to Use *The*

Use *the* before any nouns whose identity is clear to your audience and before superlatives.

▶ Mando ordered a cheeseburger and french fries and asked for *the burger* to be well done.

The article the *is used because it refers to a cheeseburger that's already been mentioned: the one that Mando ordered.*

▶ His friends had raved about *the fries* at this restaurant.

The specific fries are identified: they are the ones at this restaurant.

▶ His friends were right; these were *the best fries* he'd ever eaten.

The *is used before a superlative: these were the* best fries *ever.*

Use *the* with most plural proper nouns (*the Adirondack Mountains*, *the Philippines*, *the Dallas Cowboys*) and with singular proper nouns in the following categories.

LARGER BODIES OF WATER the Arctic Ocean, the Mississippi River

GOVERNMENT BODIES the U.S. Congress, the Canadian Parliament

HISTORICAL PERIODS the Renaissance, the Tang Dynasty

LANDMARKS the Empire State Building, the Taj Mahal

REGIONS the East Coast, the Middle East, the Mojave Desert

RELIGIOUS ENTITIES, TEXTS, AND LEADERS the Roman Catholic Church, the Qur'an, the Dalai Lama

L-8c When No Article Is Needed

No article is needed before noncount nouns (*salt, imagination, happiness*) and plural count nouns (*ideas, puppies*) when they refer to something "in general."

▶ *Milk* and *eggs* are on sale this week.

▶ *Information* wants to be free.   —Stewart Brand, *Whole Earth Review*

▶ Be less curious about people and more curious about *ideas.*
—Marie Curie

> *Brand and Curie refer to information and ideas in general, not a specific kind of information or specific ideas.*

Glossary

No article is needed with most singular **PROPER NOUNS**: *Barack Obama, Lake Titicaca, Yosemite.*

L-9 Words for Building Common Ground

A secretary objects to being called one of "the girls." The head of the English department finds the title "chairman" offensive. Why? The secretary is male, the department head is a woman, and those terms don't include them. We can build common ground with others—or not—through the words we choose, by including others or leaving them out. This chapter offers tips for using language that is positive and inclusive and that will build common ground with those we wish to reach.

L-9a Avoiding Stereotypes

Stereotypes are generalizations about groups of people and as such can offend because they presume that all members of a group are the same. The writer Geeta Kothari explains how she reacts to a seemingly neutral assumption about Indians: "Indians eat lentils. I understand this as an absolute, a decree from an unidentifiable authority that watches and judges me."

We're all familiar with stereotypes based on sex or race, but stereotypes exist about other characteristics as well: age, body type, education, income, occupation, physical ability, political affiliation, region, religion, sexual orientation, and more. Be careful not to make any broad generalizations about any group—even neutral or positive ones (that Asian students work especially hard, for example, or that Republicans are particularly patriotic).

Also be careful not to call attention to a person's group affiliation if that information is not relevant.

▶ The ~~gay~~ physical therapist who worked the morning shift knew when to let patients rest and when to push them.

L-9b Using Preferred Terms

When you are writing about a group of people, try to use terms that members of that group use themselves. This advice is sometimes easier said than done, because language changes — and words that were commonly used ten years ago may not be in wide use today. Americans of African ancestry, for example, were referred to many years ago as "colored" or "Negro" and then as "black"; today, the preferred terminology is "African American."

When you are referring to ethnicities, especially of individuals, it's usually best to be as specific as possible. Instead of saying that someone is Latina, Latino, or Hispanic, for instance, say that he or she is Puerto Rican or Dominican or Cuban, as appropriate. The same is true of religions; specify a denomination or branch of religion when you can (a Sunni Muslim, an Episcopalian, an Orthodox Jew). And while "Native American" and "American Indian" are both acceptable as general terms, it's often better to refer to a particular tribal nation (Dakota, Chippewa).

L-9c Editing Out Sexist Language

Sexist language is language that stereotypes or ignores women or men — or that unnecessarily calls attention to someone's gender. Try to eliminate such language from your writing. In particular, avoid nouns that include *man* when you're referring to people who may be either men or women.

INSTEAD OF	USE
man, mankind	humankind, humanity, humans, people
salesman	salesperson
fireman	firefighter
congressman	representative, member of Congress
male nurse	nurse
woman truck driver	truck driver

Default he

Writers once used *he, him,* and other masculine pronouns as a default to refer to people whose sex was unknown to them. Today such usage is not widely accepted—and it is no way to build common ground. Here are some alternatives.

Use *he or she* or other masculine and feminine pronouns joined by *or.* (Note, however, that using this option repeatedly may become awkward.)

▶ Before anyone can leave the country, he *or she* must have a passport or some other official documentation.

Replace a singular noun or pronoun with a plural noun

▶ Before ~~anyone~~ *travelers* can leave the country, ~~he~~ *they* must have a passport or some other official documentation.

Eliminate the pronoun altogether

▶ Before ~~anyone can leave~~ *leaving* the country, ~~he~~ *a traveler* must have a passport or some other official documentation.

L-10 Englishes

"English? Who needs that? I'm never going to England," declares Homer in an early episode of *The Simpsons*. Sorry, Homer. Anyone using this book does need English. In fact, most of us need a variety of Englishes—the "standard" English we're expected to use at school, the specialized English we use in particular academic and professional fields, and the colloquial English we use in various other communities we belong to. This chapter offers some guidance in using these many varieties of English effectively and appropriately in academic writing.

❋ academic literacies   ■ rhetorical situations   ▲ genres   ○ processes   ◆ strategies   ● research MLA / APA   ▢ media / design   ▮ readings   ▨ handbook

L-10a Standard Edited English

This is the variety used—and expected—in most academic and professional contexts, and one you need to be able to use comfortably and competently. "Standard" means that it is nearly uniform throughout the English-speaking world. Despite some minor differences—in England and Canada, for example, *labor* is *labour* and an *elevator* is a *lift*—the uniformity means that your writing has the potential to be understood by millions of people. "Edited" means that it is carefully written and polished. And "English"—well, you already know what that is.

L-10b Formal and Informal English

Some of the variation in English comes from levels of formality. Academic writing is usually formal. The tone is crisp and serious; information is stated directly. These characteristics display your competence and authority. The most informal language, on the other hand, tends to be found in the ways we talk with our close friends and relatives; those conversations are full of **IDIOMS** and slang.

HB-45–51

Words with the same basic meaning can convey very different messages when they have different levels of formality—and so the words you choose should always be guided by what's appropriate to your **AUDIENCE**, topic, and the larger context.

57–60

See, for example, two headlines that appeared in two different newspapers on the day that Pope Benedict XVI announced his resignation:

▶ Pope Resigns in Historic Move   —*Wall Street Journal*

▶ I'M OUTTA HERE, GUYS: Pope Gives God 2 Weeks' Notice
                                                     —*New York Post*

The first headline is from the *Wall Street Journal*, a newspaper dedicated to business news, with an audience of corporate and government executives. Its tone is professional and businesslike, and its English is formal. The second is from the *New York Post*, a daily tabloid newspaper known for its sensationalist headlines; its English is informal, going for laughs and marking a sharp contrast with the pomp and majesty of the papal office.

In the cartoon below the adult understands quite well what the child is saying; she's merely suggesting a more formal and polite—and appropriate—way to express his judgment of the painting.

"Instead of 'It sucks' you could say, 'It doesn't speak to me.'"

Mixing formal and informal

Occasionally mixing in an informal element—a playful image, an unexpected bit of slang—can enliven formal writing. For example, in a book about the alimentary canal, science writer Mary Roach gives detailed, well-researched descriptions of all aspects of digestion, including the anatomy of the digestive system. Although her topic is serious, she stirs in some irreverent **METAPHORS** and surprising comparisons along the way, as this description of the esophagus shows.

Glossary

▶ The esophagus is a thin, pink stretchable membrane, a biological bubble gum. —Mary Roach, *Gulp: Adventures on the Alimentary Canal*

Such everyday imagery makes a potentially dry subject come to life. What's more, the information is easier to remember. Quick: what color is your esophagus? You remembered, didn't you?

L-10c English across Fields

If you've ever listened in on a group of nurses, software designers, lawyers, or taxi drivers, you probably heard words you didn't understand, jokes you didn't think were funny. All professional fields have their own specialized language.

Restaurant staff, for example, have a shorthand for relaying food orders and seating information. In this example from an essay about blue-collar work, UCLA professor Mike Rose describes a restaurant where his mother was a waitress:

> ▶ *Fry four on two*, my mother would say as she clipped a check onto the metal wheel. Her tables were *deuces, four-tops,* or *six-tops* according to their size; seating areas also were nicknamed. The *racetrack,* for instance, was the fast-turnover front section. Lingo conferred authority and signaled know-how.   —Mike Rose, "Blue Collar Brilliance"

You might not know what *deuces* or *four-tops* are (or maybe you do), but it's language Rose's mother knows her colleagues will understand. On the one hand, specialized language allows professionals to do their work with greater ease and efficiency; on the other, it marks and helps construct a community around a certain field of work.

L-10d English across Regions

Have you ever wished that British TV shows had subtitles? The characters are definitely speaking English, but you may have a hard time understanding them. Every region has its own accent, of course, but there may also be words and expressions that are unfamiliar or mean something different to those who don't live there. In Australia (and parts of Wisconsin), for example, a *bubbler* is a drinking fountain. In India, the *hall* is the part of the house known in the United States as the living room.

In the U.S. South, *y'all* is the way many folks say *you all*. Country singer Miranda Lambert, a native of Texas, uses *y'all* frequently in her *Twitter* feed, such as in this tweet thanking a North Dakota audience after a performance:

> ▶ Thanks New Town ND! Y'all were so fun! And LOUD! Came to party and did it right!   —Miranda Lambert, @mirandalambert, June 8, 2013

In choosing to use *y'all* rather than the more standard *you*, Lambert emphasizes her southern heritage and establishes a friendly, down-home tone.

Other regions as well have their own forms of the second person plural. In Chicago and New York you might hear *youse*, and in Pittsburgh it's *yinz*. Such local language is widely understood in the regions where it is used, though it may sound strange to people from other places. Using regional language in your writing can be a good way to evoke a place—and, like Lambert, can demonstrate pride in your own regional roots.

L-10e Englishes across Cultures and Communities

Some varieties of English are associated with a particular social, ethnic, or other community. African American English is perhaps the best-known of these Englishes. Not all African Americans use it every day, and not all of its speakers are African American, but they all follow the conventions and rules that make this variety of English consistent and recognizable.

Linguist Geneva Smitherman has written extensively on this variety of English, often using the language itself to support her points. See how she shifts from standard edited English into African American English to establish her authority as an insider and drive home her point with a stylistic punch.

> ▶ Think of black speech as having two dimensions: language and style. . . . Consider [this example]. Nina Simone sing: "It bees dat way sometime." Here the language aspect is the use of the verb *be* to indicate a recurrent event or habitual condition, rather than a one-time-only occurrence. But

academic literacies · rhetorical situations · genres · processes · strategies · research MLA / APA · media / design · readings · handbook

the total expression—"It bees dat way sometime"—also reflects Black English style, for the statement suggests a point of view, a way of looking at life, and a method of adapting to life's realities. To live by the philosophy of "It bees dat way sometime" is to come to grips with the changes that life bees puttin us through, and to accept the changes and bad times as a constant, ever-present reality.

—Geneva Smitherman, *Talkin and Testifyin:*
The Language of Black America

Many other communities develop their own Englishes as well. Ethnic communities often use an English that includes words from another language. Men and women often speak differently, as Deborah Tannen and other linguists have shown. Even young people use an English that might sound very strange coming from a gray-haired elder (imagine your grandfather greeting you with "Dude!").

The differences can be subtle but sometimes a single word can make someone sound young, or old, or Texan, or Canadian—and can establish credibility with an audience. See how a simple "OMG" is enough to establish hipness with young readers of a newspaper article about a fashion show for puppies:

▶ If your pup has been good this year, it deserves a treat from Ware of the Dog, a line of luxury knits from the designer Tom Scott and his friend Jackie Rosenthal. The collection includes OMG-cute alpaca sweaters, cable-knit turtlenecks, hoodies and a geometric-pattern merino jacquard pullover.   —"Shopping Snapshots," *New York Times*

Speaking to the article's young audience, the phrase *OMG-cute* not only shows off knowledge of youth culture but also puts a little zest into an otherwise lifeless list of items.

L-10f Mixing Englishes

As a writer, you can use different varieties of English or even different languages for various purposes. Here are some examples and suggestions for doing so effectively and appropriately.

To evoke a person or represent speech

When you are describing people, you may want to quote their words, to let readers "hear" them talk—and to let them speak for themselves. Some multilingual authors flavor their English writing with words or phrases from another language to give readers an authentic sense of someone's words or thoughts. Even if some readers don't understand the non-English words, they usually add more flavor than meaning. See, for example, how Sandra Cisneros mixes English and Spanish in relating an exchange between her parents as they bicker about a trip to visit relatives. Using two languages in the dialogue adds flavor and realism, and the context makes the meaning clear even for readers who don't speak Spanish.

▶ "Zoila, why do you insist on being so stubborn?" Father shouts into the mirror, clouding the glass. "*Ya verás*. You'll see, *vieja*, it'll be fun."

"And stop calling me *vieja*," Mother shouts back. "I hate that word! Your mother's old; I'm not old." —Sandra Cisneros, *Caramelo*

When writing dialogue, you may sometimes want to use nonstandard spelling to mimic dialect or sound, as Flannery O'Connor does with the speech of a young boy questioning an outlaw.

▶ "What you got that gun for?" John Wesley asked. "Whatcha gonna do with that gun?" —Flannery O'Connor, "A Good Man Is Hard to Find"

To evoke a place or an event

In certain settings or situations—sports, auctions, math class—you will hear language you wouldn't hear anywhere else. In some cases, the topics require specialized words. There's no way to talk about golf without mentioning *par* or *putting* or *a hole in one*, or to teach math without words like *variable* or *function*. In other cases, people tend to use a certain kind of language. Think about the conversations you'd hear in a board meeting, or the ones you'd hear in a sports bar.

Such language can be used to evoke a place or an event, as in this recap of a 2013 NBA playoff game between the Los Angeles Lakers and the Dallas Mavericks.

▶ The Mavericks played Bryant aggressively, trapping him out of the pick and roll and forcing him into tough shots. He had his moments, he made his share of shots despite great defensive strategy, and ended the night right. Bryant picked up his tenth rebound to seal his triple-double and put up a beautiful hook shot to cap it off and send it home.

—Drew Garrison, *Silver Screen and Roll*

The writer can assume that his readers are familiar with the language he uses; in fact, many readers probably watched the game and just read the recap in order to relive it. His use of basketball **JARGON** helps put them back in the action. But for an audience unfamiliar with basketball, he'd need to explain terms like *pick and roll* and *triple-double*.

HB-43

To build common ground with an audience

Language is one good way to establish credibility and build common ground with readers. For example, in a feature article about how letters to the editor are chosen for publication in the daily newspaper of a city in Minnesota, the writer included the word *uff-da*, a purely local touch:

▶ We don't publish mass produced letters. There are people in these United States who like to send letters to every newspaper in the country on a weekly basis. *Uff-da!* These are easy to catch. There are also some lobbying organizations who provide forms for supporters where writers don't actually pen their own thoughts.

—Tim Engstrom, *Albert Lea Tribune*

Uff-da is a Norwegian expression that is widely used in the region. It means *wow!, whew!, no kidding!,* or even *OMG!* depending on the situation. The writer doesn't need it to convey his meaning, but using it demonstrates a sense of local knowledge and pride—and helps build common ground with his readers.

Think carefully, however, before using words from a language or variety of language that you don't speak yourself; you may offend some readers. And if by chance you use words incorrectly, you could even damage your credibility.

P Punctuation / Mechanics

academic literacies

rhetorical situations

genres

processes

strategies

research MLA / APA

media / design

readings

handbook

P-1 Commas

Commas matter. Consider the title of the best-selling book *Eats, Shoots & Leaves*. The cover shows two pandas, one with a gun in its paw, one white-washing the comma. Is the book about a panda that dines, then fires a gun and exits? Or about the panda's customary diet? In fact, it's a book about punctuation; the ambiguity of its title illustrates how commas affect meaning. This chapter shows when and where to use commas in your writing.

P-1a To Join Independent Clauses with *And, But,* and Other Coordinating Conjunctions

Put a comma before the **COORDINATING CONJUNCTIONS** *and, but, for, nor, or, so,* and *yet* when they connect two **INDEPENDENT CLAUSES**. The comma signals that one idea is ending and another is beginning.

HB-38
HB-6

> ▶ I do not love Shakespeare, but I still have those books.
> —Rick Bragg, "All Over But the Shoutin'"

> ▶ Most people think the avocado is a vegetable, yet it is actually a fruit.

> ▶ The blue ribbon went to Susanna, and Sarah got the red ribbon.
>
> *Without the comma, readers might first think both girls got blue ribbons.*

Although some writers omit the comma, especially with short independent clauses, you'll never be wrong to include it.

> ▶ I was smart, and I knew it.   —Shannon Nichols, "'Proficiency'"

No comma is needed between the verbs when a single subject performs two actions.

> ▶ Many fast-food restaurants now give calorie counts on menus and offer a variety of healthy meal options.

> ▶ Augustine wrote extensively about his mother but mentioned his father only briefly.

P-1b To Set Off Introductory Words

HB-6–7

Use a comma after an introductory word, **PHRASE**, or **CLAUSE** to mark the end of the introduction and the start of the main part of the sentence.

▶ Typically, a girl has a best friend with whom she sits and talks, frequently telling secrets. —Deborah Tannen, "Gender in the Classroom"

▶ In terms of wealth rather than income, the top 1 percent control 40 percent. —Joseph E. Stiglitz, "Of the 1%, by the 1%, for the 1%"

▶ Even ignoring the extreme poles of the economic spectrum, we find enormous class differences in the life-styles among the haves, the have-nots, and the have-littles.
—Gregory Mantsios, "Class in America—2003"

▶ When Miss Emily Grierson died, our whole town went to her funeral.
—William Faulkner, "A Rose for Emily"

Some writers don't use a comma after a short introductory word, phrase, or clause, but it's never wrong to include one.

P-1c To Separate Items in a Series

HB-6-7

Use a comma to separate the items in a series. The items may be words, **PHRASES**, or **CLAUSES**.

▶ I spend a great deal of time thinking about the power of language —the way it can evoke an emotion, a visual image, a complex idea, or a simple truth. —Amy Tan, "Mother Tongue"

Though some writers leave out the comma between the final two items in a series, this omission can confuse readers. It's never wrong to include the final comma.

▶ Nadia held a large platter of sandwiches—egg salad, peanut butter, ham, and cheese.

Without the last comma, it's not clear whether there are three or four kinds of sandwiches on the platter.

P-1d To Set Off Nonessential Elements

A nonessential (or nonrestrictive) element is one that could be deleted without changing the basic meaning of the sentence; it should be set off with commas. An essential (or restrictive) element is one that is needed to understand the sentence; therefore, it should not be set off with commas.

NONESSENTIAL

▶ Spanish, which is a Romance language, is one of six official languages at the United Nations.

The detail about being a Romance language adds information, but it is not essential to the meaning of the sentence and so is set off with a comma.

ESSENTIAL

▶ Navajo is the Athabaskan language that is spoken in the Southwest by the Navajo people.

The detail about where Navajo is spoken is essential: Navajo is not the only Athabaskan language; it is the Athabaskan language that is spoken in the Southwest.

Note that the meaning of a sentence can change depending on whether or not an element is set off with commas.

▶ My sister, Mary, just published her first novel.

The writer has only one sister.

▶ My sister Mary just published her first novel.

The writer has more than one sister; the one named Mary just published a novel.

Essential and nonessential elements can be clauses, phrases, or words.

CLAUSES

▶ He always drove Chryslers, which are made in America.

▶ He always drove cars that were made in America.

PHRASES

▶ I fumble in the dark, trying to open the mosquito netting around my bed.

▶ I see my mother clutching my baby sister.

—Chanrithy Him, "When Broken Glass Floats"

WORDS

▶ At 8:59, Flight 175 passenger Brian David Sweeney tried to call his wife, Julie.

▶ At 9:00, Lee Hanson received a second call from his son Peter.

—The 9/11 Commission, "The Hijacking of United 175"

Sweeney had only one wife, so her name provides extra but nonessential information. Hanson presumably had more than one son, so it is essential to specify which son called.

P-1e To Set Off Parenthetical Information

Information that interrupts the flow of a sentence needs to be set off with commas.

▶ Bob's conduct, most of us will immediately respond, was gravely wrong.

—Peter Singer, "The Singer Solution to World Poverty"

▶ With as little as two servings of vegetables a day, it seems to me, you can improve your eating habits.

P-1f To Set Off Transitional Expressions

TRANSITIONS such as *thus, nevertheless, for example,* and *in fact* help connect sentences or parts of sentences. They are usually set off with commas.

▶ The real world, *however,* is run by money.

—Joanna MacKay, "Organ Sales Will Save Lives"

When a transition connects two **INDEPENDENT CLAUSES** in the same sentence, it is preceded by a semicolon and is followed by a comma.

13 ❋

HB-6 ▨

academic literacies | rhetorical situations | genres | processes | strategies | research MLA / APA | media / design | readings | handbook

▶ There are few among the poor who speak of themselves as lower class; *instead,* they refer to their race, ethnic group, or geographic location.
—Gregory Mantsios, "Class in America—2003"

P-1g To Set Off Direct Quotations

Use commas to set off quoted words from the speaker or source.

▶ Pa shouts back, "I just want to know where the gunfire is coming from."
—Chanrithy Him, "When Broken Glass Floats"

▶ "You put a slick and a con man together," she said, "and you have predatory lenders."
—Peter Boyer, "Eviction: The Day They Came for Addie Polk's House"

▶ "Death and life are in the power of the tongue," says the proverb.

P-1h To Set Off Direct Address, *Yes* or *No,* Interjections, and Tag Questions

DIRECT ADDRESS	"Yes, Virginia, there really is a Santa Claus."
YES OR NO	No, you cannot replace the battery on your iPhone.
INTERJECTION	Oh, a PS4. How long did you have to wait to get it?
TAG QUESTION	That wasn't so hard, was it?

P-1i With Addresses, Place Names, and Dates

▶ Send contributions to Human Rights Campaign, 1640 Rhode Island Ave., Washington, DC 20036.

▶ Athens, Georgia, is famous for its thriving music scene.

▶ The aviator Amelia Earhart disappeared over the Pacific Ocean on July 2, 1937, while trying to make the first round-the-world flight at the equator.

Omit the commas, however, if you invert the date (on 2 July 1937) or if you give only the month and year (in July 1937).

P-1j Checking for Unnecessary Commas

Commas have so many uses that it's easy to add them unnecessarily. Here are some situations when you should not use a comma.

Between a subject and a verb

▶ What the organizers of the 1969 Woodstock concert did not anticipate, was the turnout.

▶ The event's promoters, turned down John Lennon's offer to play with his Plastic Ono Band.

Between a verb and its object

▶ Pollsters wondered, how they had so poorly predicted the winner of the 1948 presidential election.

▶ Virtually every prediction indicated, that Thomas Dewey would defeat Harry Truman.

After a coordinating conjunction

▶ The College Board reported a decline in SAT scores and, attributed the decline to changes in "student test-taking patterns."

▶ The SAT was created to provide an objective measure of academic potential, but, studies in the 1980s found racial and socioeconomic biases in some test questions.

After *like or* such as

▶ Many American-born authors, such as, Henry James, Ezra Pound, and F. Scott Fitzgerald, lived as expatriates in Europe.

After a question mark or an exclamation point

▶ Why would any nation have a monarch in an era of democracy?⁄ you might ask yourself.

▶ "O, be some other name!⁄" exclaims Juliet.

P-2 Semicolons

Semicolons offer one way to connect two closely related thoughts. Look, for example, at Martha Stewart's advice about how to tell if fruit is ripe: "A perfectly ripened fruit exudes a subtle but sweet fragrance from the stem end, appears plump, and has deeply colored skin; avoid those that have wrinkles, bruises, or tan spots." Stewart could have used a period, but the semicolon shows the connection between what to look for and what to avoid when buying peaches or plums.

P-2a Between Independent Clauses

Closely related independent clauses are most often joined with a comma plus *and* or another **COORDINATING CONJUNCTION**. If the two clauses are closely related and don't need a conjunction to signal the relationship, they may be linked with a semicolon.

HB-38

▶ The silence deepened; the room chilled.
                              —Wayson Choy, "The Ten Thousand Things"

▶ The life had not flowed out of her; it had been seized.
                              —Valerie Steiker, "Our Mother's Face"

A period would work in either of the examples above, but the semicolon suggests a stronger connection between the two independent clauses.

Another option is to use a semicolon with a **TRANSITION** that clarifies the relationship between the two independent clauses. Put a comma after the transition.

13

▶ There are no secret economies that nourish the poor; on the contrary, there are a host of special costs. —Barbara Ehrenreich, *Nickel and Dimed: On (Not) Getting By in America*

P-2b In a Series with Commas

Use semicolons to separate items in a series when one or more of the items contain commas.

▶ There are images of a few students: Erwin Petschaur, a muscular German boy with a strong accent; Dave Sanchez, who was good at math; and Sheila Wilkes, everyone's curly-haired heartthrob.
—Mike Rose, "Potato Chips and Stars"

P-2c Checking for Mistakes with Semicolons

Use a comma, not a semicolon, to set off an introductory clause.

▶ When the sun finally sets�, everyone gathers at the lake to watch the fireworks.

Use a colon, not a semicolon, to introduce a list.

▶ Every American high school student should know that the U.S. Constitution contains three sections: preamble, articles, and amendments.

P-3 End Punctuation

She married him. She married him? She married him! In each of these three sentences, the words are the same, but the end punctuation completely changes the meaning—from a simple statement to a bemused question to an emphatic exclamation. This chapter will help you use periods, question marks, and exclamation points in your writing.

P-3a Periods

Use a period to end a sentence that makes a statement.

▶ Rose Emily Meraglio came to the United States from southern Italy as a little girl in the early 1920s and settled with her family in Altoona, Pennsylvania.   —Mike Rose, "The Working Life of a Waitress"

An indirect question, which reports something that someone else has asked, ends with a period, not a question mark.

▶ Presidential candidates are often asked how they will expand the economy and create jobs?̬.

When a sentence ends with an **ABBREVIATION** that has its own period, do not add another period.

HB-104–6

▶ The Rat Pack included Frank Sinatra and Sammy Davis Jr./

P-3b Question Marks

Use a question mark to end a direct question.

▶ Did I think that because I was a minority student jobs would just come looking for me? What was I thinking?
                    —Richard Rodriguez, "None of This Is Fair"

Use a period rather than a question mark to end an indirect question.

▶ Aunt Vivian often asked what Jesus would do?̬.

P-3c Exclamation Points

Use an exclamation point to express strong emotion or add emphasis to a statement or command. Exclamation points should be used sparingly, however, or they may undercut your credibility.

▶ "Keith," we shrieked as the car drove away, "Keith, we love you!"
                    —Susan Jane Gilman, "Mick Jagger Wants Me"

When the words themselves are emotional, an exclamation point is often unnecessary, and a period is sufficient.

▶ It was so close, so low, so huge and fast, so intent on its target that I swear to you, I swear to you, I felt the vengeance and rage emanating from the plane.   —Debra Fontaine, "Witnessing"

P-4 Quotation Marks

"Girls Just Want to Have Fun" "Two thumbs up!" "Frankly, my dear, I don't give a damn." These are just some of the ways that quotation marks are used—to indicate a song title, to cite praise for a movie, to set off dialogue. In college writing, you will use quotation marks frequently to acknowledge when you've taken words from others. This chapter will show you how to use quotation marks correctly and appropriately.

P-4a Direct Quotations

Use quotation marks to enclose words spoken or written by others.

▶ "Nothing against Tom, but Johnny may be the bigger star now," says director John Waters.   —Sean Smith, "Johnny Depp: Unlikely Superstar"

▶ Newt Gringrich and Jesse Jackson have both pounded nails and raised funds for Habitat for Humanity. This is what Millard Fuller calls the "theology of the hammer."
                    —Diana George, "Changing the Face of Poverty"

When you introduce quoted words with *he said, she claimed,* or the like, use a comma between the verb and the quote. When you follow a quote with such an expression, use a comma before the closing quotation mark (unless the quote is a question or an exclamation).

▶ When my mother reported that Mr. Tomkey did not believe in television, my father said, "Well, good for him. I don't know that I believe in it either."

academic literacies rhetorical situations genres processes strategies research MLA / APA media / design readings handbook

"That's exactly how I feel," my mother said, and then my parents watched the news, and whatever came on after the news.

—David Sedaris, "Us and Them"

You do not need any punctuation between *that* and a quotation.

▶ We were assigned to write one essay agreeing or disagreeing with George Orwell's statement that, "the slovenliness of our language makes it easier for us to have foolish thoughts."

In dialogue, insert a new paragraph and a new pair of quotation marks to signal each change of speaker.

▶ "What's this?" the hospital janitor said to me as he stumbled over my right shoe.
"My shoes," I said.
That's not a shoe, brother," he replied, holding it to the light.
"That's a brick."   —Henry Louis Gates Jr., "A Giant Step"

P-4b Long Quotations

Long quotations should be set off without quotation marks as **BLOCK QUOTATIONS**. Each documentation style has distinct guidelines for the length and formatting of block quotations; you'll find more on long quotations in **MLA STYLE** and **APA STYLE**. The following example uses MLA style, which calls for setting off quotations of more than four typed lines of prose by indenting them five spaces (or one-half inch) from the left margin. Note that in the following example, the period precedes the parenthetical documentation.

481

MLA 538
APA 577

Biographer David McCullough describes Truman's railroad campaign as follows:
No president in history had ever gone so far in quest of support from the people, or with less cause for the effort, to judge by informed opinion. . . . As a test of his skills and judgment as a professional politician, not to say his stamina and disposition at age sixty-four, it would be like no other experience in his long, often difficult career, as he himself understood perfectly. (655)

P-4c Titles of Short Works

Use quotation marks to enclose the titles of articles, chapters, essays, short stories, poems, songs, and episodes of television series. Titles of books, films, newspapers, and other longer works should be in italics (or underlined) rather than enclosed in quotation marks.

▶ In "Unfriendly Skies Are No Match for El Al," Vivienne Walt, a writer for *USA Today,* describes her experience flying with this airline.
— Andie McDonie, "Airport Security"

Note that the title of the newspaper is italicized, whereas the newspaper article title takes quotation marks.

▶ With every page of Edgar Allan Poe's story "The Tell-Tale Heart," my own heart beat faster.

▶ Rita Dove's poem "Dawn Revisited" contains vivid images that appeal to the senses of sight, sound, smell, and taste.

P-4d Single Quotation Marks

When you quote a passage that already contains quotation marks, whether they enclose a quotation or a title, change the inner ones to single quotation marks.

▶ Debra Johnson notes that according to Marilyn J. Adams, "effective reading instruction is based on 'direct instruction in phonics, focusing on the orthographic regularities of English.'"

▶ Certain essays are so good (or so popular) that they are included in almost every anthology. *The Norton Reader* notes, "Some essays—Martin Luther King Jr.'s 'Letter from Birmingham Jail' and Jonathan Swift's 'Modest Proposal,' for example—are constant favorites" (xxiii).

P-4e With Other Punctuation

When other punctuation follows material in quotation marks, it should go inside the closing quotation mark in some cases and outside in others. The following guidelines are those that are conventional in the United States; they differ from those in many other countries.

Commas and periods

Put commas and periods inside closing quotation marks.

▶ "On the newsstand, the cover is acting as a poster, an ad for what's inside," she said. "The loyal reader is looking for what makes the magazine exceptional."
                    —Katharine Q. Seelye, "Lurid Numbers on Glossy Pages!"

Semicolons and colons

Put semicolons and colons outside closing quotation marks.

▶ No elder stands behind our young to say, "Folks have fought and died for your right to pierce your face, so do it right"; no community exists that can model for a young person the responsible use of the "right"; for the right, even if called self-expression, comes from no source other than desire.
                    —Stephen L. Carter, "Just Be Nice"

▶ According to James Garbarino, author of *Lost Boys: Why Our Sons Turn Violent and How We Can Save Them*, it makes no sense to talk about violent media as a direct cause of youth violence. Rather, he says, "it depends": Media violence is a risk factor that, working in concert with others, can exacerbate bad behavior.
                    —Maggie Cutler, "Whodunit—The Media?"

Question marks and exclamation points

Put question marks and exclamation points inside closing quotation marks if they are part of the quotation but outside if they apply to the whole sentence.

▶ Then she began to talk more loudly. "What he want, I come to New York tell him front of his boss, you cheating me?"
                    —Amy Tan, "Mother Tongue"

▶ How many people know the words to "Louie, Louie"?

P-4f With Parenthetical Documentation

496–99

When you provide parenthetical **DOCUMENTATION** for a quotation, put it after the closing quotation mark, and put any end punctuation that's part of your sentence after the parentheses.

▶ An avid baseball fan, Tallulah Bankhead once said, "There have been only two geniuses in the world: Willie Mays and Willie Shakespeare" (183).

P-4g Checking for Mistakes with Quotation Marks

HB-69–71

Avoid using quotation marks to identify **SLANG** or to emphasize a word. Remove the quotation marks, or substitute a better word.

SLANG Appearing /"hip/" is important to many parents in New York.

EMPHASIS The woman explained that she is /"only/" the manager, not the owner, of the health club.

Do not put quotation marks around indirect quotations, those that do not quote someone's exact words.

▶ Grandmother always said that /"meat that was any good didn't need seasoning./"

P-5 Apostrophes

McDonald's: "I'm lovin' it" proclaims an ad, demonstrating two common uses of the apostrophe: to show ownership (*McDonald's*) and to mark missing letters (*I'm, lovin'*). This chapter offers guidelines on these and other common uses for apostrophes.

P-5a Possessives

Use an apostrophe to make a word possessive: *Daniel Craig's eyes, someone else's problem, the children's playground.*

academic literacies · rhetorical situations · genres · processes · strategies · research MLA / APA · media / design · readings · handbook

Singular nouns

To make most singular nouns possessive, add an apostrophe and -s.

▶ The challenge now will be filling the park's seats.
—Michael Kimmelman, "A Ballpark Louder Than Its Fans"

▶ In Plato's *Phaedrus,* Socrates bemoaned the development of writing.
—Nicholas Carr, "Is Google Making Us Stoopid?"

▶ Bill Gates's philanthropic efforts focus on health care and education.

▶ Euripides's plays are more realistic than those of Aeschylus.

If adding -'s complicates pronunciation, some writers use only an apostrophe: *Gates', Euripides'.*

Plural nouns

To form the possessive of a plural noun not ending in -s, add an apostrophe and -s. For plural nouns that end in -s, add only an apostrophe.

▶ Are women's minds different from men's minds?
—Evelyn Fox Keller, "Women in Science"

▶ The neighbors' complaints about noise led the club owner to install soundproof insulation.

▶ Did you hear that Laurence Strauss is getting married? The reception will be at the Strausses' home.

Something, everyone, *and other indefinite pronouns*

To form the possessive of an **INDEFINITE PRONOUN**, add an apostrophe and -s.

HB-27

▶ Clarabelle was everyone's favorite clown.

Joint possession

To show that two or more individuals possess something together, use the possessive form for the last noun only.

▶ Carlson and Ventura's book is an introduction to Latino writers for English-speaking adolescents.

To show individual possession, make each noun possessive.

▶ Jan's and Al's heart transplants inspired me to become an organ donor.

Compound nouns

For nouns made up of more than one word, make the last word possessive.

▶ The surgeon general's report persuaded many people to stop smoking.

P-5b Contractions

An apostrophe in a contraction indicates where letters have been omitted.

▶ I've learned that sometimes friends and business don't mix.
—Iliana Roman, "First Job"

I've *is a contraction of* I have; don't *is a contraction of* do not.

P-5c Plurals

You'll often see apostrophes used to pluralize numbers, letters, abbreviations, and words discussed as words: 7's, A's, NGO's, *thank you's*. Usage is changing, however, and in the case of numbers, abbreviations, and words discussed as words, you should leave out the apostrophe in your own writing.

Plural of numbers

▶ The winning hand had three 8s.

▶ We were astonished to hear Grandma Eleanor say she loved the 1950**s**.

Plural of abbreviations and words discussed as words

▶ How many TV**s** does the average American family have in its home?

▶ The resolution passed when there were more *aye***s** than *nay***s**.

See that words discussed as words are italicized but the -s ending is not.

Plural of letters

MLA STYLE recommends using apostrophes to pluralize letters; **APA STYLE**, *Chicago*, and **CSE** omit these apostrophes.

MLA 500–548
APA 549–89

▶ The admissions officers spoke enthusiastically about the school's no-grades option—and then said we'd need mostly *A*'**s** to get in.

P-5d Checking for Mistakes with Apostrophes

Do not use an apostrophe in the following situations.

With plural nouns that are not possessive

▶ Both ~~cellist's~~ *cellists* played encores.

With *his, hers, ours, yours, and theirs*

▶ Look at all the lettuce. ~~Our's~~ *Ours* is organic. Is ~~your's?~~ *yours?*

With the possessive *its*

▶ It's an unusual building; ~~it's~~ *its* style has been described as postmodern, but it fits beautifully with the Gothic buildings on our campus.

It's is a contraction meaning "it is" or "it has"; its is the possessive form of it.

P-6 Other Punctuation

Some carpenters can do their jobs using only a hammer and a saw, but most rely on additional tools. The same is true of writers: you can get along with just a few punctuation marks, but having some others in your toolbox—colons, dashes, parentheses, brackets, ellipses, and slashes—can help you say what you want to more precisely—and can help readers follow what you write more easily. This chapter can help you use these other punctuation marks effectively.

P-6a Colons

Colons are used to direct attention to words that follow the colon: an explanation or elaboration, a list, a quotation, and so on.

▶ What I remember best, strangely enough, are the two things I couldn't understand and over the years grew to hate: grammar lessons and mathematics. —Mike Rose, "Potato Chips and Stars"

▶ I sized him up as fast as possible: tight black velvet pants pulled over his boots, black jacket, a red-green-yellow scarf slashed around his neck. —Susan Jane Gilman, "Mick Jagger Wants Me"

▶ She also voices some common concerns: "The product should be safe, it should be easily accessible, and it should be low-priced." —Dara Mayers, "Our Bodies, Our Lives"

▶ Fifteen years after the release of the Carnegie report, College Board surveys reveal data are no different: test scores still correlate strongly with family income. —Gregory Mantsios, "Class in America—2003"

Colons are also used after the salutation in a business letter, in ratios, between titles and subtitles, between city and publisher in bibliographies, between chapter and verse in biblical references, and between numbers that indicate hours, minutes, and seconds.

▶ Dear President Michaels:

▶ For best results, add water to the powder in a 3:1 ratio.

▶ *The Last Campaign: How Harry Truman Won the 1948 Election*

▶ New York: Norton, 2014.

▶ "Death and life are in the power of the tongue" (Proverbs 18:21).

▶ The morning shuttle departs at 6:52 AM.

P-6b Dashes

You can create a dash by typing two hyphens (--) with no spaces before or after or by selecting the em dash from the symbol menu of your word-processing program.

Use dashes to set off material you want to emphasize. Unlike colons, dashes can appear not only after an independent clause but also at other points in a sentence. To set off material at the end of a sentence, place a dash before it; to set off material in the middle of the sentence, place a dash before and after the words you want to emphasize.

▶ After that, the roller coaster rises and falls, slowing down and speeding up—all on its own.
              —Cathi Eastman and Becky Burrell, "The Science of Screams"

▶ It did not occur to me—possibly because I am an American—that there could be people anywhere who had never seen a Negro.
              —James Baldwin, "Stranger in the Village"

Dashes are often used to signal a shift in tone or thought.

▶ The best way to keep children home is to make the home atmosphere pleasant—and let the air out of the tires.   —Dorothy Parker

Keep in mind that dashes are most effective if they are used only when material needs particular emphasis. Too many dashes can interfere with the flow and clarity of your writing.

P-6c Parentheses

Use parentheses to enclose supplemental details and digressions.

▶ When I was a child, attending grade school in Washington, DC, we took classroom time to study manners. Not only the magic words "please" and "thank you" but more complicated etiquette questions, like how to answer the telephone ("Carter residence, Stephen speaking") and how to set the table (we were quizzed on whether knife blades point in or out).
—Stephen L. Carter, "Just Be Nice"

▶ In their apartments they have the material possessions that indicate success (a VCR, a color television), even if it means that they do without necessities and plunge into debt to buy these items.
—Diana George, "Changing the Face of Poverty"

▶ Before participating in the trials, Seeta and Ratna (not their real names) knew nothing about H.I.V.   —Dara Mayers, "Our Bodies, Our Lives"

P-6d Brackets

482–83

Put brackets around words that you insert in a **QUOTATION**.

▶ As Senator Reid explained, "She [Nancy Pelosi] realizes that you cannot make everyone happy."

If you are quoting a source that contains an error, put the Latin word *sic* in brackets after the error to indicate that the mistake is in the original source.

▶ Warehouse has been around for 30 years and has 263 stores, suggesting a large fan base. The chain sums up its appeal thus: "styley [*sic*], confident, sexy, glamorous, edgy, clean and individual, with it's [*sic*] finger on the fashion pulse."   —Anne Ashworth, "Chain Reaction: Warehouse"

P-6e Ellipses

482

Ellipses are three spaced dots that indicate an omission or a pause. Use ellipses to show that you have omitted words within a **QUOTATION**. If you

academic literacies ▪ rhetorical situations ▲ genres ○ processes ◆ strategies ● research MLA / APA ▫ media / design ▐ readings ◪ handbook omit a complete sentence or more in the middle of a quoted passage, add the three dots after the period.

ORIGINAL

▶ The Lux ad's visual content, like Resinol's, supports its verbal message. Several demure views of Irene Dunne emphasize her "pearly-smooth skin," the top one framed by a large heart shape. In all the photos, Dunne wears a feathery, feminine collar, giving her a birdlike appearance: she is a bird of paradise or an ornament. At the bottom of the ad, we see a happy Dunne being cuddled and admired by a man.

—Doug Lantry, " 'Stay Sweet as You Are' "

WITH ELLIPSES

▶ The Lux ad's visual content . . . supports its verbal message. Several demure views of Irene Dunne emphasize her "pearly-smooth skin," the top one framed by a large heart shape. . . . At the bottom of the ad, we see a happy Dunne being cuddled and admired by a man.

If you use parenthetical documentation after quoted material, place ellipses *before* the parentheses to indicate the deletion of words, but put the end punctuation *after* the parentheses.

▶ According to Kathleen Welch, "One can turn one's gaze away from television, but one cannot turn one's ears from it without leaving the area . . . " (102).

P-6f Slashes

When you quote two or three lines of poetry and run them in with the rest of your text, use slashes to show where one line ends and the next begins. Put a space before and after each slash.

▶ In the opening lines of the poem, he warns the reader to "Lift not the painted veil which those who live / Call Life" (1-2).

—Stephanie Huff, "Metaphor and Society in Shelley's 'Sonnet' "

P-7 Hyphens

If your mother gives you much needed advice, has she given you a great deal of advice that you needed, or advice that you needed badly? What about a psychiatry experiment that used thirty five year old subjects? Were there thirty-five subjects who were a year old? thirty subjects who were five years old? or an unspecified number of thirty-five-year-old subjects? Hyphens could clear up the confusion. This chapter provides tips for when to use hyphens and when to omit them.

P-7a Compound Words

Compound words can be two words (*ground zero*), a hyphenated word (*self-esteem*), or one word (*outsource*). Check a dictionary, and if a compound is not there, assume that it is two words.

Compound adjectives

A compound adjective is made up of two or more words. Most compound adjectives take a hyphen before a noun.

▶ a little-known trombonist

▶ a foul-smelling river

Do not use a hyphen to connect an -ly adverb and an adjective.

▶ a carefully executed plan

A compound adjective after a noun is usually easy to read without a hyphen; add a hyphen only if the compound is unclear without it.

▶ The river has become foul smelling in recent years.

academic literacies   rhetorical situations   genres   processes   strategies   research MLA / APA   media / design   readings   handbook

Prefixes and suffixes

A hyphen usually isn't needed after a prefix or before a suffix (*preschool, antislavery, counterattack, catlike, citywide*). However, hyphens are necessary in the following situations.

WITH *GREAT-*, *SELF-*, *-ELECT*   great-aunt, self-hatred, president-elect

WITH CAPITAL LETTERS   anti-American, post-Soviet literature

WITH NUMBERS   post-9/11, the mid-1960s

TO AVOID DOUBLE AND TRIPLE LETTERS   anti-intellectualism, ball-like

FOR CLARITY   re-cover (cover again) *but* recover (get well)

Numbers

Hyphenate fractions and compound numbers from twenty-one to ninety-nine.

▶   three-quarters of their income

▶   thirty-five subjects

P-7b At the End of a Line

Use a hyphen to divide a multisyllabic word that does not fit on one line. (A one-syllable word is never hyphenated.) Divide words between syllables as shown in a dictionary, after a prefix, or before a suffix. Divide compound words between the parts of the compound, if possible. Do not leave only one letter at the end or the beginning of a line.

op-er-a-tion   knot-ty   main-stream

P-8 Capitalization

Capital letters are an important signal, either that a new sentence is beginning or that a specific person, place, or brand is being discussed. Capitalize *Carol*, and it's clear that you're referring to a person; write *carol*, and readers will know you're writing about a song sung at Christmas. This chapter offers guidelines to help you know what to capitalize and when.

P-8a Proper Nouns and Common Nouns

Capitalize proper nouns, those naming specific people, places, and things. All other nouns are common nouns and should not be capitalized.

PROPER NOUNS	COMMON NOUNS
Sanjay Gupta	a doctor
Senator Schumer	a U.S. senator
Uncle Daniel	my uncle
France	a republic
the Mississippi River	a river
the West Coast	a coast
Christianity	a religion
Allah	a god
the Torah	a sacred text
Central Intelligence Agency	an agency
U.S. Congress	the U.S. government
Ohio University	a university
Composition 101	a writing course
World War II	a war
July	summer
the Middle Ages	the fourteenth century
Kleenex	tissues

Adjectives derived from proper nouns, especially the names of people and places, are usually capitalized: *Shakespearean, Swedish, Chicagoan.* There are exceptions to this rule, however, such as *french fries, roman numeral,* and *congressional.* Consult your dictionary if you are unsure whether an adjective should be capitalized.

Many dictionaries capitalize the terms *Internet, Net,* and *World Wide Web,* but you'll see variations such as *Website* and *website.* Whether you capitalize or not, be consistent throughout a paper.

P-8b Titles before a Person's Name

A professional title is capitalized when it appears before a person's name but not when it appears after a proper noun or alone.

Senator (*or* Sen.) Elizabeth Warren   Elizabeth Warren, the senator

P-8c The First Word of a Sentence

Capitalize the first word of a sentence. The first word of a quoted sentence should be capitalized, but not the first word of a quoted phrase.

▶ Speaking about acting, Clint Eastwood notes, "You can show a lot with a look.... It's punctuation."

▶ Sherry Turkle argues that we're living in "techno-enthusiastic times" and that we're inclined "to celebrate our gadgets."

Interrupted quotations

Capitalize the second part of an interrupted quotation only if it begins a new sentence.

▶ "It was just as nice," she sobbed, "as I hoped and dreamed it would be."
—Joan Didion, "Marrying Absurd"

▶ "On the newsstand, the cover is acting as a poster, an ad for what's inside," she said. "The loyal reader is looking for what makes the magazine exceptional."   —Katharine Q. Seelye, "Lurid Numbers on Glossy Pages!"

P-8d Titles and Subtitles

Capitalize the first and last words and all other important words of a title and subtitle. Do not capitalize less important words such as ARTICLES, COORDINATING CONJUNCTIONS, and PREPOSITIONS.

HB-64–66
HB-38
HB-56–58

> "Give Peace a Chance"
> *Pride and Prejudice*
> *The Shallows: What the Internet Is Doing to Our Brains*

Each documentation style has guidelines for formatting titles in notes and bibliographies. You'll find more on titles and subtitles in MLA STYLE and APA STYLE.

MLA 500–548
APA 549–89

P-9 Italics

Italic type tells us to read words a certain way. Think of the difference between the office and *The Office*, or between time and *Time*. In each case, the italicized version tells us it's a specific television show or magazine. This chapter provides guidelines on using italics in your writing.

P-9a Titles of Long Works

Titles and subtitles of long works should appear in italics (or underlined). Notable exceptions are sacred writing such as the Qur'an or the Old Testament and historical documents such as the Declaration of Independence.

BOOKS *The Norton Field Guide to Writing; War and Peace*

PERIODICALS *The Atlantic; Teen Vogue; College English*

NEWSPAPERS *Los Angeles Times*

academic literacies · rhetorical situations · genres · processes · strategies · research MLA / APA · media / design · readings · handbook

PLAYS *Medea; Six Degrees of Separation*

LONG POEMS *The Odyssey; Paradise Lost*

FILMS AND VIDEOS *Argo; Searching for Sugar Man*

MUSICAL WORKS OR ALBUMS *The Four Seasons; Rubber Soul*

RADIO AND TV SERIES *Fresh Air; Modern Family; Game of Thrones*

PAINTINGS, SCULPTURES the *Mona Lisa;* Michelangelo's *David*

DANCES BY A CHOREOGRAPHER Mark Morris's *Gloria*

SOFTWARE *Adobe Acrobat XI Standard*

SHIPS, SPACECRAFT *Queen Mary; Challenger*

WEBSITES *Salon; Etsy; IMDb*

A short work, such as a short story, an article, an episode of a series, or a song, takes quotation marks.

P-9b Words Discussed as Words

Italicize a word you are discussing as a word. The same practice applies to numbers, letters, and symbols.

▶ In those 236 words, you will hear the word *dedicate* five times.
—William Safire, "A Spirit Reborn"

▶ Most American dictionaries call for one *t* in the word *benefited*.

▶ All computer codes consist of some combination of *0*s and *1*s.

Some writers use quotation marks rather than italics to signal words discussed as words.

▶ I would learn, when I asked some people who didn't show up the next day, that "definitely attending" on Facebook means "maybe" and "maybe attending" means "likely not."
—Hal Niedzviecki, "Facebook in a Crowd"

P-9c Non-English Words

Use italics for an unfamiliar word or phrase in a language other than English. Do not italicize proper nouns.

▶ *Verstehen*, a concept often associated with Max Weber, is the sociologist's attempt to understand human actions from the actor's point of view.

If the word or phrase has become part of everyday English or has an entry in English-language dictionaries, it does not need italics.

▶ An ad hoc committee should be formed to assess the university's use of fossil fuels and ways to incorporate alternative energy sources.

▶ The plot of *Jane Eyre* follows the conventions of a bildungsroman, or a coming-of-age story.

P-9d For Emphasis

You can use italics occasionally to lend emphasis to a word or phrase, but do not overuse them.

▶ It is, perhaps, as much what Shakespeare did *not* write as what he did that seems to indicate something seriously wrong with his marriage.
　　　　　　　　　—Stephen Greenblatt, "Shakespeare on Marriage"

▶ Despite a physical beauty that had . . . hordes of teenage girls (and a few boys) dreaming of touching his hair *just once*, Depp escaped from the Hollywood star machine.
　　　　　　　　　—Sean Smith, "Johnny Depp: Unlikely Superstar"

P-10 Abbreviations

MTV. USA. OC. DNA. *fwiw.* DIY. These are some common abbreviations, shortcuts to longer words and phrases. You can use common abbreviations if you are sure your readers will recognize them. If not, spell out the

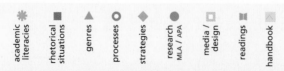

full term with the abbreviation in parentheses the first time it appears. After that, you can use the abbreviation alone.

▶ In a recent press release, officials from the international organization Médicins Sans Frontières (MSF) stressed the need for more effective tuberculosis drugs.

Periods are generally used in abbreviations of personal titles that precede a name and in Latin abbreviations such as *e.g.* or *etc.* They are not needed for state abbreviations such as CA, NY, or TX, or for most abbreviations made up of initials, like AP or YMCA. In some cases, periods are optional (BCE or B.C.E.). Be sure to use them or omit them consistently. If you're not sure about periods for a particular abbreviation, check a dictionary.

P-10a With Names

Most titles are abbreviated when they come before or after a name.

Mr. Ed Stanford	Ed Stanford Jr.
Dr. Ralph Lopez	Ralph Lopez, MD
Prof. Susan Miller	Susan Miller, PhD

Do not abbreviate job titles that are not attached to a name.

▶ The ~~RN~~ who worked with trauma victims specialized in cardiac care.
    nurse

P-10b With Numbers

The following abbreviations can be used with numbers.

632 BC ("before Christ")
344 BCE ("before the common era")
AD 800 (*"anno Domini"*)
800 CE ("common era")
10:30 AM (*or* a.m.)
7:00 PM (*or* p.m.)

Notice that *BC*, *BCE*, and *CE* follow the date, while *AD* precedes the date. Remember that the abbreviations in the list cannot be used without a date or time.

▶ By early ~~p.m.,~~ *afternoon,* all prospective subjects for the experiment had checked in.

P-10c In Notes and Documentation

With only a few exceptions, the names of months, days of the week, colleges and universities, cities, states, and countries should not be abbreviated in the body of a paper. But they often are abbreviated in footnotes and bibliographies; follow the rules of whichever documentation system you are using.

The same applies to Latin abbreviations like *ibid.*, *op. cit.*, and *et al.*: while you may use them in notes and documentation, they're not appropriate in the body of your text. Use equivalent English expressions (such as "and others" for *et al.*) instead.

▶ Being left-handed presents some challenges for writers—~~e.g.,~~ *for example,* it hurts to write in spiral notebooks and ink smears across the page and the side of your hand.

P-11 Numbers

Numbers may be written with numerals (*97*) or words (*ninety-seven*). Spell out numbers and fractions that you can write in one or two words (*thirteen, thirty-seven, thirty thousand, two-thirds*). Use numerals otherwise (*578; 5,788*). Spell out any number that begins a sentence. Be aware, however, that the conventions for writing numbers vary across disciplines.

MLA 500–548

In the humanities, **MLA STYLE** and *Chicago* recommend spelling out all numbers up to a hundred (*twenty-five*) and all round numbers (*fifty thousand*) and using numerals for specific numbers above one hundred (*101*).

academic literacies · rhetorical situations · genres · processes · strategies · research MLA / APA · media / design · readings · handbook

▶ In a survey of *two hundred* students, 135 said they spent more than two hours each day writing.

In the social sciences, **APA STYLE** recommends spelling out numbers one through nine and using numerals for all the rest.

APA 549–89

▶ *Nine 40*-minute interviews of subjects in *three* categories were conducted for this study.

In the sciences, CSE recommends using numerals in almost any situation, but spelling out zero and one to avoid confusion with l and O.

▶ The physician recommended one dose of 200 mg per day for 8 days.

In most business writing, spell out numbers one through ten and use numerals for all numbers over ten (*ten goals, 11 strategies*).

▶ We received *35* applications and identified *five* strong candidates, who we'll interview this week.

For very large numbers that include a fraction or decimal, use a combination of numerals and words.

▶ One retailer sold more than 4.5 million of its basic T-shirts last year.

In addition, numerals are generally used in the following situations.

ADDRESSES   500 Broadway; 107 175th Street

DATES   December 26, 2012; 632 BCE; the 1990s

MONEY IN EXACT AMOUNTS $3.75; $375,000; a deficit of $3.75 trillion

PARTS OF WRITTEN WORKS   volume 2; Chapter 5; page 82; act 3, scene 3

PERCENTAGES   66 percent (*or* 66%)

RATIOS   16:1 (*or* 16 to 1)

STATISTICS   a median age of 32

TIMES OF DAY   6:20 AM (*or* a.m.)

WHOLE NUMBERS WITH DECIMALS OR FRACTIONS   66.7; 66 2/3; 59½

Acknowledgments

IMAGE ACKNOWLEDGMENTS

Page 40: Courtesy of Jacob MacLeod; p. 73: Courtesy of Emily Vallowe; p. 79: Courtesy of Marjorie Agosín; p. 95: Courtesy of Hannah Berry; p. 96: Courtesy of The Clarks Companies; p. 98: Courtesy of Sorel: p. 99: Courtesy of Danielle Allen. © Laura Rose Photography; p. 105: Seth Wenig/AP; p. 117: urbanbuzz/Shutterstock.com; p. 118: TOLES © 2007 The Washington Post. Reprinted with permission of UNIVERSAL UCLICK; p. 120: AP Photo/Jeffrey Phelps; p. 121 (top): Courtesy of Ann C. Johns, Ph.D./University of Texas at Austin; p. 121 (bottom): Courtesy of Ann C. Johns, Ph.D./University of Texas at Austin: p. 129: Courtesy of Michaela Cullington; p. 137: © 2010 Larry D. Moore/Wikimedia Commons; p. 138 (left): Charles Bennett/AP; p. 138 (right): Mark Duncan/AP; p. 142 (top): Courtesy of Jon Marcus, Photo by Andrew Kubica; p. 142 (bottom): Wesley Hitt/Getty Images; p. 161: Evan Agostini/Invision/AP Photo; p. 163: © Corbis; p. 164: Courtesy of Andrew Leonard; p. 165: YouTube; p. 166: YouTube; p. 167: YouTube; p. 190: Courtesy of Jessica Ann Olson; p. 197: ConsumerReports.org; p. 198: Courtesy of Ali Heinekamp; p. 199: The Kobal Collection; p. 206: The Granger Collection, New York/The Granger Collection; p. 207: Courtesy of Stephanie Huff; p. 216: John Amis/AP; p. 224: Courtesy of Steve Hendrix/The Washington Post; p. 225: Courtesy of Heather Penney; p. 232 (left): Courtesy of Heather Penney; p. 232 (right): Courtesy of The United States Air Force; p. 235: Courtesy of Michael Granof; p. 239: Heather Ainsworth/The New York Times/Redux; p. 244: Wikimedia Commons; p. 265: Steye Raviez/Hollandse Hoogte/Redux; p. 335: Jim Mone/AP; p. 365: © Reagan Louie; p. 366: RecycleManiacs.org; p. 377: Courtesy of Michiganapples.com; p. 384 (top); © GOOGLE; p. 384 (bottom): © GOOGLE; p. 393: © Swim Ink 2, LLC/CORBIS; p. 404: The Advertising Archives; p. 405: The Advertising Archives; p. 427 (all): Courtesy of The Other Side of Fifty, othersideoffifty.com; p. 448: National Institutes of Health; p. 449: PARS/The New York Times; p. 451 (top): Houston Community College Libraries; http://library.hccs.edu/home; p. 451 (bottom): Houston Community College Libraries, http://library.hccs.edu/home; p. 453: www.wordle.net/create; p. 454: Permission to publish courtesy of EBSCO; p. 457: The University of Wyoming Library; p. 458: The University of Wyoming Library; p. 516: Jessamyn Neuhaus, "Marge Simpson, Blue-Haired Housewife Defining Domesticity on *The Simpsons*." *Journal of Popular Culture* 43.4 (2010): 761–81. Print; p. 519 (top): Michael Segal, "The Hit Book That Came from Mars." *Nautilus*. Nautilus Think, 8 January 2015. Web. 10 October 2016; p. 519 (bottom): Michael Segal, "The Hit Book That Came from Mars." *Nautilus*. Nautilus Think, 8 January 2015. Web. 10 October 2016;

p. 520: Jessamyn Neuhaus, "Marge Simpson, Blue-Haired Housewife Defining Domesticity on *The Simpsons*." *Journal of Popular Culture* 43.4 (2010): 761–81. Sport Discus with Full Text. Web. 24 Mar. 2016; p. 524 (left): Amana Fontanella-Khan, *Pink Sari Revolution: A Tale of Women and Power in India*. New York: Norton, 2013; p. 524 (right): Amana Fontanella-Khan, *Pink Sari Revolution: A Tale of Women and Power in India*. New York: Norton, 2013; p. 530: John McIlwain, Molly Simpson, and Sara Hammerschmidt. "Housing in America: Integrating Housing, Health, and Resilience in a Changing Environment." *Urban Land Institute*. Urban Land Institute, 2014. Web. 17 Sept. 2016; p. 541: Bettmann/CORBIS; p. 559 (left): Joseph E. Stiglitz, "The Great Divide: Unequal Societies and What We Can Do about Them." New York: Norton, 2015; p. 559 (right): Joseph E. Stiglitz, "The Great Divide: Unequal Societies and What We Can Do about Them." New York: Norton, 2015; p. 567: M. P. Lazette, (2015, February 25). "A Hurricane's Hit to Households." Federal Reserve Bank of Cleveland. Retrieved from www.clevelandfed.org/en/Newsroom%20and%20Events/Publications/Forefront/Katrina.aspx; p. 569: C. F. Guthrie, (2013). "Smart Technology and the Moral Life." *Ethics & Behavior*, 23, 324–37. doi: 10.1080/10508422.2013.787359; p. 570: C. F. Guthrie (2013). "Smart Technology and the Moral Life." *Ethics & Behavior*, 23(4), 324–37. doi:10.1080/10508422.2013.787359; p. 600: Ikea.com; p. 608 (left): The Philadelphia Museum of Art/Art Resource, NY; p. 608 (right): Willem de Kooning (1904–1997)/Private Collection/The Bridgeman Art Library; p. 610a: Reuters/Landov; p. 610b: Reuters/Landov; p. 610b: Reuters/Landov; p. 610d: Reuters/Landov; p. 610e: NASA/Wikimedia Commons; p. 612: ww.loc.gov/rr/record/onlinecollections; p. 613: blog.aai.si.edu; p. 618: www.nps.gov/history; p. 619: Reprinted with permission of Smithsonian Institution; p. 620: Courtesy of Ann M. Lawrence, PhD, University of South Florida; p. 623: Courtesy Richard Bullock; p. 625: Library of Congress/Wikimedia Commons; p. 626: Courtesy of Judy Davis; p. 634 (top): Prezi.com; p. 634 (bottom right): Photo by Bruce Mathews, Courtesy of the Harry S. Truman Library, Independence, Missouri.

TEXT ACKNOWLEDGMENTS

Marjorie Agosín: "Always Living in Spanish," *The Literary Life*, p. 25. Reprinted by permission of the author.

Danielle Allen: Excerpts from *Our Declaration: A Reading of the Declaration of Independence in Defense of Equality* by Danielle Allen. Copyright © 2014 by Danielle Allen. Used by permission of Liveright Publishing Corporation.

Sam Anderson: "Just One More Game . . ." from the *New York Times Magazine*, April 8, 2012. © 2012 The New York Times. All rights reserved. Used by permission and protected by the Copyright Laws of the United States. The printing, copying, redistribution, or retransmission of the Material without express written permission is prohibited.

Michael Benton et al: "Teen Film$: An Annotated Bibliography" from *Journal of Popular Film & Television*, Vol. 25, Summer 1997, pp. 83–88. Reprinted by permission of Taylor & Francis.

Erin Bilder: Bonded Together by Tailgating, copyright Erin Bilder. Reprinted with permission.

Rick Bragg: "A Man Who Buys Books Because They're Pretty" from *All Over But the Shoutin'* by Rick Bragg, copyright © 1997 by Rick Bragg. Used by permission of Pantheon Books, an imprint of the Knopf Doubleday Publishing Group, a division of Penguin Random House LLC. All rights reserved.

Matthew Bries: Warren G. Harding, Newspaperman, copyright Matthew Bries. Reprinted with permission.

Dustin Childers: Rifles and Watches, copyright Dustin Childers. Reprinted with permission.

Glossary / Index

A

a, an, HB-64

abbreviations
  overview, HB-104–106
  periods with, HB-85
  plural forms, HB-93

abstract, 183–87 A writing GENRE that summarizes a book, an article, or a paper, usually in 100–200 words. Authors in some academic fields must provide, at the top of a report submitted for publication, an abstract of its content. The abstract may then appear in a journal of abstracts, such as *Psychological Abstracts.* An *informative abstract* summarizes a complete report; a briefer *descriptive abstract* provides only a brief overview; a *proposal abstract* (also called a TOPIC PROPOSAL) requests permission to conduct research, write on a topic, or present a report at a scholarly conference. Key Features: SUMMARY of basic information • objective description • brevity
  key features, 185
  types and examples
    descriptive, 184
    informative, 183–84
    proposal, 184–85

when to use, 274
writing guide, 185–87

abstract and concrete words, HB-45
academic habits of mind, 45–52
Academic Search Complete, 459

academic writing, 3–9 Writing done in an academic or scholarly context, such as for course assignments. Key Features: evidence that you've carefully considered the subject • clear, appropriately qualified THESIS • response to what others have said • good reasons supported by evidence • acknowledgment of multiple perspectives • carefully documented sources • confident, authoritative STANCE • indication of why your topic matters • careful attention to correctness.

accept, except, HB-51
acknowledging other viewpoints. *See* multiple perspectives, incorporating
acknowledging sources, 491–94
across the board, HB-51

action verb, 256, 258, 415, HB-61 A VERB that expresses a physical or mental action (*jump, consider*).

active voice, 314, HB-19 When a VERB is in the active voice, the SUBJECT performs the action: *He sent a gift. See also* passive voice

---

Note: This glossary / index defines key terms and concepts and directs you to pages in the book where you can find specific information on these and other topics. Please note the words set in SMALL CAPITAL LETTERS are themselves defined in the glossary / index.

food into carbohydrates, proteins, and fats). Classification and/or division can serve as the ORGANIZING principle for a whole text.

clause A group of words that consists of at least a SUBJECT and a PREDICATE; a clause may be either INDEPENDENT or SUBORDINATE. *See also* independent clause; subordinate clause

cliché, 315–16, HB-43–44 An expression used so frequently that it is no longer fresh: *busy as a bee.*

clustering, 291–92 A PROCESS for GENERATING IDEAS AND TEXT, in which a writer visually connects thoughts by jotting them down and drawing lines between related items.

collaboration, 285–88 The PROCESS of working with others.

collective noun A NOUN — such as *committee, crowd, family, herd,* or *team* — that refers to a group.

comma splice, HB-10–11 Two or more INDEPENDENT CLAUSES joined with only a comma: *I came, I saw, I conquered.*

common ground, 367, HB-66–67 Shared values. Writers build common ground with AUDIENCES by acknowledging others' POINTS OF VIEW, seeking areas of compromise, and using language that includes, rather than excludes, those they aim to reach. *See also* inclusive language

of design include font, color, illustration, layout, and white space. One component of a RHETORICAL SITUATION, design plays an important part in how well a text reaches its AUDIENCE and achieves its PURPOSE.

elements of
    fonts, 601–2
    headings, 604–5
    layout, 602–3
    white space, 605
evaluating designs, 605–6
genres and
    literacy narratives, 90–91
    position papers, 180
    reports, 146, 152–53
    résumés, 259
    textual analyses, 125–26
principles of, 598–601
rhetorical situation and, 70, 598

details
in extended definitions, 394
genres and
    literacy narratives, 84
    memoirs, 220, 222–23
    profiles, 229–30
    reflections, 249
processes and
    description, 399–402
    narration, 423–25
Devlin, Keith, 363–64

dialogue, 408–13 A STRATEGY for including other people's spoken words to a text.
function of, 408–9
genres
    literacy narratives, 87
    memoirs, 223
    profiles, 229, 233

integrating, 409–10
nonstandard spelling with, HB-74
punctuation with, 92
rewriting narratives with, 310
rhetorical situation and, 412–13

Dickinson, Emily, 847
diction. *See* language
dictionaries, 455
did. See do, forms of
Didion, Joan, 426
direct quotations
    commas with, HB-81
    quotation marks with, HB-86–87

discovery drafting, 296–97 A PROCESS of DRAFTING something quickly, mostly for the purpose of discovering what one wants to say.

disinterested, uninterested, HB-53
dissertations, 459

dividing, 375–76. *See also* classifying and dividing

do, forms of, 316, HB-17, HB-44

documentation, 496–99 Publication information about the sources cited in a text. The documentation usually appears in an abbreviated form in parentheses at the point of CITATION or in an endnote or a footnote. Complete documentation usually appears as a list of WORKS CITED or REFERENCES at the end of the text. Documentation styles vary by discipline. For example, Modern Language Association (MLA) style requires an author's complete first name if it appears in a source, whereas American Psychological Association (APA) style requires only the initial of an author's first name.

evidence, 359–67 In ARGUMENT, the data you present to support your REASONS. Such data may include statistics, calculations, examples, ANECDOTES, QUOTATIONS, case studies, or anything else that will convince your reader that your reasons are compelling. Evidence should be sufficient (enough to show that the reasons have merit) and relevant (appropriate to the argument you're making).

explaining a process, 414–18 A STRATEGY for telling how something is done or how to do something. An explanation of a process can serve as the ORGANIZING principle for a whole text.

expletive, HB-5, HB-59 A word such as *it* or *there* used to introduce information provided later in a sentence: *It was difficult to drive on the icy road. There is plenty of food in the refrigerator.*

literary analysis, 206–15   A writing GENRE that examines a literary text (most often fiction, poetry, or drama) and argues for a particular INTERPRETATION of the text. Key Features: arguable THESIS • careful attention to the language of the text • attention to patterns or themes • clear interpretation • MLA style. *See also* analysis; textual analysis

literature   Literary works — including fiction, poetry, drama, and some nonfiction; also, the body of written work produced in given field.

logical appeal, 356–67   In ARGUMENT, an appeal to readers based on the use of logical reasoning and of EVIDENCE such as facts, statistics, statements from authorities on the subject, and so on.

logical fallacy. *See* fallacy, logical

logos. *See* logical appeal

metaphor, 385 A figure of speech that makes a comparison without using the word *like* or *as:* "All the world's a stage / And all the men and women merely players" (Shakespeare, *As You Like It* 2.7.138–39). *See also* figurative language; simile

modal, HB-18–19 A helping VERB — such as *can, could, may, might, must, ought to, should, will,* or *would* — that does not change form for person or number and indicates probability or necessity.

modifier A word, PHRASE, or CLAUSE that describes or specifies something about another word, phrase, or clause (*a long, informative* speech; the actors spoke *in unison;* the man *who would be king*).

N

noncount noun, HB-64 A word that names something that cannot be counted or made plural: *information, rice.*

nonessential element, 315, HB-79–80 A word, PHRASE, or CLAUSE that gives additional information but that is not necessary for understanding the basic meaning of a sentence: *I learned French, which is a Romance language, online.* Nonessential elements should be set off by commas.

noun A word that names a person, place, thing, or idea (*teacher, Zadie Smith, forest, Amazon River, notebook, democracy*).

O

object   A word or phrase that follows a PREPOSITION or that receives the action of a VERB. In the sentence *I handed him the mail on the table, him* is an indirect object and *mail* is a direct object of the verb *handed; table* is an object of the preposition *on.*

organizing   Arranging parts of a text so that the text as a whole has COHERENCE. The text may use one STRATEGY throughout or may combine several strategies to create a suitable organization.

outlining A PROCESS for GENERATING IDEAS AND TEXT or for organizing or examining a text. An *informal outline* simply lists ideas and then numbers them in the order that they will appear; a *working outline* distinguishes supporting from main ideas by indenting the former; a *formal outline* is arranged as a series of headings and indented subheadings, each on a separate line, with letters and numerals indicating relative levels of importance.

P

parallelism, HB-34–37 A writing technique that puts similar items into the same grammatical structure. For example, every item on a to-do list might begin with a command: *clean, wash, buy*; or a discussion of favorite hobbies might name each as a GERUND: running, playing basketball, writing poetry.

paraphrasing Rewording someone else's text using about the same number of words but not the phrasing or sentence structure of the original. Paraphrasing is generally called for when a writer wants to include the details of a passage but does not need to quote it word for word. Like a QUOTATION or SUMMARY, a paraphrase requires DOCUMENTATION.

passive voice, 314, HB-17, HB-19 When a VERB is in the passive voice, the subject is acted upon: *A gift was given to José. See also* active voice.

past participle A VERB form used with a HELPING VERB to create perfect tenses (*have walked*) or used alone as an ADJEC-TIVE (*processed* food). The past participle of most verbs is formed by adding *-ed* or *-d* to the base form; some past parti-ciples, though, are irregular (*the written* word).

purpose, 55–56 A writer's goal: to explore ideas, to express oneself, to entertain, to demonstrate learning, to inform, to persuade, and so on. Purpose is one element of the RHETORICAL SITUATION.

Q

questioning A PROCESS of GENERATING IDEAS AND TEXT about a topic — asking, for example, *What? Who? When? Where? How?* and *Why?* or other questions.

response, 306–7 A PROCESS of writing in which a reader gives the writer his or her thoughts about the writer's title, beginning, THESIS, support and DOCUMENTATION, ORGANIZING, STANCE, treatment of AUDIENCE, achievement of PURPOSE, handling of the GENRE, ending, and other matters.

résumé, 253–64 A GENRE that summarizes someone's academic and employment history, generally written to submit to potential employers. Key Features: organization that suits goals and experience • succinctness • design that highlights key information.

revision, 307–10 The PROCESS of making substantive changes to a draft so that it contains all the necessary content and presents it in an appropriate organization. During revision, writers generally move from whole-text issues to details with the goals of sharpening their focus and strengthening their position.

stance, 6–7, 64–67 A writer's or speaker's attitude toward his or her subject — for example, reasonable, neutral, angry, curious. Stance is conveyed through TONE. *See also* rhetorical situation

strategy, 333 A pattern for ORGANIZING text to ANALYZE CAUSE AND EFFECT, ARGUE, CLASSIFY AND DIVIDE, COMPARE AND CONTRAST, DEFINE, DESCRIBE, EXPLAIN A PROCESS, or NARRATE.

style In writing, the arrangement of sentences, CLAUSES, PHRASES, words, and punctuation to achieve a desired effect; also, the rules of capitalization, punctuation, and so on recommended for DOCUMENTATION of a source.

tone, 64–67   The way a writer's or speaker's STANCE toward the readers and subject is reflected in the text.

topic, 345–46   The specific subject written about in a text. A topic should be narrow enough to cover, not too broad or general, and needs to be developed appropriately for its AUDIENCE and PURPOSE.

topic proposal, 242–44   A statement of intent to examine a topic; also called a proposal ABSTRACT. Some instructors require a topic proposal in order to assess the feasibility of the writing project that a student has in mind. Key Features: concise discussion of the subject • clear statement of the intended focus • rationale for choosing the subject • mention of resources

topic sentence, 347–48   A sentence, often at the beginning of a paragraph, that states the paragraph's main point. The details in the rest of the paragraph should support the topic sentence.

transition, 349   A word or PHRASE that helps to connect sentences and paragraphs and to guide readers through a text. Transitions can help to show comparisons (also, similarly); contrasts (but, instead); examples (for instance, in fact); sequence (finally, next); time (at first, meanwhile); and more.

Submitting Papers for Publication by W. W. Norton & Company

We are interested in receiving writing from college students to consider including in our textbooks as examples of student writing. Please send this form with the work that you would like us to consider to Marilyn Moller, Student Writing, W. W. Norton & Company, 500 Fifth Avenue, New York NY 10110.

Text Submission Form

Student's name _____

School _____

Address _____

Department _____

Course _____

Writing assignment the text responds to _____

_____

_____

_____

_____

Instructor's name _____

(continued next page)

Please write a few sentences about what your primary purposes were for writing this text. Also, if you wish, tell us what you think you learned about writing from the experience writing it.

_____

_____

_____

_____

_____

_____

_____

Contact Information

Please provide the information below so that we can contact you if your work is selected for publication.

Name _____

Permanent address _____

Email _____

Phone _____

Revision Symbols

abbr	abbreviation **HB-105**		*ital*	italics **HB-102**
adj	adjective **HB-60**		*jarg*	jargon **HB-43**
adv	adverb **HB-60**		*lc*	lowercase letter **HB-100**
agr	agreement **HB-24, HB-29**		*mm*	misplaced modifier **HB-62**
art	article **HB-64**		*num*	number **HB-106**
awk	awkward		¶	new paragraph
cap	capitalization **HB-100**		//	parallelism **HB-34**
case	pronoun case **HB-32**		*pass*	passive voice **HB-19**
cliché	cliché **HB-43**		*ref*	pronoun reference **HB-30**
⌒	close up space		*run-on*	comma splice or fused sentence **HB-10**
cs	comma splice **HB-10**		*sexist*	sexist language **HB-67**
def	define **388–98**		*shift*	confusing shift **HB-39**
⌒	delete		*sl*	slang **HB-42**
dm	dangling modifier **HB-63**		#	insert space
doc	documentation **496–589**		*sp*	spelling
emph	emphasis **HB-104**		*trans*	transition **13**
frag	sentence fragment **HB-7**		⌣	transpose
fs	fused sentence **HB-10**		*vb*	verb **HB-12**
hyph	hyphen **HB-98**		*wrdy*	wordy **HB-59**
∧	insert		*ww*	wrong word **HB-51**

A Directory to MLA Style